D0086668

ELIZABETH
COWAN NEELD

An Instructor's Manual is available. It may be obtained through a local Scott, Foresman representative or by writing the English Editor, Higher Education Division, Scott, Foresman and Company, 1900 E. Lake Avenue, Glenview, IL 60025

Credit lines for the photos and literary materials appearing in this work are placed in the acknowledgments section on pages 633–34 of this book. The acknowledgments section is considered an extension of the copyright page.

Library of Congress Cataloging-in-Publication Data

Neeld, Elizabeth Cowan, 1940–
Writing / Elizabeth Cowan Neeld. — 3rd ed.
p. cm.
Includes bibliographical references.
ISBN 0-673-38399-7 : $17.50 (est.)
1. English language—Rhetoric. I. Title.
PE1408.N416 1990b
808′.042—dc20 89-10979
CIP

ISBN 0-673-38399-7

Printed in the United States of America.

3 4 5 6-VHJ-94 93 92 91

Preface

"There are stages in bread-making quite similar to the stages of writing." These are the words of Marguerite Yourcenar—first woman to be named a member of the French Academy and author of the beautiful *Memoirs of Hadrian*. "You begin with something shapeless which sticks to your fingers. A kind of paste. Gradually the paste becomes more and more firm. Then there comes a point where it turns rubbery, a point when you feel it's time to stop kneading. You sense that the yeast has begun to do its work: the dough is alive. Then all you have to do is let it rest."

Anyone who sits down to write recognizes the appropriateness of Marguerite Yourcenar's comparison—especially the "kind of paste" part. But writers also realize, probably with no small sigh of relief, that if the pen is kept in action, writing does not remain in the shapeless, paste stage forever; it *progresses,* through various stages of readiness, to become a completed piece of work.

Since it first appeared more than a decade ago, *Writing* has guided thousands of students through the writing process—where you begin in chaos, uncertain what form a project is going to take, and end in order, with a coherent and satisfying paper. This lastest edition supports apprentice writers even more fully and systematically than before, taking into account much that has been learned about writing in the years since the book's debut, an exciting period of growth and change. Yet *Writing* has not had to abandon its most cherished assumption because it has proven to be a sound one—*everybody can learn to write.* We may take different paths to composing well and write to diverse audiences for different purposes, but we share enough common ground to learn remarkably well from each other.

Writing *and the Writing Process*

When we make meaning out of random thoughts—shape a whole out of fragments—minds move through a sequence of operations both progressive and recursive, simultaneous and incremental. This loose sequence—the stages of the writing process—moves forward as we make finer and finer distinctions. Each set of distinctions, each movement in this process can be practiced and learned, but only by the act of composing itself. First we discover or develop ideas on a subject and set those ideas into relationships with readers; then we give them a shape that makes them familiar and a structure that makes them comprehensible; and finally we polish them into the best prose possible. *Writing* makes this incremental learning accessible by providing both general advice and a comprehensive sequence of writing assignments.

Previous editions of *Writing* have followed the writing process in sequence through three stages: creating, shaping, and completing. The third edition retains these useful categories, but presents them in a way most writers will find more supportive and practical. Part 1, appropriately titled "A Tour of the Writing Process," now quickly but thoroughly surveys all the major aspects of the composing process—including editing. It enumerates the basic principles of creating, shaping, and completing so that students can begin individual writing projects with enhanced confidence. After all, students need these essential skills as much during the first weeks of a term as during the last. The Creating section, for example, explains freewriting and brainstorming; the pages on Shaping treat such issues as audience, thesis formation, and drafting; the Completing material describes how to revise sentences for energy and punch. These topics don't represent all that composing is about, but most experienced writers will acknowledge that they are a good place to begin—a college writer's working capital.

The Portfolio

Part 2 of *Writing,* a much-expanded "Portfolio" section, challenges students with ten full writing projects. Each chapter offers guidance and support through all the stages of the composing process, and features sample essays by writers in and out of school responding to similar assignments. The assignments serve to foster discussion, collaboration, debate, peer-editing, and creative thinking. Many of them consciously invite students to explore how their writing involves them in a web of thoughts, words, and actions. Writing group activities, for example, expose students to the social, economic, and political dimensions of their thinking and encourage them to appreciate the power writing has to remake an environment and a world. The portfolio assignments cover all the basic modes of writing students are expected to master in college: the journal, the personal experience essay, the problem-solution paper, the evaluation essay, the research paper, and so on. The entire section is filled with useful tips and helpful checklists.

Becoming an Expert

As students work their way through the various portfolio assignments, they can easily enough return to the overview of the writing process in Part 1 to brush up on the basics. Or they can move ahead to Part 3 "The

Writers' Workshop," where they will find fuller or more advanced discussions of the creating, shaping, and completing stages—as well as useful information about paragraphs, sentences, and words. The workshop metaphor should be taken seriously; the portfolio assignments themselves often encourage students to dip into these later chapters on their own to find a more appropriate invention technique or a way of enlivening sentences. After all, writing can never be constrained by even the most ingenious textbook sequences. Yet instructors can also work systematically through these chapters if such a plan better fits their classroom approach. Thus the chapters in Part 3 "The Writers' Workshop" are both separate and sequential, reinforcing the overview of the writing process in Part 1 while enhancing the ability of writers to respond to assignments in Part 2.

That ability to teach without constraining is the whole point of the new structure of *Writing*. Students shouldn't have to read four hundred pages of a textbook before they grasp the "big picture"; but unfortunately, all that they can usefully learn about effective writing won't fit into a hundred pages. So *Writing* now offers it both ways: a quick review for the big picture; detailed writing sequences and "expert sections" for the finer or more complex matters.

Other Changes

Move one wall of a house, and the whole place starts to look different. That's been the case with the third edition of *Writing*. Refinements and revisions appear throughout the text, some large enough to require a new line in the table of contents—like slipping the substantially rewritten section on the research paper into the portfolio section; others are less grand, but significant in their own right—clearer headings, audience checklists and editing sheets in every portfolio assignment, and dozens of new suggestions for papers. There's also pertinent new material on audience, paragraphing, denotation and connotation, and abstract and concrete language.

Major and minor changes are particularly evident in Parts 4 and 5, "Special Applications" and "Writing Handbook," which have been subtly but significantly revised. For the first time *Writing* has a chapter on scientific writing, reflecting an augmented sensitivity throughout the text to the composing done in disciplines outside the liberal arts or humanities. As might be expected, the sections on business letters, résumés, and essay exams have been retained, but they have been carefully reworked for greater applicability. The handbook material has been fully revised too, but the section hasn't lost the clarity and style that have been its hallmarks.

As important as additions and enhancements to *Writing* are the vigorous rearrangements and cuts that have occurred within all its chapters to make them trimmer, neater, and more efficient in conveying information. The language of the text is more readable and concise, yet *Writing* retains its characteristically cordial and informal tone. Instructors familiar with previous editions of *Writing* will find most of what they have enjoyed about the book still here—and a whole lot more. Those who haven't used *Writing* will find it a comprehensive, current, and exciting invitation to college writing.

Acknowledgments

Each new edition of a book increases the debts of gratitude an author owes to the people who have made the success of the project possible. In this regard, the third edition of *Writing* is no exception.

Guiding the revision from the beginning were Anne E. Smith, Constance Rajala, and Linda Bieze at Scott, Foresman. Their commitment to this book extended not only to the quality of the revision, but to its style: they understand that there's a good deal more to a successful book than its table of contents. As a result of their efforts, *Writing* retains its distinctive character and voice while responding aggressively to important developments in composition theory and practice.

To Laurie Prossnitz fell the difficult task of seeing that the old and new editions meshed smoothly. She edited the final manuscript patiently and skillfully, catching all those embarrassing slips that occur when chapters are revised.

Gratitude is owed, too, to all the reviewers of *Writing,* especially Dorothy Bankston, Louisiana State University; Richard Batteiger, Oklahoma State University; Bonnie Braendlin, Florida State University; Linda Calendrillo, University of South Alabama; Carol David, Iowa State University; Ruth Greenberg, University of Louisville; David Mair, University of Oklahoma; and Jan Pechenik, Tufts University. Special thanks to Josephine Tarvers, Rutgers University, for her contributions to this revision.

Contents

PART 1 A Tour of the Writing Process 1

CHAPTER 1 Building an Essay 5

UNDERSTANDING THE PROCESS OF WRITING 5

SOME INITIAL CONSIDERATIONS 8

- *Procrastination* 8
- *Habits* 8
- *Taboos* 8
- *Varieties of English* 10

APPLICATION 10

CHAPTER 2 The Creating Stage 12

ENTERING THE CREATING STAGE 12

FIVE BASIC CREATING TECHNIQUES 14

- *The Reporter's Formula* 14
- *Brainstorming* 15
- *Making a List* 16
- *Chaining* 18
- *Looping* 20

STUDENT ESSAY *Confidence* 26

APPLICATION 27

CHAPTER 3 The Shaping Stage 30

PRELIMINARY AGREEMENTS 31

- *Why Are You Writing?* 32
- *To Whom Are You Writing?* 35
- *What Do You Want to Communicate?* 36

THE DISCOVERY DRAFT 39

How to Write the Discovery Draft 39
Summary of Discovery Draft 43

THESIS AS A FOCUS 43

How to Write a Good Thesis 43
Summary of Thesis 48

SHAPING STRUCTURE 51

WRITING AGAIN 52

APPLICATIONS 34, 37, 48

CHAPTER 4 *The Completing Stage* 53

REVISING 54

Revising for Flow: Transitions and Reminder Signs 54
Revising for Energy: Sentences 62
Revising for Punch: Words 66

EDITING AND MANUSCRIPT FORM 72

Why Edit? 72
The Editing Eye 74
Five Editing Steps 75

A FINAL WORD 83

PROFESSIONAL ESSAY Giving What You Say a Sense of Wholeness 55

APPLICATIONS 60, 61, 62, 65, 71

PART 2 *The Writing Portfolio: Ten Assignments* 85

PURPOSES FOR WRITING 87

Writing to Express 87
Writing to Tell 89
Writing to Change 92

CHAPTER 5 *Writing a Journal* 95

KEEPING A RECORD: YOUR JOURNAL AS A BUTTERFLY NET 96

SHARPENING YOUR SENSES: YOUR JOURNAL AS A WAKE-UP CALL 98

COLLECTING THINGS YOU LIKE: YOUR JOURNAL AS A REPOSITORY 101

IMITATING GOOD WRITING: YOUR JOURNAL AS A PRACTICE FIELD 103

MAKING MEANING, MAKING SENSE: YOUR JOURNAL AS AN ODYSSEY 107

JOURNAL WRITING AND ESSAY WRITING 109

APPLICATIONS 97, 99, 102, 104, 108

CHAPTER 6 *The Personal Experience Essay* 111

WHY WRITE THE PERSONAL EXPERIENCE ESSAY? 111

ASSIGNMENTS 112

WRITING THE PERSONAL EXPERIENCE ESSAY 113

Creating 113
Shaping/Drafting 114
Peer-Editing 116
Completing 118

STUDENT ESSAY *Stolen Kiss* 121

CHAPTER 7 *The Personal Perspective Essay* 123

WHY WRITE THE PERSONAL PERSPECTIVE ESSAY? 123

ASSIGNMENTS 124

WRITING THE PERSONAL PERSPECTIVE ESSAY 125

Creating 125
Shaping/Drafting 126
Peer-Editing 127
Completing 130

STUDENT ESSAY *Monkey See, Monkey Do* 131

CHAPTER 8 *The How-To Essay* 133

WHY WRITE THE HOW-TO ESSAY? 133

ASSIGNMENTS 134

WRITING THE HOW-TO ESSAY 135

Creating 135
Shaping/Drafting 136
Peer-Editing 138
Completing 141

STUDENT ESSAY *Teaching Star Style* 143

CHAPTER 9 *The Problem-Solution Essay* 145

WHY WRITE THE PROBLEM-SOLUTION ESSAY? 145

ASSIGNMENTS 147

WRITING THE PROBLEM-SOLUTION ESSAY 148

Creating 148
Shaping/Drafting 150
Peer-Editing 153
Completing 156

STUDENT ESSAY *Is Your Child Dyslexic?* 157

CHAPTER 10 *The Information Essay* 160

WHY WRITE THE INFORMATION ESSAY? 160

ASSIGNMENTS 161

WRITING THE INFORMATION ESSAY 163

Creating 163
Shaping/Drafting 164
Peer-Editing 165
Completing 169

STUDENT ESSAY *Stop Chewing the Fat* 173

CHAPTER 11 *The Assertion-with-Evidence Essay* 176

WHY WRITE THE ASSERTION-WITH-EVIDENCE ESSAY? 176

ASSIGNMENTS 177

WRITING THE ASSERTION-WITH-EVIDENCE ESSAY 178

Creating 179
Shaping/Drafting 179
Peer-Editing 182
Completing 185

STUDENT ESSAY *A Battle for Existence* 187

CHAPTER 12 *The Evaluation Essay* 190

WHY WRITE THE EVALUATION ESSAY? 190

ASSIGNMENTS 191

WRITING THE EVALUATION ESSAY 193

Creating 193
Shaping/Drafting 195

Peer-Editing 198
Completing 202

STUDENT ESSAY *Kidney Stone Blasting* 204

CHAPTER 13 *The Persuasion Essay* 206

WHY WRITE THE PERSUASION ESSAY? 206
ASSIGNMENTS 207
WRITING THE PERSUASION ESSAY 208
Creating 208
Shaping/Drafting 209
Peer-Editing 213
Completing 216

STUDENT ESSAY *A Young Minister to His Church* 218

CHAPTER 14 *The Research Paper* 219

PART I: CONDUCTING RESEARCH 222
THE RESEARCH PROCESS 222
Step 1: Identify Your Purpose 222
Step 2: Make a Plan 223
Step 3: Pick a Subject Area and Scout It Out 224
Step 4: Talk to People 224
Step 5: Go to the Library 225
WHAT THE LIBRARY CAN OFFER YOU 225
Starting Your Working Bibliography 237
Finding and Evaluating Your Sources 238
TAKING NOTES 239
PART II: WRITING A RESEARCH PAPER 243

A STRATEGIC APPROACH TO WRITING 243

Step 1: Do Creating Exercises to Narrow Your Subject 243
Step 2: Write a Discovery Draft 244
Step 3: Determine Your Thesis 245
Step 4: Organize Your Research into a Preliminary Outline 245
Step 5: Find the Holes and Fill Them 246
Step 6: Expand Your Discovery Draft into a Working Draft 247
Step 7: Revise the Working Draft 248
Step 8: Edit the Paper for Consistency in Form and Language 248
Step 9: Type the Final Paper—and Proofread It 250
Step 10: Release the Paper—and Yourself 250

STUDENT PAPER Paying to Dream: Has the Ohio Lottery Been a Success? 254

PART III: USING SOURCES IN YOUR WRITING 265

WHO DOCUMENTS SOURCES? 265

THE BASICS: WHAT YOU DOCUMENT 265

Documenting Direct Quotations 266
Documenting Paraphrases 266
Documenting Synthesized Information 266

WHERE IN YOUR PAPER DO YOU DOCUMENT INFORMATION? 268

Parenthetical References 268
Content Notes 269
List of Works Cited 270

FORMAT: HOW TO INCORPORATE DOCUMENTED MATERIAL 270

How to Choose Sources 271
Where to Put the Reference and What It Should Say 271
How to Tailor Sources to Fit Your Sentences 273
How to Type Quotations 274

ATTRIBUTION: HOW TO INTRODUCE SOURCES 275

MLA DOCUMENTATION: GENERAL GUIDELINES 276

Books 277
Magazines, Journals, and Newspapers 283
Reference Sources 286
Graphic and Media Arts 288
Oral and Personal Communications 290
Technological Sources 291

APA DOCUMENTATION: GENERAL GUIDELINES 292
Books 292
Periodicals 294
Reports 295
Other Written Sources 296
Nonprint Media 296
PLAGIARISM: FAILURES IN DOCUMENTATION 297
Understanding Plagiarism 297
Avoiding Plagiarism 300
APPLICATIONS 241, 301

PART 3 Crafting the Portfolio: The Writers' Workshop 305

CHAPTER 15 Quick Thoughts on Audience, Talk, and Writing 308
APPLICATION 311

CHAPTER 16 Creating: Expanded Techniques 314
FIVE EXPANDED TECHNIQUES 314
Cubing 315
Track Switching 319
Classical Invention 325
Noticing Inside Purpose 337
Reading and Researching: R&R 339
SUMMARY 342
STUDENT ESSAYS A Legacy from Prehistoric Times 318 / Jogging to a Good Job 323 / Going Back to School As an Adult 335
APPLICATIONS 319, 324, 329, 336, 339, 341, 343

CHAPTER 17 *Form and Pattern* 346

SPECIFIC PATTERNS OF ORGANIZATION 347

Time Order 348
Spatial Order 350
General-Specific Order 351
Break-Down Order 353
Relationship Order 354
Mixed Form 355

KEEPING PATTERNS OF ORGANIZATION IN PERSPECTIVE 358

STUDENT ESSAY *Try Not to Go Back: The Grist Mill, a Restaurant You Won't Forget* 356

APPLICATION 359

CHAPTER 18 *Promise and Delivery* 361

THE INTERNAL CHECK 362

Make Your Promise Clear: Have a Thesis 363
Deliver What You Promise: Stay on Track 366

THE EXTERNAL CHECK 375

The Big Picture 375
Essay Introductions 375
Essay Conclusions 377

APPLICATIONS 370, 379

CHAPTER 19 *Making Paragraphs Work* 384

WHAT A PARAGRAPH IS 384

TWO KINDS OF PARAGRAPHS 385

THE TOPIC SENTENCE PARAGRAPH 386

Checking for Flow: Looking at Topic Sentence Paragraphs 389

THE FUNCTION PARAGRAPH 408

SOME FINAL OBSERVATIONS ON PARAGRAPHING FOR FLOW 415

PROFESSIONAL ESSAY *The Living Dead Sea* 417

APPLICATIONS 388, 391, 395, 398, 406, 414

CHAPTER 20 Polishing Sentences 419

VARY SENTENCES 419

Varying Basic Patterns 420
Varying Sentence Openers 421
Varying the Order of Words 421

CHANNEL INFORMATION FOR EMPHASIS AND STYLE 423

Coordination and Subordination 423
Parallelism 427
Repetition and Rhythm 429
Avoid the Passive Voice 432

FINAL OBSERVATIONS ABOUT POLISHING SENTENCES 434

APPLICATIONS 422, 434

CHAPTER 21 Style: Words and Images 438

LEVELS OF STYLE 438

DENOTATION AND CONNOTATION 442

CONCRETE AND ABSTRACT LANGUAGE 448

TRITE DICTION 451

APPLICATIONS 441, 444, 449, 452

PART 4 Special Applications 455

CHAPTER 22 Writing the Essay Examination 458

THE PURPOSE OF THE ESSAY EXAMINATION 459

THE CREATING STAGE 460

The Reporter's Formula 461
Listing 461
Brainstorming 461

THE SHAPING STAGE 462

Audience as Shaper: Instructor as Audience 462
Start with a Thesis 462
Form 463
What to Do If You Think of a New Point While Writing 463

THE COMPLETING STAGE 464

What to Do If You Don't Know the Answer 465
What to Do If You Run Out of Time 466
Appearance 466

SUMMARY 467

APPLICATION 468

CHAPTER 23 Writing the Business Letter 472

ELEMENTS OF A BUSINESS LETTER 472

Purpose and Tone 472
Organization 472
Audience and Style 474
Appearance 475
Format 475

KINDS OF LETTERS 478

The "You" Attitude 478
Requests 479
Responses 482

APPLICATION 484

CHAPTER 24 *Writing the Job Application and Résumé* 489

CONVENTIONS OF THE JOB APPLICATION LETTER 489

- *Creating* 490
- *Shaping* 493
- *Completing* 500

RÉSUMÉ 502

- *Résumé: Model 1* 502
- *Résumé: Model 2* 504

APPLICATION 507

CHAPTER 25 *Writing About Literature* 509

PURPOSE AND AUDIENCE 509

SELECTING A STRATEGY: THE FORM YOUR WRITING WILL TAKE 510

- *Explication* 510
- *Close Reading* 510
- *Literary Criticism* 511

TERMS USED IN WRITING ABOUT LITERATURE 511

- *Plot* 511
- *Characters* 512
- *Setting* 513
- *Point of View* 513
- *Structure* 514
- *Language* 515
- *Theme* 517
- *Style* 518

STUDENT ESSAY *Hints of Reality* 522

APPLICATION 520

CHAPTER 26 *Writing for the Sciences* 525

CREATING 525

SHAPING 526

The Lab Report or Scientific Paper 526
The Abstract 527
The Review 528

COMPLETING 529

The Writing Must Be Clear 529
The Writing Must Be Concise 529
The Language Must Be Appropriate for Your Readers 530
The Writing Must Be Understandable 531
The Form of Documentation Must Be What Your Readers Expect 532

STUDENT ESSAY *Symbiosis: Parasitism, Mutualism, and Commensalism* 533

PART 5 *Writing Handbook* 539

CHAPTER 27 *Parts of Speech* 541

NOUNS 542

Noun Features 543
Noun Functions 544
Noun Identifiers 544

PRONOUNS 545

Personal Pronouns 546
Reflexive Pronouns 546
Relative Pronouns 547
Demonstrative Pronouns 547
Interrogative Pronouns 548
Indefinite Pronouns 548

VERBS 549

Auxiliary (Helping) Verbs 550
Subject-Verb-Complement (S-V-C) Combinations 553
Active and Passive Voice 555

VERBALS 556

ADJECTIVES 558
ADVERBS 560
Adverb Forms 562
PREPOSITIONS 563
Verb Particles 564
CONJUNCTIONS 564
Conjunctive Adverbs 566
INTERJECTIONS 566
SENTENCES 567
Clauses and Phrases 567
APPLICATIONS 545, 549, 553, 555, 556, 557, 562, 566, 568

CHAPTER 28 Major Sentence Errors 569
GLOSSARY OF BASIC TERMS 569
COMMA SPLICES 570
RUN-ON SENTENCES 573
FRAGMENTS 575
FAULTY PREDICATION 578
FAULTY MODIFICATION 580
AGREEMENT PROBLEMS 582
APPLICATIONS 572, 575, 577, 579, 581, 585

CHAPTER 29 Mechanics: Punctuation, Spelling, Capitalization 586
PUNCTUATION 586
Elements of Punctuation 587
SPELLING 595
What Causes Misspellings? 596

MECHANICS 600

Capitalization 600
Abbreviations and Symbols 601
Numbers 603
Apostrophe 604
Hyphen 604
Quotation Marks 605

APPLICATIONS 594, 599

CHAPTER 30 *Glossary of Usage* 607

DIALECTAL VARIETIES OF ENGLISH 609

GLOSSARY OF USAGE 610

PART 1 A Tour of the Writing Process

As you get started writing, this section will help you

- get a bird's-eye view of the entire writing process
- apply basic creating techniques to stimulate ideas for writing
- decide why you are writing, whom you are writing to, and what you want to communicate
- write a discovery draft to see where you want to go with your writing
- write a good thesis about your subject
- revise your writing for flow, energy, and punch
- edit your writing to give it the finishing touch

This is a book designed to help you write well in school, in the workplace, and in the world. Because it is intended chiefly for the classroom, *Writing* focuses on situations that produce academic writing. But schoolwork—like any other kind of writing—needs a human voice and touch. And, if you are lucky, a classroom can provide precisely the environment you need to grow as a writer—a place where you work not alone, but in a room full of writers; a place where you and your colleagues give substance and texture to ideas; a place to challenge assumptions, and probe the complex workings of life. As the twenty-first century approaches, you may discover that the most powerful tool you possess is the ability to write.

Because writing is a process, this book will introduce you to three stages through which writers move in doing their work: creating, shaping, and completing. These are *not* steps to composition or "rules for getting it right." No such simple steps, rules, or guidelines exist; both the world and writing are too complex for that. Instead, these stages—creating, shaping, completing—describe various mental and physical routines skilled writers employ to make their words work hard and well. But don't get the impression that these stages mean nothing but stern labor. Just the opposite is true, particularly when writing is going well. Controlling the process of writing means unleashing new channels of energy, finding more complex ways of engaging ideas, testing innovative structures for containing them, and learning how to bring concepts and proposals to the world in an appealing way. Like life, the process of writing breathes and moves; but, like living, it's also complicated and unpredictable. It no more follows a straight line or narrow path than you do. It depends on you to use it well, to play it like a virtuoso extracting music from a fine violin, to direct it like a Grand Prix driver negotiating an S-curve.

Writing is also about papers, articles, essays, stories, reports—what scholars of writing and language simply call *texts*. Words on a page. Stuff. This "stuff" is the end product of creating, shaping, and completing. But writing isn't simply ink pressed onto paper. It's also what happens when that ink gets read, when the world of a writer engages the culture of a reader. That exchange, so simple and impressively natural, remains one of the miracles of our existence: we reach each other through our language, our texts. We also take pride in that achievement when it is done well, knowing the energy, creativity, and effort it represents. Whether students, researchers, journalists, pipe fitters, scientists, or poets, we all want language to work for us—to help us understand ourselves better, to explain the world we live in, to improve that world.

This text will offer you a variety of opportunities for writing, probably more than you could comfortably respond to in a year, let alone an academic term. These opportunities are presented as cues for composing—a sequence of assignments intended to introduce you to specific kinds of academic writing. As always, you'll be expected to write papers in response to these prompts. To encourage you to think of your writing not as a disconnected sequence of assignments, but as a body of work—a collection of texts—the roster of assignments has a special name: "The Writing Portfolio."

Taken together at the end of a course, the papers in your portfolio will represent your involvement with the academic world. The complete set will speak more accurately and eloquently about your response to its demands than any single effort could. The portfolio may reveal the personal compromises you have made to adjust your native environment (the family, the inner city, the military, the business world) to the academic world. It may reveal your cultural identity—how your language and thinking have been shaped by particular people, places, and environments. It may reveal you as a person with many identities—with special reservoirs of knowledge, unconventional interests, an individual style, and the ability to write different roles for yourself in changing situations. If the collection exposes weaknesses in your command of academic language, chances are good it also demonstrates strengths.

In short, regarding the products of a writing course as a body of work—a portfolio—will encourage you to think of yourself as a writer who is learning and growing. Even when an instructor assigns what you must write, you can still assume responsibility for topics, revision schedules, deadlines, and other priorities based upon a reasonable assessment of your goals, skills, expertise, and ability. You need not expect to do everything well, but then no one expects you to. Because you and the world in which you live are more complex than any one paper, don't let any one text define you as a writer. Assembling a portfolio offers you the chance to explore many kinds of writing. Take advantage of this opportunity.

One last point: writing involves interactions among people. That seems clear. But the idea proves to be a challenging one, especially in a society accustomed to thinking of intellectual work as intensely private. We picture the poet sequestered in a garret, the executive in a private office, the lone journalist pounding a typewriter. Such images are not entirely inaccurate. At one level, much writing is solitary; most of us require isolation and quiet to produce an article or paper. And writers sometimes do feel like the child confined to a backroom for misbehaving while friends play tag in the street.

But good writing also requires the one-on-one exchange with friends and colleagues. We discover ideas in the world around us, not in the attic. We borrow them for a while, reshape them perhaps, and then send them back into the world. In short, writing needs people. It thrives on talk, discussion, controversy, chatter, and brainstorming. When we write about any subject (even ourselves), we interrupt a conversation already in progress; we glance behind to what's already known and leap toward what may not yet be obvious—two steps forward, one step back.

In practical terms, this means a writer needs to feel comfortable working with others throughout the writing process—creating, shaping, completing. A writer's work is no less original if a dozen colleagues contribute to its ideas, a hostile critic reshapes its structure, a special interest group refines its point of view, or an editorial staff reviews and polishes its mechanics. In fact, with much business and professional writing, the notion of single authorship is becoming an anachronism: work is usually accomplished by groups, pooling their strengths and resources to get a job done.

Working with others also means understanding better what writing can do. You already know that writing always implies an audience. But writers accustomed to working individually sometimes lose that perspective. They hear only one voice in their writing, and it's usually their own. For them, the world has narrowed and so, consequently, does the power and reach of their writing. And that's a shame because writing is a power, a way of sharing knowledge and receiving it. How one writes in part defines the cultures—academic, business, ethnic, national—one can operate in and the roles one can play in life. Thus, when you sit down with colleagues in a writing class to collaborate on an assignment or to edit each other's work, you are stepping into other worlds, beginning the process of sharing and receiving knowledge. It's a serious act with great potential. It's also exciting.

This book, then, is about the excitement and pleasures of writing. It encourages you to think of yourself as a writer crafting a body of work. It guides you through the stages of composing and invites you to invite others into your writing. It asks you to take writing seriously because our nation needs skillful writers and thinkers. But it also asks you to enjoy yourself, to open yourself up to the undeniable thrill of creativity—of using language to make something new.

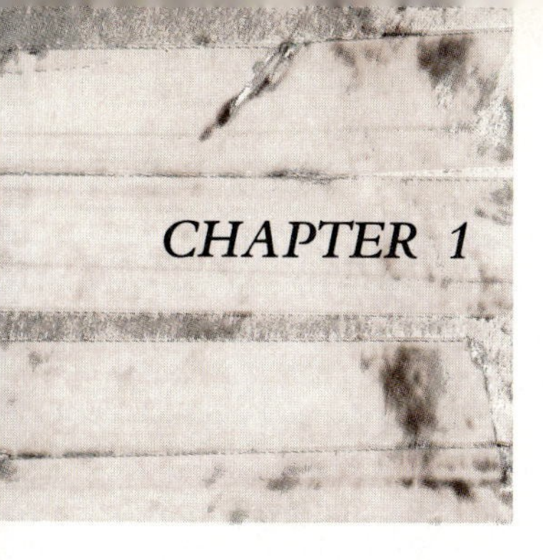

CHAPTER 1

Building an Essay

When writing an essay, you start with the intention to *make* something that wasn't there when you started. You face both opportunities and decisions—hundreds of them, some tiny, some huge. If you feel overwhelmed when you begin to write, you aren't alone. At the beginning of a project, most writers feel just as if someone has said to them: "Here's a hammer. Build a house." Most writers are nervous and usually don't know where to start—even though they feel they should. After all, everyone has been writing since second grade.

Yet most beginning writers haven't had enough experience to be familiar with the natural stages through which a piece of writing may move. They don't know what to decide when, what distinctions to make first, and what kind of activity works best at what points in the process. They find themselves thinking about everything at once while still trying to move forward, like a driver wrestling with a stickshift for the first time. They jerk, hesitate, shudder, stall. They may prefer to call it quits before breaking something.

UNDERSTANDING THE PROCESS OF WRITING

Actually, the process of writing isn't so hard to command. There is first a *creating* stage—a time to look for ideas, explore, cast about for things to say. The creating stage is ripe with possibilities. You have plenty of freedom. The things you think don't have to reveal their logic. You don't yet have to trace connections between the thoughts you put down on the page. You don't even have to know what you want to say. All you need in this first stage is a commitment to be in motion—to put words on the page or on the word-processor screen. You are collecting possibilities, exploring problems, questioning assumptions.

As you continue to move through this creating stage, you will get closer and closer to what you want to say. This doesn't mean that by the end of the creating stage you will know exactly what this is. But you are closer to it. A problem or idea has surfaced. Your thoughts have begun to array themselves into structures. You have developed a feel for your subject that is almost physical. It's time to move on to a second stage, *shaping.* But when we talk about stages in writing, we're actually describing emphases, not discrete and separable activities. So, in fact, the creating never stops; your mind is always working, inventing, perceiving new relationships as words fill up a page.

Still, writing entails action. Just as the day comes when engineers move from the planning/drawing-board stage to the fabrication of actual designs, you also advance when you write. The shaping stage progresses naturally from the creating one, yet it requires that different distinctions be made and different actions taken. The shaping stage also has a sequence, a rough progression, that goes from open to less open, from possibilities to firm commitments.

For instance, the purpose for which you are writing and the audience you are addressing form the foundation of an essay. Once that foundation is set, it determines the overall structure and approach—what you can do in that piece of writing. Change your purpose or audience, and you have to rethink the design of the entire piece. Within the audience and purpose framework, however, you still have many options. You can begin an initial or discovery draft even if you still aren't entirely clear what you want to say.

As you move through the shaping stage—writing more drafts, sharing them with colleagues, exploring the assumptions behind your thoughts—the writing evolves. With each movement in this stage, you have new decisions to make, but more grounds for making them, more experience with the topic, more points of view to inform your choices—especially if you are working with others. The closer you get to a product that seems ready to be read generally (no writing ever feels completely finished)—or the closer you get to the day when the writing *has* to be finished—the more constrained your choices become.

Like creating, however, shaping a piece of writing never simply ends. You can refine, improve, rethink as long as you have time, paper, and motive. However, if you want to be read in this lifetime, you will eventually have to call the shaping stage to a halt. You make a decision about what an acceptable level of quality is and then work to that level. At some point, you have to call it quits. When time constraints don't terminate a project, this consideration should: "I've done my best. If I haven't said everything I expected to on this subject by now, I'll wait for another opportunity." Then release the paper. Let it go. Move on.

In the third stage, *completing,* you polish, revise, edit, spiff up, check, and otherwise put the writing in showroom form. This is an extremely important stage in your writing because it is foolish to bring something to this stage and then be sloppy with the spelling or mechanics. Your readers may dismiss what you have said because of such mistakes. And you could have dealt with them easily enough.

It's critical that you *not* enter the completing stage at the very last minute. For most people, this stage—the editing, revising, polishing—is the one they are most familiar with, so they try to begin there. They put one or two sentences (or words!) down on the page and then start editing: "No, that's no good. I have to think of another way to put that." In effect, they are trying to varnish a cabinet that hasn't been built yet. No furniture maker would work that way, but writers do it all the time. And they pay for it—with writing that never develops into what it could be, with sessions at a desk that are frustrating, angry, and fruitless. The editing stage is one part of the process that shouldn't be in motion at every moment. Give yourself a break from perfection at the beginning of a project so that you can make a run for it nearer the end.

As you might expect, a large portion of this book will illustrate these stages in more detail because understanding them is what learning to write is all about. The next three chapters comprise a general survey of creating/shaping/completing, to give you a perspective from which to view all the assignments in the Writing Portfolio. Since these stages vary depending on the kind of writing, the assignments in the Portfolio section are tailored to different aspects of the writing process and different skills. But even these chapters can't render every detail about the process without losing a sense of the wholeness of the writing process itself. So the "expert-level" discussion of particular components in the process (structure, sentences, language) continues in a section entitled "Crafting the Portfolio." You can draw from these chapters at any time to enhance what you may already know about writing.

If you sense some overlap in this approach, you are right. A book about the writing process inevitably takes on some of the circular character of that process itself—moving forward, yet at the same time returning, rethinking, reconsidering. Part of the problem is that writing simply cannot be reduced to a series of simple steps. Nor can you improve your writing by practicing skills apart from the act of composing. Instead, you have to do it all at once—a seemingly impossible task, except that people manage it well every day. Given these considerations, this book is committed to the creation of full texts and to the discussion of skills only in the context of real writing—the portfolio of assignments that will represent your work. You'll learn to create, shape, and complete by going through the stages, not the motions, of writing.

SOME INITIAL CONSIDERATIONS

Before looking at the stages of writing in detail, let's deal briefly with a few important issues.

Procrastination

Peter DeVries once observed that he loved being a writer, he just hated the paperwork. Almost all writers seem to put off writing as long as they can—often to their great detriment. Who hasn't spent a nail-biting night sweating out a paper due the next morning? Yet there may be some method in the madness. Procrastination can serve the creating stage of writing if the delaying time is used to think, remember, ponder. But most writers procrastinate just to avoid writing, leaving themselves no time to finish writing. What gets cut from the process is usually the completing stage—the editing and polishing that makes the difference between sap and syrup. Writers who skip these crucial phases will rarely please readers who expect—and deserve—polished, finished writing. If you think you can't write until the dishes are done, the car is waxed, or the rerun of *Gilligan's Island* is over, think again.

Habits

Most people follow a set routine when they write. They prefer a specific location, a certain kind of pen, a particular tablet. Many people who own word processors still write first drafts on legal pads; the long yellow pages make them feel more in control. Some people can't write without coffee brewing or a can of soda within reach. A few people swear they can't compose without their stereos blasting. Others need their pencils sharpened and lined up in a row.

It makes sense to be comfortable when you write, so do what you must to create an environment congenial to wordsmithing. But don't let your preferences get in the way of composing. Writers on the job (and that includes students) rarely work under perfect conditions. They write where they must, adjusting to less than ideal conditions, background noise, inadequate lighting. They understand that demanding a perfect setup can be just another form of procrastination.

Taboos

In each American school, there seems to be a course called "Rules of Writing 101" which everyone knows about, but no one—not one living soul—has ever actually taken. Completing this course apparently makes a person a skillful and accurate writer, because almost all students attribute their difficulties in English to never having learned the rules of writing. Yet many of us cling to what we assume are the tangible artifacts of "Rules 101"—a few hoary injunctions about writing impressed upon us by a ruler-wielding teacher we'd rather forget. Knowing a few such rules—"Never begin sentences with 'And'; Avoid 'you' and 'I' in academic papers; Never end a sentence with a preposition"—convinces us that there must be at least a course full of other guidelines we missed. So the taboos linger on, shaping or distorting our writing for decades. It comes, then, as somewhat of a shock when we discover that our cherished rules often are nothing more than superstitions—clumsy conventions rusting on the ash heap of outdated usage.

Writing doesn't have rules like a sport or a lab experiment might. We cannot say, for example, that "good" essays always have five paragraphs and that "good" paragraphs have seven sentences. We cannot even claim that "good" sentences never begin with "and." Yet, you have surely heard certain "rules" applied to writing. Professor William Irmscher of the University of Washington has been collecting these "taboos"; here are some of his favorites:

Avoid general and abstract words.

Avoid slang.

Avoid big words.

Avoid colloquialisms.

Avoid foreign words.

Avoid fancy words.

Avoid using the first word that comes to mind.

Avoid using *be*-verbs.

Avoid *I think* and *In my opinion*.

Avoid turning nouns into verbs with *-ize*.

Avoid *I*, especially at the beginning of a sentence.

Avoid *There is* and *There are*.

Avoid the editorial *we*.

Avoid the casual use of *we*.

Avoid *you*.

Avoid *one*.

Avoid contractions.

Never begin more than two sentences with the same word (except *a*, *an*, and *the*).

Avoid short, choppy sentences.

Avoid long, overly involved sentences.

Avoid the passive voice.

Avoid too much punctuation.

Don't chew on your quill when writing.

Yes, some of these taboos apply in certain situations. But this tangle of rules doesn't explain what those situations are. Nor are they precise enough to offer much guidance. How much punctuation is too much? (Can you safely stop punctuating?) What makes a word fancy? (What's fancy to me may be broadcloth to you.) How big is a big word? (Is ten letters enough, eleven too many?) Just about all of the injunctions listed are, in fact, regularly and intentionally violated in academic writing by capable writers. And just about all of the injunctions make sense in other situations. At best, we are left to exercise our judgment. And that's what rules of writing usually come down to—making informed decisions and careful choices.

Varieties of English

English is English, right? Not quite. When you write, you have to choose the variety of English best suited to your purpose. Think about it for a minute. What do you call a sandwich that combines several kinds of meat and cheese and comes on a hard, torpedo-shaped roll? Depending on where you are from, it's a *hoagie, submarine, sub, grinder, poorboy,* or *muffaleta*. What's the plural of *you?* Is it *you, youse, youse guys,* or *y'all?* Do you use sentences like "Jerry working at Sears" or "Shirley, she bought me a nice present," or "Couldn't get it done nohow"? Do you flash terms like *perpetrator* or *RAM* or *ROM* or *litigant* or *transverse resection* or *polar moment of inertia?* All of these varieties of English are appropriate and correct in some situations; you'd recognize in what company they would be comfortable: with family, friends, coworkers.

But in academic writing we use a variety of English called *Standard American English* or *Edited American English*. It's not the *best* English, nor does it mean that other varieties of English you use in your life are *wrong* or *nonstandard*. Rather, Standard English is the type academic readers expect to find in their journals, papers, and books. It's the variety of language your teachers will expect you to use.

So in school, you'll use terms which others in the academic community share—not slang expressions only your close friends appreciate, not technical terms only people in your profession understand, not the colloquial terms you would use in criticizing an umpire. You'll usually expand contractions such as *can't* to *cannot*. You'll write longer sentences to make connections between ideas more precise. (You can reasonably expect your readers to pay attention to such matters.) You'll observe conventions regarding spelling, punctuation, grammar; these are outlined in the

Handbook section of this text. In short, you'll adjust your writing to the expectations of your audience—in this case, an academic audience—just as you would if you were addressing any other group. The difference is that you may have to learn more about academic style to command it easily. Very few people come to it naturally.

APPLICATION

1. You probably manage some process better than the average person—perhaps even with expertise. It may be photographing birds, mounting slides for biology experiments, building acoustical speakers, cutting a lawn, designing a dress, and so on. As an expert, you know that to acquire your skill, you probably began by following simple directions. Jot down those rules as you remember them (or as you would now give them to a novice); explain which rules still apply and which—as an expert—you now feel free to violate.
2. Write an essay explaining as carefully as possible the steps you follow as an expert in the process identified in item 1 above. Gear your essay to readers who might have some knowledge of your process, but who are not yet experts. If you can locate someone in your class with the same or a similar skill, write this essay collaboratively, comparing your processes. Try to agree on a common account of the process.
3. Think over any writing you have done recently either in school, at work, or at home. As best you can, reconstruct that process. If you are keeping a journal (see chapter 5), record your account of the writing process there.
4. Observe how people write in public places—the library, a cafeteria, a computer lab, a classroom, a lawn. Begin collecting notes for a possible report on the subject; you might examine the physical aspects of composing such as writing instruments (pens, pencils, computers), materials (legal pads, notecards, notebooks, screens), postures (straight, slouching, sprawling), expressions (grimacing, staring, talking to one's self), support materials (food, drink, music), and so on.
5. In a small group, make a list of all the rules about writing you can recall from previous instruction. Include any taboos you may have picked up outside of school as well. Discuss the validity of these guidelines. Which are worth keeping? Which might be safely discarded?

CHAPTER 2

The Creating Stage

These days the thick owner's manuals to sophisticated electronic devices often begin with a section that describes basic techniques for operating the product. Manufacturers provide this quick overview for various reasons. On the one hand, the products themselves—video recorders, cam corders, digital diaries, or (most complex of all) computers—may have so many capabilities that describing them in sequence might discourage a conscientious person from ever switching the machine on. On the other hand, people less inclined to follow detailed instructions are going to turn the products on anyway and use them—whether they know what they are doing or not. The overview helps both groups: it encourages cautious souls to explore their new devices; it deters more cavalier owners from accidentally destroying them.

The overview of the writing process in the next three chapters is designed as a sort of owner's manual for writing. It invites you to explore the features of an extraordinarily complex and powerful technology; it suggests a few cautions to prevent disasters or discouraging mistakes. This basic information about creating/shaping/completing should help any time you write.

ENTERING THE CREATING STAGE

How often have you sat down to write, only to find that you couldn't think of a thing to say? You tried two or three lines, scratched them out, crumpled up the paper, and scored two points in the circular file—the waste basket. Then you went through it again, the whole cycle. Ideas just wouldn't come.

This cycle plagues all writers at one time or another, but it occurs most often for people waiting for a "good idea." Somewhere they acquired the notion that it's possible to know what they are going to say before they begin to write—but that's not how ideas usually work. Fully developed subjects almost never pop into writers' heads—especially during those first minutes or hours of composing. Writers tend to do a lot of sitting and staring then, wondering whether thoughts will ever come. It's like waiting for a bus in the rain.

In fact, it's normal not to know what you are going to write when you first sit down. The feeling is uncomfortable for the novice; alternately terrifying and exciting for the more experienced writer. The uncertainty has benefits however.

If you write down exactly what pops into your brain you'll usually find yourself dealing in clichés or worn-out information—stuff your readers already know. After all, it has probably popped into their brains too. Yet beginning to write *before* you know what to say can also be one of the best ways of discovering what you *might* say. Like a traveler without a fixed route, you may discover fresh, out-of-the-way places you've never explored before.

Writing without a prearranged itinerary encourages you to face a subject, toe-to-toe. Suddenly what was fuzzy comes into focus. Hey! Do I really believe this? Do I want to be associated with this idea? Can I really write this? Just getting your thoughts down on paper produces insight and ideas.

"But this is catch-22," you say. "I've got to write an essay on the topic and give it to someone else, and you say it's OK to start writing before I know what I'm going to tell the person! That will go over big!"

Well, the way out of catch-22 is to realize that the writing you do in this stage is *not* the essay; it is a collection of thoughts that will lead to the essay. Don't worry whether your thoughts are good or bad; you are exploring the subject to find something to say. What you put down now is tentative. This stage, in fact, is private—just you and your subject. You aren't trying to be clear for anyone else; you aren't thinking of committing yourself to any specific subject. You are writing whatever comes into your head on the topic—maybe a list, even a heap of disjointed thoughts—so that later, with the help of others, you can read through your writing and find something you really want to say.

"But I've got a deadline," you lament. "I don't have time to waste on writing stuff that isn't my assignment."

This is the Great Paradox. Although such exploratory writing won't be an essay, it may be the most important writing you do for the essay. A good *creating* period will make the next two stages—*shaping* and *completing*—much easier, faster, and more productive. You will discover that you actually *save* time by spending it this way. It may seem strange now, but, when you've tried it once or twice, you will see. The freer you are with your labor at this stage, the more efficient you will be at the other two stages. You will have material to use when you get to the point of deciding exactly what you want to say to a reader. You will not have to stare at the sheet of paper, waiting for inspiration.

The creating stage, chaotic and unsure as it may seem, is not only efficient; it actually leads to a strong, interesting idea for your paper. You will always come up with something to say *if* you are willing to stay on the move—curious, persistent, willing to explore. The *creating stage* is truly the major source of writing power.

You have been using creating techniques for years. Remember sitting down to make a shopping list and, as you wrote, thinking of items you needed that were nowhere in your thoughts when you began the list? And when you wrote that book report in the fourth grade, your teacher told you to answer the five W's—*who, what, where, when,* and *why.* You found that these questions really *did* help you think of what to write.

Simple creating techniques like these stimulate thought; for that reason, they are sometimes described as tools of *invention*—methods of exploring subjects and your relationship to them. When you write, it helps to have these tools available; they provide the push to get you rolling.

FIVE BASIC CREATING TECHNIQUES

In this section, you'll discover some basic creating techniques, the kind you can apply in almost every writing situation. More complex invention tools are discussed in Chapter 16 "Creating: Expanded Techniques" or in separate chapters within the Writing Portfolio section.

The Reporter's Formula

Newspaper reporters ask six simple questions to discover essential information on events which they are reporting. You can use these same questions to remind yourself of details you know about a subject. Answering these questions will (1) set you up to write a complete account of your subject, (2) jog your memory to supply every detail and, (3) serve your reader. Readers always want a complete story, and this method is one way to be sure they get it.

Guides for the Reporter's Formula

Ask the following questions about your subject:

Who?	Where?	Why?
What?	When?	How?

The Best Uses for the Reporter's Formula:

For things and events you know about or have experienced

For things and events that are fresh in your mind

For things and events that do not require reflection or comment

Examples:

Reporting on an event

Answering a factual examination question

Preparing a summary memo

Presenting a proposal

Preparing a briefing on a past or future event

Brainstorming

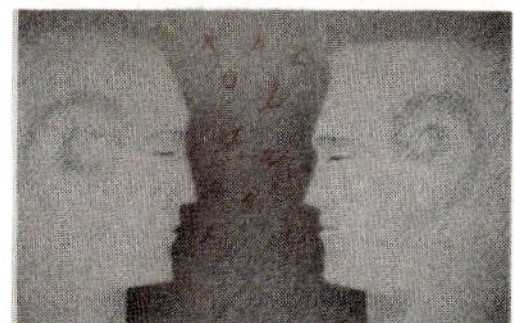

Business leaders often employ a *brainstorming* session to discover ways to solve problems, create new products, or get a fresh approach to an old situation. Brainstorming is a group activity—ideas spoken by someone else stimulate you to have ideas of your own.

You will probably have a long list of ideas when the brainstorming session is over. Now go through the list and mark out all the ideas that absolutely won't work or that you are not interested in. Then, of the remaining ideas, pick the one or two that you can imagine yourself writing on. Finally, run these ideas through one of the expanded creating techniques (see Chapter 16). When you do the actual writing, you will discover that you are well on your way to knowing what to say about this subject.

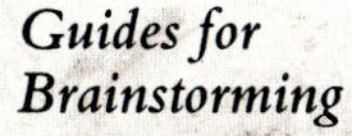

Guides for Brainstorming

1. Do it as a group activity.
2. Call out every idea you can think of. Go for quantity.
3. Freewheel. The wilder the ideas, the better.
4. Build off other people's ideas. Don't wait until you have an original thought.
5. Be completely nonjudgmental. No idea should be ridiculed, discarded, or decided upon prematurely.
6. Jot down all the ideas as they are spoken so that you will have a list to use later. Or use a tape recorder so you can devote full attention to the activity.
7. Do your own evaluating of the ideas privately, sometime after the brainstorming session.

BRAINSTORM:
A sudden and violent disturbance in the brain; a sudden clever, whimsical, or foolish idea; to freely call out ideas on a subject; to explore a topic in order to produce as many ideas as possible.

The Best Uses for Brainstorming:

For problem/solution topics

For tired subjects that seem unlikely to interest anyone

For topics assigned to the class as a whole

Examples:

Finding an original solution to a problem

Answering an examination question that requires discussion or analysis

Discussing with others something that everyone has read or studied

Analyzing a picture, chart, graph, or table

Planning an event

Visualizing the uses of an object, product, or idea

Making a List

LIST:
An item-by-item printed or written entry of persons or things, often arranged in a particular order, and usually of a specified nature or category; a guest list; a shopping list; to itemize; to catalog.

We all make lists in order not to forget. What about making lists in order to discover?

List-making can be a valuable first step in many writing situations, especially those that require you to recall something you already know or realize something new about a familiar subject. For example, you might list the steps in a process—how to make a bookshelf—or the arguments for or against drinking.

As you settle down to write, a list can (1) give you a definite purpose and activity to get you started; (2) cause you to have associations and thereby to think of something you might not have thought of before; (3) provide you with a framework for your thinking at that moment.

When you have finished the list, you can do several things: select the items on the list that have the most promise for your writing; put the items on the list in some order—say, most important to least important; cross out items you don't like; expand one or two items; add new items. The important thing is for the list to serve as a source of ideas. The most valuable use of the list will be what it reveals to you—what you see when you review it.

The Best Uses for Making a List:

For seeing the bits and pieces of your thoughts form a picture

For putting things or ideas in sequence

For seeing the way entries sort themselves into groups

For exploring alternatives

For jogging your memory

Guides for Making a List

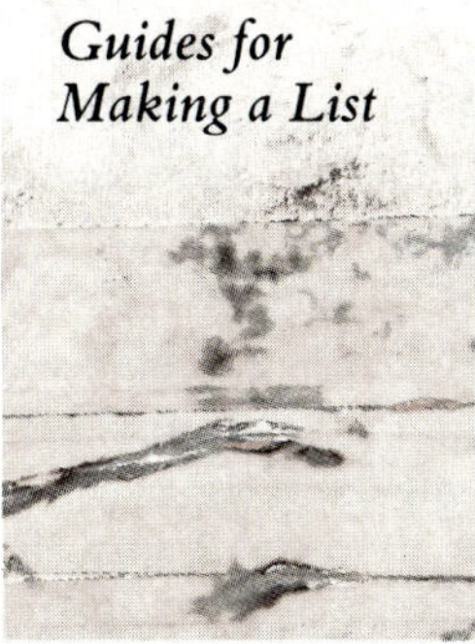

1. Put a title at the top of your list so you will stay on purpose and always know why you are making the list. ("Why I deserve a raise" or "Things our town could do for young adults.")
2. Write as fast as possible and use single words or short phrases.
3. Don't be critical of any item on the list at this point; just collect as many entries on the list as you possibly can in a limited time.
4. Set a time limit. Force yourself to concentrate.

Examples:

Doing a quick review of a subject

Preparing an impromptu discussion

Writing on a subject that you already have ideas about

Ordering or arranging your ideas or plans

Practicing Making a List. Elizabeth Cade is president of the local Chamber of Commerce. She must prepare a report to mail to the membership in which she outlines new directions for the organization for the coming year. She dreads this writing task because she isn't sure what she wants to say. She sits down and begins a *creating stage,* and finds that ideas emerge that give her confidence that the report can be done. Here is the *creating stage* for the report:

What do I want the Chamber of Commerce to do next year?

1. Get new business and industry into our town.
2. Sponsor a series of symphony concerts for young people.
3. Have more meetings.
4. Get a government grant to set up a tutoring center for adults in the community.
5. Buy the old Mansard House and convert it into a library and reception hall for the organization.

That list seemed to be everything she could think of right off the bat, so she reread what she had written and had this talk with herself:

What does this list reveal to me?

1. That I have long- and short-range goals for the chamber.
2. That I need to decide which of my goals I want the most.
3. That I have lots of ideas on things to do but not many on where to get the money to do them.

So I'd better do some serious thinking on this before I start my report. Serious thinking about what? About arranging goals into short- and long-term groups. About arranging goals in order of importance. About places to get money. Great. So now you know exactly what you need to think about. Right.

In this example you can see how Ms. Cade uses the creating stage to make list of things she'd like to do in order to organize her thoughts and direct her energies. And you can also quite clearly see that she is discovering what she thinks as she goes along. She is spotting areas she needs to concentrate on and seeing problems that she hadn't thought of until she sat down to put words on paper. Her final report will be much better because she goes through a creating stage *before* she begins writing the report.

Chaining

CHAIN:
A series of things linked, connected, or associated together.

CHAINING:
A series of thoughts so related to each other that each one initiates the next.

Chaining is a simple creating technique that uses questions and answers in order to stimulate connections and relationships. Chaining is particularly valuable as a method that allows you to build one thought off another and, through this, produce something new.

Chaining works like this: The first question becomes the first "link" in the chain. The answer to that question then becomes the second "link." Then a question related to the answer becomes the third. And so on. By asking and answering your own questions, you can produce a chain of thought that builds on itself.

Here is an example of how a student used chaining to get ideas on a subject:

Investing Money

Q: How do I get enough money to invest?

A: You work.

Q: What kind of work will earn me enough money to invest?

A: Something that pays a lot.

Q: How do I get a job that pays a lot?

A: You go out and look for it.

Q: Well, what if I can't find it?

A: You keep looking.

Q: Well, what if investing money has nothing to do with working or with the job you have at all?

A: Well, that's possible.

Q: But, see, how can I *get* the money to invest if I don't work?

A: You could borrow it.

Q: Well, how am I going to borrow it?

A: From a banker or a friend or a broker.

Q: Well, what would I use for collateral?

A: I don't know.

Q: Well, what can I do now about investing money?

A: You could read up on the subject and learn it thoroughly—or as thoroughly as possible until you had the money.

Q: But why can't I begin investing now and learn as I go?

A: Well, you don't have money of your own. It doesn't look as if you could borrow any now.

Q: But what if I could borrow some?

A: Perhaps you are afraid of losing the money you borrow from someone else.

Q: Is that really it? Am I afraid to move into investing money because I am afraid I will lose at the game?

A: Sounds like a real possibility.

Q: What does this show me?

A: How about this—that you could find lots of ways to get the money and invest it, if you were willing to risk losing it.

As you can see from this example, chaining can throw light on a subject that has reached a dead end. Asking and answering questions like these often helps you get at the truth of a subject that you need to explore.

The Best Uses for Chaining:

For getting unstuck on a subject

For coming upon an insight by indirect action or surprise

For finding out what your personal approach or position is on this topic or subject

For following a thought through to its conclusion

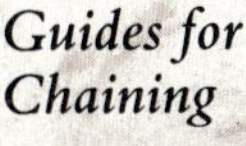

Guides for Chaining

1. At the top of your paper write the subject to be explored.
2. Begin by asking a question about this subject.
3. Let the answer to the first question lead to the next question.
4. Keep asking and answering questions until you get an insight into the topic.

Examples:

Writing your personal viewpoint on a subject

Preparing a position paper

Presenting a reasoned argument on a subject

Describing a process or a procedure

Looping

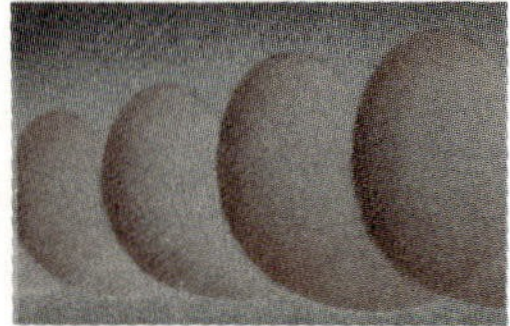

Looping is a writing activity in which you start with a subject and, without planning or consciously thinking, write anything that comes into your mind on the topic. This technique lets you explore a subject to see what you know about it without deciding whether the ideas are good or bad, or whether they are important enough to do a paper on. The looping activity also gets other things that are on your mind out on paper so they don't block your mind as you work. (This technique is based on an approach Peter Elbow discusses in his book *Writing Without Teachers;* you would enjoy reading his version.)

The dog that trots about finds the bone.
—Spanish proverb

Begin with a Specific Topic. At the top of the page, put down the subject (topic) you are going to write on in the loop. This allows your mind to focus at the beginning. As you write, you may discover that your mind gets off the subject and you are writing about something else entirely. When this happens, go ahead and finish what you are writing about and then go back to the subject you listed at the top of the page and concentrate on *that* subject. Often what you write *off* the subject will be something that is *on* your mind, perhaps worrying you. Or what you write may look as if it were off the subject but is actually connected somehow. Either way, "off-the-subject" writing is valuable because either it gets whatever is on your mind (and in the way of your thoughts on the subject) out onto paper, or it gives you an idea that you didn't at first think was connected to the topic. The aim of looping, however, is to come up with some idea on a specific subject for a paper; staying on that subject as closely as possible is the best thing to do.

Guides for Looping

1. Begin with a specific topic.
2. Write nonstop for x number of minutes.
3. Make no changes or corrections.
4. Write a center of gravity sentence for each loop before going on to the next one.

Write Nonstop for* x *Minutes. This rule is simple but crucial. Allow five minutes for each loop when you are first learning the technique. Later, you will want to vary the time, depending on the subject and on the time you have. You *must* keep writing. Do not lift your pencil or pen off the page. Keep it moving the whole five minutes. You can write things like "I can't think of anything on this topic," or "This topic is dumb," or "I despise this looping activity." You may even draw circles or make chicken-scratch marks on the paper, but *you must keep the pen moving*. This is to keep your thoughts stirred up and your mind open to whatever ideas occur.

Make No Corrections. Whether a writer follows this rule or breaks it will determine the success of looping. It is just that simple. You absolutely cannot stop to think about whether a word is spelled right or whether a comma is in the wrong place. You cannot stop to judge whether a statement you have just written is stupid or smart. You cannot stop to decide whether or not you want to say something. *Any kind of correcting or deliberating will cause the looping activity to fail.* (There is, of course, a time to correct your work; however, it isn't during the *creating stage*.) The purpose of looping is to scare up ideas, and to do that you need to forge ahead, not to pause or polish. So don't mark anything out; don't change anything. Just keep writing.

We can't use our minds at full capacity unless we have some idea of how much of what we think we're thinking is really thought, and how much is just familiar words running along their own familiar tracks. There's always the danger of automatic fluency, turning on a tap and letting a lot of . . . bumble emerge.
—Northrop Frye

Write Center of Gravity Sentences. When you have finished each loop, scan what you have written. What are you most drawn to in this loop? What did your mind go back to as you wrote? What do you seem to be drifting toward in this group of sentences? If you had to pick out the thing that "weighs" the most—that has the most interest, the most potential for you—what would that be? This is your center of gravity for the loop.

The center of gravity may appear, perfectly stated, in the loop. Or you may have written around it, rather than stating it directly in a single sentence. Look over what you have written and make a quick, unstudied decision about what your center of gravity is. If you don't find it or can't think of what it might be, make one up. This isn't a test—it is merely a way to come back to home base after exploring uncharted territory. The center of gravity will ground your thinking for a few seconds before you begin to loop out again.

After you have written the center of gravity sentence for the first loop, do two additional loops to complete the creating activity. (Be sure to include a center of gravity sentence after the second and third loops.)

Practicing Looping. To be sure that you understand how looping helps you have ideas on a subject, do a dry run. Take an unspecific subject, a very broad one, and see how the technique leads you to have something quite specific and focused to say about the topic. Run through the creating stage on the subject of *opportunity*.

Topic: Opportunity

To write a five-minute loop on the subject of opportunity, you will need some clean paper (be sure you have plenty) and a pen that won't run out of ink (you may want to have a spare handy). Write the word *opportunity* at the top of the first sheet. Have a clock, watch, or timer so that you know when the five minutes are up. Be clear about the rules: **no stopping, no changing, no correcting.**

OK. Ready?

Write the first five-minute loop on **Opportunity.**

What happened during that five minutes of writing? Did you write much on the subject itself? Did you find that your thoughts mostly rambled and didn't stay on the subject at all? Did you get bored? Did your hand hurt from writing?

Whatever you wrote about in this first loop is right! In the *creating stage* there is no wrong way; every word you write will contribute to your finding something to say. You will see later exactly why this is so.

Find the center of gravity in this first loop on **Opportunity.**

Reread it. Your writing probably moved in several directions and raised a number of different points. But if you *had* to write a single sentence that caught the thing you would most like to discuss, what would that sentence be? This center of gravity sentence may not be the thing you *wrote the most* about; it may instead be the thing you *like most* in the writing or the thing you find the *most interesting*. Or it might be the idea or subject you *returned to* several times in the loop. Just make a decision. If you can't determine the center of gravity in that loop, just make up what you *think* it is.

Write this center of gravity sentence at the end of your first loop.

Now you are ready for the second loop. The rules are the same: Your pen can't stop on the page. You can't correct. You can't make judgments about whether or not your writing is good. You are just writing to see what there is to think about this subject.

One thing to note about the second and third loops is that they begin wherever they begin. They do not have to be connected to the loop that came ahead of them. They may turn out to start exactly where the last loop left off. But they may also start someplace totally unrelated to the loop before. Looping is like taking a snapshot of your mind at the moment you are writing—whatever is in that "picture" is what the loop will contain. *There is no way to do this wrong.*

Write the second five-minute loop on **Opportunity.**

Now, read over what you wrote this time. Did anything pop up that didn't surface last time? Anything absolutely new? Or did you write about the same thing you wrote about last time? This loop may be closely related to the first one, may be something that *grew out of* the first loop, or may be *completely different from* the first loop. Any of these outcomes is all right.

Find the center of gravity in the second loop on **Opportunity.**

Remember that the center of gravity sentence is whatever you think it is. It can be what you *wrote* about the most, what you *liked* the most, what you are drawn to the most. Anything you think is the center of gravity *is* the center of gravity.

Write one sentence expressing that.

Get ready to repeat the process one more time. Set your timer for five minutes, and begin.

Write the third five-minute loop on **Opportunity.**

When you finish this third loop, read it. *Then write the center of gravity sentence at the bottom of the page.*

Congratulations! You have finished the complete cycle. And you are probably tired. Get up and stretch.

Usually by the end of the third loop you have come up with an idea that could be developed into an essay, something you could share with another person. Something will have stirred you or excited you or interested you; it may have just barely cropped up in the loop writings, but there are strong odds that you do see *something* to use as a slightly more focused subject than the broad word *opportunity.* If so, you are ready at the end of the third loop to move on to the next step in the writing process, the *shaping stage,* in which you make a discovery draft of a piece of writing that you will give to another person. If an idea has not surfaced by the end of the third loop, you might try writing an extra loop or two, or you might switch to another creating technique to see if it will work better.

STUDENT EXAMPLE & ESSAY Looping

Here are the loops and the essay that one student wrote.

Loop 1

This may be the start of a bad habit. I bought this new pen today so I could write neater and now I'm doing a looping with it. Oh, well, I'll just be careful of my pen. First of all, to get some things off my mind before I write on opportunity (which is a very dumb topic). Excuse me, but my pen's messing up. First of all, the coach of the football team resigned today and that's pretty sad because he's a human being and what will he do and where will he go from here. Also, I'm mad at my best friend because I was taking a nap and she turned the television on. Later I found out she wasn't even watching anything. Now, to zero in on opportunity. I have had opportunities to sing, to dance, to jog, to be me. I've had lots of opportunities throughout my life. I was brought up in a nice home with neat parents who never fought in front of me and who will be married for 25 years this August. I went to a great high school with a rotten football team, but that's OK because I guess I learned a lot about people while I was there. I learned a lot about boys anyway! Ha. In high school they were all nerds. Oh, well, what will be will be. I also went to a nice church and we had lots of kids and a fabulous choir director. We put on musicals and went all over the United States. I almost didn't take that opportunity, though, because I hated choir at first. I never did want to go to rehearsals. I really didn't want to spend my Saturdays all day practicing music and choreography. I'm glad I did, though. That was a neat opportunity my parents *made* me do.

Center of gravity sentence: *I've had lots of opportunities in my life, and some of them my parents made me take when I didn't want to.*

Loop 2

I really have . . . I guess I'm glad my parents made me do those things. In fact, I'm more than glad; I'm ecstatic. Really, I think my best opportunity is myself, though, how I am. I owe it to my parents for bringing me up the way they did, though. They instilled values and personality into me. But right now going to college, planning my biggest opportunity is about myself—*is* myself. I guess that sounds conceited but . . . I'm thinking about something a former teacher of mine told me, that writing was an art and a writer didn't have to paint by number or follow lines. Well, that's the way I feel about my opportunities to get out there and make something of my life. See, I'm the artist; I hold the brushes and the oils and my parents' training is the. . . . I have the opportunity to be anybody I want this person to be. Conceit, conceit, conceit. I better narrow this thing down further. I have grabbed opportunities and created opportunities by all the things I've done. One way that I've realized this and changed my attitude about myself in the world is by working in Colorado this summer cleaning cabins. I've always thought of myself as a city girl, but I've always loved the mountains, so when the opportunity came, I went to clean cabins. I look back on it now and think, man, what all different opportunities there were. I learned how to fly fish, how to flip gas refrigerators to make the freon circulate. I think, most of all, I had the opportunity to learn that it's people who make a feeling, not a place. A place can bring back memories, but it can't make you feel things. I don't know, I thought I was just going to clean cabins, and I ended up learning lots about business.

Center of gravity sentence: *My biggest opportunity is MYSELF, and I proved this by working in Colorado this summer.*

Loop 3

When I was a little girl, we used to go to Taylor Park, Colorado, for vacation, and we found this rickety place called Holt's Guest Ranch. I'll never know what made me love that place so much except maybe it was the childhood memories I feel there. Fishing with my dad. Dancing at family night. Anyway, Mr. and Mrs. Holt always hired two college girls to work with them. I used to tag along behind them, and Mrs. Holt would always say, "Debbi, someday when you're in college, maybe you can come work for us." I had all my plans made when I was nine. . . . I realize as I write this that what looked like an opportunity last summer wasn't just a fluke or just good luck. I, myself, brought that opportunity about by keeping in touch with Mrs. Holt, even after they sold the ranch to the Speers who almost ruined it, and then when they bought it back. And, especially, I caused that opportunity to happen when I told Mrs. Holt last year to call me if they kept the cabins. I wonder how many things we call opportunities are really like this; we do things that make the opportunities happen. I feel real encouraged by thinking about this. If I—*myself*—made that opportunity happen last summer, can I do it again? And I am really proud of what I learned by taking advantage of that opportunity. I remember that first night there. I slept in Dad's flannel pajamas, long Fruit-of-the-Loom underwear and lined ski socks. We had two beds, but the thermal coupling in the heater was broken, so my roommate and I slept in the same bed to keep warm. Also, I didn't want to sleep in my bed because there was a dead mouse in it. [Squiggles] I don't know what else to write. I'm tired of thinking about opportunities. I wish the timer would go off and I could stop this loop. Great, there it is.

Center of gravity sentence: *I made my own opportunity.*

When Debbi finished these three loops, she had a subject for her essay. She decided to write on the idea that occurred in her second loop. "My biggest opportunity is *MYSELF,* and I proved this by working in

Colorado this summer." Now read the essay she wrote on this subject. You will easily see the connection between her creating activity and the content of the essay itself.

CONFIDENCE

Last April my telephone rang early in the morning, and it took me a full thirty seconds to recognize Mrs. Holt's voice. She wanted me to come to Colorado that summer and clean the guest cabins at her ranch. I thought about it a while and decided to go. I told myself, "This is a great opportunity to make money." What I learned during the summer, however, was that there is a bigger opportunity than making money. That opportunity is having confidence in yourself.

I flew from my hometown on May 19. When we arrived in Colorado, the temperature was 38 degrees. I got off the plane and realized that I had to carry both my suitcases and my clothes bag myself. This was just one of the things I was to discover during the summer that I had to do for myself. All the way up the drive in the canyon to the ranch, I kept thinking, "Don't forget how much money you are going to make. It will be worth it all." I was really scared.

It is true that the summer was a great opportunity to make money. I saved $500. My salary was $250 a month plus room and board. With all the baked potatoes and gravy and even some boiled cabbage that I finally learned to swallow, I felt I came out on the good end of the room and board part of the deal. I was able to save almost all my salary because there was nothing to spend it on except maybe an occasional tube of toothpaste at Sherm Cranor's Taylor Park Trading Post.

Sometime during the early summer, I quit thinking about the opportunity to make money. I began to experience the opportunity of proving myself and accomplishing hard and new things by myself. It was really rough running a guest ranch. There was always a pilot light that had gone out or a toilet that wouldn't flush. There was always a beaver to clog up the irrigation ditch or a guest who needed dry bath towels at the strangest moment. I learned all about leaky pipes and the parts of a toilet. I spent hours plunging with my plumber's friend. I even learned how to run a "snake" through sewer pipes. I made beds in three minutes flat, and I washed three million dirty bath and tea towels every day. I set thousands of mouse traps. I learned how to light the pilot on cooking and heating stoves. I helped flip refrigerators so their freon would circulate, and I exploded them when they wouldn't draw the air up. I painted signs and cleaned the fireplace and dusted furniture and even helped lay linoleum in the laundry room. (It got a big wrinkle down the middle. We nicknamed it the Continental Divide.)

So, what I had thought would be just an opportunity to make money turned out to be an opportunity to grow with myself. I found out so many things about me. I became very proud of myself and what I was able to learn and do. I found out I really liked people. It made me feel good to work hard and accomplish things. I even learned to like cabbage.

Someday, I'll go back. By then I am sure that I will have grabbed a lot more opportunities to make myself proud of me. And I will probably even make money on top of it.

APPLICATION

1. Apply one or more of the basic creating techniques (Reporter's Formula; Brainstorming; Listing; Chaining; Looping) to one of the following writing situations (see the table summarizing these techniques on page 28). Write the creating stage and then discuss it with a group of classmates.
   A. You are a student whose teacher has just assigned a first essay: a description of your home town. What would you write in the creating stage for this assignment?
   B. You are looking for a job; the employment counselor tells you to write a short paper in which you describe the jobs you have had in the past and the skills you developed as a result. What would you write in the creating stage for this assignment?
   C. You are a member of a sports or social club that will be listed in a newspaper supplement on "Things to Do." You are the person who will prepare the information on your club for the newspaper. Write the creating stage for this short newspaper article.
2. Work with several other students brainstorming, listing, or chaining to explore one of the following writing situations.
   A. An administrator at your school wants your team to prepare a guidebook for new students on campus. What would you write in the creating stage for this job?
   B. A local government official has challenged your group to prepare a problem-solution paper on homelessness in your town, city, or county. What would you write in the creating stage for this assignment?
   C. Your local government is considering a ban on bicycles and motorcycles on roads in the area of your campus. Your group has been asked by fellow students to suggest reasons for opposing this ban. What would you write in the creating stage for this assignment?
3. Select one of the following topics and do three five-minute loops on it:

Families	Work
Music	Travel
Women (or Men)	Time

Technique	*Characteristic*	*Works Best For*	*Strengths*	*Weaknesses*
Reporter's Formula 	familiar, a set pattern	viewing subject as "thing" or separate entity; giving clear, objective information	produces factual information, detail; can suggest actual order/organization of finished writing	can be routine, unimaginative; can be applied only to *some* subjects (not all); separates writer from subject
Brainstorming 	group activity	breaking mental blocks, getting fresh approaches	ranges widely; uncritical; works off other people's ideas	may seem merely silly, horseplay
Listing 	simple, direct	gathering facts, details, points which already exist	quick, easy	limited application; requires the previous information to be there and within reach
Chaining 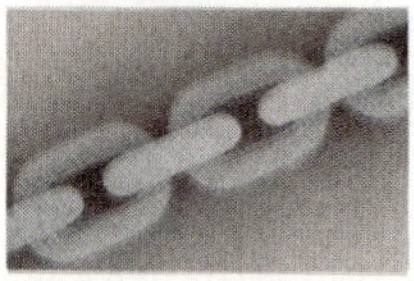	linking thoughts	getting unstuck; finding own personal position	takes advantage of mind's natural tendency to relate thoughts; familiar format; provides structure for revealing surprise connections	can remain at a superficial level indefinitely; may seem like an artificial device; can go on forever
Looping 	unstructured; a fishing expedition	exploring in a free, wide-range way	brings surprises and pleasures; lets the strongest thing emerge	usually takes several loops to work; may not always give depth

When you have completed all three loops, review what you have written. If you were required to write a paper on some idea that occurred to you during this creating stage, what would you write about?

4. Discuss the topic you arrived at in application 3 with several of your colleagues. Were you surprised by the topic? Was it something you hadn't thought about for a long time? What did you like about it? What makes it seem like a good subject for a paper?

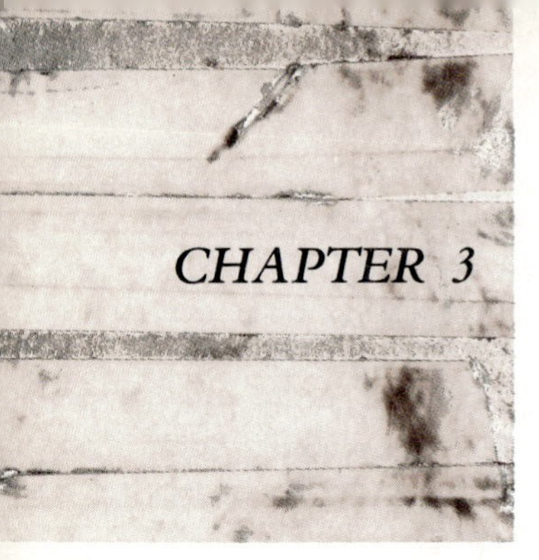

The Shaping Stage

In the creating stage of writing you can lose yourself in ideas; at this early point, nothing matters but the project you are working on. When creating is going well, a project may absorb you and your colleagues completely. You talk, write, think, discover for what seems like minutes, only to discover that an hour has gone or that you've skipped lunch—and you didn't even miss it.

If you set out to discover only what you think about a subject, then you might be finished when you've done the creating. But the value and power of ideas comes in sharing them with others—putting them in circulation, making them part of the conversation. To accomplish that, you move on to the second stage in the writing process, one determined by the world around you.

Writing for the world assumes a relationship between a writer and readers based upon common ideas and assumptions; we write for communities we understand, want to join, want to learn from, or want to address. Even in our most private moments and thoughts, we are part of larger worlds that have shaped us—our families, our neighborhoods, our ethnic heritage, our religion, our country. Writing is one way we respond to all these worlds. Each of them may evoke a different response from us or compel us to shape our ideas in a particular way. These worlds—our audiences—participate in our life by receiving, reading, engaging, and criticizing what we have written. It's this partnership, this mutual engagement of self and other, that makes writing one of the most powerful ways we have of knowing our world. But the communication doesn't always work.

You can't do much about the audience's role in the communication partnership directly. The writer's role—your role—you can do everything about. That is why you shape what you write and involve others in the shaping process: you do whatever is possible to make the communication clear, focused, sensible, and recognizable to the community you are addressing. You don't shape because rules in an English book tell you to; you shape because you want to be read. You want the audiences you respect to respect the work you do.

For most students using this book, the shaping force for their writing is something called the "academic community." That's a technical term for school, for "college writing." It is the standard evoked when someone suggests that an idea isn't college-level or that a paper doesn't read like university material, or that a point is vague or unsupported by convincing evidence. But you won't find a short checklist of academic standards anywhere; it's something you absorb gradually through taking courses, doing your school work, reading your assignments, and following the recommendations made in texts like this for writing public or professional prose. It's the shaping force behind words like *clarity, organization, focus, evidence, reasonableness*—qualities that are identified with academic writing. The "audience" referred to in this text will be a kind of reader who is comfortable with the assumptions of academic writing.

Shaping any writing—but especially academic writing—is a complex process with many paths and byways. In this chapter, we'll review the most basic considerations in shaping a paper: how to assess purpose, how to write for an audience, how to write a discovery draft, and how to shape a thesis. More detailed aspects of shaping are covered in Part 3 of this book, "Crafting the Portfolio."

PRELIMINARY AGREEMENTS

Long before you write your first drafts of the communication you intend to give to someone else, shaping begins. Shaping is already starting when you make certain preliminary agreements with yourself.

The shape of what you are going to say begins to form itself as you consider the following questions: "Why am I writing?" "To whom am I writing?" "What do I want to communicate?"

In this early shaping stage, your answers to these questions will be tentative. Only as you do the "first cut" on paper—as you write your early discovery draft—will you "see" distinctly what your purpose is, who your specific audience is, and exactly what you want to write.

Many people have trouble getting started in the shaping stage because they want these answers too early. They are impatient to know exactly what the message is going to be, exactly how the first words of the writing are going to begin, and exactly what approach they are going to take. However, these are things a writer finds out only in the act of writing itself.

Why Are You Writing?

To help you decide on your preliminary purpose and intention for your chosen piece of writing, here are two ways of looking at the act of communicating.

The Transmission Model. Your intention might be to *transmit* something you think or know to someone else. The model for this kind of communication would look like this:

> From your past experience/reading/discussion/knowledge, you choose an idea to transmit to another person. Using words on paper, you select and sort to encode this message.
>
> From the reader's past experience/reading/discussion/knowledge, he or she decodes the message you have transmitted, and selects and sorts in order to reconstruct your idea in his or her thinking, to recreate what you have said.

If your purpose in writing is to transmit a message, then you are satisfied when the reader "gets the message," understands what you meant, and "hears" what you had to say. Thus, your purpose in this model of communication is something like this:

> I am writing to give information about . . .
>
> I am writing to share an insight I have had . . .
>
> I am writing to get this off my chest . . .
>
> I am writing to answer a request . . .

The Transformation Model. Another way to approach the communication of information through writing is as *transformation,* rather than simply as *transmission.* In this communication model, you write to change and/or affect the reader's actions. The transformation model of communication looks like this:

> The writer begins with an intention or a commitment to have the reader think about a thing in a certain way, to do a certain thing, or to act in a certain way. From the writer's knowledge/experience/reading, he or she chooses those words that bring about the transformation that the writing intends to accomplish. The writer knows that the communication works when the reader changes or acts in the ways the writer intended.

> The reader begins by considering the possibility of being affected by the writing seriously enough to read what has been written. Then, from past experience/reading/knowledge, he or she chooses whether to accept what has been written and to do what the writer has requested, suggested, or recommended.

When your purpose is to spur the reader into action, you write with the *intention* that your communication will produce the intended action. Whereas the transmission model requires simply that you organize and pass on information in a readable, engaging form, the transformation model requires that, as the writer, you be *responsible* for what you say and for what you urge the reader to do; that is, you must be open and aboveboard about what it is that you are urging the reader to do or think. Unlike subliminal advertisements, which present one idea or product in the foreground while actually selling another in the background (for example, a woman in a bikini leaning against a particular make of car), the transformation model makes a direct, action-oriented presentation. The reader is a partner, with the responsibility to read and consider the communication directly.

Of course, you cannot *make* the reader join you in this partnership, and you need to remember that the final acceptance of your request or idea is strictly up to the reader. But if you write in the responsible manner described here, your written communication will have the ring of authenticity that will engage the reader's willingness to enter into the partnership.

If you are writing to *transform,* your purpose might be phrased like this:

> I am writing to persuade my reader that . . .
>
> I am writing to get my reader to . . .
>
> I am writing to direct people to do . . .
>
> I am writing to argue that . . .
>
> I am writing to require that . . .
>
> I am writing to propose that . . .
>
> I am writing to make the distinction . . .

Virtually any subject can be written about in terms of the transmission model or the transformation model. Take, for example, the following subject:

SUBJECT: VOTING FOR A PRESIDENTIAL CANDIDATE

Transmission Model	*Transformation Model*
Purpose: To let the reader know what you think or know.	Purpose: To get the reader to do something.
Emphasis: Explain how the electoral college works.	Emphasis: Convince the reader that a free society depends on the participation of all its citizens.
End Result: The reader should understand the voting process.	End Result: The reader should go out and vote.

APPLICATION

1. Imagine that a group of friends is taking a trip together next summer. What preliminary agreements would they need to make, far in advance of taking the trip?
2. Choose one of the following topics:

   Watching the Superbowl

   Paying for school

   Dealing with crime

   Dealing with poverty

Speak to a classmate first with an intention to use the transmission model. Then, in a separate conversation, use the transformation model. Which was easier? What kind of shift did you find yourself making between the two conversations?

3. Read the following paragraphs first as if they were written from the transmission model of communication. Then read the paragraphs as if they were written from the transformation model.

   Four million people are facing starvation in Mozambique, Africa, out of a population of 13.4 million. According to a *New York Times* correspondent, "Maputo (the capital of Mozambique) is a city of tired and listless people and silent, patient food lines."

   While most of Mozambique is experiencing food shortages, the three provinces in which hunger is most widespread are Tete, Sofala, and Manica in the central and northwestern parts of the country.

Certain types of leaves and fruit found in Mozambique are believed by the people to be more harmful than nourishing, and are therefore eaten only at times of distress. Many people in Mozambique are now eating these leaves and fruits as their only food.

Last year, famine in Mozambique killed more than 100,000 people. A similar situation is now said to be "unavoidable" for the 1990s.

What kind of shift did you make in reading these paragraphs from two different communication models? From which communication model would you guess the writer wrote the paragraphs? Discuss these questions with your classmates.

4. Look at this list of subjects and identify the communication model—transmission or transformation—that most obviously fits the topic:

How to stay alive in the Arctic

When to plant onions

How to clean up the air

Where to find the best bargains on tires in town

Why your heart is broken

Why your heart is strong

Why you like physical education

To Whom Are You Writing?

When you talk, you don't have to invent an audience because an audience is there. You may have to *analyze* your audience when you talk—for example, find out what age they are, what they already know about your subject, etc.—but you don't have to make up an audience. In writing, however, because the audience is not actually present in the room with you, you must both visualize and analyze the audience. But what if you don't visualize and know your audience before you start writing?

Well, if you write a paper to no one, then the only audience you are likely to attract are people who like papers written with no particular audience in mind. How many people like that can there be? If you choose to write an essay with no audience in mind, or "forget" about the audience, or write for a general audience, it all comes to the same thing: you are actually deciding that your audience will be those few souls in the universe who like dull prose. If you know your audience in advance, however, you can plan the whole essay around this group of people. You gain enormously by having your audience in mind from the very start.

The problem with writing to a general audience is that you tend to scatter your efforts broadly rather than focus them on real people. It's the difference between sunlight falling broadly on the earth and sunlight focused through a lens—one can light a fire; the other can't.

It is crucial to note who your specific audience is at the outset (or to select an audience if the choice is yours) because your approach to the subject will be determined by who this audience is. Just suppose that you were writing an essay to inform your readers about the attractiveness of the town you live in as a vacation spot. Sure, why not? People always think they have to go *somewhere* to have a vacation. What might happen if they came to your town? Of course, the question has more obvious answers if you live in a place like San Francisco or Las Vegas, but even the most unpromising places can be appealing—if you bother to work out the appeal.

If you were to explain the attractions of your town to potential tourists, what would you say? What would the differences be in how you approached the subject if your audience were:

people your own age	foreign travelers
people with small children	retired people
out-of-state visitors	

You can see right away how many decisions would turn out one way for one group of people, another way for other people. Almost everything would depend on which audience you wanted to attract.

If you are writing for a "college audience," you would probably emphasize the qualities respected in an academic community—sober, reasoned arguments; well-organized ideas; conventional language and usage. You would need to be fairly formal in tone; your sentences could not sound like ordinary conversation. You would be unusually careful about defining terms, providing ample evidence, and citing your sources because you expect that academic readers will be concerned with such matters: they tend to admire precision and clarity. In many situations, you would be writing simultaneously for people at your own level of expertise—that is, other students—and those with an expert's level of knowledge, your instructors. And you would be shaping your writing according to the nature of individual courses and assignments. A one-page "position paper" in a literature class might allow you to be more free-wheeling and speculative than a formal term paper in philosophy.

As you can see, not only the approach and purpose in writing are influenced by your preliminary sense of audience, but also the content of the writing itself. Understanding the nature of the community you are addressing and of the typical reader in that community gives you a perspective from which to shape your writing.

What Do You Want to Communicate?

You will know only vaguely what you want to communicate when you begin the *shaping stage* of writing—in fact, you will know mostly what you think you want to say at this point. Sometime in the *creating stage* the

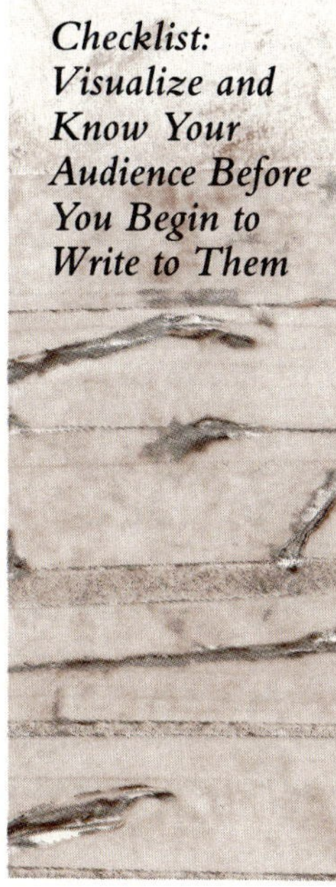

Checklist: Visualize and Know Your Audience Before You Begin to Write to Them

1. Know the truth about *all* audiences.
   They do not like to be bored; they do like to be stimulated.
   They want a feeling of achievement or accomplishment.
   They want to get something out of what they read.
   They are busy and don't want their time wasted.
   They often have things to do besides read.
   They need explanations and details.
   They like order and hate chaos.
2. Picture a *specific* audience.
   Who is the audience?
   What do you know about this audience?
   How old? What educational background? What kind of work?
   What is the audience's attitude toward the subject?
   How much does the audience already know about the subject?
   Will they already be interested in the subject? Why?
3. Decide what your audience is like and what it is likely to understand, find stimulating, need to know, enjoy . . . and
4. Deliver that.

idea you wanted to communicate began to emerge. Now you have to communicate this idea to someone else to see what you do think and what you want that person to know. So, it is a case of both knowing and not knowing: you have an idea of what you want to communicate, and yet you won't really know what you want to communicate about that idea and just how you are going to present that idea until you put it down on paper. Eventually, this will become a clear thesis for your paper. But at this point, the idea of what you want to say will be a starting point for discovering what that thesis will be. The only thing for you to do at this point, when you know vaguely what you want to say, is to *get started.* And the way to do that is just to jump right in and begin writing your first discovery draft.

APPLICATION

1. Turn to the chart comparing the two models of communication—writing to transmit and writing to transform—that appears earlier in this section. Prepare a similar chart on one of the following subjects, showing how the purpose determines what will be emphasized in the writing and what the end result of the writing will be.

a movie you have seen
a holiday celebration
a sport you like
a place you have been

2. Think of writing an essay that would describe your town as an attractive vacation spot. Make a list of things you would talk about for each of the following audiences:

people with small children	out-of-state visitors
retired people	a group you make up

When you finish your five lists, look at the ways each list differs from the others because of what is needed for the specific readers. Which audience seems to you easiest to write for? Which is hardest? Why? Which would you most enjoy writing for? Why? (Do you see, now, how having a *specific* set of readers in mind at the outset of your writing process takes care of a lot of those initial decisions?)

3. Choose one of the following writing contexts. After you have completed a creating technique for the subject, decide what you would write about if you were going to do an essay or an article. State what you would say on the subject in a sentence or two and discuss it with your classmates. (Naturally, this idea will be tentative and may change completely when you start the shaping stage.)
   A. You have been asked to speak to a group of parents whose children will begin their first year of college in the fall. Do the creating stage for this speech, and then summarize in one or two sentences what you think you would say if you were going to write the speech.
   B. You have lived (a) in the country and now live in town, (b) in town and now live in the country, (c) the same place all your life.

      For a class assignment you have been asked to write about the advantages of living in place *x* (choose one of the above). Do the creating stage for this essay, and then summarize what you would want to say if you were going to begin a discovery draft of the essay.
   C. You have been asked by the school's science fiction club to write the club's newsletter about (a) *Star Trek,* (b) *Star Wars,* or (c) *Aliens.* Do a creating stage on this article, and then summarize in one or two sentences what your main idea would be for the essay were you to begin a discovery draft.

THE DISCOVERY DRAFT

You are now ready to start writing the paper. You have made tentative agreements about what your purpose is for writing, who your audience is, and what you want to say. You still don't have any idea, however, of how you want to begin.

That's the beauty of doing a discovery draft.

You get to write a version of the paper before you are smart. Before you know how the paper is going to develop. Before you know what specific points you are going to make.

You write to see how the paper is going to turn out. And while you are doing this discovery draft, you will see—probably for the first time—what you are saying and how you want to say it. You will also get a clearer sense—with almost every line you write—about the relationship between what you are writing and the people to whom you will be communicating.

The voyage of the best ship is a zigzag line of a hundred tacks. See the line from a sufficient distance, and it straightens itself [out].
—Emerson, "Self Reliance"

You will find this is a very natural process. In the process of getting something, anything, down on paper, your thoughts will develop under your very eyes, your purpose will become even clearer, and even the way you want to organize the writing may become apparent.

Or something else may occur: during the process of your thoughts developing, you may find that you want to start over completely because you don't have nearly as much to say as you thought you did on this subject. You may feel that you sound absolutely stupid. You may be certain by the end of the second or third paragraph that no person in the universe would be interested in what you have to say.

All these experiences and feelings are legitimate: the times when you do a discovery draft and find that the paper is almost writing itself, and the times when you do a discovery draft and find that nothing is working. In every case, the important thing is that you have begun. Until you have begun, no paper will ever be written. And, as an old French philosopher said, until you are willing to put black on white, you won't *have* anything to change, refine, improve, or fix. So jump in and write the first draft of the essay.

How to Write the Discovery Draft

Draft: Preliminary version of a document.

Begin your discovery draft by putting three things at the top of the first page: your **purpose** for writing, a short **description** of your audience, and the general **idea** you want to communicate. These won't appear on the final paper itself, of course, but for now they will remind you of the *reason* you are writing, the person or persons *to whom* you are writing, and the *message* you intend to deliver. They will set your mind in the right channel as you begin. If worse comes to worst—you still aren't sure of exactly what you want to tell the readers and you have no time left for creating activities—just put down your best guess and start the draft anyway. The shaping process will probably chase some good ideas out of hiding, and you can rewrite more purposefully later.

THE BIG THREE:
Beginning
Middle
End

Keep in Mind the Basic Arrangement of All Essays. The basic arrangement for all essays is beginning/middle/end. Sooner or later, the opening paragraph or paragraphs of your paper will have to:

- Get your readers' attention.
- Reveal or suggest the message you intend to send in the essay.
- Ease your readers into the very aspect/perspective of your subject you want them to think about.

The beginning (it may be one paragraph or several) provides a rationale both for writer and readers. For the writer, the opening explains what is to be attempted in the paper—the thesis. It spells out the scope and the limits of the effort so that a writer knows how to proceed, what he or she is responsible for. For the reader, the opening must provide the incentive for reading and a rationale for spending time with the writer. This doesn't mean that every opening paragraph must promise a Mardi Gras, only that the writer must supply some good reason for expecting readers—particularly in an academic setting—to take seriously what is written.

The middle of the essay must deliver on the promises made by the opening, arranging information or events coherently so that readers can follow them easily enough; it must expand upon the thesis in significant ways without losing readers in thickets of detail. Yet it must supply enough details to persuade, convince, inform—even amuse readers, if that is the paper's purpose. The middle must also be shapely; its coverage of various aspects of a subject should be in proportion to their importance. Consequently significant ideas get more attention and more dramatic placement than less important ones. And the middle should be replete with signposts that explain the relationships between ideas and keep readers headed in the right direction.

The middle paragraphs or body of the essay will have to:

- Stick to a thesis.
- Deliver the message as promised.
- Get the idea that was in your head into your readers' heads.

The ending of the paper will have to:

- Remind your readers of what you said.

- Give your readers at least one new thing or twist on the subject to consider.
- Provide a gentle landing so that your readers are not left hanging in mid-air.

"How do I know what I think until I see what I say?"—E. M. Forster

It isn't likely that you will be able to accomplish all of these in the discovery draft, but keeping in mind the purposes of each basic part of the essay will often feed your creativity and help you make spontaneous, even unconscious, decisions about what you want to say and how you want to say it.

Get Started on the Draft Itself. Actually start putting words on the page. Don't get caught in the cycle of writing and crossing out. And don't think of the hundred other things you could be doing—cleaning out your bureau drawers, washing the top of the refrigerator, calling a friend you haven't seen in four years. Handle this draft the way you handle swimming in cold water—just jump in! Start writing even if what you are putting down seems so obviously stupid that you are embarrassed to see it on the page. **Put it down.**

You already know that an essay always opens with some kind of introduction, so start there. Think of *anything* that can serve as an introduction. Tell a story; give a quote; ask some questions—anything that leads into what you want to discuss with the reader. Aim, if you can, for something interesting and catchy (since an introduction must be both). If you produce a workable introduction this time around, fine. If not, don't let that stop you. Keep moving; keep writing. The point is to start the draft, not to get stuck at the very beginning. If all else fails just write *Introduction* across the page and go on to the middle.

Involve the Reader from the Start. Remind yourself that you are writing to a person. You will be amazed at how many decisions you can make about what details to put into your paper and how to arrange them if you will only keep *this* reader and *this* situation in mind. On the other hand, remember that your reader won't be reading your discovery draft, so don't worry too much about writing correctly. If the idea of an audience begins to hinder instead of help you, just concentrate on expressing your ideas. You can get back to audience later.

Write More Instead of Less. Write every idea you can think of to communicate what you want your reader to know. This is the main part of your discovery draft. Your reader has very likely *not* been thinking about your subject and certainly hasn't done the creating activities you have done. And the reader probably has a different background and set of experiences from yours, too. So write plenty. Make all the points you can think of to convince or inform or explain. And when you suppose you have given enough information for your message to be very clear, add about 10 percent.

Don't Get Bogged Down! Don't worry at this point whether *this* example should come before *that* one. Don't worry if you can't spell some of the words, or if you can't recall a specific thing you are trying to think of. *You have to keep moving.* You can worry about all the rest later—you can take out, put in, fix up, skim down. Right now, however, you have to get the material onto the paper. Until you do, there simply isn't anything to revise.

Wrap Up the Essay. Go on and finish it, even if you think it is the worst thing you ever wrote. What was the main idea you wanted to leave in your readers' heads—even if you are sure you didn't achieve your intention? Put that idea down again now. Having written the discovery draft, you may have a better idea of what you actually do want to communicate than you did when you began writing. This restatement will help you revise later on. Some writers have to write the last paragraph of the discovery draft before they really know what they want to say in the opening paragraph of the revised draft. (This often happens because the idea actually grows and perhaps even changes during the discovery draft.) What value is your reader likely to find in what you have communicated? Write that down too. You may have insights now that you didn't have when you started. So don't lose them. They may be the inspirations that will encourage you to do the hard work of transforming this "diamond in the rough"—your first draft—into a polished gem.

When you think you have given the reader enough information so that he or she can understand exactly what you have been saying, it's time to bring the writing to a close. Maybe you do nothing more than write "Amen!" and let it go at that. Or "The End." But you *do* come to a close.

Put Your Discovery Draft Aside to Cool. When you have completed the discovery draft, you will probably feel wonderful, and you're entitled to. Whatever the faults of this draft, you have at least tested your idea and done a preliminary version of your writing. Sure, it looks rough. But you do have a complete paper, something you can work on later, and having *that* is exactly what you set out to achieve. Put the paper aside with a sigh of contentment—or at least of relief. Leave it for several hours or more. Set it on the windowsill to cool.

If you are working on a tight schedule and don't have time to let the paper cool for a few hours, at least do this: find a friend and read the paper out loud to him or her. Ask what message the person hears in

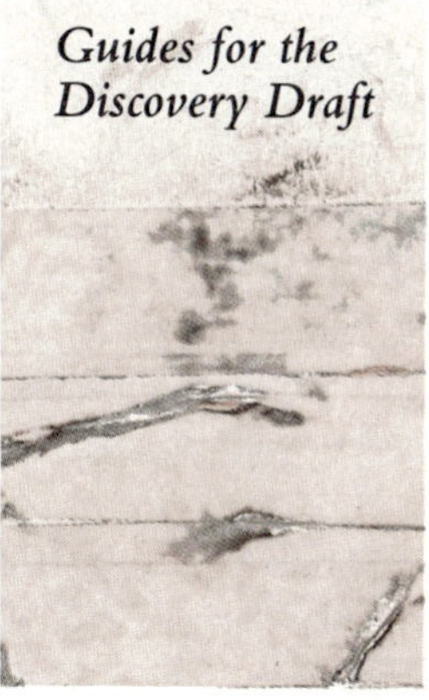

1. Recall why, to whom, and about what you are writing the essay.
2. Keep in mind the basic arrangement of all essays—beginning/middle/end.
3. Get started on the draft itself.
4. Involve the reader from the start.
5. Write more instead of less.
6. Don't get bogged down.
7. Wrap up the essay.
8. Put the discovery draft aside to cool.

the paper. Watch your listener's face and see if he or she looks confused as you read the paper. Listen to yourself and notice if you stumble anywhere as you read it. (*Research shows that wherever you stumble there is usually something that can stand to be changed in the writing.*) Ask your listener if the paper was boring. In general, get another person's response to what you have written.

Summary of Discovery Draft

Your discovery draft may be uneven, imperfect, and rough. But it can also be revelatory and exciting—it can make you see new things you are thinking. No matter how the first draft is turning out, remember that most of us do not know *what* we think on a subject until we write about it. And most of us need to continue to write to see how we want to say what we find out.

Discovery comes from taking chances, but the risks in writing a discovery draft are minimal compared to the results: getting something, anything, down on paper; learning what we really feel about a subject; seeing how our minds approach a certain issue.

THESIS AS A FOCUS

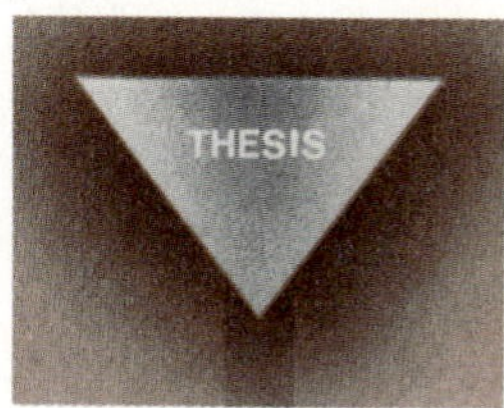

You might think it odd that little has been said about a thesis statement until now. That's because worrying about a specific thesis too early in the production of a paper can shut down the whole process faster than a blown fuse. It's usually better to start with a subject you are willing to explore and then allow the thesis to grow out of that topic during the creating stage and in the discovery draft.

For the sake of clarity, make sure you understand the difference between topic and thesis. The thesis is always much more definite than the topic or general subject of a paper. The thesis is, in fact, a specific statement about the topic—the central point you want to make about it. Consider the topic as a *thing;* the thesis as an *action.*

How to Write a Good Thesis

THESIS:
A setting down; something set down; a proposition stated or put forward for consideration, especially to be discussed or proved or maintained.

When you wrote your discovery draft, a thesis—or some hint of one—probably showed up. (Maybe even three or four!) But the thesis in a discovery draft is rarely developed enough to serve readers well; it may not even be identifiable.

If this is the case, you probably did your discovery draft right. You weren't supposed to be concerned about stating a clear thesis. In a true discovery draft, you are just getting words on a page. But with a draft completed, the time has come to define a thesis so that it gives focus to what you want to say.

Assertion: A statement that says "This is so."

Make an Assertion About Your Subject. Unless it is one of those truly rare occasions, your writing in the first discovery draft probably wanders around a good deal. The thesis is probably not a pointed assertion. And that's natural. But to make the writing really zing right into your reader's attention, you need to focus the subject into a clear, sharp assertion.

Look at the opening paragraph of this student's discovery draft on tourist attractions:

> What can I say about tourist attractions? Well, tourist attractions are famous, or people wouldn't go to see them. And some are interesting (although some are boring). Many are in cities, although small towns have them, too—not only museums and tall buildings but also old forts, monuments. Elementary school field trips are often to tourist attractions—I've had my share! They are often so crowded, and people are bustling around with their cameras and soda bottles—sometimes it's hard to get to *see* the attraction for the crowds. Sometimes the crowd itself *becomes* the attraction.

Now, this is fine for a discovery draft. But it is also clear that this student doesn't yet recognize the *point* of what she wants to say. She has a subject without an assertion.

For the writing in this discovery draft to be transformed into a thesis, and for the reader to read along with interest and with value received, the question "What *about* tourists?" must be answered. One way to do this is to read the discovery draft with an eye to a likely candidate for an assertion—something on which to focus everything else you have to say.

When Carla, the student who wrote the paper on tourist attractions, looked over her discovery draft to spot a possible assertion, she realized that what interested her most in the writing was the statement about how tourists themselves can be the attraction.

Eureka! There was a thesis, something to *set forth,* to put out to the reader. She would write about how you can get the benefits of traveling just by being with tourists. Her new introduction looked like this:

> Ever find yourself squiring out-of-town relatives to your local tourist attractions? Ever find yourself waiting in line just to squeeze into some dark museum and see rusted-away eating utensils from some insignificant dynasty? Ever get elbowed black and blue by all the *other* tourists snapping their photos and buying their souvenirs? Well, if the museum, monument, or scenic sandlot doesn't thrill you the way it does your Aunt Sally, try focusing your lens on the tourists themselves. Sometimes they're the ones who really provide the interest. Visiting a local museum, for example, I've had the pleasure of eavesdropping on people from France, Sweden, England, Mexico, and Ethiopia. Even though in most cases I had no idea what they were talking about, just listening to the sounds of their languages, and looking at their clothes, movements, and gestures, gave me the sense that *I* was the tourist—that I could see the world right from where I was. The people don't have to be from far-away places, either, to enrich the touring-in-your-hometown experience—listen for a Southern drawl, New York quick speech. See what you can notice—tourists let you do a bit of traveling without hardly leaving your doorstep.

This time the reader knows exactly what the thesis is—even if the thesis sentence doesn't appear, per se, in the paragraph. The subject "tourists" has been further narrowed to "tourists who visit tourist attractions in your hometown." And the assertion is clear, too: Tourists are attractions in themselves. And why will the reader be interested? In this paragraph, unlike the first, *there is a point to the whole thing,* and the point is perfectly clear to the reader. The writer has made an *assertion.*

Be an Insider. After coming up with a clear thesis to discuss in an essay, you must ask this crucial question: "Am I an insider in this matter?" The answer is "maybe" if you know something about the subject or thesis that the reader doesn't know, or have a special expertise in the matter.

Figure out and establish your own special qualifications as an expert. Be certain that *you* are *the* appropriate person to write on this thesis. If that sounds too hard, you may need to look for another subject or another thesis, since you obviously don't want to waste your reader's time by latching onto a thesis and writing on it simply to have something to turn in. And, in fact, it wouldn't be a good preparation for life after school, where "turning in assignments" means more than merely going through the motions.

It's a point that can't be emphasized too much: if you can't write about something you're an expert on, if you can't give the reader the insider's view, you'll be staying on the surface and you'll wind up with a rehash of what you both already know. The way to get past that is to do some more work in the creating stage until something turns up that you *are* an insider on, *or* until you discover how to get the inside edge on the subject you want to write on. *Communication* begins when you're giving the reader your special, expert, inside view of the matter, your unique perception or special appreciation.

State the Thesis Clearly. After deciding on a thesis for the paper and determining if you are an insider on the matter and can give a personal approach to the topic, make sure the reader knows *exactly what your message is going to be.* Somewhere early in the writing you should get that message out clearly. Sometimes the message is expressed in the thesis sentence; other times it may come across to the reader through several sentences or even a whole paragraph, as it did in the example about tourists. But whether the thesis is expressed explicitly in one unmistakable sentence or whether it is imbedded in several sentences or a paragraph, *let the reader know clearly what the rest of the essay is going to be about.*

Here's an opening paragraph that shows who the audience is, what the subject is, what the paper will say about the subject, and what the value to the reader will be:

> This last summer thousands of people stamped up and down hundreds of miles of backpacking and hiking trails all across the United States and Canada, putting their feet through such punishment and pain as they never had felt before. Blisters, corns, and painful swelling of joints plagued nearly everyone, including both the novice and the experienced trail guide. There is no sure way to prevent these discomforts, but the right type and fit of hiking boot can help make it a great deal easier, as I learned this last summer.

Who is the audience? Anyone who hikes or is planning to hike.

What is the subject? How to get the right type of fit in hiking boots.

What will the writer concentrate on? Giving the reader information on how to choose hiking boots.

What is the value to the reader? Information and, perhaps, more comfortable feet.

The thesis is expressed in the last sentence. The rest of the paper will expand on this thesis. A particular "thing to discuss" has been set up, and the rest of the paper will be devoted to discussing the thesis that the writer has selected.

Here is another example, the first two paragraphs of a student theme:

> Soft, intriguing music plays in the background. Martha, a pretty brunette, walks into the living room. Her husband, Paul, is sitting

> anxiously on the couch. "Martha, where have you been?"; then taking a closer look he adds, "You haven't been down at Ted's nightclub again, have you?" She remains silent for a moment and then speaks defensively: "What difference does it make to you? You spend every night working at the clinic! What do you expect me to do, stay home and watch TV by myself?" And so another dramatic episode begins.
>
> Each weekday, many stories similar to this one are broadcast on TV. These soap operas are viewed by thousands of people across the country. Men are also enjoying what used to be considered shows for women only, and new soap operas are appearing during evening hours. "The soaps" have become an American pastime. Why do people watch soap operas? Why have they become so popular?

Here the writer defers any hint of a thesis until the end of the second paragraph—and by so doing she generates a certain measure of suspense for the reader. However, it's clear at the end of the second paragraph that the topic is soap operas, that the paper will explore the reasons why people like them, and that the reader is probably someone who knows about soap operas and will be interested in an analysis of their appeal.

Make the Thesis Matter to the Reader. It's always tempting to assume that anything interesting to *you* will also be interesting to the reader—but that's not always the case. You're interested in something simply because you're interested. And so you start out interested. The reader, though, starts wherever *he* or *she* starts from, and that may or may not be in alignment with what interests you. Is it something that the reader will gain value from? What's in it for the reader? Checking your thesis in advance can help you present a subject and approach that are exciting and satisfactory to you and also that really connect with the reader.

Knowing clearly who the reader is, having a detailed image of the audience, will let you realize whether you're likely to connect. Here is where the person who wrote about tourists can take measures to guarantee her success. Her thesis clearly meets the first three requirements:

1. She does come up with one particular aspect of her subject and makes a statement about it;
2. She is an insider on the subject (we assume);
3. She clearly puts the thesis in the opening of her essay.

Now, the next question is: *Who will care?* If the writer can think of readers who would be interested in the message, she can develop a strategy that will help her connect. If, for instance, she decides to write for a travel magazine, she could certainly make the thesis matter to her readers. And if she writes for her English classmates right before school is out

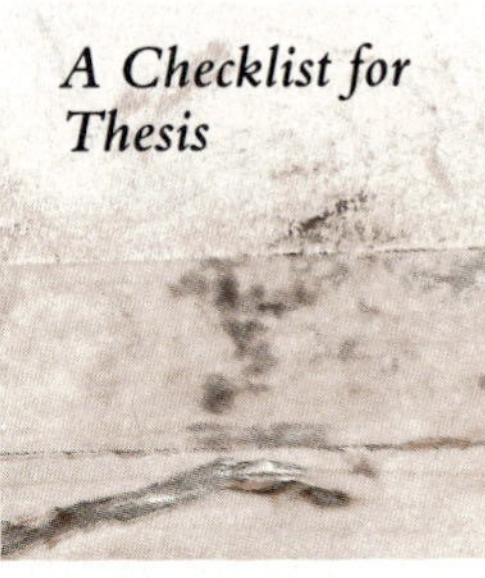

A Checklist for Thesis

1. Have I made an assertion about my subject?
2. Have I said something about the subject that the reader doesn't already know or hasn't already thought about—in other words, am I an insider?
3. Did I state the thesis clearly?
4. Am I reasonably sure this thesis is something that will *matter* to the reader?

for the summer (when many will be traveling), she will also know exactly what to do with *that* audience.

The point, though, is that you have to make the message matter.

Summary of Thesis

Asking yourself exactly what the paper is going to assert is absolutely necessary. To be sure that readers will take time to read your writing, to be sure they'll get something out of your work, to be sure that they will be interested and that you'll tell them something they don't already know, ask these questions:

Am I writing on a *single aspect* of the subject?

Am I writing as an *insider* in the matter?

Have I stated the thesis *early* and *clearly?*

Is the reader likely to *care?*

When you can answer *yes* to these questions, you will know your purpose for writing and the specific message you want to send. Since there are hundreds of things you are an insider on, hundreds of subjects you can write about and thereby contribute to a reader's enjoyment, knowledge, and awareness, don't waste your time and theirs writing on some blah subject that doesn't matter to anybody. If you are keen on a subject, if you really have something to say about it, you can make it matter to anybody.

APPLICATION

1. Look at these opening paragraphs from student essays and see if the writers seem to be *insiders* on the subject. What passages, words, sentences, establish them as *insiders* (or *outsiders,* as the case may be)? Be able to discuss these paragraphs in class.
   A. I came to college with high and mighty, yet customary, goals. The excitement of everything about college seemed enough to keep me

propelled forward forever. But, after two months, I'm worried. The excitement flew out the window, and I was left amidst the crowds of students sharing the same problem. Instead of something flashy and fairly easy, I found that college is dingy clothes and a D in Biology.

B. Racquetball is the youngest of the racquet sports. And, in many ways, it is the best. The game can be enjoyed at any level of competition. Almost anyone can hit a rubber ball against the wall, but few can do it with the power, velocity, and finesse of a racquetball champion.

C. "You know that class is awful. I never learn anything from it, but it seems to last for hours."
"I know what you mean. The lectures are so disorganized. He doesn't even know what he's talking about."
"Well, I won't be there next class. I have better ways to spend my time."

This conversation is often heard after many college classes. However, this attitude can be reversed through the efforts of the professor. By inspiring confidence in the student and through an organized and knowledgeable presentation of the material, a professor can make any class interesting as well as instructive.

2. Which of the following paragraphs convinces you the writer can give some unique *value* on the *thesis?* When you've finished making your decision, look closely at the convincing paragraph(s) and examine it (them) for features that suggest the writer has the reader in mind. Explain what techniques a writer can use to convince the reader that there is value in the writing.

A. Have you ever had the courage to work with little kids and not only try to teach them how to play soccer, but, at the same time, have them enjoy what you are teaching? Chances are your answer is no, but then again you probably never thought about it quite like that. This act of bravery is not a subject to be taken lightly, mainly because teaching is one of the hardest ways to relate to kids. While you are teaching them, you need to do it in such a manner that they can enjoy what they are learning. Some people just do not understand that kids can enjoy what they are being taught.

B. The American way has always been toward progress but not always toward every aspect of the future ahead. Americans in their race for progressive happiness have damaged one integral part of their future—their own lands. Now the people are beginning to see their wrongs and are correcting these problems. The only natural wild lands they have left to save are those in the national parks and forests, and their time for repenting their ways grows short.

3. Read the following paragraphs. Answer these questions about them: Does each paragraph have a clear thesis statement? If so, what is it? If a thesis statement is present, what assertion is the writer making? How has the writer shown or indicated that he or she is an insider in the matter? Can the reader know what he or she is going to get from reading the paper? Be able to discuss your answers for each paragraph in class.
   A. "Gee, Mom, it smells good in here! What's cooking?" asks a boy as he walks through the kitchen. Slam! Mom watches her son come in and walk by without even noticing her presence. In tears she looks on as he hunts through the refrigerator for a mid-afternoon snack and thinks, "You call this a family."
   B. It took me twelve years of school to finally realize that I did not know how to study. When I was in high school, I did about twenty minutes of studying a night (of course, excluding Fridays and Saturdays). Plus, for a test, I kicked in about thirty extra minutes. Despite the lack of study I still pulled out a 3.325. Then came the shock of my life, college.
   C. I cannot believe that it is all over. When I was little, all I ever wanted to be was a teenager. I longed for the days when I would do nothing but chase boys, talk on the telephone and blast my stereo. I wonder now, if I had not talked quite so long on the phone and had not listened to my loud stereo quite so avidly, if my high school years would have gone by any slower. I never really took the time to stop and say "Hey! I am now one normal, 100-percent, full-fledged teenager!" Instead, it seems as if I made a transition straight from babydoll little girl life into womanhood without even stopping to think twice.
   D. The serene atmosphere surrounding the neighborhood was pierced by an echoing scream. A teenager turned and ran in the direction of the noise. Rounding a corner he was confronted by a mother and father standing over their son. The teenager took note of the situation and immediately began artificial respiration. Within a few minutes the child was conscious and active. Why was the teenager able to save the child while the mother and father stood helplessly by? Were they overcome by the shock of seeing their son in trouble, or did they not know how to administer first aid? In either case their son might have died if it had not been for a total stranger. The teenager was able to save the child's life because he had been taught first aid.
4. All of the following paragraphs fail to meet the conditions for effective thesis development, effective adaptation to audience, or both. Read them carefully; then be prepared to discuss exactly how each fails and what could be done to improve them. When you've finished, pick two and rewrite them.

A. Man is, at heart, a cruel animal, injuring and attacking not for food or protection but for enjoyment. What is more, men do this fighting with each other. Those of the species who do not participate watch and cheer on their favorite, wishing all the time that they had the skill to be in his place. Of course I am speaking of man's sports, his vicious ways of recreating.

B. For many people, the idea of a restaurant brings to mind a place where one can relax and eat the food of his or her choice. Some people go to a restaurant to relax, have a few drinks and eat a good meal. After a hard day, nothing is better than to go a quiet restaurant and let someone else, who is probably better than you anyway, cook the meal of your choice. You can also listen to the quiet music while you eat your delicious meal. With no interruptions like a telephone or a doorbell ringing, you can probably enjoy your meal more. You can take your time eating and enjoy every morsel of your delectable meal. Someone else will cook your meal to your specifications and will also serve it to you quietly and politely. The dishes will be taken away and you will not even have to clean them up.

C. There are many restaurants that specialize in certain types of food. My favorite varieties of food are seafood and Mexican food. One thing that annoys me is some people who go into a restaurant that specializes in one particular food and they order something completely off the menu. The customer should show some courtesy to the establishment. He could show this by leaving a tip for the waiter. A tip shows the customer's appreciation of a service which he considers the waiter deserved. In a few cases, I have encountered rude waiters who give no or very poor service. But these cases have been very few as I have been satisfied with most of the service I have received. A restaurant is still a good place to go to relax and enjoy the best food possible.

SHAPING STRUCTURE

After you have refined your thesis, you are ready to consider how the materials you've generated in the creating stage and in the discovery draft fit together. That means thinking about organization and structure. In writing, organization describes the order in which you present ideas and the amount of coverage you give them. Ordinarily your thesis makes a promise that the rest of the essay must deliver on. Organization follows from that promise, that is, from the type of writing you are doing—from your purpose, audience, topic, and main point.

Because organization is so closely related to the type of writing you do, you'll find detailed advice on patterns of organization in the separate

Portfolio chapters. In addition, methods for assessing the effectiveness of your structure are presented in Chapter 17, "Form and Pattern." Here let it suffice to say that a good paper works quite deliberately to lead readers through its ideas, examples, illustrations, and arguments. The reader has a definite sense of passing through a beginning, middle, and end.

If everything works well, readers wind up at the conclusion, a very good place to end. Like the opening, the conclusion can be one or more paragraphs; it is that portion of the essay responsible for taking stock, either summarizing what's been said (without simply rehashing it), drawing out the implications, or hammering home the consequences. Endings also help readers exit the writing gracefully, suggesting subtly that it may be time to ponder what's been offered in the paper. Readers generally don't like conclusions that drop them off a cliff.

WRITING AGAIN

With the confidence that comes from a clear sense of purpose, a realistic appreciation of audience, an intriguing thesis, and a general sense of the essay's shape, you are ready to move beyond the discovery draft toward a more consciously crafted version of an essay. We might call this the *drafting stage,* but a more accurate description might simply be *work*. There's no getting around it. This is the time that makes you grateful for the cushion on your seat—the mornings, afternoons, and evenings when you sit and think and write and write and write toward some conclusion. That conclusion might be a world-class draft almost ready to edit, or (more likely) one that still needs more revision and more work—which means more drafts, more creating, more shaping, more appreciation for that cushion.

People who teach writing often describe the process of composing as *recursive*. By that they mean exactly what you discover every time you find yourself lurching back and forth in your composing, thinking you have claimed a subject and shaped it well enough to write about it, and then finding that you have to pause at some point in the draft to rethink an idea—and so you enter the creating stage again to brainstorm, perhaps, or loop. Then it's back to shaping, forward to revising, back to creating, and on and on. The overall movement may be forward, but you are tracking like a puppy who's lapped beer instead of water. Finally, however, even the most committed writer has to say, "No more new ideas, no more revisions for better development and flow. That's it. I'm out of here. Fini." But before you can say that, you have to know how to bring your writing to the completing stage. Enter the next chapter.

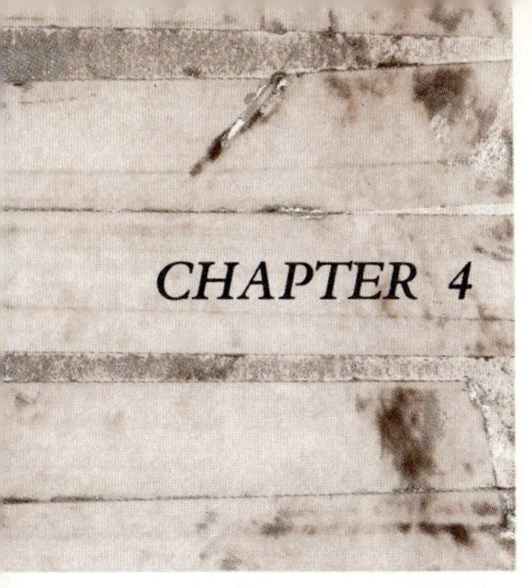

CHAPTER 4

The Completing Stage

Perhaps you've taken up a new sport in the last few years. Remember the way your instruction went? First you learned the fundamentals of the game—how to score, how to use the equipment, how to move. Then after you handled the essentials, your instructor moved to the skills that make the difference between the bush leagues and the majors. You "progressed" in the sport to the extent that you concentrated on these specifics, mastering single parts of the game.

This is the way you might think of the *completing* stage of the writing process. There are things you have to do to complete your work responsibly (the fundamentals) and there are things in the completing stage that will make the difference between adequate and good writing (the fine points).

What do you *have* to do in the completing stage?

You *must* edit what you have written and prepare a *clean, correct* manuscript.

What else can you do in the completing stage to polish your writing and add to the reader's pleasure?

You can revise your writing with careful attention to individual, refinable parts—paragraphs, sentences, words.

In the best of all possible worlds, of course, you would do both: revise and edit. Certainly by the time you have added two or three papers to your portfolio, you will want to know what you can do to take your work to a higher level and will want to revise thoroughly. Or perhaps your instructor will see reasons for having you concentrate on matters of flow, energy, and punch quite early in a term. What this chapter provides are basic guidelines on revision and full directions for editing and preparing a manuscript. In short, this is the material you need to control the fundamentals of writing. When you are ready for advanced play, you can consult more detailed advice on mastering paragraphs, sentences, and words in Chapters 19, 20, and 21.

REVISING

The writing process is a little like Chinese boxes—one fits inside the other and then a smaller one inside that and then a smaller one inside that. When you start the creating stage of the writing process you, in effect, make the big box. Then inside that box you keep writing—the discovery draft, the middle drafts, the late draft. And the organic evolution of the process produces a tighter and tighter piece of writing, the next size box and then the next.

First you get a clear idea of what you want to say. Then you start thinking about your reader and the writing comes closer to matching the readers' needs. Next you home in on a thesis sentence, and that sentence carries in it the form, the development, that the writing is going to take. And on and on.

Now you have arrived at the completing stage and are ready to polish what you have produced. Here's where the advice of readers can direct you to necessary changes, particularly in flow, energy, and punch. Attend carefully to the comments colleagues have made on your drafts; ask questions about their remarks. Assume that criticisms are made in good faith and don't be defensive about problems. If a peer finds your paper hard to follow, don't blame him or her for not reading carefully enough; instead, take a second look at your transitions. If another reader describes your draft as dull or slow-moving, don't attribute the problems to the difficulty of your topic. Consider the possibility that the paper may, in fact, be wordy, or plagued with dull verbs and vague nouns.

Then take action. The three brief revision sections that follow concentrate on some common problems in student writing: inattention to transitions, sentences that lack energy, and wordiness. Take care of these problems in every paper you write and you'll serve your readers well. Recognize these faults in papers you read, and you will be an especially helpful and respected editor.

Revising for Flow: Transitions and Reminder Signs

To be sure your writing moves smoothly along for readers, you need to give them signals that indicate your direction (*transitions*) and reminder signs that help them recall what you are writing about. You have probably heard about *transitions* from high school courses. *Reminder signs* might be a newer concept, but you probably use them at least occasionally.

Transitions. One meaning of the word *transition* is "a passage from one place to another." Transitions in your writing help readers move from one point to the next. Transitions may be whole paragraphs in length, or they may be only a sentence or even a few words—anything that indicates to readers that you are shifting lanes or turning onto another highway. Although forms may vary, it's the concept of "transitioning" you want to learn. Once you understand the principle, you will be able to insert transitions into your work in any form—paragraphs, sentences, or single words. You'll develop a feel for just how much direction your readers need. Not enough and your readers drift away; too much, and you seem like an overzealous crossing guard.

Let's begin by examining the work of other writers to see how they indicate transitions, how they show the movement from thought to thought. Once you can spot the transitions in someone else's writing and understand how they function (regardless of form), you'll be in good shape to look at your own writing to see whether there are enough (and adequate) transitions. In the essay that follows, the transition signals are marked.

GIVING WHAT YOU SAY A SENSE OF WHOLENESS

John Stewart and Gary d'Angelo

Key word repeated.

(1) If your experience is anything like ours, people have been telling you to "get organized" ever since you were in diapers. Your toy box was to help you learn to organize your room. School and work taught you to organize your time. And invariably, one goal of English, speech, philosophy, and science classes is to teach you to organize your thinking and the ways to express yourself. Sometimes, I wonder whether we tend to go a little overboard. Gary's got a cartoon on his office door that shows a high-school-age girl deep in thought, and the caption is: "Sometimes they teach things out of me. And I feel like saying, 'I wanted to keep that.'" We sometimes wonder whether spontaneous chaos is one of those things that schools "teach out of us" that we might enjoy—and profit from—keeping.

Signals contrast.

Signals contrast.

(2) On the other hand, most psychologists believe that we *naturally* structure our world, i.e., that order is more characteristically human than is disorder. But whether structure is natural or is an artifact of Western culture, it's here. We *do* tend to see things and people in wholes made up

Signals conclusion.
Shift from conclusion to how people act.

of parts that are somehow related to one another. Therefore, communication that has a sense of wholeness is usually easier for us to comprehend clearly than is communication that doesn't.

Signals example.
Signals similarity.
Signals summary.

(3) When people perceive something that's "incomplete" or "disordered," they sometimes fill in or add details so that it makes more sense to them. For example, as you watch a television program you may see an actor put a coffee cup to his lips and make drinking movements. Even though you don't actually see the coffee itself, you mentally "put" coffee in the cup—you fill in the detail. This same kind of process can occur when you're talking with another person. If you don't provide a "whole" message, the other person may fill in missing details or examples and in so doing may make your message into something you didn't intend. To the extent that you don't come across as a "whole" person, the other person may fill in or infer things about you that don't adequately characterize you as an individual. In short, giving a sense of wholeness and some structure to your communication gives you some control over how *you* and your *ideas* are perceived by others.

Shift to general principle about formal/informal contexts.
Signals contrast.
Signals contrast.

(4) The more formal the communication context, the more obvious that sense of wholeness can be. Persons listening to a public speech usually expect the talk to be clearly structured. A public speech doesn't have to sound as if it's coming from a robot; the speaker can still promote some person-to-person contact. But the speech should usually be pretty clearly organized. Your contribution to a group discussion should also have fairly clear structure, although it can be less formal than the organization of a speech.

Signals contrast.
Key word repeated.

(5) An informal conversation, however, is obviously different from both a speech and a group discussion. You don't sit down beforehand to organize a conversation—not usually, anyway. (Your first date might have been an exception to that rule. I remember frantically trying to plan topics of conversation for my first major boy-girl social engagements. You know how well that worked.)

Signals reassertion.
Signals example.

(6) Yet structure is important, even in conversational communication. For example, have you ever had a conversation like this?

Fred: How many Christmas presents do we have left to get?
Wilma: Just a couple. You have any ideas for your brother? I don't remember what we got him last year.
Fred: That reminds me, I forgot to call that woman.
Wilma: Huh? Should we call Ann and ask her? I always feel like . . . .
Fred: Damn, that makes me mad! Oh, well, he still does a lot of hunting.
Wilma: She remembers *Halloween* even.
Fred: Who?
Wilma: Was it you who told me about that guy who killed one of the six remaining animals of that one species?
Fred: Yeah, but how does *that* relate to Sam's present?

Reminds readers of example.

(7) In a conversation like that, the problem is *not* that there's a total lack of structure. Fred's contributions make all kinds of sense to him, and so do Wilma's—to Wilma. *The problem is that the implicit structure is not made explicit.* Fred knows the connections among his own statements, but he doesn't bother to show Wilma those relationships, and Wilma doesn't bother to explain anything to Fred.

Signals example.

(8) For example, when Wilma mentions Fred's brother (Sam), Fred pictures Sam on the job—Sam counsels handicapped children—which reminds Fred that he forgot to call a psychologist he works with—"that woman." Wilma hears "that woman" and assumes that Fred is talking about Sam's wife, Ann. Wilma feels uncomfortable around Ann and so begins to say to Fred, "I always feel like . . ." Fred doesn't even hear her. He's thinking that they might get Sam something he can use while hunting; when Wilma hears the word "hunting," she remembers a story Fred told her that she's been wanting to share with a friend, but forgot about until now, and so on.

Signals point.
Signals summary.
Signals conclusion.
Signals condition.

(9) The point we're trying to make is that there's structure even in an informal conversation, in the sense that each person's contributions "fit in" or "follow logically" or "make sense"—in short, connect—*for that person.* Problems arise when two (or more) persons' structures don't merge or fit together. Then you get the kind of confusing exchange Fred and Wilma had. You can avoid such confusion by thinking of the other person as unique, as someone who doesn't structure the world or the conversation as you do. Your thought patterns, the connections you see between ideas, are different from his or hers. So if you reveal your thought patterns, if you make them explicit by bringing them to the surface with verbal cues, then the structure of each person's contributions to the conversation becomes apparent to the other, and there will be less room for misinterpretation.

Signals rephrasing.
Signals contrast.

(10) In other words, there are ways to structure even informal conversation so that it makes sense. You don't necessarily have to give your conversation a beginning (introduction), middle (body), and end (conclusion). It would sound a little phony if you said to someone in an informal conversation: "Hi, I'm really glad to be talking with you today. As our conversation progresses I'd like to talk about three things: (1) the weather, (2) the movie I saw last night, and (3) our relationship." That kind of organization or structure fits many public speeches, but most people prefer spontaneity in informal conversation.

Signals qualification.
Signals rephrasing.
Contrasts conditions.
Signals rephrasing.

(11) Even in an informal conversation, however, you can verbalize the implicit structure, that is, talk about the links you're seeing between ideas. When you don't, you leave open the possibility for all kinds of misinterpretation. When you do, you significantly improve your chances of adequately limiting the range of interpretations, i.e., you improve your chances of "being clear."

"The labor of writing and rewriting, correcting and recorrecting, is the due exacted by every good book from its author. . . . The easily flowing connection of sentence with sentence and paragraph with paragraph has always been won by the sweat of the brow."
—G. M. Trevelyan

This selection is rich with connectors that act as a map to guide the reader from major point to major point, and also as a blueprint of structure even within the sentences themselves. The reader appreciates this wealth of clues, too, even though some of them may not register in the conscious level. In fact, sometimes clues work best when they are so smooth and subtle that the reader doesn't notice them. However, by means of such clues the writer's ideas are made to flow smoothly and steadily for the reader. Without the clues, the reader's head bobs from point to point hopelessly.

This essay, with its signals marked in the margins, makes clear exactly how these signals work. They *do* help the reader see where the writer is going at all times. And you will probably find that *you* usually put transitions into your own writing quite naturally and automatically, without thinking much about it. Yet sometimes as you're writing, your mind twists, turns, and shifts so fast that you forget to tell the reader where you have gone—or where you're headed. So it is always worthwhile to look over your paper to check if the transition signals are there. If they are, you are in good shape (and probably haven't lost much time in checking). If they are not, you can provide a thoughtful service—a courtesy—for your reader by inserting enough transition signal words so that he or she will always know exactly where you are going.

Reminder Signs. People generally have a short memory of what they read. In fact, recent research indicates that within twenty seconds they forget the *form* of the message and remember only its *gist*. (Of course that's a good reason to be sure that you do have a message in there in the first place!) Since we have considered this aspect of the message in the *creating* and *shaping* stages, what bearing has this for us in the *completing stage?* Just this: since a reader will tend to forget the order of the words themselves so easily, you must use reminder signs all along the way in your writing to refresh the reader's memory and to keep your subject clearly visible.

What are reminder signs in writing? They are simply *key words* or *phrases* repeated throughout the writing. Sometimes it is the same word repeated exactly (as the word *organize* was repeated in the last sample essay); other times it is a *variation* of that word, a *synonym* for the word, or a *pronoun* that stands for the word. The important thing about this repeating is that it keeps the reader pointed in a straight line without looking back to rediscover what you're talking about. It's the principle of "courteous repetition."

Here's a paragraph that illustrates the principle.

> Leaves fall in an annual *cycle,* and there is a natural *cyclical pattern* of *normal hair loss* on the human head, too. The greatest amount of *hair loss* occurs in November; the least amount in May. A single *hair*

Transition Signal Words

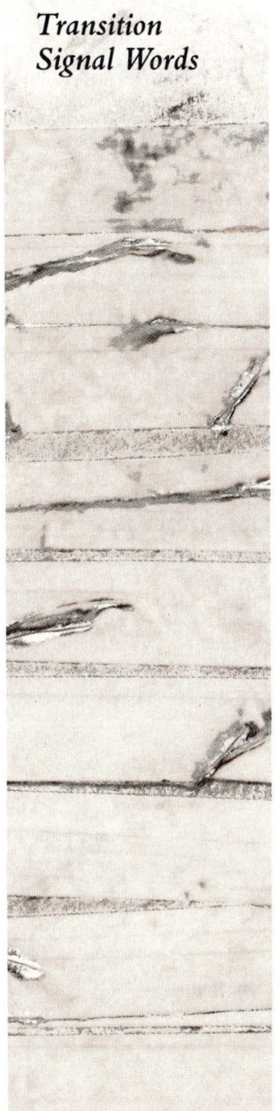

A short list of words and phrases mainly used to indicate relationships between one piece of writing and another. (Although there are many such words and phrases, this is an illustrative list.)

Transition Signal Words	***Meaning***
for example, for instance, e.g.	"Here's an example of that principle or generalization."
because, consequently, since, therefore	"This caused that, or is a reason for that."
in other words, that is, so, i.e.	"Here is a restatement or a clarification."
but, however, on the other hand, yet, nevertheless, on the contrary	"This is different from that."
similarly, likewise, in the same manner, in the same way	"This is similar to that."
also, too, in addition, and, furthermore, moreover	"Here comes another one, just like the other one."
first, next, then, last, before, prior, subsequently, earlier, later	"These exist in time relationship."
aboard, above, beyond, on top of, under, alongside, upon, beneath, to the left	"These are related in space."
finally, at last, after all, in conclusion, to conclude, to sum up	"This wraps it up. The end is in sight."

grows on your head for a little less than three years. Then *it rests.* After about three months of *rest, it* falls out and a new *hair* grows in its place in the same *hair* follicle, and the *cycle* begins again. *This* is the end of that *resting period* for old *hair,* so you can expect heavier accumulations than usual in your brush and comb. Up to *one hundred hairs* a day may fall out in the *normal* course of things, but healthy new *hairs* are growing as you read this. If you suspect that your *hair loss* is greater than *normal* count the *hairs* that come out in your comb. If the total is higher than *one hundred,* take measures. See the hairologist at a good salon for treatments.

—Vidal and Beverly Sassoon

Use Transitions and Reminder Signs Because

1. Your readers forget easily, within twenty seconds.
2. You have a lot of competition for your reader's attention.
3. The best way to keep your readers with you is to keep them moving in a straight line, never causing them to double back to see what you are talking about.

Examining this paragraph, you can see that the key words are *cycle, normal hair loss, rest,* and *one hundred.* These key words are repeated all the way through the paragraph, and the reader is never allowed to forget what the subject is, never is obliged to double back to pick up the thought. In your own writing, you naturally have to beware of sounding monotonous, and so you will want to vary the wording, using pronouns or synonyms. However, you *will* need to do a certain amount of repeating of the main word or words in your message if you are going to keep the idea directly before your reader. This may finally—with the transitions—be the most important thing in your writing that causes it to really flow. A reader can't move in a straight line toward the goal—your total message—unless all along the way you give reminder signs to help overcome that twenty-second memory risk.

"One should not aim at being possible to understand, but at being impossible to misunderstand."
—Quintilian

APPLICATION

1. In the two samples below, find all the *transitions* and *reminder signs.* List them and be prepared to explain how they keep the reader moving smoothly through the paragraph and how they keep the subject at the front of the reader's attention.
   A. Shopping around for a car loan is not as much fun as shopping for the car. But just as the savvy shopper checks out several car dealers before that final handshake, he should also check out competing lenders. To help him, the Federal Trade Commission has prepared a handy pocket *Credit Shopping Guide.* It includes tips on borrowing and a series of tables so you can compare the cost of car loans, home improvement loans and mortgages at various interest rates and over different time periods.

      The total finance charge on a loan can depend on where you borrow. Let's say you need $3,000 for three years to buy a new car. If you finance it through the car dealer, where the average annual percentage rate—the true rate of interest—is 13½%, that $3,000 loan is likely to cost you $665. But if you go to a bank, where the average rate is 11%, the loan may cost $536; and if you can borrow against your life insurance, the rate will average 6%—for a cost of $286. . . .

To get a copy of the free credit guide, write the Public Reference Branch, Federal Trade Commission, Washington, D.C. 20580.

—Money Magazine

B. Samuel Johnson has fascinated more people than any other writer except Shakespeare. Statesmen, lawyers, and physicians quote him, as do writers and scientists, philosophers and farmers, manufacturers and leaders of labor unions. For generations people have been discovering new details about him and reexamining and correcting old ones. Interest in Johnson is by no means confined to the English-speaking world, though naturally it is strongest there. In Asia, Africa, and South America, groups of Johnsonians meet every year to talk about every aspect of him. The reason why Johnson has always fascinated so many people of different kinds is not simply that Johnson is so vividly picturesque and quotable, though these are the qualities that first catch our attention. The deeper secret of his hypnotic attraction, especially during our own generation, lies in the immense reassurance he gives to human nature, which needs—and quickly begins to value—every friend it can get.

—Walter Jackson Bate

2. Here are two examples that show just how effective your writing can be when you constantly keep the subject before the reader by using reminder signs. The first is by Chief Joseph of the Nez Percé Indians (published in 1879). What are the key terms? How often are they repeated? How does this contribute to the force of this paragraph?

   The second example, by Don Fabun, is about the ways people use space to communicate. Examine this one for two things: the way Fabun *repeats* the key terms (which he is discussing) and the way he *signals* the reader at the beginning of each sentence. Underline both devices: *repeated key terms* and *signals,* and be prepared to discuss how Fabun uses each to lead the reader from sentence to sentence and to keep the main point always before the reader.

A. I have heard talk and talk, but nothing is done. Good words do not last long unless they amount to something. Words do not pay for my dead people. They do not pay for my country, now overrun by white men. . . . Good words will not give my people good health and stop them from dying. Good words will not get my people a home where they can live in peace and take care of themselves. I am tired of talk that comes to nothing. It makes my heart sick when I remember all the good words and broken promises. . . .

—Chief Joseph

B. The way we use space is another way that we communicate with one another. The distance between you and someone else may determine the nature of the communication. If you are a few inches away from someone's ear, chances are that you will whisper and the nature of the communication will be "secret." At a distance of several feet, the communication may still be private, but its tone and nature will have changed. The change is even greater if you are speaking to a large audience. Here the nature of the message may be determined in part by the distance between you and the most distant members of the audience.

—Don Fabun

Revising for Energy: Sentences

How can you put energy into your writing? In this section we will suggest three immediate ways: by combining choppy sentences, by adding details, and by placing description in the right place for emphasis. Along with what you'll learn in the next section about eliminating wordiness, you should be able to produce solid, readable writing. In Chapter 20, "Polishing Sentences," we'll explore the fine points of sentence construction—sentence types and variation; coordination and subordination; parallelism; repetition; rhythm—to give your writing grace and style.

Combining Choppy Sentences. You don't get energy in writing by sounding monotonous. Here is a passage from a third-grade reader that shows how sentences that are too short and choppy put one to sleep rather than energize.

> Most of the ways to turn salt water into fresh water cost a lot of money. The Symi factory on an island in Greece uses a way that costs very little.
>
> Right in the middle of the town are some long ponds. They are only a few inches deep. The men of Symi dug out earth to make the ponds.
>
> Over each pond is a low tent. It is made of plastic that you can see through.
>
> At night, sea water is pumped into the ponds. The next day, the hot sun shines through the tents. The sun's heat turns the water into vapor that rises from the ponds. The salt is left behind.

Of course, the short paragraphs and the elementary vocabulary also contribute to the too-simple effect. But it is the repetition of sentence after sentence, each in the same pattern, each containing only a single unit of information, that makes that passage sound so childlike and undeveloped. The deadness, for adult readers, comes from dragging on and on through sentence after sentence, picking up only one lifeless bit of message per sentence. *Combining* those informational bits into longer, more varied sentences, would make them much more attractive and effective.

Now look at this passage from a college-level government book:

> John F. Kennedy's assassination on November 21, 1963, probably evoked—in the period that followed his death—greater feeling on the part of more people than the death of any other American. His assassination was as close to formal tragedy as is conceivable in a democracy. Kennedy had all the attributes of a hero: power, prestige, presence, the heroism of the warrior, affability, social standing, youth, physical attraction, religious belief, and wealth. He embodied all of these qualities with a special grace, and his death seemed associated with the death of youth in America.
>
> —Theodore Gross

By comparing this passage with the earlier one, you can see immediately the effect of short, simple sentences and the effect of longer, more varied sentences. The short little sentences are perfect for third graders, but unless that is your audience, you may insult your readers with sentences that sound as though they were written for eight-year-olds. The more you combine short, simple sentences together, the more sophisticated your writing seems to the reader—and the more information units the reader gets per sentence, too—which really facilitates communication by making it seem effortless. For example, take these two sentences:

> Over each pond is a low tent.
> It is made of plastic that you can see through.

Each one offers a niggling bit of information, yet the reader has to come to a complete stop at the end of each, and do all the work a reader does in beginning and ending sentences. However, *combining* them allows the information to come together in a neat and orderly way, and the reader is spared unnecessary effort:

> Over each pond is a low plastic tent that you can see through.

What's happened? You've produced some variation on that same dreary repeated sentence pattern, *and* you've shown what really *is* important—that there is a tent over each pond. The information about what material the tent is made of is clearly less important, and the combined sentence helps the reader to keep clear what's important and what isn't.

In much the same way, you could perversely create dreariness out of the Kennedy passage by uncoupling the sentences and separating the items out into single bits.

Kennedy had all the attributes of a hero.
He had power.
He had prestige.
He had presence.
Etc. Yawn, yawn, and ho-hum!

No, it is not the *separation,* but the *combination* of those bits that makes the sense of the passage easier to follow. And that's how sentence combining works: it lets you send complex thoughts in an easy-to-follow form.

Adding Details. To get more energy *into* a sentence—so that your reader can get more energy *out of* the sentence—you need to provide more than just a flat statement. Just as five sticks of wood in a fireplace give more heat than one stick of wood, so a sentence that provides description gives more genergy than a sentence that gives only the bland, general facts. When you add—judiciously—descriptive words to a sentence, you make it come alive for the reader. And there's energy in being alive!

For example, take this one-firewood-stick sentence:

The woman carried her attaché.

This does tell the reader something, to be sure. But how much more energy is provided by the descriptive words added to the sentence:

The weary woman carried her battered attaché with a hopeless resignation.

Already, we know a great deal more from the addition of the descriptive words. They set up questions that can provoke the reader: Why is the woman weary? How did her attaché get battered? Why does she react with resignation? And so on. When you give enough descriptive information, the reader wants to keep moving—the writing has energy.

Putting Descriptive Words in the Right Place. It's great to use descriptive words, but it's not enough just to throw them in anywhere. It makes sense to put a lamp *on* the livingroom table, but it doesn't make sense to put it *under* the livingroom table. To make your energetic words fire up sentences, put them where they will do the most good.

The places for descriptors in sentences are: before the subject, between the subject and verb, and after the verb. For example:

before the subject	*After I turned out the lights,*
between the subject and verb	the child, *who was scared of nightmares,*
after the verb	tossed and turned *with stiff, open eyes.*

Use this as a guideline, not a rule, however. Don't put descriptors in all these places. You want to give the reader enough information to get excited about your sentence; you don't want to give so much information that the reader feels swamped and confused.

> After I had completed my banking transactions, which I typically do at the branch nearest my home, although, from time to time, I utilize the branch nearest my office, which actually, is in the same building, an architectural concept that, as an office worker, I find admirable but, as an appreciator of beauty, I find often quite deplorable, I walked home.

This sentence is technically correct, but descriptive words have been put in far too many (and not the right) places.

APPLICATION

1. Rewrite the following paragraphs by combining the choppy sentences into sentences with energy:

   I was fortunate enough to be able to travel to Europe during my senior year in high school. We went during our spring break, March 17–26. The travelers consisted of eighteen students and two teachers. We traveled in a group known as the American Leadership Study Group.

   There was question of whether or not I would be able to go. During the Christmas holidays we had a family reunion. My parents asked me if I wanted to go on the European trip. I said no immediately because I thought it was out of the question. The trip was too expensive. I began thinking about the trip more and more, and I finally decided I wanted to go. I had done quite a bit of baby-sitting and saved the money.

   We proceeded to find out more information about the trip. My mother and I thought the only obstacle would be getting the passport in time. However, my teacher told me there was a waiting list for the trip. He told me he was an area representative for ALSG and that a friend of his owed him a favor. That information lifted our spirits. I would probably be first on the waiting list. My mother and I went to the post office to apply for a passport. We learned that we could receive a passport very quickly if we paid an extra fee. We paid the fee and received the passport in a week.
2. The sentences below are unrevealing, flat statements. Add descriptive words that put life into these sentences.

A. The man left home.
B. By noon it was empty.
C. Hereafter, I will not go.
D. The bell rang.
E. The woman held the door.
F. The children looked out.

3. Choose the best locations for adding descriptive words to the following sentences. Consider both what words to add *and* where to add them for the most energy in the writing.
A. The game was over.
B. The night ended.
C. Boys came over.
D. The check bounced.
E. The return was not audited.
F. The candles sparkled.
G. We saw stars.

Revising for Punch: Words

Getting punch in your writing comes down to four simple things:

1. Replace vague, general words with specific, exact words.
2. Cut out every word you don't absolutely need.
3. Use action verbs.
4. Avoid circumlocutions.

These four will just about do it. If you revise your words with these principles in mind, you will have *power* and *punch* in your writing. Here are some specific examples to illustrate the four principles:

Replace Vague Words with Specific, Concrete Words. Look at the difference in these sentences:

VAGUE: The landscape is quite varied.
SPECIFIC: The landscape changes from high, old mountains in the east to flat, horse-raising country in the middle to river-bottom delta land in the west.

VAGUE: The people living in the housing project are diverse.
SPECIFIC: The people living in the housing project come from ten different countries on four different continents.

VAGUE: The pizza was great.
SPECIFIC: The pizza started with a crust made of fresh-baked dough on which was piled a layer of cheddar cheese, ground beef,

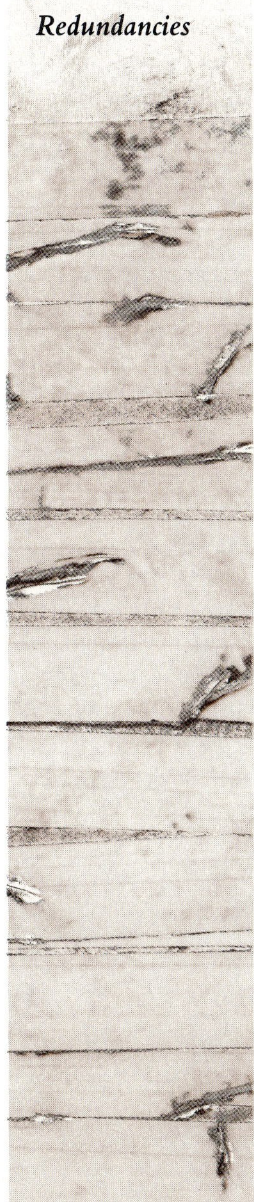

Redundancies

If you describe an object as red in color and round in shape, you're really nailing it down, taking no chance on being misunderstood. But you're also betraying insecurity and will bore readers to tears. This kind of writing lacks crispness. It's limp.

The following list gives examples of redundancies to avoid. The words in parentheses can (and should) be omitted.

Because (of the fact that)
The maximum (possible) amount
A range (all the way) from
A (time) interval or period
An (innumerable) number of
(Final) climax
(Capping) the climax
Assemble (together)
Connect (together)
Add (together)
Connect (up)
Fuse (together)
Square (in shape)
Few (in number)
Big (in size)
Adequate (enough)
(Entirely) completed
Atop (of)
Inside (of)
All (of)
(And) moreover
This (same) program
Equally (as) willing
The same (identical) meaning
Throughout (the whole of)
Bisect (into two parts)
Halved (in two parts)
(Most) unique
Bald (-headed) man
The modern man (of today)
(Every) now and then
Total effect of (all) this
Mutual advantage (of both)
(Surrounding) circumstances
Endorse (on the back)
They are (both) alike
Favorable condition for warping (to occur)
Necessary (requisite)
(True) facts
(Successful) achievements
Recoil (back)
Repeat (again)
Return (back)
Each (and every)
Thus (as a result)
Continue (on)
Termed (as)
Blue (in color)
(Still) persists
Might (possibly)
(As) yet
(But) nevertheless
(As to) whether
2 P.M. (in the afternoon)
(New) beginners

—Ernst Jacobi

mushrooms, anchovies, sliced meatballs, sausage, baloney, pepper, onions, green pepper, and finally another layer of cheese: mozzarella.

Whenever you supply a specific for a general word, you will add power and punch to what you write.

Cut Out Every Word You Don't Absolutely Need. Save your reader time and energy; cut the flab. Make your writing lean. Nothing will steal your power sooner than words that the reader has to wade through and climb over to get to your message. See the difference for yourself.

> FAT: There are many people alive in the world today who are living strange and unusual lives.
> LEAN: Many people live strange lives.
> FAT: Modern men and women of today are both alike in similar ways; they repeat again and again their messages after they have already said them once.
> LEAN: Both men and women tend to repeat their messages.

> FAT: Because of the fact that I don't have any money and am therefore flat broke, I don't go inside a restaurant.
> LEAN: Because I don't have any money, I don't go inside a restaurant.

Use Action Verbs. Most texts take an unyielding position against passive verbs. That's because students often use the passive voice to avoid taking a stand about anything, or because excessive use of passives makes business and technical writing characterless. Occasionally, though, the passive is useful to the writer—as when a cause or agent is unknown. However, for now it will probably do more good to take the traditional stand *against* passive verbs—and then later allow them into writing in just—and only—the places where they actually are appropriate.

Bureaucratic Phrases and Alternatives

Bureaucratic	*Direct*
by means of	by
in the event of	if
along the lines of	like, as
with the result that designed so that	so that
in order to with a view toward for the purpose of	to
for the reason that on the grounds that on the basis of	because, since
in connection with in relation to, with regard to, with respect to, in the matter of	about

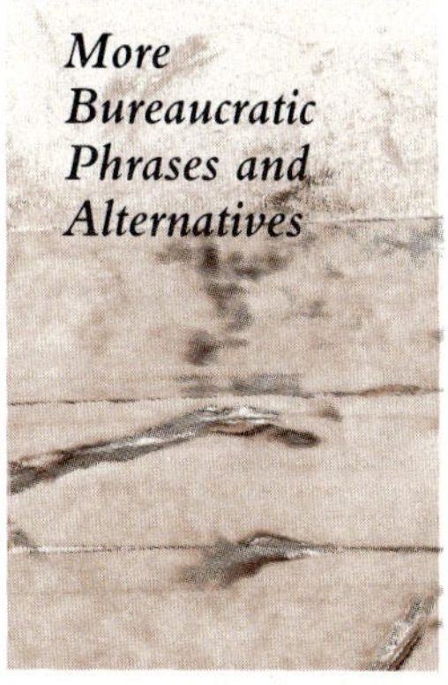

More Bureaucratic Phrases and Alternatives

The words in parentheses are stereotyped business jargon—chatter that should be eliminated.

(This is to inform you that) Mr. Broadbeam will call on you at your office (as) soon (as possible).

(We are pleased to direct your attention to) paragraph 8 (which) indicates that . . .

Please (feel free to) write (to this office) if you (find yourself in) need (of) additional details.

(Data obtained during) flight tests indicated that . . .

—Ernst Jacobi

Let your reader *see* what is happening. Passive verb forms kill writing, and nobody knows "who dunnit." It's a classic way of concealing the evidence or hiding the responsibility, but it usually makes for dull reading.

Avoid Circumlocutions. Circumlocution—the deliberate use of roundabout expressions—creates wordiness and obscurity. The objective of writers who use circumlocutions is to sound impressive, not to communicate efficiently and directly. Ironically, when you recognize circumlocutions in a piece of writing, you are struck not by its impressiveness, but by its absurdity. In the passage below, circumlocutions are underlined. Notice how they obscure meaning and make communication difficult.

(1) As silent tears flowed down my cheeks in diamond-filled rivulets, I reflected on the presumptuous attitudes of society's "young adults." (2) Of course, generalization during a period of severe depression is opted for, and I consider myself no failure!

(3) It appeared to me that the feelings of humans aged eleven to nineteen towards the humans that had survived on this planet for the longest number of years ranged from bothersome to useless. (4) Sporting a different opinion, and allowed to exclude myself from this degrading category for the sole reason that I was the inventor of the horrible thought, I began to defend this misconception possessed by the multitudes.

(5) My attitude, I must admit, ran the gamut from bothersome to surprisingly capable and extremely helpful, so I cannot debate the reasoning behind the depicting of "old people" as bothersome. (6) In order to clear my records, I must reveal that I consider almost every age of our species bothersome! (7) I believe that to be a predominant human characteristic, perhaps even a prerequisite!

Vitiated Verbs

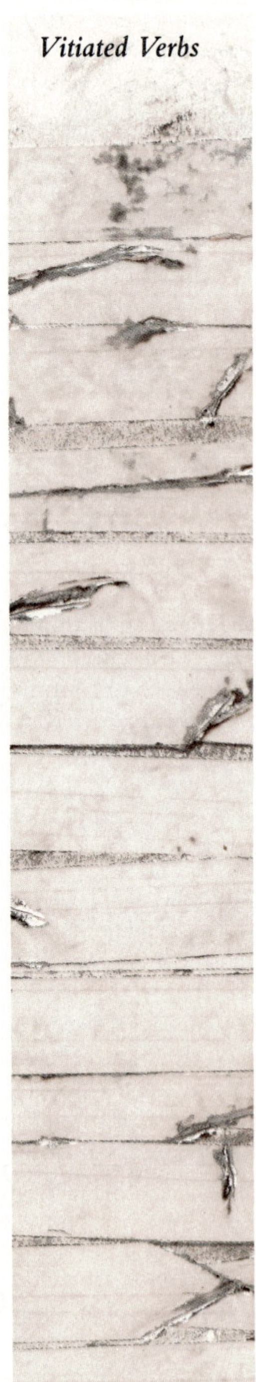

An undesirable by-product of the passive voice is the use of vitiated, or debased, verbs. A vitiated verb is one that has been turned into a noun but continues to take the place of the verb by appearing in combination with an auxiliary or some other "weak" verb. Examples:

Vitiated	*Active/Strong*
An indication of . . . is provided by . . .	The . . . indicates that . . .
Repayment will be made . . .	We will repay . . .
Consideration is given to . . .	We are considering . . .
Make an adjustment of . . .	Adjust . . .
An evaluation has been made . . .	We have evaluated . . .
The writer has an appreciation of . . .	We appreciate/like . . .
An inclination is shown by . . .	. . . inclines
The operation was performed . . .	The doctor operated . . .
Attribution of the remarks was made to . . .	He attributed the remarks to . . .
An investigation has been undertaken of . . .	We have investigated/ studied . . .
A positive rating was arrived at by . . .	We rated . . . positive because . . .
An analysis has been made of . . .	We have analyzed . . .
A report has been released by . . .	XYZ has reported that . . .
Emphasis should be placed on . . .	. . . should be emphasized
An improvement has been made in . . .	. . . has been improved

Verbs are the muscles and sinews of language. They move your sentences forward and make your words flow. Each time you change a verb into a noun you slow your cadence and lower the pressure. You break your stride when you vitiate verbs.

—Ernst Jacobi

The writer reveals other problems—the use of trite diction and errors in denotation, but circumlocution is the problem that interferes with communication the most. The roundabout words confuse the reader. Sentence (3) is particularly obscure. It seems that it is the feelings of young people that are bothersome and useless, but it becomes clear later that "bothersome and useless" refers to older people. In sentence (4), circumlocutions reverse the author's intended meaning. The writer says he will *defend* the misconception when he actually means that he will prove it wrong.

By rewriting the circumlocutions as direct expressions, the writer's message becomes clearer, shorter, and much easier to understand:

> As I sat crying, I reflected on the presumptuous attitudes of young people. We all tend to generalize when we are depressed, and that's what I was doing then. As I saw it, teenagers consider older people bothersome and useless. I, of course, excluded myself from this generalization, and I tried to prove that prevalent attitudes toward older people were founded on misconceptions.
>
> I believe older people can be productive, but I admit that I sometimes consider them bothersome. I cannot defend that attitude; however, I consider people of almost any age bothersome, and I think most people feel this way at one time or another.

As you revise for *specifics, lean sentences, active verb forms,* and *direct expressions,* you will put punch in your writing that will help your readers to remember for a long time what you had to say.

APPLICATION

Each of the sentences below contains problems in word use. Identify the problem and revise the sentence to correct it. If possible, do this activity in groups.

1. The air smelled good, the trees looked nice, the breeze was just right, and we felt great.
2. Exercise is something that should be tried by everyone.
3. In my estimation, the requirement of additional classrooms is an unwise move undertaken by the school board.
4. It is expected by most of the members of the community that the abandonment of the drive to retain the trees will be detrimental to the city.
5. The old house on the corner was in sad need of repair: the porch was falling, most of windows were broken, the paint was peeling all over, the roof looked terrible.

6. The Congress's insistence on backing up the budgetary demands by the President only resulted in the creation of an atmosphere of resentment and mistrust among the voters.
7. It was agreed by everyone that a good time was enjoyed at the great movie last night.

EDITING AND MANUSCRIPT FORM

Have you ever been getting dressed for some big event—and for hours it seems you are experimenting with this outfit, trying on that combination, changing this color, adding that? Then, finally, you look at the clock and know that you have to decide. You have to choose something and start getting ready.

Well, often that is the way you have to behave regarding your writing. You could do discovery drafts forever; you could always make some improvements in what you are working on in the shaping stage. But you just have to call a halt. (Not, of course, before you have a discovery draft that communicates to the reader, hangs together, and has form.) Perhaps it is the timeline that provokes your calling a halt; perhaps it is your own decision that "this one is going to be it." Whatever the instigation to say, "Yep, now I'm moving into the completing stage with this writing," there comes a time when you have to move.

When you do move into the completing stage, you can either revise the paper and then edit it or move directly from shaping to editing. But you must take the paper through the editing phase of the completing stage. It is irresponsible—and dumb—not to edit your paper after you have put as much of yourself as you have into it and worked on it as hard as you have to be sure that readers enjoy the writing. But let's look at some specific reasons why you must edit. You'll see for yourself that editing is the smart writer's last act.

Why Edit?

NO SHIRT
NO SHOES
NO SERVICE

Certain rules of correctness and propriety are associated with writing. If you violate these established principles—say, have no margins or write in choppy, incomplete thoughts—then you are asking for the same kind of rebuff received by a barefoot person who tries to go into a roadside restaurant that clearly has a sign on the door: NO SHOES, NO SHIRT, NO SERVICE. There may be something to be proved by going against the rules, but in the case of writing, it's just plain smart to know the rules and to go by them. *"It's easier to ride the horse in the direction it's going."*

NOT CORRECT
NOT POLISHED
NOT READ

Editing Makes the Reader More Receptive to Your Message. Going through the editing phase of the completing stage makes life easier for your *message*. People do have certain expectations of a paper—they want it to be neat, to make sense, to be readable, to be correctly spelled and punctuated, and to have an order that they can follow. Because that's so, many people see only the errors or weakness—the smudge, the misspelled words, the awkward sentence—and fail to see anything else in the paper, no matter how important that "anything else" might be. You may not think it is fair to equate mistakes in papers with sloppy thinking, but many people do just that. They pay so much attention to one or two faults that they miss the whole message. To give your message the best chance possible, you have to make it free of blemishes.

Editing Removes the Last Sources of Confusion. Things written in haste sometimes confuse a reader because the message is actually blocked by gaps in the organization, too little development of the main points, or a lack of coherence. The completing stage gives you a final chance to make the message totally clear. Perhaps the reader is tolerant, maybe he or she doesn't mind a smudge or is "understanding" about the misspelled word (although it's dangerous to count on that). But even if the errors or weaknesses don't upset the reader, they may still steal the punch or cloud the clarity of the message you are trying to get across. It is a shame to spend hours on a piece of writing, only to have it less effective than it could be simply because you didn't do a thorough completing stage and remove the last sources of confusion. The completing stage lets you find those things that could weaken the message; you have the leisure to sit back, relaxed and objective, and revise so that there is no confusion in your writing.

Novelist June Flaum Singer:

"*I work!* I'm a dedicated worker. I don't go in for fancy excuses. I never moan and groan that I'm blocked. So some days it doesn't come. But you write anyway and fix it the next day. You work and you labor because you want to see the results."

Editing Lets You Say What You Mean in a Way You Can Really Be Proud of. There is nothing like the feeling you get when you say something important in *just* the way you want it said. But it's impossible to check on the *way* it is said while the thoughts are still hot and rolling in. It's only after the words are "cold" that you can do the fine tuning that turns work from "OK" into "Good" or "Good" into "Best." Going back over your work gives you a chance to (1) say what you mean, (2) put on any finishing touches that you want to make, (3) rearrange for better effect, and (4) put your best foot forward. *It's your final chance to make the writing something you are proud of—both for* what *you say and* how *you say it.*

Editing Releases Your Paper and You. Of the three stages of writing, the third one is valuable to you symbolically because it says, "*I'm finished!* It is the final act of this project in my life. I started it; I worked on it; I've finished it. I'm now ready to move on to something else." There is a sense of liberation in this act. You've in effect said, "This is the best I can do on this at the moment. I've finished it. I'm ready for a new project." Skipping the third stage will always leave you feeling that you did not give the writing your best.

The Editing Eye

Editing does not mean condemning. The critical faculty of your mind allows you to evaluate and discriminate in the editing phase. You are able to turn a critical eye—an editing eye—on your writing and spot the possibilities that are still there for making the writing better.

When you turn a *critical eye* on your work, you are doing something you do in life many times a day. Have you ever hung posters or pictures on a wall and then stepped back to see how they looked? "That one is too high . . . no, a little too low, put it back up just an inch or so . . . that's right; hold it while I get the hammer." That is turning a critical eye on your work.

You do a similar assessment of your writing in the editing phase of the completing stage. You take a critical—but constructive—look. You aren't looking to blame yourself for what you did badly—you merely want to see how your writing might appear to someone else. Then, after you have found some ways to make your writing not only say what you want it to but also read better, you make those changes that will cause your readers to keep on reading.

What kinds of questions might you ask yourself in order to make this critical evaluation? Here are some evocative ones:

> Have I made everything clear? Do I give enough information, and do I relate the various elements to my main idea and to one another?
>
> Can the reader always see where I am going in this piece of writing?
>
> Do I have enough variety?
>
> What kinds of improvement and polish can I give this so that it is the very best writing I can possibly do?

We need our critical faculty if we are to write really satisfying pieces. The problem with this critic is that it usually shows up too soon—in the creating stage, for example, when we are nowhere near a re-vision or editing stage (it's all we can do just to see at all, much less re-see). Because the critic can get so strident and so pushy in the early stages, where it is counterproductive, we may lean too much in the other direction and assume that we don't need a critical eye at all.

But our critic really helps us in the editing phase. This is the perfect time to give your writing the once-over—but not lightly. And there is nothing negative about it. It is absolutely a golden opportunity for you to sit back—almost like a person who didn't write the paper—and see what can be done to make it the best it can be.

Although you might suppose that nobody would send out a paper without polishing, editing, and correcting it, experience shows that almost all beginning writers tend to skip this stage. Perhaps they lack the special skills required to do the job, or maybe they feel so burdened throughout the creating and shaping stages they figure that *any* kind of first draft is victory enough. Whatever the cause, many people omit this final stage. They shouldn't, however, and neither should you.

Five Editing Steps

There are five steps to take in the editing phase of the completing stage; each takes you closer to the goal of a perfect paper. Here are the five steps:

1. The Get Distance Step
2. The Read Aloud Step
3. The Find-the-Errors Step
4. The Make-It-Look-Good Step
5. The Proofread Step

Let's look at what you need to do to complete this five-step approach to editing your work.

The Get Distance Step

It happens to most writers, including professionals: they fall in love with what they have just finished writing. They can't tear themselves away from it. In fact, they read and reread each word, each gem of a phrase, each brilliantly wrought paragraph. How ever could they have doubted their ability to carry it off? It may well be the best-written work on the subject—anywhere—ever—or on any subject, for that matter.

Well, this euphoria is well deserved—but *not* particularly trustworthy. The relief of finally being finished may get in the way of your ability to see your creation as others might see it. When love is blind, disappointment may lurk in the wings: "I never knew you snored," might be the complaint of a honeymoon-is-over couple. More likely, they *did* know—but, being in the hypnotic fog of romantic love, ignored what they noticed later on, once the fog lifted. Similarly, writers who are "in love" with their latest creation are not likely to be entirely objective.

What to do? Love your writing all you want. But get some distance. There are several ways to get distance, and although you'll get by using only one of them, you'll really profit by using all of them. Here they are:

Let the writing cool before you edit it. Of course you will be entranced by each well-chosen word if you read your piece when it's hot off the typewriter or computer. That's why you need to let at least a day go by—

preferably two—before you get back to it. Waiting that length of time will make a "new reader" out of you—your approach will be more like a *reader's* and less like the *author's*. You will detect weaknesses and errors you simply couldn't see before.

Pretend you are a (skeptical) reader. This is another way to give you some distance from your writing. You didn't want a hostile critic peering over your shoulder in the creating and shaping stages—it might have wrecked all your explorations and discoveries. Well, here's a place where a critic does belong—and can actually help you. Pretend that you are the most disbelieving, skeptical, "show me!" reader you can dream up. Ask the writer (who, for the moment, is someone other than you) to prove *everything:* "Oh yeah? Why should I believe that? What's the connection between this paragraph and the ones that follow? What's the point?" And so on. This isn't the kindest way, granted; but it will provide you with a rigorous critique.

Read your writing backwards. No, not from right to left (unless you write in Hebrew or Arabic)—from last sentence to first sentence. This odd exercise is actually an aid to becoming objective. It gives you distance from your writing by disengaging you from the familiarity of it, from the flow of one line to another. Each sentence stands out, alone and naked, unprotected by its neighbors. If it's weak, or incomplete, or boring, you'll know. (This procedure works only with sentences, not with larger elements such as organization and structure of paragraphs.)

Make marginal notes to yourself. Use symbols to make quick, shorthand notes in the margins as you edit. (Obviously, leave wide margins on your draft.) You need to see your writing as a whole, and you can't do so if you are constantly stopping to correct errors and make changes as you read it. When you are all done, then you can go back to your symbols and make the needed changes. You can make up your own symbols. Or you can use these:

? a passage seems unclear

SS sentence seems awkward

ℊ delete a word, sentence, or passage

* insertion needed for further explanation or similar reason

Get a second (and third) opinion. The easiest way to assure critical distance in revising a paper is to let others read it and give you feedback. The more readers the better. That's what professionals do all the time: they share their work with friends, colleagues, and editors, trusting them to point out both strengths and weaknesses. It's important to know what readers consider your strengths so you don't accidentally purge them in revision; it also helps to hear several opinions about weaknesses to give you perspective. Readers and editors won't always agree about your work; two readers may give you completely different feedback. But at least you know what elements of a given paper are evoking reactions. If it's the reaction you want, keep things as they are. If not, you'll need to revise.

Remember that responsible editing is a two-way street. If you expect others to read your work sensitively, you owe them the same courtesy.

The Read Aloud Step

This sounds like a small thing, but it could actually be the secret to finding errors and mistakes in your work before you turn it in for final evaluation. You can just about be certain that if you stumble over something when you are reading it, there *is* something there to fix. Countless times students, when they are reading their papers out loud to other members of the class, are overheard to say something like "Oh, I left part of that sentence out" or "I didn't say what I thought I did or meant to say there; I'll fix it before I turn it in." Reading out loud will catch a lot of your mistakes. The best way is to read it aloud to someone else—you tend to really notice what doesn't work when someone else is listening! But you can even read it out loud to yourself (preferably into a tape recorder), and your ear will catch what your eye may have missed. If you find yourself listening with only half an ear and becoming bored, read the paragraphs out of order. That will perk up your attention and help your ear catch inconsistencies in development as well as weaknesses in word choice and rhythm.

The Find-the-Errors Step

True, there are a million errors you might make in putting together a paper, but some errors seem to occur more frequently than others. In this case, as in many others, knowledge is power—if you know what kinds of errors to look for, you are likely to find (and fix) them. So if you are simply aware—awake and conscious—of the problems you *typically* have with grammar mistakes, spelling errors, and so on, you will be ahead of about half of all people who are studying how to write.

Here are some places where errors like to lurk:

Misspelled words or typos. Includes typing or handwriting errors.

Punctuation errors and omissions. For example, commas left out or in the wrong place; apostrophes left out or in the wrong place; one quotation mark missing (in a set of two); one parenthesis missing (in a set of two).

Punctuation out of place. Commas and periods should *precede* quotation marks. For example: *She complained, "I don't know why he spilled the beans."* Colons and semicolons should be placed *outside* quotation marks.

Confused and inaccurate use of punctuation. When do you use a comma? When do you use a semicolon? What about colons and dashes? Here are some rules of thumb to choose punctuation:

Commas

(1) before a coordinating conjunction (and, but, or, so, yet, and the rest) in a compound sentence. For example: *The boy loved to swing, so he bypassed the seesaw.*

(2) with introductory words, phrases, or clauses that need to be separated from the main idea. For example: *Inside, the house looked more elegant than it did on the outside.*

(3) to separate a series of nouns. For example: *The man, the boy, and the dog loved to run together.*

Semicolons

(1) when there's an independent clause on both sides of the semicolon. For example: *He liked her smile; she liked his style.*

(2) in a compound sentence, instead of a coordinating conjunction. For example: *This example is not the only one possible; however, it is one that works.*

Colons

(1) after a grammatically complete sentence, to lead into an enumeration, explanation, illustration, or long quotation. For example: *Here's how the gadget works: it extracts the liquid by means of pressure and rotation.*

Dashes

(1) after a word or group of words that summarizes, amplifies, or reverses what goes before it. For example: *Seeing a black cat near his path, he took a deep breath, chided himself for being silly—and crossed the street as rapidly as possible.*

(2) to enclose parenthetical statements (an alternative to parentheses—has more presence within the sentence than parentheses do. They are more of an aside). For example: *I, too—although I am embarrassed to admit it—voted for that candidate.*

Words that are commonly confused. Similarities in spelling and meaning often cause writers to misuse the following words.

It's/Its	*It's* a contraction of "it is"—***It's** a nice day today. Its* has to do with possession—*The book rested on **its** special shelf* (that is, the shelf "belonged" to the book).
To/Too/Two	*Too* means also—*I prefer chocolate, **too**. Two* is the number—*I want **two** identical shirts. To* is everything else—*I want **to** go **to** the store.*
Advise/Advice	*Advise* is a verb—*It's important to **advise** people who come to you for help. Advice* is a noun—*That's good **advice,** but I won't be taking it.*
Affect/Effect	*Affect* is a verb meaning "to influence"—*The movie **affects** everyone who sees it. Effect* is a noun meaning "a result"—*The **effect** of this perfume will not be legendary.*
Fewer/Less	*Fewer* is for amounts that can be counted separately—*There are **fewer** flies today than yesterday. Less* is for amounts that can't be compared separately—*There's **less** rain today than yesterday.*

Inconsistencies. When you choose a way of expressing something, use that way consistently throughout your paper. Examples include: **percent** *vs.* **per cent** *vs.* **%;** spelling out numbers under 10 *vs.* under 100; hyphenation of prefixes, such as **nonverbal** *vs.* **non-verbal.**

Insufficient use of writing tools. Use the dictionary as often as you need to (maybe more). It will tell you about spelling, hyphenation, and what the best word might be for a particular application. You may also want to use a thesaurus for finding synonyms.

Sentence fragments. Be sure that you have a subject and verb for every sentence—or be sure that you intended not to have. Sentence fragments are sometimes used intentionally for emphasis. Just be certain if you have sentence fragments that they are appropriate to the writing and are intentional. Otherwise, pack a verb for every subject—don't leave home without one!

Run-on sentences. Don't do this: Don't have one complete sentence like this, the next sentence will look like that. (See that run-on? how confusing it is?) Put a period at the end of a complete sentence and start the next sentence with a capital letter. Or put a comma or semicolon between the two sentences.

Consistent tense and person. If you are writing in the present tense (The congressional staff is now in training), don't change suddenly to past tense (It was studied by several citizen groups this week.) Also, if you are writing about a single person (She looks for a dancing partner every week), don't use a plural verb or plural pronoun (but they can't find one.) Stick with what you start out with—same tense, same person—all the way through.

The Make-It-Look-Good Step

Manuscript form. When you have checked your paper for errors and oversights, you are ready to write or type the final copy. Now you want to think about the way the writing is going to look on the page. Be alert to this! As in editing, don't let carelessness or laziness cause you to do a halfway job. Nobody would spend hours building a beautiful walnut bookcase and then display it at a craft fair with sawdust all over it. The way your paper *looks* will have a considerable psychological effect on the reader. And while a good-looking paper with no content won't get you anywhere, a paper with excellent content but a sloppy appearance usually won't either. You can't win *either* way on this one. It has to be *both*. Good content + good appearance = success with reader.

The total is equal to the *sum* of its parts. Period! Parts alone don't make it.

Whether your paper is handwritten or typewritten, there are some conventions that you should always observe:

1. Make your paper as neat as possible. Erase carefully, and whenever possible, use correction fluid instead of an eraser. Correction fluid is especially good for long corrections.

2. Use one side of the paper only.

3. Use standard size (8″ × 10½″ or 8½″ × 11″) ruled paper if you are handwriting, or 8½″ × 11″ unruled paper if you are typing. Do not use legal size, colored, or spiral-notebook paper or cheap typing paper.

4. Always number your pages.

Making a Handwritten Paper as Attractive as Possible

1. Always use a black or blue ballpoint pen. Do not use felt tip markers; they tend to make your writing too bold and unattractive. Never use pencil for the final copy. It suggests that the paper is not yet in final form and is hard to read.

2. Write neatly and legibly. Remember that if your reader doesn't understand your writing, he or she is not likely to pay attention to your message. If double spacing makes your handwriting easier to read, then double-space—but make sure your teacher doesn't object to this.

3. If you have a title for the writing, put it on the top line of the first page. Skip at least one line, preferably two or three, before beginning the

text of your paper. If you don't have a title, begin on the second or third line of the page.

4. Follow the margin on the left side of the paper and leave at least a half-inch margin on the right. Don't write on the last line of the page. Your words should neither bleed off the right nor fall off the bottom edge of the page.

Making a Typewritten Paper Look Professional

1. Always double-space when you type. Single spacing is difficult to read.

2. Use good quality paper. It is difficult to read material typed on cheap typing paper or onion skin paper. Do not use erasable bond. Its finish, which makes erasures easy, also makes smudging more likely. Besides, unless you erase carefully, erasures will still be noticeable and will often be messy. If you plan to type most of your papers, invest in several hundred sheets of good quality typing paper bought at a book or office supply store, not at the local grocery store.

3. Use a good black or blue ribbon. Change your ribbon when it begins to look faint. A paper typed using a worn-out ribbon is difficult to read. Do not use italics or script characters except for special effects. See that the type in your typewriter is clean.

4. Leave at least one-inch margins all around. If you will bind your paper in a folder, the left margin should be slightly wider to avoid making that side of the page look cramped once it is in the folder. The top margin on the first page should always be about two inches. Type the title; then triple space before beginning the body of the paper.

Making a Computer-Printed Paper Look Professional

1. Always double-space when you put the final version of the writing into your word processor.

2. Establish good margins by formatting and be certain that the top and bottom of your computer formatting pagination is what you will want for your finished product.

3. Type in upper and lower case; don't put the CAP key down on the computer keyboard for convenience and forget to let it up when you are editing the final version before printing it off.

4. Use a letter-quality printer, if at all possible. No matter what printer you use, be certain that it makes a legible page. Don't turn in an essay that looks like a spread sheet with funny computer marks all over it and signs and symbols nobody but you would understand.

5. If at all possible, photocopy the paper and turn in the copy. This will allow you to avoid turning in computer paper which may be of a

lesser quality than copy paper. If you must turn in the copy directly off your printer, be sure that you tear off the perforations on each side of the page. And tear the sheets apart! Don't give your professor a running computer printout. Make sure the piece of writing looks like a piece of writing, not a laboratory inventory sheet.

6. If your computer and/or printer allows for varying fonts, use a font that resembles typing. Don't justify your copy or use unusual characters or fonts. Keep it simple.

The Proofread Step

Your paper can be proofread by you or by someone else, but the important thing is that it gets done. A well-written, good-looking page replete with typographical and other errors is a little hard to take seriously.

It's worth your while to become familiar with proofreading concerns and symbols, but for extra insurance have another person proofread on top of your proofreading. It is *very* difficult for the person who has written a paper to see mistakes in it. For one thing, the eye compensates for letters left out or words missing, and your brain will just fill in the blanks. Since you, the writer, *know* what you are saying, the words don't actually have to be there on the page for you to *think* them as you read. Also, you may not know certain principles of correctness (like commas or apostrophes) and it may take you a few weeks to learn these rules. In the meantime, your papers may be evaluated. So get someone adept at catching errors to go over your paper with you before you turn it in.

What *is* proofreading? It is the final read-through for the purpose of catching careless *errors*. At this stage, you are looking only for typographical errors, omitted letters or words, sometimes even omitted sentences, misspellings, incorrect punctuation, and similar minor errors. Use the following symbols to indicate to yourself or to your typist the necessary change.

k capitalization needed
K no capitalization
^, insert comma
^; insert semicolon
⊙ insert period
⊙: insert colon
delete
⁀‿ close up
^ insert a word or sentence
# insert a space
bak transpose letters

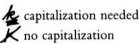

Here is an example of what a manuscript with proofreader's marks can look like:

> The task of finding good in bad, or in beauty in ugliness, is one that I find most interesting but difficult. The first thought of any intelligent person is that's ridiculus! But many tasks look ridiculus at first, and then turn out to be really interesting.
>
> So here is what I looked at insomnia.
>
> You might think, what could be good about insomhia? Isn't it bad for your health? Isn't sleep improtant? What about all the over the counter drgs (and the perscrition drugs) that get people with insomnia addicted? What about the shortempers in the daytime? Yes, all this is true and statisticly documented. But here is one advantige of insomnia: You get time to do what you have to do, and nobody bothers you! The phone doesn't ring, and the dppr bell doesnt ring, and no one needs you to do anything for them. YOU ARE LEFT ALONE! You can concntrate!
>
> In fact, I am writing this at 2 am right now.

A FINAL WORD

Don't spend time trying to be perfect, unless you are superhuman. None of us is able to learn or do everything at once; what counts is steady progress and growing confidence that you and your classmates know what good writing feels and looks like.

You've worked hard to get this far. Now it is time to apply what you have learned in this general discussion of the writing process—Part 1: A Tour of the Writing Process—to specific writing assignments that follow in the next part, The Writing Portfolio. Don't hesitate to return to these chapters as necessary to review. And remember that more detailed discussions of the topics introduced here follow The Writing Portfolio, in Part 3: Crafting the Portfolio.

Best of luck!

PART 2 The Writing Portfolio: Ten Assignments

As you delve more deeply into the writing process, this section will help you

- assemble a portfolio of writing that represents the range of your skills
- understand the three general writing purposes: writing to express, writing to tell, and writing to change
- identify the particular emphasis, purpose, motivation, situation, circumstance, and writer-reader relationship of each writing purpose
- practice employing each writing purpose through several assignments

Students and teachers alike tend to treat papers submitted in an academic course as individual products dropping off an assembly line: the instructor assigns a paper; the students write it; the teacher marks, grades, and returns the work; then the assembly line clatters on to the next job. When a grade is given for the writing course, it is usually the average of the marks earned by the individual assignments.

This familiar procedure makes a certain sense, but it can leave the impression that learning about writing is like a two-week tour through Europe. By the end of the trip, your passport has accumulated perhaps a dozen stamps but you've gained little feel for the continent itself. It's all a blur, just a kaleidoscope of languages, shapes, and people seen through a tour bus window. Similarly, a writing course can seem like a travelogue of separate assignments, each a bit different in tone, organization, audience, and purpose. They keep you engaged for a while, but by the end of a course, you may find it hard to distinguish one paper from another. You're confident you've learned something from the experience, but just aren't sure what.

To break down the impression that a writing course is a sequence of unrelated assignments, try looking upon what you produce as a body of work—as material that contributes to a writing portfolio. This portfolio will represent your "collected works," what you have produced over the course of a school term. In some classes, you may be allowed to hone and polish selected pieces in the portfolio right up to the conclusion of the course. In other cases, you will work on the papers one at a time and add them in sequence to your collection. In either case, what you finally have is a body of work that represents a range of writing experiences unified by your authorship. Some items in the portfolio may be stronger than others; some you will give more attention to; some will simply interest you more. And that is precisely the point of building a portfolio rather than seeing your essays as separate products. The portfolio allows you to highlight your strengths and put your weaknesses into context. It builds an individual portrait of you as a writer—much the way a collection of anyone's work presents a fuller picture than does an individual piece. *Macbeth* is a great play, good enough in itself to assure us that Shakespeare, its author, was a genius; but if *Macbeth* were Shakespeare's only surviving work, we'd have a much more restricted view of his ability than we in fact do from his existing "portfolio" of thirty-seven plays. What if the only Beatles' song recorded were "I Want to Hold Your Hand" or the only Steven Spielberg movie made were *1941?*

More important, looking at your papers as a body of work might encourage you to see the relationships among them—how your tone changed when you moved from a personal essay to a persuasive one; how you shifted patterns of organization from essay to essay; how much easier it was for you to write critically than expressively. These shifts tell you something both about the nature of writing (different writing assignments require different tactics) and about yourself (different people have different abilities and interests).

So as you survey the chapters that follow, either writing the papers your instructor selects or making the choice of assignments yourself, work toward assembling a package that represents a broad range of skills. Express yourself as fully and competently as you can in the time available. Strive for diversity too. Don't play it safe by choosing or emphasizing only those kinds of writing you already know how to manage. Broaden your portfolio to include samples of writing to express, writing to tell, writing to change. You needn't apologize, however, if you don't master each category—few writers do.

And that's what the portfolio makes you—a *writer* with something to show for your efforts. The portfolio is something to look back on and something to grow from. So make the most of this opportunity.

Guides for Collecting a Writing Portfolio

1. Provide a one- or two-page survey of the contents of your portfolio: list the name of each writing assignment and the title of the essay you wrote in response to it.
2. For each assignment, include your final version of the essay.
3. Following each essay, include its corresponding creating activities, discovery draft, and intermediate drafts.

PURPOSES FOR WRITING

The assignments in the Portfolio section are grouped according to three general writing purposes which are important for you to understand: writing to express, writing to tell, and writing to change. To build confidence as a writer you need to know what you are doing, and, where writing is concerned, knowing what to do means understanding *purpose*. Once you understand the purpose of a given piece of work, you've got a collar on it. You can lead it in directions that suit you. Of course, people write for many specific reasons (to apologize for an angry remark, to describe a new roommate, to ask the IRS for an extension), but even situations such as these can be roughly classified into these three general purposes.

Writing to Express

In Writing to Tell, the writer's intention is to convey information; in Writing to Change, the intention is to make something happen—to have the reader see, think, or do something differently as a result of reading that piece of writing. But although Writing to Express may involve certain information and offer the reader a certain perspective, its major focus is on the writer. In other words, you yourself are the subject. It is your own sensibilities, experiences, thoughts, feelings, realizations, and so on that take center stage. This is a subjective mode—you are educating your reader about yourself.

This is a risk, of course, "Here I am," you tell the reader, "this is what I have done/thought/felt." Whether you are writing about something that is intensely personal or about your intellectual reaction to something, you take the risk that the subject—you—will be judged. The readers may not like what you write, or they may judge it as stupid, or they may not even respond at all. In the face of this admittedly unnerving risk, why do people write to express?

Some people may do it to show off, to be arrogant, to dominate, to be right, or to push individual ideas off on the reader. But this is writing to hide, not to express—and readers can tell the difference between a person and an act. When you write to express, you tell the truth as you know it; and the readers know this because they find themselves in what you write—their own lives, thoughts, and experiences. Honest expressive writing has the ring of truth; the reader is touched.

The form in which you express is fairly open-ended. Writing to Express takes no customary, predictable form. Instead, the form springs from the writer's sensibilities—some expressive writings come out as books, others as essays, others as journals, letters, editorials, sermons, prefaces, aphorisms, and more. But no matter what the form, the writing will have a personal voice—the reader can hear and know the person behind that writing. So although you can't count on a predictable form, you can count on there always being a voice.

All Writing to Express has a particular emphasis, motivation, situation, circumstance, and writer-reader relationship.

Emphasis. The focus is on the writer's sensibilities, experiences, and/or thoughts. You, the writer, are the star.

Motivation. What would make you want to write for expression? You might have:

- some inner need.
- some stimulation of ideas.
- some stirring of your emotions.
- some desire to share yourself.
- a dedication to others' quality of life.
- a love for personal form.
- a love for words.

Any or all of these reasons is enough motivation to get the juices flowing.

Situation. Unlike other forms, where the writing often is requested by an employer, publisher, or editor, Writing to Express may not be written for publication at all. Many letters, journals, and diaries are written only for the writer, or to one or several particular people, and only get published long after the time of writing.

Circumstance. This mode usually has no timelines (although sometimes an expressive piece is requested by a publisher or editor, if the writer is famous already). The writer usually determines the writing's length and time—it is organic to the writing itself.

Writer-Reader Relationship. Unlike Writing to Tell, where the relationship is "informed person" to "less informed person," and Writing to Change, where the relationship is "person who wants *X*" to "person who could do *X*," here the relationship is friend to friend, or host to guest.

The Portfolio offers three expressive assignments:

Chapter 5: Writing a Journal

Chapter 6: The Personal Experience Essay

Chapter 7: The Personal Perspective Essay

Writing to Tell

Writing to Tell means that you have some valuable information that the reader probably does not have, and that you want to relate this information to the reader. This is different from Writing to Express, where the intention is to educate the reader about the writer—your personal feelings, experiences, and perspectives. It is also different from Writing to Change, where the intention is to make the reader see or do something in a certain way and take action. In Writing to Tell, the intention is to lay out or teach the reader something you know—to convey facts rather than opinions, hypotheses, positions, or personal experiences. Therefore, in Writing to Tell, what takes center stage is not what you think or how you feel about the subject, but the subject itself.

This means that you need to write about a subject you know well. And this, in turn, means that your writer-reader relationship is one of "informed person" to "less informed person." This doesn't imply that you are superior to the reader; it just means that you know something that might be of value, and that you wish to make this information available to your reader.

Therefore, if you choose a subject and a style appropriate for your audience, you are likely to have a grateful reader, rather than one who feels patronized, resentful, or bored. In short, you will be performing a genuine service by making available what you know.

The *form* in which you convey your information depends on what it is you want to tell, and what kind of result you intend to get. If you want to teach the reader how to do something—build a birdhouse, begin a stamp collection, solve an algebra problem—you will write a *how-to* essay. If you want to alert the reader to a particular problem and to suggest a solution, you will write a *problem-solution* essay. And if you want simply to let the reader know about the existence of something, you'll write an *information* essay. Each of these forms will be discussed in up-coming chapters. But whether you choose the *how-to*, the *problem-solving*, or the *information* essay, the following points are true of all three forms.

All Writing to Tell essays have a particular emphasis, purpose, motivation, situation, circumstance, and writer-reader relationship.

Emphasis. The *emphasis* of a piece of writing is what takes center stage. Anything that is not the information itself—your opinions, the flavor of your personality, your personal experience and perspective—must take a back seat. These aspects may be present in the writing, but they will be in the background. The reason for this is that emphasizing the content allows your writing to fulfill its purpose.

Purpose. And what *is* the purpose of a Writing to Tell essay? To do one or more of the following:

- to report.
- to inform.
- to convey facts or details.
- to announce.
- to instruct.
- to make known.
- to make available.

Motivation. All writers (whether aware of it or not) always have a reason for writing a particular piece. While the initial motivation may be less than inspiring (for example, your instructor requires you to write an assignment, or you want to publish an article to make some money), the writing doesn't really get going until you find your own motivation. The main question to ask is "What really interests me about this subject?" There is no such thing as a "right" or "wrong" motivation, only one that gets the juices flowing. For example, if two people were asked to write about the Empire State Building, the first person might focus on the structural techniques for building safe skyscrapers (perhaps she loved to play with blocks as a child), while the second one might choose to discuss the phenomenon of vertigo (perhaps he always had a secret fear of heights). Both pieces of writing would be legitimate responses to the assignment—they would differ because of the writer's unique motivation.

Situation. It makes a difference where your essay will appear. A Writing to Tell piece is appropriate for any publication that conveys facts and information. Thus it is appropriate to use the Writing to Tell form if your essay will appears in a newspaper; it is not appropriate to use this form if the destination of the essay is a political leaflet that showcases opinions. Typical Writing to Tell pieces appear in:

- work-related writing (memos, reports, analyses, letters).
- articles in magazines and newspapers.
- texts and other educational books (like this one).
- manuals.
- essays for college courses (like the ones you will be doing).

Circumstance. What are the practical conditions—the terms—that govern a Writing to Tell essay? In short, how long should it be? Who wants you to write it? And how much time do you have in which to write it?

> Length: This is proscribed by the publication or the person requesting the piece (for example, "under 500 words").
>
> Who wants it written: Someone requests or demands it (for example, a teacher, an editor, a publisher, or an employer).
>
> Time value: Writing to Tell pieces usually have what's called a "short shelf-life"—that is, it may be important to be the first one to tell about the subject, or the subject may become outdated and need to be updated. On the other hand, some Writing to Tell essays are so well done that they remain the best on the subject no matter how many additional articles are written by others.

Writer-Reader Relationship. Writing to Tell assumes that you know something that the reader will want to know (providing you do your job well). You are the "informed person" to the reader's "less informed person." This gives you some real authority. So use it appropriately. Don't be overly modest about your expertise, but don't look down on the reader for not knowing what you know. After all, it's what the reader does not know that creates a market for your writing in the first place.

These points in Writing to Tell—emphasis, purpose, motivation, situation, circumstance, and writer-reader relationship—"go together" in a way that will soon become familiar to you as you write. For instance, in Writing to Tell the place of possible publication is extremely important because where you want to see the writing printed will determine a lot about how you write it. Also, knowing that there is almost always a set or standard length for Writing to Tell, you will find yourself writing into that constraint naturally. (When you practice Writing to Change and

Writing to Express, on the other hand, you will see a different "configuration" or "pattern" that the points of the writing take.)

The Portfolio offers these assignments that involve Writing to Tell:

Chapter 8: The How-To Essay

Chapter 9: The Problem-Solution Essay

Chapter 10: The Information Essay

Writing to Change

What distinguishes Writing to Change from other forms is that it intends to make something happen—to have the reader look, think, or act in a certain way as a result of reading the writer's words. By contrast, the focus in Writing to Tell is on the information to be conveyed, while in Writing to Express, the focus is on the writer's own experiences and perspective. Writing to Change uses some aspects of each of the other modes. Like Writing to Tell, it conveys information, and like Writing to Express, it speaks in the writer's own distinct voice. But its purpose in delivering the information is not merely to inform but to convince the reader to do something differently, and its purpose in revealing the writer's voice is not to share experiences but to support the writer's assertions about what needs to be changed, and how to make those changes.

Implicit in Writing to Change is the conviction that words have real power—that they can change how people see themselves, each other, societal institutions and relationships, and the world. We find examples of this kind of writing throughout history, from the Ten Commandments to the Declaration of Independence and beyond. You probably have written many Writing to Change communications already, whether you know it or not; certainly, grade-school essays on "Why We Should Save Animals from Extinction" fall into this category, but so do letters to the editor, slips of paper dropped in "Suggestion" or "Complaint" boxes, and "Dear John" or "Marry me" letters. So for as long as you have been writing anything, at least some of that writing has been to change something. You are not, therefore, a stranger to this mode.

What may be new to you, though, is a knowledge of how best to use Writing to Change. You will use it when you want to: (1) Cause action, movement, or transformation of some sort or (2) Take a new position or stand by asserting something in a new way, judging something in a new way, evaluating something in a new way, or acting in a new way.

A Writing to Change essay may take several forms. If you want to change what the reader knows, thinks, or believes about a particular thing, then you will write an *assertion-with-evidence* essay. If you want to change the readers' ability to judge by helping them be informed, then you will write an *evaluation* essay. If you want to change the reader's mind and perhaps persuade the reader to act, then you will write a *persuasion* essay or a *research report*. Each form will be discussed separately, but the following points apply for all four.

All Writing to Change essays have a particular *emphasis, motivation, situation, circumstance,* and *writer-reader relationship*.

Emphasis. Some modes emphasize the content over the purpose or the purpose over the content, but Writing to Change emphasizes both. It is the combination of the writer's intention and the information being communicated that causes the reader to take the action necessary for bringing about the desired change. In other words, the writer's emphasis is on what the reader will say, know, do, or believe after reading the essay. This does not mean that the reader is expected to literally *do* something immediately—how many of us slam down the morning paper and rush out to put the editorials into practice? But when the reader does act, he or she will (the writer hopes) take the substance of the essay into account. So while the writer-as-a-person does not appear on center stage, the writer's view, assertion, position, judgment, or vision is the major focus, since it becomes part of what the reader will (if the essay fulfills its intention) think or do. The emphasis is on the dynamics between the writer's intention, the content of the writing, and the readers' response.

The purpose of a Writing to Change essay is for your words to make the reader do one or more of the following, on the basis of those words: know something; accept something; act upon something; believe something; or make a decision.

Motivation. What would make you want to write a Writing to Change essay? You might be motivated by direct experience, or by personal research and investigation that you've done, or a vision you have, or a commitment you feel, or insights you perceive.

Purpose. Because of how you, uniquely, perceive, filter, and assimilate the facts, you are able to take a stand, position, or viewpoint. Sometimes this will simply mean that you want the reader to look at a situation in a different way, in order to see new implications or possibilities. Other times, your position will be that you want the reader to make a commitment or a lifelong change. When you write to change, you usually have a deep-rooted interest in the matter, rather than a passing or intellectual interest. So you would use the Writing to Change essay if you wanted to:

- state your own interests, commitments, visions, and experience.
- get the reader to look at a situation in a different way, see the possibilities and implications or share your vision.
- move the reader from one position to another.
- persuade or convince the reader.
- get a commitment from the reader.

Situation. Some Writing to Change pieces are called forth externally, such as by a publisher, editor, employer, or teacher. Others are called forth internally, by the writer's own vision and commitment. Both kinds can appear in any of the following forms:

essays	evaluations
articles	letters
books	memos
reviews	manifestos
critiques	tracts
research papers	position papers

Circumstance. As with other types of essay assignments, the terms that govern a Writing to Change essay vary, depending on whether the piece comes out of an external demand or an internal requirement.

Length: If the stimulus is external, the length depends on the need of the publication or person requesting the piece (for example, "500 words or less"). If the stimulus is internal, the length is whatever the writer decides.

Who wants it written: An external demand is made by a publisher, an editor, an employer, or a teacher; an internal demand is self-imposed by the writer in order to fulfill a personal desire, vision, or commitment.

Time value: Writing to Change essays may meet an external deadline determined by: the requirements of the publication; the date of an important event; the completion of an experiment, an evaluation, or a data-collection process. If the deadline is internal, the essay gets written according to the writer's personal time-schedule.

Writer-Reader Relationship. In Writing to Change, the writer's relation to the reader is "person who wants *x*" to "person who can do *x*." But it isn't just information with which the writer is equipped—it is also experience, vision, insight, or expertise. This is what the writer shares with the reader. Therefore, the writer is a person who is calling on the reader to bring forth a certain action, or to accept a certain body of evidence, or to acknowledge a particular evaluation.

The Portfolio offers four assignments that involve writing to change:

Chapter 11: The Assertion-With-Evidence Essay

Chapter 12: The Evaluation Essay

Chapter 13: The Persuasion Essay

Chapter 14: The Research Paper

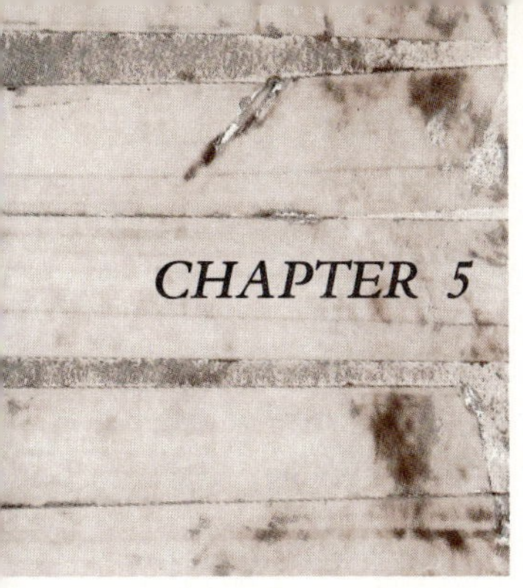

CHAPTER 5

Writing a Journal

KEEP A JOURNAL:

To record events and thoughts

To sharpen powers of observation

To collect things you like

To imitate writing that pleases you

To make sense of your life

Most of the academic writing you'll do will involve essays, reports, analyses, and research. Such writing demands that your thoughts be clearly ordered, logically arranged, and coherently expressed. You're expected to organize, plan, clarify, and polish. The proof is in the next nine chapters.

This chapter, however, is a bit different. It encourages you to write a journal—a type of writing that's usually better if it's *not* polished to a bootcamp shine. Yet there are at least five good reasons for writing regularly in a journal, and all of them contribute significantly to your skill, range, control, ease, and strength as a writer.

First, writing a journal preserves a *record of events, scenes, thoughts, activities, and experiences that you might otherwise forget* and that may be valuable to you in the future. Second, your journal entries can be *an opportunity to deliberately sharpen your senses*—to wake yourself up to smells, sights, sounds, tastes, touches that you are ordinarily unaware of. Third, a journal *provides you with a repository*—a catch-all basket—in which to put quotations you like, lines from poems, things a five-year-old said that you want to remember, names of books you want to read, sections of articles you want to keep. A fourth plus for a journal is that it *encourages you to imitate* models of writing that you like. By doing short imitations you can learn how writing gets put together, and you discover that your own writing style begins to show new possibilities. Finally, a fifth reason for keeping a journal is that in a journal you can *make sense of events, see patterns and connections among seemingly unrelated thoughts and experiences, follow the movement of your life, make discoveries, and have insights.*

KEEPING A RECORD: YOUR JOURNAL AS A BUTTERFLY NET

We all know how quickly we forget specifics, the little details, of our lives. Yet it is often remembering these details that will bring an entire experience or period of our lives rushing back.

When you write in a journal, you will discover for yourself the pleasure, the joy, of having a record of times that were important in your life. And catching the details "in the moment" will let you remember things that even photographs would not recall. People who write a lot can't do without this resource. Reporters jot down every detail they notice. Novelists taking a trip will record "unimportant" details even if what they are currently writing has nothing to do with the place they are traveling through. You never know when you might want to remember the specifics later. Whether or not you plan to be a reporter or novelist, you can have the same rich resource available to you for supplementing your memory, even if you do nothing with it except go back and read it now and again.

The journal as a record keeper—as a butterfly net—works the same for fleeting thoughts, ideas, and recognitions, as it does for actual events. Since good ideas, flashes of insight, or new realizations usually occur when we least expect them, your journal can catch these before they disappear. You will soon accumulate lots of thoughts, ideas, and impressions which will be valuable as time goes on.

So, write a journal to record the events and details of your life and to accumulate your thoughts. You'll never regret that you did.

My mother would say abrupt things, reckless things, liberating things. I remember her saying of some people in town, "*They are so boring you get tired of them, even when they are not around.*"

Two little ones were pretending a telephone conversation:
"How are your children?"
"They're dead."
"Chicken pox?"
"No, the hear-ache."
These are just samples recollected.—William Stafford
Writing the Australian Crawl

APPLICATION

Keep your journal with you at all times and use it to catch events and thoughts. Try some of these specific recommendations to get a sense of how enjoyable writing a journal can be:

1. Sit in a favorite eating place by yourself. Record the details of the restaurant and your thoughts while you are sitting there.
2. Record some conversation you overheard during the day.
3. The next time your family is together for a holiday, a meal, or a special event, record every detail you can get down on paper.
4. Listen to a preschooler talk and record what you hear.
5. Pretend you are a reporter at a sports event. In your journal, record every detail you can remember about the event.
6. Pick a place that you like to visit—say, an aquarium to watch the dolphins, a cathedral, a park—and record your thoughts while you are there.
7. Go look at the latest model of a new car and record what you remember in exact details.
8. When you notice a resemblance between two things, write it in your journal. You can even do the comparison game by thinking of the most unlikely pair of things that you can think of: a brick and a banana, a flea and an elephant, a toaster and a pencil, a piece of yarn and a telephone. Or take two very similar things—two nickels, two tires, two drummers, two blades of grass—and list all the differences you can think of. The point of the game is to go *beyond* the obvious.
9. Describe a picture that has special meaning for you. A photo of your grandfather in front of his workbench, your mother with her hands held as she always holds them, two friends with arms around each other's shoulders. Maybe a snapshot that catches your brother looking thoughtful, your sister in a baseball uniform, somebody looking through a window or standing in line. Describe the picture in a way that explains what it means to you.

   You can do the same for a painting, a billboard, poster, song, dance program, movie, sculpture, trophy, pottery, and so on.
10. Write a letter to someone you don't know—maybe someone famous or dead or both. What would you say to Bill Cosby? to Winston Churchill? to Attila the Hun? to Florence Nightingale? Helen Keller? Joan of Arc? Shakespeare? Madonna? Coretta King? Billy Graham? Pope John Paul II? Tell the person whatever you want to. Admire, sympathize, scold—whatever.

11. Write about something you've changed your mind about. As we live, our attitudes change. Tell what you used to think about something, what happened to change your mind, or what happened when you realized you no longer thought the old way about it, and what you think now. Perhaps something like a political party, or something you used to collect—stamps, dolls, model cars—that doesn't seem interesting or worthwhile now. Perhaps your attitude toward some food that you used to eat but don't eat now, or vice-versa. Perhaps your attitude toward people who lived in a certain place or dressed or spoke in a certain way.
12. Write about something you used to love as a child. Marbles? Cars? Doing tricks with a yo-yo? Skipping rope? Riding a trike? Playing dolls? Splashing in rain puddles? Eating popsicles in the summer? Building a snowman? Describe how good it used to be.

SHARPENING YOUR SENSES: YOUR JOURNAL AS A WAKE-UP CALL

Journal writing can cause you to see the world with fresh eyes; you look closer and sharper and clearer. It can make you more aware of each sense, and that awareness in turn will expand your perception and response.

Developing the senses will provide new materials to write about. For example, if one day you're sitting and wondering what to write for your journal entry and you see an ant walking across your table, you can either dismiss that ("Oh, that's just an ant"), as sometimes language dismisses things, or you can focus your attention on observing the ant—not just looking at it, but really *seeing* it in full detail. How large is it? How is its body shaped? How many legs? Does it have antennae? Where are they located, exactly? How does it walk—what is the pattern of movement with the legs? Does it go along at a steady pace or in a series of darting movements? Does it keep to the same direction, or move here and there? What happens when it comes to an obstacle (your pencil, your paper, your finger)? What color is it? What exactly is it doing? How long have you observed it? What happened between when you first *saw* it and when you began to *observe* it? All this can make for interesting writing.

We must learn to reawaken and keep ourselves awake, not by mechanical aids, but by an infinite expectation of the dawn, which does not forsake us in our soundest sleep.

—Thoreau

Strangely enough, there is considerable evidence that people live much of their lives in their heads, talking to themselves about things they remember from the past or things they imagine. Cultivating awareness of the senses and the ability to observe and respond to what is here and now is a way of getting in touch with reality and gives great energy, a sense of well-being, and a sense of importance and excitement to ordinary moments. These are *sharpening* activities, and they are a way of waking you up and making your senses work.

APPLICATION

Sharpening Seeing

1. Look at something you don't understand—a circuit diagram, a topographical map, a complicated machine (sewing machine, car engine). Notice what you *see* when you look at it. Then have someone who knows about it explain it to you. *Now* what do you see?
2. Look at the pattern of the cross section of a lemon, apple, orange, cucumber, tomato, grapefruit. Note the patterns carefully, then put the object out of sight and draw it from memory. When you've finished your drawing, get the object out and look again. Then write about the difference between looking at a thing and observing it.
3. Draw some familiar object from memory: lamp, telephone, housekey. When you've finished drawing it from memory, put that drawing aside. Then with the object in front of you, draw from direct observation. When you finish the second drawing, get everything out of sight—things, drawings—and make a third drawing, again from memory. What did you "learn"?
4. Write about seeing something (or somebody) for the first time. When you become aware of something for the first time, what do you notice? After a while, do you notice different things—that is, does your attention shift to other visual qualities? Do some things matter more in the beginning than they do later on? ("The first time we saw a beautiful California sunset behind the campus watertower, it literally took our breath away; later, though it remained spectacular, it no longer had the power to stop us in our tracks. And the more familiar we became with the sky, the more our seeing shifted from the sky to the things on the ground: the walks, buildings, trees, grass.")

Sharpening Hearing

1. Watch TV with the sound off. What do you notice as different?
2. Watch TV with the sound on but the picture blacked out. Again, what happens?
3. Why do people take portable radios to the beach, to the mountains?
4. Neon lights, traffic, talk in a lunchroom, machines in a laundromat—what rhythms are there?
5. What memories of sounds do you have? (creak of a wicker chair, creak in floor, way a door slams, early morning farm sounds, street sounds, sounds of familiar footsteps coming upstairs)
6. What can you hear when it's "quiet"?
7. What can you hear when it's "noisy"?

Sharpening Smell

1. Try tasting something while you're holding your nose.
2. Really smell something *before* you taste it—coffee, dried fruit, sliced tomato, pizza. Get down close to it and sniff! Pick out all the smells that you can separate. Really enjoy the experience of smelling your food. *Then* taste it. Well?
3. Think of places that have special smells. "This smells like a cabin ought to smell." "I don't like the way this hotel smells." Beaches, woodyards, gymnasiums, locker rooms, poolhalls, perfume counters, basketball courts, clothing stores, candy shops, leather stores, hayfields, tobacco barns, bakeries. How far away can you pick up that first whiff? As you approach? Through the door?
4. Think of things that have special smells. Your father's chair smelled different from your mother's. Closets? Bureau drawers? Attics? Trunks? Old books? Cedar chests? How do they smell? What special associations do they have?
5. What smells are associated with certain days: Christmas, Chanukah, 4th of July, Labor Day, family reunion, picnic, Thanksgiving, birthday.
6. Did you ever get used to a smell, take it for granted, and be surprised by it later? For example, a whiff of sagebrush that reminded you of a place you visited as a child. The smell of wet dirt after a rain. The smell of the factory in town. Apples on the ground. Neighborhood grocery store. What smells trigger memories?

Sharpening Taste

1. Buy something new to eat at the grocery store, something brand new to you. Bring it home and eat it. Describe the experience. Order a brand-new dish at a new restaurant. When you get home, describe that ordering/eating/tasting experience.
2. Discuss tasting something new at somebody's house—chili? raki? taramosalata? grits? pheasant? venison? rabbit? strawberry cake? Did you know it was new before you tasted it? How did you feel about trying it? (Does that keep you from trying new things?)
3. Discuss something *you* really like to taste—a particular flavor of ice cream, steak fixed a special way, fresh creamed corn, omelettes, hot spiced sausage.
4. Taste memories. Remember the taste of wood tongue depressors? Cafeteria silverware? Library paste? Crayons? Remember something you used to taste long ago—a table top, doorknob, water faucet—and let the memories flow from that remembered taste. Cinnamon toothpicks, chlorine pool water, grass stems, a yellow pencil, an eraser.

Sharpening Touch

1. What exactly is the difference in feeling between sandpaper and a feather?
2. People like to rub old coins, an old watch, a worn medal, or a new shiny bolt. What accounts for the satisfaction we get from touching such things?
3. Consider things that you dislike touching. Make a list. Get some friends to make a list. How many items appear on *many* lists? How many appear on only one or two? What does that suggest about where we develop our preferences about touching things?
4. Round up a golf ball, a marble, a ping-pong ball, and a steel ball bearing. Carefully explore them by touch—any two of them, or all four. Consider such things as density and temperature, as well as rough/smooth, heavy/light, and so on.
5. What can you feel with your feet? Put on wet shoes. Stand barefoot on a cold floor, on a carpet, on gravel, on boards, on grass.

COLLECTING THINGS YOU LIKE: YOUR JOURNAL AS A REPOSITORY

When you begin writing a journal, you will be participating in an ancient activity. At least as far back as Plato, people have been keeping "copybooks" or "notebooks"—called *hypomnemata* by the Greeks. Michael Foucault gives an excellent summary of the uses made of these early journals:

> *In the technical sense,* hypomnemata *could be account books, public registers, individual notebooks serving as memoranda. Their use as books of life and guides for conduct seems to have become a current thing for a whole cultivated public. Into them one entered quotations, fragments of works, examples, and actions which one had witnessed or of which one had read. . . . They constituted a material memory of things read, heard, or thought; they were an accumulated treasure for rereading and later meditation.*

Using your journal, then, to collect quotations, statements, sections of articles, lines from books—to collect the "already said"—can provide you with rich material to look back on later. When you reread what you have collected, you can reflect on what it meant—or means—to you, meditate on the applicability of the excerpts to your life, or laugh at the humor of one-liners which you could not refrain from inserting into your journal. You will find this use of your journal a convenient way to keep in one place those things you come across that you don't want to lose track of or don't want to forget.

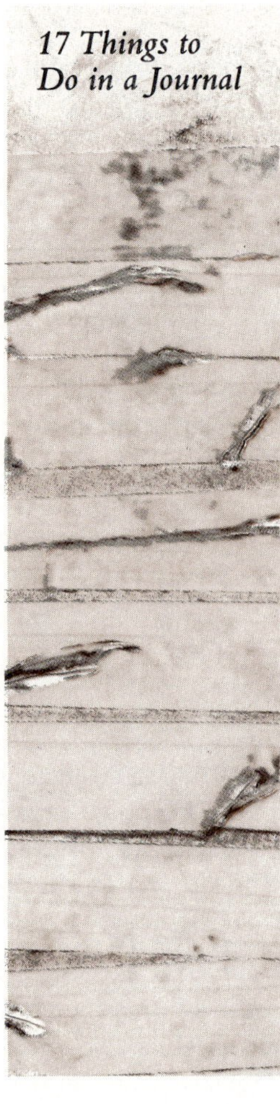

17 Things to Do in a Journal

1. Copy poems, sentences, paragraphs, graffiti, cemetery road signs, sayings.
2. Write first drafts of letters.
3. Write about how hard, irritating, absurd, impossible, it is to write in a journal.
4. Make word associations.
5. Note things from classes and reading that catch your fancy.
6. Make pen or pencil sketches (draw a leaf).
7. Describe things. What is the color of a pine trunk?
8. Describe people. (What do they do? What are they aware of? What *would* they do in specific situations? What do they seem to feel? What do you feel about them?)
9. *Where* are you?
10. Search for questions.
11. Explain the difference between living in the town and living in the country. (Where are *they?*)
12. Explain the difference between having an education and making an education.
13. Tell lies.
14. Record: dreams, weather, drinks, replies you made or should have, intentions.
15. Give commands!
16. List books you want to read later.
17. Write "Kilroy was here."

—Walter Clark, University of Michigan

APPLICATION

1. If you have a place where you put things that you want to keep—like a shoebox, a little wooden cedar chest, a desk drawer—go through the things you find there and choose five things you want to copy into your journal. These may include the message on a card someone special gave you, a fortune cookie message, a Bible verse, a particularly relevant cartoon, a quote about you from an article in a newspaper—

anything that is an "already-said" which you would like to incorporate into your journal collection.

2. The next time you get a letter, choose a few lines from the letter to copy into your journal.
3. Under a heading in your journal called "Sayings I Remember from My Childhood," write down every nursery rhyme, ditty, adage, etc., that you can think of from your early life. Make the list as long as you can.
   (Example: "I see the moon/The moon sees me/God bless the moon/ God bless me" or "Now I lay me down to sleep . . ." or "Hickory, dickory, dock, the mouse ran up the clock . . ." or "A bird in the hand is worth two in the bush.")
4. Locate two or three printed items that describe the code you have lived by—that are part of your "philosophy about life"—and copy these into your journal.
5. Listen to people talking around you—at home, at school, at church, at social events—and copy into your journal ways they said things that struck you as interesting.
6. Copy into your journal a paragraph from a writer that you really like. Do this every week until you have a collection of examples of writing that you enjoy.
7. Collect the lyrics from three songs that are among your favorites.

IMITATING GOOD WRITING: YOUR JOURNAL AS A PRACTICE FIELD

We all know someone who talks in such a predictable style that we can guess how every sentence will begin: "Well, you know, we went to the store, you know . . ." or "Now, for all practical purposes . . . Yes, for all practical purposes . . ." We find these broken-record ways of talking amusing sometimes and aggravating most of the time.

What we may not realize, however, is that we probably write in a way that, repeated over and over again, becomes boring or, at best, predictable. While having a personal style is one of the things you want to accomplish as a writer, you don't want this style to be by default—the style you adopted unconsciously just because you don't know any options or can't come up with any alternatives.

One of the best ways to add possibilities to your own writing style is to imitate, consciously and deliberately, sentences and paragraphs of writers you enjoy. This doesn't mean that you will copy them in your own writing later, but by imitating them you will teach yourself varieties in language, possibilities in how words are put together, so that you naturally make them a part of how you write. By imitating, you can breathe life into an old pattern of writing that you were unaware you had.

Here is a beautiful passage from *Death Comes for the Archbishop* written by Willa Cather.

> *When he opened his eyes again, his glance immediately fell upon one juniper which differed in shape from the others. It was not a thick-growing cone, but a naked, twisted trunk, perhaps ten feet high, and at the top it parted into two lateral, flat-lying branches, with a little crest of green in the centre, just above the cleavage. Living vegetation could not present more faithfully the form of the Cross.*

Here is how the passage might be imitated:

> *As she touched the child again, her thoughts unexpectedly went to one gift which stood out in memory from the others. It was not a well-known book, but a small, worn pamphlet, perhaps twenty years old, and within the covers it divided into three separate, bright-colored sections, with a small image of gold on each page, very near the top. Printed words could never depict more beautifully the coming of the Wisemen.*

Here is another excerpt—this one from the best-selling novel, *The Laurels of Lake Constance,* written by one of the most popular novelists in France today, Marie Chaix:

> *One night after she had given up waiting for him but was lying awake, with her bedside lamp turned low, he came in exhausted, but his eyes were shining as he said to her, "It's time to put on your white gown and golden slippers. I'm taking you to Germany."*

Here is how Marie's style might be imitated:

> *Two hours after she had let go looking for him but was sitting alone, with her television sound turned off, he sauntered in arrogantly, but his hands were perspiring as he spoke to her, "It's time to take off my dandy coat and dancing shoes. I'm marrying you for life."*

Even if you are not pleased with your imitations, you benefit anyway. It's not in the perfection of the imitation that the value lies—it's in the doing of it. You're learning more than you realize.

APPLICATION

Begin practicing imitation by modeling these:

1. The wind by now was more than redoubled. The shutters were bulging as if tired elephants were leaning against them, and Father was trying to tie the fastening with that handkerchief. But to push against this

wind was like pushing against rock. The handkerchief, shutters, everything burst: the rain poured in like the sea into a sinking ship, the wind occupied the room, snatching pictures from the wall, sweeping the table bare.

—Richard Hughes, *A High Wind in Jamaica*

2. You could expect many things of God at night when the campfire burned before the tents. You could look through and beyond the veils of scarlet and see shadows of the world as God first made it and hear the voices of the beasts He put there. It was a world as old as Time, but as new as Creation's hour had left it.

   In a sense it was formless. When the low stars shone over it and the moon clothed it in silver fog, it was the way the firmament must have been when the waters had gone and the night of the Fifth Day had fallen on creatures still bewildered by the wonder of their being. It was an empty world because no man had yet joined sticks to make a house or scratched the earth to make a road or embedded the transient symbols of his artifice in the clean horizon. But it was not a sterile world. It held the genesis of life and lay deep and anticipant under the sky.

   You were alone when you sat and talked with the others—and they were alone. This is so wherever you are if it is night and a fire burns in free flames rising to a free wind. What you say has no ready ear but your own, and what you think is nothing except to yourself. The world is there, and you are here—and these are the only poles, the only realities.

   You talk, but who listens? You listen, but who talks? Is it someone you know? And do the things he says explain the stars or give an answer to the quiet questions of a single sleepless bird? Think of these questions, fold your arms across your knees and stare at the firelight and at the embers waning on its margin. The questions are your questions too.

   —Beryl Markham, *West with the Night*

3. 26 February 58
   The elegant paper was provided by my aunt Mary so that I could write my few feeble lines. We just got out of the place Monday—one week in there. My mother after being cured of the disease had to be cured of the medicine . . . At six o'clock in the morning I heard the following conversation from two nurses in the hall. What have you done with them sheets? I ain't done nothing with them. Well I tole you what to do with them. You ain't never done no suchofva thing. I know what I done. I know what you done too. You may know what you done but you don't know what I done. This went on for some

time. It was the first vacation my mother has had in years, this being in the hospital for a week . . .

All my goose eggs froze, popped, and were eaten by the Muscovy drake. We begin again.

—Flannery O'Connor, *The Habit of Being*

4. Ten miles this side of Bidwell's Bar, the road, hitherto so smooth and level, became stony and hilly. For more than a mile we drove along the edge of a precipice, and so near, that it seemed to me, should the horses deviate a hair's breadth from their usual track, we must be dashed into eternity. Wonderful to relate, I did not oh! nor ah! nor shriek *once;* but remained crouched in the back of the wagon as silent as death. When we were again in safety, the driver exclaimed in the classic *patois* of New England, "Wall, I guess yer the fust woman that ever rode over that are hill without hollering." He evidently did not know that it was the intensity of my *fear* that kept me so still.

—"Dame Shirley," *The Shirley Letters*

5. While I was standing in quiet, shady water, I half noticed that no stone flies were hatching, and I should have thought longer about what I saw but instead I found myself thinking about character. It seems somehow natural to start thinking about character when you get ahead of somebody, especially about the character of the one who is behind. I was thinking of how, when things got tough, my brother looked to himself to get himself out of trouble. He never looked for any flies from me. I had a whole round of thoughts on this subject before I returned to reality and yellow stone flies. I started by thinking that, though he was my brother, he was sometimes knot-headed. I pursued this line of thought back to the Greeks who believed that not wanting any help might even get you killed. Then I suddenly remembered that my brother was almost always a winner and often because he didn't borrow flies. So I decided that the response we make to character on any given day depends largely on the response fish are making to character on the same day. And thinking of the response of fish, I shifted rapidly back to reality, and said to myself, "I still have one more hole to go."

—Norman Maclean, *A River Runs Through It*

6. Robinson was seated in front of the fire. "I knew Johns," he said. "I met him in Detroit in '38. We were trapped together in a bar by the great blizzard of that winter. It was the only time he ever spoke to me of his past life—of his adventures as sailor and shepherd, of the extraordinary enterprises he had founded in various parts of the world, and of that encounter with Rouxinol you just mentioned, when he lay sick with yellow fever in New Guinea."

—Harry Mathews, *The Novel as History*

MAKING MEANING, MAKING SENSE: YOUR JOURNAL AS AN ODYSSEY

Someone once compared life to a river, starting out at a spring or a trickle at the edge of a snowfield, becoming larger and deeper as more currents feed in, joining larger currents still, moving swiftly sometimes, slowly sometimes, with occasional shallow spots, rapids, snags—but always in motion, always changing. One reason journal writing is so pleasurable and so important is that you are able to mark your path, chart where you've been, what you were doing at a particular time, what you thought. *It is a record of the path your life takes, a record of your progress.* You experience the pleasure of saying things on paper, expanding yourself, taking measure. Looking back you see how life passes on, how all things work out, how everything is just a spot in the entire continuum.

In that sense, everything you write in your journal captures and reflects one person's way of seeing the world. So no matter what you write about, it gives you a sense of history and perspective about your life. Whatever you choose to put in there is a picture of *you* simply because it is something that *you* chose out of all the welter of stuff there is in the world. Rereading your journal, you can probably make some interesting discoveries about your life from those things alone even if you said nothing else, made no remarks about them. (On the TV program "60 Minutes," experts claimed the ability to reconstruct your life from just your checkbook!) So a journal, even if it's limited to objective events, can be a chart of where you were in your personal growth at a particular time.

I went to the woods because I wished to live deliberately, . . .
—Thoreau

Using a journal to make sense, to look for meaning, is an invaluable activity. You're able to be a philosopher without claiming to be one. You're able to probe for connections in what looks like unrelated events in your life. You can also use the journal to record your movement through crisis, through a struggle to overcome some trait that haunts you (like anger or fear or suspicion), through some difficult circumstance in your life (such as losing your job, mourning a death, or getting over a broken heart).

There's a river somewhere, flows through the lives of everyone; And it flows through the valleys and the mountains and the meadows of Time.
—Eugene McDaniels, *River*

What's at stake for you as a writer is that the use of language is one of the most important means of expression that a human being possesses with which to construct the self. The self is always defined by its doing something to achieve its intentions. Humans use language to achieve the projects that they value. What's significant about journal writing is that there is a personal stake in it for the writer. The focus is on you, the writer. You dominate this writing, and it is by this writing that you achieve new aspects of your individuality. In the discovery of self is the discovery of style, and vice-versa. But by translating self into written language, you objectify the self, put it outside your head and onto paper;

you "stop the river" at that place. You look at the river from a fresh viewpoint, imagining how someone else might view it; you see it from above the surface and below, from before and after. This translation of experience for yourself alone is, of course, a preliminary for the translation of experience for others. *Private writing is a valuable prelude to public writing.*

APPLICATION

Making Meaning/Making Sense

READ A JOURNAL TODAY:
Pepys
George Sand
Samuel Johnson
Ninn
Anne Frank
Lewis & Clark
Holt
Coleridge
Terkel
Sarton
Mark Twain

1. Record something important to you. Begin it by writing, "Right now what's important to me is ______." Then explain what it is and the ways it is important.
2. How do you feel in different kinds of weather? When you're aware of particularly strong reactions to weather—say, after five days of rain—write about that. Is it too hot, too cold, too wet, too dry? For what? Does your attitude toward the weather have anything to do with the rest of your life—for example, are you more likely to gripe about the weather if you have a big test coming up or if you're having a squabble with somebody important? Check it out.
3. Experiment with feeling a new way about the weather. If you always hate the rain, see if you can find *anything* at all to like about it. Even to be happy about. You can't control the weather, but maybe you can learn to enjoy all of it.
4. Prepare for a critical situation that is likely to happen fairly soon. Imagine exactly what will happen and write a description of it. List all the possible outcomes and figure out what you'll do about each. When you've finished writing about it, how do you feel about that situation?
5. On a day you feel really down and lacking energy, write about that. Really get into it, and be as specific as you can about exactly how you feel. Get all the details you can—how your body feels, how the world looks, how you look at the rest of the world. When you finish writing that description, see if you still feel the same.
6. Next time your inner voice says, "No you can't, you're not strong enough, smart enough, good-looking enough etc.," write a dialogue between you and the little voice in which you argue back. Really put that little voice in its place. Do this activity as often as you like—that little voice has had free reign for possibly your whole life, and it deserves a lot of answering back.
7. Learn five new things every day for a week. At the end of each day list the five things. At the end of the week, look over your lists. What

can you say about the things you learned? What did you learn from doing the activity? Did you let anyone know about what you were doing? What was the reaction? What did you say? What would you say now? Would you do it again? Why or why not?

8. Tell the truth. Do it for every situation. Do not lie, fudge, fib, weasel, prevaricate, bend the truth, or tell even a little white lie. Tell the truth. At the end of each day, record incidents that made this activity easy or hard, frustrating or rewarding. At the end of the week, write whether the truth helps or hinders your growth. What is the truth about telling the truth?
9. For a week, keep every agreement you make. Absolutely. If that means you don't have time to sleep, don't sleep. If that means you have to cut down the number of things you try to get done, cut them down. If that means you have to miss a meal of two, miss them. After a week of keeping your agreements, how is your life running?
10. Respond to what you read. Copy it, comment on it, criticize it, praise it.

JOURNAL WRITING AND ESSAY WRITING

Journal writing differs from essay writing because there is much less composing. There's almost no concern whatever about selecting, ordering, arranging, fitting the writing to the audience. Journal writing is much freer, and many people find it more fun because there's no censorship. There's no one way it *has* to be—and there are no rules. It can be any length on any subject, as serious or as silly as you want. It doesn't even have to be in sentences; sentence fragments, or lists of words, will do as well. You can draw in your journal, too, doodle and sketch away if you want to.

There's simply the pleasure of developing, the joy of discovery, the satisfaction of working out the significance of something, for yourself. Journal writing gives you a quiet place to withdraw to, where you can get in touch with yourself, give yourself a breathing spell—just you and your journal in your corner of the world.

Journal writing is also a way of keeping your writing loose, fluent, and free from self-consciousness. The rhythms and conventions of private writing are much different from those of public writing, usually—so let your journal writing be natural, *your* way of doing it.

Journal writing will automatically stimulate ideas and *serve as a "file" or "reference desk"* where good ideas are kept. Often good ideas can be developed into powerful and effective essays—but the journal serves perfectly well, even if *none* of the entries finds its way into any of your formal writing: the journal develops facility with thinking and writing. And it is also its own reward; there's *no obligation* to do anything with the journal except to enjoy it (and, of course, write in it regularly). That alone will produce amazing results and is worth the time and effort even if there weren't other benefits (and, of course, there *are* other benefits).

As you use the journal to develop your capacity to observe, to respond, to catch the wonder and joy and marvel of life, you don't need to *do* anything with it. Just let the observations accumulate. Sometimes you simply record an event and use it as an excuse to flex your language and contact something real—an excuse to become observant and thoughtful. If that turns out to be something that you later want to work up into an essay, fine. If you can take a piece of it—an image, phrase, insight, comparison—and use that bit in an essay, more power to you. Some entries will seem to have more "essay potential" than others. What's important, though, for you as a writer is that *you are getting into the habit of linking writing to thinking*. You'll also have a store of written thoughts you can draw upon, depart from, develop. And if you've been one of those who have always churned out the unthought-out 500-word theme, you'll appreciate the advance here.

One way of becoming a person who *has* something to say is to notice how language can put you in contact with a thing—or how it prevents contact. For example, think of all the words and expressions for *rain* that country people are likely to have, and how few city people are likely to have. If *rain* is the only word for it, it's clear that language is not providing much contact. Anthropologists report that Eskimos have nearly 30 words for *snow,* that desert nomads have more than 20 words for *sandstorm,* and Trobriand Islanders have more than 40 words for *sweet potato*. Well, if you're an Eskimo, a desert nomad, or a Trobriander, you pretty well grow up without much noticing that variety, the way a fish grows up without noticing that it's in water. However, there can be moments of noticing, and those moments can start the insight rolling.

One way we use language to dismiss a thing, to box it up and ship it off, is to oversimplify the thing. "That's just a penny." "That's just a teapot." The *journal attitude* invites you to notice when words are being used to stop thought, to take something for granted, to dismiss it. Then you can break through those dull, dismissing boxes and discover the riches within. Break through by thinking of all the *other* words there might be for that thing. Think of all the possible significances that thing might have for you, for someone else in your time, for someone in the past, for someone in the future. You'll see yourself having quite a lot to say, interesting things, things only *you* could have come up with, things that will help other people get in contact with experience, life, existence, significance, wonder.

Or break through by *really* seeing what you're only looking at. That is, go beyond mere looking at it, and experience it fully, openly, as it really might be.

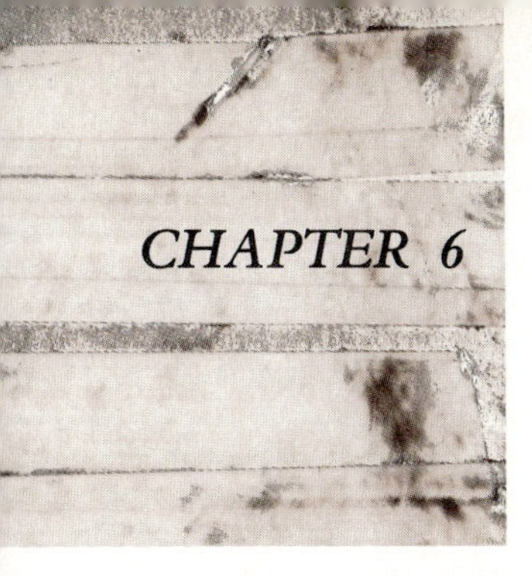

CHAPTER 6

The Personal Experience Essay

Everyone has a story to tell. The urge to recall one's experiences is certainly older than written history. And since the invention of writing, people have been recording either what they have seen and experienced themselves, or learned from others—warriors, pilgrims, nomads, traders, and so on.

WHY WRITE THE PERSONAL EXPERIENCE ESSAY?

What might prompt *you* to tell a part of your story—your history—to the world? Possible motives may be to understand how you came to be who you are; to identify the forces and influences that shaped your identity, morality, culture, and voice; to connect your individual experiences to wider political, social, or cultural roles—you want to discover how you fit in and how you differ; to get something out of your system—you may not understand what has been bothering you until you have seen it in written language.

You may also write a personal experience to make sense of a troubling or difficult experience—with the benefits of greater maturity and hindsight, you can narrate the past to understand how it has shaped your present and future; to share something remarkable that has happened to you; to tell a good story—you want readers to share the pleasures of an amusing, enlightening, suspenseful, scary, or illuminating experience; to put down words that will endure; to suggest something about life that you feel is true and worth preserving.

Checklist for writing a Personal Experience essay:

- Think of a Personal Experience essay as an opportunity to tell readers about yourself.

- Choose an incident, occasion, event, or situation that you recall vividly enough to write about in detail. Don't bore your readers.
- Tell a story worth the effort—one that you might want to put into words even if no one would ever read it.
- Use examples, illustrations, and details to put readers inside the story.
- Locate the incidents carefully. Make sure readers know *who* is doing *what* to *whom* and *when*. Describe important locations.
- Select the incidents you talk about carefully. Give the lengthiest coverage and heaviest emphasis to the most important events.
- Take a moment to characterize the important people in your story. Be sure to mention their names.
- Use vivid language and, when appropriate, dialogue.
- Build toward a climax, either in the events themselves or in the emotional lives of those involved.

ASSIGNMENTS

Select one of the following situations to serve as the basis of a Personal Experience essay—then develop this essay as you work through the rest of the chapter.

1. Select a difficult or traumatic event from your not-so-recent past which you can now write about with a sense of perspective. Think of it as an event that changed you or altered your outlook on life. The incident may have been as simple as getting cut from an athletic squad or as painful as a forced separation from a parent. Retell the story now with an emphasis on what you have learned and how you have developed.

2. Write a humorous or entertaining travel narrative, describing what you learned (not what you saw or where you stayed) on a trip. Don't bore readers with a day-by-day itinerary of your travels; instead, provide a candid and thoughtful narrative of your mental adventures and explorations of different people, attitudes, and assumptions. One point—you don't have to travel to an exotic locale to tell an intriguing story.

3. Your family is assembling a history and each member is to contribute an anecdote about his or her life. Write a Personal Experience essay for this collection based upon some incident you would like your family to know about or remember you by.

4. Form a writing group with four or five students and decide upon a theme to link your separate narratives into a profile of the group. A group may consist of individuals who share a similar ethnic background, religious training, economic level, sports experience, family situation (only child, youngest child, divorced parents), or any other commonal-

ity. Define the structure and scope of your narratives, making sure these self-portraits contribute to the larger theme. As a group, assemble the collection of personal narratives, linking them with a suitable introduction and conclusion.

5. Suppose that for a long time you have been wondering why the relationships between men and women are often so rocky. Write an essay in which you explore this problem through an incident that has occurred to you recently.

6. An international education magazine is inviting its readers to submit a short Personal Experience essay on "The First Time I Ever . . .," in the interest of exploring how people from different cultures approach learning. You might write about the first time you drove a car, operated a computer, kissed a date, made a speech, flew on a plane, got married, and so on. Use the incident to explain something about the traditions and assumptions of the culture in which you were raised.

WRITING THE PERSONAL EXPERIENCE ESSAY

In writing a Personal Experience essay, the object of the creating/shaping/completing process is to select a personal experience that you can share with an audience in such a way that it will have meaning for them as well.

Creating

Since the emphasis in a Personal Experience essay is on you, the best way to locate a topic is to examine your own experiences. Did a childhood event—such as a bicycle accident when you were in the third grade—shape your later attitudes toward taking risks? Did you have an illuminating insight about "life in the fast lane" while driving on a freeway? Did you ever witness an ugly incident or vicious prank that unexpectedly reformed your moral outlook? If so, consider writing about these sorts of events. But remember what you owe readers—a paper worth their time and attention. Your third-grade trauma will be pointless unless readers feel it has some connection to their lives.

Making a list is one way of finding a topic. Just list all the incidents you can think of that might satisfy the requirements of a Personal Experience essay. It may help to generate a chronological list, beginning at some specific time or repeated event (the first grade, spring breaks, annual family reunions) and working forward. *Looping* is also a good creating tool to work with. Put "What has happened to me?" at the top of a blank sheet of paper or computer screen. Then do a few loops of 5 to 10 minutes each; remember to write non-stop for the entire time.

Once you have a topic, flesh it out both with lists and the *reporter's formula*. Use the lists to recall specific details about the characters and events in the narrative, creating a new list for each important location and

Recommended Creating Techniques

1. Making a List (See pp. 16–17)
2. Looping (See pp. 20–21)
3. Reporter's Formula (See pp. 14–15)

person. Be as specific as possible—right down to the color of the necktie your Uncle Roland wore nearly every day. Answer the *who, what, where, when, how,* and *why* queries to be sure that you have given readers the points of reference they need to follow your story. (The closer you are to an event, the more likely you are to omit the specifics that make it come alive to readers; because you recall the details, you may wrongly assume that readers are aware of them too.)

Shaping/Drafting

In writing the Personal Experience essay, you want readers to share an event from your life, to understand what you learned from it, to appreciate your reactions to it. You also want them to enjoy or value what you've composed. In order to accomplish this, you need to consider your audience, the thesis of your essay, and the organization of elements in the essay.

Audience. The items on this audience checklist may help you attain your goals:

- Know precisely for whom you are writing. Fill in background information according to the needs of your audience. Too much background can be as bad as too little.
- Connect your particular experience to experiences readers might have shared. Look for social and cultural similarities and differences.
- If readers are likely to assume that your life resembles theirs, highlight the unexpected contrasts between your worlds; if readers are likely to assume differences between you and them, surprise them by pointing out similarities.
- Assure readers that your experience is valuable by crafting your narrative with care. Fill the paper with lustrous, memorable details that only an insider would know.
- Remember that people like to read about people. Give all the persons in a paper—including yourself—a breathing presence. Names and faces are important.
- To thine own self be true. Writing a personal essay may be an important emotional release; pleasing an audience is not the only goal of this form of writing.

Thesis/Promise/Delivery. Your Personal Experience essay may not have an explicit thesis statement. Instead, the point of the paper may unfold gradually as the narrative itself advances. But be sure that the essay *does* have a point over and above presenting the experience itself. Even thirty-second television commercials often have stories that build to a climax.

When you do have an explicit thesis, it should relate directly to the incident: evaluate it, judge it, explain its importance. "I had a great time in the mountains" is not a thesis; "Climbing mountains made me aware of strengths I never knew I had" is more to the point—though it too might be refined.

An explicit thesis can require some finesse in placement. If you put it up front in an introductory paragraph, it can look like the prologue to a parable. After the narrative, a thesis may sound like the moral of a tale—something tacked on to justify telling the story. There's no easy solution to this problem except to relate your thesis clearly to the incident you are expounding. The more abstract or pious your thesis, the more likely it will sound like a moral. So avoid any thesis that begins: "From this incident, I learned . . ."

The promise you make to readers in a Personal Experience essay is this: "I will describe an event so that you can appreciate its significance to me." That may seem like a simple job, but it is not. True, erecting the framework of a narrative is relatively straightforward; but it's another matter to provide substance and shape. To check whether your personal essay delivers on its promise, see whether you can locate specific points—words, phrases, sentences—in your narrative where events reveal their significance. These points would occur at moments when something happens in the *minds* of your characters (or your readers) *as a result* of the incidents narrated. If your essay has no emotional or intellectual moments of discovery, it probably has not delivered on its promise.

Organization. The narrative form is the basic structure for this kind of writing. The basic shape can be extraordinarily simple (for variations, see Chapter 17, "Form and Pattern"):

Introduction
Happening One
Happening Two
Happening Three ———→ building to a climax
Conclusion

To tell a good story, you need to be sure to give the reader a clear time order. Provide a clear sequence of events. Often this sequence will be *chronological*—first this happened, then this, then that. . . . You may, however, use a *flashback* technique in which you show an earlier scene and then relate that scene to the main story you are telling at the moment. You also want to let your readers feel the *action* of your story. Don't just tell them *about* what happened. Let them *live* through what happened. Make a movie of the sequence of actions. The more *immediate* the details and the more *descriptive* the scenes, the more your readers will feel a part of what is going on in the story.

Be very *selective* in the details you choose. Don't give the readers a lot of information they don't need to understand or see your story. Stick to details that are directly related to your purpose in telling the story. Also, make sure you decide on a *point of view*. Point of view is how the story is told. Very likely the *first person point of view* (when the author is a character in the story) will be the easiest way to tell a story that has happened to you. Later, however, when you are using narration as part of other pieces of writing, you may want to adopt the *omniscient point of view,* in which the writer knows everything and gives an objective, outside account of the sequence of events.

Peer-Editing

When you have completed a draft of your essay (based on one of the situations presented earlier), ask one or more classmates to review the paper using the following form for guidance.

PEER-EDITING SHEET Personal Experience Essay

Essay writer's name ______________ Reader's name ______________

Please answer each question briefly. Be sure to explain your answer in terms of specific examples from the essay you are reading.

1. List some initial thoughts you had while reading the essay.

2. Is the context (the real world purpose for writing and the audience) clear to you, the reader of the draft? YES NO NOT SURE (circle one)
   a. What do you see as the purpose of this essay?

b. To what specific audience do you think the essay is directed?

3. Is the main point of the essay clear to you? YES NO (circle one) In either case, try to write out in *one* sentence what you think is the main point, or thesis, of the essay.

4. Did the essay hold your interest? YES NO PARTLY (circle one) Please list *three* interesting details, descriptions, or situations in it:
   a.

   b.

   c.

5. If the essay didn't completely hold your interest, try to explain why and at what point you lost interest.

6. Circle the paragraphs in which you didn't feel involved in the action of the story: 1 2 3 4 5 6 7 8 9 10 11

7. Circle the paragraphs where you became confused, or couldn't follow the story: 1 2 3 4 5 6 7 8 9 10 11

8. Was the time order clear and easy to follow? YES NO PARTLY
   If you answer no, or partly, explain why.

9. One paragraph that was especially full of good detail or drama begins with the line:

10. Please write out any sentences that you found either hard to understand or confusing.

11. a. Is this paper physically neat? YES NO
    b. Is there a cover sheet? YES NO
    c. Is there a title? YES NO
    d. Is the title appropriate? YES NO
       Why?

12. Overall, what do you remember best from the essay?

Completing

Once you've got a draft of your personal experience and have reviewed the comments of your classmates and peers, you are ready for the completing stage. It's time to do the fine tuning that will make your writing memorable. Four key elements deserve your attention: paragraphs, sentences, words, and editing.

Paragraphs. There are two kinds of paragraphs—*topic sentence* and *function*. (Both types are explained in detail in Chapter 19, "Making Paragraphs Work.") Topic sentence paragraphs tell what the paper is about—they relate to the thesis, or topic. If you were writing an essay that had a specific message—for instance, "Everyone should be vaccinated against certain diseases"—then it would be important to put that message right up front, where your readers could see it clearly. But since you are writing about your own personal experience, you have the choice of putting your "Here is my thesis" paragraph at the beginning, at the end—or nowhere (see "Thesis/Promise/Delivery earlier in this chapter).

The function paragraph is particularly important in personal writing. This paragraph tells your readers *how* to read what you are writing. A function paragraph can say, "Okay, now get excited" (i.e., it can add drama), or "time to move on" (i.e., it can provide transitions from one paragraph to another), or "take a breather" (i.e., it can break up long paragraphs), or "see what I mean?" (i.e., it can explain or emphasize a point or detail), and so on. Of these functions, adding *detail* and *drama* are the ones that provide the real heart of the *personal experience* essay. Drama makes the difference between a "who cares" response in the reader, and a lively, hanging-in-there response. Consider the difference between the following two sentences:

> "Going to school was always boring. I always hated it. I'm glad I don't go to school anymore."

> "I'd stay under the covers as long as I could, trying to ignore the sounds of my mom banging the saucepans on the stove. Finally, she'd call out for maybe the fourth or fifth time, 'I said, it's time to get up for school!' and I'd groan and force myself out from under those toasty-warm covers and face the prospect of another day at school."

In both cases, the basic point—"I hate going to school"—comes across. But the second example puts the reader where you were—showing instead of telling. So use vivid language—words and phrases that would give the reader clear or striking mental images. You do this in two ways:

1. Appeal to all the reader's senses—sight, smell, touch, hearing, taste. Be specific.
2. Select the details you want to include in the description so that they give one main impression of the object, person, or scene. Don't try to describe everything at once—choose details that suit your purpose at that time.

Sentences. Has anyone ever told you his or her life story without your expecting it, like on a bus or a plane, or in a hospital? If so, were you bored and annoyed or fascinated and eager? What could make the difference between one kind of personal experience telling and the other?

One factor is the energy with which the story is told. It's just hard to care about a story that begins, "Well, I was born in that city, and then I went to school, and then. . . ." So what? What *about* that city, or that school? One way to get to the "what aboutness" is to give the reader enough information—enough, that is, to put the reader in the experience. There is a difference between "I jumped into the water and swam" and "I jumped numbly into the ice-capped water, and swam." You will notice that what make the difference here are simply adjectives ("ice-capped") and adverbs ("numbly"). Isn't your curiosity aroused more by the second sentence than by the first? What was the person doing, jumping into ice-capped water? Was it a dare? Was someone drowning? Was the person running away from something even worse? And why was the person numb, rather than terrified or confident? (You see how this works?)

Another way to make energetic sentences is to combine short, choppy ones into longer, more flowing ones (unless you deliberately want short, choppy ones). Compare "The boy was hungry. He knocked on the door. He asked for bread. The man gave him a piece,' with "The hungry boy knocked on the door and asked for bread. The man gave him a piece."

Also, pay attention to *coordination* (words of equal weight) and *subordination* (words of lesser weight). When you do the work of linking up words within a sentence in this way, your reader has a clear sense of what goes with what. (And since readers love to understand and hate to be confused, you are doing both of you a favor.)

In this kind of writing, *parallelism, balance and repetition,* and *rhythm* go a long way toward making your writing come alive. When you use parallel constructions, you establish a sense of expectation that brings satisfaction. Balance and repetition emphasize similarity and create contrast; the first gives an experience of unity, the second of individuality. And rhythm is the music, the pattern, the heartbeat of a piece of writing.

Words. It can't be said often enough—if you use other people's words in other people's ways, your writing won't have as much punch as if you find your own words. Why are clichés clichés? Once upon a time (a cliché in itself) they were new and fresh, and caught our attention; with repeated use, however, they lost their punch—we stopped paying attention to them. "Love thy neighbor as thyself" still has a lot to tell us, but we are so used to those words put together in that way that we find it hard to really listen. So look for words that are specific, exact, precise, detailed, picture-making, and image-making.

Editing. Almost done—hang in there! This is the almost-final stage, and it involves looking over your paper for basic errors—typos, misspelled words, absent apostrophes, inconsistent tenses, and so on. If you find an error, fix it. The written expression of your personal experience deserves to be treated with total respect—including editorial respect.

EXAMPLE The Personal Experience Essay

Troyce Nolan, a freshman, wrote this personal narrative for his English class, addressing it to his classmates.

Emphasis: On a change that occurred in the writer, although readers are carefully and deliberately addressed.

Purpose: To provide insight into a young man's first encounter with romance.

Situation: A paper for an English composition course.

Circumstance: Length: About 500 words. Deadline: ten days.

Writer-Reader Relationship: Writer sharing an incident that should evoke similar events in the readers' lives.

STOLEN KISS

Sigmund Freud, the eminent psychiatrist, believed that a man's world revolves around sexual attraction. I think he was right. Like most college-aged men, I now pattern my lifestyle around what is appealing to the opposite sex, from what I wear to the route I take to the library (the one that passes by the women's dormitories). I was not always like this. I can recall many recess breaks when I found myself running for my life from a group of little girls intent upon stealing a kiss.

My disinclination toward romance did not alter gradually. Instead, I can point to the exact moment when my attitude changed—an afternoon during my third grade year when I made a trip to the park. My next door neighbor, Sharon P., asked if I would be willing to walk to the park with her because her parents would not allow her to go on her own. As far as I was concerned Sharon was a typical girl. She always wore dresses, played with dolls, and for some unknown reason did not like football or baseball.

Going against what I then considered my best instincts, I reluctantly agreed to let her walk with me. I assumed that we would go our separate ways when we got to the park, and meet later to walk home. Little did I know that that was not her plan; she intended that we play together. After we had tried all the various pieces of playground equipment, we decided to get a drink of water. Not yet understanding any need for chivalry, I took my drink from the fountain first and then sat on a bench nearby. The next thing I knew, Sharon was sitting on the bench next to me with just about enough room to slide a dollar bill between us. As I turned to face her to ask her to move away, she reached up and kissed me on the lips.

I was so mad I could have punched her. But

I knew better than to punch a girl; my mother had taught me that. Unable to control my emotions, I got up from the bench and stormed out of the park, leaving Sharon sitting alone on the bench. I was so upset I turned down my best friend's offer to join him on the see-saw. As I walked home, I thought over what had happened to me just minutes before. Was it really all that awful? The more I thought about the kiss, the more appealing it seemed. Heck, I figured if my dad kisses my mom, how bad can it be?

I never kissed Sharon again because my family moved shortly after this incident and it was several years later before I really had my first experience with a girl. It was Sharon, though, who made me begin to appreciate that what made girls different from boys was more than their reluctance to play football and climb trees. Soon after, I began to develop strong friendships with girls, some of which I still have today. Slowly my understanding of girls grew, and I actually began to pattern my lifestyle, dress, and mannerisms around what would please them. As I look back upon that day in the park, I understand that I owe a debt of gratitude to Sharon P. and her stolen kiss.

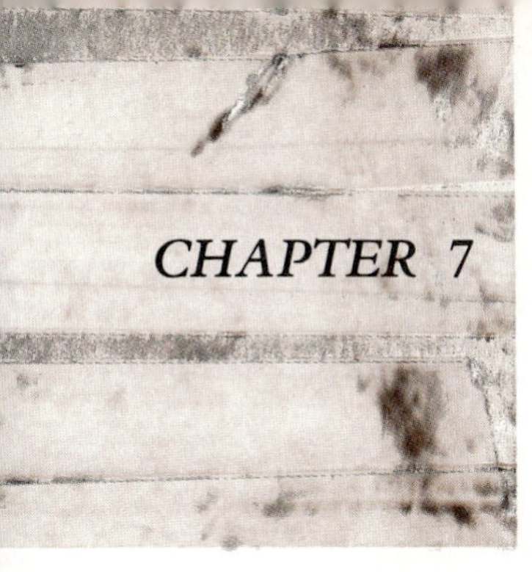

CHAPTER 7

The Personal Perspective Essay

A Personal Perspective essay focuses on a writer's opinion or point of view. For that reason, it differs from a Personal Experience essay (see Chapter 6) which tends to focus on events. When a Personal Perspective essay stakes out a particularly strong position, it may seem like a persuasive or argumentative effort. But it differs from a true persuasive essay in that it is not written first and foremost to change the opinion of readers. The writer wants to be understood more than supported or followed.

WHY WRITE THE PERSONAL PERSPECTIVE ESSAY?

Why would you write a Personal Perspective piece? A few possible reasons are to explain what you think or how you view the world; to affirm what you already believe and to understand better the premises of those beliefs; to challenge what you believe—this means that you question your basic assumptions or look for new ways of understanding the world (politically, socially, economically, religiously, personally); to see the world through someone else's eyes—you consciously assume the perspective of a friend, an enemy, an opposite; to provide others with a look into your world.

Checklist for writing a Personal Perspective essay:

- Write about something that's been on your mind for a while.
- Stake out your own position. Don't borrow the opinions, views, or positions of others.
- Help the readers understand your point of view. Be engaging and entertaining.

- Find a style suited to your subject but distinctly in your own voice. Use the first person: *I*.
- Use many examples, illustrations, and details to involve readers in the paper.

ASSIGNMENTS

Select one of the following situations to serve as the basis of a Personal Perspective essay—then develop this essay as you work through the rest of the chapter.

1. You've been offered the chance to write an "In My Opinion" column for the campus paper. The editor, however, wants you to avoid controversial social and political issues and to focus, instead, on some annoying or amusing foible of human nature or American culture—the way Andy Rooney would on *60 Minutes*. Complain about people who talk too much, treatment you receive in the registrar's office, containers that automatically spill their contents, ugly postage stamps, implausible movies, and so on.

2. Write a humorous or entertaining personal perspective essay explaining your opinion of a place you have visited—foreign or domestic. Don't describe your travels; instead, provide a thoughtful critique of the people, attitudes, and assumptions evident in that strange locale. You may want to use a brief anecdote as the focal point of your story—how losing your wallet in Minneapolis gave you special insight into the efficiency of the local police, or how accidentally stopping in an off-the-beaten-path town made you rethink the value of traveling on interstate highways.

3. Your public health class has been discussing the "other victims of illness"—the family members and friends of someone who is seriously injured or ill. Your professor asks each of you to write a personal perspective paper about a time when you or someone you know has been one of these "other victims."

4. You are the victim of some form of harassment at work. Nothing major has happened but enough minor incidents have occurred and you are fed up. Write a letter about what's happened to put in your company's anonymous "Suggestions and Complaints" box in the lunchroom. Make your opinion clear.

5. An examination came back with a lower grade than you anticipated. You are furious! You have every intention of arguing with your teacher about the mark—vehemently if need be. You walk to the teacher's office, thinking about how it's *her* fault, blaming *her* for asking such impossible questions. But a thought suddenly strikes you, one so surprising

that your hand actually pauses in mid-knock just centimeters from the instructor's office door. You really *didn't* study. You are so surprised by the admission that you return home to think about it. You discover a pattern, not only in your own behavior but in that of other people as well, to shift the blame for personal failures onto others. You are so intrigued by this insight that you decide to write a paper about it.

6. Something about a "younger" or "older" generation really bugs you. Explain in detail what the problem is and why it upsets you so. If appropriate, suggest what might be done about it or how a sensible person of your generation should react.

WRITING THE PERSONAL PERSPECTIVE ESSAY

In writing a Personal Perspective essay, the creating/shaping/completing process focuses on exploring your opinions and reactions, developing your essay to gain readers' understanding, and editing so that it is personal and casual, but polished.

Creating

As is true of a Personal Experience essay, the emphasis in a Personal Perspective essay is *you*. Therefore, the best way to locate a topic is to explore your own opinions and your reactions to ideas. Why do you believe what you do? Did a particular person influence your moral development—a friend who constantly got into trouble, a sensitive pastor, a patient grandparent? What makes you laugh with amusement or chuckle with a sense of superiority? What sets you off—angers you, excites you, makes you want to speak up? Consider writing about these sorts of subjects and reactions. But remember that you owe readers a paper worth the time they'll spend with it. You want your unique point of view to be recognized by your readers. "Yes," they should nod, "I know the feeling exactly."

Looping is the creating technique of choice for Personal Perspective essays. At the top of a blank sheet of paper, write "What do I care about strongly and know enough about to discuss intelligently?" Then write three 5 to 10 minute loops. You are likely to hit on at least one promising subject by the end of the third loop. Once you have a topic, develop or explore it further through *listing* and *cubing*.

Recommended Creating Techniques

1. Looping (See pp. 20–21)
2. Making a List (See pp. 16–17)
3. Cubing (See pp. 315–316)

Shaping/Drafting

In this stage of the writing process you need to turn your attention to audience, thesis, and organization.

Audience. In writing the Personal Perspective essay, you don't necessarily want readers to agree with you, but you do want their understanding and identification—perhaps even their sympathy. You also want them to enjoy what you've composed—to consider it important or entertaining. The items on this audience checklist may suggest ways of stimulating such reactions:

- Make your audience sympathetic to your point of view. Give them details that enable them to appreciate why you feel as you do. Help them understand what it's like to be in (or to take) your position.
- Connect your particular opinion to related opinions readers might share. (For example, people who own pets might better understand your refusal to use cosmetics that are tested on animals.)
- Anticipate what your readers need to know. Give them numbers, dates, and facts as needed, brief descriptions of locales, quick rundowns of relevant situations.
- Remember that people like to read about people. Give all the people in the essay—including yourself—an identity. Names and faces are important.
- Ask yourself, "What sort of person would be interested in what I have to say?" Then tailor your paper to that reader.

Thesis/Promise/Delivery. Your Personal Perspective essay will probably have a definite thesis. The clearer and more unique your thesis, the better. It's too broad to write "Education in this country stinks." By narrowing your focus, you arrive at a statement that is more truly a thesis: "Schools are teaching students to doubt their own creativity by boring them with endless rote exercises and drills." With this thesis you've given readers something they recognize (boring exercises and drills) and might even care about. Now you have to prove that you care.

A thesis for a Personal Perspective essay might look like this:

Thesis: I believe X because . . . .

Variations, of course, are numerous. Here are just two:

Thesis: Although X might be the case, I still believe that Y is possible (desirable).

Thesis: If we don't do (believe in, support) X, then we'll have to deal with Y.

Organization. Even though you don't have to support your arguments as rigorously in a Personal Perspective paper as you might in a persuasive essay, you can still borrow patterns of development suited to more formal demonstration: induction, deduction, analysis, even analogy. These patterns are presented in Chapter 17, "Form and Pattern." An even simpler way to visualize how you can arrange the Personal Perspective essay is outlined in the Statement/Proof pattern shown below. If you want readers to understand your point of view (statement) and why you believe what you do (proof), consider this model:

Introduction: who you are
Statement: what you believe
Proof: why you believe it
Examples and illustrations
Conclusion

The commitment you have to fulfill in a Personal Perspective essay is to make readers understand your point of view: "I will explain an opinion or idea so that you can appreciate its significance to me." This requires that you make readers believe that your opinion is worth hearing. In a sense, the real commitment you make is to be honest. Because people are social creatures, they want to hear what their neighbors, friends, classmates, and fellow citizens have to say. But they'll give your ideas serious consideration only if they believe you are delivering them in good faith, that you've spent time thinking about your subject, and that you have made an effort to present it fairly, intelligently, and skillfully.

Peer-Editing

When you have completed a draft of your essay (based on one of the situations presented earlier) ask one or more classmates to review the paper using the following form for guidance.

PEER-EDITING SHEET The Personal Perspective Essay

Essay writer's name ______________ Reader's name ______________

Please answer each question briefly, but thoughtfully, responding to the draft with useful comments. Be sure to explain your answer using specific, clear examples.

1. List some initial thoughts you had while reading the draft.

2. What do you see as the purpose of this essay?

3. To what specific audience do you think the essay is directed?

4. Point out three specific examples showing how the needs of this essay's particular audience helped to shape it; that is, cite particular choices of tone, kind or level of words, kinds of details given, format, and so on.
   a.

   b.

   c.

5. Write out the sentence or sentences near the beginning of the essay that best express its thesis.

6. Generally, does the essay supply vivid, concrete details, examples, and illustrations that give its audience a clear picture of what is being discussed? YES NO Cite three of its most helpful, most interesting details, examples and illustrations:
   a.

b.

c.

7. In which paragraphs would you like to see more details, examples, and illustrations? 1 2 3 4 5 6 7 8 9 10 Why?

8. Does the essay present its perspective so that the reader can hear a "voice," so that it seems written for real people? Explain:

9. Overall, did the writer come across to you as an insider about the information provided in the paper? YES NO If not, briefly explain why.

10. Is there a clear beginning, middle, and end to this draft? Summarize briefly where each of the three parts begins and ends.
    Beginning:

    Middle:

    End:

11. Were there any paragraphs in which you became confused or couldn't follow the essay? 1 2 3 4 5 6 7 8 9 10 Explain:

12. Is there more than enough material here to convey the personal perspective asserted in the thesis so that you could thoroughly understand it? YES NO If not, what didn't you understand?

Completing

Even though a Personal Perspective paper will feel more casual than some other kinds of writing, readers still expect it to be polished. You don't create an informal and personal tone by appearing careless, but by deliberately lending words and sentences your own voice.

You can do that by selecting the first person point of view, *I,* though it is possible to write a paper from the third person. Use contractions to make your writing move more quickly and sound like speech. Address readers as *you* where it's natural to do so, and fill the paper with recognizable details from everyday life so that readers feel at home. Give names to things. Don't write "a car" when you know it to be a "rusty Mustang"; don't say "my younger brother" when you could describe him as "my nine-year-old brother Mikey with the broken tooth and black eye." Pay attention to sentences, words, and editing.

Sentences. The difference between a dead sentence and a live one is *energy*—that which moves from your mind onto the page and into the reader's mind. To move your reader, you must first be moved yourself. How can you accomplish this?

One way is to find new and interesting ways to put sentences together. *Sentence combining* is one such way—if you find yourself with many short, choppy sentences that don't seem to have much connection to their neighbors, try combining them to make one long, flowing sentence. (This doesn't mean that it's wrong to use short, choppy sentences when you really *want* them.)

Checking for *coordinate* and *subordinate* clauses might be helpful too. This means clarifying which words are of equal weight, and which are of lesser weight. When you make the priorities clear to the reader, you help the reader follow your meaning more easily. And a reader who is not confused is a reader who *is* hanging in there.

The devices of *parallelism, balance and repetition,* and *rhythm* can serve you well and energetically. *Parallelism* involves repeating certain words, phrases, or constructions. This sets up a pleasing sense of expectation (a tension between what is familiar and what is unknown). *Balance and repetition* makes use of similarity and contrast. And *rhythm* provides the undertone, the drumbeat, the heartbeat of a piece. (See Chapter 20 "Polishing Sentences" for more details.)

Words. Perhaps because personal essays are typically casual and informal, they seem to encourage the use of clichés. Clichés are the stock phrases and predictable comparisons that come to a writer's mind immediately. Precisely because they are so predictable, you should avoid using them. Find fresh or interesting ways of expressing yourself.

Editing. Neatness counts. Don't forget to polish the drafts carefully. Type or write it on good quality paper. Leave ample margins and check the title. Does it invite a reader into the paper? If not, you still have time to improve it.

EXAMPLE The Personal Perspective Essay

Susan wrote the following essay after some class discussions and a lively brainstorming session about the comments teachers write on student papers. She wanted to share with her fellow students her confusion about the signals she felt her teachers were sending her, and to express the frustration this confusion made her feel. She chose a third-person point of view and an implied thesis for her paper.

Emphasis: On expressing her opinions

Purpose: To express her (and her classmates') frustrations with comments they'd received on their papers for other courses

Situation: An essay for class circulation

Circumstance: Self-imposed length. Deadline: next class

Writer-Reader Relationship: Person with an opinion to like-thinking readers

MONKEY SEE, MONKEY DO

During a recent workshop on grammar, a sentence—"I am going bananas"—was introduced for comment. A short poll of this class has rendered some suggestions about the kinds of responses a teacher would give if a student dared to write such a sentence.

"I am going bananas." The teacher will write "Slang. Please rewrite" in the margin.

The student will obviously know what's slangy about the sentence, so no further comment is needed. This approach avoids the sticky question of verbs altogether and especially avoids discussion of intransitive, transitive, and linking verbs.

The teacher will probably get "I am going crazy" as the rewritten sentence. If this does indeed occur, the teacher can choose between two attacks: (1) Ignore it and go on, or (2) Mark "Too colloquial for Standard English models. Please rewrite." The latter is the more common, and certainly the preferred teacher response, since it affords her the opportunity to explain what colloquialisms are and why Standard English is *so* much better. After she has explained how "crazy" can be improved upon, she'll probably get the following rewrite: "I am losing my mind."

This sentence will really allow the teacher to deliver the *coup de grace* to the student! She'll simply write "Idiom" next to the sentence. After all, everyone knows you don't *really* lose your mind unless you have a particularly leaky cranium. If people really could lose their minds, others of us would find them lying around, wouldn't we? The student, of course, will believe this to be another error, and take one of two courses. He'll either give up, or produce an unsolicited rewrite.

The result might look like this: "As a response to certain unfavorable stimuli in an increasingly complex and hostile environment, this subject is developing a labile personality and is rapidly approaching an irrational state of mind." This, fellow writers, is a teacher's gold mine. She might begin with wordiness and jargon, but the majority of students polled (99.9%) felt that the following teacher comment would be most fitting and would help the student understand the intricacies of the English language more fully: "Jargon. Be concise and clear. Why don't you just write, 'I'm going bananas'?"

CHAPTER 8

The How-To Essay

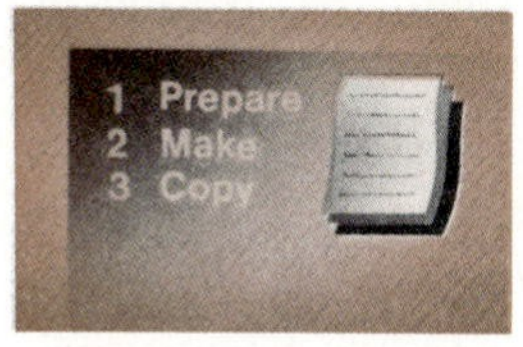

Writing that explains how something works is writing we couldn't do without. It can be as simple as the directions on a package of microwave popcorn or as complex as the manuals NASA uses to explain Shuttle launch procedures. At first glance, writing a set of instructions may seem easy: you just list what to do first, second, third, fourth until "how in the world . . . ?" becomes "how about that!" But anyone who has tried to repair a car, operate a computer, or assemble a child's toy from "easy-to-follow directions" realizes that writing clear and helpful instructions is an art. Fortunately, it's one that can be learned.

WHY WRITE THE HOW-TO ESSAY?

The reasons for writing a How-To essay primarily are to explain how something is done; to explain how something is not done; to explain how something works.

Checklist for writing a How-To essay:

- Choose a subject or process you understand thoroughly.
- Choose a subject readers need to learn more about.
- Understand your readers; tailor explanations to their level of knowledge and skill.
- Anticipate what readers don't know.
- Anticipate what may confuse readers.
- Define each step in your explanation clearly and distinctly.
- Link the steps within an interesting framework.

- Use vivid details.
- Be consistent.
- Be accurate.

ASSIGNMENTS

Select one of the following situations to serve as the basis of a How-To essay—then develop this essay as you work through the rest of the chapter.

1. Registration at your school this year was chaotic: freshmen and transfer students milled around for hours with little idea of what to do. The campus student association, to which you belong, decides to develop a Freshman Survival Guide to be mailed to next year's new students. You are asked to write the part on "Surviving Registration and Drop-Add." Your four-page section is due in a week. (This is an excellent assignment to work on in a group: ask your classmates to share their registration experiences and frustrations; later, test the advice in your survival guide on the same group.)

2. Identify some skill you have acquired in school during the last few semesters—conducting a physics experiment, writing a lab report, handling a spreadsheet in an accounting course, blocking a scene from a play, taking a scientific survey. Then write a short (three to four pages) paper explaining that skill to other students so clearly that they might reasonably acquire it. Be sure to convey the nuances of the accomplishment in your paper; give your colleagues your insider's point-of-view.

3. Most of us have managed to fail spectacularly at one thing or another. Write a humorous essay for your campus paper on how *not* to do something—how not to keep a job, how not to impress your date, how not to endear yourself to your teacher, or so on.

4. You are seeing a career counselor to find out what kinds of job skills you have, and she suggests that you review your experiences to see what you have expertise in. By "experiences," she explains, she means not only paid jobs but also volunteer jobs—and also skills you develop without realizing that you developed them. For example, if you are a working parent, you are in a position to write "How to Interview a Babysitter." Or if you have helped out at church dinners, you are in a position to write "How to Cook for 100." Find a skill you had that you never looked at as a skill, and write a *How-To* essay about it.

5. You have worked at the same summer camp for the last few years, and this year the director approaches you with a request: the camp wants to start a file of camping skills so that new counselors can benefit from the expertise of the more experienced counselors. Subjects include teach-

ing arts and crafts, swimming, making fires, music, and so on. Pick an area you know something about, and write a *How-To* guide for counselors to help them teach the subject to their campers.

WRITING THE HOW-TO ESSAY

In writing a How-To essay, the emphasis of the creating/shaping/completing process is on selecting a subject or skill about which you are an expert, explaining it completely to your audience, and polishing the essay to ensure that all essential information and details are provided.

Creating

Even when a How-To essay covers familiar territory, you'll want to review the subject thoroughly in the creating stage. In fact, a subject you know very well may pose the greatest challenge simply because the process is so familiar that you hardly notice the individual steps any longer. So one goal of the creating stage is to make the steps in a How-To process stand out. *Listing* is the obvious creating method to employ in this situation. Fill a page with all the steps or considerations that go into course registration, generating oxygen, or changing an oil filter. Don't worry about the order of the items yet. Just get down all of the steps that help answer the question—*How?* For example:

CHANGING OIL

Get plenty of rags

Find a pan for collecting the oil

Warm the engine enough to circulate oil through the oil filter

Buy oil and a good quality oil filter

Locate the drain plug

Check the owner's manual for recommended grade of oil

Loosen the oil filter carefully so as not to break it off

Once the list is under way, you'll usually find that one detail quickly suggests a second, and a third. Only after you've got what feels like a complete list should you think about ordering the items. Try to organize the original items around several key items or steps. These steps may subsequently become paragraphs in the draft of the paper.

When you don't know what your subject will be, the creating stage must start a step further back. Use *looping* to answer the question "What do I know how to do well?" Three loops of five to ten minutes each should help you find an intriguing topic. *Chaining, track-switching,* or just talking can also lead you into a subject. You might consider, too, what sorts of topics your readers might benefit from knowing more about.

Recommended Creating Techniques

1. Making a List (See pp. 16–17)
2. Looping (See pp. 20–21)
3. Chaining (See pp. 18–19)
4. Track Switching (See pp. 319–321)

Whatever topic you decide upon, it should be something you know *thoroughly*. In the How-To essay, you will present yourself as an expert, so you must have the knowledge to claim that authority or the ability to acquire such expertise quickly through research. You don't have to be Mario Andretti to write about oil changes or Carl Sagan to describe the mechanics of a telescope. But by the same token you shouldn't discuss how to make fine wine if you can't tell the difference between champagne and cider: readers won't take advice from a writer who seems to know less than they do about a subject.

Be careful, however, not to overestimate the value of what you do know. It's possible that a skill you have—folding paper airplanes, coaxing poinsettias to bloom a second time, restoring old clocks—may appeal to only a limited audience. But it's just as challenging to consider how to make your specialty appeal to a wider audience.

Shaping/Drafting

Once you've focused on a particular skill or process, you need to turn your attention to audience, thesis, and organization.

Audience. Your rationale for writing the How-To paper is to convey your knowledge so thoroughly that readers will learn how to do this skill themselves. To accomplish that, you'll need to consider the items on this audience checklist:

- Try to gauge the level of your reader's knowledge. Adjust your writing to whatever that level is: rank beginner, enthusiastic amateur, skilled practitioner.
- Be sure your subject suits your audience: don't teach chefs to heat microwave pizzas or children to make dynamite.
- When dealing with uninformed readers, realize that more information is usually better than less. Define all key terms.
- Unless you are writing a very basic manual, look for ways to humanize the details so readers enjoy them. Use memorable examples, details, or illustrations.
- Assume that if readers *can* go off track, they probably *will*. Use lots of transitions.

- Give readers clear signals. If a step or procedure is likely to be difficult, admit that.
- Don't bore your readers. Look for places to cut the verbiage without reducing clarity.

Thesis/Promise/Delivery. The thesis of a How-To essay is usually some version of the following:

> *Thesis:* Readers will benefit from knowing how to do *X,* and so here are the steps for doing it.

Your version of an actual how-to thesis may include an incentive:

> *Thesis:* If you want to lengthen your life by about four years, here's how to cut cholesterol from your diet.

> *Thesis:* The average family *can save over $100* on income tax just by following these record-keeping routines during the next tax year.

The promise in the How-To essay is that you will teach readers to do *X*. The delivery you make on that commitment is easy to measure—can readers do what you promised to explain to them? To be sure you deliver, you need to keep asking yourself: Am I furnishing enough information? Am I explaining key terms? Am I focusing on the process or am I rambling? Would readers benefit from an example or a diagram? Am I leaving things out that an expert takes for granted?

Organization. The shape of a How-To essay is largely determined by its message. The basic design can be remarkably simple:

Introduction
Step One
Step Two
Step Three
Conclusion

This basic outline can be modified and reshaped to fit your treatment of the subject. Step Two, for example, might require a lengthy digression or a discussion of a subroutine—how to diagnose engine troubles from the color of the oil pouring into the drip pan, how to prune poinsettias correctly, how to flip an omelette. But readers following a process will expect an eventual return to the major steps.

Be sure readers can distinguish clearly between steps and follow the procedures you've set down. We've all experienced the frustration of trying to follow directions that omitted a crucial step or weren't written in plain English. Garbled instructions anger readers; understandable directions make them grateful.

Therefore it's important to divide the process you are detailing into clear, logical steps. Simply telling readers to "loosen and carefully remove the oil filter" won't help them much if they don't know where to locate that filter or what a filter looks like. Fill in the gap:

> The oil filter is a canister about the size of a large soup can mounted near the back of the engine.

Basic steps (which tend to be *actions*) quite often need to be fleshed out with *descriptions:*

> Cut the plant at the first node below the bloom. The node is the joint where a leaf meets the main stem.

Your words on the page take the place of in-person instruction, so describe every step the reader will need to know. Remember that the reader can't interrupt to ask questions.

Peer-Editing

When you have completed a draft of your essay (based on one of the situations presented earlier), ask one or more classmates to review it using the following form for guidance.

PEER-EDITING SHEET *The How-To Essay*

Essay writer's name ______________ Reader's name ______________

Please answer each question briefly, but thoughtfully, responding to the draft with useful comments. Be sure to explain your answers using specific, clear examples.

1. List some initial thoughts you had while reading the draft.

2. Is there a clear beginning, middle, and end to this draft? Summarize briefly where each of the three parts begins and ends.
   Beginning:

Middle:

End:

3. Briefly, write out what you think is this essay's purpose.

4. For what specific audience do you think the essay is written?

5. Point out three specific examples showing how the needs of this essay's particular audience helped to shape it; that is, cite particular choices of tone, kind or level of words, kinds of information given, format, and so on.
   a.

   b.

   c.

6. Does the paper, especially at the beginning, make you feel as if a person has written it to appeal to you as another person (your interests, your feelings, your imagination, your concerns)? Or does it come across as a mechanical recitation of facts or instructions? Explain.

7. Is the how-to information presented in an interesting framework, or does it seem mechanical? Explain which one and why.

8. Would you say that the writer comes across as an insider, that the writer thoroughly knows the process he or she is trying to explain? YES NO PARTLY. (The problem may merely be a matter of unclear writing, but it will be important for the writer to know if he or she *seems* not to know enough.) If you said that the writer *doesn't* always seem like an insider, circle the paragraph number(s) that struck you as not showing enough knowledge or insight into the process. 1 2 3 4 5 6 7 8 9 10 Briefly, why did you circle these paragraphs?

9. Does the essay make every step clear? YES NO If not, where does it fall short? Paragraph 1 2 3 4 5 6 7 8 9 10 Briefly explain why.

10. Does the essay present each step so you can follow the process? YES NO If not, where does it fall short? Paragraph 1 2 3 4 5 6 7 8 9 10 Briefly explain why.

11. Does the essay define its terms? YES NO If not, where does it fall short? Paragraph 1 2 3 4 5 6 7 8 9 10 Which terms need explaining?

12. Generally, does the essay use vivid details that are relevant to the point and which give readers a clear picture of what is being discussed? YES NO Cite your favorite details:

13. Has the essay successfully instructed you how to do something?

Completing

If an essay is to interest readers as well as to teach them, give the completing stage full attention. The following suggestions will make sure that you do.

Paragraphs. A key principle in the How-To essay is to *give the reader enough information.* Often we've done something so many times that we take the obvious for granted. Consider how you'd explain the making of a peanut-butter-and-jelly sandwich. You'd probably start with "spread the peanut butter on one piece of bread." But what kind of bread? And what do you spread it with? Your fingers? Be sure to look over your essay in the completing stage to make sure you've furnished all the instructions and details your readers will need.

Likewise, the more details you provide in your paragraphs, the more interested your reader will be. Colors, pictures, analogies—these all make concepts and procedures easier to understand than do accurate but lifeless words. Compare the following two instructions: which do you think would help novice plasterers more?

> Mix the spackling compound with water until you have a fairly thick paste.

or

> Gradually stir warm water into the white spackling compound until you have a paste thick enough to hold your mixing stick straight up.

Use visual aids to back up complicated instructions. If you're trying to tell readers how to install the mouse in their computers, a diagram of the internal board connections showing exactly where to plug in the controller card can help a reader follow your written instructions.

Transitions such as "first," "then," "now," "for example" and so forth help you move from one point to the next. Key words can be repeated throughout the essay in order to provide continuity for the reader. For example,

> Warm the *Erlenmeyer flask* in warm water. Then fill the *flask* with the NaCl solution. Put the *Erlenmeyer flask* on the heating ring and light the burner below it. Slowly rotate the *flask* with tongs to ensure even heating. Don't touch the *flask* with your hands; it retains heat and will burn you.

Sentences. In writing a How-To paper, clear, well-constructed sentences are essential. Giving enough information—particularly in the form of adjectives and adverbs—will make your writing more interesting and informative. "A survey" provides some information; "a survey of forty-one respondents" provides more; and "a survey taken by telephone of 41 randomly chosen respondents in Manville" provides even more. Also consider the matters of *coordination* and *subordination,* to show your readers what words are of equal weight and what words are less important. And combine sentences to connect related ideas.

Words. Even though you need to be precise, you can still use vivid, punchy words to instruct your readers. Keep your eyes open and your ears tuned for the most lively words you can find to describe your skill. *Consistency* is also important in the How-To essay. Establish guidelines and keep to them. If you're numbering your steps #1, #2, #3 and so on, don't suddenly switch to letters. If you're writing about eggplants, don't suddenly begin calling them aubergines. And resist the urge to use creative synonyms for important information: if you call a wire *red* in one sentence, don't make it *vermilion* in the next, *scarlet* in the next, and *cherry* halfway down the page.

Editing. Precision is important in writing the How-To essay, so make sure you don't have any typos, omissions, or misleading constructions. Try to avoid sentences such as "The red and yellow wires are crossed; connect the green wire to the top one." Review the Five Editing Steps in Chapter 4 to make sure you've got everything in perfect form. If possible, have a friend or writing partner read the instructions to see if they find any gaps. Once you're confident you've revised and edited your paper thoroughly, type a final draft to be turned in.

EXAMPLE The How-To Essay

The following essay was written by a student in an expository writing class. She had just been promoted to chief instructor at the exercise studio where she worked.

Emphasis: On the information her new exercise instructors need

Purpose: To obtain the exercise system her studio uses

Situation: The opening lecture at instructor orientation

Circumstance: A fifteen-minute talk; self-imposed deadline

Writer-Reader Relationship: Informed person to less-informed person

TEACHING STAR STYLE

The Star Exercise System is designed to accommodate three target areas of fitness: strength, flexibility, and stress reduction. As aerobics teachers, you're aware of all these areas; now we want you to know how they're integrated in the Star System. It's designed to control the heart rate and stroke-volume conditions of the heart in order to protect against traumatic injury during vigorous activity such as workouts. The advantages of the system are significant improvements in flexibility and a reduced chance of potential injury. It works to alleviate soreness, lower back pain, and neck and shoulder stiffness. The slow rate of movement in a narrow range of motion—the trademark of the Star Exercise system—helps prevent common injuries such as groin pulls, hamstring pulls, Charley horses, and lower back aches. Moreover, because clients using our system experience a minimal amount of soreness, they'll find it an extremely beneficial workout. They'll consistently progress in both flexibility and strength. As future Star System trainers, you'll be our best example of how well the system works.

As a Star System trainee, you'll need to concentrate on all three areas of the system. Let's take strength first. Three hours a day will be devoted to physical training. You'll have a one-hour group lesson on techniques, a second hour for a private lesson in choreography, and a third hour for studio practice. Here you can work on developing your own creative, coherent, and artistically pleasing routine for the hour-long classes you'll teach. We want our classes to have a light and jovial atmosphere, which is why you have to train so hard. There's no chatter, no wasting of time. Right now, training *is* your job.

In the Star System Exercise program, we use several strength training methods, the predominant one being continuous isokinetic contractions counterbalanced by static stretches in specific muscle areas. Star System Isokinetics allow for a constant resistance to movement at a constant rate of movement; this is different from the traditional aerobic workouts most of you are used to. The low resistance and high number of repetitions we use contribute to the rapid increase in muscle strength we advertise.

You'll need academic strength, too. So at night, you'll have lectures from doctors, researchers, and physiotherapists on medicine, nutrition, physical therapy, and exercise physiology. You'll receive a set of textbooks and videotapes put together by the Studio to accompany these lectures. They cover anatomy, the neuromuscular system and exercise, cardiovascular and respiratory responses to different kinds of exercise, and injury protection. Every day, try to learn a little more. Star instructors make it a point to become a little stronger and a little smarter every day. At the end of the three-week training period you'll have to pass a written exam on the lectures and instructional materials, so you'll need to master this material thoroughly.

You also can't neglect the second important aspect of the Star System, the stretch work which increases flexibility. Isokinetics must immediately be followed by stretching the same muscle area, since the heat produced from highly contracted muscles allows muscle fibers to extend beyond their normal capacity. It's this combination of contracting and stretching which improves our clients' flexibility. The static stretches should be slow, elongated, graceful movements. Furthermore, we add deep breathing to the stretching to reinforce the constant oppositions of contractions and stretches; this is the most effective means of dispersing built-up lactic acid in our clients' muscles, reducing their fatigue.

Finally, as in most forms of exercise, the Star System workout provides an outlet for stress, caused by the release of the hormone epinephrine in the brain after exercise. In addition, the adrenal glands are stimulated during this workout, producing high levels of energy; oxygen intake increases, and its high density in the bloodstream produces that wonderful euphoria we call an "exercise high." The pressures and tensions of stress from everyday living build up in us like water boiling in a closed kettle; you want to design a workout which releases that stress, minimizing the chances of suffering from anxiety, neurosis, depression, and "burnout." You'll have to work hard to help your students relax.

In our system for building strength and flexibility while reducing stress, there are a few moves that we never recommend. Leg lifts with full extension are terrible, especially if both legs are lifted simultaneously; such exercises are a chief cause of back pain. Deep knee bends stretch the lateral ligaments of the knees dangerously; if the stretching is excessive, the stability of the knee can be severely weakened. Moreover, prolonged daily repetitions of deep knee bends can lead to pinched cartilages, which often require surgical correction. Toe-touching also forces the knees to over-extend. Repeated toe-touching can also have a detrimental effect on the lumbar disks, leading to slipped or ruptured disks, or worse! Finally, straight-leg sit-ups are a no-no; they can cause hyper-extension of the back.

As you know, teaching an exercise class isn't as easy as it looks. The burden of a good class is on the teacher; she must think through every move, tying each to our three goals. She owes her customers not only good health and relaxation, but protection from injury. After all, that's what they're paying her for! If a teacher conducts her class with smoothness, confidence, imagination, and command over her body, and at the same time maintains a level of difficulty that gives her students a good workout each and every time, you can bet that the teacher has had many hours of practice. That's why you're working on these three areas. At the end of these three weeks, you'll be the product, the sale, the success or failure of the studio. You'll have a carefully thought-out class routine to teach, and know what you're doing and why. In short, you'll be able to live up to the motto of the Star Exercise System—you'll "do it with style!"

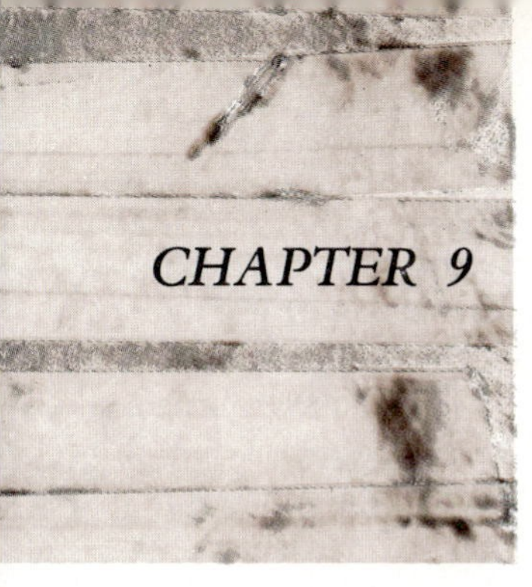

CHAPTER 9

The Problem-Solution Essay

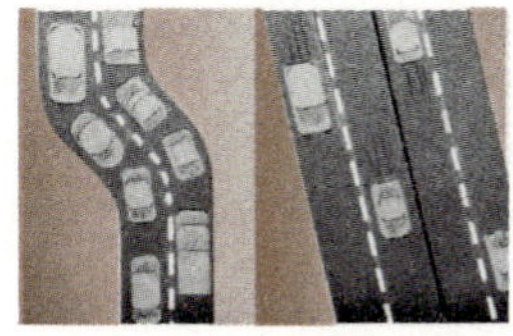

A great part of the political and social energies of any group—school, business, nation—are typically spent defining problems and proposing solutions. Such activities help these groups achieve their purpose.

WHY WRITE THE PROBLEM-SOLUTION ESSAY?

Problem-Solution essays are written to provide solutions to an identified problem; for instance, the administration of a university realizes that its minority retention projects have been neglecting Asian-American students; it will propose programs to correct that omission. Such essays also explore the nature of a problem and then offer a program of action; for example, a manufacturer, hurt by product liability suits that have tarnished its formerly solid reputation, experiences a sharp decline in sales; the company must do a thorough market analysis and then propose ways to upgrade its products and refine its image to recapture market share.

A Problem-Solution essay may acknowledge an existing set of problems and, while conceding difficulties, offer solutions to at least some of the problems; for instance, the federal government, strapped by budget problems, still realizes that education in the United States must improve if the country is to compete internationally; federal agencies seek ways of supporting education without increasing pressures on the budget. Or, it may argue for a particular approach to a problem—perhaps officers of the student government at a community college have found they have lost the backing of the campus population; at their next executive meeting, each officer presents an approach to regaining campus-wide support.

Situations like these inspire the kind of thinking and action that define the Problem-Solution essay.

Certainly there's no scarcity of problems in our world, nation, local communities, or personal lives. Notice, however, that the Problem-Solution paper has two parts: *problem* and *solution*. The second half of the paper often gets all the attention because we are—almost by nature—a society that believes in solutions. Give us a problem; we're sure we can handle it, whether it's curing polio, landing a man on the moon, or slimming our bulging waistlines. Such confidence is not a bad thing. Yet occasionally we wind up proposing solutions to problems that have not been adequately defined or understood. For example, when the AIDS crisis first became known, some scientists were confident that the virus would quickly succumb to a technological solution—most likely in the form of a vaccine that would control the virus. As the condition (the *problem*) became more fully understood, the likelihood of a quick cure receded and far more complex approaches to the disease were instituted.

So the first part of a Problem-Solution paper cannot be taken for granted or ignored. A worthwhile solution can be offered only when you understand the implications and dimensions of the problems you face—in depth and in context. And this may be the case even with what seem like petty problems. If this sounds pessimistic, it really shouldn't. Sometimes looking at a complex problem in depth helps you realize that all along you've been asking the wrong questions or tracking the wrong conclusions. The real answer turns out to be simple.

Checklist for writing a Problem-Solution essay:

- Attack a problem manageable within the length and time constraints of your paper.
- Choose a problem you know something about and can discuss from firsthand experience or as a knowledgeable observer.
- Define the problem carefully. Make sure readers understand the *who, what, where, when, how,* and (most important) *why* of the situation.
- Understand your readers; be sure you can make the problem mean something to them.
- Use many examples and illustrations.
- Choose details and incidents that will move your readers. Get them involved.
- Don't oversimplify the problem.
- Don't dismiss alternative solutions without giving them a fair hearing.
- Don't rush to judgment.
- Admit any limitations in the solution you propose.
- Suggest how readers ought to act in response to your solution. What action makes sense after they read your paper?

ASSIGNMENTS

Select one of the following situations to serve as the basis of a Problem-Solution essay—then develop this essay as you work through the rest of the chapter.

1. You're a student who comes from a different background (older-than-average, ethnic minority, religious minority, foreign, handicapped, and so on) than most students at your institution. Some of the programs aimed at your group seem off target, or perhaps you believe your special needs aren't being met in useful or creative ways. Write an article for your campus paper identifying an area where the school's efforts to meet the needs of your group fall short, and suggest what might be done about it. Be sure to define the problem carefully as you see it and to be sensitive and reasonable in the solutions you offer. (You might team up on this project with a classmate who you believe represents the "majority." Let the final version of the paper include a definition of the problem and a proposal for action that you both can support. Discuss and negotiate both the problem and solution fully. Write the paper together.)

2. Your (history, political science, psychology, or economics) class has been studying how recent national trends or actions will affect American citizens. Pick one such trend (economic development, trade policy, quality of education, labor concerns, race relations, church and state conflicts, and so on) and narrow it to a more specific problem or issue. Write an essay precisely defining that conflict and offering what you believe is a reasonable approach to it. (This paper might be done with a single subject—selected and agreed upon by the whole class—as the topic for a series of position papers written by groups of students with differing viewpoints. After the papers have been written and revised in the groups, they might be read aloud in class and debated.)

3. Explore a significant problem in your local community. (*Community* would include dormitories, apartments, co-ops, fraternity and sorority houses, and so on.) Choose a problem with implications for readers who don't live in your community (crime, adequate security, rowdy or sexist behavior, heavy drinking, lack of fire safety precautions), not a mere irritant (broken washing machine, eccentric landlord, snoring roommate). Provide a reasonable solution.

4. You've held your current job long enough to realize that many things could be improved if you were in charge: other workers' skills aren't used as fully as they might be; maintenance on expensive equipment is neglected; time is managed poorly; customers are ignored or mistreated. Write a letter to your supervisor identifying one of these problems and offering a solution. Be tactful. Remember that your supervisor probably should have been the one to diagnose the problem.

5. You have just returned to a familiar environment after being away for a while. (You could be returning to the United States after studying abroad, returning to your high school after a semester at college, returning home after spending time in another town, returning to school after a summer break, and so on.) Suddenly your old territory seems a little strange to you. Places that had always looked just fine now appear dilapidated, perhaps a little provincial. Before you readjust and settle back into comfortable routines, write an essay about a problem now apparent to you. Offer a possible solution. This essay might be written for a campus paper, a hometown paper, a travel magazine, or even as a letter to a friend.

WRITING THE PROBLEM-SOLUTION ESSAY

In writing a Problem-Solution essay, the focus of the creating/shaping/completing process is on defining a specific problem and solution(s), convincing readers that the problem is legitimate and the solutions logical, and editing to make sure the information is presented in a compelling manner.

Creating

When problems occur at the creating stage of a Problem-Solution paper, it's often because a writer has taken on too large or too abstract a subject:

> *Freedom is something that everybody wants, because freedom is a political and economic right, which our forebears put down in writing. No one doesn't want freedom, and all sociologists and historians can attest to this. Freedom is the basis of everything, and no one wants to be oppressed. Slaves didn't want it, or Lincoln either, and inflation makes freedom harder to get but even more necessary than before, during the Revolutionary War and after.*

What in the world is this writer talking about? It makes no sense at all. The subject is too large and too unfocused; the writer doesn't pinpoint a specific problem or solution. Nor does she indicate any expertise about the subject, or even any interest. Without insights into the real-life problem of "freedom," the writer has reduced the topic to boring, unrelated platitudes. You've heard it all before.

So although you may be tempted to tackle the big problems—conservation, the environment, health care, war, world peace—the truth is that you are apt to flounder in these deep waters of abstraction. If you don't know a good solution for the problem from first-hand experience, your own second-hand experience, or your reading—don't write about that problem. If you write what you know—what is real to you—then you are an expert, and therefore you have something of value to offer your reader.

1. Brainstorming (See pp. 15–16)
2. Looping (See pp. 20–21)
3. Reporter's Formula (See pp. 14–15)
4. Cubing (See pp. 315–316)
5. Track Switching (See pp. 319–321)

So the creating stage for a Problem-Solution essay actually has two parts: one process of discovery for finding and defining a problem and a second for exploring potential solutions. A *brainstorming* session with some classmates or *looping* exercises may be the best techniques for discovering subjects worth writing about. In these exercises, you need to give size and dimension to what may be persistent but shadowy annoyances:

> *"What's been getting under my skin lately? . . . It's been raining too much—but I can't do anything about that. . . . So what else? How about the way cars are always zooming and screeching down my street? . . . What if I write about the problem of inappropriate traffic in residential areas? . . . What are the consequences of fast-lane traffic on a slow-lane street? Not safe for kids—noise—accidents. . . . Okay, I could pursue that line of thought. And what solutions are there? . . . I don't know—wait, my friend in Berkeley, California, told me about these concrete barriers—with flowers planted at the top—that were put up around the city to slow down traffic. . . . That's one possible solution. Maybe I can think of others. . . . So what if I write about this problem, and suggest one or more solutions . . . and what if I decide to write this for my local neighborhood association . . . and what if I decide to write it within one week, so that they can have this information before the City Board meets in three weeks . . . and what if I keep it short—like, 50 words—so that a lot of people will be willing to spend time reading it . . . and what if my motive is that I'm tired of being awakened by the screeching of brakes . . . and what if the form is 'here's the problem, and a possible solution' . . . and what if my intention is to get local residents interested in slowing down residential traffic . . . then how do I start writing?"*

Indeed, this is how Problem-Solution papers typically begin, with the sense that something could be different, improved, or changed.

Once you decide upon a subject, you must examine it in detail. To do that, you might employ the reporter's formula to be certain you have enumerated all the material facts: who is involved; what exactly has happened; what locations or places are affected; what periods of time are involved, either in the development of the problem or its potential solution; how the situation came about; and why.

The *why* question may be the most important because understanding a problem means knowing how it came about—both its immediate and underlying causes. The cliché about getting to the "root of a problem" presents exactly the right focus. Serious problems are like stubborn weeds: there's usually a great deal of foliage above ground that can be hacked away easily enough. But there are always tangled, well-developed roots ready to sprout new weeds (problems) if fundamental causes and conflicts (roots) aren't taken care of. A writer preparing a Problem-Solution paper cannot afford to ignore the question *why?* or to answer it in crude and simplistic terms.

Once a problem is defined, there's no guarantee that a solution will be available. The most useful creating techniques in such a situation are those that compel a writer to look at a subject from different points of view, most notably *cubing* and *track switching* (see Chapter 16). Problems often persist because people insist on applying conventional or convenient remedies—the way a cook tries to douse a grease fire with water, only to spread the flames. What worked in one situation does not necessarily apply to another. So writers need to change perspective, alter their point of view, see things through the eyes of others. Cubing and track-switching encourage you to do this.

Shaping/Drafting

Your job in writing the Problem-Solution paper is twofold: (1) to describe a problem clearly and compellingly enough to persuade readers that a solution is needed and (2) to offer a reasonable and convincing solution. To do that, you'll need to consider audience, thesis, and organization.

Audience. The following checklist highlights key concerns with respect to focusing on your intended audience.

- Show how the problem you are presenting will affect readers. Don't allow them to suspect that your concern serves only your personal interests.
- Be sure the subject suits your readers: don't expect the poor to feel sympathy for the tax problems of the rich, or students to display interest in the retirement problems of military personnel.
- When dealing with an unfamiliar problem, realize that more information is usually better than less. Define all key terms and provide a clear narrative of events.
- Establish your authority. Give readers good reasons for regarding you as an expert on the subject. Establish your credentials.

- Be sure readers can distinguish between your statement of the problem and your solutions.
- Don't bore your readers. Look for places to cut the verbiage without reducing clarity.

Thesis/Promise/Delivery. The thesis of a Problem-Solution essay is usually a complex statement that sometimes takes a full paragraph to express. It names the problem and suggests the standards by which any solution will have to be judged. However complex an actual thesis turns out to be, its basic structure will likely contain these core elements:

Thesis: X is a problem requiring the following action: ________.

As usual, a good thesis will be carefully focused. You may feel that you want to develop the idea that "The whole world is a mess these days," but you'll be better off facing one crisis at a time: "The Electoral College constitutionally delegated to choose a President of the United States needs to be reformed or eliminated before it seriously disrupts the democratic process."

The promise in the Problem-Solution essay is to show readers a problem and offer an intelligent and reasonable solution. The delivery you make on that commitment is measured by how willing your readers are to entertain your ideas—not necessarily how readily they accept them. Very few Problem-Solution papers can be expected to move readers to immediate action. You've done a good job when you've simply gotten people to think about and debate your proposal.

Organization. The shape of a Problem-Solution essay is determined by its *focus*—whether on the problem, on the solution, or on both. Here are the building blocks for three kinds of Problem-Solution essays:

Emphasis on the Problem

Introduction
The problem
Why readers should care
Description of the problem
Examples
Illustrations
What readers should know
Conclusions

Emphasis on the Solution

- Introduction
  - The basic problem
  - The solution
    - What the solution involves
      - Examples
      - Illustrations
    - Assessment: will it work?
    - What the reader should do
- Conclusions

Emphasis on both Problem and Solution

- Introduction
  - The problem
    - Why readers should care
    - Description of the problem
      - Examples
      - Illustrations
  - The solution
    - What the solution involves
      - Examples
      - Illustrations
  - What the reader should do
- Conclusions

These outlines will need to be modified and reshaped in ways appropriate to a subject. Quite often, the Problem-Solution essay will follow a particular pattern within its various sections. Four common patterns of presenting information within such essays include:

> Cause-and-Effect: "Because of the massive disappearance of shopping carts, the Big Food Supermarket has taken to raising its prices by 10 percent." *Principle:* First *x* happened, then *y* happened.

Deduction: "Children are less literate than they were 25 years ago. Bookstore sales to people under age 15 are down by __% since the early 1950s, and polls show that most children watch TV an average of __ hours per day." *Principle:* General statement, supported by specifics.

Induction: "Within a single week, the local movie theaters ran films that sported chain-saw murders, beheadings, grisly hackings, and similar violent crimes. Clearly, society has become numbed to the pervasiveness of violence." *Principle:* Specifics leading to generalization.

Analysis: "Let's take a look at why the same party always gets voted in. For one thing, people are just plain used to it. (Exploration of familiarity as a motivation for voting.) For another thing, people are reluctant to take chances on an unknown quantity. (Exploration of don't-rock-the-boat phenomenon.)" *Principle:* Break down larger subject into parts, discuss the parts and relate them, then put the parts back together into a whole.

Peer-Editing

When you have completed a draft of your essay (based on one of the situations presented earlier), ask one or more classmates to review it using the following form for guidance.

PEER-EDITING SHEET The Problem-Solution Essay

Essay writer's name ______________ Reader's name ______________

Please answer each question briefly, but thoughtfully, responding to the draft with useful comments. Be sure to explain your answer using specific, clear examples.

1. List some initial thoughts you had while reading the draft.

2. What do you see as the purpose of this essay?

3. Circle one: Does this essay focus on a problem, a solution, or both?

4. Does the essay explain why the reader should care about the problem/solution? YES NO

5. Are the problem, the solution, or both fully described, with several detailed examples? YES NO Comment:

6. To what specific audience do you think the essay is directed?

7. Point out three specific examples showing how the needs of this essay's particular audience helped to shape it; that is, cite particular choices of tone, kind or level of words, kinds of information given, format, and so on.

   a.

   b.

   c.

8. Does the paper, especially at the beginning, make you feel as if the writer has written it to appeal to another person (his or her interests, feelings, imagination, concerns)?

9. Overall, did the writer come across to you as an insider about the problem treated in the paper? YES NO If not, briefly explain why.

10. Please write out the sentence or sentences near the beginning of the essay that best express its thesis.

11. Does this thesis make a clear assertion about the subject? YES NO Comment:

12. Identify the paper's thesis. Then please re-read each paragraph, noting if it is clearly related to the overall thesis of the essay.

Par. 1	Yes	No	Par. 4	Yes	No	Par. 7	Yes	No
Par. 2	Yes	No	Par. 5	Yes	No	Par. 8	Yes	No
Par. 3	Yes	No	Par. 6	Yes	No			

13. Is each point about the thesis developed fully enough for you to understand why it was brought up and used to explain or support the thesis?

Point 1	Yes	No	Point 4	Yes	No	Point 7	Yes	No
Point 2	Yes	No	Point 5	Yes	No	Point 8	Yes	No
Point 3	Yes	No	Point 6	Yes	No			

14. Does the introduction:
    a. Get the reader's attention? YES NO
    b. Reveal the thesis or message of the essay? Yes No
    c. Ease the reader into the very aspect/perspective of the subject on which the paper is focused? Yes No

15. Does the conclusion:
    a. Remind you of what's been said? Yes No
    b. Give you at least one new thing to think about? YES NO
    c. Provide a smooth ending so you are not left hanging in mid-air? YES NO

16. Is there enough material here to explain the problem fully? YES NO If not, what didn't you understand?

17. Honestly, did you end up caring about the problem/solution discussed?

Completing

Since a Problem-Solution paper focuses on the content of your writing and not its presentation, you don't want any minor problems to distract your readers or weaken their confidence in you. So spend extra effort polishing your paragraphs, sentences, and words.

Paragraphs. As you'll see in Chapter 19, paragraphs can be divided into two broad classes—*topic sentence* paragraphs, which convey your message, and *function* paragraphs, which help readers move from one point to the next. In writing the Problem-Solution essay, you'll want to make sure that your topic sentence paragraphs include explanation, analysis, facts and figures, illustrations, examples, and details to convince your reader that you really are an expert on this subject. Your function paragraphs should be laden with transitions such as "For instance," "To summarize," "Let's consider some examples" and so forth to provide a road map through your text for readers to follow. And both kinds of paragraphs can repeat key words and synonyms to knit the essay together.

Sentences. A sentence can sit passively on the page or leap up and grab your readers. The second kind, of course, is more likely to get your audience's attention. So how can you write interesting sentences? One way is to use adverbs and adjectives to convey necessary information. If you're talking about campaign rhetoric, for instance, "accusations" carries less weight than "stunning accusations of incompetence and graft lodged by his opponent." The latter tells your readers a great deal more than the former.

Coordination and *subordination* can help your readers identify your priorities, recognize the ways in which elements are related, and follow your logic. *Parallelism* allows you to establish a rhythm and help your readers predict what will follow. *Balance* and *repetition* provide unity or highlight contrasts. All these techniques can add energy and life to your writing. For a fuller explanation, see Chapter 20 in The Writers' Workshop section.

Words. Even if you're writing about serious subjects—perhaps especially then—connotative and suggestive words can help you convince your readers. Our minds see in pictures, and the clearer the word pictures you paint for your readers, the more likely they'll see what you see. But don't overuse descriptive language and become too wordy: quantity of words doesn't equal the quality of the words you select. Try to avoid preaching or scolding your readers; they're far less likely to respond appropriately to your proposals.

Editing. Mechanical correctness conveys a psychological message to your readers that you, the writer, are knowledgeable and in charge. A perfectly presented essay will go a long way toward convincing readers to see the problem/solution from your perspective.

EXAMPLE The Problem-Solution Essay

Anita wrote the following essay for her expository writing class. In it she assumes the persona of an experienced educator.

Emphasis: On an analysis of the problem

Purpose: To alert parents to a potential learning disability

Situation: An article for the PTA newsletter

Circumstance: Length: About 1,000 words; self-imposed deadline

Writer-Reader Relationship: Concerned writer to willing readers

IS YOUR CHILD DYSLEXIC?

Although much has been written recently for teachers on the subject of dyslexia, little has been done to educate parents about this crucial learning disability. The parents of the dyslexic student may sense that "something is wrong" when their child rebels; the overworked teacher may relegate the student to the slow track or scold him or her for not trying hard enough.

But dyslexia isn't a behavior problem, or caused by mental insufficiency or apathy. It's important for parents to recognize the differences in order to tackle this problem.

What is dyslexia? The term, from Greek, means an inability to read, caused by neurological disabilities or emotional traumas. But it doesn't mean the student is weak in oral or written language abilities. Rather, the student's brain is conveying confused messages from the eyes to the cerebellum. Letters may appear backwards, upside down, or in scrambled sequences; a *b* may look like a *d, god* may look like *dog,* or *pop* may look like *dod,* for instance. These scrambled messages, though, don't suggest that the student lacks intelligence; many dyslexics, in fact, have above-average IQs. Their "slowness" usually results from their frustration: dyslexic students often lack motivation because they feel "I'll be laughed at by the other kids; I'll never get it right."

Children with dyslexia are often not diagnosed until the later grades, when their inability to keep up with classmates can no longer be excused. Teachers who don't recognize the root of the problem or who are overwhelmed by the demands of large classes may label the student as "slow" or "unmotivated," and the student may find her- or himself in a class with developmentally disabled or even mentally retarded students. Parents, frustrated with the student's lack of progress, may scold or condemn instead of understanding the problem.

As concerned parents, how do you recognize this serious problem in your children and get appropriate help for them?

First, many dyslexic children are hyperactive and have distinct behavior patterns which cause them trouble at home and at school. In the household, the child's hyperactivity typically manifests itself as constant mischief, resulting in punishments, "groundings," and "time-out" for discipline. Minor infractions of house rules keep the child constantly in trouble, and parents tend to lack sympathy because the child's behavior seems so inexplicable. For instance, dyslexic children never seem to pick up their rooms or remember to stop at the store when asked to. And dyslexic students tend to have faulty memories, inciting parental frustrations when they can't find their homework or possessions, or remember to perform chores. They may even forget which house on the block is theirs. To add to the problem, many dyslexics lack physical coordination, which leads to spilled paint, broken valuables (or limbs), dropped food, and inevitable punishments. Since all of these symptoms are out of the child's control, the parents must practice patience and compassion to protect the student's self-image.

In the classroom, dyslexics tend to behave in one of three ways. The first behavioral category is the class clown. These students' antics keep their classmates laughing with them, not at them, and the teacher's attention off their schoolwork. The second category is the antisocial student, who uses isolation as a way of hiding this disability from the scrutiny (and ridicule) of others. Typically these students are the ones playing alone at recess or avoiding group games. The third category is the bully, who uses physical or verbal aggression as a way of avoiding the accusation of stupidity or the recognition of his or her problem. All three of these behaviors are aggravated by the teasing—often unintentionally cruel—of the students' peers.

Dyslexic students' problems usually become evident only when they reach the age for graded written work. The student's grades will be low, typically; but frequently an even more telling symptom is the teacher's comment "Did not follow directions." Because of their problems in perceiving letters, dyslexic students also have problems with handwriting; their difficulties in producing the correct letters leads them to write extremely slowly, to malform letters, to spell poorly, and even to fail to finish writing assignments. The reading level will usually lag behind the grade level, because the students have extreme difficulty reading aloud, omitting words, mispronouncing words, or guessing at what they see. Not all dyslexic students show all these symptoms, but the presence of two or three will cause trouble in school and should signal the parent to seek professional evaluation for the child.

What are the effects of dyslexia on children afflicted by it? They often lack self-esteem and self-confidence; they're likely to believe what the other children say, that they're the class dummies. They're intimidated and humiliated by the teasing of their peers, for frequently they can't tell what they're doing wrong. They just know that no matter how hard they try, they always seem to mess up. New experiences are dreaded because they lead to new occasions of failure. Eventually, these students may give up trying at all, or find some forum where their disability won't be noticed. Greg Louganis, an Olympic diver, is a good example; he compensated for his dyslexia by applying himself to sports.

If your child has some of these behavioral or academic problems, it's worth your while—and his or her future—to investigate further. All students have behavior problems at some time, and lots of them have trouble initially with learning to read and write. These problems don't necessarily mean that you have a dyslexic in the family. But if your child shows several of these symptoms, or if the symptoms persist, ask your school's guidance counselor or evaluator to test your child for dyslexia at the earliest possible date. Dyslexics can master their problems with hard work, counselling, and lots of positive reinforcement; and the sooner these remedies are applied, the better. Don't let your children suffer for a problem they didn't cause and can't cure without your help. Those behavioral problems and low grades can be a cry for help; don't let it go unanswered.

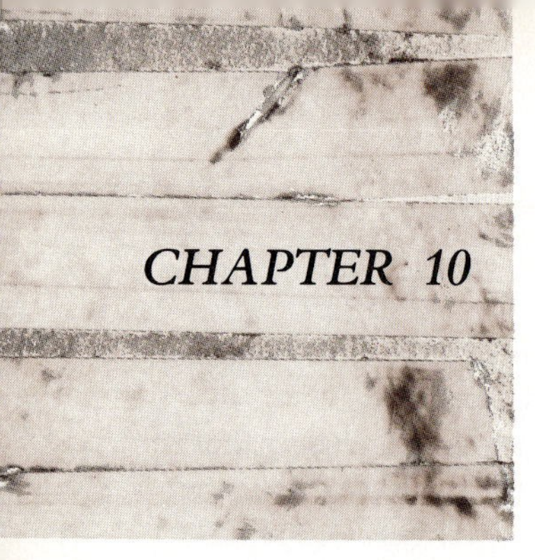

CHAPTER 10

The Information Essay

Ours is an "information society"—one that thrives on collecting and distributing facts, figures, new ideas, and new knowledge as completely and quickly as possible. Every day, people routinely gather information from dozens of printed sources: newspapers, magazines, books, manuals, journals, memos, encyclopedias. They scan this material on the printed page and the computer screen—compare it, contrast it, evaluate it, classify it, act upon it. For many people, informative writing is the writing that counts.

WHY WRITE THE INFORMATION ESSAY?

The reasons for preparing an informative paper are almost as numerous as the topics in an encyclopedia. These reasons include telling readers something they don't already know—something they might find educational (the composition of Mars' atmosphere), important (the IRS' latest tax decision), interesting (a biography of Henry Ford), or entertaining (a history of horror movies)—and enlarging readers' knowledge about something they might already appreciate (the origins of rock music, the influence of advertising on American culture). You might supply inside information, obscure but interesting facts, newly discovered material, and so on. Another motive for writing such a paper is to record events happening in the present or that occurred in the past (the current mayoral election, the rise and fall of the Dallas Cowboys).

Informative papers also are written to provide new information that readers want to have promptly (the latest trends in computer architecture, the results of public opinion surveys); to explain ideas, concepts, principles, or situations that readers might otherwise find hard to understand without special training or education (a non-specialist's guide to quantum theory, principles of post-modern architecture; a guide to business law); to summarize or report a current state of affairs (a corporation's annual report, a yearbook, a news summary); to present facts and information that will add to or broaden readers' general knowledge (a history of Western art, a survey of world religions).

Informative papers are the purest form of "writing to tell." You are not explaining how to do something, pinpointing a difficulty, suggesting solutions to problems, or offering an opinion. Instead you are describing your subject so that readers come away from the paper as well informed as you are.

Checklist for writing an Information essay:

- Make the information the center of attention, not your opinions, thoughts, insights, or feelings.
- Present the information so that readers can hear a "voice"—you are writing for people, not machines.
- Be faithful to the facts, but present the subject in its most compelling light.
- Focus your subject carefully. Choose a topic you can define and discuss in intriguing detail within the limits of your assignment.
- Make sure your coverage of the topic is comprehensive. Discuss the *who, what, where, when, how,* and *why* of the topic.
- Make sure your coverage is accurate. Check your facts and use reliable sources.
- Make sure your information is surprising. Don't bore readers with information they already have or could assume on their own.
- Relate new material, especially any complicated ideas and concepts, to what readers already know.
- Organize the paper well. Use headings to guide readers through the material and to provide easy access and be consistent.
- Use images—both verbal and visual—to enhance the presentation. Label all figures and diagrams.
- Use examples and illustrations freely.
- Use clear, nontechnical language. Define all unfamiliar terms.

ASSIGNMENTS

Select one of the following situations as the basis of an Information essay—then develop this essay as you work through the rest of the chapter.

1. Using newspaper or magazine indexes, spend a few hours in the library listing some of the major events that occurred during the month

or year of your birth. Select one major event, research it more thoroughly, and write an informative paper about it.

2. Select a historical figure whose name you have heard often, but whose accomplishments are unknown to you. (Be sure to choose a person you really want to learn more about and whose achievements can be researched in the library.) Then write an informative paper about *one* event or *one* accomplishment in that person's life. In discussing this single event or achievement, you'll probably have to supply some background information. But do *not* write a complete biography of your subject—just provide those facts about the individual's life essential to understanding the particular event you are discussing. Explore that topic in depth. Use several sources in constructing your Information essay; relying on only one or two sources, no matter how comprehensive or authoritative, is a mistake. You will be tempted to borrow too much of your sources' organization and point of view rather than finding a structure of your own.

3. Pick a challenging and important concept you have mastered in one of your other classes and explain it to students not currently enrolled in that course. Or, if you have selected a major, choose a theory or concept central to that discipline and explain it to your classmates. For either paper, be sure to use many examples, illustrations, or comparisons.

4. Form a writing group with four or five students and decide upon a subject to explore collaboratively. Pick a topic of mutual interest that can be conveniently divided into parts: dominant theories in psychology; the conservative Justices of the Supreme Court; the outer planets; major American romantic poets. Divide up the research assignments among members of the group. Then define the scope of the research: how much information of what sort should each member of your research task force collect? Be as specific as you can in defining the project. When the data have been collected, write a paper based on the information gathered. Establish a pattern for the information, have each member contribute to the effort, and then edit the paper for consistency in organization and style. (This is a lengthy project, not something that can be done in a few days.)

5. When discussions among your friends and classmates center on current events, you may occasionally hear someone complain, "I just don't understand why . . ." or "Does anybody know what X is?" Pick up on one of these remarks and write a paper to clear up the speaker's confusion.

6. Write an article for a major geography journal about a place where you have lived. Beginning with the assumption that the city, town, or area is a worthy place to learn about, make the piece both informative and entertaining. Explore aspects of the geographic, architectural, cultural, social, religious, ethnic, and/or political brew. If you are from a

familiar spot (New York, Los Angeles, Chicago, Houston), don't emphasize conventional tourist traps. Give readers an insider's perspective on your stomping grounds. If you are from a small town or an "ordinary" suburb, it may help if you consider how exotic a place like Parma, Ohio; Normal, Illinois; or Arlington, Texas, might seem to someone from Addis Ababa, Poznan, or Nagpur (cities in Ethiopia, Poland, and India).

7. There's probably an activity you have always loved (drag racing, going to the opera, playing the stock market), perhaps to the point of boring your friends. Your best friend finally confesses an interest in understanding your hobby. Write an informative essay to explain the source of your fascination.

WRITING THE INFORMATION ESSAY

In writing an Information essay, the creating/shaping/completing process involves choosing a topic you are knowledgeable on or are willing to research; presenting your information in an interesting and authoritative manner; and editing to make sure that the flow and language are appropriate to the topic and the audience.

Creating

Since the emphasis in an Information essay is on the information itself, rather than on what you think, feel, or perceive, you need a subject that (1) interests you and (2) you can write about with authority. Consequently you either have to know something about the topic when you start or be willing to research it within the time available.

Looping is always a good creating tool to begin with, especially if you are having trouble finding a subject. Just put "What information do I have that other people might find interesting or useful?" at the top of a blank sheet of paper or computer screen. Then do three loops of 5 to 10 minutes each. You will probably discover an intriguing subject, perhaps even a surprising one.

Once you have a topic, you can begin to flesh it out with the *reporter's formula*. Responding to the *who, what, where, when, how,* and *why* inquiries will make sure you have touched all the bases and give your paper the comprehensiveness expected of an informative project. For locating more facts on a subject, you'll need to use one of the advanced invention techniques—*reading and research* (see Chapter 16 or refer to Chapter 14 on the research paper for more details about library research). The research paper, after all, is often just an extended and carefully documented Information essay.

If you will be writing an Information essay that explains something, use the technique of *classical invention,* explained fully in Chapter 16. Not

Recommended Creating Techniques

1. Looping (See pp. 20–21)
2. Reporter's Formula (See pp. 14–15)
3. Reading and Researching (See pp. 339–341)
4. Classical Invention (See pp. 325–329)

only will it draw out information on your topic, but it will also clarify important relationships within the subject—specifically, between causes and effects. And these cause-and-effect relationships are often the foundation of explanatory writing.

Shaping/Drafting

Your job in writing the Information essay is to present a subject comprehensively, accurately, surprisingly, and clearly enough to teach an audience something they didn't know.

Audience. To accomplish this goal, you'll need to consider the items on this audience checklist:

- Assess the level of your audience. How much do they already know about your subject? How much do you have to explain?
- Be sure the subject suits your readers.
- When dealing with an unfamiliar subject, realize that more information is usually better than less. Define all key terms and provide a clear narrative of events.
- Define all key terms and give an explanation of background items: persons, places, and things your readers might not recognize.
- Establish your authority. Give readers good reasons for regarding you as an expert on the subject. Explain your credentials.
- Don't belabor obvious points. Look for places to cut the verbiage without reducing clarity.

Thesis/Promise/Delivery. A strong thesis is essential in an Information essay. Readers need to understand precisely the point you are trying to make or the topic you intend to cover. The need for precision rules out any thesis that simply identifies a topic area: "Here is some information about the U.S. House of Representatives." Readers need to know more exactly what they will be told about the subject and perhaps why: "The U.S. House of Representatives operates under elaborate protocols that give the Speaker of the House enormous power to influence legislation." Because of the great variety of information papers, it is difficult to provide a thesis blueprint, but here are some core elements:

Thesis: X is (size, shape, color, weight, distance, other properties).

Thesis: X does (function, purpose, aim).

Thesis: X did (history, biography).

Thesis: X consists of these parts: _____, _____, and _____.

Thesis: X can be classified according to _____, _____, and _____.

Thesis: X is the result of _____, _____, and _____.

Thesis: The causes of X are _____, _____, and _____.

Thesis: X is (un)like _____.

At the creating stage, before you had gathered information or decided precisely what portion of a topic to cover, the preliminary thesis may have been somewhat general. But in the shaping stage, you should gradually sharpen the focus until the thesis is more interesting and authoritative:

First version of thesis: Bunratty is a castle in County Clare, Ireland.

Second version of thesis: Bunratty, a castle in County Clare Ireland, is a fascinating location.

Third version of thesis: Bunratty, a castle in County Clare Ireland, provides tourists with a haunting glimpse into its medieval past.

In writing an Information paper, you make your readers this promise: "I will tell you, teach you, or explain to you about X so that you understand X and its importance to you." To deliver on your promise, ask yourself, "Have I provided information that is complete, accurate, and surprising? Does the information follow in the order suggested by my thesis or opening paragraph?" If so, you've done your job.

Organization. The shape of an Information paper is determined by its *thesis*—and the patterns that follow from it. The various patterns available to you when shaping such a project are presented in detail in Chapter 17, "Form and Pattern." Any particular organizational design will need to be modified and reshaped in ways appropriate to a given subject. The Information essay will often combine patterns within its various sections, moving rapidly from narration to description, or description to comparison with the aid of a transitional phrase or paragraph.

Peer-Editing

When you have completed a draft of your essay (based on one of the situations presented earlier), ask one or more classmates to review it using the following form for guidance.

PEER-EDITING SHEET The Information Essay

Essay writer's name ______________ Reader's name ______________

Please answer each question briefly, but thoroughly, responding to the draft with useful comments. Be sure to explain your answer using specific, clear examples.

1. List some initial thoughts you had while reading the draft.

2. What do you see as the purpose of this essay?

3. To what specific audience do you think the essay is directed?

4. Point out three specific examples showing how the needs of this essay's particular audience helped to shape it; that is, cite particular choices of tone, kind or level of words, kinds of information given, format, and so on.

   a.

   b.

   c.

5. Please write out here the sentence or sentences near the beginning of the essay that best express its thesis.

6. Does this thesis make a clear assertion about the subject? YES NO Comment:

7. Identify the paper's thesis. Then please re-read each paragraph, noting if it is clearly related to the overall thesis of the essay.

Par. 1	Yes	No	Par. 4	Yes	No	Par. 7	Yes	No
Par. 2	Yes	No	Par. 5	Yes	No	Par. 8	Yes	No
Par. 3	Yes	No	Par. 6	Yes	No			

8. Generally, does the essay supply vivid facts that are relevant to the point and which give its audience a clear picture of what is being discussed? YES NO Cite three of its best, most helpful, and most interesting facts:

   a.

   b.

   c.

9. In which paragraphs would you like to see more facts? 1 2 3 4 5 6 7 8 9 10

10. Overall, are the essay's facts interesting? YES NO PARTLY Please note those facts you found uninteresting:

11. Is the new information understandable to you? Is it presented so that the audience can relate it easily to what it might already know? YES NO PARTLY Explain:

12. Does the essay make clear to you why this information is significant? YES NO UNSURE Explain:

13. Circle an answer for each. Does the introduction:
    a. Get the reader's attention? YES NO
    b. Reveal the thesis or message of the essay? YES NO
    c. Ease the reader into the very aspect/perspective of the subject on which the paper is focused? YES NO

14. Does the conclusion:
    a. Remind you of what's been said? YES NO
    b. Give you at least one new thing to think about? YES NO
    c. Provide a smooth ending so that you are not left hanging in midair? YES NO

15. Overall, did the writer come across to you as an insider about the information provided in the paper? YES NO If not, briefly explain why.

16. Has the essay provided you with information that you think is worth knowing?

Completing

In the Information essay, the structure (how the ideas relate and flow) is very important—and so is the particular language you choose. Take a look at the following details to give your readers an Information essay that will interest as well as inform them.

Paragraphs. Make sure that your Topic Sentence paragraphs relate clearly to the topic—they should tell the reader what your essay is about. Function paragraphs tell the reader how to read the essay: they provide drama, connect one part to another (transition), break up long paragraphs, accommodate your personal style, emphasize a point, develop an example, add detail, and so on. Be sure you have both kinds of paragraphs. (See Chapter 19.)

Particularly in an Information essay, it's important to give enough information. Does the reader have all the details, illustrations, examples, facts, figures, and explanations required to really get the message you are sending? The mind accepts pictures more readily than abstract statements, so back up all your abstractions with specific examples. To make your writing more powerful, illustrate a general statement such as "California offers a delightfully varied landscape" with specifics such as "Within the one state you can ski in the Sierra Mountains, swim in the coastal waters, pick fruits from the lush farmland orchards, and camp in the desert of Death Valley."

Just because your audience wants information doesn't mean that it wants to be bored. (Nor do you, when *you* are the reader.) So you need to offer more than just a solemn recitation of facts and figures—give the audience a significant and valuable piece of writing. Revise your paragraphs so that *every* detail, every piece of the development, is right. Here are some things to think about as you complete the revision of your paper.

- You've heard the saying, "A picture is worth a thousand words." This is particularly true for the Information essay—throwing dry facts at a reader is more likely to produce a headache than an ache for knowledge. Since we all think in mental pictures, use description (colorful words, analogies, images, and so on) and, when appropriate, actual illustrations and diagrams.
- The way you present facts has a bearing on how interesting readers will find them. It's not too interesting to read, "Columbus discovered America in 1492"—that's for encyclopedias. So offer something more than a fact book. For example, isn't it more interesting to read this about Columbus? "Nowadays we think nothing of crossing the ocean; we have all sorts of navigational aids—

including state-of-the-art technology and the entire U.S. Coast Guard—at our disposal, not to mention haute cuisine and chlorinated pools. But imagine the state of things in the late 15th century, when Columbus was trying to acquire a crew and some backing from the Queen of Spain for a foolhardy voyage to find the Indies—a voyage that would waste both money and lives when the ships fell off the edge of the earth."

- Even the smartest reader will find it hard to understand totally foreign material. To assist your readers, do all you can to relate the new information to something with which they already are familiar. This means giving familiar examples or references, as well as specific details and colorful word-pictures.
- Readers will want to know why it is important to know this information you are presenting. When you draw comparisons and contrasts between the new material and what the readers already know, you help them understand the significance of what they are reading.
- Readers always want value for the time, attention, and effort they put into reading. So let the readers know that you are taking them somewhere worth going—stick to the point, refrain from rambling, and avoid unnecessary details.

Don't forget transitions (if necessary, review "Transitions" in Chapter 4). Transitions and reminder signs are like bridges and traffic signs for the reader. Transitions connect separate ideas or paragraphs, and reminder signs tell the reader what is important. Examples of transition words include *for example, because, therefore,* and *similarly.* Reminder signs are key words or phrases that you repeat to let the reader know what the essay is all about. If you were writing about the Civil War, you might repeat the two words *Civil War,* several times or more, for emphasis and continuity. Or you might use synonyms, or otherwise refer to the Civil War without directly mentioning it.

Sentences. You want live, energetic sentences, not dead weight. So check to make sure your sentences are as alive as they can be. Would you gain anything by combining sentences? Is it clear which sentences are coordinate and which are subordinate? The clearer these internal relationships are, the more easily your reader will get the picture.

Be sure to give the reader the full picture. This doesn't necessarily mean more data—it may simply mean enough adjectives and adverbs to paint a picture. Contrast the plain description, "The summer hills" with the more evocative "The maize-colored summer hills"; the second description gives you more actual information (color, climate, appearance).

Words. You've all heard the *Dragnet* bromide "Just the facts, ma'am. I just want the facts." But readers of Information essays aren't Joe Friday, Badge 714; they want a lot more than names, dates, facts, and figures. So you need to provide your information in ways which will engage their interest, pique their curiosity, stimulate their intellects—in other words, in ways which will encourage them to keep reading. How can you do this?

First, remember that you're *showing,* not just *telling*. So you'll need to think like an artist when you convey your message. Compare these two informative passages. Both have the same basic information, but which do you think will engage the readers' interest more effectively?

> The presence of certain levels of chemicals in the soil, rather than the falling temperature, is responsible for the many different colors of leaves we see in the autumn.

> Our schoolday notion of Jack Frost painting the autumn leaves with his icy brush is romantic—but scientifically wrong. Studies show that the levels of iron and copper in the soil are the real reasons why leaves turn so many shades of amber, gold, sienna, pumpkin, scarlet, and vermilion in the fall.

Next, consider your audience and pick your words—particularly adjectives and adverbs—with them in mind. For instance, a doctor or pharmacist would probably have no trouble with this passage, because the words chosen come from the specific vocabulary of medicine. They expect to receive information in this way:

> A gel may be a colloidal suspension of a drug—for example, aluminum hydroxide—or a solution or suspension of a drug in a thickened vehicle. In the latter case, the design may be to keep the drug in contact with the oral or pharyngeal mucosa or to achieve a demulcent effect. In the past gums were used and the preparation called a mucilage.

But average readers—even experts in other fields—would be bewildered by the passage. So to present this information to them, you'd need to rewrite it using words the new audience can cope with:

> Some prescription drugs, such as aluminum hydroxide, come in thick, semi-liquid forms called gels. Such forms can also be used to dissolve a drug and administer it by spoon, making it easier for patients to take. Gels are also useful when the drug must remain in contact with the linings of the mouth or throat; they coat the tissues, administering the medicine where it's needed. In your grandparents' time, these gels were made from vegetable gums and called mucilages—the same term used for library paste.

Third, you need to choose words which help your readers understand your subject. How many times do you hear a term you don't understand used in a lecture? And if you don't ask for clarification, how confused do you become? So include definitions and explanations as well as familiar examples to help your readers follow. Consider these two instances:

> Bankruptcy court rules require that debtors regularly amortize their debts.
>
> Bankruptcy court rules require that debtors amortize their debts, keeping up a regular schedule of payments.

Both examples use the same technical term, *amortize,* but the second clarifies it with a participal phrase so that readers know that *amortization* is the process of paying back a debt with regular payments. Note that it isn't necessary to fuss over the definition with such constructions as "Amortize may be defined as" or "according to Webster;" rather, the definition is subordinated to the main information about court requirements.

Editing. Though you've worked hard to find interesting and lively ways to present your material, your focus in the Information essay is on the content of your material. So once you've finished revising, you need to check the accuracy of the information you convey. Make sure that numbers haven't been transposed or decimal points omitted; that key words haven't been omitted (for instance, what's the difference between "Try to cut the wires" and "Try not to cut the wires"); and that spelling or punctuation inaccuracies haven't inadvertently changed or obscured your meaning (for instance, typing "Use the Spell function" for "Use the Shell function"). This attention to detail ensures you'll keep your promise to your readers and reinforces your readers' perception of your care and competence.

EXAMPLE The Information Essay

The following essay was written by Ruth Blumenthal for her freshman composition class.

> ***Emphasis:*** On informing the reader about healthful diet alternatives
>
> ***Purpose:*** To give the reader enough information to make his or her own decision about diet

Context: A class assignment, completed in two weeks

Circumstances: Written late in the semester

Writer-Reader Relationship: Knowledgeable expert to open-minded reader

STOP CHEWING THE FAT

Would you change your lifestyle to add fifteen years to your life? I think you might. All of your life you have been taught to eat from the four basic food groups: milk, bread, meat, and fruits and vegetables. Yet some of these foods have been proven to be high in fat and cholesterol and should be eaten in moderation, if not omitted entirely from your diet. Until recently, it was thought that all of the foods from the four basic food groups were nutritious, but research has proven that high fats from the above mentioned typical American diet are contributing factors to several diseases.

Some foods in the American diet are not as nutritious as you might believe. For example, red meats, including beef, pork, and hamburger, and dairy products, such as butter, whole milk, sour cream, and cheeses, are heavy with fats. These foods are harmful because they are fattening and they are loaded with cholesterol.

What is cholesterol and how does it pose a threat to you? Cholesterol, a fatty, wax-like substance found in all body cells, circulates in the blood, but is most concentrated in the brain, spinal cord, adrenal glands, liver, gallbladder, and skin. It is essential to life because the body needs cholesterol to manufacture hormones, to help in the formation of vitamin D, and to insulate nerve tissue. Cholesterol is produced in the body, a large amount being manufactured by the liver. When the extra cholesterol from the high fat foods you eat is added to what the body is already producing, too much cholesterol is absorbed in the blood.

Too much cholesterol in the blood is associated with three serious health problems: coronary heart disease—the number one killer in America; stroke, which afflicts nearly two million Americans; and high blood pressure, which leads to stroke, heart attack, and kidney failure. Some of your parents may have these diseases now and you may inherit them in the future. But there is still hope. Because these problems are affiliated with a high-fat diet, you can help prevent them by eating a low-fat, high-carbohydrate diet.

Studies indicate that a low-fat, low-cholesterol diet lowers blood cholesterol levels in most people, and reduces the risks of developing heart disease and high blood pressure. To help lower blood cholesterol levels, physicians recommend these changes in diet:

1. Cut down on saturated fats.
2. Substitute polyunsaturated fats for saturated fats.
3. Eat fewer foods high in cholesterol.
4. Combine a low-fat diet with a high-carbohydrate one.

Saturated fats, which are found in foods of animal origin (eggs, meat, butter, cream), are the primary cause of high cholesterol in the body. Such fats are usually hard at room temperature. When you must eat fats, substitute polyunsaturated fats, which are found in most vegetable oils (safflower, soybean, corn), nuts (walnuts, pecans, almonds), and seeds (sunflower, pumpkin), for saturated fats. Polyunsaturated fats are usually liquid at room temperature. Unlike saturated fats, they have little effect on cholesterol levels. Substituting polyunsaturated for saturated fats will cause your cholesterol intake to decrease. To eat a healthy diet, cholesterol intake should not exceed a total of three hundred milligrams a day. Once you have established a low-fat diet, combine it with one that is high in carbohydrates.

Combining a low-fat diet with a high-carbohydrate diet is important because carbohydrates help keep you healthy. Fat calories cause more weight gain than do calories from carbohydrates. So, while you should limit your fat intake, carbohydrate intake should rise. Carbohydrates come in two types: simple and complex. Simple carbohydrates are syrup, sugars, and honey, which break down into glucose and are too fattening. Simple carbohydrates are the type most people think of when speaking about carbohydrates, and that is why people think all carbohydrates are fattening. On the other hand, complex carbohydrates, which include fruit, vegetables, and starches (pasta), are better for you than simple because they break down slower and have fewer calories.

Not only do complex carbohydrates have fewer calories than simple carbohydrates, but they are a great source of protein, which is essential to the body. Beef is a source of protein, but it contains too much fat and cholesterol. It is better to get protein from complex carbohydrates. But remember, anything eaten to excess will cause you to gain weight. Just because they are better for you does not mean you can pig out on complex carbohydrates.

Once you cut-down on your fat and/or cholesterol intake, your calorie intake is also reduced, because foods high in fats are also high in calories. This may surprise you, but the average full grown person needs to eat only 1200–1500 calories per day to stay healthy. In order to stay thin, you must limit calorie intake, while also keeping aware of fats. (See the two sample meals at the end of this essay: the first one shows a low-fat, low-cholesterol meal and the second is an example of a "typical American" meal high in fat and cholesterol).

Notice that, in the high calorie meal, you have used up all of your calories and cholesterol for the day in only one meal. Now, what will you do for the other two meals in the day? Nibble on carrot sticks? The important thing to remember is that, while the number of calories you eat are important, what is in those calories, such as fats, cholesterol, and carbohydrates, is equally significant.

Growing bodies consume more calories, but when your body stops growing and you continue to eat a high-fat diet, you gain about 3–5 pounds per year, which you may ignore until three or four years go by. Once you reach the age of thirty or thirty-five, you may develop high blood pressure and high cholesterol because of your added pounds, which can progress into a stroke or a heart attack.

Today, people over age thirty-five who have experienced heart attacks and strokes are being taught to reverse the disease process by sensible eating and exercise. Thirty is not that far away. Don't you think it would be better if you took care of your health and body now, and not face these diseases in the future? If they are reversible, then certainly they can be prevented.

Just remember:

1. Concentrate on eating a diet low in fats and/or cholesterol.
2. Combine your low-fat diet with one high in complex carbohydrates.
3. Combine your good diet with a planned program of exercise.

The time to start is now, while you are young, so smarten-up, eat right, and live longer.

Example of meal with 300 calories:

3½ ounces of chicken or fish—broiled or baked without the skin	120 calories	99 mg. cholesterol
1 cup of vegetables steamed with no butter	80 calories	0 mg. cholesterol
As much lettuce salad (without dressing) as you want	40 calories	0 mg. cholesterol
Jello, fruit, or angelfood cake	60 calories	0 mg. cholesterol
	300 calories	99 mg. cholesterol

Example of "typical American" meal:

At least 3½ ounces of steak	260 calories	107 mg. cholesterol
Baked potato with sour cream and butter	440 calories	197 mg. cholesterol
Vegetables with butter	110 calories	35 mg. cholesterol
Salad with creamy dressing	160 calories	6 mg. cholesterol
Ice cream (2 scoops)	220 calories	106 mg. cholesterol
	1190 calories	451 mg. cholesterol

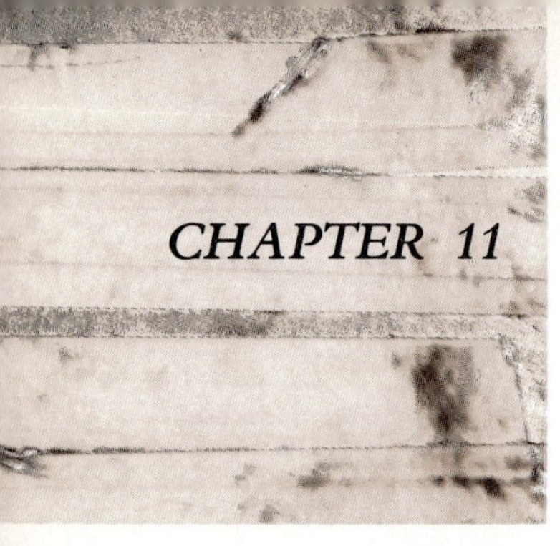

CHAPTER 11

The Assertion-with-Evidence Essay

The Assertion-with-Evidence essay goes a step beyond the Information essay (see Chapter 10), which presents readers with facts, ideas, and concepts for their own sake. In the Assertion-with-Evidence essay, you use the facts to support a more definite position—an assertion that you intend to prove logically and clearly. You can, of course, state an opinion without bothering to back it up, but informed readers will simply dismiss such writing as annoying, self-righteous, or unimportant. If you want an idea to change the thinking and behavior of your readers, you need to back it up with good reasons and strong evidence. Good reasons are logical, powerful, consistent, and engaging; strong evidence is authoritative, accurate, and fully researched.

WHY WRITE THE ASSERTION-WITH-EVIDENCE ESSAY?

The reasons for preparing an Assertion-with-Evidence essay are simple—to persuade readers that something is true or false, right or wrong; to present the evidence in favor of some assertion; to dissuade readers from a position they already hold; and to encourage readers to consider a new position based on facts they may not have. Assertion-with-Evidence papers are the most straightforward kind of "writing to change." They go directly to the point, even more so than Personal Perspective essays (see Chapter 7). While Personal Perspective essays tend to emphasize the writer as much as the idea, Assertion-with-Evidence papers are concerned with facts.

Checklist for writing an Assertion-with-Evidence essay:

- Make your assertion—not your opinions, thoughts, insights, or feelings—the center of attention.

- State your thesis (your assertion) as carefully as possible. Qualify all general statements. Be sure you are prepared to define or explain the meaning of all key terms, especially abstractions.
- If helpful, break your assertion into parts that can be proven sequentially.
- Provide clear evidence to support your assertion.
- Break the evidence into parts. Make one key point at a time.
- Show the relationship between each link in your chain of evidence.
- Make sure your evidence is clear to the audience you are addressing.
- Provide concrete evidence: examples, graphs, charts, illustrations. As necessary, quote authorities.
- Organize the paper carefully. Be sure the opening introduces the subject and the conclusion summarizes what you have demonstrated.
- Keep the tone of the paper serious and low-key. But be clear, direct, and reader-oriented.

ASSIGNMENTS

Select one of the following situations to serve as the basis of an Assertion-with-Evidence essay—then develop this essay as you work through the rest of the chapter.

1. In an Assertion-with-Evidence essay, prove that some widely held and repeated generalization that you believe to be incorrect is *in fact* incorrect—or at least inaccurate in some or most cases. You may want to question local stereotypes—that campus athletes live a privileged life. Or your focus may be larger—on such controversial national issues as defense spending, education, or welfare. In all cases, start with what the general public believes and give good reasons to doubt that belief.

2. Examine a political, military, cultural, or social phenomenon or event of the past which people today tend to regard differently than when it occurred (the dropping of atomic bombs on Japan; the Civil Rights Movement; the decision to land astronauts on the moon; the building of nuclear power plants; the Vietnam War; the establishment of Social Security; the beginnings of rock and roll). In a writing group, discuss several such issues before agreeing on one that might furnish material for a collaborative paper. When you have reached a decision, divide responsibility for research among members of the group, either according to subtopics (persons, events, political conditions) or potential sources of information (magazines, newspapers, books, journal articles). When this preliminary research is complete, meet to discuss what you each have discovered. Sum-

marize, assess, and debate the evidence thoroughly and then write a group paper explaining (1) why public opinion has changed and (2) whether current opinion is based upon accurate knowledge of the past.

3. Study a group of persons, places, or things to prove or disprove an opinion or assumption you have about them:

A. Men are better at mathematics than women, but women outperform men in the language arts.
B. Japanese cars are better built than comparable products from Europe.
C. Asian students outperform other minority groups academically.

If appropriate, construct a survey or poll as a means of testing your assumption. Do whatever reading or research is required to furnish additional evidence. Throughout your research, keep an open mind. Your paper should support what the facts lead you to believe, not what you'd like to believe. In your paper, be careful to define all critical terms.

4. Make a generalization about television programs (talk shows, dramas, soap operas), printed advertisements, radio programming, or movies (comedies, serious dramas, teen films) that you can test by studying a reasonable sample. Make sure your assertion is clear and reasonably specific:

A. Most teen horror/slasher films make women the chief targets and victims of violence.
B. TV talk shows are less responsible and factual in discussing political issues than sexual ones.

Whatever your assertion, collect ample evidence to support it. Then write an Assertion-with-Evidence essay. Be sure to provide clear, detailed, and specific illustrations and examples.

5. Choose a controversial topic in your major field of study and write a paper for an audience of nonspecialists (people outside the field) that takes a stand on that issue. Be sure to provide clear evidence that nonspecialists can assess.

WRITING THE ASSERTION-WITH-EVIDENCE ESSAY

In writing an Assertion-with-Evidence essay, the focus of the creating/shaping/completing process is on selecting a topic you feel strongly about, making an assertion that you support with evidence, and polishing your essay to ensure that it is clear, factual, and influential.

Creating

Even though the emphasis in an Assertion-with-Evidence essay is on the assertion itself and the facts supporting it, you should begin with an issue or topic that moves *you* to write—something you believe in enough to investigate and present conscientiously. As is true in an Information paper, you either have to know something about your subject when you start or be willing to research it within the time available.

Looping is always a good creating tool to begin with, especially when you are casting about for a topic. *Cubing* is good for tracking an elusive subject out to its logical conclusion. *Track Switching* will help you explore various sides of an issue; by seeing other sides and discovering what the objections to your assertion may be, you can build counter-arguments for your side. Finally, *Reading and Researching* plays a key role in many Assertion-with-Evidence essays because an entire argument can be destroyed by one figure overlooked or one fact not properly interpreted.

Shaping/Drafting

In this stage of the process you need to be thinking about audience, thesis, and organization.

Audience. In proving your assertion, keep your audience in mind. Understand what kind of evidence is appropriate to the subject and to the audience you are addressing. Quite obviously, a scientific research article must meet different standards of proof than an Assertion-with-Evidence article for the campus newspaper or a position paper for a literature or political science course.

You must also have reasonable expectations about what you can achieve with a given subject. No logical arguments might convince jobless factory employees that robots are better workers than humans; you might, however, make a case that robots are better suited to hazardous or extremely repetitive duties. To develop a sense of your particular audience, consider the items in the audience checklist:

- Don't argue an impossible case. Be sure the facts you've gathered are sufficient to move the audience you are addressing.

Recommended Creating Techniques

1. Looping (See pp. 20–21)
2. Cubing (See pp. 315–316)
3. Track Switching (See pp. 319–321)
4. Reading and Researching (See pp. 339–341)

- Assess the expertise of your audience. How much do they already know about your subject? How much do you have to explain?
- Assess the attitude of your audience. Are your potential readers likely to be friendly, hostile, or neutral toward your assertion?
- Consider what you expect your readers to do as a result of your paper. Would accepting your assertion require them then to act differently or change their perspectives on a subject? If so, do you need to state that or merely imply it?
- Get readers to identify with a subject as you see it. Explain what's in it for them.
- Make your readers trust your authority and honesty. Use clear, relatively neutral language to avoid suspicion of bias.

Thesis/Promise/Delivery. A clear thesis is essential in an Assertion-with-Evidence essay. Readers need to understand precisely the point you intend to prove.

Recall that a thesis is a particular aspect of a subject; both you and the reader must be able to grasp the assertion made in the thesis, and understand what is required to prove it. For example, "Something is wrong with modern civilization" would hardly qualify as a thesis. How would you know when and if you have proven that "something" is out of joint in civilization. What civilization? Which something?

Clarity is crucial too. The Assertion-with-Evidence paper cannot introduce elusive concepts and ambiguous terms; the reader will expect you to have sorted out all the difficulties in explaining the issue. So while the thesis itself can be quite specific and complex, it should offer what is suggested by this general pattern:

Thesis: This is the way X is, and here is why.

In writing an Assertion-with-Evidence essay, you are making a promise to your reader: "I will tell you what, in my way of thinking, is so, and I will do all that I can by means of words to get you to consider my assertions seriously." If you have seriously considered your purpose, your audience, and your thesis, then you have done yourself what you are asking your readers to do. And that makes you an authority—your word is good, and you make good on your word.

Organization. The various patterns available to you when shaping an Assertion-with-Evidence essay are presented in detail in Chapter 17, "Form and Pattern." But it is possible to sketch out a general design for such an essay:

1. State your assertion clearly, early in the essay: "Television is giving viewers an unrealistic view of life."

2. Give your evidence quickly, and make sure it really supports your assertion: "A survey of prime-time TV shows reveals that __% present at least one violent crime per episode, __% present casual sex, and __% take place in congested urban areas."
3. To offer the reader further convincing evidence, follow up with facts, examples, illustrations, or other information that the reader can check, if desired. Or present a discussion that is so logical and convincing that the reader is willing to accept it without argument: "There are a lot of un-squeaky wheels watching TV—people who do not make big waves in the areas of violent crimes, sexual exploitation, or unconcern with love, loyalty, and all those other seemingly outmoded values. But how often do they get portrayed as subjects? Perhaps they are not exciting enough—yet they are real, and plentiful. Iowa farmers, Maryland families, California dairymen—all live lives as real—more real—than anything shown nightly on TV."
4. Acknowledge any weaknesses your evidence might have (or at least be aware of them yourself): "I confess that I speak as one who is fed up with this lopsided view. As a child, I noted that the evening news only told the *bad* news, never the mundane *good* news—'A father played happily with his son, today'—and I don't think the situation has changed much."
5. Conclude with a commitment to what you say—"The truth is, it's gotten so bad that I have stashed my boob tube in the closet. I only take it out for very special events, like the Olympics."

As with other kinds of essay writing, to a large extent the form of the Assertion-with-Evidence paper is contained within the thesis itself. Since you are out to change your readers' perceptions or actions, you'll use a form that shows the relationship of component parts. After all, the basic premise of this kind of writing is "I say that something is so, and here is why you should see it this way, too." Depending on your intention, thesis, and audience, you have several choices of form.

Deduction involves going from the general to the specific. If your generalization is "The credit-card system doesn't work very well," you could back that up with specific examples of evidence: "On October 10, 1985, a Missouri man was billed for $40,000 worth of purchases he never made. After many months of persistence on the man's part, the company finally admitted to a computer error."

Induction is the opposite—starting with specifics and ending up with a larger generalization. "Hospital A paints its walls a sickly green, and the recovery rate of its patients is three months" is one piece of specific evidence; "Hospital B paints its walls a cheery yellow, and the recovery rate of its patients is only two months" is another. The generalization—

"There is a relationship between the colors of hospital walls and the rate of recovery of patients"—is built up to logically.

The *example* form is just what it sounds like—you back up your assertion with examples that prove the point. Say you began with the assertion, "The members of the board of directors are too heterogeneous." You would simply give relevant examples: "Mr. X. is a pharmacist; Ms. Y. is a dancer; Mrs. Z. is a banker." By the time the readers reach your summary—"Therefore we need board members who have more in common with one another"—they should have plenty of information about why your assertion is a solid one.

Analysis is yet another form that works well here. To analyze means to separate a whole into its parts. You approach a large subject by dividing it into smaller parts. Then you discuss these parts one at a time, show their relation to each other, and then put them back into a whole. Suppose that your assertion is "The school building needs to be modernized." You could then address the specific parts: the windows are too high; the desks are too cramped; the desks are rooted to the floor, thus preventing more imaginative groupings of children; the walls are too thin. By the summary, the reader should understand the component parts, as well as the whole, of the subject that you analyzed.

No matter what form your essay finally takes, you'll find it was inherently present—and perhaps even revealed outright—in your thesis sentence.

Peer-Editing

When you have completed a draft of your essay (based on one of the situations presented earlier), ask one or more classmates to review it using the following form for guidance.

PEER-EDITING SHEET The Assertion-with-Evidence Essay

Essay writer's name ______________ Reader's name ______________

Please answer each question briefly, but thoughtfully. Be sure to explain your answer using specific, clear examples.

1. List some initial thoughts you had while reading the draft.

2. What do you see as the purpose of this essay?

3. To what specific audience do you think the essay is directed?

4. Point out three specific examples showing how the needs of this essay's particular audience helped to shape it; that is, cite particular choices of tone, kind or level of words, kinds of information given, format, and so on.

   a.

   b.

   c.

5. Please write out here the sentence or sentences near the beginning of the essay that best express its thesis.

6. Does this thesis make a clear assertion about the subject?
   YES NO Comment:

7. Identify the paper's thesis. Then please re-read each paragraph, noting if it is clearly related to the overall thesis of the essay.

Par. 1	Yes	No	Par. 4	Yes	No	Par. 7	Yes	No
Par. 2	Yes	No	Par. 5	Yes	No	Par. 8	Yes	No
Par. 3	Yes	No	Par. 6	Yes	No			

8. Does the essay give plenty of evidence, and give it quickly? YES NO

9. Evaluate the effectiveness of the essay's evidence:
   a. logic ___ clear & convincing ___ unclear & unconvincing
   b. examples & illustrations ___ clear & convincing ___ unclear & unconvincing
   c. documentation & references ___ clear & convincing ___ unclear & unconvincing

   Briefly explain any unfavorable evaluations of the evidence:

10. Does the essay acknowledge the weaknesses in its evidence? YES NO Do you see any weaknesses it doesn't acknowledge?

11. Which form would you say this essay takes? (Circle one)

    Deduction (general-to-specific development)
    Induction (specific-to-general development)
    Examples
    Analysis (separating the whole into parts)

12. Does the essay present its assertion and its evidence so that the reader can hear a "voice," so that it seems written for specific people?

13. Does the introduction:
    a. Get the reader's attention? YES NO
    b. Reveal the thesis or message of the essay? YES NO
    c. Ease the reader into the very aspect/perspective of the subject on which the paper is focused? YES NO

14. Does the conclusion:
    a. Remind you of what's been said? YES NO
    b. Give you at least one new thing to think about? YES NO
    c. Provide a smooth ending so that you are not left hanging in mid-air? YES NO

15. Are the transitions between paragraphs smooth and clear? YES NO SOME Between which paragraphs were the transitions hard to follow? (Please circle them.) 1 2 3 4 5 6 7 8 9 10

16. Has the essay succeeded in changing you in some way? Explain.

Completing

This is the stage where you perfect and polish your draft. Your proper and logical outline turns into a piece of writing with style and energy.

Paragraphs. Revise your paragraphs to deliver on promises you've made to supply readers with information. This may mean quoting facts and figures—but it may also mean providing concrete details—examples, illustrations, analogies, even anecdotes that hammer home a basic point. While Assertion-with-Evidence papers tend to be sober and factual, they can also show spirit and emotion. Compare these two passages:

> Route 101 has terrible bumps and holes. It is a danger to all drivers, including careful drivers. We pay taxes! These taxes should be used to fix public roads.

> I had just shelled out $360.86 to get brand-new radial tires and I was feeling the pinch—payday was a week off. Still, I depend a lot on my car—it takes me to my job, to my girlfriend's house, to the hub of the city for a night on the town, to the sanctuary of nature when the city's getting to me. It's worth spending my hard-earned bucks to keep my car in good shape so it can help keep *me* in good shape.
>
> So you know I wasn't exactly overjoyed when—on its maiden voyage, mind you!—my brand-new right front tire hit a pothole the size of a crater. Good old Route 101!

The difference is obvious: in the first statement, the assertion may be true and totally supported with facts, but in terms of the reader's interest, who cares? In the second statement, there is a wealth of concrete detail that the reader can identify with—having to spend money you don't really have on necessities like tires; depending on your car; experiencing unfortunate timing; being angry about the state of the public roads. Paradoxically, by describing his experience in such a particular way, the writer has made his experience universal. Almost anyone can relate to his experience. Therefore, the focus wouldn't even have to be the poor condition of public Route 101—it could be, but it doesn't have to be. It could now be about the condition of public roads in general, with Route 101 as an illustrative example. So the moral is: Use details, details, and more details—there's nothing like the concrete to make abstractions understandable.

It is also important that you check to see that all your paragraphs are connected in a way that will be sensible to the reader. You can actually orchestrate the way your evidence is presented. Use a particular strategy in placing your evidence as you prove your assertion. And see that your topic sentences, in the Topic Sentence Paragraphs, clearly state the new evidence you are about to present.

Transitions and *reminder signs* are useful to keep the reader on track. Think of them as bridges and road signs. Transitions will help the reader bridge the ideas from one paragraph to another by means of such words as "because," "consequently," "therefore," "on the other hand," and so on. Reminder signs occur when you repeat a key word or phrase to let the reader keep in mind what is important.

Sentences. You are more apt to convince your reader of the strength and rightness of your assertion if you write sentences that are lively and energetic. How do you do this? One way is by *sentence combining*—linking together several short, choppy sentences to make one longer rhythmic one.

Another is by giving a full picture—adding those adjectives and adverbs that will really make the scene come alive for your readers. Consider the difference between "The traffic was terrible" and "The traffic was backed up for three miles in the noonday sun. All around me, drivers were wiping their faces with handkerchiefs, loosening their collars, cursing, and honking their horns."

Also pay attention to *coordination* and *subordination* within sentences—that is, which words have equal weight, and which have less weight. When you set your priorities in this way, so does your (grateful) reader. ("Grateful" because readers like to understand what they read—they get frustrated when the writer is unclear, and unless they are particularly dedicated to the subject or the writer, they are apt to throw down the essay in disgust. So the more you do your work, the longer you will hold your grateful reader's interest.)

Words. The more specific your words, the more liveliness—punch—your writing will have. The problem with cliches is not that they are wrong, but that we are so used to them that they evoke no surprise. The more exact, pictorial, concrete, and specific your words, the more you will surprise the reader—enable the reader to see things in a new way. And this is one essential element of keeping your reader interested.

Editing. Now is the time to look over your writing for any possible inaccuracies—misspelled words, typos, incorrect usage, inconsistent tenses, and punctuation. It's not the creative part of the work, but it is a necessary part. After all, you wouldn't cook a terrific meal and then serve it to guests on cardboard, would you?

EXAMPLE The Assertion-with-Evidence Essay

Troyce Nolan wrote the following essay in his composition class. He supports his assertion with evidence from expert sources which he carefully documents following Modern Language Association style (see Chapter 14 for an explanation of MLA documentation style).

Emphasis: On constructing a convincing case

Purpose: To construct an argument that the writer endorses and to support it with expert evidence

Context: A class assignment, completed in three weeks

Circumstances: Written late in the semester

Writer-Reader-Relationship: Well-informed expert to an open-minded reader

A BATTLE FOR EXISTENCE

Because cities across the nation are growing, more and more land once occupied by wild animals is being developed from wilderness to metropolis. Developing the animals' wild habitat is causing over-crowding and a shortage of food and shelter. Because of the crowding and shortages, many animals are dwindling in numbers and others are becoming extinct. *Editorial*

Research Reports estimates nearly 250,000 species are endangered in the world today. According to the same report, "In this country, no fewer than 181 species—including 36 mammals, 68 birds, 30 fishes, 10 reptiles, and 4 amphibians—fall into the endangered species category" (Gimlin et al. 683). According to the Endangered Species Act of 1973, an animal is considered endangered when it appears close to extinction throughout its livable habitat (Gimlin et al. 683). One such endangered animal is the whooping crane. With the help of man and a cross-fostering program, however, the number of whooping cranes can be replenished.

Scientifically known as the *Grus americana,* the whooper is "the rarest North American species" (Peterson 79). The bird gets its name from its most distinguishing characteristic, its call, which resembles a loud whoop, and it is easily recognized by its white body feathers, red skin around the face, and black wing feathers (Peterson 79). The whooping crane is America's largest bird, averaging from four to five feet high and having a seven-foot wingspan (Harmon 41).

The whooping crane's summer habitat once covered much of northern Canada, and a section of the United States including northern Illinois, Minnesota, and North Dakota. Their wintering grounds were found all along the Gulf of Mexico. Also, there was a non-migratory flock in southwestern Louisiana. The population within this entire range peaked between 1,300 and 1,500 whoopers (Hamilton 56). But, between 1800 and 1920 the whoopers began to disappear (Drewein 682). Construction in the prairie wetlands and hunting quickly thinned out the crane's population. Also, in 1940, a hurricane wiped out the Louisiana flock. Of the thirteen birds in the flock, seven of them were killed during the storm, and the remaining six had all disappeared by 1949 (Mackenzie 124).

By 1936 man was trying to help the struggling cranes because of their inability to reproduce steadily in the wild (Zimmerman, *Peril* 75). During 1936 the U.S. Fish and Wildlife Service established a 47,000 acre refuge near Aransas pass in Texas called the Aransas Pass National Wildlife Refuge, where the last surviving flock spends its winters (Zimmerman, "Technique" 54). But, because their nesting grounds had not been discovered, the flock dwindled down to a record low of fifteen in 1948 (Harmon 41). Finally, the long-sought-after nesting grounds were found at Wood Buffalo National Park (W.B.N.P.) in a remote section of Canada's Northwest Territories (Drewein 682).

Once scientists discovered Wood Buffalo, they began attempts to rebuild the whooper's population. Scientists working for the Endangered Wildlife Research Program first attempted to form a captive flock at Patuxent Wildlife Research Center in Laural, Maryland (Zimmerman, *Peril* 75–76). These captive cranes failed to mate on their own, so artificial insemination was used. Fertile eggs were produced through this technique, but the chicks did not survive because of physical disorders. The next attempt at helping the whoopers was to collect eggs from W.B.N.P. and let the Patuxent whoopers hatch and raise them. Unfortunately, the results of this experiment were much the same as those from earlier attempts (Drewein 683).

Still using the egg collecting idea, scientists decided to try having sandhill cranes acting much like foster parents hatch and raise the eggs (Drewein 683). As Lee Harmon explains in *Sunset:*

> The foster parent plan is a joint American-Canadian experiment. It uses the sandhill cranes as foster parents. For three years now, eggs of northern California whoopers have been transferred to sandhill nests at Gray's Lake National Wildlife Refuge in southeastern Idaho. The sandhill cranes have adopted the whoopers, even bringing

them along their own 800 mile winter migration to Bosque del Apache (41).

In the *National Geographic* Roderick Drewein reports that the foster parent sandhill cranes behaved much like the whoopers. Like whoopers, sandhills lay two eggs that require a thirty day incubation period, the chicks are identical to those of the whooper, and the adult cranes did not abandon the nest if an egg was taken or switched. Also, like the whoopers, of the two layed eggs, very seldom do two offspring survive due to sibling rivalries. Therefore, even if the collected eggs do not hatch, the birds' normal evolutionary cycle is not upset. In fact, the number of chicks that reached maturity increased during the egg collection process (684).

The first trial with egg-fostering produced ten chicks from fourteen transported eggs. Three died at birth, two were lost, and five migrated south to winter in Bosque del Apache with their fostering sandhills (Zimmerman, "Cranes" 132). The whoopers were compatible with their foster parents, but were very aggressive towards sandhill chicks, a sign of species recognition that will help them when they begin mating (Zimmerman, "Cranes" 132).

Bruce Hamilton writing in *Sierra* reports that, "To date the foster parent program is highly successful. However, it will be several years before researchers know if the fostered juveniles will mate, breed and establish a second stable flock" (58). The wait is because whooping cranes do not become sexually mature until the age of five or six (Drewein 692). Despite the wait for maturity, progress can already be seen. In 1980 there were just over 90 whoopers wintering on the Gulf Coast (Jansgard 74). Maybe, with the help of man and the cross-fostering program, the whooping crane can once again live without the danger of extinction.

Works Cited

Derwein, Roderick C. "Teamwork Helps the Whooping Crane." *National Geographic* May 1979: 680+.

Gimlin, Hoyt et al. *Editorial Research Reports*. Washington, D.C.: Congressional Quarterly, 1977.

Hamilton, Druce. "The Whooping Crane a Success Story." *Sierra* May/June 1979: 56.

Harmon, Lee. "The Whoopers at Bosque del Apache." *Sunset* Dec. 1978: 41.

Jonsgard, Paul A. "Whooper Recount." *Natural History* Feb. 1982: 70.

Mackenzie, John. *Birds in Peril*. Boston: Houghton, 1977.

Peterson, Roger Torey. *A Field Guide to the Birds of Texas*. Boston: Houghton, 1960.

Zimmerman, David R. "A Technique Called Cross-Fostering May Help to Save the Whooping Crane." *Smithsonian* Sept. 1978: 52.

———. *To Save a Bird in Peril*. New York: Coward, 1975.

———. "Whooping Cranes." *Audubon* Mar. 1976: 132.

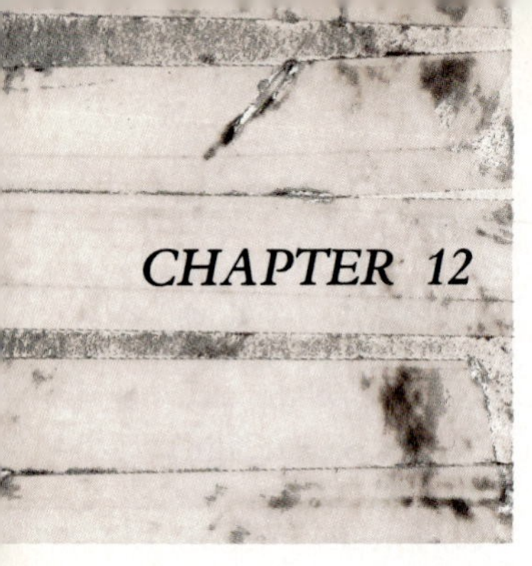

CHAPTER 12

The Evaluation Essay

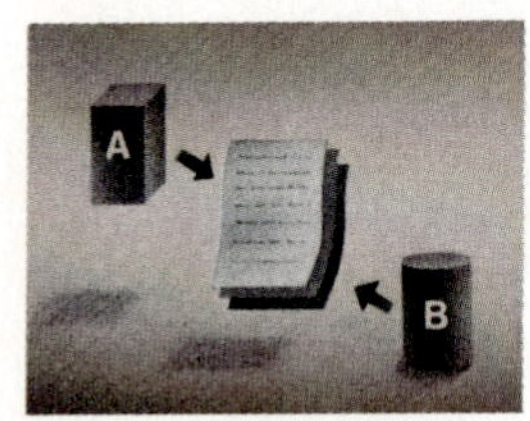

When you write an Evaluation essay, you compare and contrast one thing with another: which manufacturer offers the best CD player? Is the movie playing in the student union any good? Which car is a better deal for the money, the foreign model or the domestic? You probably evaluate many things—people, products, ideas, and experiences—in a single day. When you put evaluations into written words, it's usually to persuade readers to make a choice based upon your assessment and recommendations.

WHY WRITE THE EVALUATION ESSAY?

The reasons for writing an Evaluation essay are not complicated—to persuade readers that something is good or bad; to persuade readers that one thing is better than another; to indicate what your preferences or tastes are; and to recommend your tastes or preferences to readers. Evaluations, of course, can be flip and casual: "That novel isn't worth the effort to throw it in the garbage—don't buy it." But the kind of evaluation you will write in professional and academic circumstances requires careful evidence and support.

Checklist for writing an Evaluation essay:

- Make sure you identify precisely what you are evaluating.
- When you make an evaluation, be sure you contrast comparable items. Don't compare cabbages and computers.
- Make sure your criteria of evaluation are relevant to your topic: don't expect a snowblower to cut grass.
- Be certain your readers know what criteria you are applying in your evaluation.

- Be fair to all sides. When appropriate, admit the strengths in an opposing view.
- Provide detailed evidence or arguments in support of your evaluations. Show exactly how the subject under scrutiny measures up to the standards you have defined. Use examples, facts, figures, charts, and graphs and cite authorities as necessary.
- Develop one point at a time.
- Arrange your arguments to build toward the strongest evidence that supports your assessment.
- Make sure your evidence is significant. Don't make a major judgment on the basis of a minor issue.
- Be sure the tone of the paper conveys fairness. A biased opinion won't be respected.

ASSIGNMENTS

Select one of the following situations to serve as the basis of an Evaluation essay—then develop this essay as you work through the rest of the chapter.

1. If you've held a job for some years while attending school, write a letter of recommendation for an employee whom you have supervised or with whom you have worked closely. Assume that your colleague is looking for a job similar to the one he or she is now doing.

2. You have been invited to be the guest (book, music, dance, food, or film) reviewer for the local newspaper while the regular reviewer goes on vacation. This delights you because you have been wanting to see a variety of types of ________ reviewed, and you welcome the chance to see your own standards and preferences reflected on the review page. The editor has just called to say the first review is due Tuesday. Write the essay that will put *you* in the public eye!

3. You have a friend who resisted the idea of using computers for a long time. Now, however, he decides that he is ready to buy a personal computer. But when he glances at the ads, he feels overwhelmed by the amount and variety of brands, types, and configurations of computers that are sold. He really wants to take this step, but he doesn't know where to begin. He thinks of you as a person who knows how to judge things, and he asks you to help him buy the right computer. You have had a computer for some time and decide to help him by evaluating several models you think will suit his needs. Write the Evaluation essay you would give him.

4. A cousin who lives in another state is almost ready to apply to college. You have been requested—by your aunt, uncle, mother, and fa-

ther—to help your cousin choose a school. She wants to go to a school that will fit her personality and interests; her parents are concerned that she not go too far away and that the school actually teach her something. With the characteristics of your cousin's personality in mind, write her a letter about your recommendations.

5. You belong to a lively young adults' group that has its own monthly newsletter. The editor has asked you to write a piece for the next issue about the comparative advantages and disadvantages of living in a dormitory versus an apartment. Since you have done both—and, in fact, have had pleasant experiences with both living situations—you are a good choice to give a balanced evaluation.

6. The principal (or your favorite teacher) from your elementary (or high) school is retiring. You have been asked to come to the banquet in this person's honor and give an evaluation of the value this person has given to the school and the students. You know this will be a hard assignment, but you are looking forward to paying this tribute to a person who has meant a lot to you and your friends. You sit down to prepare the remarks you will deliver, and the evaluation of this person's worth and value comes more easily than you think. Remember to keep your praise specific, not vague—it will be a more interesting tribute that way, and it will also mean more to the recipient.

7. You are president of an organization and in this capacity must serve on a national committee which selects the next site of the annual convention of the club. You and the group have visited more than a half dozen possible sites for the convention, and each of you has been asked to narrow your choices to two. You must write an evaluation of these two cities to give to the chair of the committee. Write an evaluation of the two cities you liked best as convention sites, emphasizing the advantages and disadvantages of each. (Be sure to write about two places you know well—they need not be major urban centers.)

8. Form a small writing group with classmates who share a taste for some particular form of art or entertainment: music (rock, classical, jazz, gospel, easy listening); film (suspense, horror, science fiction, comedy, drama); sports (football, baseball, auto racing, golf); theater (classical, musicals, opera, light opera), and so on. Discuss the qualities that define excellence in that form: what makes an opera great; what does a classic horror film do; what characterizes a first-class baseball team? When your group has agreed upon these general criteria of evaluation, choose a controversial figure or work in the area and, individually, write evaluation essays based on your agreed-upon criteria. When the essays are complete, read them aloud in the group and then discuss how well each member of the group has applied the original criteria of evaluation.

WRITING THE EVALUATION ESSAY

In writing an Evaluation essay, the creating/shaping/completing process focuses on selecting a topic and establishing its evaluative criteria and the features to be evaluated, and presenting a clear, fair, and authoritative comparison.

Creating

The Evaluation essay requires two kinds of creating that occur after you've decided what, in general, you are evaluating—whether a form of government, an athlete's performance, a book, a camera, and so on. The first type of creating establishes the criteria of evaluation to be applied in a given situation; the second defines the features to be judged in a given comparison or evaluation.

Standards of evaluation are of two kinds: external and internal. *External standards* are specific, objective, measurable reasons for making a judgment. For instance, a reviewer might claim that Car A is a better family vehicle than Car B because it gets better fuel mileage, costs less, has a bigger trunk, and offers more interior space. Such features can be observed and measured by anyone who makes the effort to gather the data. Thus the standards are external or objective. A subjective element remains, however, in the evaluator's assumption that most readers will accept these features as valid measures of the car's usefulness to families.

At the creating stage, you can look for external standards by establishing what the purposes of an object are and then defining criteria to measure performance; that is, how well purposes are met. In many cases, success has to be measured by several criteria. A Mercedes-Benz may handle very well, but it may be a less than perfect automobile for a family when price is factored into the evaluative equation. So, in establishing external criteria, you might try *listing* as a means of discovering all the relevant criteria. Even something as simple as a cantaloup, for example, quickly suggests the following list of standards:

size	firmness
shape	smell
texture	taste
weight	juiciness

Internal standards of evaluation come from a writer's own values. Consider a casual (and common) evaluation like this one—"Thumbs down on that movie; there's too much action, too little plot, and the dialogue is awful." It's not easy to measure the thinness of a plot or the awfulness of dialogue. So the writer is relying on readers believing, first, that thick plots and good dialogue are fair expectations for a good movie and, second, that it is possible to provide reasonable (though not measurable) evidence of deficiencies in these areas. The reader must either be willing to grant the writer the expertise to make such judgments or be reasonably agreeable to the internal criteria.

Not surprisingly, most viewers *would* consider plot and dialogue as factors important to the success or failure of a movie. If a reviewer, however, claimed that a movie was terrible because its credits sequence at the beginning was dull, most readers would question that internal measure of assessment. They aren't willing to accept or reject a film on the basis of its titles alone. So internal criteria, though they reflect the thinking of an evaluator, must also be shared by readers to some extent. Otherwise, readers can easily disagree with an assessment. The only way to counter potential disagreement over a controversial internal standard is to explain clearly to readers why the criteria are important.

Looping can sometimes help expose the rationale behind evaluative assumptions. On a blank sheet of paper, write the question: "Exactly why do I think X is good (bad)?" Write nonstop for five or ten minutes, and then loop any important criteria revealed in the first exercise. This exercise should reveal arguments in support of strong criteria or cracks in weaker ones.

Once a particular subject has been targeted for evaluation and criteria have been established, *listing* can again help in finding elements that can be evaluated. For example, if you were comparing cities as possible convention sites a list might look like this:

New Orleans	*Santa Fe*
great food	Old-World atmosphere
distinct Cajun culture	few hotels
many hotels	reasonable prices
high prices	distinctive New Mexican food
Mississippi River	great opera
Dixieland jazz	Chimayo weaving nearby
French Market	fascinating history
great shopping	breathtaking scenery
Bourbon Street	not easily accessible by air
hard to get around in car because of traffic	pueblos nearby
easy to get to by air	high quality arts and crafts available
plantations nearby	

Recommended Creating Techniques

1. Listing (See pp. 16–17)
2. Looping (See pp. 20–21)
3. Classical Invention (See pp. 325–329)
4. Track Switching (See pp. 319–321)

Two other creating techniques well suited to Evaluation essays are *classical invention* and *track switching* (which is particularly helpful with comparisons).

Shaping/Drafting

Once you've determined your criteria of evaluation and the features to be evaluated, you need to think about audience, thesis, and organization.

Audience. One of the most important aspects shaping the Evaluation essay for a particular group of readers is establishing criteria that readers can understand and believe. Let readers know right away what criteria you are using in making an evaluation so that they can intelligently compare their standards to yours and accept (or reject) your assertions. It makes sense, of course, to present standards that are fair, logical, and consistent; if your standards are unreasonably high or low or inappropriate, readers won't grant you the authority needed to be convincing.

In some cases, you may have to tell readers how to use the criteria. For instance, what is a reader to make of a statement such as this: "The treads on tire A are 3/4″ thicker than the treads on tire B"? Are thick treads desirable? A simple sentence like the following would clarify the criteria: "The thicker the treads, the longer the life of the tire."

Don't confuse readers by presenting too many criteria. Pick the ones most likely to influence a given audience. In evaluating a French film for an American audience, the legibility of subtitles might be a persuasive factor; for a French-speaking audience it would be irrelevant.

Be sure to assure readers that you are qualified to make a particular evaluation. With external standards, your qualifications might resemble those listed in a résumé: "As an apprentice chef at a major downtown restaurant, I find that Blippo's Burgers. . . ." With internal standards, you may have to be willing to disclose more of your subjective feelings and judgments: "I sit in a chair all week—I don't go to a movie to see my own predictable life replayed on the screen."

The following checklist will help you zero in on your audience:

- Evaluate your readers carefully to determine which criteria of evaluation they are likely to accept and which you will have to prove.
- Use criteria that readers can identify with or might apply themselves.
- Take into account the attitude of the audience toward the person, place, or thing you are evaluating. Are your potential readers likely to be friendly, hostile, or neutral toward your evaluation?
- Be fair or your readers will mistrust you. Don't distort the evidence.

No matter whether your standards are internal or external, the ultimate value in this kind of writing has to do with the relationship between the writer and what the writer is evaluating. The reader is left with the interface (or friction) between the person doing the judging and the thing or experience being judged, rather than an absolute truth or proof. Even if the standards are external, the writer's own human nature still intrudes on the evaluation—how many cars were tested the day this particular one was judged as the best? Does the evaluator work for the company whose car won? Do other cars have outstanding features that are more important than mileage, cost, and serviceability?

This doesn't mean, of course, that the evaluation should be separated from the evaluator. What the writer brings to the evaluation—even including biases and vested interests—makes the evaluations interesting, variable, and eclectic. But when writing or reading evaluations, we do need to be aware that we are observing not only the subject being evaluated but also the person making the evaluation. And this creates a most stimulating tension.

Thesis/Promise/Delivery. Writing a thesis for an Evaluation paper is relatively easy once you've decided on a subject. It should be stated clearly and follow a pattern somewhat like the following:

> *Thesis:* In comparing X, Y, and Z, I find that the best one is ______ because ______.
>
> *Thesis:* X is better than Y for these reasons: ______.
>
> *Thesis:* X is a successful ______ because ______.

In writing an Evaluation essay, you make your readers this promise: "I will explain to you why X is better than Y." To judge whether you have delivered on your promise, you need only check that you have made your thesis clear, that you've presented and defended reasonable standards of evaluation, that you've chosen a subject you can write on intelligently, and that you've shaped your ideas to suit the readers you anticipate.

Organization. Since in many Evaluation essays you are comparing two or more things, experiences, or ideas, you have a choice of two basic forms—comparison/contrast and analogy.

Comparison/contrast means that you show how two things, ideas, methods, or whatever, are *alike* and how they are *different*. "Both cars are in the *XXX* price range. However, Car A gets 35 miles per gallon, while Car B gets 28 miles per gallon." In writing an essay that uses this form, you compare and contrast the relevant characteristics point by point. Another method you could use to compare and contrast Car A and Car B is to discuss Car A fully, and then discuss Car B fully.

Analogy involves finding likenesses between two or more things—"*This* is like *that*" (having a pet is like having a child; windsurfing is like flying; and so on). In this form, you make your analogy and then give examples; that is, you show how windsurfing is like flying—what characteristics are common to each?

Focus on Comparison/Contrast (two basic patterns)

Item by Item

Introduction: Thesis
Item #1 evaluated
Criteria #1
Criteria #2
Criteria #3
Item #2 evaluated
Criteria #1
Criteria #2
Criteria #3
Conclusions: Assessment

CHAPTER 13

The Persuasion Essay

Persuasion is among the most potent and important responsibilities of writing. Our world—in political, social, and legal terms—is shaped by persuasion. Some persuasive efforts influence the electorate to choose candidates for office, others convince judges and juries to make specific decisions, and still others move ordinary citizens to think or act in new ways. In all such cases, successful persuasion implies a change in thinking or behavior. That's what persuasive writing is all about—change.

WHY WRITE THE PERSUASION ESSAY?

The purposes of the Persuasion essay are easy to state, but hard to achieve—to persuade readers to believe something and to persuade readers to do something.

All of us have ideas or beliefs that we hold valuable. Whether it's a profound idea about how people should prepare for the afterlife or simply a fervent wish that our friends would go see a movie we just enjoyed, the usual result of strong feeling is that we want others to share that feeling and do something to show they share it. Since we usually can't force people to believe as we do, we must often persuade them; and since their response is important to us, we want to know the best ways to do that persuading.

Checklist for writing a Persuasion essay:

- Choose a subject you care about strongly enough to urge others to act upon.
- Choose an audience in a position to take action.
- Be sure your thesis is clear. Readers must know where you stand.
- Argue to the point. Don't get involved in side issues.

- Develop one point at a time.
- Argue logically, providing ample evidence to appeal to a reader's mind.
- Argue emotionally, using legitimate appeals to the reader's heart.
- Establish your authority and credibility: make readers want to share your convictions.
- Be fair to all sides. When appropriate, concede the strengths in an opposing view.
- Arrange your arguments to build toward the strongest evidence in support of your cause.
- Use clear and powerful language.
- Tell the readers exactly what action you want them to take.

ASSIGNMENTS

Select one of the following situations to serve as the basis of a Persuasion essay—then develop this essay as you work through the rest of the chapter.

1. In a small writing group, hold a discussion to debate what single action members of your class or students at your institution could most profitably take to improve the local community. Perhaps nighttime assaults on campus suggest the need to establish a volunteer security escort service; maybe you see a need to raise funds through a booksale to assist the homeless who dwell on campus streets; perhaps a demonstration to protest questionable university priorities. When (and if) your group is able to agree on one best course of action, write a short persuasive article urging classmates in other groups and the student body in general to take the action your group recommends. Design the article to fit a guest editorial slot in your campus paper.

2. You've just purchased a used car, appliance, or other product. It had a six-month warranty. But the purchase has been a lemon; you've had nothing but trouble with it. To add to your frustration, your dealer now claims that the warranty doesn't cover the broken parts of your purchase. You're furious. You need this product in working order, and you want it fixed, now, free of charge. Present your case to the Consumer Rights reporter at your local TV station.

3. Your university is suffering from budget problems. Today the student newspaper reports that library hours will be reduced and several librarian positions will be eliminated as part of the budget cutbacks. You agree that the budget must be trimmed, but think the library is the wrong place to start. Write an editorial column for your student newspaper galvanizing student support to keep the library at its current strength.

4. Your sister or brother, who is well informed and well qualified, is running in the primary election for a seat on the town council. You've agreed to help her or him gather support. In a short, informal essay, persuade the members of your class, church or social group, or the people with whom you work to vote for your brother or sister.

5. A number of students in one of your classes don't speak English as their first language. Although their English is good, they are still having trouble following class discussions and doing the readings in their texts. Convince the head of that department to arrange for tutoring for these students.

6. In one of your classes, you've studied two completely different approaches (critical, experimental, or theoretical) to the subject matter. In a well-reasoned essay, convince your classmates which approach is best.

WRITING THE PERSUASION ESSAY

In writing a Persuasion essay, the creating/shaping/completing process focuses on selecting a topic you are committed to, targeting your message to your audience through logical and emotional appeals, and offering an interesting and compelling presentation.

Creating

The best way to find a context for the Persuasion essay is to find something that you believe should be changed—that requires action to be taken. Of course this can't be something frivolous, something you don't really care about—you can't mobilize much interest in yourself (and therefore in your reader) if you write about "Why supermarkets should sell packages of all-green jellybeans."

It is caring about your cause—commitment to it—that allows you to move your readers to act. If you received a leaflet that said "Vote for Joe Schmoe, um, because, well, he's kinda good on the basic issues," you would not be inspired to vote for Joe Schmoe. In order to convince the reader, the writer must be convinced.

If you are having a difficult time finding a subject, you might try

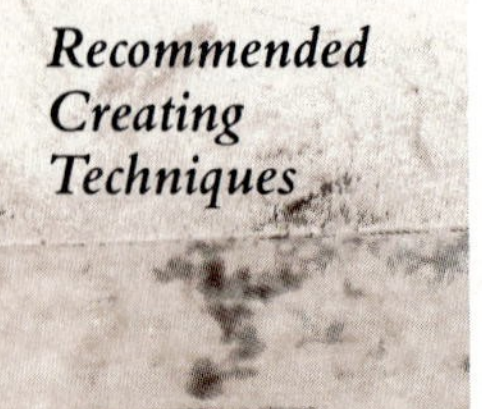

1. Brainstorming (See pp. 15–16)
2. Looping (See pp. 20–21)
3. Classical Invention (See pp. 325–329)
4. Cubing (See pp. 315–316)
5. Reading and Researching (See pp. 339–341)

looping to discover what's on your mind. Write for five or ten minutes on a sheet of paper with the heading "What do I really care about?" Or, working in a group, you might *brainstorm* a list of problems to be addressed in a collaborative paper (see Assignment #1). For any subject you come up with, you must be able to answer *yes* to these two questions:

1. Do I (we) really care about this subject?
2. Do I (we) really know enough about this subject to present it intelligently?

When you actually have a topic, the best creating techniques for exploring possible angles of argument are *Classical Invention* and *Cubing*. Because convincing arguments rely upon accurate and overwhelming information, consider doing some *Reading and Researching*.

Shaping/Drafting

In writing a Persuasion essay, you are not proclaiming your message before a faceless crowd; you are writing for real people. But even more so than with other kinds of essays, the reader of the persuasive paper determines the success of the effort. If the reader is not challenged, stimulated, and moved, the essay—no matter how intelligent or well written—will be judged a failure.

Audience. The better you understand your readers, the more likely you are to find a way of reaching them. In a Persuasion essay, the writer/reader relationship begins like this:

Writer	*Reader*
Person who sees	Person who hasn't yet seen
Person who is committed	Person who isn't yet committed
Person who has a vision	Person who doesn't have a vision, or who has a different vision

In addition, your audience is likely to fall into one of these categories:

- The general public
- People who have authority in the area you are writing about
- People who can take the kind of action you are urging

So if you are writing about the advantages of speed-reading, you can aim your arrow toward the general public (because nearly everybody reads). And if you are writing about defective seat belts, your audience might be someone who already is an authority (the president of the seat-belt company), or it might be car owners (you could urge them to write to their representatives in Congress to outlaw defective seat belts). Which audience you choose will depend on what action you want as a result, and on who you want to do the acting.

The following checklist will help you tailor your essay to your audience:

- Tell your readers right away what you want them to do, believe, or act on.
- Present your argument through situations and circumstances readers can identify with or imagine themselves in.
- Identify your readers' needs and appeal to those needs.
- Convince readers that you know your subject well. Use personal experiences to validate your authority.
- Convince readers that you are trustworthy, fair, and accountable for your facts and figures.
- Choose a tone that is concerned but not overly emotional. Don't scream at your readers or demean their intelligence.
- Don't overload your reader with suggestions and proposals. Whenever possible, keep the argument simple and direct.
- Take into account the attitude of the audience toward the person, place, or thing you are proposing. Are your potential readers likely to be friendly, hostile, or neutral? If friendly, don't take their goodwill for granted; if hostile, attain their goodwill by acknowledging the legitimacy of their initial stance; if neutral, emphasize the reasonableness of your position and the ease with which they can support it.

There is, of course, always the problem in persuasive writing that readers have mixed feelings about being told what to think or do. On the one hand, they may be willing to see things in a new light. On the other hand, they don't want to be told that they hold unreasonable or idiotic viewpoints. In short, they need to trust the persuader, and the only way to do that is if the persuader—you, the writer—treats them with respect. How do you do that? One way is to write as an insider about something you know from real experience. There is an inherent authority—a right to tell—that comes with speaking from experience. For example, would you have the same reaction to the following two pieces of persuasive writing?

> People should learn to cooperate. Why don't they learn? Life would be so much better if they did. I can hardly believe what idiots people are, refusing to cooperate as much as they do. Really, they're crazy. Life would be so much easier. Why don't you cooperate?

> Clearly, there are benefits to be gained by cooperating, and the lack of cooperation is undoubtedly behind many of the world's ills. But how are we to help this happen? We all use the same word—"cooperation"—as if we all meant the same thing by it. But perhaps we are not speaking the same language. When I was in second grade, there was a boy named Bobby who was always being yelled at by the teacher. "Why won't you cooperate!" she screamed every time he refused to join hands or color inside the lines of the coloring book or sing and dance on cue. What that overworked, underpaid, underappreciated lady meant was, "I'm already overwhelmed, and I need things to go smoothly. Don't make things hard for me." But the message that Bobby got (and took with him, through high school truancy and minor thefts) was, "You are different, and you are bad, and you are not one of us." So clearly "cooperation"—while a good and necessary thing—must be defined before it can be put into practice.

Thesis/Promise/Delivery. Without a thesis either stated or implied, a Persuasion essay is like a rifle without a shell or a bow without an arrow. It can only miss the target. A well-focused thesis is the projectile that advances the whole project. Consider the difference between a banal statement and a sharp assertion:

> "People should treat their pets right."
>
> "If people really wanted to be good to their pets, they would have them neutered."

The first is bland and unappealing; the second has some fiber to it. It gives the writer a point to argue and a place to begin.

The thesis sentence of a Persuasion essay can take many forms. Here are just three:

> *Thesis:* We ought to do X because . . .
>
> *Thesis:* We ought to support X because . . .
>
> *Thesis:* We ought to believe X because . . .

In writing a Persuasion essay, you make your readers this promise: "I will do my best to show you why I think you should believe what I do." The success of your promise is measured by the result you achieve. Do readers find your paper readable enough and sufficiently well argued to make their way through it from beginning to end? Are they persuaded to at least consider acting upon your recommendations?

Organization. The form of a Persuasion essay is often contained in the thesis itself. Consider the thesis:

> *Thesis:* If people really wanted to be good to their pets, they would have them neutered.

This suggests a simple pattern of development:

1. What are the results of *not* having pets neutered?
   a. Example 1.
   b. Example 2.
2. What are the results of having pets neutered?
   a. In terms of the pet.
   b. In terms of the owner.
   c. In terms of society.
3. Conclusion

A different thesis might dictate a different form, but you can see how once you know your thesis and your audience, the shape begins to emerge. The following forms particularly lend themselves to the Persuasion essay.

Analysis: It's no good telling a reader, "End war"—that's too big a bite. The reader can't grab hold of the concept in concrete, experiential terms. Therefore, you need to *analyze* the subject—to break it down into its individual components—so that the reader can understand it, assimilate it, and use it.

Cause-and-Effect: It doesn't work to tell the reader to do something just because you say so. (When you were little and your parents gave you that reason, did you do the required action willingly or unwillingly?) You need to let your readers know the *relationship*—the causes and effects—of what you want them to do and the results that you foresee.

You can also use *deduction* (start with a generalization, then back it up with specifics), *induction* (start with specifics and build up to a generalization), or *comparison/contrast* (show how two or more things are alike and different). For fuller descriptions of these patterns, see Chapter 17, "Form and Pattern."

Perhaps the most familiar persuasive organization is the all-purpose one you learned in high school. Though it oversimplifies the shape of this kind of writing, it can provide a starting point when you find yourself confused or uncertain about form:

Introduction: Builds to a Thesis Statement

Argument #1 (Strong)

Proof

Examples/illustrations

Argument #2 (Stronger)

Proof

Examples/illustrations

Final argument (Strongest)

Proof

Examples/illustrations

Conclusions and implications

Peer-Editing

Write a complete first draft of your essay (based on one of the situations presented earlier), then ask one or more classmates to review the paper using the following form for guidance.

PEER-EDITING SHEET The Persuasion Essay

Essay writer's name ______________ Reader's name ______________

Please answer each question briefly, but thoughtfully, responding to the draft with useful comments. Be sure to explain your answer using specific, clear examples.

1. List some initial thoughts you had while reading the draft.

2. What do you see as the purpose of this essay?

3. To what specific audience do you think the essay is directed?

4. Overall, is the essay presented in a tone that (circle one):
   Attracts and includes you
   Repels you
   Leaves you indifferent
   Why?

5. Does the essay clearly express its thesis right away? YES NO Please write out here the sentence or sentences near the beginning of the essay that best express its thesis.

6. Does the thesis focus on a single area to be changed? YES NO If not, how is it too broad?

7. Identify the paper's thesis. Then please re-read each paragraph, noting if it is clearly related to the overall thesis of the essay.

   Par. 1 Yes No
   Par. 2 Yes No
   Par. 3 Yes No
   Par. 4 Yes No
   Par. 5 Yes No
   Par. 6 Yes No
   Par. 7 Yes No
   Par. 8 Yes No

8. Generally, does the essay supply vivid details, facts, and examples to help the reader identify with the situation and to help the reader see the writer's viewpoint? YES NO Cite three of its most helpful and vivid details, facts, and examples:

   a.

   b.

   c.

9. In which paragraphs would you like to see more details, facts, examples? 1 2 3 4 5 6 7 8 9 10 Why?

10. Which form would you say this essay takes? (Circle one)
    Deduction (general-to-specific development)
    Induction (specific-to-general development)
    Comparison and Contrast
    Cause-and-Effect
    Analysis (separating the whole into parts)

11. Overall, did the writer come across to you as an insider about the issue at stake in the essay? YES NO If not, briefly explain why not.

12. Does the introduction:
    a. Get the reader's attention? YES NO
    b. Reveal the thesis or message of the essay? YES NO
    c. Ease the reader into the very aspect/perspective of the subject on which the paper is focused? YES NO

13. Does the conclusion:
    a. Remind you of what's been said? YES NO
    b. Give you at least one new thing to think about? YES NO
    c. Provide a smooth ending so that you are not left hanging in midair? YES NO

14. Are the transitions between paragraphs smooth and clear? YES NO SOME Between which paragraphs were the transitions hard to follow? (Please circle them) 1 2 3 4 5 6 7 8 9 10

15. Does the essay make you care about its subject? YES NO Why?

16. Does the essay make clear what you should do as a result of reading it? YES NO If not, why?

Completing

Before you offer a Persuasion essay to your readers, you need to do everything possible to make sure that your paragraphs, sentences, and words reinforce the assertions you make.

Paragraphs. If you haven't paid attention to function paragraphs before, you should do so now. These will get your readers' attention, keep them interested, and add drama to your arguments. In a Persuasion essay, you'll want to use every possible tool to grab your readers' attention, and function paragraphs can make points really stand out for your readers.

Like this.

Remember?

Function paragraphs can also break up long paragraphs, sum up points before moving on, or raise provocative new questions which advance your argument.

As in the other kinds of writing to persuade, your paragraphs will also need substance: plenty of development to help the readers see matters your way. Examples and illustrations help them identify with your beliefs; anecdotes can illuminate a situation; facts and figures provide touchstones. For example, the need for young, athletic people to have regular physical checkups could be illustrated by the case of Arthur Ashe, the tennis champion who underwent cardiac bypass surgery before the age of forty. Who'd expect such a relatively young man to have a heart attack? His example could surprise your readers into reconsidering their health plans.

Choose illustrations and analogies that appeal to your readers. A good example of this is in Martin Luther King's letter written from the Birmingham jail to a group of clergy; it is full of references to the Bible and to martyrdom. If your readers are sports fans, use sporting metaphors; if they're scientists, use scientific examples. Customize your paragraphs for best effect.

Sentences. What makes the difference between a boring speech and a rousing call to action? One answer is the energy the writer invests in the language. Since calls to action—the heart of persuasion—are emotional, you'll want to use rhythm and repetition, the most effective sentence strategies for inspiring an audience. Two noteworthy examples are Abraham Lincoln's Gettysburg Address, which uses "government of the people, by the people, and for the people" to conclude his oration; and John F. Kennedy's "Ask not what your country can do for you; ask what you can do for your country." It's the rhythm, the cadence, the repetition with slight variations that make these lines endure in our memories.

Words. If you want people to act, you need inspiring words. Generalizations won't motivate couch potatoes; you must find specific, connotative words. Which campaign slogan do you think would get more applause? "I support traditional American values" or "I stand foursquare behind the American flag, the American family, and the freedom to go to ballgames, eat hot dogs, and criticize the umpire."

Be as colorful, descriptive, and detailed as you can. Think of your words as photographs: what conveys the horror of the harp seal slaughter better than those pictures of seal pups with their large, luminous, friendly eyes? And what tells the horror of war to children better than Nicholas Ut's picture of the Vietnamese children who had just been napalmed? "Save the seals" or "War is hell" just don't carry the same punch. So draw pictures with your words.

Again, you'll want to eliminate any surface errors before you present your Persuasion essay, because you don't want even the slightest bobble to distract your readers from the results you want to achieve.

EXAMPLE The Persuasion Essay

The following essay was written by a student, using the persona of a young, male minister.

Emphasis: On action that the reader should take.

Purpose: To get the congregation to treat a local minority group with fairness and love.

Situation: A letter to the members of his congregation.

Circumstance: Length: 1–2 pages. Deadline: 1 day.

Writer-Reader Relationship: Visionary to those who do not share the same vision.

A YOUNG MINISTER TO HIS CHURCH

Gentlemen:

You knew when you hired me that I was 26 years old, had a wife and new son, and that I had just graduated from the seminary. Let me tell you some other things about me. I made a C in the conjugation of Hebrew verbs. I don't know how to tell when wheat is "in the dough." I ruined a pipe on the church's hot water heater trying to fix it. So, I'm looking forward to learning a lot of new things.

Now, however, one thing I do know is that when we have love, God said we should share it. I've seen a lot of love demonstrated since I've been here. I've seen people helping each other work cattle and keeping each other's kids and making quilts together and taking sick folks to the doctor. I want us to think about extending that love.

Since I've been here, I've also heard a lot of statements about the minority group that lives in our town, statements like these:

"They are lazy." (except for the laborers)

"They drink too much."

"They don't know how to plan for the future."

"They won't tell the truth."

"They steal."

"They have too many kids."

These ideas seem to be believed for two reasons: (1) they were taught to us by our parents, and (2) they have, in fact, been true about some of these people we know personally.

May I tell you something I learned when I studied history? *These characteristics have always been shown by people who don't know they can control their own lives.*

Your community has just lived through some history. In the last few years things have happened that have caused this minority group to see themselves in a different way, and from now on they're going to behave differently. Our church stands right now in a position to direct them toward brotherhood and community spirit or, by what we do or don't do in the next few years, cause hostility. What we decide to do may determine whether our children will be able to raise their families in this country. You have seen how much harm can be done by a few people preaching hate and hostility; why don't we see how much healing we can get out of tolerance and love?

I don't have in mind a campaign to see how many people we can corral into our worship services. In fact, I'm not talking about an organized program of any kind. I'm talking about a feeling that God really meant it when He said, "There is no difference between the Jew and the Greek." As the spiritual leaders of this town, you can make that feeling happen.

I'm putting this in a letter to you for two reasons. First, I am very serious about this. The Christian conscience cannot ignore the circumstances we are living with. Second, I want you to do what may seem like a strange thing. I want you to read [this letter] every day between now and next Sunday. Discuss it with each other every day, if possible. Notice if what you say and feel changes any during the week.

I will appreciate hearing your comments next Sunday. I hope you will begin to think of ways our church can present itself as a spiritual welcome to everybody in our town.

(signed)

CHAPTER 14

The Research Paper

You've just heard that one of the major requirements of a course you are taking is a research paper, and you groan. You *know* what hard work that kind of writing is. Probably the first thing you think of is how difficult it will be to type and how many hours it takes to find the material in the library. Well, cheer up: much of the drudgery can be taken out of the activity. What you will need, and what you are about to be shown, is a *system*—a system that moves step by step, making the paper a manageable job. This chapter will teach you a system that should work for all the research projects you are likely to do. It has three major divisions: Part I—Conducting Research; Part II—Writing a Research Paper; and Part III—Using Sources in Your Writing.

But why does doing a research paper seem like such a job?

Several things account for it, which, summed up, come to this: while you have to exercise all the ordinary and regular skills involved in the writing process—getting ideas, deciding about audience, shaping, revising, completing—you also have to exercise several *new* nonwriting skills simultaneously. And it is this load-on-load that makes it seem like so much work.

What are the nonwriting skills that you have to master in order to do a good research paper?

1. First of all, the creating stage for a research paper is different from the creating stage in other kinds of writing. Most of the creating techniques that you have learned to use call for information and knowledge that you already possess. When you did the creating technique, you pulled out this old information—or discovered new thoughts that emerged from the interaction of facts, experiences, and information that you had already possessed.

With the research paper, however, it's different. To do your initial creating for this kind of writing, you begin by putting information *into* your head, not taking it out. The two creating techniques that will most serve these purposes are Noticing Inside Purpose and Reading and Researching (see Chapter 16). Noticing Inside Purpose allows you to gather information about a subject as you go, and to see the underlying theme, or surprising interconnections, that a one-time-only glance at a subject would not reveal. Reading and Researching (R & R) is a way to obtain information from the library and other outside sources, and to mine it for possible ideas and topics. In both cases, you end up using new information later on (whether days, weeks, or months later), when you are planning and writing the paper itself. The assumption in doing a research paper is that you don't already possess much knowledge or information on the subject of your paper. (If you did, there wouldn't be a need to research the topic.) The idea in *research* paper writing is that you must gather new information from outside sources *before* you can have anything to say on the subject. Going to the library is actually *the creating technique* for this kind of writing. You may, of course, loop or cube some part of the new information later in a secondary creating activity, but the first step to finding an idea in this case is to discover what other people have said on the subject.

Reading and Researching and Noticing Inside Purpose require a skill that you may not have used in other essays: *finding material in the library.* Learning how to use the library is an extra technique to master (very valuable, of course, but still *extra*), so it is no wonder that you may feel from the start that doing a research paper is more work.

2. Another "extra" in research paper writing is learning how to take notes, how to incorporate these notes into the body of an essay, and how to give credit for the information. Without question, it is tedious. Deciding when to give credit to an author and when not to requires some thought. Getting the paragraphs based on your notes to sound like coherent, flowing sentences instead of separate items from your notecards requires much rewriting. But these skills of notetaking, incorporating notes into your own writing, and documenting notes correctly are essential to an acceptable research paper. So, that's another skill to learn—on top of all the skills necessary in the writing process itself.

3. Finally, there's the *form* of the paper itself. All the outside sources must be documented where they occur in the paper, and also collected in a bibliography—and knowing how to cite and to format is a big job. Anyone who has ever forgotten to indent the second line of the *Works Cited* after already completing one-third of the page knows the frustration that the *form* of a research paper can bring. This, then, is a third nonwriting skill that you have to know how to do.

To do a good research paper, therefore, you have to have a large number of skills—some writing skills, some nonwriting.

Writing Skills	*Nonwriting Skills*
Finding an angle or thesis	Learning how to use the library
Writing to a particular audience	Learning how to take notes
Fully developing the points	Learning how to incorporate notes into an essay
Shaping the essay for the reader	Learning how to document
Revising	Learning proper research paper forms
Editing and correcting	

Is it any wonder, then, that the project looks big?

But, you may say, if it's all this much work why do it? Is *anything* worth that much time and effort? Here are some reasons that may help you answer *yes*.

1. Learning to use the library is a skill that will stay with you for life. And it is a skill transferable to any kind of research you will ever want to do, in any career.

2. Once you learn the system for notetaking, citing information, and documenting sources, you'll know it for good. And the same system that you learn now will work when you do research projects for your company, when you look up legal briefs for an appearance in court, or when you search for the latest information on the income tax laws in order to handle an IRS audit.

3. Learning correct documentation form means simply learning what style and format practices to follow in order to make reading your research paper as easy as possible. Good documentation also serves the readers by letting them know what books, articles, and other reference materials they could consult if they wanted to know more about your subject.

4. Finally, however, more than any of these others, the reason the research paper is worth doing is the sheer power it gives you: *personal power.* Once you know *how* to find information, you can find information on *anything*. No worldly knowledge can be kept from you. And this is power—the power to be knowledgeable, to find out things, and to communicate your findings to others. You may never have to write a formal research paper again once you leave college—or you may spend the rest of your life conducting and publishing research. But no matter what you do, you *will* have plenty of opportunities to use your researching skills.

As mentioned earlier, this chapter divides the process of writing a research paper into three parts. Part I shows you how you might conduct your research—how to gather your raw materials. Part II shows you how to assemble those raw materials into a fluent paper. And Part III reviews everything you need to know about documentation and incorporating sources into your paper. This step-by-step approach should clarify the process of writing a research paper—and put *you* in charge.

PART I: CONDUCTING RESEARCH

Research—the very word suggests musty libraries, piles of notecards, stacks of journals. Boring! But if you ask people who conduct research for a living, they'll say it's exciting and fascinating. Do they know something you don't know? Yes. Professional researchers know that the library is their *last* stop on the road to a successful search. They start long before they open the library doors; you can, too.

THE RESEARCH PROCESS

In nearly every circumstance, your instructor will give you *some* information about the kind of research paper you're expected to write. The following steps will help you expand on this information in order to develop a topic for your paper.

Step 1: Identify Your Purpose

Generally, you'll need to answer two questions:

1. Is my purpose to *describe* some subject (a survey) or to *persuade* my readers to feel some way about a subject (argument)? If you're describing, you'll be using the techniques for writing to inform; if you're persuading, you'll be using the techniques for writing to change.
2. Am I supposed to do *primary* research that I conduct myself (such as interviews, fieldwork, and questionnaires), secondary research (such as finding information in the library), or a combination of both? If you're conducting primary research, you may need to use basic and expanded creating techniques such as the Reporter's Formula and Classical Invention (see Chapters 2 and 16, respectively); if you're using secondary research you'll probably use other expanded creating techniques such as Noticing Inside Purpose and Reading and Researching (see Chapter 16).

Before you start your research make sure you can answer both of these questions; they will prevent you from wasting time and energy.

Step 2: Make a Plan

You may be one of those writers for whom starting a research assignment is very difficult. Because the job looks so overwhelming, you may delay or stall or run around in circles—all of which defeat your purpose. So as soon as you're given your assignment and its due date, set up a tentative schedule for completing it. Work backward from the due date. If you're a slow typist, allow the last three days for typing, proofreading, and making corrections. Allow at least three days before that for revising; it takes time to get the documentation forms in perfect shape. Allow about a week before that for writing a first draft and shaping, since you'll probably have to go back to your sources to find material to fill in the gaps in your paper. Whatever time you have left before that—let's hope it's *at least* a week—is your researching time. Remember, too, that other students may be using the materials you want; you may have to recall books or borrow them through an interlibrary loan, or find other sources to replace missing materials. Copy this schedule on a calendar and post it prominently where you'll have to look at it every day—by your desk, on the bathroom mirror, on the refrigerator door. Look at it daily and make yourself do the day's assigned work.

Usually the biggest problem in writing research papers is time management; you may let tasks slide until it's too late, then pull all-nighters trying to get the paper in some kind of acceptable shape. The results are those C+ papers you swore you'd never write again. If you stick to your schedule, you won't run out of time.

As soon as you make your schedule, motivate yourself to start researching by getting organized. Go to the bookstore and load up on supplies:

1. Get 3 × 5 notecards for recording bibliographical information. (Why not buy some in color? They may make sorting your material easier.)
2. Get 4 × 6 or 5 × 8 notecards for the notes themselves. These give you more room to write. (Again, go for the color.)
3. Stock up on a bag of strong rubber bands to hold the cards together. If you can afford it, buy one of those plastic boxes or an expanding file to hold your cards.
4. Get several pens, in different colors, and reserve them just for your research project.

Merely buying these supplies will move you one step closer to the library. You'll feel that you've done *something* about the assignment, and that's a great first step. And then you'll be prepared when you do go to the library.

Step 3: Pick a Subject Area and Scout It Out

In many classes, instructors will give you a subject or list of subjects from which you can choose your research paper topic. On some campuses, the reference librarians will also provide such a list. (These are invaluable, because the librarians pick subjects on which they *know* the library holds plenty of information.) If you're left to choose your own topic, however, you need to do a little creating.

You might try brainstorming on one of these topics, for instance:

I've always wanted to know . . .

In my future profession or career, I'll need to know about . . .

I'm already pretty knowledgeable about . . .

I spend most of my free time . . .

I have to write a research paper in one of my other classes about . . .

I think people should really be concerned about . . .

If I could change just one thing in the world, I'd . . .

The answers you get to each of these questions ought to provide plenty of subject areas. You can also try the other creating techniques you've mastered: listing, cubing, looping, and so forth. At this point, you need to find a subject to work with. Remember that a subject is just a general frame—it's not your actual thesis. There'll be time to narrow your focus after you've done some more searching.

Step 4: Talk to People

On a college campus, nearly every instructor is an expert on *something*. So no matter what subject you pick, you should be able to find someone who can give you some professional help on your subject. Suppose you want to write about the special effects used in movies; check the film courses in your school's catalog and make an appointment to see the professors who teach courses in film making. If you're interested in South Africa seek out professors who teach courses in political science, African or Black studies, or history. Do you wonder if your state lottery is a financial success? Look for an expert in the political science, economics, or finance departments.

And, of course, you can use off-campus resources. The manager of a local computer store might fill you in on the latest developments in operating systems; a gynecologist can tell you the pros and cons of birth control pill use. A local golf pro can tell you about square-grooved clubs; the local historical society can provide you with background on your community's development.

When you talk to these experts, let them know what you're doing. Six questions you want to ask are:

1. Is there sufficient information out there which a non-expert can understand?
2. What are some of the key issues in this field right now?
3. Who or what are the most authoritative sources on this subject?
4. Could you recommend two or three good sources that provide a general overview of this subject?
5. Once I do my research, may I call you to ask a few specific follow-up questions?
6. What kinds of non-library research should I do for this subject?

Most experts can give you this information in five or ten minutes—or send you to someone who can help you find the information. Take notes and transfer them to notecards as soon as you get home, before you forget anything. If you can't find an expert in your subject area, ask your reference librarians to suggest some starting places. Librarians, remember, have extensive professional training in finding source material. In fact, sometimes they're more up to date on certain subjects than are experts in the field!

Step 5: Go to the Library

Once you've chosen a subject and gotten some expert advice, head for the library, taking your research supplies and the notes from your informational interview with you. The first thing you'll want to do is to find a workspace; try to find a desk or table where you can spread out several pages or books at once. Good lighting helps. Next, get a library guide or map from the main desk if you need it, but be sure you can find all these key places:

the reference librarians' desk

the card catalogs

the reference book section

the library's list of periodicals

the location for bound periodicals

the location for microfilms and other microforms

the location of the photocopying machines

Every one of these will be important in writing a good research paper.

WHAT THE LIBRARY CAN OFFER YOU

The heart of nearly every library is its *card catalog,* a collection of small file drawers which contain information on anywhere from 50 to 100 percent of the library's texts. (In some libraries this may also be available on computer, but since these data bases tend to be limited—and since computers tend to "go down"—we'll talk here about using the cards.) Card catalogs are generally organized along three principles: the names of authors, the titles of works, and subject headings. Of these, the *subject headings* will probably be the most useful to you at this point.

The Library of Congress publishes a large catalog of subject headings which lists all the ways in which a subject might be described in a card catalog. So, for instance, if you were working on a paper on state lotteries, you'd look under *Lottery* in the subject headings and find the following:

Lotteries *(May Subd Geog)*
[HG6105-6270]
BT Criminal law
Gambling
NT Lottery winners
—Advertising
USE Advertising—Lotteries
—Law and legislation *(May Subd Geog)*
Lottery winners *(May Subd Geog)*
[HV6105-6270.9]
USE Loucks family
Loucks family *(Not Subd Geog)*
UF Louck family
Louk family
Louks family
Lowk family
Lowks family
Loud family *(Not Subd Geog)*
UF Leod family
Lowd family

This passage gives you a number of useful tips. The word *Lotteries* in boldface type tells you that books on this topic will be listed under the subject "Lotteries." *May Subd Geog* says that the card catalog *may subdivide* the category by *geography*—region, state, or country. *BT* means information can also be found under the *broader topics* "Criminal Law" and "Gambling." *NT* tells you to search also under the *narrower topic* "Lottery Winners." And *USE* tells you that lottery advertising *uses* the subject heading "Advertising—Lotteries." One heading—lotteries—has already yielded four new directions for your search.

Now you can look under all these subjects alphabetically in the card catalog to find material on lotteries. As you skim the cards you find, look especially for books with bibliographies. These will save you a great deal of time since they already list a collection of sources relevant to your topic. You shouldn't *just* look at the contents of those bibliographies; newer works, or works written from different perspectives, may be listed in the card catalog as well. Still, if time is of the essence, these pre-made checklists are essential. An example of a *subject card* found under "Lotteries" appears at the top of page 227.

This card gives you a great deal of information. It tells you not only how long the book is (208 pages), but that it's illustrated and that it has a 24-page bibliography. It's a little out of date (1974) but probably worth looking at just for the bibliography alone. It also tells you that more books on the subject are listed under "Gambling—United States" and "Lotteries—United States." The subject card here is valuable, because you probably wouldn't have thought to look under "Impact" or "Weinstein" to find information on lotteries.

Subject Card

ALEX LOTTERIES - UNITED STATES.

HV Weinstein, David, 1938–
6715 The impact of legalized gambling: the socio-economic
.W43 consequences of lotteries and off-track betting [by] David
Weinstein [and] Lillian Deitch. New York, Praeger [1974]
xii, 208 p. illus. 24 cm.
(Praeger special studies in U.S. economic, social, and political issues)
Bibliography: p. 180–204.
1. Gambling - United States. 2. Lotteries - United States. I. Deitch, Lillian, joint author. II. Title.

R01 0–275–08980–6 74–004012 750329

If your information interview yielded titles of books on your subject, now's the time to look them up. In most libraries, they will be listed under both author and title. When you find the card for these books, note the location—and also check the subject headings listed at the bottom of the card, to make sure they're on your master list of subject headings.

Here are the author and title cards for David Weinstein's book. Notice that they have the same information as the subject card; it's just the first line that varies.

Author Card

ALEX Weinstein, David, 1938–
The impact of legalized gambling: the socio-economic
HV consequences of lotteries and off-track betting [by]
6715 David Weinstein [and] Lillian Deitch. New York, Praeger [1974]
.W43 xii, 208 p. illus. 24 cm.
(Praeger special studies in U.S. economic, social, and political issues)
Bibliography: p. 180–204.
1. Gambling - United States. 2. Lotteries - United States. I. Deitch, Lillian, joint author. II. Title.

R01 0–275–08980–6 74–004012 750329

Title Card

ALEX The impact of legalized gambling

HV Weinstein, David, 1938–
6715 The impact of legalized gambling: the socio-economic
.W43 consequences of lotteries and off-track betting [by] David
Weinstein [and] Lillian Deitch. New York, Praeger [1974]
xii, 208 p. illus. 24 cm.
(Praeger special studies in U.S. economic, social, and political issues)
Bibliography: p. 180–204.
1. Gambling - United States. 2. Lotteries - United States. I. Deitch, Lillian, joint author. II. Title.

R01 0–275–08980–6 74–004012 750329

Card catalogs, of course, list the names of *books;* but libraries contain many other sources of information which you may want to consult. After all, books take several years to write, another year or more to be published, and possibly as long as three years for your library to catalog and shelve. More recent information—such as magazine and journal articles, government documents, and recordings—are listed elsewhere in the library. Here's where the *reference area* in the library comes in handy. In it you'll find a collection of works, including atlases, yearbooks, almanacs, biographical sources, bibliographies and library guides, booklists, dictionaries, encyclopedias (both general and specific), and indexes (both general and specific). On the next several pages you'll find a descriptive list of many of these works. To save yourself time, skim it once and put checks next to the titles of those which you think may apply to your topic, and write the location of each source in the margin next to it. Then you can easily find all the sources when you need them. Notice that several sources are now available on computer; if your library subscribes to such services as *InfoTech* or *The Business Index,* you'll be able to locate several years' worth of sources in one sitting.

Reference Material

Atlases, Yearbooks, and Almanacs

Atlas of World History, Rand McNally, 1970
Britannica Atlas: Geography Edition, 1980
The CBS News Almanac, 1976–present

Demographic Yearbook, 1949–present

Facts on File, 1940–present

The Geographical Digest, 1963

Information Please Almanac, 1947–present

National Geographic Atlas of the World, 1981

The Negro Almanac, 1967–present

The New Cambridge Modern History, 1970

The New York Times Atlas of the World, 1983

The Oxford Bible Atlas, 1984

Rand McNally Commercial Atlas and Marketing Guide, 1876–present

The Statesman's Yearbook, 1864–present

Statistical Abstract of the United States, 1878–present

The Times Atlas of the World: Comprehensive Edition, 1980

Webster's New Geographical Dictionary, rev. ed., 1984

The World Almanac and Book of Facts, 1868–present

Yearbook of the United Nations, 1947–present

Yearbook of World Affairs, 1947–present

Bibliographies and Library Guides*

Basic Reference Sources: An Introduction to Materials and Methods, Louis Shores, Chicago, American Library Association, 1954

Bibliographic Index: A Cumulative Bibliography of Bibliographies, New York, H. W. Wilson Co., 1937–present

Bibliography of Agriculture, Washington, U.S. National Agricultural Library, 1942–present

Guide to Reference Books, Eugene P. Sheehy, Chicago, American Library Association, 10th ed., 1986

Guide to the Use of Books and Libraries, Jean K. Gates, New York, McGraw-Hill, 4th ed., 1979

Historical Abstracts: Bibliography of the World's Periodical Literature, Eric H. Boehm, ed., Santa Barbara, Clio Press, 1955–present

MLA International Bibliography of Books and Articles on the Modern Languages and Literatures, MLA, New York, 1922–present

The Modern Researcher, Jacques Barzun and Henry F. Graff, New York, Harcourt, 3rd ed., 1977

The New Cambridge Bibliography of English Literature, George Watson, ed., Cambridge University Press, 4 vols., 1969–74

The New York Times Guide to Reference Materials, Mona McCormick, New York, Popular Library, 1978

Reference Books: A Brief Guide, Baltimore, Enoch Pratt Free Library, 7th ed., 1978

Science Reference Sources, Frances B. Jenkins, Cambridge, MIT Press, 5th ed., 1969

Sources of Information in the Social Sciences: A Guide to the Literature, Carl M. White et al., eds., Chicago, American Library Association, 2nd ed., 1973

The Use of Books and Libraries, Minneapolis, University of Minnesota, 10 vols., 1933–1963

A World Bibliography of Bibliographies, Theodore A. Besterman, Lausanne, Societas Bibliographica, 4th ed., 5 vols., 1963

Year's Work in English Studies, London, English Association, 1919–present

*Some of these sources are now available for searching by computer or CD-ROM. Ask your reference librarian if you can get access to such facilities.

Biographical References

Biography Index, 1946–present

Chambers's Biographical Dictionary, 1974

Contemporary Authors: A Bio-bibliographical Guide to Current Authors and Their Works, 1967–present

Dictionary of American Biography, 16 vols. & supplements, 1944–1981

Dictionary of National Biography, 22 vols. & supplements, 1882–1953

Directory of American Scholars, 7th ed., 4 vols., 1978

International Who's Who, 1935–present

Twentieth Century Authors, 1942, supplement (1955)

Webster's Biographical Dictionary, 1976

Who's Who (Great Britain), 1897–present

Who's Who in America, 1899–present

Who's Who in [. . .] (Regions such as West, East, South, Midwest, etc., and professions such as theatre, football, jazz, insurance, etc.)

Who's Who of American Women, 1958–present

Booklists

Books in Print, 1948–present. All books currently in print in U.S. Author and title.

Cumulative Book Index, 1898–present. Author, subject, and title index of all books printed in English.

Paperbound Books in Print, 1955–present. All books in U.S. printed in paperback.

Subject Guide to Books in Print, 1957–present. All books currently in print in U.S. by subject.

Dictionaries

The American Heritage Dictionary of the English Language, 1984

The Basic Dictionary of Science, Macmillan, 1965

Dictionary of American Slang, 2nd ed., 1975

Dictionary of the Bible, John L. McKenzie, Macmillan, 1965

Dictionary of Geological Terms, rev. ed., 1984

Groves' Dictionary of Music and Musicians, 5th ed., 9 vols. and supplement, 1981

The Interpreter's Dictionary of the Bible, 5 vols., 1976

McGraw-Hill Dictionary of Modern Economics, 1973

McGraw-Hill Dictionary of Scientific and Technical Terms, 2nd ed., 1978

The Oxford English Dictionary, 12 vols. and supplements, 1933–1987

The Random House Dictionary of the English Language (Unabridged 2nd Edition), 1987

Roget's International Thesaurus, 1984

Webster's Third New International Dictionary Unabridged: The Great Library of the English Language, 1981

Encyclopedias (General)

Chambers' Encyclopedia

Collier's Encyclopedia

Encyclopaedia Britannica

Encyclopedia Americana

New Columbia Encyclopedia

The Random House Encyclopedia

Encyclopedias (Specialized)

Cassell's Encyclopaedia of World Literature, rev. ed., 1973

Encyclopedia of American History, 5th ed., 1976

Encyclopedia of Banking and Finance, 8th rev. ed., 1983

The Encyclopedia of the Biological Sciences, 2nd ed., 1970

The Encyclopedia of Education, 10 vols., 1971

The Encyclopedia of Educational Research, 5th ed., 1982

Encyclopedia of Painting, Bernard S. Myers, ed., 4th ed., 1979

The Encyclopedia of Philosophy, 4 vols., 1973

The Encyclopedia of Physics, Robert M. Besancon, ed., 2nd ed., 1974

Encyclopedia of Psychology, H. J. Eysenck et al., eds., 2nd ed., 1979

Encyclopedia of Religion and Ethics, 13 vols., 1961

Encyclopedia of World Art, 16 vols., 1959–1983

An Encyclopedia of World History, 5th ed., 1972

International Encyclopedia of Social Sciences, 17 vols., 1967

The Larousse Encyclopedia of World Geography, 1965

McGraw-Hill Encyclopedia of Science and Technology, 4th ed., 1977

The Mythology of All Races, 13 vols., 1932

The Negro in American History, 3 vols., 1972

The New Catholic Encyclopedia, 17 vols., 1981

New Larousse Encyclopedia of Mythology, 1974

The Oxford Companion to American History, 5th ed., 1983

The Oxford Companion to Music, 1970

The Reader's Encyclopedia, William R. Benet, ed., 2nd ed., 1965

The Reader's Encyclopedia of World Drama, 1969

Universal Jewish Encyclopedia and Readers Guide, 11 vols., 1944

Van Nostrand's Scientific Encyclopedia, 5th ed., 1976

Indexes (General)*

Book Review Digest, 1905–present. Summarizes reviews of books from a large number of periodicals. Gives critical reception of books reviewed.

The Business Index, 1986–present. Author, title, and subject index of more than 810 business periodicals and newspapers. Available on computer.

Humanities Index, 1974–present. Periodical articles about the humanities. Author and subject entries. (See *Social Sciences and Humanities Index* for 1965–1974. See *International Index to Periodicals* for 1907–1965.)

Info Trac, 1985–present. On-line searches of author, title, and subject for most general periodicals and newspapers, with extensive cross-referencing abilities. Some systems can access government documents as well.

The Magazine Index, 1985–present. On-line searches for author, title, and subject in most general periodicals and selected newspapers.

New York Times Index, 1851–present. Subject index in alphabetical order. Includes abstracts of newspaper articles. Every article appearing in this newspaper will be included by subject in the index.

Nineteenth Century Reader's Guide, 1890–1899. Periodicals for the last ten years of the 1800s.

Poole's Index to Periodical Literature, 1802–1906. Indexed by subject. Author index in supplemental volume.

Reader's Guide to Periodical Literature, 1900–present. An excellent guide for general purpose reading. Lists articles from a broad range of periodicals. Entries by author, subject, and cross listing. Most articles appearing in this index written for general public.

Social Sciences Index, 1974–present. Periodical articles in the social sciences. Indexed by author and subject. (See *Social Sciences and Humanities Index* for 1965–1974 and *International Index to Periodicals* for 1907–1965.)

* Many of these sources are now available for searching by computer or CD-ROM. Ask your reference librarian if you can get access to such facilities.

Indexes (Specialized)

Accountants Index, 1921–present. Author and subject index of books, pamphlets, and periodical articles.

Applied Science and Technology Index, 1958–present. Subject index. (Before 1958, see *Industrial Arts Index.*)

Architectural Periodicals Index, 1972–present. Covers architecture and allied arts, constructional technology, design, landscape, etc. Indexed by subject and architect/project.

The Art Index, 1929–present. By author and subject. Indexes periodicals and museum bulletins.

Biographical Dictionaries Master Index, Gale Research Co., 1975. Subject index. Guide to *Who's Who* and collective biographies.

Biography Index, 1946–present. Indexes information about people, dead and alive. Indexed by biographee and profession.

Biological Abstracts, 1926–present. References, abstracts, and indexes to world's life sciences research literature. Indexed by subject, author, and keyword.

Biological and Agricultural Index, 1964–present. Subject index to periodicals in these and related fields.

Business Periodicals Index, 1958–present. Subject index. Covers such fields as accounting, economics, advertising, public relations, and so on.

Chemical Abstracts, 1907–present. Index to periodical articles, papers, conferences. Indexed by subject, keyword, author.

Congressional Information Service Index of Publications of the United States Congress, 1970–present. Lists all written material from Senate and Congress.

Dramatic Index, 1909–1949. Articles on theatre and plays.

Education Index, 1929–present. Indexed by author and subject. Articles in magazines, books, and other sources discussing the entire field of education.

Engineering Index, 1906–present. Subject index. Includes reports of technical societies, government agencies, laboratories, as well as engineering periodicals.

Essay and General Literature Index, 1900–present. Essays and articles which have appeared in books.

Film Literature Index, 1973–present. Indexed by title of movie and by director.

Index of Economic Articles, 1961–present. Subject and author indexes. (For 1886–1965, see *Index of Economic Journals.*)

Index to London Times, 1906–present. By subject.

The Monthly Catalog of United States Government, 1898–present. Lists all government publications by title, date, and purpose. States availability of material.

Music Index, 1949–present. By subject and author.

The Newspaper Index, 1972–present. Subject listings from the *Chicago Tribune,* the *Los Angeles Times,* the *New Orleans Times-Picayune,* and the *Washington Post.*

Nuclear Science Abstracts, 1947–present. Indexed by personal author, corporate author, and report number.

The Philosopher's Index, 1967–present. By subject and author. Includes American and foreign periodicals and journals.

Psychological Abstracts, 1927–present. Author and subject indexes.

Public Affairs Information Service Bulletin, 1915–present. Subject index for areas such as government, international relations, economics, etc.

Religion Index, 1977–present. Indexed by author and subject. Index of book reviews by author. (See *Index to Religious Periodical Literature* for 1949–1976.)

Television News Index and Abstracts, 1972–present. Indexes subject by topic, institution, and personality.

Theatre, Film and TV Biographies Master Index, Gale Research Co.,

1979. Subject index to biographical sketches of people in performing arts found in biographical directories and dictionaries.

Ulrich's International Periodicals Directory, new editions periodically. Lists all periodicals available in various fields.

Vertical File Index, 1932–present. Subject and title. Includes pamphlets, leaflets, mimeographed materials, and so on.

Quotations

Dictionary of Quotations, Larousse, 1981

Familiar Quotations, John Bartlett, 16th ed., 1988

The Home Book of Quotations, Classical and Modern, 11th ed., 1984

The Oxford Dictionary of Quotations, 3rd ed., 1979

Two of the most commonly used reference sources are *The Reader's Guide to Periodical Literature* and *The New York Times Index*. Both are arranged using nearly the same subject headings as in the card catalog, so you can consult the same list. For the topic of state lotteries, here are examples of what references in the *Reader's Guide* and *The New York Times Index* look like.

The Reader's Guide

Lott, Trent

Lessons of the Iran-contra affair. por *Read Dig* 130:75–6 Je '87

Lotteries

See also

Television broadcasting—Lottery results

As drama it was a waste, but financially, Michigan's first cow-drop raffle was no flop, il *People Wkly* 28:85 Jl 6 '87

From the publisher [major magazine subscription promotional offers] D. K. Graham. *Antiques Collect Hobbies* 92:6+ O '87

Lottery foes target public policy [proposed Indiana state lottery] B. L. Rohrig. *Christ Century* 104:396–7 Ap 29 '87

The lottery luster [educational funds raised in state lotteries] C. Pipho. *Phi Delta Kappan* 69:254–5 D '87

The myth of the money tree [state lotteries] C. W. Colson. il *Christ Today* 31:64 Jl 10 '87

Automation

Can Gtech keep winning at the lottery? [designing and installing state lottery systems] L. Helm. il *Bus Week* p93–4 My 18 '87

Lottery winners

$3 million lotto win 'numbs' Queens man [U. Hosang] il por *Jet* 72:24 Ag 24 '87

Black millionaire lottery winners party aboard ship. il *Jet* 73:16+ O 5 '87

Blacks hit lottery for $7.5 million in New York and $2 million in Illinois. il por *Jet* 72:12 Jl 20 '87

Blind D.C. woman wins $1.2 million in lottery [J. Saunders] *Jet* 71:7 Ja 19 '87

The listing includes the title, the author, and the source of the article. Listings are arranged alphabetically. Brackets sometimes surround a phrase describing the subject of the article. *See also* and subheads like *Automation* help you find and sort information. Notice that months are abbreviated as one or two letters: *O* for *October;* very few spaces are left between numbers. This is compact, concise information.

The New York Times Index

LOTTE COMPANY OF JAPAN. See also
Candy, Je 14
LOTTERIES. See also
Athletics and Sports, Je 21
Day Care Centers, S 6
Education and Schools, Ja 4
Elsmere (Del), Ja 11
Housing, Mr 29
Immigration and Emigration, F 23

Winning numbers in $19 million New York Lotto drawing are announced (S), Ja 4, I,27:5

Swampscott, Mass, whose town committee members bought two season lottery tickets in hopes of ending $450,000 budget deficit, finds it is not in such terrible financial straits and manages to balance its budget (S), Ja 4,I,33:2

Ballot proposals to help finance public education through state lotteries, which swept across Northeast in last decade, are now making inroads in South and West; some analysts believe, however, that when it comes to education funding, lotteries have only partly paid off; drawing (special section, Education Life), Ja 4,XII,14:2

Four ticket-holders will each get $4.75-million of $19-million New York State lottery prize (S), Ja 5,II,6:6

New York State lottery prizes worth $4.75 million each are claimed by Mah-Jongg group of friends from Brooklyn, as well as by three other winners (S), Ja 6,II,2:1

Dr Marvin Steinberg, president of Connecticut Council on Compulsive Gambling, has complained that stepped-up advertising of State Lottery has enabled state to go too far trying to get more people to gamble; says he believes state has failed to own up to fact that legalized gambling can lead to compulsive gambling (M), Ja 11,XXIII,1:5

New York Lottery adds new daily Win-10 drawing (S), Ja 20,II,8:1

Group of workers from Shuttle Meadow Country Club in Berlin, Conn, has twice won million-dollar jackpots in Connecticut Lotto game; chief of State Lottery, J Blaine Lewis Jr, comments; photo (M), Ja 25,XXII,3:1

Three and half months after her number was drawn in Lotto 48, Melanie Richards, business student at Baruch College, emerges from protective anonymity to claim her $12 million prize; Richards expresses concern about having to face the sudden celebrity and new demands of wealth;

The listing includes the title of the article, a date, page, and column reference, a one-sentence summary of the article, and an indication if the article is *short (S), medium (M),* or *long (L).* They are arranged chronologically. *See also* refers to articles on other subjects, with the dates on which the relevant articles appeared. Notice again the one-letter abbreviations for months and the compacted spacing in numbers.

Your library may also hold a number of information sources on microforms (either microfilms or microfiches) or on computer. Ask your reference librarian what is available in your library; the library may also provide handouts or guides to using this material.

Starting Your Working Bibliography

To save yourself time and frustration, make a habit of recording complete bibliographical information for every source that looks promising to you. (Look under "Works Cited" in Part II of this Chapter to know what constitutes complete information for each source.) Using 3 × 5 note-cards, write down all the information you'd need to find those sources again. (Use a separate card for *every* source. This is an important step; don't skimp.) If you make a full bibliography card for every source you find, you'll save an enormous amount of time. When you're typing the final paper at 2:00 AM and the library is closed, for instance, you'll need that year of publication or the correct spelling of an author's name.

Make sure every card has at least these elements:

- name of the author(s) spelled correctly
- full title
- place of publication and publisher (either a town and publisher's name, or the name of a journal and source)
- date of publication (either the year, for books, or the year, volume number, month, day, and pages for journals or magazines)
- any special identifying numbers (government document number, series number, and so on)
- library call number or location
- a quick note to yourself about the source

Here's what some sample bibliography cards look like:

Bibliography Cards

Weinstein, David, and Lillian Deitch. The Impact of Legalized Gambling: The Socio-Economic Consequences of Lotteries and Off-Track Betting. New York: Praeger, 1974. HV 6715. W43 2nd floor
Great (20+ pp) biblio; lots of tables and statistics; very good historical background. Sort of old but still useful.

Rohrig, Byron L.
"Lottery Foes Target Public Policy."
Christian Century Apr. 1987: 396-7.
Periodicals
Moral and religious objections to lotteries in gen'l. and Indiana lottery in particular. Interesting figures on $$ to advertise lotteries on TV, compares lottery & bookie's payoffs.

Eichenwald, Kurt.
"Are Lotteries Really the Ticket?"
New York Times 4 Jan. 1987: sec. XII: 14-15. Microforms
Good article, focuses on education funding, solid facts & figures, several specific refs. to Ohio.

Your working bibliography will probably be much bigger than the list of works cited in your final paper. Don't worry; your goal is to generate enough material so that you can pick and choose *the best* for the final product. It's far better to have too much information than too little.

Finding and Evaluating Your Sources

It's simply not possible to read every source you might find on your topic—and frankly, it's not necessary. Don't waste time at this stage trying to cover all the bases in search of that one perfect fact or quote—even though you may not yet know what your focus is. You can avoid such time-consuming mistakes if you follow these suggestions.

First, decide whether the source is *informative* with respect to your subject. Titles can be misleading: a book called *Gambling on Education* may or may not be about financing schools through public lotteries. Glance quickly at the source; skim its table of contents, preface, introduction, and conclusion. These will tell you whether the source's information is in your ballpark. Check for a bibliography, and look at the index.

If the source doesn't look promising for your paper—no matter how intrinsically interesting it sounds—put the card aside. You can read the item later if you have time.

Second, decide whether the source is *up-to-date* about your subject. When was it published? How old is the information it presents? (You can get a good idea for the second question by looking at the dates of works in the source's bibliography.) A source on the space shuttle program written before the *Challenger* disaster will lack some of the perspective you'll find in sources written after that date. Try to find the most current information you can on your topic. While some older sources may be classics, many of them have been superseded by newer research.

Third, look for sources that are *comprehensive*. At this stage of your research, you're trying to put together a big picture, so you want sources that provide an overview of your subject if these are available. Put the cards for sources that seem more narrowly focused in a separate stack; you'll want these later.

Finally, look for sources that *provide new directions*. Summary or review articles may direct you to several other sources where primary material may be found; works with bibliographies or extensive notes can be gold mines for suggesting new leads. You're trying to save time here, so look for sources that do your legwork for you by presenting information about as many other sources as possible.

TAKING NOTES

Your notes are essential: they're the backbone of the material you'll need to shape into your final paper. So it's worthwhile to take good notes. Two sample note cards appear on the following page.

Note Cards

code words

Eichenwald (p. 14)

Reminder that this is boiled down — (Synth): States vary in lottery funding for education; 28% in New Hampshire to 45% in New York. Ohio 40% to education in 1985; enough funds to keep the school systems running for only 9 days. (Nine Days!)

Reminder that this is source material — (Paraphrase): Many states are turning to lotteries because politicians have found that lotteries raise revenue so that no new taxes are needed. This is politically expedient; it keeps the voters happy. (14)

#16

Page number of source easily found

Slotnick (p. 302)

People prefer lotteries because they leave no "paper trail" (302).

Quotation marks for direct quotation — "(. . .) nearly 37% of those I surveyed who buy tickets (even though these lotteries are legal) still think there is something wrong with spending their money this way. Even more revealing, 43% of those who now play regularly told me they wouldnt if giving their name [sic] and Social Security number [sic] were ~~allowed~~ required" (302).

Ellipsis indicates a trimmed quote

neatly corrected error

MORAL OBJECT. #41

index word for the card

This was the forty-first notecard

Brackets mark a possible error in source

When you reach this stage in your own research project, you're ready to look ahead to Part III of this chapter for information about the correct way to quote, paraphrase, and synthesize your sources. Make sure it's clear on your note cards which of the three techniques you're using. (Notice how the student made those distinctions on the cards above.) Some students use different colored cards for each technique; others use multicolored highlighting pens to mark quotes, paraphrases, and syntheses. (This second method works well if you decide to quote part of a source and paraphrase or synthesize the rest.) But no matter what method you choose, *stick with it consistently.* A great deal of unintentional plagiarism occurs as a result of sloppy note taking.

A note here about photocopying. Many students like to photocopy articles or passages from books so that they can take a full copy of the source home from the library to work with. And some instructors require that students turn in copies of all their sources so that the instructor can check the handling and documenting of this material. But three warnings are in order. First, *photocopying can't replace note taking.* At some point you must decide what's important and what's not. Second, *photocopying gets expensive;* try not to copy *everything* ever written on your subject, just what you need. Third, *excessive photocopying—even for your own use—can violate copyright laws.* If you do photocopy your sources, *make a bibliography card for every source you photocopy.* Just because you have the pages from the magazine, for instance, doesn't mean you'll automatically remember the year or volume number in which the article appeared.

And finally, a note about note cards. Some students find note cards very confining. If you're one of them, try using the larger 5 × 8 note cards, or don't use them at all. Individual sheets of notebook paper work just as well—they just take up more space on your desk and floor. Whether you use note cards or regular paper, though, follow these hints:

- write only on one side
- number the cards or sheets in case you drop them
- keep them together in a folder, box, or envelope so that you don't lose key information while traveling from library to residence to class.

APPLICATION

1. Brainstorm, do some looping, talk, ransack your journal, and then make a list of at least five subjects that you might be interested in researching for a paper. For each subject, find the names of two people who might be able to give you expert information.

2. Discuss in a small group the following ideas for research papers. Which seem like they'd be good subjects to write about? Which need more work? Which wouldn't work at all?
   A. The problem of affordable housing
   B. Which brand of ice cream is better—Dove bars or Haagen-Daz?
   C. The causes of the energy crisis
   D. Financing a new car
   E. How did the world begin?
   F. The "grand unification" theory of creation
   G. Ways to make a company run more efficiently
   H. Fish oil will make you healthier
   I. Good places to buy computers
   J. Television shows based on children's toys
   K. Explanation of commodities trading
   L. How to invest your nest egg
   M. Television game shows
3. These are some subjects students want to use for their research papers. What purposes do the subjects seem to fit best? Mark *A* for *Assertion-with-Evidence, P/S* for *Problem-Solution, I* for *Information,* and *H* for *How-To.* (See Chapters 11, 9, 10, and 8.)
   A. Advancement of women in government jobs
   B. The English-only constitutional amendment
   C. Waste disposal for metropolitan areas
   D. Trends in movie attendance
   E. Role of diet in cancer prevention
   F. The importance of televising political conventions
4. Review the list of library sources on pages 228–235, and for each of the topics below identify three or four likely sources of information on them.
   A. Benefits of aerobics
   B. Solar batteries for cars
   C. Donald Trump
   D. Liquid-protein diets
   E. Problems with the Social Security system
   F. How new drugs are developed and tested
   G. Reviews of the movie *X* (you choose one)
   H. The greenhouse effect
   I. Recent political developments in the Middle East
   J. The speaker, occasion, and circumstance when these words were spoken: "I have a dream."
   K. Corporate-financed child care
   L. Latch-key children
   M. Hostile takeovers of corporations

5. With your group choose two of the subjects from number 4, go to the library, and find three books, articles, or references that you would read if you were going to do a research project on those topics. Make bibliography cards for each source. Compare your results to see how many different sources you've found.
6. Consult with a reference librarian and find two sources for the research paper you are developing that are in the library's reference section but which are not listed under the *Reference Material* section in this chapter. Add them to the list of *Reference Material* and jot down a brief summary of what they contain.

PART II: WRITING A RESEARCH PAPER

Once you've gathered an initial harvest of information about a topic, it's time to begin putting that information through the writing process and turning it into a paper. It's not necessary to have completed *all* your research before you put together a discovery draft; in fact, you may save time by drafting a portion of your paper before you're through in the library. Once again, though, you need a plan, a strategic set of steps to follow.

A STRATEGIC APPROACH TO WRITING

Many writers develop their own research/writing strategy; you can adjust the one that follows to suit your own needs and working habits. We'll show you the work of one student, Jennifer Corwin, as she follows the process, so that you can see how a research paper is shaped.

Step 1: Do Creating Exercises to Narrow Your Subject

At this point you probably have information about many facets of your topic, and may have begun to despair of molding it into any recognizable shape. Don't panic. Now's the time to try brainstorming, listing, and especially cubing and looping to help find a center to your material. What are the hot spots, the points of interest, the controversies to which many of your sources refer? You can also try the old "stacking" technique: sort your note cards into stacks on each aspect of your topic. The tallest stack—that is, the aspect about which you have the most information—is your most likely topic.

Here's part of Jennifer's looping activity for her paper:

> Money for the school? for Ohio? what am I going to write about. I wish I had a million dollars then I wouldn't have to write this paper!

> I wouldn't have to go to school, I wouldn't have to do anything, I could buy things for my kid, Dr. Harper is looking at me funny, back to work. Where could I get a million dollars? Maybe I'll hit the lottery. Ha. I hear the commercials all the time in my car but I never buy tickets. Still it would be funny if I won because lotteries are supposed to fund education and I'd use the money not to go to school, I wonder what they use the lottery money for really? They must make a bundle. Kenny Rogers? Do gamblers make money?

When Jennifer looked back at what she had written, two ideas caught her attention: that winning a million dollars in the Ohio Lottery could make her dreams come true, and that the Lottery must be very profitable. These were the hot spots she decided to explore through a discovery draft.

Step 2: Write a Discovery Draft

When your creating produces an idea that you think might be worth developing, you can begin to roughly shape your paper. Write a very rough discovery draft summarizing the information you've found. Don't worry at this point about an introduction, a conclusion, or documenting your sources—you just want a draft you can revise and reshape. You might not even refer to your note cards at this stage; draft following the picture of the subject you've created in your head, allowing a shape and angle on the subject to emerge. Don't worry if this draft is short, or if it's not written in full sentences. Amplification and polishing will come later.

Here's what Jennifer's discovery draft looked like. You'll notice that it's not really a paper at this point; it's the beginnings of a road map that she wanted to follow.

> Money can't buy me love, but I bet it could buy me some happiness. Look at all those commercials of lottery winners driving around in limos and smiling all the time. Winning the Lottery sure seems to have made them happy.
>
> And I guess the Lottery has made the state happy. From all the ads and hoopla, I'd say Ohio was making out okay. There sure are a lot of games—daily number, lotto, pick six—every store you go into has a ticket machine for the Lottery.
>
> I know some people object to lotteries on religious/moral grounds—gambling. And some people claim that lotteries damage the state's economy (how)? I think I remember hearing that they had lotteries during the Revolutionary War, so I guess this fight has been going on for a long time.
>
> Where does this get me?

Jennifer is still confused here, but there's a growing sense of a topic. Having come this far, she knew she had to find a focus.

Step 3: Determine Your Thesis

Once you have developed a preliminary sense of your paper's shape through creating and drafting, it's time to limit your focus. As you've read, thought, and written about your topic, it's likely that you've already begun to develop the controlling idea for your paper. In Jennifer's case, she'd reached the conclusion that she wanted to write about the real value of the Ohio Lottery, but she hadn't gotten any more specific than this.

When she discussed her subject with her classmates, she made a breakthrough. They helped her realize that her thoughts kept coming back to the notion of lottery money buying happiness—for the winners, for the merchants who sell tickets, and for the state. After this brainstorming session, she wrote a preliminary thesis statement:

> *Thesis:* The Ohio Lottery hasn't succeeded in accomplishing all it was intended to.

Note that this isn't as sharp a thesis as it will finally be; she hasn't defined *succeeded* or *intended.* Nonetheless, it predicts a structure for her essay (background on the lottery, what the criteria for success will be, how the lottery fails to meet those criteria) and gets her ready to shape the information she's found in her research.

At this stage your thesis need not be any more specific than Jennifer's. Once you've developed it, write it on a big piece of paper and post it over your desk. That way you can keep glancing up at it to keep you on track.

Step 4: Organize Your Research into a Preliminary Outline

At this point you should be ready to revise your discovery draft into a more coherent shape. You can begin by making a rough outline of the parts you think that you will need to develop your overview or argument. This outline isn't set in concrete; you should feel free to change it if your writing and research take you in other directions. The key information that your preliminary outline should provide, however, is a list of your *major sections or divisions* and a sense of what *support* you need to fill those parts out.

Here's Jennifer's preliminary outline for her paper on the Ohio Lottery:

```
Intro

History of Lotteries
    Elsewhere
    In Ohio

The Players
    The Losers
    The Winners

What Lotteries are Supposed to Do
    For Education
    For the Elderly
    For Public Transportation

Who Opposes Lotteries?
    Religious
    Moral
    Economic

Conclusion
```

Notice that Jennifer hasn't bothered at this point to copy in sources from her notes; rather, she's identified the kinds of information she might discuss, and has sketched a picture for herself of what kinds of sources she needs. Some of this material will eventually have to be cut, but she's not worrying about that now. From this outline she can begin revising her discovery draft and start to incorporate the reading and researching she's done.

Step 5: Find the Holes and Fill Them

Once you've composed a preliminary picture of your paper, it's time to test it for comprehensiveness. Now you can sort your stacks of note cards and bibliography cards into piles corresponding to each heading on the outline. At this stage, you'll find holes in your research coverage; you'll probably have piles of information on some points, but no information on others. Now's the time to go back to the library, either to find some of those more narrowly focused sources you skipped on your first search or to look for new material. Because you are looking for specific material—and because you're familiar with the research techniques you need to use—this second search can probably be accomplished in a much shorter time than your first. Here's Jennifer's annotated outline, showing the gaps she needed to fill:

I. Introduction

II. History of the lottery
 a. First existence of lotteries
  1. Why lotteries began *need*
  2. Why lotteries did not succeed
 b. Rejuvenation of lotteries (1964) *when lotteries were revived*
  1. Why lotteries were revived *have*
  2. How the lottery works
III. → a. The Commission *b. disbursement of funds*
  ~~b. The games~~
  c. The sales agent *need*
  d. The games
  e. The odds

IV. About the people that play
 a. Who plays
 b. The reason people play *need*

V. About the people that win *Have*
 a. Individual winners *not all they hoped it would be*
 b. Lottery sales agent *w/cost of extra employees it has not been as profitable for small agents*
 c. Big Investors *Big winners!*
 d. Advertisers *to keep up public interest*

VI. Are the lotteries succeeding?
 a. For education purposes *need*
 b. To subsidize government funds instead of raise taxes
 c. Illegal gambling
 d. Moral issue? is there one?

VII. Conclusion
 a. Lotteries have been run as fairly as possible, but
  1. They have not lived up to their expectations *for school, gov't revenue, elderly*
  2. Still exploits the poor
  3. No different than gambling

In 1878
~~The lottery in 1988 is not so different from the lottery in 1878. The public,~~ the government and taxpaying citizens determined the lottery to be swindles, exploiting the poor, and generally not what it was expected to be. Is it so different in 1988?

Step 6: Expand Your Discovery Draft into a Working Draft

Finally—you're ready to complete the paper. At this point, you'll be surprised at how much information you've gathered and at how easily the paper begins to come together. Writing the research paper at this stage is like writing any other paper—with one *major* exception. As you begin to incorporate your note cards into your text, make sure you mark every

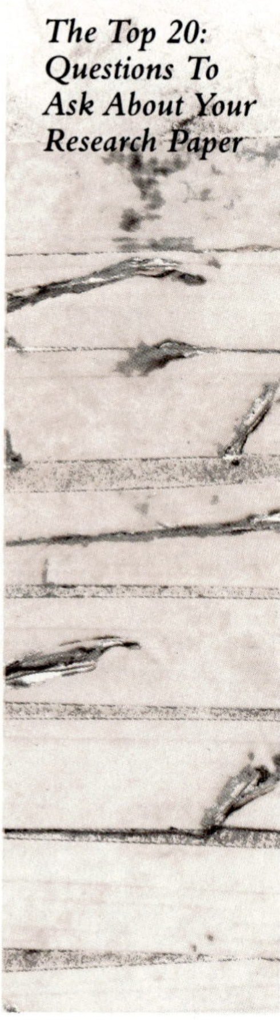

General

1. Is the paper easy to read even if the subject is unfamiliar?
2. Have I given some of my own thoughts, ideas, or opinions in addition to the information I got from my sources?

Title

3. Does the title arouse curiosity and accurately reflect the content of the paper?

Outline or Abstract

4. Is it in proper form?
5. Does it reflect the actual organization and intention of the paper?

Thesis Statement

6. Is the thesis of the paper clear to the reader at the very start?
7. Does the thesis statement limit and focus the paper as well as illustrate the purpose of the paper?
8. Does the thesis statement do one of the following: (a) clearly state the assertion to be proven in the paper, (b) present the problem that the paper is going to concentrate on and suggest the solutions to be given, (c) give relevant information, (d) pose the question that the research paper sets out to answer?

place you use material from a source. At this draft stage, you may wish to use big asterisks in the margin, or different colored pens, or some other technique to remind yourself that you are using source material. Some students like to use big sheets of computer paper at this point, writing on one half and taping or stapling their note cards alongside the places where the information is used. The important thing is to find a technique and stick with it.

Step 7: Revise the Working Draft

Now you're ready to rework your draft, just as you would any other piece of writing. If you haven't already done so, you can begin to work on an introduction that will help draw your audience into the paper and a conclusion that puts your writing in perspective for your readers. Spend

Development and Organization

9. Does everything in the paper relate to the thesis?
10. Is there a logical order in the development of the paper?
11. Are all the main points adequately supported with quotes and references? Are they fully developed?

Conclusion

12. Do the final paragraphs pull the paper together by giving the reader a sense of completeness and closure? Is the thesis reviewed, summarized, or referred to?

Documentation

13. Have I introduced and documented any sources I've used?
14. Have I integrated my research material into the essay so that it doesn't sound like a paste-up job of my note cards? Did I use enough sources?
15. Are the parenthetical references in proper form? Is there a Works Cited entry for each source cited in a footnote?
16. Is the list of Works Cited in correct form?

Mechanics

17. Do I have transitions connecting the sections of the essay?
18. Are there any spelling errors?
19. Did I punctuate correctly?
20. Did I use accepted grammatical forms?

some time, too, picking out a title; try to avoid boring, obvious ones like "A Research Paper on Gun Control." Pick a title that will intrigue or inform your readers. You needn't get too artistic in choosing your title; just remember it's the first thing your readers will see. You want it to invite the audience to read what follows.

In the revision stage, you're also ready to make sure your sources are handled properly. Make sure that you have clearly identified all uses of source material in your paper, and that you've used attribution to introduce the sources smoothly into the flow of your writing. Set aside the bibliography cards for all the sources you've actually used in your paper; you'll need them for the final bibliography, now usually called *Works Cited*. If your paper must have a formal outline or brief abstract, now is the time to prepare it.

Step 8: Edit the Paper for Consistency in Form and Language

In the final days prior to handing the paper in you'll want to do everything possible to ensure that your hard work will earn a good grade. So now you must *edit* the paper scrupulously. Carefully prepare the entries for the *Works Cited* or *References* page, using the forms shown in Part III of this chapter.

Step 9: Type the Final Paper—and Proofread It

At last the time has come. You're ready to prepare the final copy of your research paper. Type it carefully. Make sure you put in documentation for your sources; don't stint on this stage! If you hire someone else (your roommate, spouse, friend, secretary, or local typist) to handle this stage for you, remember that *you alone are responsible for the final product.* Make sure your typist understands the format conventions that are required.

When you are through typing, allow a mandatory overnight "cooling" period before proofreading the paper (even if someone else has typed it). Then, when you can bring fresh attention to bear on the paper, proofread it carefully, one word at a time. Make sure that key words or paragraphs or parenthetical references appear where they're supposed to, just as they did in your draft.

Step 10: Release the Paper—and Yourself

Finally you are ready to turn the paper in and go on with your life. You've made yourself into an insider on the subject, and you're ready to get your readers' response to your work. First, make a copy of the paper to protect your sanity in case of disaster. Submit the paper to your instructor in the form he or she requires—some instructors prefer that you turn in copies of your sources and all your notes and drafts as well. If your instructor doesn't ask for your sources and drafts, store them safely in your room until the paper is returned to you; this precaution will help you if the instructor asks to see some of your preliminary material to resolve questions about your paper. You may be able to use these source materials for other projects as well.

EXAMPLE The Research Paper

This is the final paper Jennifer wrote about the Ohio Lottery. The paper begins with an outline and an abstract. Generally, a paper with one or both of these elements before the body of the paper also has a title page.

Though the Modern Language Association prefers that research papers do not include title pages, many instructors disagree—and *require* their students to provide a title page.

The safest solution to this dilemma is to ask your instructors about their preferences and then follow them. When preparing a title page, include the title of your paper, your name, your class section, your instructor's name, and the date. This information should be centered on the page, side-to-side and top-to-bottom. Each element should appear on a separate line. Double-space between elements—or triple space if you find that it looks better. Remember that your title page will provide the first impression your reader has of what is to come.

Jennifer's paper is documented in Modern Language Association style; at the end of the paper is a sample page done in American Psychological Association style and a copy of the *References* list done in APA style. (These style forms are explained in Part III of this chapter.) Key features of Jennifer's paper are highlighted.

Emphasis: Writing to Tell

Purpose: To inform the voters of Marion, Ohio, about the Ohio Lottery's success

Context: Research paper for a freshman composition class.

Circumstances: Students had one month from the initial assignment to complete and turn in the paper.

Writer-Reader Relationship: Jennifer is a well-informed and politically active member of her community. Her readers are members of the same community, but spend less time thinking about and becoming active in public affairs.

No page # on pages with a title

Outline

Thesis

Although the Ohio Lottery was designed to provide financial support for education, state government, and the elderly, it cannot be considered a complete success.

} 2 doublespaces

I. Introduction

II. When and why lotteries have been popular
   A. Used in colonial America to raise money for government and nonprofit institutions
   B. Discontinued over the course of the nineteenth century because they were either rigged or offered too small a chance of winning
   C. Reinstituted in recent history
      1. In New Hampshire in 1964 to avoid new taxes
      2. In Ohio in 1974 to benefit state revenues
      3. Proposed in 1987 to remedy the Federal deficit

This is a topic outline

III. Kinds of lottery games available
   A. Instant lotteries
   B. Numbers
   C. Lotto

IV. Lottery players and lottery profiteers
   A. Lower-income players who spend more than they can afford with little return on their investment
   B. Investors who hold stock in companies making lottery supplies and get greater return on their investment
   C. Lottery Sales Partners who pay minimal licensing fees and make a profit on the number of tickets sold
   D. Television stations which sell $23.3 million dollars in lottery advertisements a year

V. Successes and failures of the lottery
   A. In funding education
      1. Supposed to supplement already-allocated funds
      2. Has replaced allocated funds for no net gain
   B. In deterring crime
      1. Supposed to curtail illegal gambling
      2. Has apparently not replaced bookmaking and other illegal operations
   C. In helping overcome moral reservations about gambling
      1. State sanctions it
      2. Many users are still uncomfortable about it

VI. Conclusion

Abstract

This research paper explores the history and workings of state lotteries and argues that although the Ohio Lottery was designed to provide financial support for education, state government, and the elderly, it cannot be considered a complete success. The paper examines the history and functions of lotteries in America and focuses on their modern reemergence. It then examines the kinds of people who play and profit from lotteries. It concludes by examining the claims made on the Ohio Lottery's behalf and evaluates their validity.

Jennifer Corwin
English 101:K4
Dr. Harper
December 15, 1988

Title uses a phrase which will be quoted in the body of the paper

Paying to Dream:

Has the Ohio Lottery Been a Success?

Introduction developed through narration, moving into problem-solution form

One day as I jumped into my car, turned on the radio, and drove toward my intended destination, a disc jockey on the radio announced that the Ohio Lottery jackpot had accumulated $21,000,000. I fought an irresistible urge to go buy a lottery ticket. Logically, I knew I would not win the Lottery; and yet, I could not stop myself from daydreaming about actually winning and spending all that money! I knew that the Lottery had not brought happiness to all who have played it and won. But had the lottery issue been proposed and passed to bring happiness to its participants? I had to answer this question, "Yes, indirectly;" the Lottery was designed to be a "painless tax" in which players voluntarily contribute funds to provide financial support for educational programs, the state government, and the elderly (Rohrig 397). However, the painful reality is that the Ohio Lottery cannot be considered a complete success. thesis

Opening uses large jackpot to symbolize lottery appeal

History of lottery in the U.S.

Many people think of the lottery as being a relatively new idea, occurring within the past two decades. In fact, lotteries in America date as far back as the Jamestown Colony ("Wheels"). Early lotteries were considered easy sources of revenues by the government. Lottery proceeds were used to help finance the French and Indian wars, the Revolutionary War, and many colleges including Harvard and Yale (Brammer 1). However, many of the early lotteries were misrepresented to the players and lottery "winners" were in fact prearranged. Middlemen who served as ticket brokers skimmed a considerable portion of the profits (Weinstein and Deitch 9-10). Many people felt that lotteries were unfair because they encouraged people to spend their

The history of U.S. lotteries is synthesized into this summary ¶ in which she cites 3 separate sources: an editorial, a journal article, and a book

Corwin 2

miniscule incomes on a chance to become instantly wealthy. As a result of these problems, most state lotteries were discontinued by 1878 (Brammer 2).

In 1964, New Hampshire began the revival of lotteries to avoid assessing new taxes upon the public. The state government needed more money to maintain services to which the public had become accustomed and to enable the government to provide better services and meet public demands. It was determined that the lottery would offer a voluntary source of revenue; therefore, the state would avoid controversy over new tax proposals (Brammer 2).

Summarizing information from a government document

In 1974, the state of Ohio loaned two million dollars from the general revenue fund to the Lottery Commission to begin the Ohio Lottery. By legal agreement, the first two million dollars earned from lottery sales would be repaid to Ohio's general revenue fund (U.S. Govt. 407). Although, legally, no less than thirty percent of the Lottery's total revenue is supposed to be deposited into Ohio's state treasury ("Page's" sec. 3770.06), the Ohio Lottery Commission deposits approximately forty percent of its total lottery revenue into Ohio's general revenue fund instead. Another ten percent of the Lottery's total revenue is used for administrative expenses. Finally, approximately fifty percent of the total Lottery revenue is returned to the public in the form of prizes (Mooney 1).[1]

Since this figure seemed questionable, she added a footnote to discuss the problem.

In 1987, a National Lottery was proposed to decrease the Federal deficit. However, according to Richard Mooney of the New York Times, the operational expenses of such a lottery would be so extensive that a National Lottery would not be worthwhile. Likewise, state governments say that lotteries have not produced nearly as much profit as was originally anticipated (Brammer 4). Why do the lotteries continue if the states are not making an adequate profit? The answer may be that if the states wish to continue operating on their existing budgets, a uniform tax would have to be imposed to replace the funds provided voluntarily by the lotteries. Politically, lotteries make better sense than tax increases.

Paraphrased source is introduced with attribution

Corwin 3

Content ¶

The Ohio Lottery Commission, which currently consists of nine appointed members, has created several ways of allowing individuals opportunities to win prizes and contribute voluntary revenue to the state. Dana B. Brammer of the University of Mississippi describes the available lottery games as follows:

Attribution introduces the direct quote

No quotation marks used for a blocked quote

> 1. The instant lottery. Instant lottery games offer individuals the opportunity to win prizes immediately without risking large sums of money. Tickets usually sell for $1.00 each and contain a latex coating which obscures numbers or symbols (e.g. a tic-tac-toe game, a poker hand, or some other arrangement). Simply by scratching off the latex, a player can learn whether or not he has a winning ticket.
>
> 2. Numbers games. Where numbers are legalized . . . a bettor chooses his own number—sometimes two-digit, sometimes three-digit, and sometimes four-digit, rather than purchasing a prenumbered ticket, as is the case in passive games [such as the Instant Lottery]. The chosen number is then compared with a winning number.
>
> 3. Lotto. In this centuries-old game that is now legal in a growing number of states, player select a group of numbers from a larger field, typically, six numbers from a field of forty. Drawings are held weekly, and a player must match the combination of numbers drawn. If the winning combination is matched by more than one player, the prize is shared. If the winning combination has not been chosen by any player, the purse is added to the next game, causing the jackpot—and thus the excitement—to grow. (3)

Content ¶

Ellipsis show omission from her source

Buried in her research Jennifer found the odds for winning at Lotto & noted their source.

Pagination for a blocked quote goes outside the punctuation

The voluntary revenue that is collected by the state from these games has been justified to the public by convincing them that the Lottery would provide many benefits. In fact, many property owners were led to believe that the need to assess new property taxes to support the schools would practically be eliminated by the state Lottery. As a result, public support for the Ohio Lottery has steadily strengthened.

2 Function ¶s sum up Jennifer's overview & plunge her into an evaluation

Corwin 4

2nd function ¶

Authorities report lottery betting has quadrupled since 1975, grossing more than $20 billion dollars annually—$88 per person per year ("Dream"). Who are the bettors? And who are the beneficiaries?

Mixed paragraph developed using comparison-contrast, facts & figures, and narration

Content ¶

Although there is no proof that low-income persons play the lottery more often than middle-income persons, statistics indicate that low-income bettors invest a larger percentage of their total income than do other economic groups (Brammer 4). One California study reported that people who earn less than ten thousand dollars per year spend an average of 1.4 percent of their total income on lottery tickets. People earning an income over fifty thousand dollars annually bet only 0.1 percent of their income on lottery tickets ("Dream"). Nancy Fletcher, who manages the Short Stop Convenience Store in Marion, Ohio, says that the majority of the people who purchase lottery tickets from her store cannot afford to spend money on the Lottery. In fact, very often, customers will purchase groceries with food stamps; then, these people will spend $10 to $20 in cash on lottery games. Certainly, in Mrs. Fletcher's experience, low-income persons are the main group of lottery customers. Obviously, if this is true, the state has not succeeded in voluntarily taxing the individuals it intended to—those who are in the middle- and upper-income brackets.

Wealthier investors are still betting on the lotteries, but not by standing in line to buy a chance at a jackpot. Many of these people invest in the corporations such as G. tech that supply the computers and software to the Lottery's Sales Partners (Marcial).[3] By doing this, investors' "winnings" are greater and they have greater control over investment losses.

Again, Jennifer has a comment to offer which is relevant but doesn't belong in this ¶.

Lottery Sales Partners are also betting on the Lottery's continued success. Anyone may apply to become a Sales Partner as long as lottery sales are not his or her sole business ("Page's" sec. 3770.05). The cost involved in becoming a Sales Partner is minimal. In return, Sales Partners receive five cents of every dollar they take in from lottery sales. In addition, if a Partner sells the only winning jackpot ticket in a game, he or she earns ten thousand dollars. If more than one person has chosen the

Jennifer continues to paraphrase her sources, the language of which is not vivid enough to merit quoting directly.

Corwin 5

winning numbers, the Lottery Sales Partners involved in the sale of those winning tickets divide the ten thousand dollars (Fletcher). Therefore, by putting a computer terminal in their retail businesses, Partners enjoy increased sales and receive a portion of the profits from Lottery revenues.

Partners also acquire an enticing advertising gimmick. The Lottery uses game variations and advertising to maintain the public's interest and motivation to buy tickets from the Partners (Brammer 3). In fact, according to the Television Bureau of Advertising Statistics, in 1984 lotteries spent $23.3 million dollars on television advertisements (Rohrig 397). These advertisements not only increase lottery sales and the television networks' revenues, but also provide free advertising for the Partners.

In summary, many more people than those who hold the winning tickets collect money from the Lottery. As the New York Times put it in an editorial, "The rich get richer and the poor pay to dream about it" ("Dream").

Here is the direct quotation which is the source of the title

But what dreams does the lottery actually fulfill? Ohio's Lottery advertisements concentrate on the statement "Help the Ohio Lottery continue to be a source of fun for many, and increased opportunities for our children" (Compulsive 3). Of course, the Lottery officials are referring to the funds that the Lottery supplies to our educational programs. But there's a catch. Although the state does actually contribute the amount of revenue for educational purposes that is advertised, many Lottery supporters assume that the Lottery's contribution is in addition to already-allocated government funds. But in reality, funds collected from the public in the form of taxes and appropriated by the legislature for educational purposes are reduced by an amount equalling the Lottery's contribution. The Lottery's annual contribution to Ohio education would only keep the state education going for nine days (Eichenwald 15). In addition, many taxpayers mistakenly assume that the Lottery provides all additional monies needed for education; therefore, voters justify the defeat of proposed school levies (Eichenwald).

Another direct quote—this one's the Lottery's earnest slogan

Use of shocking statistic gets readers' attention

Corwin 6

Another argument made in support of the Lottery is that it would deter illegal gambling (Janson). But law enforcement officials agree that illegal gambling continues to flourish for several reasons:

Three paraphrased sources are presented as an inset list. Note that paren. ref. goes after period

Illegal bookmakers pay off at a better rate. (Rohrig 397)

Illegal casinos are less regulated and winnings are not reported as taxable income. (Janson)

Lotteries provide an untraceable way of disposing of illegally-earned income. (Blotnick)

In fact, Michael Bozza, Assistant Director of the Organized Crime section of New Jersey's Division of Criminal Justice, states, "There is no logic to arguing that bets should be placed with the state lottery rather than with a man with a pad in his hand" (quoted in Janson).

Lively language merits direct quote

Since Bozza's name isn't on the list of Works Cited, Jennifer helps her readers find the source more easily

The gambling element has led some Lottery opponents to insist that lotteries be discontinued because gambling is immoral (Brammer 5). One survey, in fact, reported that nearly 37 percent of its respondents thought that there was "something wrong with spending their money this way," and that "43 percent of those who now play regularly" would not play if they had to fill out forms to indicate they were participating (Blotnick 302). I am not sure if they are right; nonetheless, I find it ironic that, because gambling leads to corruption, many states make it illegal except when it takes place in state-sanctioned forms such as lotteries. In other words, gambling is excusable if the state approves of it—but only as long as the state doesn't inquire too closely about who's playing. This situation parallels the lottery itself—people seem to approve of the lottery as long as they don't ask too many questions about where the money's going.

Direct quotations give immediacy to these surprising statistics

a personal perspective

As I reached to turn off my radio and prepared to step out of my car, I thought of the words in a song entitled "The Gambler," in which Kenny Rogers sings, "You've got to know when to hold 'em—know when to fold 'em. . . ." The dream of instant wealth dies hard; people don't seem ready to fold on the Lottery. Nonetheless, al-

Conclusion developed by analogy drawn from a song

though we don't know who'll eventually hold the winning hand in the Ohio Lottery game, we're already beginning to see who's gotten a bad deal. For our schools, our elderly, our poor—for our society—the Ohio Lottery hasn't yet proved worth the gamble.

Notes

[1]Several articles use this approximation, but none give a source for their figures.

[2]The odds of selecting five correct numbers out of sixty are 1:30, 961. The odds of selecting six correct numbers out of sixty are 1:7,059,052 (Lottery Annual Report 9).

[3]G.tech, the corporation which has supplied computer equipment for the Lottery's use since 1986, has experienced a 41 percent rise in profits since that time (Helm).

MLA Format

Works Cited

Blotnick, Srully. "The Lure of the Lottery." Forbes Jan. 1986: 302–3. a magazine

Brammer, Dana B. "State Lotteries: Promise But No Panacea." Public Administration Survey Spring/Summer 1987: 1–5.

Compulsive Gambling: First It Takes Your Money; Then It Takes Your Dignity. Ohio Lottery Commission, 1987. a pamphlet

"Dream Tax." Editorial. New York Times 17 July 1987: sec. 1: 34. an editorial

Eichenwald, Kurt. "Are Lotteries Really the Ticket?" New York Times 4 Jan. 1987: sec. XII: 14–15. a newspaper article

Fletcher, Nancy E. Personal Interview. 2 Nov. 1988.

Helm, Lillian. "Can Gtech Keep Winning at the Lottery?" Business Week 18 May 1987: 93–94.

Janson, Donald. "Casinos Help Illegal Gambling Thrive in Jersey, Officials Say." New York Times 17 Oct. 1986: sec. 1: 33.

Marcial, Gene G. "A Lottery Play for High Rollers." Business Week 23 June 1986: 122.

Mooney, Richard. "Federal Gamblers." New York Times 22 May 1987: I: 30.

"Ohio Lottery Annual Report—1985." Ohio Lottery Commission 1985: 1–16. a published report

Rogers, Kenny. "The Gambler." Kenny Rogers' Greatest Hits. Liberty Records, Inc., 1980. a record

Rohrig, Byron L. "Lottery Foes Target Public Policy." Christian Century Apr. 1987: 396–7.

U. S. Government, State of Ohio. 1974: 407–12.

U. S. Government, State of Ohio. Page's Ohio Revised Code Annotated. Cincinnati, OH: Anderson Publishing Co., 1988. government publications

Weinstein, David, and Lillian Deitch. The Impact of Legalized Gambling: The Socio-Economic Consequences of Lotteries and Off-Track Betting. New York: Praeger, 1974. book, 2 authors

"Wheels of Fortune." Forbes June 1985: 15.

Sample page in APA style

Corwin 3

parenthetical reference when author is not named in text

its total lottery revenue into Ohio's general revenue fund instead. Another ten percent of the Lottery's total revenue is used for administrative expenses. Finally, approximately fifty percent of the total Lottery revenue is returned to the public in the form of prizes (Mooney, 1987, p. 30).[1]

APA notes are identical to the MLA notes. The writer can put them at the foot of the page if he or she so desires.

In 1987, a National Lottery was proposed to decrease the Federal deficit. However, according to Richard Mooney (1987, p. 30) of the New York Times, the operational expenses of such a lottery would be so extensive that a National Lottery would not be worthwhile. Likewise, state governments say that lotteries have not produced nearly as much profit as was originally anticipated (Brammer, 1987, p. 4). Why do the lotteries continue if the states are not making an adequate profit? The answer may be that if the states wish to continue operating on their existing budgets, a uniform tax would have to be imposed to replace the funds provided voluntarily by the lotteries. Politically, lotteries make better sense than tax increases.

The Ohio Lottery offers several ways of allowing individuals opportunities to win prizes and contribute voluntary revenue to the state. Dana B. Brammer of the University of Mississippi (1987, p. 3) describes the available lottery games as follows:

parenthetical reference when author is named in text

1. The instant lottery. Instant lottery games offer individuals the opportunity to win prizes immediately without risking large sums. Tickets usually sell for $1.00 each.

Sample reference page in APA style

date follows author, not publisher

References — Note that APA uses this term instead of Works Cited

Journal article — Brammer, D. (1987). State lotteries: Promise but no panacea. Public Administration Survey, Spring/Summer, 1–5.

Mooney, R. (1987, May). Federal gamblers. The New York Times, p. 30I. — newspaper article

Book, 2 authors — Weinstein, D. & Deitch, L. (1974). The impact of legalized gambling: The socio-economic consequences of lotteries and off-track betting. New York: Praeger.

PART III: USING SOURCES IN YOUR WRITING

Many students dislike writing research papers, not because they don't enjoy finding out and writing about new ideas, but because they're intimidated by the seemingly complex methods they need to learn to show what sources they've used. These methods are called *documentation* in academic writing, and learning these techniques is one of the major steps in becoming a successful academic writer.

WHO DOCUMENTS SOURCES?

Academic writing isn't the only place where documentation plays an important role. Writers composing biographies or fact-based books need to include sections of *Notes* to document their sources of information (partly to inform interested readers and partly to protect themselves against possible legal action).

Researchers in the natural, physical, and social sciences publish long lists of references with their articles. These references not only provide background and source material, but also save time; for instance, such researchers may write "Protein was purified using the method of Lundblad (21)," and then provide in reference 21 the documentation for Lundblad's article describing the purification process in detail. Engineers cite reports and stress studies; politicians and bureaucrats refer to laws and government documents. Lawyers are perhaps the most prolific documenters of all: they usually cite numerous published cases to establish precedents for their own arguments.

Almost every field of professional writing has its own requirements for documentation. The two most common systems of documentation used in academic writing are Modern Language Association (MLA) style and American Psychological Association (APA) style. The following sections will show you how to document your writing using both of these styles. If your instructor asks you to complete your documentation following another style, be sure to ask for a reference which shows you the requirements for that format.

THE BASICS: WHAT YOU DOCUMENT

The purpose of documentation is to let all readers judge the quality of your research, to help interested readers find out more about your subject, and to allow skeptical readers to judge the authority and accuracy of your sources. The point of researched writing is to *demonstrate* your research. But documentation can get overwhelming: do you need to cite a source for every sentence? What goes in those citations? Are footnotes still used?

You need not document your own argument, the superstructure of your paper. The introduction, conclusion, introductory and summary sentences of each section, and your interpretation of the sources are your own work; since they're original in your paper, they don't get documented. Some material you use to support your paper, such as names, dates, and facts in *common knowledge* (described later), are also not documented. What you do need to document is source material taken directly from your research. It usually falls into one of three categories: *direct quotations, paraphrases,* or *synthesized information.*

Documenting Direct Quotations

You must provide a reference for any *direct quotation* you copy exactly from some source. The quotation can be words (phrases, sentences, whole paragraphs), numbers (statistics, calculations, tables, and so on), or graphics (charts, diagrams, pictures, and so on).

MLA: Arrowsmith claims that many dictionary users are "semiliterate klutzes" (8).

APA: Arrowsmith (1988) claims that many dictionary users are "semiliterate klützes."

Sometimes you'll want to quote a famous saying or biblical reference ("Money is the root of all evil"; "Let there be light"); these don't require documentation. If you use a brief quote as an *epigram* at the beginning of your paper or one of its sections, it's usually sufficient to list the author's name below it as a credit. (Such epigrams do not need to be listed in your final list of works cited.) For example:

> You don't have to be a weatherman to know which way the wind blows.
>
> —Bob Dylan

Documenting Paraphrases

When you *paraphrase,* you recast an author's ideas in *your own* words and sentence structure. Since you're taking the ideas from a source, you must give the original author credit by citing a reference.

MLA: Arrowsmith contends that most dictionary users are uneducated and not very talented (8).

APA: Arrowsmith (1988) contends that most dictionary users are uneducated and not very talented.

Documenting Synthesized Information

Sometimes you'll want to use ideas, facts, statistics, thoughts, verbal echoes, lines of argument, or general concepts from your reading in your research paper. How do you decide which of these you must document? A common test is the rule of *common knowledge*. Basically this means that you need not document anything that is generally known by your readership: facts, dates, names, and so forth. Most educated readers know (or could easily discover) that Elvis Presley died in 1977, that Pete Rose holds the major league career record for base hits, that Vatican City has no coastline; and that Franklin D. Roosevelt was elected to four terms as President. These facts can be easily checked in an encyclopedia or almanac, the chief repositories of common knowledge.

If your audience has a particular body of knowledge in common, you need not document information from that common body; a passing reference is generally all that is needed. Most scientists know what Planck's constant and Einstein's theory of relativity are; most linguists know what Grimm's and Verner's Laws are; most educators are familiar with Piaget's theories of child development; most public health officials are familiar with the diseases most commonly associated with the AIDS virus. When writing for such audiences, you don't need to document the common knowledge and assumptions you and they share.

What you must document, no matter who the audience, are those ideas, statistics, and thoughts that are not commonly known or that might be challenged by a reader. For instance, the Centers for Disease Control, the National Institutes of Health, the Department of Health and Human Services, the World Health Organization, and several independent researchers have each predicted how many people will be infected with AIDS in the next ten years. But these numbers vary widely, so if you quote one of these estimates in your paper, you must give a source so that readers can tell *which* estimate you're using.

While most scientists know $e = mc^2$, they probably would need a reference to Einstein's letters on the dangers of nuclear weapons, since those opinions are less well known. Likewise, most people know that Gene Kelly starred in *Singin' In The Rain;* even film buffs would probably want to know where you found out that Brick Sullivan played the police officer in the famous rain scene. A good rule of thumb is that if your audience can ask "Sez who?" or "How do you know that?" you should provide documentation.

Sometimes you'll be tempted to use information in your paper that you half-remember from school or a television program. Such information is called *hearsay,* because you've heard it said, or read it somewhere. If you can confirm the information, use it with a source cited (after all, *you* had to look it up!); if you can't confirm it, no matter how good it seems, don't use it. If a reader challenged you on that evidence, you couldn't back it up; that would undermine a reader's confidence in the rest of your paper.

WHERE IN YOUR PAPER DO YOU DOCUMENT INFORMATION?

The formats for documentation can vary widely. Some of you may have learned a style that included footnotes or endnotes and a bibliography. Most systems of documentation now use a three-part system: *parenthetical references* within the text, *content notes* numbered in the text and written out after the body of the main text, and a list of *Works Cited* at the end of the paper.

Parenthetical References

Parenthetical references replace the old system of footnotes or endnotes within the body of the paper. Now when you use a source in your paper, you include in parentheses a reference which will enable the reader to identify it on the list of *Works Cited*. MLA style emphasizes the author's name and the page number of the reference in the parenthesis; APA emphasizes the author's name and the year in which the reference was published.

Rules for Including Parenthetical References (MLA Style)

1. If you refer to an entire work of an author, not just part of it, you should include the author's name in your text:

   Fraser says the Chinese are "far more complicated" than Westerners think.

2. If you decide not to use the author's name in your text, then it must be given in a parenthetical reference:

   The Chinese are "far more complicated" than Westerners think (Fraser).

3. If, however, you are citing only a specific part of an author's work, you must give page numbers to that part in a parenthetical reference. If the author's name is not mentioned in your text, it must go in the parenthetical reference as well:

   Fraser says the Chinese are "far more complicated" than Westerners think (18).

   The Chinese are "far more complicated" than Westerners think (Fraser 18).

Later in this chapter you will find a listing of the correct MLA bibliography forms for many common kinds of reference sources and the appropriate parenthetical reference form for each.

Rules for Including Parenthetical References (APA Style)

1. When possible, the author's name and the date of the source's publication should be woven into the text:

   In 1965, Pauling hypothesized . . .
   In the first published article on the subject (Pauling 1965) . . .
   Pauling (1965) argued . . .

2. If the source has no identified author, a brief form of the title is used in the parenthetical reference:

   A recent survey of scholarship ("Research in Writing," 1984) . . .

3. If you refer only to specific pages of a source, add page or chapter numbers after the date. (Page numbers must always be used for a direct quotation.)

   Pauling (1965, pp. 345–347) . . .
   Samuelson (1983, Chap. 6) suggests . . .

Later in this chapter you will find the correct APA bibliographical forms for more than fifty sources, and the appropriate parenthetical reference for each.

You can also use parenthetical information to help readers identify people, dates, and literary references. (Such parenthetical references are not included in your list of *Works Cited*.)

> Geoffrey Chaucer (c. 1340–1400) naturalized many French words. (The *c.* stands for "circa," the Latin word meaning "approximately," and is used when scholars are unsure about a particular date.)
>
> The miracle of the burning bush (Exodus 3:1–14) is widely debated.
>
> Henry's supremacy was established at the Battle of Agincourt (1415).

Content Notes

Content notes are used sparingly in the MLA and APA systems. They provide important material, extra explanations, or references that would distract readers if placed in the main text. Keep them brief; if the material must be discussed at length, it probably belongs in the main text. These notes are numbered in sequence with raised (superscript) numerals in your text, in the style of old footnotes or endnotes. The text of the notes appears between the end of your paper and the list of *Works Cited*.

Some reasons for including such notes might be:

1. To acknowledge assistance you've received in writing the paper.

   [1]Robert Shore of Alarmtronics, Inc., Flemington, NJ, provided the alarms used in this survey.

2. To define a specialized term or abbreviation.

   [2]DSP is dithiobis-succinimidyl propionate.

3. To name a work or source used throughout the paper.

   [3]All quotations from *Paradise Lost* will be taken from the New Edition, ed. Merritt Y. Hughes (NY: Macmillan, 1962), and cited by book and line numbers in the text.

4. To explain a calculation or statistic.

   [4]The estimate of ESL students in 1995 was taken from a speech by Saul Cooperman, Commissioner of Education for New Jersey, at Livingston College, April 17, 1987, and modified by statistics released by the Rutgers University Admissions Office.

5. To give a survey of the scholarship on a point.

   [5]Guinevere's guilt is examined by Moore (81) and Silver (204–211).

6. To direct readers to background information.

   [6]These terms are defined in Passmore's *Philosophy of Teaching* (17–38).

Any works referred to in content notes must also be cited in the list of *Works Cited.*

List of Works Cited

At the end of your paper, you should provide a list (in alphabetical order) of all the sources referred to in your paper. In MLA style it is called *Works Cited;* in APA style it is called *References.* These titles replace the old term "bibliography." In this list you should provide the full reference to all sources mentioned in the parenthetical references and content notes of your paper. An example of such a list in both styles is shown in Part II of this chapter as part of the sample research paper.

FORMAT: HOW TO INCORPORATE DOCUMENTED MATERIAL

One of the greatest difficulties in research writing is that of maintaining control over your paper. Unless you take care, your finished product may resemble no more than a neatly typed stack of index cards taped in a row with a few hastily cobbled sentences holding them together. But if you choose your sources well, introduce them smoothly, and tailor them to fit your own sentences, you should have a professional-looking research paper.

How to Choose Sources

The sources you choose should support the points *you* are making. So you'll want to look at a wide variety of materials to find the information that best backs up your ideas. This means you must pick and choose among the sources you find; you simply can't use everything, or just the first things you find, in your paper. Look for sources that do at least one of the following:

- provide key information (facts, figures, insights, explanations). This will be the "meat" you put on the skeleton of your ideas.
- provide authoritative reinforcement for your position (for example, Henry Kissinger for foreign policy, Stephen Hawking for relativity). The names should either be immediately recognizable or the person's or organization's title should carry authoritative weight. (Beware of "celebrity endorsements;" the celebrity may not be an expert on the matter at hand.)
- provide a vivid phrasing that best expresses the idea you are trying to convey (for example, Kennedy's "Ask not what your country can do for you," Nixon's "Silent Majority," Alice Walker's "Every time I see a rock I throw it.").
- explain how a representative portion or majority feels on a particular issue (for example, official statements from organizations, overview articles, and so on). These sources are particularly good for introductions and general background.

Use direct quotes sparingly to avoid the pasted-together effect. In general, use them only if they are vivid or particularly authoritative. If the information or authority is very important but the phrasing is not memorable, paraphrase the source in your own words and word order. Finally, if the sense of the information is important but the source is rather ordinary, synthesize the information you need from it into your own text and provide documentation.

Where to Put the Reference and What It Should Say

It takes practice to work parenthetical references smoothly into your text; at first, all those parentheses will look awkward and intrusive. Here are some tips to help you make the writing read more smoothly.

1. *When the author's name is mentioned in the text:*
   MLA: Put the page reference at the end of the clause in which the reference is used. (In MLA style you must give page numbers for all citations.) The reference precedes the punctuation.

> Baugh says "Milton's language is more complex than his Heaven" (xxvi).

> Although Milton's language has been called "more complex than that of his contemporaries" (xxvi), it is nonetheless understandable to a modern reader.

APA: Put the year reference after the author's name.

> Baugh (1962) says "Milton's language is more complex than that of his contemporaries (p. xxvi)."

In APA style you need not give the page number for a paraphrase. You can also separate the name/date and page number information (as the above example shows) if it makes the reading easier.

2. *When the author's name is not mentioned in the text:*
   MLA and APA: Put the reference at the end of the clause following the source.

   > Milton's language has been called "more complex than that of his contemporaries" (Baugh xxvi). [In APA this would read (Baugh, 1962, p. xxvi).]

3. *When the quotation is set off in a block:*
   MLA: The citation goes outside the punctuation mark. (The rules for deciding when to block quotations are explained later.)

   > Scholars in the 19th century made the first leap back in hypothetical ancestral languages. By comparing archaic words of modern languages and analyzing internal vowel changes and common word endings, they established the probable common root of Latin, Greek, Sanskrit, Germanic, Balto-Slavic and Indo-Iranian. Called Indo-European, its daughter languages constitute today's most widely spoken linguistic family. (Wilford B5)

4. *If the work has more than one author:*
   MLA: List either all the authors (Carter and Skates 41) or use the Latin abbreviation *et al.* ("and others") (Carter et al. 41).
   APA: If the work has only two authors, both names must be used in all references (Carter and Skates 41). If there are three or more authors all three names must be used in the first reference (Tarvers, Roberts and Lundblad 1175); in subsequent references *et al.* may be used (Tarvers et al. 1181).

5. *If more than one work by an author is cited:*
   MLA: Use a short form of the title preceding the page reference.

(Clancy, *Red October,* 28)

(Clancy, *Cardinal,* 119)

APA: Use the year to clarify the reference.

(Tarvers, 1983, p. 1175)

(Tarvers, 1984, p. 2034)

If both works were published in the same year, assign them letters of the alphabet corresponding to the alphabetical order of the titles. Thus Tarvers, "Sources . . ." becomes 1983a and Tarvers, "Technological . . ." becomes 1983b.

How to Tailor Sources to Fit Your Sentences

Unfortunately, writers don't always set out to write quotable material which fits neatly into your sentences. So sometimes you must smooth quotes to incorporate them into your writing.

Cutting Material Out. If you need to cut words or phrases from a quotation, you must show the omission using the punctuation called *ellipsis,* three typed dots with spaces between them: . . .

Original:

> Nelson's long rumination on the history and motives of IBM (whose "fall" he continues to predict, with considerable persuasiveness) is one of those models of historical clearheadedness that so rarely find their way into print (Manes 85).

Ellipsis in beginning, middle, and end:

> Manes calls Nelson's book ". . . on the history and motives of IBM . . . one of those models of historical clearheadedness . . . (85)."

You needn't use ellipsis at the beginning of every quote if the sentence reads more smoothly without it:

> Manes calls Nelson's book "one of those models of historical clearheadedness that so rarely find their way into print (85)."

If you omit anything with end punctuation (periods, question marks, exclamation points) or whole sentences or paragraphs, the ellipsis is made with four dots, not three. This signals readers that a larger chunk of context has been removed. Such four-dot ellipses come only at the end of your own sentences.

Adding Material. If you add new words or letters to a quote, indicate the changes in square brackets:

> Manes calls Nelson's book "[a] model . . . of historical clearheadedness (85)."
>
> Nelson "ruminat[es] . . . on the history and motives of IBM (85)."
>
> [Ted] Nelson is still predicting the fall of IBM (85).

Recording Mistakes in Your Sources. If there is a mistake in your source, indicate it with the Latin word *sic* ("it appears so") in square brackets. If the mistake is itself in quotation marks or italics, *sic* may be placed in parentheses.

> Jones insists that "The cat protects it's [sic] young fiercely" (54).
>
> Her paper's title was misprinted as "Love and Punishment in *Romeo and Joliet* (sic)."

How to Type Quotations

Short quotations of prose and poetry (up to four lines of prose or three lines of poetry) can be incorporated directly into your doublespaced text with quotation marks, so that they fit more smoothly into your own writing.

> Hughes points out that "Arthur's regulations permitted the informer to 'have his discharge from the ship should he require it'" (211).

Note that in the above example the double quotation marks in the original are converted to single quotation marks in an incorporated quotation.

> Satan rationalizes that "Here we may reign secure, and in my choice / To reign is worth ambition though in Hell: / Better to reign in Hell, than serve in Heav'n" (I:261–264).

Note that the slashes marking line ends have spaces on either side, and that the punctuation and spelling of the original are copied exactly.

In both MLA and APA style, long prose quotations (more than four typed lines) or poetry quotations (more than three typed lines) are indented ten spaces. Such quotations are called *block quotations*. Quotation marks are not used, and the reference is placed after the last punctuation mark. If the prose quotation extends more than one paragraph, the first lines of subsequent paragraphs are indented an additional three spaces (thirteen total).

> It is not known how many escaped convicts ended up as beachcombers on the sandalwood islands. Hundreds of them must have been scattered in remote parts of the Pacific. "Strangers in their new societies and scandals to their old,"

> they contributed their own violence and opportunism, incubated and hardened by the System, to the ruin of the island cultures. By 1850 there was no part of the Pacific where the name of Botany Bay did not carry a sour infected reek—the breath of England, gone carious in double exile.
>
> It was much harder for convicts to steal a boat for themselves than to stow away on someone else's; but that did not prevent some from trying. (Hughes 212)

Note that quotation marks in the original are copied directly into the blocked prose quotation.

If the original has any special typographical arrangement, spelling or punctuation (as, for example, in the poetry of e. e. cummings), you should reproduce it as nearly as possible in the text of your paper.

ATTRIBUTION: HOW TO INTRODUCE SOURCES

Some research papers seem pasted together because the sources are placed in the body of the paper without any introduction. The name we give to such introductions is *attribution,* and it is an important part of documenting your sources. Attribution not only smooths the reader's way into your source material, but also can add more authority to your source. For instance, a study saying that massive servings of tuna fish cure the common cold would be more convincing if it appeared in *The Journal of the American Medical Association* than if it appeared in *The Journal of Tuna Fishing;* a reader would have less reason to think the source was biased. A statement on the costs of national defense might not sound impressive if it came from Janet Doakes, but if it was attributed to "Janet Doakes, costs-benefits analyst for defense at the General Accounting Office," a reader would have better cause to trust Ms. Doakes' expertise.

When you first give attribution to a source in your paper, you usually give the source's name and title:

> Former Transportation Secretary Elizabeth Dole argued . . .

You needn't, however, give the source's title if it's well known:

> In *Mein Kampf,* Hitler asserts . . .

In subsequent references, a shortened attribution will usually suffice:

> Dole also contended . . .
>
> Hitler makes clear that . . .

If it has been several pages since you referred to this source, however, readers may appreciate a fuller attribution to jog their memory:

Former Secretary Dole was quoted . . .

The GAO's Doakes cites figures . . .

You may find yourself introducing all your sources with the verb "says," even when it doesn't fit the syntax. But with more practice, you'll find many ways to smoothe your attribution into the paper. Try some of these:

Gilder believes that . . .

One critic suggests that . . .

As one author remarks, . . .

An article in *Consumer Reports* recommends three solutions. First, . . .

"The difficulties," according to Fraser, include ". . ."

McCoy's comment on this charge is that . . .

In a critical article, Stanley Fish concludes . . .

In this sense Carl Sagan proposes that we . . .

He also stipulates that . . .

She went on to argue . . .

Her theory also suggests . . .

He further claims that . . .

Marshall cites statistics showing . . .

The government insists . . .

Industry spokespersons contend . . .

Remember that the attribution can also come at the end of the source:

". . . ," Baker suggests.

". . . ," says the GAO's Doakes.

". . . !" he ended his speech.

Other good attribution verbs include *accept, affirm, add, admit, assert, believe, confirm, contend, declare, deny, emphasize, mention, propose, rely on, reveal, state, submit, think, allege, regard, verify, point out, think,* and *insist.* Use the one that works best with each source for the greatest effect.

MLA DOCUMENTATION: GENERAL GUIDELINES

In preparing your list of *Works Cited* in the MLA style, you need to include three general categories of information: author information, title information, and publication information. The division between each category is marked by a *period and two spaces*. If other subcategories of information are added, such as the name of a translator, editor, or series, these are also followed by a *period and two spaces*. Various kinds of sources are documented slightly differently, so this section covers them by type: books; magazines, journals, and newspapers; reference sources; graphic and media arts; oral and personal communications; and technological sources.

Books

There are many parts of books you may wish to document, each requiring a slight adjustment of the standard book form to give full information to your readers. When you cite a book, the normal arrangement and punctuation for information is:

1. Author's name.
2. "Title of the part of the book."
3. Title of the book.
4. Name of the editor, translator, or compiler.
5. Edition used.
6. Number of volumes.
7. Name of the series.
8. Place of publication: name of the publisher, date of publication.
9. Volume and page numbers.

What are the conventions for recording each of these?

1. Author's name. This is used either for the author or the editor, if the work is a compilation. Reverse the last and first names for alphabetizing, adding a comma after the last name: Keillor, Garrison. (Remember that information is entered in the list of *Works Cited* alphabetically by the last name of the author.) Record the name exactly as it appears on the title page: T. S. Eliot, not Thomas Stearns Eliot; John Milton, not J. Milton. If the author's name is a pseudonym and you wish to indicate the author's real name, you can use brackets: Peters, Elizabeth [Barbara Michaels].
2. "Title of the part of the book." When you use only a part of a book (an essay from a collection, a work from an anthology, and so on), cite the title of the part in quotation marks *exactly* as it appears in the book.
3. Title of the book. Give the book's full title, including any subtitles; use a colon and one space to set subtitles off from the full title, unless the full title ends in a question mark or exclamation point:

Teaching Writing: Theories and Practices

Is There a Text in This Class? The Authority of Interpretive Communities.

Underline the entire title, but not the period which sets this category off from the information that follows it. If part of the title is itself underlined or italicized, *do not* underline it when you retype it:

A Preface to Paradise Lost.

The absence of underlining tells readers what was underlined in the original.

4. Name of the editor, translator, or compiler. If the name of an editor, translator, or compiler appears on the title page, it should follow the full title in your list of *Works Cited*. It can be abbreviated as follows:

   The Divine Comedy. Trans. John Ciardi.

   The Fire of Love. Ed. Betty Radice.

5. Edition used. Many books have appeared in more than one edition. Since the information they contain changes from edition to edition, it's important to tell your readers what edition you took your source from. If the title page or the copyright page (which contains the Library of Congress copyright information) indicates that the book is not a first edition, you should reflect this information in your *Works Cited*. You may indicate the edition by number (2nd ed.), by name (Rev. ed. for "revised edition"), by year (1989 ed.), or by a combination of these elements (2nd rev. ed.), depending on what the title and copyright pages tell you.
6. Number of volumes. Always cite the complete number of volumes when citing a multivolume work.
7. Name of the series. If a book is part of a publication series, give the name of the series and the Arabic numeral which indicates the book's place in the series: Chaucer Studies 2. If the series has been going on for a long time, it may have several sets of numbers. In this case, use the information on the title page to indicate which series numeration you are using: Early English Text Society n.s. 23 (for "New Series 23").
8. Place of publication: Name of the publisher, date of publication. Use the book itself to determine the place of publication, name of the publisher, and the date of publication. (Bibliographies and library catalogs have been known to be wrong.) The place of publication should be indicated first: New York. If the place is not well known or may be confused, you can add qualifying information following a comma and a space: Glenview, IL; Cambridge, MA. If the place of publication is

spelled in a foreign language, you may add a translation following it in brackets: Praha [Prague]. The place of publication is followed immediately (no spaces) by a colon.

Next comes the name of the publisher. This is usually abbreviated to the shortest *easily*-recognized form: Scott for Scott Foresman; Prentice for Prentice-Hall; Harcourt for Harcourt, Brace, Jovanovich. Articles, business abbreviations such as Co., Corp., and Ltd., and descriptive words (books, press, etc.) are omitted. If the publisher's name is a person's name, abbreviate it to the last name alone: Brewer for D. S. Brewer. Abbreviate the phrase "University Press" as UP. If no publisher is named, write n.p. (no spaces) after the colon. The name of the publisher is followed by a comma and one space.

The date of publication should be taken from the title or copyright page. If the book is a reprint, give the dates of both the original edition and the reprint: 1972. New York: Avon, 1983. (Note that there's no need to use the abbreviation *rpt.* for "reprint" when both dates are given.) If you are citing a multivolume work that has been completed over the years, give the inclusive dates: 1981–86.

9. Volume and page numbers. When you cite *part* of a book, such as an essay or a work from an anthology, give the page (and, if necessary, volume) numbers for the *entire* work, not just the individual pages you referenced in your paper. The abbreviations *pp.* for pages and *vol.* for volume are not used.

Sample Works Cited Forms for Books

1. One author

Keillor, Garrison. Lake Wobegon Days. New York: Viking, 1985.

Fish, Stanley. Is There a Text in This Class? The Authority of Interpretive Communities. Cambridge: Harvard, 1980.

If you cite more than one work by the same author, list them alphabetically by title. Type the author's full name for only the first citation; in subsequent citations, begin with three hyphens, a period, and two spaces.

Keillor, Garrison. Lake Wobegon Days. New York: Viking, 1985.

---. Leaving Home. New York: Viking, 1987.

If you cite more than one work *edited* or *translated* by the same author, the principle is the same; however, the three hyphens are followed by a comma and the correct abbreviation:

Berthoff, Ann. The Making of Meaning. Upper Montclair, NJ: Boynton, 1981.

---, ed. Reclaiming the Imagination: Philosophical Perspectives for Writers and Teachers of Writing. Upper Montclair, NJ: Boynton, 1984.

2. Two or three authors

Note here that only the name of the first author or editor is reversed for alphabetizing; the other authors' names follow the first, separated by a comma and one space.

Summerfield, Judith, and Geoffrey Summerfield. Texts and Contexts: A Contribution to the Theory and Practice of Teaching Composition. New York: Random, 1986.

Kennedy, Edward Donald, Ronald Waldron, and Joseph S. Wittig, eds. Medieval English Studies Presented to George Kane. Wolfeboro, NH: Brewer, 1988.

3. Four or more authors

Here the Latin abbreviation *et al.* ("and others") is useful. Only the first author's name is used when *et al.* is employed.

Edens, Walter, et al., eds. Teaching Shakespeare. Princeton: Princeton UP, 1977.

4. A book edited or compiled by the author

Berthoff, Ann E., ed. Reclaiming the Imagination: Philosophical Perspectives for Writers and Teachers of Writing. Upper Montclair, NJ: Boynton, 1984.

5. A book edited by another author

Malory, Thomas. Le Morte D'Arthur. Ed. Janet Cowan. 2 vols. Baltimore: Penguin, 1969.

If you were focusing on Cowan's work in preparing this edition, you could list it under her name:

Cowan, Janet, ed. Le Morte D'Arthur. By Thomas Malory. 2 vols. Baltimore: Penguin, 1969.

6. A chapter or section in a book

First, cite the author and title of the chapter or essay you are citing, enclosing the title in quotation marks. Next, give the full title of the book and the name(s) of the editor(s), and the publication information. Finally give the complete page numbers for the chapter or essay you are citing.

Winterowd, W. Ross. "Literacy, Linguistics, and Rhetoric." Teaching Composition: Twelve Bibliographic Essays. Ed. Gary Tate. Rev. ed. Fort Worth: Texas Christian UP, 1987. 265–290.

The exceptions to this rule are prefaces, introductions, forewords, and afterwords. Only the descriptive term, without underlining, is used to name the section. If these explanatory sections are written by another writer, use "By" and the author's full name in the citation; if the author wrote the explanatory section, only write "By" and the last name.

Keillor, Garrison. Preface. Lake Wobegon Days. By Keillor. New York: Viking, 1985. vii–x.

Popkin, Henry. Introduction. The Importance of Being Earnest. By Oscar Wilde. New York: Avon, 1965. 9–21.

7. A book published by a group or association

Associations and corporations often publish their own materials. Cite them as the authors as well as the publishers, but do not reverse the order of words in their names.

American Heart Association. Advanced Cardiac Life Support Manual. Rev. ed. Washington: American Heart Assoc., 1987.

8. A book with no named author

If a book has no author's name on the title page, alphabetize it under the first word of the title that is not an article. Do not alphabetize it under "anonymous" or "anon."

New Cassell's German-English Dictionary. New York: Funk, 1971.

9. A book published in more than one volume

If you use a multivolume work, cite all the volumes, not just the one(s) you use. If the volumes were published over a span of years, include all those at the end of the citation; if the work is still in progress, use "to date" after the number of volumes and do not include a closing date of publication.

Miller, John H. General Anesthesia. 3 vols. New Haven: Mosby, 1987.

Wing, Donald, et al., eds. Short-Title Catalogue of Books Printed in England, Scotland, Ireland, Wales, and British America and of English Books Printed in Other Countries, 1641–1700. 2nd ed. 3 vols. to date. New York: MLA, 1972–

10. A book in translation

If your focus is on the work itself, cite the original author of the work first; if your focus is on the translator's effort, cite the translator's name first.

Alighieri, Dante. The Divine Comedy. Trans. John Ciardi. New York: Norton, 1977.

Ciardi, John, trans. The Divine Comedy. By Dante Alighieri. New York: Norton, 1977.

11. A reprint of an older book

When you cite a book that has appeared previously in some other form (for example, as a hard-bound book before a paperback), give the original publication date, followed by a period and two spaces, then the complete publication information for the form in which you found the source. Do not use the abbreviation *rpt.*

Bunyan, John. The Pilgrim's Progress. 1957. New York: Washington Square, 1973.

12. A book in a series

When a book you cite is part of a series, it's important to include that information in the *Works Cited* list, since some libraries may reference the work by series rather than by title. Include the full name of the series and the Arabic volume number between the title and the publication category.

Pantin, W. A. The English Church in the Fourteenth Century. Medieval Academy Reprints for Teaching 5. 1955. Toronto: U Toronto P, 1980.

13. An anthology

When you include an entire anthology, begin with the name of the editor(s) or compiler(s) as you would for a book with that many authors.

Abrams, M. H., et al. The Norton Anthology of English Literature. 5th ed. 2 vols. New York: Norton, 1986.

14. Individual works from an anthology

First, cite the author and title of the piece you are using as if they appeared independently. Then include the title of the anthology, the name(s) of any editors, translators, or compilers, the publication information, and the complete inclusive pages for the work you are citing.

Sidney, Philip. The Defense of Poesy. The Norton Anthology of English Literature. Ed. M. H. Abrams et al. 5th ed. 2 vols. New York: Norton, 1986. I: 505–526.

Or you can cross-reference the individual works to avoid repetition, as long as the *Works Cited* contains a full reference to the anthology:

Sidney, Philip. The Defense of Poesy. Abrams I: 505–526.

Traherne, Thomas. "Wonder." Abrams I: 1666–67.

15. A book whose title includes another title in quotes or italics

If the work you are citing contains a title normally enclosed within quotation marks, retain the quotation marks in your citation and underline the entire title:

Danzig, Allan, ed. Twentieth Century Interpretations of "The Eve of St. Agnes." Englewood Cliffs, NJ: Prentice, 1971.

If the work you are citing contains a title normally italicized or underlined, do not underline it.

Lewis, C. S. A Preface to Paradise Lost. Oxford: Oxford UP, 1956.

Magazines, Journals, and Newspapers

Magazines, journals, and newspapers are generally classed by libraries as "periodicals;" that is, they appear at regular intervals (daily, weekly, monthly, yearly). Because they appear in so many formats, however, it's necessary to use several different documentation forms. However, all include these characteristics, and these punctuations:

1. Author's name.
2. "Title of the article."
3. Name of the periodical
4. Series number or name
5. Volume number
6. (Date of publication)
7. Page numbers.

Here are the requirements for these elements:

1. Author's name. Take this from the beginning or end of the article, and follow the rules for the names of authors of books.
2. "Title of the article." Cite the full title of the article, and enclose it in quotation marks. The end punctuation (period, question mark, or exclamation point) goes inside the quotation marks.
3. Name of the periodical. Cite the full name, but omit any articles (National Review, not The National Review). Underline the full title. If there are several periodicals with the same name, give the place of origin in brackets following the title to clear up confusion: Quarterly Review [Amherst]. No punctuation follows the name of the periodical.
4. Series number or name. If the periodical has appeared in more than one series, state it or abbreviate it after the name of the periodical: Notes and Queries 3rd ser.; Kenyon Review n.s. (for "new series"). No punctuation goes after the series number.
5. Volume number. Give the volume number for a scholarly journal, but not for a magazine that appears monthly or more frequently, and not for a newspaper. Your teacher or librarian can help you determine what is a magazine and what is a scholarly journal. One rule of thumb is that publications you can buy at newsstands are magazines, not journals. Don't let the presence or absence of the word Journal in the title mislead you; for instance, Ladies' Home Journal is a magazine.

No punctuation follows the volume number, and the abbreviations *v.* and *vol.* do not appear.

6. (Date of publication). Leave a space after the volume number, name of series, or title of the periodical, then include the date of publication within parentheses, followed by a colon, a space, and the inclusive page numbers of the article, followed by a period. Abbreviate all months except June, July, and May. Use full abbreviations (Jan., Nov.), not the one-letter abbreviations you may find in The Readers' Guide or similar sources:

   PC Magazine (31 Jan. 1988): 77–78.
   Freshman English News 17.1 (1988): 33–36.

7. Page numbers. Give the complete page numbers for the articles you cite, not just the individual pages to which you referred in your paper. If the article is not printed on consecutive pages, but rather skips pages, it is permissible to write only the first page number, followed immediately by a plus sign, rather than writing out all the pages: 78+, rather than 78, 81–84, 89.

   The following are the most common forms for listing periodicals in your list of *Works Cited.*

Sample Works Cited Forms for Magazines

1. An article in a weekly or biweekly magazine

Give the author, title, name of the periodical, and date of publication. Give the complete date, but abbreviate the month. Do not give the volume and issue numbers even if they are listed:

> Morrow, Lance. "1968: Like a Knife Blade, the Year Severed Past from Future." Time 11 Jan. 1988: 16+.

2. An article in a monthly magazine

Give the month and year, but do not give the volume and issue numbers, even if they are listed.

> Hoberman, Barry. "Translating the Bible." Atlantic Monthly Feb. 1985: 67+.

Sample Works Cited Forms for Journals

1. An article in a journal with issue-by-issue pagination

Scholarly journals usually publish less frequently than do magazines, so the volume and issue numbers, not the month of publication, are usually cited for reference. If each issue of the journal starts with page 1, follow the rules for monthly magazine citations, but include the volume and issue number in place of the month.

Harris, Jeannette. "Rethinking Invention." Freshman English News 17.1 (1988): 13–19.

2. An article whose pagination is continuous for the year or volume

Some scholarly journals continue their pagination from one issue to another within a volume; for instance, volume 1 may contain pages 1–212, and volume 2 will begin with page 213. In such cases you may ignore the issue number when citing your reference:

Corbett, Edward P. J. "Teaching Composition: Where We've Been and Where We're Going." College Composition and Communication 38 (1987): 444–452.

Sample Works Cited Forms for Newspapers

In citing a newspaper, give the title as it appears on the first page (the "masthead"), but omit articles (Washington Post, not The Washington Post). If the city of publication is not indicated in the title, add it in brackets following the title: Advocate [Provincetown, MA]. For nationally published newspapers such as USA Today or the Wall Street Journal, no city is needed. Add the complete date (day first, followed by the abbreviated month and the year) and the edition, if any is indicated: city, national, final, and so on.

If each section is paginated separately, treat it as you would the volume numbers for a multivolume book: II: 1+. If the sections are identified by letters, give the page number *before* the section letter: 19B. If, as is sometimes the case in Sunday papers, the section is identified only by name, give it before the page number: Sports 22. If the newspaper is paginated continuously, treat the pages as you would for a weekly magazine.

Here are the *Works Cited* forms for some of the most commonly cited newspaper elements:

1. A by-lined article

If the author of the article is indicated, treat it as you would for an article in a magazine:

Hirsch, E. D., Jr. "Kissinger Views Talks With Caution." New York Times 17 June 1988, natl. ed.: A18.

2. An unsigned article

If no author is given for the article you are citing, begin your citation with the title and alphabetize it under the first word which is not an article:

"The Perils of Fashion." Courier-Post [Camden, NJ] 9 July 1987, Style 6. (This would be alphabetized under *P.*)

3. An editorial

If the editorial you cite is signed, treat it as you would a by-lined article, but include the word "Editorial" after the title and before the name of the publication. If the editorial is unsigned, treat it as you would an unsigned article, but again include the word "Editorial" after the title.

Rinke, Carlotta M., M. D. "CPR 1986: What's New." Editorial. Journal of the American Medical Association 255.21 (1986): 2991–92.

"Reagan's Dangerous Task." Editorial. New Orleans Times-Picayune 26 June 1987: A8.

4. A letter to the editor

Identify the writer of the letter and add the descriptive label "Letter" after the name. Use no title, and give the appropriate place of publication reference.

Muskie, Edmund S. Letter. Time 28 Feb. 1987: 25.

Reference Sources

There are a variety of forms for reference works depending on what the works are and how they are arranged.

Sample Works Cited Forms for Reference Sources

1. Reference works

Treat an entry in an encyclopedia or dictionary as you would a piece in a collection, but do not cite the editor of the complete work. Unsigned entries are treated as unsigned articles. If entries in the reference book are alphabetical, give only the entry label in quotation marks; no volume or page numbers are needed. Familiar reference works need only have the edition and year cited; less familiar references need a fuller citation.

"Honest." Oxford English Dictionary (1933).

"O'Connor, Sandra Day." Who's Who of American Women. 15th ed. 1987–88.

Lundblad, Roger L. "Hemostasis." Encyclopedia of Hematology and Oncology. Ed. Harold R. Roberts et al. 4 vols. Chapel Hill: U North Carolina P, 1988.

2. A dissertation

If the dissertation has been published, cite it as a book, but add the relevant dissertation information, and, if included, the University Microfilms catalog number.

Moon, Helen M., ed. The Life of the Soul: An Edition with Commentary. Diss. Fordham U, 1975. Elizabethan and Renaissance

Studies 75. Salzburg: Institut fur Englische Sprache und Literature, 1978.

If the dissertation has not been published, place the title in quotation marks. Follow it with the label "Diss.", preceded and followed by two spaces, and add the name of the university where it was written, a comma, one space, the year, and a period:

Hall, William Lincoln. "Personification in Middle English Religious Poetry, c. 1200–1400." Diss. U of North Carolina, 1987.

3. A pamphlet

Treat a pamphlet as you would a book.

Ohio Lottery Commission. Gambling and the Problem Gambler. Cleveland: Ohio Lottery Commission, 1985.

4. The Bible

The Bible is cited by giving the name of the Biblical book (without underlining or quotation marks) followed by a space, the chapter number, a period, and the verse number(s) either directly or parenthetically within your text. If you use the King James (Standard Version) Bible there is no need to include the Bible on your list of *Works Cited*. If you use any other edition, treat it as you would a book with no named author in your list of *Works Cited*.

5. A government document

Because government documents come from so many different sources, they are sometimes particularly hard to cite. If the individual author of a document is not known, treat the issuing government agency as the author. If the issuing agency is part of a larger agency, you may have to break up the author's name:

United States. Department of Education. Commission on Testing and Reform.

The title of the publication should follow a period and two spaces. Underline it, and include all information needed to identify it: session of Congress, name or number of bill or resolution, document number, or date. Abbreviate "Senate" as "S" and "House of Representatives" as "H":

99th Congress
H 197

S. Rept. 18

The usual publication information comes next. Most federal publications are issued by the Government Printing Office (GPO) in Washington; however, check the title page for contradictory information.

Cong. Rec. 28 Feb. 1987: 3822–26. (This is the appropriate form for the Congressional Record).

United States. Internal Revenue Service. Your Federal Income Tax. Washington: GPO, 1987.

New Jersey. Department of Motor Vehicles. Instructions for Obtaining a Motor Vehicle License. Trenton: State of New Jersey, 1968.

---. Department of Revenue. Information for Taxpayers. Trenton: State of New Jersey, 1987.

6. A published review

Reviews of sources appear in many places: in books, magazines, journals, on television and radio, in newspapers, and the like. Give the reviewer's name and title (if these appear); then write *Rev. of* (neither underlined nor in quotes), the title of the work reviewed, a comma and one space, the word *by* (or, if appropriate *ed.* or *trans.* or *dir.* or *cond.*), pertinent performance information if needed, and the publication information appropriate to the place where the review appeared.

Simon, John. Rev. of Into the Woods, Mark Hellinger Theatre, New York. New York (May 1987): 36+.

"The Cooling of an Admiration." Rev. of Pound/Joyce: The Letters of Ezra Pound to James Joyce, with Pound's Essays on Joyce, ed. Forrest Read. Times Literary Supplement 6 Mar. 1969: 239–40.

Graphic and Media Arts

Sources you take from the graphic and media arts are generally treated as you would a book or article, but descriptive labels are included to help readers understand the nature of the sources.

Sample Works Cited Forms for Graphic Arts

1. A cartoon

Give the artist's name, the title of the cartoon (if any) in quotation marks, and the descriptive label *Cartoon* neither underlined nor in quotation marks. Follow with the correct citation for the form where the cartoon appeared.

Larson, Gary. "The Far Side." Cartoon. Washington Post 23 May 1986: B5.

Addams, Charles. Cartoon. New Yorker 14 Feb. 1987: 38.

2. A map or chart

Treat a map or chart like an anonymous book, but add the descriptive label that fits it:

Illinois. Map. New York: American Automobile Assoc., 1987.

Periodic Table of the Elements. Chart. Boston: Heath, 1951.

3. A work of art

Give the artist's name first; underline the title of the work; name the institution where the work is preserved, followed by a comma and the city.

Buonnarrotti, Michaelangelo. Pieta. St. Peter's Basilica, Rome.

Monet, Claude. Waterlilies. Philadelphia Museum of Art, Philadelphia.

If you cite the work from a photograph, be sure to give a full citation for the source in which you found the work:

DaVinci, Leonardo. La Gioconda [Mona Lisa]. The Louvre, Paris. Illus. 234 in Art through the Ages. By James Gardner et al. 6th ed. New York: Hambledon, 1981.

4. An advertisement

When you cite an advertisement, use the sponsoring company as the author, and follow it with the label *Advertisement*. Follow with the complete publication information.

American Airlines. Advertisement. Time 11 Jan. 1988: 52.

Sample Works Cited Forms for Media Arts

1. A television program or radio broadcast

The order of presentation is the name of the individual program, the name(s) of people who had responsibility for the program or appeared in it, the name of the continuing program, the broadcast source, the name of the station broadcasting the program, and the date.

"Comrades in Arms." By Larry Gelbart and Alan Alda. M*A*S*H. CBS Television. WCAU, Philadelphia. 17–24 Nov. 1981.

War of the Worlds. Dir. Orson Welles. Mercury Theatre on the Air, CBS Radio. WCBS, New York. 30 Oct. 1938.

If you wish to emphasize the writers' or director's effort, you could cite it thus:

Gelbart, Larry, and Alan Alda. "Comrades in Arms." M*A*S*H. CBS Television. WCAU, Philadelphia. 17–24 Nov. 1981.

Welles, Orson, dir. War of the Worlds. Mercury Theatre on the Air, CBS Radio. WCBS, New York. 30 Oct. 1938.

2. A movie or videotape

Excalibur. Dir. John Boorman. With Nicol Williamson. Orion, 1981.

If you wish to emphasize the director's effort, you could cite it thus:

Boorman, John, dir. Excalibur. With Nicol Williamson. Orion, 1981.

3. A tape recording

The person cited first (performer, composer, conductor) will vary depending on the emphasis you gave the source in your paper. Follow it with the title of the tape, the artist(s), the manufacturer, the catalog number (if there is one), and the year of issue (write "n.d." if none is listed):

Bach, Johann Sebastian. Brandenburg Concertos Nos. 1, 3, and 6, BMV 1046, 1048, 1051. Cond. Karl Richter. Munich Bach Orchestra. Deutsche Grammaphon, 415 910–4, n.d.

For privately produced tapes, the name of the program is not underlined. The size and nature of the tape and the archival reference number for the tape are included:

Hankins, Elizabeth. Traditional Children's Stories. Audiotape. Rec. 19–22 April 1974. U of California, Los Angeles, Archives of Folklore. F.56 82. 7 1/2 ips, 7" reel.

4. A record, cassette, or compact disc

These entries follow the rules for tape recordings.

Beethoven, Ludwig van. Symphony no. 7 in A, op. 92. Cond. Herbert von Karajan. Vienna Philharmonic Orch. London, STS 15107, 1966.

Clapton, Eric. Crossroads. Disc 2. Polydor, 835 269–2, 1988.

5. Musical composition

These entries begin with the composer's name. If the work has a named title (e.g. 1812 Overture), underline it; otherwise do not underline works identified only by form, numbers, keys, or opus or standard catalog numbers.

Strauss, Johann. Die Fledermaus.

Beethoven, Ludwig van. Symphony no. 7 in A, op. 92.

Oral and Personal Communications

1. A letter

Published letters are treated like works in an anthology; add the date of the letter and the number (if the editor has assigned one).

Unpublished letters include the writer's name, the receiver's name, the date of the letter, and the location where the letter is currently kept.

Fitzgerald, F. Scott. Letter to Maxwell Perkins. 24 Dec. 1933. F. Scott Fitzgerald Papers. Firestone Library, Princeton.

King, Coretta Scott. Letter to the author, 5 June 1987.

2. An interview

If the interview has been broadcast or published, give the relevant information in the form appropriate for the source of broadcast or publication:

Dole, Elizabeth Hanford. Interview. All Things Considered. Natl. Public Radio. WNYC, New York. 17 Nov. 1988.

If you conducted the interview, cite it:

Jackson, Rev. Jesse. Telephone interview. 9 July 1988.

Dussinger, Prof. Elizabeth. Personal interview. 5 May 1981.

3. A lecture

Give the speaker's name, the occasion, and the date. If the lecture has a title, it may be included.

Richards, Ann. Address. Opening General Sess. Democratic Natl. Convention. Atlanta, 12 July 1988.

Asimov, Isaac. "We'll Never Conquer Space." Lecture. Penn State U. University Park, PA, 9 Sept. 1987.

Technological Sources

1. Computer software

Give the name of the program, the publisher if there is one, the date of publication, and any pertinent information about the operating system or computer for which it was designed. If you know the author's name, it may be included.

Sidekick Plus. Computer software. Borland International, 1987. DOS 3.1, 5-1/4" disk.

Brandt, Richard. C-Turbo Debugger, 1988. OS-2, 3-1/2" disk.

2. Material from a database or computer service

These forms are somewhat problematic, as nearly every service provides different information. However, give the publication information as you would for the form you find (an article, an editorial, a report) and add a reference at the end identifying the service which provided it and the accession or identifying number from the service.

National Commission on Student Financial Assistance. Access and Choice: Equitable Financing of Postsecondary Education. Rept. 7, rev. ed. ERIC, 1987 ED 388 931.

Greene, Bob. "Love and Money." Washington Post 23 May 1988, B2. InfoTrac, 1988 23-D-98742.

APA DOCUMENTATION: GENERAL GUIDELINES

The American Psychological Association (APA) has developed the system of documentation used widely throughout the social sciences. It is explained completely in *Publication Manual of the American Psychological Association,* 3rd edition (1983), which is available in the reference section of your library. This section will outline in general the guidelines used for documenting sources according to APA style.

The sources are listed at the end of your paper in alphabetical order; however, in APA style they are called *References* rather than *Works Cited.* Like MLA style, APA style lists anonymous sources by the first word of the title which is not an article. If sources with multiple authors have the same first author but different second or third authors, they are then separated by the first letter of the second name: Smith, Cochran, and Ruiz comes before Smith, Ruiz, and Weber, for instance.

APA style abbreviates the names of authors, but retains most other elements (titles, names of periodicals, names of publishers) in their entirety. It also emphasizes the date, placing it before the title of the source. Almost all elements in APA references conclude with a period and one space. The special typographic requirements of APA style are explained in this section.

APA style has fewer variations than does MLA style. However, that sometimes means that APA form does not contain an exact model for the source you are trying to reference. Here's the APA's advice on what to do if APA style does not provide an exact model for your source: "Choose the example . . . that is most like your source and follow that format. When in doubt, provide more information rather than less" (117).

Books

1. An entire book

Treat the authors of books as you do the authors of articles in periodicals. If the book is compiled by editors, follow the name(s) of the editor(s) with a space, and the abbreviation *Ed.* or *Eds.* in parentheses. Follow the parentheses with a period. The date of publication is handled as it is for a periodical. Book titles are underlined; capitalize only the first word of the main title and the first word of the subtitle, and any proper nouns, no matter how the typography appears on the first page. Enclose additional information needed for identity and retrieval, such as edition or volume numbers, in parentheses after the title. Follow this with a period.

Give the city, and, if the location is not well known, the U.S. Postal Service abbreviation for the state, followed by a colon and one space, and the name of the publisher, abbreviated as briefly as can be understood. Spell out the names of associations and university presses, but omit superfluous corporate terms like *Inc.*

Cremins, E. T. (1982). The art of abstracting. Philadelphia: ISI.

Strub, R. L., & Black, F. W. (1985). The mental status examination in neurology (2nd ed.). Philadelphia: Davis.

2. A chapter or article in an edited book

When you cite a chapter or article from an edited book, begin with the author, date, and title as above. Then follow the title with a period, one space, and *In,* followed by the name of the editor(s) in normal order, a comma and one space, an underlined book title, a space, and the complete page numbers in parentheses. Follow these with a period, one space, and the publishers' information.

Fishman, M. C. (1981). Coronary Artery Disease. In A. R. Hoffman et al. (Ed.), Medicine (pp. 11–25). Philadelphia: Lippincott.

3. A book with a corporate author

Treat the corporate author as a single author, but do not reverse any of the words in the corporate title:

American Psychological Association. (1983). Publication manual of the American Psychological Association (3rd ed.). Washington: American Psychological Assoc.

4. A multivolume work

Place the volume numbers in parentheses after the title, before the period; if the work was published over more than one year, indicate that in the date parenthesis.

Wilson, J. G., & Finlay, R. (Eds.). (1984–1985) Handbook of hemostasis (Vols. 1–3). Durham: Duke University Press.

5. A translated book

If you used the English translation of a work, cite it and give the information on original publication in parentheses without punctuation:

Hippocrates. (1978). Hippocratic writings (G. E. R. Lloyd, Trans.). Baltimore: Penguin. (Original works published c. 430 B.C.)

6. A book with no named author

Alphabetize such works by the first significant word in the title:

The college bound senior. (1985). Princeton, NJ: College Board Publications.

7. *An edited book*

Tate, G. (Ed.). (1987). Teaching writing: Twelve bibliographical essays (rev. ed.). Fort Worth: Texas Christian University Press.

Periodicals

1. *A journal article*

When you cite an article, give all the authors' names last name first; reduce first names to initials. Use an & instead of the word "and" in references. If there are six or more authors, use *et al.* after the first author's name. The list of names ends with a period and one space.

The date of publication appears after the authors' names in parentheses, followed by a period and one space. If more than one work is cited by these authors from one year, letters are assigned to the articles (which are alphabetized by title): 1985a, 1985b, etc.

The title of the article is reproduced as it appears. Capitalize only the first letter of the main title and the first letter of the subtitle, unless proper nouns appear within the title. Any qualifying information important for identification and retrieval is placed in brackets after the title but before the period (e.g. [Letter to the editor].) The title is neither underlined nor put in quotation marks. It is followed by a period and one space.

The journal title is given in full, in upper and lowercase letters as it appears on the title page, and is underlined; include all articles. It is followed by a comma and a space. Next comes the volume number, also underlined. If the individual issues are separately paginated, the issue number in parentheses follows the volume number without any spaces: 45(3). The volume and issue number are followed by a comma and a space. Finally, the inclusive page numbers are given, followed by a period. You must cite all the pages in APA style; do not use + to indicate discontinuous pages.

Tarvers, Richard C. (1985). Purification of human prothrombin fragment 1 using hydrophobic chromatography. Thrombosis Research, 40, 235–421.

2. *A magazine article*

When you cite a magazine article, treat the author and article title information as you would for a journal article, except that a month or specific date is added to the year. Spell the month out:

Hickson, C., & Selig, W. (1981, October).

Shelly, C., & Seelbinder, E. (1981, September 23).

No volume number or issue number is included, even if one appears on the masthead. Use *pp.* before the page numbers:

Hickson, C., & Selig, W. (1981, October). The psychology of testing. Psychology Today, pp. 78–84.

3. A newspaper article

The newspaper's full title is cited, along with the section of the paper in which the article appears:

> Brody, J. (1987, November 7). Elisa test proves expensive, unreliable. The New York Times, p. 18B.

Unsigned articles are alphabetized by the first word which is not an article; page numbers are indicated with *p.* or *pp.*:

> On idle: The unemployed shun work. (1980, December 5). The Wall Street Journal, pp. 1, 25.

4. A letter to the editor

Cite letters to the editor by typing the descriptive phrase in brackets immediately after a short phrase describing the letter (if no title is given) but before the period following the title.

> Viskup, R. W. (1987, December). In support of mandatory HLV-II testing [Letter to the Editor]. FDA Consumer, p. 3.

5. An abstract

When you cite only an abstract, first give the full reference to where the article originally appeared, then follow with the reference for the source of the abstract in parentheses without following punctuation:

> Misumi, J., & Fujita, M. (1982). Effects of PM organizational development in supermarket organization. Japanese Journal of Experimental Social Psychology, 21, 93–111. (From Psychological Abstracts, 1982, 68, Abstract No. 11474)

Reports

1. An edited report

The authors and date of publication for reports are treated as they are for periodicals. The title follows the form for the title of an entire book; any code number or issuing number follows the title, unitalicized, in parentheses, before the period. The publication information follows that for books; if the report was obtained from a document retrieval service, enclose the retrieval number after the publication information, but do not follow it with a period.

> Wislowski, A., and Kyle, M. (1987). Automobile safety statistics (C-4577). Cherry Hill, NJ: Cigna Foundation.

2. A government report

List the issuing agency as the author, but do not reverse any elements in the issuing agency's name.

National Institute of Mental Health. (1982). Television and behavior: Ten years of scientific progress and implications for the eighties (DHHS Publication No. ADM 82–1195). Washington, DC: U.S. Government Printing Office.

3. A report from a university or private organization

Ben Yishay, Y. (Ed.). (1981). Working approaches to remediation of cognitive deficits in brain damaged persons (Rehabilitation Monograph No. 62). New York: New York University Medical Center, Institute of Rehabilitation Medicine. (NTIS No. P881-298841)

Other Written Sources

1. A lecture or paper given at a professional meeting

Use the form for a magazine article, but replace the publication information with a description of the forum where the paper was presented.

Monroe, D. (1986, June). Genetic investigation of human coagulation proteins. Paper presented at the American Society of Biological Chemists Meeting, St. Louis, MO.

2. A master's thesis or doctoral dissertation

List unpublished theses or dissertations as entire books, but replace the place of publication and name of the publisher with the name and location of the university awarding the degree:

Featherstone, G. L. (1985). Analysis of substrate interactions. Unpublished master's thesis, University of North Carolina, Chapel Hill.

Treat published dissertations and theses as journal articles. If the dissertation was obtained by microfilm, list the University Microfilms reference in parentheses at the end of the reference; do not follow it with a period.

Kyle, J. A. (1988). Effects of musical and dance therapy on autistic teenagers (Doctoral dissertation, Rutgers University). Dissertation Abstracts International, 49, 4370B. (University Microfilms No. 88-25436)

3. A review

Follow the form for a journal article, but include in brackets after the title the phrase *Review of* followed by the title of the work being reviewed.

Gould, S. J. (1988, October) Sticks and bones [Review of Archaeology and Language]. American Speech, 34, 219–220.

Nonprint Media

1. A film, videotape, audiotape, chart, slide, or photograph

Give the names of the originator or primary contributors, the medium in brackets immediately following the title, and the location and name of the distributor.

Peters, L. M. (Producer). (1985). The Coagulation Cascade [Film]. St. Louis: Sigma.

2. A record, tape, cassette recording, or other audio source

Coghill, N., Davis, N., Davis, L., & Burrow, J. (1962). Geoffrey Chaucer: Excerpts from The Canterbury Tales (Record No. PLP 1002). London: Decca.

3. A computer program or program manual

Give, if known, the primary contributor's name as the author. In brackets after the title, indicate the source as a computer program or program manual. Give the location and title of the organization that produced the material, as well as any additional information needed to identify or retrieve it (the latter in parentheses).

Sidekick Plus [Computer software]. (1987). Borland International. (DOS 3.1, 5-1/4" disk)

Brandt, Richard. (1988). C-Turbo Debugger On-Line Manual [Computer Program Manual]. (OS-2, 3-1/2" disk)

PLAGIARISM: FAILURES IN DOCUMENTATION

If you haven't already discovered so, you'll eventually find out that you can get away with nearly anything in the academic environment—experiment with alternate lifestyles, study exotica, read the most obscure works, spend years working on experiments that only twelve people in the world will understand—as long as you tell the truth. That's because the free and truthful exchange of ideas is the very foundation of the academic life. So it stands to reason that failure to tell the truth about your sources—*plagiarism*—is one of the most serious "sins" in the academic community.

It's not just in school, however, that plagiarism causes trouble; in the last several years, one famous musician was convicted of plagiarizing a melody (George Harrison) while another was acquitted of plagiarizing words (Mick Jagger). A famous author published an apology in *The New Yorker* for cribbing from another book review. Several prominent scientists and researchers, including a prominent faculty member at Harvard Medical School, lost their jobs and government funding for publishing work that wasn't theirs. A reporter for the *Washington Post* was fired for making up sources. This is serious business, and you need to take it seriously not only in college but in whatever you do.

Understanding Plagiarism

First of all, what is plagiarism? It is the use—unintentional or intentional—of someone else's words, thoughts, or ideas in your own writing without documentation. It occurs when you misrepresent someone else's work as your own. It doesn't matter if you *really* meant to put a parenthetical reference in and forgot to, or if you intended to "snow" the instructor—it's plagiarism in both cases. Now this may be different from what you practiced in high school, where anything short of photocopying an encyclopedia page and signing your name to it may have been acceptable. But in academic papers the goal is to get you to *use* the material you find; that's why it's important you learn to use it correctly.

As this chapter has emphasized, any material you take from a source, be it quoted, paraphrased, or synthesized, must be documented with *both* a parenthetical reference in the text and a full citation in *Works Cited* or *References*. Attribution by itself isn't adequate documentation, but its presence helps readers believe in your honesty; if you attribute a source, most readers assume you mean to acknowledge it.

Writers sometimes have difficulty working the documentation in; let's look at five original sources and then see how they were used by students. The original material is as follows:

1. [Bertrand] Russell and others, including Albert Einstein, urged full, global disarmament. Instead, the world set about building the arsenals we possess today. The period of grace we had in which to ward off the nuclear peril before it became a reality—the time between the moment of the invention of the weapons and the construction of the full-scale machinery for extinction—was squandered and now the peril that Russell foresaw is upon us. Indeed, if we are honest with ourselves we have to admit that unless we rid ourselves of our nuclear arsenals a holocaust not only *might* occur but *will* occur—if not today, then tomorrow; if not this year, then the next. We have come to live on borrowed time: every year of continued human life is a borrowed year, every day a borrowed day.

   —Jonathan Schell, "The Fate of the Earth." *The New Yorker* 15 Feb. 1982: 45.

2. ". . . nudging Washington was the point of the vote. With an almost quaint, civics-class formality, the antinuclear proposition called on the state legislature to pass a resolution directing Vermont's three-man congressional delegation to urge President Reagan to propose a mutual arms freeze with the Soviet Union. On Friday in the Vermont state legislature, the house passed the resolution, 103 to 26. Similar measures have been approved by six other states, and town meetings in Maine and New Hampshire are about to address the issue. . . ."

   —"Vermont Bans the Bomb." *Time* 15 March 1982: 16.

3. . . . The new movement is far more broadly based; it includes more bishops than Berrigans, doctors and lawyers with impeccable Establishment credentials, archconservatives as well as diehard liberals, and such knowledgeable experts as retired Admiral Noel Gayler, former director of the supersecret National Security Agency, and former

SALT II Negotiator Paul Warnke. Says Rabbi Alexander Schindler, head of the Union of American Hebrew Congregations: "Nuclear disarmament is going to become the central moral issue of the '80s, just as Vietnam was in the '60s." . . .

—James B. Kelly, "Thinking About The Unthinkable." *Time* 29 March 1982:10.

4. . . . Although the Kennedy-Hatfield resolution has attracted only 20 supporters in the Senate, it has a better chance of passage in the House, which last week held an extraordinary eight-hour arms-control debate. The most recent comparable session was a discussion of the Vietnam War in 1969. In somber tones Speaker [of the House] Tip O'Neill spoke of the overabundance of warheads possessed by the U.S. and U.S.S.R. Said he: "What is happening to us? What is causing this madness? I hope and pray the [freeze resolution] will provide the vehicle to stop this arms race." Republican Leader Robert Michel disagreed: "The major issue confronting the world today is not the possession of nuclear arms by the U.S., but the defense and preservation of freedom. If freedom cannot be defended by any other means but by the possession of a nuclear deterrent by the U.S., the possession of such a deterrent is a political and moral imperative." . . .

   —Walter Isaacson, "A Deadly Dilemma." *Time* 12 April 1982:13.

5. "Look and listen to what's going on, to what you see on TV and hear on the radio, see in the newspapers. It's the new rhetoric. Instead of slinging mud in the nuclear arms debate, politicians are playing with people's emotions. It's turning out to be a very valuable campaign technique in some cases, playing on people's fear of being—whooom!—blown up."

   —Professor Peter McLeod, Department of Political Science, Western Jersey University. Personal Interview, 22 April 1988.

Now, let's look at how some students used these sources.

A. A great deal of emotional language is used in the nuclear arms debate, which is called madness, rhetoric, and the defense and preservation of freedom by the various sides. Some people threaten a holocaust, if not today, then tomorrow or this year or the next, while others say nukes are the Vietnam of the '80s. All of this plays on people's fear of being blown up.

B. The controversy over the proposed nuclear arms freeze has been emotional for years. Tip O'Neill used to call nuclear defense madness, while his opponents called it defending and preserving freedom. A leading rabbi called it "The central moral issue of the '80s" (Kelly 10), while Jonathan Schell compared it to the Holocaust. Such highly charged terms blur the issue, even when people talk about it as if they would in a civics class.

C. The opponents in the nuclear arms battle like to use loaded words to impress their audiences. Tip O'Neill called the arms race "madness" while his Congressional opponents called it "the defense and preservation of freedom" and "a moral imperative" (Isaacson 13). Rabbi Alexander Schindler, a leader of the Union of American Hebrew Congregations, compares the political battle to the one that went on in this country at the time of Vietnam (Kelly 10). Jonathan Schell, in the article which led to his best-selling book *The Fate of the Earth,* raised the specter of the Holocaust, predicting it would come "if not today then tomorrow; if not this year, then the next" (45). Politicians, "[i]nstead of slinging mud in the nuclear arms debate, . . . are playing with people's emotions" as "a very valuable campaign technique" (McLeod). It's almost as if advertising copywriters had taken over—the language is almost the same as that used by the smoking/anti-smoking or abortion/birthrights battles.

The first student is in *serious* trouble. Look at all the information cribbed from the sources word-for-word or nearly so: *madness, the defense and preservation of freedom, holocaust if not today then tomorrow or this year or the next, plays on people's fear of being blown up*. This student—intentionally or not—has plagiarized by writing as if the sources' words are his. All of the direct quotes and paraphrases must be indicated by parenthetical references.

The second student has committed a more common kind of plagiarism, by documenting some but not all of the sources she used. The words *madness* and *civics class* were definitely inspired by her source; in fact, the whole second sentence is paraphrased from Isaacson's article and needs a parenthetical reference at the end. If *civics class* is meant to echo the source, she should put quotes around it and give a reference; otherwise she should rewrite that clause to eliminate the echo.

The third student, though, has handled her documentation well. All of her sources are clearly indicated with documentation and attribution. Yet it's also clear *she's* in charge; she has decided what evidence best supports her argument, picked the key phrases to quote, and paraphrased and synthesized the rest. A reader can clearly tell what her ideas are, and how her sources support those ideas. This is what well-documented writing can look like, if you take the time to do it right.

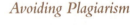

Avoiding Plagiarism

Plagiarism is easily avoided if you keep four points in mind:

1. Leave yourself enough time to do the work right. Most plagiarisms occur because a time-strapped writer was cutting corners. If you really get pressed for time, consider throwing yourself on the mercy of the instructor. Most instructors would far rather give you a little extra

time to put in the correct documentation than to deal with a plagiarized paper.

2. Remember there's no easy way, just the right way. Buying papers, borrowing one from a friend or dorm file or sorority sister may look like an easy out—but it's not *your* writing or research; you're being dishonest, and the odds are strong you'll be discovered anyhow. (Your teacher knows what your style looks like; who wants to forge note cards and drafts for an acquired paper; the sources on purchased papers are frequently fifteen years out of date anyway [recently one instructor saw a paper on the U.S. space program which talked about the *proposed* space shuttle program! You get what you pay for.])

3. Learn to keep good records of your sources, as suggested in Part II of this chapter. It may be tiresome, but no matter what you end up doing with your life—accountant or CEO or doctor or lawyer or farmer or model or Indian chief—you're going to have to do paperwork. Get used to it now.

4. When in doubt, document. If you start early enough you can consult your instructor if questions arise; if the question comes up at 3:00 AM and the paper is due at 8:00 AM, put in the reference and preserve your honesty.

Documentation, then, is a matter of telling the truth—and, as a higher authority reminded us—the truth *shall* set you free.

APPLICATION

1. The following is a list of sources for an anthropology paper on taboos in various cultures. With the members of a group:
   A. Work out the forms in which they would appear for both MLA and APA styles and prepare a *Works Cited* and *References* page. (If there is no specific APA form for a particular kind of source, invent one which conforms to APA style.)
   B. Pick any five and work out the forms, in both MLA and APA styles, for the first and subsequent parenthetical references.
      —A book was published by Doubleday and Co. in New York in 1953. It's called *The People Called Shakers* and it's by Edward Deming Andrews.
      —James Strachey translated Sigmund Freud's classic book *Totem and Taboo.* The translation appeared in London in 1961 and was published by Faber & Faber.
      —An unsigned entry from *Funk and Wagnall's Encyclopedia,* published by them in 1973 in New York, is on the subject *Hinduism.*
      —An article appeared on pages 231–237 of the *Journal of Anthropo-*

logical Research in the summer of 1979. It was by Nancy McDowell; it occurred in volume 35 of the journal; and it was called "The Significance of Cultural Context: A Note on Food Taboos in Bun."

—Leo Trepp published an article in the magazine *Psychology and Culture* in October 1979. It was called "Dreidls and Dread: What Jews May Not Do." It started on pages 19–20, and concluded on pages 86–91.

—The *Washington Post* runs an article in its first section on Sunday, January 1, 1985, called "New Year's Day Around the World." It appears on page 6, in columns 5 and 6. The authors were Linda Bieze and Marisa L'Heureux.

—You conducted an interview with Christopher Davey who is the Avery Professor of Anthropology at the University of Wallamalloo, on November 28th, 1987.

—Margaret Mead wrote you a letter on November 17th, 1987.

—You cite an essay, "The Moon-Eyed Horse," by Edward Abbey. It was originally published in 1968, but you found it in a book Abbey edited called *The Best of Edward Abbey,* published in San Francisco in 1984 by Sierra Club Books.

—An essay by John Dewitt appears in *A Christian Scientist's Life,* a book edited by Ervin D. Canrahan and published in 1962 by Prentice-Hall & Co. in Englewood Cliffs, New Jersey. Mr. Dewitt's essay is called "The Christian Science Way of Life."

2. The following are five references to the film *The Wizard of Oz,* collected by Professor Kathleen Reuter. (If you've forgotten, Ray Bolger played the Scarecrow, Billie Burke played Glynda the Good Witch, Margaret Hamilton played the Wicked Witch of the West, and Bert Lahr played the Cowardly Lion. Mervyn LeRoy directed the film.) With the members of your group, discuss three different paragraphs you could write based on these sources. Which do you find yourselves using most often: direct quotes, paraphrases or synthesis?

A. I was pleased to be working with Ray Bolger because his dancing was so enjoyable to watch. Day after day the shooting went on, and I waited in vain for him to dance. Finally I asked him when his dancing scene would be shot. "Dance?" he said, amazed. "Dance? Billie, that's what I do. I was given a Hollywood contract because I'm a dancer. So of course I don't dance."

—Billie Burke, *With a Feather on My Nose.*
New York: Appleton, Crofts, 1949, p. 301.

B. MGM balked at the guarantee Margaret Hamilton's agent demanded. "I never did work for less than a two-week guarantee, which was not extravagant, not beyond the pale, but respectable.

This time Jess asked the studio for six weeks, and they didn't want to give it to him. They were perfectly willing to guarantee three weeks, but they were adamant about six. And I begged my agent, 'Jess, don't lose this part. You know nobody gives six weeks unless they're sure it's going to be eight. Don't hold out, Jess. I *want* this part.' But he insisted on holding out. . . ." Margaret Hamilton got her six week guarantee. It was, as it turned out, hardly worth fighting about, since she worked on the picture for four months, earning a salary of $18,541.68.

—Aljean Harmetz, *The Making of* The Wizard of Oz. New York: Alfred A. Knopf, Inc., 1977, p. 126.

C. Although [Bert] Lahr wanted to do the picture immediately, Metro wanted his services for only three weeks at $2,500 per week. Lahr balked. "I said I wanted a five week guarantee. When they wouldn't give it to me I said 'The hell with this, I'll go back East and do a show.' I wasn't getting the right parts. Nobody knew what to do with my comedy." It took Metro a month to accept Lahr's terms. Its prediction was significantly unrealistic. Lahr worked five weeks on one number, "The Jitterbug," which never got into the picture. The studio exhibited little understanding of the complexity of the undertaking or of the future of their venture into realistic fantasy. Lahr spent twenty-six weeks as the Cowardly Lion.

—John Lahr, *Notes on a Cowardly Lion.* New York: Knopf, 1975, p. 173.

D. It took six months to prepare the picture, six more months to shoot it, and then a lengthy post-production schedule for editing and scoring. Altogether, *Wizard of Oz* was many months in the making.

—Mervyn LeRoy, *Take One.* New York: Hawthorn, 1974, p. 138.

E. The preparations for that film were enormous. Nothing like it had ever been done before. For Munchkinland, Cedric Gibbons and his team built a model that was one-fourth life size. They fabricated an entire model town, 122 buildings. It took months to finish that alone, and some of the statistics boggle the mind. There were 150 painters, and they used 62 shades of paint. When the full set was built, it covered 25 acres on the studio backlot. We had 65 sets in the picture.

—Mervyn LeRoy, *Take One*. New York: Hawthorn, 1974, p. 138.

3. In your journal write one of the paragraphs you planned with your group in application 2. Take care to document what you take from the sources, and practice different styles of attribution in your paragraphs. For practice, work out both the MLA and APA documentation for your sources.

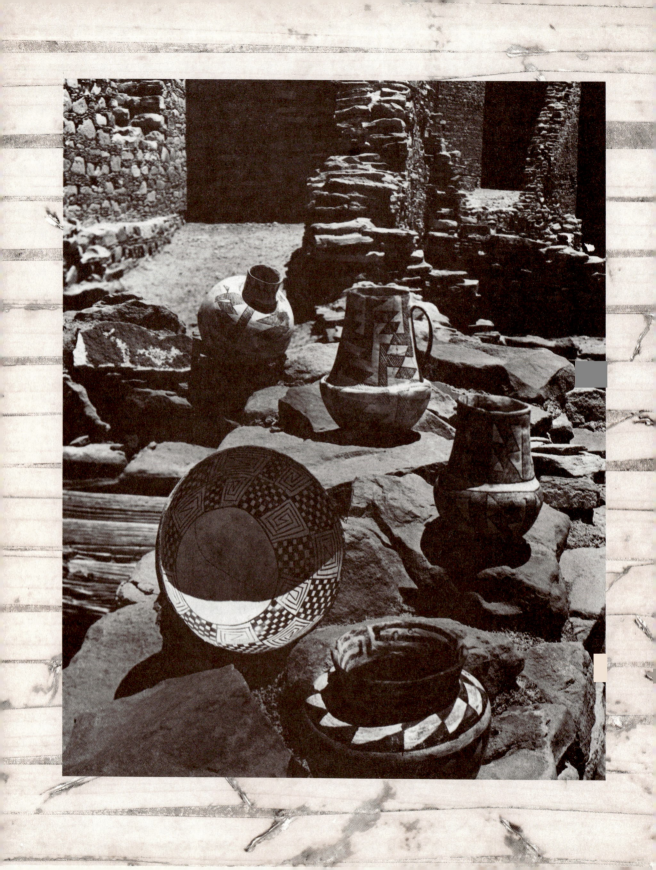

PART 3 Crafting the Portfolio: The Writers' Workshop

As you focus on refining your writing skills, this section will help you

- gain a clearer notion of who your audience is and how they will respond to you
- apply expanded creating techniques to develop useful ideas for academic writing
- practice patterns of organization that grow organically from particular types of theses
- evaluate the internal unity of your writing through examining promise and delivery in practice
- develop the finer points of shaping and completing by examining paragraphs, sentences, and words in depth

In an article written for *The New York Times Magazine* (August 21, 1983), Marvin Minsky—a researcher in the field of artificial intelligence—uses a simple example to explain a major problem in teaching machines how to think: "Nobody's ever tried to make a machine that could build a bird's nest. . . . Instead they're all out there in factories assembling motors. People say, oh yes, the bird gets straws and sticks them in the nest and glues them in. But a motor is designed to be put together. The debris lying around the floor of a forest isn't designed to be made into nests."

What Minsky means is that programmers can make computers and robots do increasingly complicated tasks by writing ever more sophisticated sets of rules to direct their actions. But they have yet to endow their machines with that spark of life which would enable them to take random objects, the sticks and straw on the floor of the forest, and turn the debris into a satisfying piece of work—something as seemingly ordinary as a bird's nest. As you might suspect, there's an analogy here to be made about writing.

People can make thousands of rules about writing and apply them to the millions of situations requiring words on paper or on a screen. Dozens of guidelines can be established for any specific job—composing research papers for example. You need only glance at Chapter 14 to recall how complicated they can be to write. You're expected to include a title page, an outline, an introductory paragraph, a thesis statement, a full discussion, graphs, charts, a concluding paragraph, a *Works Cited* page, and so on. You may be asked to use a minimum of, let's say, ten sources, at least three of which are magazine articles. You must document all information that is not common knowledge, and your documentation must follow a specific form that dictates everything, right down to the placement of commas, colons, and capital letters. The body of the paper itself, your teacher insists, should be lively, filled with examples, and coherent. You should avoid comma splices, unnecessary passives, dangling modifiers, misspelled words—and three dozen other things.

As you can see, people can make a lot of rules about writing. They can make a million. But the rules don't make writing. If you think of writing only as rules, you'll become a robot assembling motors.

What can't be invented are rules for creativity, rules to show you how your ideas fit together, or rules for finding the best word every time. More important, you shouldn't want such rigid guides. Some jobs, perhaps, can be reduced to formulas: repetitive tasks like welding joints or typing statistics. But even the *simplest* writing takes a spark of creativity—the human mind searches the world for the random sticks and straws it will turn into a memo, a research paper, or *Hamlet*.

Offered here instead is what you've seen so far in this book, a description of the process of writing in its richness and diversity. We've already described a process meant to guide you in your interactions with colleagues, teachers, friends, and even adversaries as you attempt to shape a world *in* and *through* langauge. In the chapters that follow you'll enter the Writers' Workshop, a special series of chapters that challenge you to consider subtler, more complex aspects of writing.

The process outlined in Part 1 of this text covered a good deal more than the basics of writing; but as you write, you'll discover that you still need to stop now and then to consult a specialist about certain problems or opportunities. Perhaps you need a clearer notion of "audience" or have a subject that requires more sophisticated treatment at the creating stage. Perhaps you are beginning to wonder what exactly makes a paragraph work well. Or you want a common sense method for checking how well a piece of writing is shaping up—a way of making sentences more energetic, a way of testing the commitments you've made to readers.

All this and a great deal more is filed away in the chapters that follow. Use the materials as you need them or as your instructor directs. But don't consider these chapters as just more rules about writing, more stuff to be crammed into your head after a tough day at school. What's in here can't be learned that way; it will make sense only when you are engaged in writing. So the one requirement of the Writers' Workshop is that you be writing when you drop in. Then these chapters really can make a difference. They can help you and your classmates feel more confident about your work, more professional, more in control. The Writers' Workshop is only paper until you and your classmates do something more with it—but then consider what a creative spark and a little paper might start.

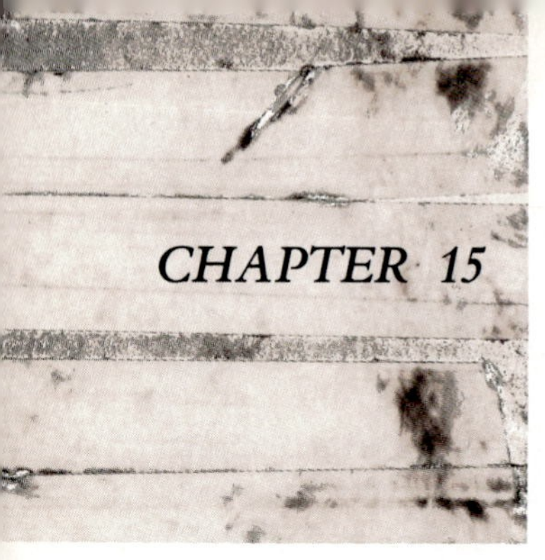

CHAPTER 15

Quick Thoughts on Audience, Talk, and Writing

Audience, as you learned in Part 1 of *Writing,* is a major consideration for any writer beginning a project. That audience is ordinarily made up of readers whom a writer chooses to address—classmates, teachers, professional colleagues, the readership of an editorial page. An audience may also be the readers a writer hopes to find.

In adapting to an audience, particularly an academic one, a writer can be saying many things, not all of them polite: "I think you need to listen to what I've got to say"; or "I want my work to prove to you that I'm someone who should be included in your group"; or "I want you to take my work seriously"; or "I'm different from you, but we can still discuss these issues"; or "I could care less what you think of me or my work." What a writer feels about an audience makes a world of difference in writing—in fact, addressing audience is one way writers represent the world in their writing.

What does this have to do with the process of writing? To some extent, when you are in the creating stage, you may be in a private world, completely lost in your thoughts, totally unaware of everything else. It's like spending a Saturday afternoon reading Agatha Christie or Tom Clancy, building a model, or making a skirt. You suddenly look up and find that it's dinnertime or it has started snowing or you've missed an appointment. You've been absorbed by your project to the detriment of everything else. During the creating stage of writing you may feel the same way initially: nothing outside matters except you and your ideas. It seems a time only for learning what you think about something, for finding ideas, for discovering connections among the things you know already. You explore your mind and consider what you want to say.

Such isolation is valuable as a way of identifying subjects and feelings. But it's like playing basketball with yourself; don't expect thundering achievements. Even in the creating stage, you need an audience—a sense of communication with people who can discuss, challenge, or expand the ideas you have. (It is amazing how long and how easily people can harbor false ideas or questionable assumptions just because they've never tested them in the public arena.) You can begin shaping your sense of audience at the creating stage if you have the confidence to make at least some of your ideas public.

AUDIENCE:
The readers, hearers, or viewers reached by a book, broadcast, or performance; an opportunity to be heard or to express one's views.

PUBLIC:
Open to the knowledge or judgment of all; participated in by the people or community; connected with or acting on behalf of the people or community.

PRIVATE:
Of or confined to one person; not available for public use or participation.

Writing to communicate with someone else allows—even requires—a partnership to develop between you and your reader. You shape what you have to say out of an awareness and a respect for the audience. The audience participates with you by receiving, reading, and engaging with what you have written. If either side of the partnership breaks down, communication does not occur. For instance, if the person receiving the communication attempts to "read" what you have written while talking on the phone or watching television, you can be fairly sure that there is not much communication going on.

What can you do about this? What resources do you, as a writer, have to reach an audience, to break through to that couch potato watching *Letterman* and say "Pay attention!" the way you would if you were in that room yourself?

Not many.

If you are there, talking, you can get your point across by using gestures (try a fist) and facial expressions (look mean) or by changing the tone of your voice. These mannerisms and inflections can have immediate impact on your listener. That person responds in kind—with words, gestures, and particular tones of voice—and this feedback will let you know that you are being understood. (Or not understood—in which case you will make unconscious shifts in your approach until your listener lets you know that you are getting your point across.)

But in writing you have a different situation altogether. What's missing in writing, contrasted to speaking, are all these:

an audience you can see

feedback as you write

any indication about whether your communication is working

any hint about whether your reader finds the communication appropriate

some clue about whether the reader is still interested, or even whether the reader is still reading

Because there is a big difference between the liveliness of talking to someone who is right there and the act of writing on blank paper, it's no surprise to learn that many people don't really think of writing as *commu-*

Writing to Communicate to Oneself	*Writing to Communicate with Someone Else*
The writer	The writer
has to think only of himself or herself	thinks always of another person, the reader
is under no obligation to explain or connect or make clear	must explain, connect, and make clear so that another person can understand what is being said
can be uninterested in whether anyone else would like the writing	considers at all points whether the reader will start and complete the piece of writing
can ramble and roam wherever the mind travels	must decide what exactly is to be communicated to the reader and stick to that
can write things that would be totally insignificant or trivial to another person	cannot waste the reader's time or insult the reader by writing about things, without thinking about their significance to other people
rules supreme	is a partner with the reader in causing communication to happen

nicating at all. But if writing isn't *communicating,* it is merely an empty and unsatisfactory activity to the writer, not to mention the reader.

Why is it important to recognize that writing differs from talking? Because those differences also underscore some of the strengths of writing: its subtlety, permanence, and convenience. A gesture or grimace may emphasize a point now, but the next instant, it's gone, perhaps never to be delivered the same way again. Was it presented exactly as the speaker intended; did he or she have control over the physical movement? Perhaps not with the surety that enables a writer to choose a word like a weapon or to command a sentence to dance.

When the talker is gone, so too is the talk. Of course it's possible to record voices and images easily now, but those images are as fixed as writing. In fact, they are often too fixed: they became historical artifacts rather than living pieces of conversation. A conversation in written words arguably has greater reach and staying power. We still read Plato on good government, but find Franklin Roosevelt on film a bit grainy and hoarse.

Support Systems Available for Speaking and Writing

	For Speaking	*For Writing*
words	yes	yes
paper	no	yes
pen	no	yes
audience present	yes	no
immediate feedback	yes	no
facial expression	yes	no
voice tone	yes	no
pitch	yes	no
loudness	yes	no
ability to switch as you go along	yes	yes
gestures	yes	no
location known	yes	no
situation known	yes	perhaps

Talk is lively, but writing is solid—it's there when you need it. That's because it is remarkably convenient. You can carry writing with you—with all its attendant audiences—in your pocket, briefcase, gym bag. Even on a plane, pull down the tray table, unfold the sheets of paper, and the conversation with your audience begins again, complete and remarkably whole, just where you left off. The experience of addressing an audience couldn't be more real if you had chartered the entire plane for your friends.

APPLICATION

1. Choose someone in your class to be your listener. Then tell that person how to get from one specific place to another specific place—how to get from a building on one end of the campus to a fountain at the other end, how to get from the campus to the bus station, or how to get from the dorm to the new pizza house.

Check how many things besides words you use to communicate this information. Also check how many things the listener does to make the communication clear.

Speaker	*Listener*
_______ used hands to gesture or point	_______ used hands to indicate understanding or lack of understanding
_______ started over again when listener did not understand	_______ showed by look on face that she or he did not understand
_______ asked listener questions in order to determine what information to give	_______ asked speaker questions to clarify information
_______ others	_______ others

2. Now, write out the directions you gave orally just a little while ago, telling someone how to get from one specific place to another. (Use the same two places that you used in number 1.) Give these written directions to someone else in class, not the person you gave the oral directions to.

   Then, make a list of all the ways writing the directions was harder for you than talking. Get as complete a list as you can. If it was easier in any ways, list those too.

   Next, after your classmate has read the directions, talk with that person about how well he or she understood them. Notice what wasn't clear that you thought would be. Notice what you assumed the reader would know that he or she didn't know.
3. Write a paragraph in which you summarize the differences you experienced between telling a message and writing it.
4. Write a paragraph in which you describe the preferences and dislikes of the typical "academic audience." Then, meet with a group of four or five classmates and compare your separate impressions of this special group of readers (the people you write for in college viewed collectively), and agree upon a general description of this academic audience.
5. What characteristics would writing designed to engage an academic audience have? Can you think of any kind of writing that has these characteristics? What are the virtues of such writing?
6. Write a short review (one or two paragraphs) of something you disliked very much (book, movie, TV show, teacher, sports team, designer). In this review, consider how you might convey the verbal

equivalent of facial expressions, voice tones, loudness, and gestures. Have a little fun with the assignment.

7. Now write another, somewhat more serious review, perhaps on something other than what you dealt with in Application 6. Give this more tempered review to a classmate, and ask him or her to read it with appropriate intonation, expressions, and gestures. How does reading the review aloud add to the composition?

CHAPTER 16

Creating: Expanded Techniques

Chapter 2 introduced five basic techniques for exploring a subject—the reporter's formula, brainstorming, listing, chaining, and looping. Like "C" cell batteries, these techniques supply the juice for many different writing situations; they are easy to use, convenient, and simple to remember.

But just as a "C" battery can't power every electrical device (try starting a car with one), neither will the basic methods work for every kind of writing. Sometimes you may need to push your ideas beyond what you can learn from a series of straightforward questions or a brainstorming session. The basic techniques are your starting blocks, but if the race is a long one, you'll need help all around the course. That help can be furnished by a catalog of invention techniques that direct your writing purposefully and intelligently.

FIVE EXPANDED TECHNIQUES

The techniques outlined in this chapter are designed to help a writer move deliberately and creatively toward a conclusion in writing a paper—particularly an academic piece. The Application section suggests how these techniques apply in a variety of situations, including writing term papers, memos, and letters. Some of the methods outlined here—Classical Invention, in particular—are quite complex; others—like Reading and Researching—require time in the library. You can't run through them as easily as *Who? What? Where? When? How?* and *Why?* So it's important to make the effort to discover what's in this chapter; then you can decide which technique is most appropriate for you whenever you are in the creating stage. You need never worry about dead batteries again.

The techniques outlined are Cubing, Track Switching, Classical Invention, Noticing Inside Purpose, and Reading and Researching.

Cubing

Cubing is a technique for swiftly considering a subject from six points of view. The emphasis is on *swiftly* and on *six*.

Often writers can't get going on a subject because they are locked in on a single way of looking at the topic, and that's where Cubing works well. Cubing lets you have a single point of view for only 3 to 5 minutes, then moves you on to the next point of view. When you've finished cubing, you've spent 18 to 30 minutes deliberately varying your point of view. This technique moves very swiftly and is quite structured.

Use All Six Sides of the Cube. Imagine a cube—think of it as a solid block. Now imagine that each side has something different written on it.

One side of the cube says: **Describe it.**

Another side says: **Compare it.**

A third side says: **Associate it.**

The fourth says: **Analyze it.**

The fifth says: **Apply it.**

The sixth side says: **Argue for or against it.**

For the Cubing technique, you need to use *all six sides*. This is *not* an exercise in describing, analyzing, or arguing. It *is* a technique to help you learn to look at a subject from a variety of perspectives. Consequently, doing just one of the sides won't work. Doing just one side is like a mechanical assignment—"describe this picture." You may decide after doing all six sides that you *do* want to describe it; but by then your decision will be meaningful and intelligent, based on your recognizing that describing it will be better than doing anything else. So remember, cubing takes all six sides.

Do each of the six steps in order, spending no more than 3 to 5 minutes on each.

1. **Describe it.** Look at the subject closely and describe what you see. Colors, shapes, sizes, and so forth.

Guides for Cubing

1. Use all six sides of the cube.
2. Move fast. Don't allow yourself more than 3 to 5 minutes on each side of the cube.

destroy many years of tree growth in the woods—in only a matter of hours it can take away that beauty. Fire in the hands of a pyromaniac puts people and buildings in danger of destruction. Fire is too potentially destructive.

A LEGACY FROM PREHISTORIC TIMES

At first, it's a little bit like wandering into a landscape on another planet: the valleys are orange, the mountains tipped with incandescent blue. In that strange clime, bodies and other solid things undergo a kind of metamorphosis; they shimmer in the air. At the valley's base is something primitive, urgent, like ancient dancers swaying in the wind, leaping wild, leaping high, climbing endlessly up the blue-tipped spires. Who, in this eerie terrain, can survive?

Our ancestors survived it—and, for the most part, tamed it, used it for warmth in winter, light during night, fuel for cooking, a place for gathering, a fortress against wild animals.

Fire. Without it, our society would not be what it is.

Our ancestors began thinking about how to harness fire's energy, and we have been thinking along the same lines ever since. Many of our inventions have fire as their basis, in one form or another. Given the existence of fire and the presence of their desire to warm their homes, early humans put those two things together. The wood-burning stove emerged as a refinement of that original idea. Later on came floor furnaces and space heaters. The notion that fire could be used to heat an area was behind these relatively recent inventions as well as their older prototypes.

And then there was cooking. Early humans got the notion that most food tasted better cooked than raw—a notion they probably got when someone's raw dinosaur chop fell into the fire by accident and emerged not ruined but actually tasty. Later on, the wood-burning stove improved on the fire pit as a dual-purpose heating/cooking apparatus. Nowadays, gas and electric stoves, and even microwave ovens, use modern technology to produce heat; and certainly they are safer than an open fire. Yet we need to recall the origin of even our fanciest cooking devices.

The fireplace, too, has its origin in times past. Where once it was the campfire that functioned as a central gathering spot, today the fireplace is where people get together. They cozy up in front of the fire in couples, they congregate in groups for cheery drinks and Christmas carols, and they even cozy up to their thoughts and reveries while staring at the flames. And, as realtors can attest, the presence of a fireplace (all other things being equal) can make or break the sale of a new home. So in both tangible and symbolic ways, the fireplace is a status symbol in our society.

Fire continues to provide us with light, as well. Camping trips depend on kerosene lamps to light the way back to the tent. And the candle, while no longer essential to the persistence of civilization past sundown, still lightens our nights during stormy blackouts, inevitable power failures, or romantic dinners.

In this day of high technology, it's probably worth our while to remember the humble beginnings of so many of our current heating, cooking, socializing, and lighting conveniences. From fireplaces to space heaters, from wood-burning stoves to microwave ovens, fire continues to influence our lives and society, just as it did for our ancestors. We can appreciate the warmth, fuel, cooked food, and beauty that fire offers us. And perhaps our ancestors, once they were warmed and well fed, also had the luxury and ability to appreciate the strange, intense, multicolored beauty of that soaring, wind-dancing, spire-climbing element: fire.

APPLICATION

1. Pick a topic very familiar to you: A family holiday celebration; the personality of your sister, brother, aunt, best friend; the den in your house. *Cube* this subject; you will be surprised at the "new" thoughts you have during this creating activity about a very "old" subject.
2. Using the topic you chose in the looping application in Chapter 2—families, music, women (or men), work, time, or travel—put that same subject through the cubing creating technique. This is one of the best ways to discover what each activity has to offer—how each differs in bringing ideas to your mind. In light of what you discover, what can you say about the kinds of subjects you think cubing might be most useful to you in finding out what you know or think on the topic?
3. Cube one of the subjects you are taking in school: chemistry; world religions; abnormal psychology; European economic policy since WW II; handball for beginners, and so on. What perspectives on the subject does cubing reveal that the course perhaps has not?
4. Cube some societal issue or problem currently in the news: toxic waste; child abuse; Medicare fraud; drug use; disintegration of the family; prison crowding; immigration policy. When you are alone, make a list of the different kinds of papers you might write on the subject. Discuss your list with members of your class.
5. Cube an abstraction valued by some segment of our culture: liberty, freedom, free enterprise, equality, fairness, initiative, honesty, caring, rigor. Use the cubing to give specific features and dimension to the abstraction. Then use it as a way of initiating a discussion of society's values and morals.

Track Switching

When beginning to explore a paper, all writers tend to put down familiar words running along a familiar track. Track Switching actually makes use of this automatic tendency. When it works, track switching can enlarge our world by making us ponder the assumptions and premises of worlds and cultures other than our own. Whether exploring topics as

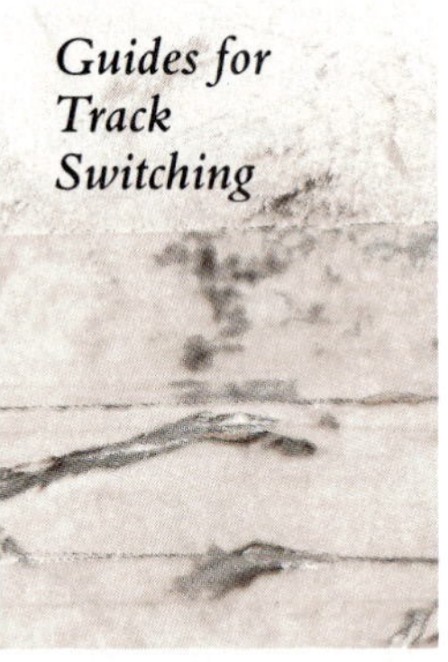

1. Begin by making any statement on your subject.
2. Write on that track for five minutes.
3. Switch to Track #2. Make another statement about your subject, as different as possible from the one you just made.
4. Write on this track for five minutes. Stay on the track.
5. Repeat the process until you have five tracks.
6. Write a fresh idea track, in which you trace the fresh idea you see emerging from or standing around the fringe of the tracks you've just written.

simple as jogging or as complex as human nature, we naturally tend to channel thoughts down familiar paths. We might acknowledge that others may see matters differently than we do, but we rarely take those differences seriously. We suspect, down deep, that our own views are not only right, but also natural and inevitable—as natural as driving in the righthand lane of the street, reading from the top of the page to the bottom, or eating turkey on Thanksgiving Day. Track Switching challenges you to be courageous in your thinking, to engage momentarily with the improbable, to speculate about difference, to say, "What if. . . ?" It makes you realize that not everyone eats turkey on Thanksgiving, speaks the language you do, or shares the same ideas about order, virtue, and beauty.

In school, a willingness to explore differences ought to be a normal part of the process of education. Track Switching should lead to speculation about why *things* (institutions, governments, even people) are the way they are. It also ought to question the process of questioning. In this method of creating, no statement is assumed to be final or right or beyond further exploration. What counts is possibility: the movement from one concept to another.

In order to direct your thinking about a subject in ways that are not automatic, you can begin wherever your mind wants to begin—no matter how ordinary or automatic or unoriginal that place is—and then you can deliberately switch tracks. You can intentionally change the angle or approach you took originally by writing about the subject from an entirely different viewpoint.

Switching tracks works like this:

Begin by making a statement about your subject—any statement. This statement does not have to be anything you believe in or care to be held to. It's just a place to start. Each time you *switch tracks,* you make a new statement about your subject—again, any statement. Each time you change to another statement, you use whatever pops into your head. You do not have to say deliberately the opposite of what you have just written or say something connected with any angle you have taken so far.

As you are writing along on each track, don't worry about saying anything smart. If you can't think of something new to write, just repeat what you have already said until you do think of something else to put on the paper. Don't try to be profound. Just let the words run along the track and see what turns up.

At some point in writing these variations on your subject, a fresh idea will come—something you do want to say.

When you have finished *switching tracks,* look to see what you've uncovered for yourself. Write a capsule *fresh idea track* statement at the conclusion of the last track.

Let's look at this student example to see how *Track Switching* turns up something fresh and interesting on a potentially over-used subject.

STUDENT EXAMPLE & ESSAY Track Switching

Topic: Jogging

Track #1

Jogging is boring.

Have you ever run by yourself around a track? Such monotony. Nothing to see but the same old thing. Putting one foot in front of another. You stay on the track. You do the same thing over and over again. And it's just the same thing day after day. Put on your shoes—go outside—run. No variety, unlike tennis in which the ball might go any way any time it comes toward you. Or football, during which you always have to anticipate what other people are going to do. You don't even have the variety of swimming—you can vary your strokes in that exercise—how much variation can you put into the way you run? Yes, jogging is about as boring as any sport can be.

Track #2

Jogging is an exciting sport.

The challenge of jogging is all inside you. You can make up the game—how long will you run—how far—how fast? When you just start to jog, you can make up a game called "get out the door." The excitement in jogging is internal, not external. You can get excited about how much better shape you're getting into. You can create excitement when you jog by changing your route and changing the time of day you run. You can become very excited about learning how your body functions in different circumstances—how long can you run in the heat—how long in the cold. Jogging is a very exciting sport if you make it that way.

Track #3 Jogging is not something everyone can do.

Babies can't jog. People in wheelchairs can't jog. People riding in cars can't jog. People sitting in chairs can't jog. People with no discipline over themselves can't jog. Anybody not intending to jog or not aware enough to jog or not physically able to jog can't jog. Looks like all other people can jog, if they want to.

Track #4 Jogging is a lifetime opportunity.

One of the great things about jogging is that you never get too old to jog. And by getting in shape at one stage in life and continuing to jog, you can only build on being in shape. Contrasted with some sports, age is not a factor. So you can make it a sport for the rest of your life.

Track #5 Jogging is a national phenomenon.

Why? It is easy to do. You don't need equipment. You can be any age. You can do it on the road. You can run everywhere. It also shows the spirit of individual responsibility and choice. You can be yourself. Is there anything else? Are we learning to be with ourselves more?

Fresh Idea Track

In these five tracks I see this idea emerging: jogging allows people to be in charge of their own lives, to play alone, to take themselves as a project. People can build a sense of control over their own lives by jogging and can display commitment at the same time they are doing something valuable for their health.

Do you see how much more individuality and freshness is potentially present in this *fresh idea track* than was present on the first track the student wrote—a track that began with a very automatic, unoriginal idea? As you read through the tracks you may not see a clear statement of the fresh idea. You may see only the fringe of the idea—a faint shape of the idea—the hints and first appearances. With careful reading, however, you can watch the mind at work, beginning to think for itself rather than just running along on an automatic track.

Here is the essay which resulted from the track switching.

JOGGING TO A GOOD JOB

It was the spring of 1988, my last months in high school. All of us seniors were counting the hours until the senior prom, graduation day—and then freedom. None of us had much to do in our last quarter's classes, so we were mostly breezing through.

Then Coach Marshall had his bright idea. Our boys' physical education class would take up jogging. Serious jogging. We *started* at two miles and went up from there. Coach Marshall had never heard of running some and walking some. He certainly had never heard of starting with something as simple as one mile.

We jogged five days a week, rain or shine. The two miles soon became four and then five and then six. Every day, I hated it when it was time to get out on the track. I hated every step of the way. The only thing I didn't hate was the feeling of pride and satisfaction I had at the end of every gym period when I had completed the jog.

It wasn't until the summer after we graduated that I found out how valuable that last quarter's physical education class had been. I needed a job to help pay my college tuition in the fall. I had been planning all year long to work at the docks, unloading fish and shrimp from the trawlers. High school kids had always been able to get summer work doing that.

When I started making the rounds of the fishing fleet in early June, though, there was no job to be found. The red tide had come in and ruined fishing. Nobody had any jobs on the docks. This meant that I had to find some other work, and in a town where fishing is the main economic activity, that wasn't easy.

I went out every day that first week. Everytime somebody told me "no," I screwed up my courage and just knew that the next place would be better. But day after day I had no success. By the second week I was ready to call it quits—but I really didn't have the choice to do that. I had to find a job.

Then I remembered jogging. I knew that if I had gone out jogging day after day when I didn't want to that I could keep looking for work. I also knew from that jogging class that things didn't have to start out easy, that I was capable of doing more than I would have ever believed if left on my own. I also remembered the satisfaction I got from jogging—even though I would never in a million years let Coach Marshall know that.

I guess the most important realization that really kept me looking for work was that hating something didn't have anything to do with doing it, even doing it well. So, I put what I had learned from jogging to good use. I went out every day that second week and then the third.

It was on Thursday of the third week that I got work in a place where I would probably never have thought to look if things hadn't been the way they were. Almost as a last resort I went to the police station to see if they had any kind of summer work. They did—helping clean the beaches of the dead fish and scum from the red tide. So, I got to do something that made me feel good inside—cleaning up the environment—and something that paid me well.

I guess you might say I jogged myself to a good job.

APPLICATION

1. Choose one of the following subjects for practicing Track Switching:

Parent/child relationships	Religion in America
Staying in shape	Exploring outer space
The value of a college degree	Illiteracy

2. Imagine that you are applying for a job. You need to write a letter about yourself to accompany your resume. Do a Track Switching exercise to discover something fresh to say about yourself and your work capabilities.
3. At one of the commercial times during televised college football games there is a spot on each of the colleges playing that day in the game. Sometimes this college description is about how many students go to the school, what the school is noted for, where the school is located, and so on. Imagine that your school is playing in a game and will be featured in one of the commercial spots. Do a Track Switching exercise to find something provocative and interesting to say about your school.
4. Use Track Switching for one of the following:

   A paper to persuade

   An advertisement

   An annual report for a company

   A resume and an application letter to get a job

5. Try team Track Switching. Divide a group of six to eight people into two teams dealing with the same general subject area. Choose a subject of some immediate interest, preferably one likely to evoke strong opinions; if possible, divide the teams according to their positions. Let one team make a statement and work for a minute or two to support it. Then the second team should respond, switching the track established by the first team, writing for a few minutes as a group and then reading their statement to the first team. Then the first team switches tracks again. But the team's movement should be clearly in a new direction—not a return to their original position. And the response of

the second team should similarly break new ground so that everyone is compelled during the course of the exercise to see their topic and position from innovative perspectives. Use the team exercise as a possible stimulus for a group paper.

Classical Invention

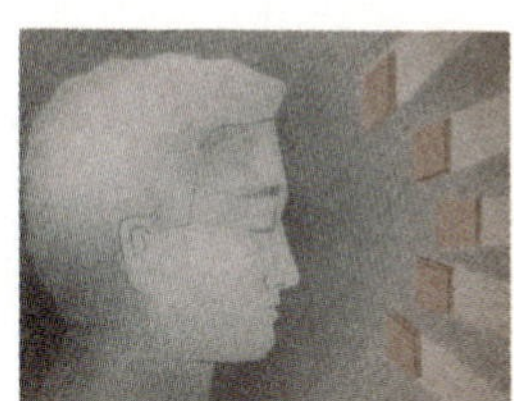

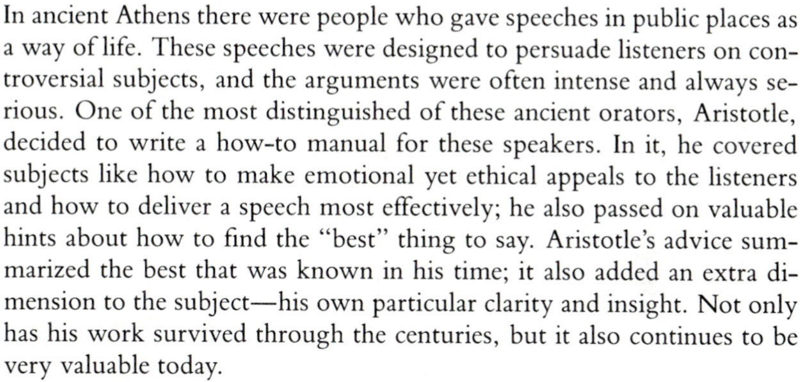

In ancient Athens there were people who gave speeches in public places as a way of life. These speeches were designed to persuade listeners on controversial subjects, and the arguments were often intense and always serious. One of the most distinguished of these ancient orators, Aristotle, decided to write a how-to manual for these speakers. In it, he covered subjects like how to make emotional yet ethical appeals to the listeners and how to deliver a speech most effectively; he also passed on valuable hints about how to find the "best" thing to say. Aristotle's advice summarized the best that was known in his time; it also added an extra dimension to the subject—his own particular clarity and insight. Not only has his work survived through the centuries, but it also continues to be very valuable today.

Although Aristotle's advice was aimed at speakers, not writers, his principles can easily be applied to writing. In fact, many of his original guidelines for organizing and presenting a speech still appear in current textbooks on writing, even though Aristotle himself may not be mentioned. Let's look at Aristotle's original advice on finding ideas, and then see how we can use this for our modern-day purposes.

INVENT:
To conceive of or devise first; originate.
To fabricate; to make up.
(From Middle English *enventen*, to come upon, to find.)

To invent is to extend a system . . . already present in the mind.
—Frank D'Angelo

When you sit down to think of content for a speech, Aristotle suggested, picture your mind as a land with several kinds of places or regions in it. These places (called *topoi* in Greek; "topics" in modern times) stand for different ways to view or think of a subject. Just as each part of the country—desert or mountains—would have a climate of its own, so each area of the mind has its characteristic way of thinking.

Obviously, this is merely a figurative, picturesque way of describing different mental processes—and, of course, Aristotle lived many centuries before modern brain research. Nevertheless, thinking of these different areas of the mind can provide a way of seeing what ideas might occur to you as you examine a subject from each different perspective, or place.

With your subject in mind, look at the *topoi*. The first one is *definition*, so ask questions like "Does this subject *need* to be defined?" "If I define it, what do I do with the definition?" "What if I broke my subject down into parts; what parts do I have?" "Is there any problem about my subject that would be uncovered through defining?"—and so on until you feel you have asked enough questions about defining your subject. Then go to the next topic, *comparison*, and ask the questions that the topic makes you think of. Somewhere along the line, this methodical search for ideas will pay off; you will think of something you want to write.

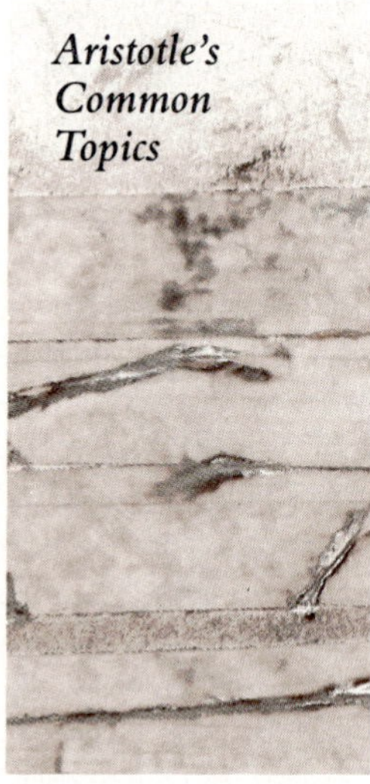

Definition

A. Genus

B. Division

Comparison

A. Similarity

B. Difference

C. Degree

Relationship

A. Cause and effect

B. Antecedent and consequence

C. Contraries

D. Contradictions

Circumstance

A. Possible and impossible

B. Past fact and future fact

Testimony

A. Authority

B. Testimonial

C. Statistics

D. Maxims

E. Law

F. Precedents

After a little practice you'll find that, as soon as you know your subject, you instinctively go directly to the *topoi* that will work best with that subject, the *topoi* most likely to give you ideas. Until then, however, you will need to go through all five *topoi,* checking each to see if, using that perspective, you can think of something to say.

Take the Questions One at a Time, Thoughtfully. Following this rule is the key to using Classical Invention successfully. The power of Classical Invention comes from its relationship to common patterns of human thought. A number of times each day you discover the meaning of a new term (definition), compare one thing to another, consider relationships, decide whether to accept or reject some advertiser's claim, or weigh whether some action will or won't be possible (circumstance). Taking the questions one at a time and thinking about the answers will strengthen that particular way of examining the subject. Be kind to yourself, and allow each new mental skill to develop at its own rate, even if it means slowly, thoughtfully.

Write Brief Notes About the Answers. It will be necessary to have some kind of notes so that you can recreate your thinking later. Also, because our minds range widely—especially on a question that seems particularly appropriate to our subject—we need notes, *outlines, key words* or *phrases* that will let us retrace our thoughts. But keep the notes brief—otherwise, you'll be writing long, sometimes exhaustive (and exhausting!) answers.

If You Get Stuck or Have Nothing to Say, Move On. Although it takes time to come up with an answer for every question—and sometimes several answers—some questions simply don't apply. For example, Question 5, *testimony,* asks what sources you've looked into. That's a useful question if you need ideas on places to look for testimony, or if it jogs your memory about something recently read or heard. But unless you intend to do research on a subject, it's best to use Question 5 as a memory aid and let it go at that. If other questions clearly don't apply, pass them by. Remember, though, that surprises *can* happen; sometimes a seemingly useless question *can* provide a subject.

Reread Your Answers and Star Those That Are Useful in Generating Material, Information, or Energy. Make a list of points that emerged after doing Classical Invention. Your brief notes will have already started to reveal thought patterns connected with each of the *topoi* or questions. By starring the answers that promise the most for your future writing and listing the major points that emerged in this activity, you will be ready to take the ideas to their next level. You can follow up, perhaps by looping, to develop in more detail the questions that hold strong possibility for your writing.

Practicing Classical Invention

Let's practice the creating technique of Classical Invention by using the subject *Romantic Love*. Don't groan! Deliberately choosing an unpromising subject will demonstrate how Classical Invention helps you come up with something to say on any topic. According to the Roman orator Cicero, a speaker relies on three things to find appropriate subject matter: native genius, diligence, and method (or art). As for genius, you're already operating on whatever level of genius you've got; and as for diligence: you owe it to yourself, right? And method, fortunately, is something you *can* learn. That's comforting. Given your level of native genius

Guides for Classical Invention

1. Take the questions one at a time, thoughtfully.
2. Write brief notes about the answers.
3. If you get stuck or have nothing to say, move on.
4. When you finish the questions, reread the answers and star those that are most useful in generating material, information, or energy. Make a list of the major points that emerged from the classical invention.

and your willingness to look for ideas diligently, you can learn methods that will *always* work to find content for your writing.

Here are the questions to use in practicing this modern version of Classical Invention. Go through these questions, seeing what ideas emerge about romantic love. Remember, too, that these same questions will work for any subject you might encounter at a later time.

Definition

1. How does the dictionary define _______?
2. What earlier words did _______ come from?
3. What do *I* mean by _______?
4. What group of things does _______ seem to belong to? How is _______ different from other things in this group?
5. What parts can _______ be divided into?
6. Did _______ mean something in the past that it doesn't mean now? If so, what? What does this former meaning tell us about how the idea grew and developed?
7. Does _______ mean something now that it didn't years ago? If so, what?
8. What other words mean approximately the same as _______?
9. What are some concrete examples of _______?
10. When is the meaning of _______ misunderstood?

Comparison

1. What is _______ similar to? In what ways?
2. What is _______ different from? In what ways?
3. _______ is superior to what? In what ways?
4. _______ is inferior to what? In what ways?
5. _______ is most unlike what? (What is it opposite to?) In what ways?
6. _______ is most like what? In what ways?

Relationship

1. What causes _______?
2. What is the purpose of _______?
3. Why does _______ happen?
4. What is the consequence of _______?
5. What comes before _______?
6. What comes after _______?

Circumstance

1. Is _______ possible or impossible?
2. What qualities, conditions, or circumstances make _______ possible or impossible?
3. Supposing that _______ is possible, is it also desirable? Why?
4. When did _______ happen previously?
5. Who has done or experienced _______?
6. Who can do _______?
7. If _______ starts, what makes it end?
8. What would it take for _______ to happen now?
9. What would prevent _______ from happening?

Testimony

1. What have I heard people say about _______?
2. Do I know any facts or statistics about _______? If so, what?
3. Have I talked with anyone about _______?
4. Do I know any famous or well-known saying (e.g. "A bird in the hand is worth two in the bush") about _______?
5. Can I quote any proverbs or any poems about _______?
6. Are there any laws about _______?
7. Do I remember any songs about _______? Do I remember anything I've read about _______ in books or magazines? Anything I've seen in a movie or on television?
8. Do I want to do any research on _______?

APPLICATION

Begin. Go through each of the questions in each of the *topoi* groups, using *Romantic Love* as your subject. Write your answers to the questions in brief notes. If other questions occur to you, make a note of them, too. If you get stuck or have nothing to say on any particular question, move on. When you've finished all the questions, reread your answers and star the ones that you think will be the most useful in giving you something to say on the subject of romantic love. Make a list of the major points that emerged during classical invention.

At the end of this process, you will have used several ways of thinking to consider your subject. Having a method like Classical Invention to know how to switch deliberately from one thought pattern to another lets you do a systematic, *thorough* investigation of your subject and arrive at ideas that have depth and potential for your writing.

Let's look at what one student discovered by using the Classical Invention creating technique.

STUDENT EXAMPLE & ESSAY
Classical Invention

Topic: Going Back to School as an Adult

Definition

1. How does the dictionary define this?
   (I have to find one word for this concept. The closest I can come up with is "reentry" student.)
   Reentry: (1) A retaking possession;
   (2) a second, or new entry;
   (3) a playing card that will enable the player to regain the lead;
   * (4) the action of reentering the earth's atmosphere after *travel in space*.
2. What earlier words did _______ come from?
   Middle English *entre,* Old French *entree*—both mean "to enter."
3. What do *I* mean by _______?
   Going back to something after an absence. Doing something else in between.
4. What group of things does _______ seem to belong to?
   Animals that go back to a certain place—birds migrating south in winter, salmon swimming upstream to spawn; the prodigal son in Bible story.
   How is _______ different from other things in this group?
   Different from animals—for them it's biological; for people, re- * entry is a *choice.* Different from prodigal son—reentry students didn't necessarily do anything wrong by leaving.
5. What parts can _______ be divided into?
   Older students who return, after their kids are grown, to continue their original path of education; older students who return in order to change careers; younger students who took time out, or * dropped out, to travel or work, etc. and are *ready to be serious about getting an education.*

6. Does _______ mean something now that it didn't years ago? If so, what?
   What's new is that the term "reentry student" applies now to many students. There are enough reentry students that this group of people gets to have a category all its own.
7. What other words mean approximately the same as _______?
   Return; come back; (and, making "re" words of synonyms for
   * "entry") repenetrate; repierce, *reprobe.*
8. What are some concrete examples of _______?
   Me! (and many others)
9. When is the meaning of _______ misunderstood?
   When people accept a stereotype instead of finding out the facts. Many people think the typical reentry student is in her mid-40s, has two boring, obnoxious teenage kids, and has kept her mind totally submerged in dirty dishwater since leaving school.

Comparison

1. What is _______ similar to? In what ways?
   It's similar to coming home, coming back to church, attending a family reunion—returning to something larger than just yourself,
   * something that connects you to others. Being *welcomed back* into the fold.
2. What is _______ different from? In what ways?
   It's different from being a rebel; from being a provincial who never ventures out of your territory; from being in a rut; from giving up.
3. _______ is superior to what? In what ways?
   * *Superior to never having left*—leaving for "real life" gives you valuable life experiences not obtainable by perpetual students, and gives you a chance to clarify what you really want to learn. *Superior to never coming back*—reentry students are more *mature,* and they learn in more mature, goal-directed ways.
4. _______ is inferior to what? In what ways?
   Inferior to going all the way through school when quite young, and thereby having the knowledge and degree to use earlier (more expertise, professionalism, status, money in one's career).
5. _______ is most unlike what? In what ways?
   (I'm blanking here) Most unlike a 16-year-old college freshman; a moss-covered stone (opposite of a rolling stone); an anti-intellectual.
6. _______ is most like what? In what ways?
   Most like a rolling stone; a ripe fruit; a Talmudic scholar; a knight seeking the Holy Grail; a smart cookie.

Relationship

1. What causes ______?
   Eagerness to learn; dissatisfaction with present job and/or state of knowledge; boredom; curiosity.
2. What are the effects of ______?
   * Excitement; disorientation; *fears of inadequacy; feelings of confidence;*
   * appreciation for learning; *appreciation for one's own experience.*
3. What is the purpose of ______?
   To get knowledge of a particular field of study; to get a degree.
4. Why does ______ happen?
   It happened to me because I only discovered my real interest after spending many years doing something else.
5. What is the consequence of ______?
   A degree; new job skills.
6. What comes before ______?
   Leaving school; other jobs (including the job of homemaker and mother).
7. What comes after ______?
   Staying in school; persisting; getting the degree.

Circumstance

1. Is ______ possible or impossible?
   Possible.
2. What qualities, conditions, or circumstances make ______ possible or impossible?
   Having a high school diploma; having decent grades your last
   * stint in school; having time and *money* to go back to school; having good babysitters (and/or a spouse, parent, friends who'll sit and maybe even cook).
3. Supposing that ______ is possible, is it also feasible? Why?
   Yes, for me. I have the time, the money (student loan), and a husband who is willing to do childcare and defrost TV dinners.
4. When did ______ happen previously?
   Never for me. For others, it's probably been happening since there have been colleges. (A guess—I don't know for how long, but certainly it *has* happened before.)
5. Who has done or experienced ______?
   Many people from all walks of life, all races, all ethnic backgrounds, both sexes.
6. Who can do ______?
   Anyone with a high school diploma, decent college grades (if they
   * went to college), and the *motivation* and stamina to return to school.

7. If _______ starts, what makes it end?
   Getting the degree, or dropping out again.
8. What would it take for _______ to happen now?
   For people to want to return to school, and for them to be accepted by a school of their choice.
9. What would prevent _______ from happening?
   Thinking it's too hard to get accepted, to get financing (loans, etc.), to keep up with the work; undefined learning and/or career goals; lack of interest.

Testimony

1. What have I heard people say about _______?
   That it's sometimes hard at first; that it can take time to adjust;
   * that in some ways it's *easier* to be in school as a reentry student than it was the first time around.
2. Do I know any facts or statistics about _______? If so, what?
   I don't know any exact figures, but there are many more reentry students now than there used to be. Some schools even have "over-40" programs for reentry students.
3. Have I talked with anyone about _______?
   Yes—several friends who've done it; college deans and advisors; my family.
4. Do I know any famous or well-known saying about _______?
   "It's better the second time around."
5. Can I quote any proverbs or poems about _______?
   "'Tis better to have loved and lost than never to have loved at all." (This isn't exactly on the subject, but if you substitute "gone to school" for "love" it sort of works.)
   "Experience is the best teacher."
   "A little bit of knowledge is a dangerous thing."
   "I am woman; I am invincible."
6. Are there any laws about _______?
   You have to pay the tuition, attend most of the classes, turn in assignments on time, take the exams.
7. Do I remember any songs about _______?
   "The Whiffenpoof Song"
   "Sweetheart of Sigma Chi"
   "Sock Hop"
   "Varsity Rag"
   "Teacher's Pet"
   Any books or magazines I've read?
   Books: *Ella Price's Journal*, by Dorothy Bryant. Magazines: Prob-

ably some articles in *Ms., Redbook* (don't remember distinctly).
Anything I've seen in a movie or on television?
No, but I sure would like to. Maybe Shirley MacLaine would play the lead . . . ?

8. Do I want to do any research on ______?
Not really, although maybe a few statistics on how this population has grown in the last ten or so years wouldn't hurt.

Major Points That Emerged

- A reentry student has been somewhere and done something in between (something of value, although student may not see this right away).
- Going back to school as an adult is a *choice*. Kids who go to college straight from high school aren't always acting from pure, voluntary choice. Older people usually are.
- Reentry students are serious about getting an education. They usually are there for more defined reasons (having to do with career or what they wish to learn) than for ambiguous or social reasons.
- "Reentry" carries a subtle stigma, as if people have been wasting time in between, or doing nothing important, or didn't have what it took to persevere through college for four straight years in their teens and early twenties. But in fact this usually isn't true; reentry students are often more mature, more insightful, more able to learn, more able to make practical use of what they learn.
- "Reentry" means *reprobe*—to explore again, this time from a different vantage point.
- Does one reenter school as a prodigal son (sinner) or as a confident, valuable person who is shifting focus? Does the reentry student feel stigmatized or welcomed back?
- There is a value in having left school, and in coming back to school.
- Reentry students don't always appreciate their own contributions to the teacher and the rest of the students. They need to see and appreciate the value of their life experiences in a school setting.
- It's harder to be in school when an adult, in some ways, but in other ways it's easier.
- Motivation gets you through obstacles in coming back to school.

GOING BACK TO SCHOOL AS AN ADULT

Some people may think of reentry students as befuddled-looking, middle-aged women wandering dazedly around a campus, trying to keep their books in their arms and a mess of facts in their brains, while all around them younger students in designer jeans and off-the-shoulder sweatshirts cavort in the cafeteria and still manage to pull straight A's. But this is the Hollywood, Grade-B view of adults who come back to school. In truth, the situation is very different.

There are two categories of reentry students: those who never completed their undergraduate work and return to get a B.A. or B.S., and those who completed their undergraduate work, spent time out of school, and are now coming back to graduate school. The majority of adults in either category return to school not because they couldn't make it in the world—often, they have been quite successful as lawyers, homemakers, teachers, secretaries, and social workers—but because the experience of living and maturing has helped them realize what they really want to do with their lives. As one woman in her late thirties said, "When I was eighteen and starting college, all I knew was that I *didn't* want to get a blue-collar job, I *didn't* want to be different from my friends (all of whom were going to college), I *didn't* want to be out in the world yet, forced to fly before my wings were quite dry. However, I didn't know what I *did* want—being in college was just marking time. So I dropped out—I went out into the wide world, tested my wings, fell down some, and flew some. Now here I am, ready to be serious about school."

This is a common story. Many people, who left school (or who stopped with their B.A. or B.S.) because they didn't really have the motivation to continue, find that when they return to school as adults it's by *choice*. The act of *choosing* to return to school seems to go a long way: Reentry students are full of enthusiasm, motivation, stamina, and a wealth of life experience that can enrich discussions of many subjects, in many classes.

Unfortunately, reentry students don't always realize their own value. They sometimes feel too old (compared with energetic teenagers), too insignificant ("*All* I did was raise two children."), too rusty ("I haven't taken an exam in 14 years—I've forgotten how!"), and too disoriented ("How can I tell one classroom from another? They all look exactly alike!"). This "reentry shock" afflicts even very bright and competent students. It's a bit like the "culture shock" experienced by travelers returning to their own country: Suddenly the native language sounds foreign, the customs seem odd, the normal routines seem, at best, anthropological. So during this reentry period, adult students must bridge the gap between their earlier experiences of school and the nonschool, adult world they have been living in. Experiencing confusion, anxiety, and feelings of inadequacy during this period is not pleasant; but it is normal, and it eventually does pass.

One thing that helps to shorten this awkward period is for reentry students to realize that for all they have yet to learn, there's a lot they already know. This knowledge isn't limited to facts, either. Reentry students tend also to know:

1. *The relative importance of things.* For example, they can now tolerate getting a B rather than an A. The "failure to be perfect" is no longer a cause for thoughts of the Foreign Legion.

2. *How to learn what they don't yet know.* Teenagers don't have the experience to evaluate what is and isn't important to them. This can make being in school an overwhelming experience; young students may *accept* all the information (and end up feeling stuffed or confused) or *reject* it all (and end up feeling angry and isolated). Adult students, however, have lived through, and survived, real-life events—from losing loved ones through getting the mortgage paid. This experience of surviving the normal vicissitudes of life can make adult students more able to take in and evaluate new information.
3. *How to pursue a goal.* Nobody forces adults to come back to school; reentry students are inner-directed. They already have some idea of what they want and how to get it. School isn't molding shapeless clay—it's helping the adults refine and challenge their already developed notions and fill in the holes.
4. *How to satisfy themselves, instead of worrying about what others think of them.* Teenagers inevitably care so much about how others see them. While this preoccupation never goes away entirely, by adulthood it has receded into a more realistic perspective. Adults tend to be more concerned about whether an activity satisfies them than about whether it gets the approval of someone else. This inner-directedness makes it easier to be in a classroom, to risk offering the wrong answer, to study with interest, to write papers, and, in general, to have the experience of becoming educated.

So adults who go back to school have both a harder time and an easier time. And they enrich not only themselves by being back in school but also the people around them—by their experience, their sense of priorities, and their ability to hone in on their goal. Reentry students have nothing to be ashamed of; they are not prodigal children. We do ourselves a service by welcoming them back into the fold.

APPLICATION

1. Using the topic questions for Classical Invention, explore one of the following subjects to see what might be said about it:

   budget deficits (local, state, federal)
   required courses in college
   labor unions
   prayer in school
   loneliness
   contemporary architecture
   using animals in research
   sexism

the NCAA and college athletes

neo-Nazi groups in the U.S.

Use the student example in this section as a guide to your work.

2. Use the method of Classical Invention in a group to develop a possible subject for a collaborative paper or to provoke discussion. Pick one of the subjects listed above or agree on a subject within the group.
3. Following the group work in #2 above, discuss what occurred as you used the Classical Invention technique. Was there a point where the group suddenly became interested in the subject? What question sparked that interest? What part of the technique evoked the most surprising responses?

Noticing Inside Purpose

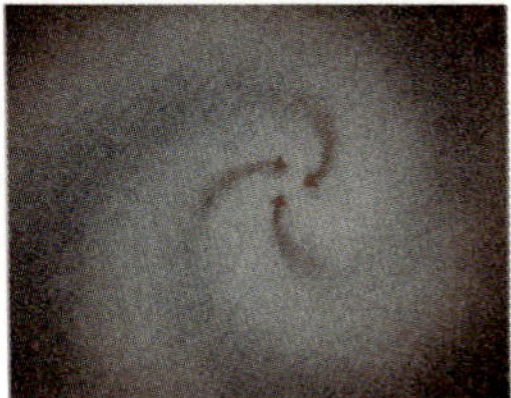

If you were building a birdhouse, someone has said, you would have more thoughts about carpentering than you would if you were putting together a stamp collection. This is how the human mind works—where there is a particular purpose or focus, the mind pulls in thoughts, sights, ideas, memories, and connections that are related to that purpose. The purpose—the focus—serves as a magnet for what your mind and eye no-

Guides for Noticing Inside Purpose

1. Buy a small (pocket-size) notebook and label it "Notebook to Record Noticing."
2. Write the purpose and subject of the things you are going to be noticing about (the subject of your future writing) at the top of the page. (Important: This is the purpose of the assignment, not the purpose of the paper you will write later. You won't know the purpose of the paper itself until after you've done the creating technique.)
3. Keep a running record of everything you notice that is connected with the subject on which you are going to write.
4. Every time you notice something new connected with this subject or assignment—or have an idea associated with it—turn to the next page in your notebook and record the observation or idea.
5. At least once before beginning the discovery draft of the shaping stage, deliberately go on a "noticing expedition." Have as your express intention to observe and watch your subject and to take notes of your watching and observation.

tice. You can deliberately use this tendency of the mind to your advantage: getting ideas for something you want to write.

Noticing Inside Purpose works like this: imagine that your assignment is to write about the economy of a Third World country. You would set up Noticing Inside Purpose as part of the creating stage for this assignment. Setting up involves, at first, simply writing the purpose of your assignment at the top of the page. Then, over time, you fill up the page with things you noticed as you went about your daily activities. The list might include such things as:

1. I noticed two articles in the newspaper today about the economy in Argentina and Brazil. (I've cut these out to read later.)
2. I noticed there was a guy from Brazil in my geometry class. I've set up a time to meet with him tomorrow to discuss the economy of his country.
3. I noticed today, much to my surprise, that the school library subscribes to a Brazilian newspaper that is in English!

This creating technique allows us to pay attention to and keep a record of what usually goes unnoticed. When we have a particular purpose, we naturally and automatically see things connected with that purpose that we never would have noticed otherwise.

You can use Noticing Inside Purpose intentionally. Set aside *X* time on *X* day to go out noticing or observing your subject, and then record your observations on paper. When you set out to notice things related to your subject, you will be surprised just how much there is to see. Noticing is a simple act of the mind, yet one worth cultivating.

The creating technique Noticing Inside Purpose lets you hold onto observations in written form—observations that you otherwise might lose record of. The notes serve as a structure to hold the particles of information, ideas, plans, and possibilities for this piece of writing.

The Best Uses of Noticing Inside Purpose:

For projects that you have several days or longer to mull over, plan for, and think about

For writing assignments that require you to make fresh connections with, see relationships among, or pull together your own version of the information

For topics that, at the outset, suggest nothing about which you already know that relates to them

For writing assignments that require description

Examples:

Writing a paper that describes a particular location, object, or work of art

Preparing a research paper or report

Doing a synthesis article or report

Writing on a subject from a personal viewpoint, from personal experience, or from exposure to the subject or topic

Preparing a technical or scientific report

APPLICATION

1. Practice this creating technique even before you are assigned a paper in advance. You will be astonished at how many things seem to show up when you deliberately focus on one particular topic. Choose a purpose like one of these:

   Finding out how to save on energy bills

   Discovering what the current styles are in clothes

   Learning about Middle Eastern cooking

   Knowing what stocks are hot now on the stock market

   Start keeping your Noticing Inside Purpose notebook, even though you are not planning to write a paper on this subject. It will seem almost like magic how many times you see and hear something about this subject—just because you have set yourself a purpose that focuses what passes through your awareness.

2. Use this creating technique for a paper you need to write for some other class. Test the technique out on far-fetched subjects like "the beginning of the Second World War," or "styles of architecture in medieval Europe" and discover how and what you notice even on topics like these.

Reading and Researching: R&R

You already know that reading and researching are necessary for many types of writing, particularly research papers and technical reports. However, you may be surprised to think of these common activities as techniques for the creating stage of the writing process, not as something you do *prior* to the writing process. Once you start thinking of reading and

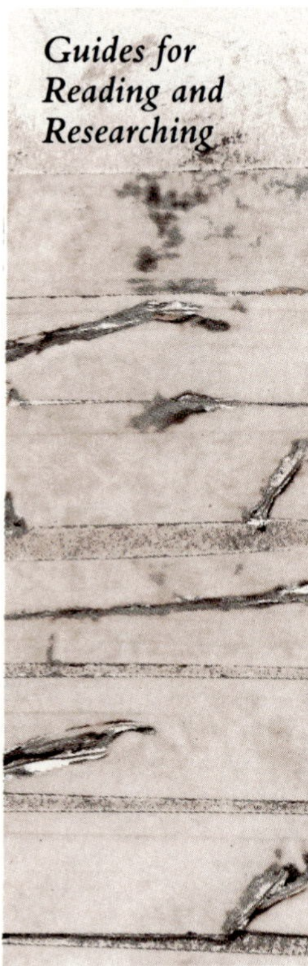

1. Consider each time period you spend reading and doing research as a distinct creating session for the paper or report you are going to write.
2. For each R&R session, answer both the advance and the concluding questions in writing.
3. Keeping a running log for these R&R sessions:

   R&R Session #________

   Date ________

   Advance Questions:

   What is my specific purpose or intention in doing this R&R today?

   How is this R&R session I am about to do a part of my writing the paper or report?

   Concluding Questions:

   What specific ideas do I now have for writing my paper?

   What is the big win out of this R&R time period—what did I come upon in the R&R that will probably be the most valuable in my writing?

   What are at least five points/facts/ideas I got out of this R&R period for my writing?

researching as part of the writing process, your mind will start connecting ideas long before you sit down to do a discovery draft.

The time frame for Reading and Researching is based not on "This is separate from the term paper or report I have to write" but rather on "This is actually part of the writing of my term paper or report."

To set up reading and researching as a technique, put your R&R (as well as the note taking that is part of it) into a "writing the paper framework." To do this, ask yourself questions immediately before doing the reading and researching, and then again afterwards. So the R&R technique looks like this:

"Keep on going and the chances are you will stumble on something, perhaps when you are least expecting it. I have never heard of anyone stumbling on something sitting down."
—Charles Kettering

Questions to Answer Prior to Starting Reading and Researching

1. What is my specific purpose in doing this reading and researching?
2. How is the reading and researching I am about to do a part of writing the paper or report?

Questions to Answer Immediately After Reading and Researching

1. What specific ideas do I now have for writing my paper?
2. What is the big win out of this period of reading and researching—what did I come upon in the R&R that will probably be the most valuable in my writing?
3. What are points/facts/ideas I got out of this reading and researching for my writing?

The power in Reading and Researching is that, from the start, you relate each reading and researching period to writing the paper. Each R&R period will yield different types of information, some more valuable than others; you identify the information that is most valuable. You may not hit the jackpot every time you read or do research, but putting these activities inside a creating technique will ensure that you get the most out of every session. (For an excellent demonstration, see the section on writing a research paper earlier in this book.)

The Best Uses for R&R:

For getting optimal value from your reading and researching activity

For beginning a research or term paper

For structuring your reading and researching as a first stage in the writing process

For checking as you go to see where your reading and researching is leading you

Examples:

Writing a term paper or research paper

Writing a technical report

Doing the research for an article or factual essay

Writing a speech

Gathering material for a long-range project or for projects with undetermined or indefinite time lines

APPLICATION

1. Think about how unfocused and time-consuming your library research may have been in the past. Then, to prove to yourself, even

before you have a research paper to do, that there has to be a better way, do one Reading and Researching session on a topic like this:

A person I admire

A current career interest

Sports in the 1800's

A place you would enjoy going on vacation during spring break

Be able to discuss questions like these with your classmates when the activity is complete: how was this creating technique a time-saver? In what ways did focusing happen even in this first visit to the library? In what direction did this first Reading and Researching point me for my next visit to the library?

2. Use Reading and Researching to prepare a laboratory report in a science, computer, or engineering class—even though all your research is going to be done in the laboratory or in your room (rather than the library). How does this creating technique work with material that is in your text or other supplementary sources?

SUMMARY

Between this section and Chapter 2, you have now practiced several distinctly different creating techniques; you may already have your favorite among them, the one that works best when you are searching for ideas. You will certainly have noticed the ways the techniques are different. Some work like a fishing expedition—you lower a net and catch whatever thoughts you have on the subject. Some work like a reminder or checklist to help you think of things you already knew but had forgotten. Some actually let you invent something new by rubbing together thoughts, ideas, and information you already had to come up with new combinations, insights, and relationships. Some work best when you don't have a single thing to say; others work best when you already have several ideas on a subject and need to decide which is the most promising. Some of the techniques are unstructured and loose; some are tightly controlled. No single one is inherently better than another.

Learning what each technique will do for you may be trial and error at the beginning, but as you become more familiar with the ways to create, you will develop a feel for which to use when.

The important thing to remember is that there is a *creating stage* in the writing process—that you need to let yourself hunt for ideas before you begin writing a paper. Now you know how to get started, no matter what the writing task or assignment is. You know something you *can* do. You know how to get *some* words on the page. You will never again have to say, "But I can't think of anything to say. I don't know how to start."

Because now you do know how to start. *You start by creating. You don't start by writing the piece of writing itself.* In fact, you don't worry at all in this stage about the essay or report or whatever you must write; you just set yourself to have ideas on the subject of that essay, report, or whatever by using a creating technique.

And there is a bonus for you when you create—even if you never write the essay or the report, even if you never go a step further, the creating activity clarifies by letting you see and know something. During the creating stage you find out what you think about this subject, what you believe, what you know, what questions can be asked about it. What is more, you not only come to *know* the subject by writing about it, but you also have *words on a page* to use as a starting point for sending your ideas to someone else. The *creating stage* serves both purposes. You find out what you know, and you get ideas that you can shape into a coherent message for another person.

APPLICATION

Taking the same subject through more than one creating technique is an excellent way to see which techniques you find most beneficial for which kinds of subjects. To get practice in knowing the characteristics of various creating techniques, choose one of the following topics and *run it through two different creating techniques.* (Review Chapter 2 as necessary.) Be ready to discuss with the class what you discovered in this process, what one technique did that the other didn't, which you found most beneficial, what idea(s) you came up with that you could write on if you were required to do so, and so on.

1. **Choose One**
   Getting along with (parents, children)
   Finding work
   Problems of growing up
   What you want in a relationship

   Choose Two
   Cubing
   Looping
   Classical Invention
   Chaining
   Track Switching

2. **Choose one**
   Things wrong with holidays
   A skill you have and are proud of
   A problem you had and how you solved it
   Ways people act that you don't like
   A movie you just saw
   A book you just read
   Soap operas

   Choose Two
   Cubing
   Looping
   Classical Invention
   Reporter's Formula
   Brainstorming
   Writing a List

Technique	*Characteristic*	*Works Best For*	*Strengths*	*Weaknesses*
Cubing	fast-moving, structured; combination of fishing expedition and planned search	considering subject from six points of view to set up a variety of perspectives	"loosens the soil" of your mind; corresponds to way people usually think about subjects; shows writer perspective most likely to yield ideas for the essay	doesn't work on all classroom assignments; may not give enough depth
Track Switching	structured; changing direction on the same subject many times	breaking habit of writing what is on top of head; finding a fresh approach for understanding your own position by probing opposite ones	lets you begin with any quality of thought, from mundane to profound; lets you look at the same subject from a variety of angles; moves quickly	requires toleration for surface thinking for a time; dependent on coming up with five different points
Classical Invention	structured; a planned search; goes into depth	exploring regions of the mind; handling subjects that benefit from logical, planned investigation	well-developed; traditionally useful, corresponds to human thought processes	can result in mechanical writing or writing that is more interesting in form than in content; takes considerable time

3. **Choose One**

   A landscape that appeals to you

   A figure from history who inspires or repels you

   How writing assignments are useful to you personally

   What people have in common with animals

   An incident that molded your life

   Choose Two

   Cubing

   Noticing Inside Purpose

   Looping

   Reading and Researching

   Track Switching

Technique	*Characteristic*	*Works Best For*	*Strengths*	*Weaknesses*
Noticing Inside Purpose 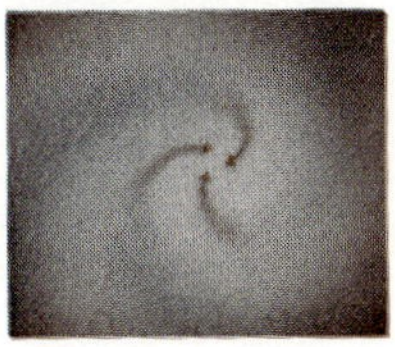	structured; increasing how much you notice on a subject by recording what you notice	producing fresh connections; generating material on subjects you have not thought much about; subjects to be explored over time	lets you pin down and preserve back-of-the-mind observations that you might otherwise ignore; allows ongoing creating in any setting	not good for in-class assignments; requires availability of notebook at all times; might restrict your awareness of other topics
Reading and Researching (R&R) 	structured; using the usual R&R time prior to writing a paper as part of the creating stage answering defining-type questions before and after doing the R&R	getting most value from R&R; getting a head start by using R&R as creating for the final piece of writing	can help you feel very productive; makes the usual R&R process more interesting and focused; makes each R&R period a distinct event	may force too much structure too quickly; adds another step to research time

Discussion

1. What is the direct connection between the writing you do during the *creating stage* and the completely finished final essay?
2. What are some possible disadvantages of creating techniques?
3. What arguments would you give to a friend who said he or she didn't have to do a *creating stage* for a piece of writing?
4. What state of mind should you be in as you near the *creating stage?*
5. Which technique works best for a subject you already know something about? Which works best for a subject you are absolutely blank on?
6. When would a quick technique, such as a list, work best?

Form and Pattern

Nobody is sure exactly how writers decide the form their writing will take. Often a writer doesn't consciously select a plan of organization. Instead, the form of a paper may develop organically from its subject matter or thesis—the writer arranges materials in a way naturally suited to the aim, purpose, and audience of the piece. Or the paper may follow a preexisting pattern that requires little variation once it is learned—as might be the case with a lab report, a memo, or a résumé. Or a paper takes shape the way an off-the-rack suit is fitted. A basic size, a rough fit, is found for the customer; then the garment is tailored again to mold to the individual more accurately. So too a writer may begin with a rough design—a narrative, a comparison/contrast pattern—but then tailor it to suit a particular subject. That makes sense. A writer's larger purposes, not a pattern of organization, should determine the form of an essay. With experienced writers, form is often subconscious or automatic.

Let's look at an example to see how *form* comes organically from a writer's *purpose* and *thesis*. Suppose that a student in an economics class intends to explain why the U.S. budget deficit increased dramatically in the 1980s. The thesis might look something like this:

> *Thesis:* The enormous increase in the size of the U.S. federal budget deficit in the 1980s began with actions to cut federal taxes that were not followed by cuts in overall spending.

This purpose and thesis contain within themselves the shape—the form—the essay will take. For instance, the form is *not* going to be a comparison of U.S. and Japanese budget policies. The form is *not* going to be an extended definition of deficits or taxes. It is *not* going to classify accounting methods used in handling federal revenues.

Rather, the form organically contained in this thesis will be something like "First, the President and Congress agreed to do this . . . then they did this . . . but they did not follow up and do this," and so on, until the writer has finished narrating the decisions that ultimately triggered the budget deficits. This is the design both topic and thesis suggest; it is also the form readers will expect as a result of having read the thesis. You have set up an expectation that you must fulfill (see Chapter 18).

So when you consider how to organize a paper, don't expect to be guided by an abstract rule imposed from outside your work. Your ideas themselves contain the best suggestions for structure. If you've done a thorough job at the creating stage, your purpose and thesis will offer a form to you.

What then is the purpose of this chapter if form is as natural as breathing? What can you do to make yourself more confident that a paper you are writing has an organization that both you and your readers will find satisfactory? You can study form consciously—look at the patterns a thesis lends itself to, experiment with them, enter them into the vocabulary of your writing process now so that eventually you can call them up automatically.

Each of the patterns of organization offered in this chapter will seem to arise naturally and organically from your thinking. They seem like "natural" patterns of thought because most of us have been using them since we were children: we have been trained to look for orderly sequences, for similarities, for differences. We expect actions to have traceable causes; we rely on the stability of definitions ("*Webster's* says . . ."); we love to break complex masses into more manageable categories. The patterns express our cultural habits; they are so characteristic of the way we think and behave that it takes a conscious effort to imagine societies that might not share the same patterns and assumptions. In our world, especially the academic one, these patterns serve as guides and reference points that give shape and coherence to our writing.

The point of studying these patterns, then, is to grow more conscious of the design you need to write appropriately and to become aware of relationships between thesis and pattern. You need to know when telling a story is an appropriate way of delivering information and when it isn't, when description is more helpful than classification. The more you write, the more proficient you will be in recognizing potential patterns of organization within your topic and thesis.

SPECIFIC PATTERNS OF ORGANIZATION

The patterns of organization explored in this chapter are Time Order, Spatial Order, General-Specific Order, Break-Down Order, and Relationship Order. Mixed Form—that is, a combination of patterns within a single work, is also discussed.

Time Order

TIME ORDER
Narration
Process
Cause and Effect

The first of these patterns of organization is the *chronological* or *time order.* Within the time order are more specific categories: narration, process, and cause and effect.

Narration. If you have a thesis like this one, the time order in your essay will be *narration.*

> *Thesis:* The story of the rescue of Apollo 13 reads like a thriller.

Here, your purpose in writing the essay is to tell this story and to capture the drama of the rescue. You, therefore, naturally begin:

> First, the mission was launched . . .
>
> Then, the trouble developed . . .
>
> After that, the team . . .
>
> Next, this happened . . .
>
> Finally, . . .

and on to the end of the story. You close off the essay with some discussion of the significance of this story for the reader, and there you have your specific pattern of organization—*time order: narration*—which you have not imposed arbitrarily. The pattern of organization has emerged from the thesis of your essay.

Narration:

Introduction

Body: (choice of pattern)

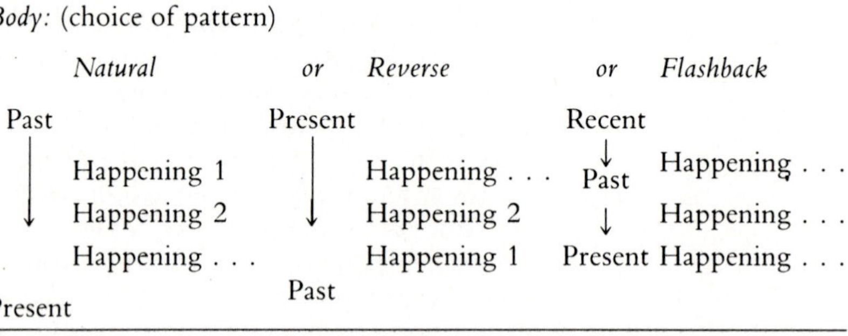

Conclusion

Process. Here is another thesis that leads naturally to time order as a pattern of organization in an essay. In this instance, the time order is one that we can call *process.*

> *Thesis:* Following these steps, a person can learn to operate a computer file program.

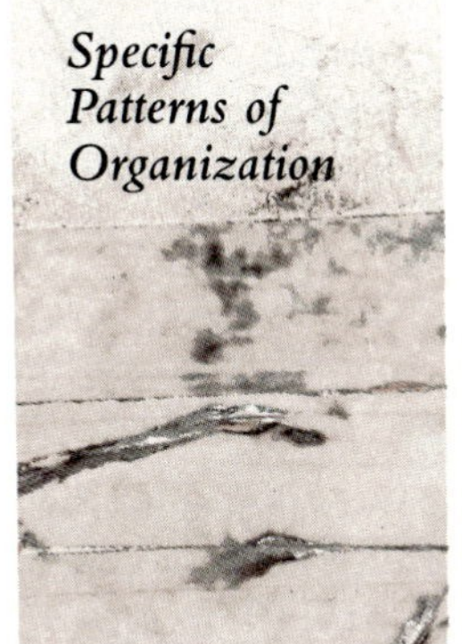

Time Order
Narration
Process
Cause and Effect

Spatial Order
Description

General-Specific Order
Definition
Deduction
Induction

Break-Down Order
Analysis
Classification
Examples

Relationship Order
Comparison/Contrast
Analogy

Do you see how the development that follows a process thesis will automatically take a chronological shape?

First, you do this . . .

Then, you do that . . .

After that, you do . . .

Another thing you can do is . . .

and so on to the end of the steps.

Process:

Introduction

Body: (choice of pattern)

Enumeration	or	Steps	or	Sequence
1		Step one		First
2		Step two		Next
3		Step three		Then
4		Step four		After that
				Finally

Conclusion

Cause and Effect. Here is another thesis that would naturally produce a time-order pattern of organization in an essay. This time order is known as *cause and effect.*

Thesis: The 1954 Supreme Court decision in *Oliver Brown et al.* v. *Board of Education of Topeka* caused American education to change.

To develop this thesis, follow a *time order* again because first there is this cause—a court decision—and after that there are these effects—a historic shift in a nation's attitude. If x hadn't happened before, y wouldn't have happened afterwards. It is an organic organization pattern for this thesis, then, when you discuss first the cause and then the effects.

Sometimes the pattern might be reversed; you might want to discuss the effects first and then the cause, as in a paper written on a thesis like this:

> *Thesis:* Although common in America today, integrated education began in 1954 with the famous Supreme Court "Brown" decision.

Then your paper would fall into a discussion of the effect first and then a longer discussion of the causes of this effect. You would still be moving in *time order,* however, because the cause occurred first and the effects second.

Cause and Effect:

Introduction

Body: (choice of pattern)

Cause	*or*	Effect
1		1
2		2
3		3
4		4
. . .		. . .
Effect		Cause
1		1
2		2
3		3
4		4
. . .		. . .

Conclusion

Spatial Order

SPATIAL ORDER
Description

Spatial order is another specific pattern of organization that occurs again and again in writing. Just as we all think in time order, we experience objects in the world arranged in various predictable ways.

Description. The following thesis would result in a paper organized on the spatial-order principles of *description.*

> *Thesis:* Robots have been designed to work on automobile assembly lines.

It isn't hard to see how this thesis would have as its organic development a description of the new machines. The writer might describe the robots from *top* to *bottom, inside* to *outside, in action* or *not in action*. The important thing is that the writer's pattern of organization is in some way "built into" the thesis of the paper.

Description:

Introduction

Body: (choice of pattern)

North	Top	Near	Inside	Left	Active
↓	↓	↓	↓	↓	↓
South	Bottom	Far	Outside	Right	Inactive

Conclusion

General-Specific Order

GENERAL-SPECIFIC ORDER
Definition
Deduction
Induction

A general statement is one that applies to many things and includes several instances or examples. A specific statement gives one particular example or incident. Thought patterns that move from the general to the specific help us understand new terms or concepts. Categories included in the general-specific order are definition, deduction, and induction.

Definition. A thesis like this would lead to a general-specific order of definition.

Thesis: Cajun cooking is not like other southern food.

This thesis leads organically to a definition of Cajun food. The essay would begin with a discussion of the general subject, southern cooking, of which Cajun food is one type, and then move to a definition of the specific subject, Cajun cooking.

In this flow from the general to the specific, it will be necessary to place Cajun cooking in the larger context of southern cooking in order to identify its different characteristics. The definition of Cajun cooking will result in general-specific order because you are moving from a general category (southern cooking) to a specific topic within that general category (Cajun cooking) to show how the specific stands out from the general.

Definition:

Introduction

Body: (choice of pattern)

Define by synonym. Define by class. Define by origin. Define by details, description, and so on.

Conclusion

Deduction. Here is another thesis that would result in a general-specific order of *deduction* for an essay:

> *Thesis:* CPAs are expected not to advertise, but some accountants are making millions by breaking this rule.

An essay written on this thesis would begin with a discussion of the generalization contained in the first part of the thesis: that CPAs are expected not to advertise. After this discussion, the writer would move to something more specific: evidence that some CPAs are now getting rich from the business they bring in through ads. The shape and form of the essay is actually "predicted" and contained in the thesis sentence itself.

Deduction:

Introduction

Body:

General

Specific

Conclusion

Induction. The general-specific order can appear as *induction,* an arrangement that moves from particular observations to general conclusions. You might have a thesis like this:

> *Thesis:* Just because hunger and starvation have existed a long time is no reason to suppose that death by starvation will always be with us.

You could develop that thesis with a series of specific examples of things that people used to believe but that are no longer true. You might use beliefs about the world being flat (which ended around 1492), that humans couldn't fly (which ended in 1903), that running a mile in under four minutes was physically impossible (which ended in 1954), that traveling to the moon was an unattainable dream (which ended in 1969). From those specifics you could move to a generalization: other "impossible" things have been achieved; there is evidence now that we can also achieve an end to starvation within our lifetime.

And the shape of the paper emerges effortlessly from the thesis.

Induction:

Introduction

Body:

Specific 1

Specific 2

Specific 3

Specific . . .

Generalization

Conclusion

Break-Down Order

BREAK-DOWN ORDER
Analysis
Classification
Examples

Another common thought pattern of organization is the *break-down order.* This pattern includes the categories of analysis, classification, and examples.

Analysis.

The break-down order of analysis is illustrated by this thesis:

Thesis: All good businesses have some characteristics in common.

As you wrote the essay that developed this thesis, you would naturally discuss the specific characteristics—you would *analyze* good businesses to see what they shared in common.

Analysis:

Introduction

Body: (choice of pattern)

Part 1	Characteristic 1
Part 2	Characteristic 2
Part 3	Characteristic 3
Part . . .	Characteristic . . .

Conclusion

Classification.

Another kind of thesis that results in a break-down pattern of organization—this time *classification*—is one like this:

Thesis: Television shows can be divided into those that are produced to entertain and those that are produced to educate.

If you were going to develop this thesis, you would not even have to think about what organization pattern to use. The parts of the essay would be the classification of television shows, the two divisions that were identified. The thesis itself produces the break-down organizational pattern of classification.

Classification:

Introduction

Body:

Group 1
Group 2
Group 3
Group . . .

Conclusion

Examples. A third kind of break-down shape—*examples*—appears in this thesis sentence:

> *Thesis:* The Oregon coast is a great vacation spot, even in the winter.

To develop this thesis, you would give examples. Your aim in this essay would be to convince your reader by citing specifics you think prove that the coast is a good place to take a vacation. You wouldn't have to worry about the overall shape of the essay because it's organically present in your thesis.

Examples:

Introduction

Body:

Example 1
Example 2
Example 3
Example . . .

Conclusion

Relationship Order

RELATIONSHIP ORDER
Comparison/Contrast
Analogy

The final thought pattern of organization is the *relationship order.* The two categories in this pattern are comparison/contrast and analogy.

Comparison/Contrast. Imagine that the thesis of your essay was this:

> *Thesis:* City dwellers often dream about living in the country, but these dreams are very different from actually living the rural life.

You would set up your paper to discuss two things: dreams about living in the country and the reality of living there. The kind of *comparison/contrast* present in the thesis gives the writer his or her organizational pattern.

Here is another example of the relationship order of *comparison/contrast.*

> *Thesis:* The decision to rent or to buy your own home is becoming more complex every day.

The organization pattern for this essay would be to discuss renting and to discuss owning. The only decision you would have to make is whether to say everything you want to say about renting before going on to owning, or whether to talk about a *particular aspect* of the thesis—say, tax relief—and, in the discussion of tax relief, talk about *both* renting and owning, and then go on to *another aspect* of the thesis—say, initial investment—and talk about both renting and owning under that. No matter which variation you choose, the basic pattern of organization—*comparison/contrast*—is an organic part of the thesis itself.

Comparison/Contrast:

Introduction

Body: (choice of pattern)

I	*or*	II
Item A		Point 1
Point 1		Item A
2		B
. . .		. . .
Item B		Point 2
Point 1		Item A
2		B
Item . . .		Point . . .
Point 1		Item A
2		B

Conclusion

Analogy. Another relationship pattern—*analogy*—is organically present in this thesis:

> *Thesis:* Business partnership is a legal arrangement something like marriage.

The organization pattern comes directly out of the thesis: a discussion of something perhaps less familiar to the reader (partnership) by comparing it to something familiar (marriage). This is a form of comparison that carries *one point extended all the way through the essay* with examples or details to show how the comparison is accurate.

Analogy:

Introduction

Body:

Example 1: _______ is like _______ in this way
Example 2: _______ is like _______ in this way
Example . . .

Conclusion

Mixed Form

If you studied a group of essays in a collection introduced as *Essays of Definition*, you might notice that they did many things in addition to defining—for instance, *contrasting, comparing,* and *narrating.* This inconsistency in form shouldn't surprise you. Most essays combine several patterns of organization in the course of making a point. A definition paper, for example, may open with a short narrative—an anecdote to gain the reader's attention. Then, in the process of providing a definition, it might divide and classify key concepts. The classifications might then be illustrated through a series of examples—which could be narrative or descriptive in approach. The overall purpose of the essay might be defined by the pattern of definition, but that pattern, in turn, is supported by other forms. Just as one handsome building may reflect a variety of architectural themes and elements, one paper may display a host of forms and still prove coherent.

Read the following student essay and notice (1) how the writer's thesis determines its overall shape and (2) how other forms of thinking also appear within the overall pattern.

EXAMPLE Mixed Form

Ron was asked to review an excellent restaurant within driving distance of his apartment. This review appeared in a restaurant review column in the local newspaper.

> Student's Purpose: To describe a restaurant—The Grist Mill—in such a way that the reader will want to eat there.
>
> *Thesis:* You won't quickly forget an evening you spend eating at The Grist Mill.

TRY NOT *TO GO BACK: THE GRIST MILL, A RESTAURANT YOU WON'T FORGET*

Thesis + Form = Description

Have you ever stumbled onto an unbelievably good restaurant in the middle of nowhere? Have you ever searched for a restaurant someone told you about, and that search took you hours? If you have, then you will have some reference for understanding about The Grist Mill. Hidden away in an old German settlement, The Grist Mill is not an easy place to find. But, believe me, it is well worth the search. Established in the ghost town of Gruene, Texas, The Grist Mill has to be one of the best restaurants anywhere. You won't forget an evening you spend eating at The Grist Mill. It's a restaurant to which you'll have to go back.

Narration

After parking the car, as you are walking up the long gravel and dirt road to The Grist Mill, the strains of country and western music hit you. The music is coming from the oldest dance hall in Texas, which is located right next to the restaurant. The dance hall is huge and is made out of stone and thick wooden planks, which were painted dark green years ago. Inside, the live band plays to a large crowd.

Description

Just past the dance hall is The Grist Mill. It is three stories tall and also made out of stones and wooden planks. The big front doors are thrown wide open, and you can see all the people enjoying their meals on the first floor. The upper two floors have windows that extend from about 3½ feet up, up to the ceilings, and these windows are propped wide open to catch the evening breeze.

Narration

After giving your name to the hostess, you can walk over and get some lemonade or beer from the outside bar and sit down with everyone else who is waiting. They are all sitting on split-log benches, facing an entertainer who will sing or play a guitar for you. As you wait, you can go over and look at the river. It is just a few feet to the right. If you stand on the edge of the bluff that the mill sits on, you can see the greenish-blue water of the Guadalupe River rolling by.

Soon you are called to take a table. If you are really lucky, the table is on the third floor, facing the river. You can see miles of trees that seem to form a bushy green carpet below your eyes. Hectic life seems a thousand miles away.

Now it is time to order.

Definition

For appetizers, you must order bratwurst and potatoes. Fried bratwurst, cubed, on toothpicks. (Bratwurst is a spicy, thick German stuffed sausage, which squirts its delicious juices into your mouth.) The potatoes are fried like chips, but the slices are thick enough to still be moist inside, instead of crunchy. For the main course, I recommend the chicken-fried steak: a tender cut of beef, marinated all night long in a wine marinade, then dipped into a delicious batter and deep fried.

Description

After the meal, it is time for dessert. For the best dessert, order the strawberry shortcake. It comes on about a 6- or 8-inch platter, but you won't be able to see the platter—it is too obscured by all the whipped cream and strawberries. There is a soft, spongy cake with the center taken out, in the middle of this delight. In place of the center, there is a scoop of vanilla ice cream, on top of the ice cream comes the whipped cream and strawberries, piled about 6 inches high, and topped off with a maraschino cherry.

Analysis

Finally, it is time for coffee. The Grist Mill grinds its own beans, so the coffee is always fresh and strong. If you don't have to be rolled out of The Grist Mill, you might want to go to the dance hall and dance off some of the weight you have just gained.

Conclusion

Then again, you might just want to go on home, in a contented stuffed stupor, wondering how soon you will be coming back. The evening at The Grist Mill—from the sounds of the tumbleweed and the music in the air to the melancholy sigh of the ancient river rolling by to the testimony of the old German building where you eat and the food you put in your mouth—will be an evening you will not forget. I bet you won't be able not to go back.

You can see in Ron's essay that the form is the spatial order of description. His thesis—you won't forget an evening you spend eating at The Grist Mill; it's a restaurant to which you will have to go back—organically and naturally contains the form of description.

Yet, inside this over-all ordering form of description, Ron does many other things. For instance, he narrates: the walk up to the restaurant, the wait before the meal, the parts of the meal itself, and the ending of the evening spent at the mill. He defines: the bratwurst and chicken-fried steak. He analyzes: the reasons why this will have been an evening you will never forget. He has written an essay that has mixed form. The overall form flowing organically from the thesis is the spatial order of description. Inside this form, however, other types of thinking emerge.

KEEPING PATTERNS OF ORGANIZATION IN PERSPECTIVE

Here are some suggestions for you to remember about patterns of organization:

1. Be confident that a thesis will suggest its own pattern of organization.
2. Realize that although the overall pattern of organization may be defined as one word (*classification, definition,* etc.), many patterns of thinking will appear in the essay. The form of most essays is a *mixed form.*
3. Become familiar with and conscious of the basic patterns of organization, but don't make these patterns the reason you write.

Writing in order to fit a pattern is writing backwards. Always begin with a *purpose,* an *audience,* and a *message.* Write because you have something to say to someone, and then be aware after that of the variety of methods of organization you might use for that message. Be confident, though, that if you have a *purpose* for writing, a particular *audience* in mind, and a *message* you really want to send, then an *organizing principle* will naturally and organically follow. Your essay will have a shape.

APPLICATION

1. Read these thesis sentences and decide what organizational patterns are organically present in them:
   A. The movie *Casablanca* is as popular today as it was when it first came out.
   B. There are only three basic types of running shoes.
   C. Sally Ride's trip into space was inspiring for all women.
   D. The new office building has a very unusual shape.
   E. The book *The Accidental Tourist* is extremely well written.
   F. *Occurred* is a word everybody ought to learn to spell.
   G. The story of Shirley MacLaine's forty-ninth year is fascinating.
   H. People are eating better all over the country; this is causing some significant changes in health, illness, and death.
   I. The schools in this state are losing students every year.
   J. *The Entrepreneurial Life* tells readers how to be out on their own.
   K. Everything the reporter said on the news points to one fact.
   L. Stories abound about the danger of high-fat diets.
   M. Our new senator is a flamboyant person.
   N. *Poetry* is a hard word to pin down.
   O. Swimming doesn't use the same muscles that tennis does.
   P. Subways are picturesque.
2. Here are two lists of thesis sentences. Choose one from Group 1 and its corresponding number in Group 2. When you've chosen, begin *at once* to write an essay on the subject in Group 1 and then the subject in Group 2.

   The point is to notice how each thesis carries with it an organic shape. Therefore, deliberately avoid thinking about shape for the essay. (Bypass the creating stage, too, since you're only going to write the opening of the essay.)

   You don't need to write two whole essays. Just write enough of each essay to experience how the form is contained within the thesis.

Group 1	*Group 2*
1. Black is not a good color to wear on a hot day.	1. Black is a better color to wear than white for anyone who is overweight.

2. Organizing recipes requires some kind of system.
3. Artificial respiration saved the life of a friend of mine.
4. The mountains were breathtaking.
5. You can recognize my neighborhood by its distinct boundaries.
6. My father's (mother's) face is a record of his (her) life.
7. Although my mother and father are both parents, each has a different role.

2. This recipe for making pie dough is easy to follow.
3. Artificial respiration causes a victim's lungs to resume functioning.
4. The mountains have interesting geological features.
5. My neighborhood has a feeling all its own.
6. There is more to fatherhood (or motherhood) than just producing offspring.
7. Although my mother and father each have very different roles, they both are described by the word *parent*.

3. Find a short article you've enjoyed that you'd like to share with your classmates. Bring enough copies to class for the members of your editing or writing group. Go through the piece carefully. First determine the thesis of the piece. Then try to decide upon its dominant form or pattern of organization. If you cannot agree on the pattern, list the major patterns you do find. If you can agree on one dominant design, then go over the piece carefully to identify as many other patterns within the essay as you can.

Promise and Delivery

When you put on a garment that doesn't fit, you know it immediately: it hangs loose like a sack or constricts like a sausage casing. Either you make adjustments in the item or you select another garment.

When shaping an essay, you also need a sense of fit and proportion. Unfortunately, criteria for judging how well an essay hangs together are not easy to establish. You can't size up a paper simply by reading it, especially after you have been deeply involved in its composition. You are too close to the work to see it objectively. So you need a more precise way of checking the structure of your writing, one that provides standards to help you make adjustments in a paper or realize when you might be better off beginning all over again.

This chapter provides a two-pronged approach to testing work produced during the shaping stage—after you have developed a full draft. Both approaches are based upon a single design principle: an effective paper makes a chain of agreements with its readers. The links in this chain of agreement are:

- Your *promise to the reader*—your *thesis,* which you prominently and clearly display at the beginning of the writing;
- Your *delivery* of that promise, which you accomplish by staying on the subject you have promised to discuss—by sticking to your thesis—all the way through the piece of writing.

By actually writing to send a message to someone else, you have tacitly made an agreement with your readers. The agreement goes something like this:

> If you will read this essay, I promise to tell you this particular message so clearly and thoroughly that you will know exactly what I mean.

The readers can then decide whether they choose to join in the agreement with you or not—by continuing to read or by stopping. If you want them to keep on reading, you are obliged to *deliver what you promised* and to *keep your agreement.*

If you do, a paper will be coherent and well-organized. To be sure you've kept your promise, you need to evaluate a paper both *internally* and *externally.*

The *internal check* lets you look at the links in your promise-and-delivery chain of agreements.

Link #1: Did you make a clear *promise*—a thesis that is an assertion?

Link #2: Is every point you made clearly related to the thesis—did you *deliver* on your promise?

The *external check* lets you look at your writing to see if its structure highlights the promise-and-delivery agreement system and makes it easy for the reader to see. In the external check you examine these parts of the writing structure:

The three-part framework: beginning, middle, and end

The introduction's development

The conclusion's completeness

You need to do both the internal and the external check. The internal check lets you know that you stayed focused and are clear about what you were saying all the way through the paper. The external check lets you know that all the necessary parts of the essay's structure are there—your readers don't wander off, then, looking for some missing part. Let's look now at these two ways to make the late shaping stage worth your while.

THE INTERNAL CHECK

This process allows you to do two things:

- Determine that you do have a promise—a thesis—that readers cannot miss when they begin to read your writing.
- Examine every point you have made in the writing to be certain that you have stayed on the thesis—that you have delivered what you promised.

The internal check tests every part of a paper against the standard set by its thesis. Quite often, writers will have a topic—a general subject they want to explore—but they will not have refined it to a central concern. As a result, they tinker with a subject rather than develop it, presenting idea after idea in no discernable order. Obviously, if a paper doesn't have a thesis or clear central point to develop, it's in deep trouble. It will meander like a stream, losing readers at every bend. In academic writing especially, readers expect a paper to have a sense of purpose and direction. Both are established by the thesis. An essay without a point is disjointed and confusing—difficult for a writer to compose because there are no limits to what must be covered; difficult for a reader to understand because there's no predicting what comes next or how the piece might develop. If a paper you're evaluating states no thesis or makes no clear promise to readers, it needs to be revised. What readers want—in almost every kind of writing—is to have the subject clearly set down and to have it stuck to from beginning to end.

Make Your Promise Clear: Have a Thesis

One of the best ways to sharpen your eye for focusing on a thesis is to look at an essay that lacks a specific promise and to notice the results of not having had a chain of agreements.

Here is an essay on growing asparagus. Let's look at the opening paragraph to see whether the writer makes us, the readers, a promise:

A LIFETIME OF ASPARAGUS

> As asparagus came into season this year, I watched eager gourmets grab the tender stalks out of their icy beds, while penny-conscious shoppers watched wistfully, then moved to the broccoli in the next bin. If the latter only knew how easily they could grow the spears, and have a bed to last them 20 years! It occurred to me then that there are some things they might want to know that would help them grow asparagus, and some things that won't help them grow it but might be of interest.

The closest thing to a promise in this introduction to the essay is the sentence, "It occurred to me then that there are some things they might want to know that would help them grow asparagus, and some things that won't help them grow it but might be of interest."

What kind of a promise is this?

Is it a clear link in a chain to which the rest of the essay can be linked? Is it a firm promise? (And how much *value* does this thesis promise the reader?)

The writer assumes that you will keep on reading: he depends on the weak promise that he will write about some things that "occurred to him" in which you might be interested. He is also assuming that you *want* to grow asparagus. A dangerous assumption on the writer's part, right?

It's clear that this writer did not seriously make a promise of real value to the reader. The extent of his promise is that the subject of asparagus will hook you enough to have you read on. Let's read more of the essay and see how much you are interested in what "occurred" to this writer:

> Botanically, garden asparagus (*Asparagus officinalis*), is in the genus of the lily family (*Liliaceae*), with about 300 species of largely desert herbs and vines. The family comprises such unlike plants as "smilax" of the florist, the common garden asparagus, and the so-called asparagus fern, used for trimming countless bouquets. Asparagus is the Greek name for the vegetable.

> As a vegetable, asparagus has been prized by epicures since Roman times. It is the most permanent of all vegetable crops. Once established, it used to be assumed—and still is, in England—that it will last a lifetime. It is grown extensively in France, Italy, and the United States, where California and Washington are its leading commercial growers.

Here the writer first discusses the botanical side of asparagus, then moves right into the history of asparagus and the places it is grown—all in the same paragraph. You may already detect the absence of a chain of agreements, a promise-and-delivery system. Since he did not promise anything specific to begin with, he has no guide, no rationale, for what to include and what not to include. You can almost imagine this writer with a pile of notecards in front of him, picking up one stack and writing about this aspect of asparagus, and then picking up the next stack and writing about that. Contrast this with a writer who agrees to deliver on a specific promise of value to the reader, and whose writing is then shaped by delivering on that promise.

What does the writer do next?

> Asparagus is a perennial, which means that once planted, it will produce again and again without replanting. It bears its first main crop three years after planting if grown from seeds, or in its second season if started from year-old roots. It may remain productive for 20 years or more. However, it requires a dormant period during

> winter months and grows only where dormancy is induced naturally by climate or can be forced artificially by cultivation methods. It grows well anywhere in the United States and southern Canada, except Florida and the Gulf Coast, where the moist soil and mild temperatures prevent it from getting its necessary period of rest.
>
> Asparagus may be erect or climbing, and are more or less woodsy. The rhizome-like, or sometimes tuberous roots, give rise to conspicuous, leaf-like branchlets; true leaves are reduced to small scales. The plant has a fine, fernlike foliage and would grow four to six feet tall if left unpicked, but it should be harvested when the stems are only about half a foot tall.

Here he returns to presenting botanical information about asparagus—information that belongs with the second paragraph in the essay. Why does he make such disjointed points? Because he doesn't have a clear thesis, a firm promise. The writer is not forging a chain of linked thoughts.

Next he moves on to *kinds* of asparagus:

> Dozens of asparagus varieties are known. Of these only a few have survived the ravages of various pests and the test of public taste. One of the best varieties for most areas is Waltham, Washington. In the midwest, a widely used improved form is Viking, sometimes called Mary Washington Improved. In California, a variety called 500W is especially productive: a 12-foot row yields about six pounds of asparagus over a period of six to ten weeks.

Here is the next point:

> No soil is too rich for asparagus. It will grow in any ordinary good garden soil, but it will not produce tender stalks without liberal supplies of stable manure, plenty of moisture, and good drainage. Since it is a perennial, it is best to plant it in its own space—traditionally an "asparagus bed," so it will not interfere with annual crops. A family of five will need about 100 feet of rows to assure ample quantities, assuming asparagus is served twice a week.

Now, while some of these facts about asparagus are interesting, what do they have to do with anything? What promise are they fulfilling? Where is the writer going with this essay? Did he prepare us for the random salad of facts about asparagus?

The next paragraph begins with "You can sow seeds indoors in midwinter or in hotbeds in early spring," and it is followed by a number of paragraphs telling the reader how to plant and tend asparagus. After this group of paragraphs, the writer says, "I do a couple of things to keep disease and insect problems on asparagus to a minimum."

With no transition and no connection, the essay then moves on to a discussion of when you should cut and eat the asparagus you have grown.

Following this section, the next two paragraphs bring the essay to a close.

> A true asparagus lover measures the year not by the calendar, but by the beginning and end of the asparagus season. The vegetable is served steamed, boiled, or baked, hot or cold: creamed, au gratin, in omelettes or salads, accompanied by a variety of sauces and other garnishes—mayonnaise, vinaigrette, melted butter, and hollandaise sauce.
>
> Preparing the stalks has developed into a fine culinary art in some circles. A French chef demonstrating it on television shows how to break the stalk at precisely the right place—where it snaps without resistance. Below the break the stalk is tough and stringy; above it, soft and tender. A vegetable peeler helps to pare brown spots and immature scales.

The writer has to stop writing in mid-air. Since there was no point to it to begin with, there is no appropriate place to end. When you don't make a promise to your reader, you don't have anything by which to judge whether you are finished. You have no links in a chain of agreements, and the promise-and-delivery system falls apart.

Deliver What You Promise: Stay on Track

Words trigger ideas as effortlessly as smiles beget smiles. At the creating stage, these powers of association help writers see subtle relationships or make unexpected connections. At the shaping stage, however, the fertility of language can lead to disaster if writers wander off too easily, following every suggestion like a bee through a field of wildflowers. Writers may tend to wander not because they are inept, but because most people are naturally curious, appreciating variety and change.

But late in the process of writing a paper, there comes a point (usually under the pressure of a deadline) when you've got to give more attention to the shape of ideas than to their scope. It is time for *screening* thoughts, keeping only those that relate to what you've promised to communicate to a reader. It's also time to be sure the thoughts you have assembled link up intelligently.

The following essay illustrates what happens when a writer forgets what she has promised:

TEST OF LIFE

Context: Personal experience essay written as part of college application process
Audience: College admission officials

"Ya'll, I'm scared of heights. I can't do this!"
"We're here for support; you can trust us, Mary."

I still remember this conversation vividly. It happened during summer camp in 1979, and it was during this camp that I learned the importance of trust and support.

(Now, here is Sandy's thesis. She is promising the reader that she will write about a camp experience that taught her the importance of trust and support. This is her first link in the chain of the promise-and-delivery system.)

First example of importance of trust and support

The reason Mary needed to trust us was that she was standing on top of a pole which was six feet high, and her back was facing about ten people, in two rows, with their arms held tightly together. The frightening part of it all was that she was supposed to fall back into our arms.

No, this wasn't some kind of torture.

This was a game, actually, a group effort, in which the object was for everyone in the group to complete everything on an obstacle course. This wasn't just any obstacle course, either. It didn't even stress physical strength or ability but, instead, caused everyone who passed it to have to work together.

To do this special obstacle course you had to go beyond fears which you might have had all your life. The one Mary was having trouble with was trusting that, when she fell off this pole backwards, the people below her would catch her and put her down to safety. Earlier in the game she had similar trouble crawling through a long, narrow tunnel which required you to let other people in the group support you completely in getting through the tunnel.

Mary finally jumped. Backwards she came into our arms. And we caught her. Everybody laughed and everybody cried. We all knew at that moment what it is to trust and support each other.

Transition

I think that everyone who went to that camp learned many lessons that can be applied to life. Throughout life, all of us experience many hardships, and it is during these times that we often have to trust our friends to give us support. During that two-week period, my eyes opened up to see all of the times in my life when people came to my aid.

I will discuss one of these times, though there are many I would like to tell about.

(*What is happening here? Sandy's thoughts on her experience at camp have triggered other memories she has of other times that her eyes opened up to incidents when people had come to her aid. It is easy to see, isn't it, how the thoughts are related; how one has led to another. So, the thoughts aren't unconnected. They just aren't links in the chain of the promise-and-delivery system that Sandy has set up. She promised to discuss a time at camp when she learned the importance of trust and support—this was her opening link in the chain of agreements. Therefore, she cannot wander away from this link, no matter how easily her mind has moved to the incident she is now about to relate. She has to deliver what she promised, because that was the agreement she made with the reader.*)

Off on another subject

There was a day that my family was the victim of a frightening accident, and we are lucky to have lived through it.

Living through an accident

I still remember looking up at the sliding glass door, and thinking what a big, funny-looking bug was on the window. (I was only four—what can you expect.) What it really was was the headlight of a riderless motorcycle. The rider had jumped off a block away, but the bike kept going. It turned two corners and went between two parked cars in our driveway before it entered our house and turned our lives upside down.

When the ambulance finally arrived, it seemed as if all the work was already done. My father had lifted the motorcycle up off of me, and my mother picked me up and carried me outside. My father also picked up my sister Cindy and carried her out of the burning house. The ambulance attendant pronounced Cindy dead, but my mother wasn't going to believe that. She started to use C.P.R. and saved Cindy's life. The miracle of it all was that the only demonstration my mother had ever seen of C.P.R. had been the week before on "Romper Room." My sister and I were destined to spend over a month in the hospital.

In the fire caused by the accident we lost almost all of our possessions to smoke damage and everything was a complete mess. This was a time that my parents needed physical and emotional support, and their friends were nearby to give it. Cases like this are seen constantly in the news.

Many times, without friends and family to help us, it would be much more difficult for us to make it through a crisis. We all need to learn to trust our friends enough to lean on them when we need to, because they are always willing to help out. Just as we are willing to support them.

Because Sandy's essay falls into two parts, the focus of the communication is lost and the essay is less effective than if she had used a thesis that would have let her tell both stories as a unit, or if she had delivered on the thesis that she set up.

In contrast, look at this next example. Julie's essay makes a clear promise at the beginning—to discuss why people watch soap operas and why soap operas are so popular. After she makes this promise, there is no point where Julie fails to deliver on what she said. Her thesis, and the points that follow it, are all links in the chain of agreement that she set up.

AS THE SOAP TURNS

Context: Analysis essay written as part of college admission process
Audience: College admission administrators

Dramatic beginning, to get readers' attention.

Soft, intriguing music plays in the background. Martha, a pretty brunette, walks into the living room. Her husband, Paul, is sitting anxiously on the couch. "Martha, where have you been?"; then, taking a closer look he adds, "You haven't been down at Ted's Nightclub again, have you?" She remains silent for a moment and then speaks defensively, "What difference does it make to you? You spend every night at the clinic! What do you expect me to do, stay home and watch T.V. by myself?" And so another dramatic episode begins.

Transition to essay.

Generalization from the specific example.

Questions: an indirect way of putting the thesis.

Each weekday, many stories similar to this one are broadcast on T.V. Soap operas are viewed by thousands of people across the country. Now soap operas are also shown at night. Men are also enjoying what used to be considered shows for women. They have become an American pastime. Why do people watch soap operas? Why have they become so popular?

First reason: people identify with the characters.

Conclusion ties example back to main point: the watchers identify with characters.

Many people watch soap operas because they can identify with the characters. They can relate their own problems to those of the characters in the show. Maggie, on *Falcon's Crest,* has become a single mother, while at the same time pursuing a career. Her situation often occurs in the lives of real women. Their decisions, as well as Maggie's, will affect them for the rest of their lives.

Second example: divorce.

Tying this example to the point.

Divorce is a common situation in soap operas. Recently on *All My Children,* Adam and Brooke got a divorce. Before it happened, both of them wondered if divorce was what they really wanted. Men and women can see themselves in Adam and Brooke. The frustrations of indecision, the agonies encountered while carrying out a decision and the enjoyments of later realizing that the right decision was made are felt by the

Tying example to point again.

viewer in his or her own personal experiences. Seeing the same thing happening to someone else is comforting to the viewer.

Third point: dream world fantasy.

Soap operas also provide a dream world in which an individual can fantasize. You can imagine what you might do if the same situation confronted you. If you were pregnant, or getting a divorce, or experiencing any one of the number of things that happen to the characters, would you make the same decision they did? Soap operas allow you to forget your own worries and momentarily focus on something else. Thinking about the character's problem creates a distraction from your own. This distraction sometimes makes your problems easier to take in stride.

Tying example to point.

Tying example to point.

Fourth point: related to paragraph above, but slightly different.

Soap operas are also beneficial in helping viewers see that their own life isn't as bad as it may seem. After watching a soap opera, you might find that the character's life is more complicated than your own. Almost any soap opera character's life could be considered complicated when compared to real life. For example, on *All My Children,* Adam Chandler, a wealthy businessman, was married to Brooke, but is now married to Dixie. While married to Brooke, Adam had had an affair with Dixie, who became pregnant and agreed to let Adam and Brooke adopt the child since Brooke could no longer have children. But, Dixie later changed her mind. Realizing that your life is not worse than theirs can encourage you. You have living evidence that things are much worse on the other side of the street.

Specific example.

Tying example to point.

Soap operas will remain part of American life. They are unending stories that are enjoyed by men and women alike. Martha and Paul may have reconciled their differences for today, but what will happen tomorrow? Will another argument arise? Why does Martha like to go to Ted's Nightclub? Does Paul really have to work nights at the clinic? The questions about the soap opera characters' lives never end. This is also true for people who watch the programs. Their lives are filled with questions needing to be answered.

Return to examples used in introduction.

Somehow it seems reassuring to think that all these questions and more might be answered in tomorrow's episode.

Again tying it to point.

APPLICATION

The following essays have defective promise-and-delivery systems. Select someone to read each aloud for your group. Then work together to apply an internal check to determine where in the essay the writer could have made a promise but didn't or provides an unsatisfactory thesis. Annotate the essay in the margin, showing where and how the failure to provide a focus affects other parts of the paper. The first essay is annotated to help you see its problems. Treat the other essays similarly.

FAMILY CLOSENESS

Title says that general subject is family closeness.

1. **Context:** Written for a freshman class assignment
 Audience: Classmates; professor

Can you find a main statement that the essay will discuss, consider, or prove?

Special occasions, Christmas, relatives, small families, dinner, presents.

Special occasions seem to bring families together. There is usually a party consisting of the whole family during Christmas. Relatives from far away always come together to eat and enjoy each other's company. I have a relatively small family; my father has only one brother and my mother has none. Small families seem to be closer knit. During Christmas, nobody at the dinner table is shy to talk to one another because everybody is so closely related. It is a wonderful time of year; presents are passed about. Imagine yourself as a little kid and think about how excited you were when you opened the beautiful presents.

Parents' work, vacations, trips.

My father is a hard worker. He owns a restaurant, and my mother is a housewife. They are usually very busy, and it is a shame that they do not have time to enjoy themselves more. Another time that we are all together is the two weeks in June when my father takes off for a vacation. We usually go to a different part of the United States.

Trip to New York, grandfather, toy stores, streets, ice cream, June.

My first time to New York was when I was a child of six. Things seemed so big. That was my first impression of New York. I can remember the time when my grandfather took me shopping at toy stores. We walked on endless streets and we went into all the shops. To close off the day, we would go to a drugstore and have ice cream. I always got chocolate and my grandpa got strawberry. In the month of June in New York, things are bright and warm.

Grandparents' apartment, grandfather's character.

I can still picture my grandparents' apartment. It consisted of four rooms, a kitchen, restroom, living room, and bedroom. It was an old beat-up place. Walls were torn, and on one of the walls were two pictures, one of my grandmother and one of my grandfather. My grandfather is an outgoing person. He was the one who took my brother and me to see the streets of New York.

Most recent trip to New York.

Last year was the last time I went to New York. This time the city gave me a drab feeling. It was cold and there was snow at least two feet high. New York did not feel the same as the time before.

MEXICO CITY

2. Context: Written for a travel article to describe a destination vacationers would enjoy visiting
Audience: Readers of travel magazines; adults with some money to spend

After visiting Mexico City in the summer of 1985, I found that it is a very large city centrally located between the Sierra mountain ranges of Mexico. It is approximately 3500 feet above sea level, which provides the city with a daily climate of 72° F. The city is known throughout the world for its beauty because of the mountains that are part of the city's scenic background. The city has a multitude of rainbow colors which help contribute to its beauty. The culture of the city is also rich in color and tradition. I found after touring the downtown area and suburbs of the city that most of the people were similar in family background and religion. Every one of the native countrymen was able to speak Spanish very fluently. Each family also possessed a very unified bond toward the Catholic church of the city. After carefully analyzing the churches within the city, I found that the majority of the people were Roman Catholic. This is due to the fact that Spanish explorers settled in Mexico many centuries ago. The Roman Catholic church has always been a predominant church within the city and throughout the country. I had the golden opportunity of attending mass at the cathedral in which the Pope of the Catholic church had said mass. After quietly entering the church, I suddenly was astonished by the beauty of the church's interior. As I slowly walked down the center aisle toward the altar I could not help but admire the delicate inlaid gold on the walls of the church. There were also numerous paintings hanging on the walls of the church which were painted by famous Mexican artists of the past decades. Located at the rear of the church on the upper deck was the choir podium and a massive pipe organ. After listening to this organ, I truly believe I have never heard such a fine instrument as this one.

The architecture throughout Mexico City has been influenced mainly by the European Spanish explorers who came to the country around 1500 A.D. These explorers brought with them architectural ideas which they had seen implemented in their own country. All of the old buildings and churches built throughout the city have been constructed under the influence of Spanish architecture. When I toured the downtown area, many of the buildings we visited certainly resembled the structures throughout Spain.

The one experience I undoubtedly enjoyed while I was in Mexico City was the nightly entertainment that Mexico City had to offer. Mexico City has always offered unlimited amounts of live entertainment such as discos, bars, and restaurants. Or perhaps if you desire a little romantic touch for yourself and your date you can have dinner in a small cafe in the downtown area where live *mariache* bands (band trio) perform at your table upon request. I can assure you that after a bottle of fine wine and a platter of *cabritol* (Bar-B-Qued goat), a couple will be full for the rest of the evening and ready to hit the discos. If you are a romantic person like myself, you would probably prefer a horse-drawn carriage to transport you to a disco. This is exactly what I did. I was able to rent a two-person carriage for the evening. After arriving at the disco, I was ready to boogie!

Mexico City has a unique market place. The Mexican vendors in the market will bargain prices with the customer down to the last *peso* (Mexican dollar). I myself found many exceptional bargains at the market on items such as jewelry, shirts, candy, pottery, books, records, knives, piñatas, etc. One piece of advice I will surely mention to the American tourist is to be careful while bargaining with the vendors because they will make every effort to overcharge you, especially if you do not speak the native tongue. Mexico City also has many other fine shops besides the market place to shop at. But I preferred the more economical places to shop at while I was in Mexico. I preferred to shop at places where I could actually bargain with the vendors myself.

Finally, after returning to the United States I learned many important differences between the U.S. and Mexico. I found that I could compare Mexico City to New York City in numerous ways. I found that each city has a very common culture and tradition. Each city is very much involved in its religious belief and traditions. Both cities have very interesting museums, restaurants, nightly entertainment and exciting places to shop at. Although I have visited both cities over the past few years, I found Mexico City to be a very romantic and educational city to visit. I wish that every young student from the United States could have the opportunity to visit such an exciting city as I have done.

A FIVE-LETTER WORD

3. **Context:** Written for a freshman economics class assignment
   Audience: Classmates; professor

It is thin and crinkles when you handle it. It is just white paper with green printing on it. It is a small collection of silver and copper discs which jingle in your pocket when you walk. It is a commodity certain people say they cannot live without. How much of it one has determines a person's social status. "It" is a five-letter word—*money*.

According to certain theories, our present-day monetary system evolved from Primitive Man using seashells or coconuts or some other article in exchange for something that he wanted. Someone would trade a bunch of seashells for a piece of fruit someone else grew. This person would then give the seashells to someone else for a cutting utensil and so on. The amount of seashells one had determined one's wealth or social position. Over the years the seashells became gold and silver coins and finally evolved into the system we use today. As with the seashells, the amount of money one has determines one's social position.

There are three main social divisions in this country: the rich, who are few; the poor, who are many; and the middle class, who pay all the taxes and bear the brunt of every social crunch. The rich have more money than you can shake a stick at. They always have high-salaried lawyers who find every loophole they can to prevent their employer from paying "more than he or she truly owes" in taxes. The rich can also afford to hire people to lobby for those issues they feel will benefit themselves either immediately or in the long run. The rich also have benefits people do not usually think of, such as being well known if one is rich enough, and having the opportunity to rub elbows with other well-known individuals, like movie stars. But, then, what can you expect from someone whose main worry is how to spend $50,000 just to keep from paying that amount in taxes.

Then there are the poor. These are generally those people who live in what is referred to as the "inner city," "the ghetto," or the "poverty pocket." Whatever name you like, it all means the same. It means that these people have very little income and, subsequently, a lesser amount of money. These are the people who can really stretch a dollar, mainly because they usually have to. The poor also benefit in some ways from today's society, in a form of relief, i.e., welfare, medicare, and medicaid. Despite all the drawbacks, some of the happiest people in the world fall into this category of social status.

Last, but not least, there is the middle class. These people are the backbone and make up the fiber of today's society. These are the people that have to pay for the programs which give relief to the poor and the class that answers "How high" when the rich yell "Jump." The middle class is more mobile, in that one can still improve one's stature in society. This can be done many ways, but the main way is hard work. Some advantages for the middle class are that big business is set up to satisfy the average middle-class person; one can set up a small business with relatively little capital and move up in position; and the government is starting to swing toward the side of the average citizen. All things considered, middle class is pretty well off.

In going from seashells to dollar bills, the economic setup has changed and stayed the same. The rich have certain advantages over the other classes. The rich and poor can be more easily defined and distinguished now. There are three main classes with several divisions in each class. This is the main difference between now and seashells. People are still judged by how much they have.

THE EXTERNAL CHECK

This process allows you to do three things:

- Check the overall structure of the piece—the big picture.
- Check that the introduction is successful.
- Check that the conclusion does its job.

The Big Picture

Regardless of what shape the thesis gives the body of a paper, the basic arrangement for all papers is *beginning/middle/end*. This sounds easy, but as you'll soon learn, beginnings and endings must be consciously created. They don't just appear where they are needed. They aren't already present in a thesis—you have to think them up. When you've done that, you want to be sure that the whole essay reads correctly—that a reader will have a sense that you've started in an appropriate place, developed the point you promised fully, and concluded with firmness and authority. That's the big picture. The introduction can't drag on too long, the conclusion shouldn't lamely repeat the opening, the middle has got to justify the time spent getting from beginning to end. In short, the essay must feel complete. If you sense problems, gaps, unexpected shifts and lapses, you can bet your reader will too. You'll need to spend a bit more time in the shaping stage.

Essay Introductions

The opening paragraphs of your paper should do three things:

- Get your readers' attention.
- State the promise you are making to readers—the thesis.
- Ease the readers into a perspective on the subject you want them to adopt.

Get Your Reader's Attention. Powerful introductions are crucial to successful papers for two reasons: (1) boredom is a writer's worst enemy and (2) competition for a reader's attention is enormous.

Never assume you've got a patient reader who will examine your paper the way a conscientious teacher or classmate might. Most readers turn away from a piece the moment they've lost interest and look for something else. It's said that a successful movie has to grab a viewer within its first ten minutes. As a writer, you don't have nearly that much time. Figure on about two lines or twenty *seconds.* That's right: twenty seconds. One-third the time Michael Jackson has to sell you a Diet Pepsi. The lesson is *don't dawdle.*

State the Promise You Are Making to the Reader. You can almost always *get* anybody's attention for a second or two, but you won't *keep* it long if there isn't something in what you say that seems clear and valuable. So after you have gotten your readers' attention, you must let them know what your purpose is, what you are going to write about; you must point them in the direction you want them to follow. They can't simply be left in mid-air, entertained with some snazzy opening; they have also got to see what you are promising to discuss in the essay.

Some students are inclined to write at the end of their introductions, "The purpose of this paper is . . ." or "In this paper I will. . . ." Readers usually enjoy an approach that is less stiff and mechanical. Don't leave a gap between the attention-getting part of the introduction and the point-telling part; but don't jar your reader with some klunky and obvious "I'm going to tell you about . . ." statement, either. Gaps and jars are hard on readers. Remember, though, that the introduction must contain, either explicitly or implicitly, the thesis of the writing, the promise you are making. Readers must know or be able to sense your point. Be sure they can.

Ease the Readers into a Perspective on Your Subject That You Want Them to Adopt. This is a more subtle task for your introduction, but it allows you to use the opening of the paper for double duty. You could spend the entire introduction talking about your subject in general, but it is more efficient to go directly to the subject as you are going to be discussing it. The following two examples show the difference. Both deal with the same message—telling the reader that canning one's own pickles offers two advantages: the fun of canning and the pleasure of having healthy food. Here is the first version, which begins—as you can see—far, far too wide.

> Health foods. Do those words make you think of seaweed cookies and sawdust-tasting soup? More and more people are beginning to learn that health foods can look and even taste just like ordinary food, yet they can really make a difference in length and quality of life. Health foods may be nothing more than ordinary foods grown or prepared in an organic and pure way, such as apples grown with no insecticide or peaches canned without additives. Realizing this,

> many people are more receptive to health foods and are willing to give them a try. A lot of people are beginning to do home canning. Pickles are a favorite thing to put up.

Well, this introduction finally *does* get to talking about canning pickles, but the reader has to wade through too much brine about health food in general. The writer is taking far too long to get to the subject and is not directing the reader's attention enough—or soon enough—to the specific subject of the essay. She has to jump awkwardly from health food to home canning. The reader feels stretched and senses too big a gap there.

Let's look at the second version:

> Home canning used to be a drag. Women would slave over a hot stove, heaving large pots of boiling water and taking all day to put up perhaps just one batch of beans. Home canning now is a hobby for men and women alike, and a lot of the pleasure comes from the ease of modern canning processes and the satisfaction of knowing that you are putting up clean, healthy food with no additives or preservatives. The new inexpensive equipment available for canners and the new awareness of the dangers of many commercially canned products makes even a job like making pickles a real pleasure. . . .

Here the writer gets into the subject of home canning immediately. It gives the reader a clear focus on the area to be concentrated on; it lets the reader know right away why the essay was written and what the reader ought to be thinking about. The more a writer can do this for a reader, the better the writing will be received.

Essay Conclusions

The ending of your paper ought to do three things:

- Remind readers of what you've said.
- Give readers one new thing to think about.
- Land readers gently—don't leave them hanging in the air.

Remind Readers of What You've Said. The whole purpose of your essay was to convey an idea to your readers. You gave them information, shared an opinion, argued a case. Now it makes sense to underscore your accomplishment with a brief flourish. Don't bore readers by replaying your entire theme—just hit the high notes. Reprise the tunes you want your audience to walk away from the paper whistling.

Sum up your main points. Pull together all that you've written into one tight statement that the reader can remember. That's all you need to do.

Give the Readers One New Thing to Think About. How can this be sound advice? Shouldn't you be concentrating on that "one tight statement" described in the previous paragraph? Won't readers be distracted if you give them something *new* to think about at the end of a paper? No, not if the idea spins off of your original thesis. Let it be some shrewd extra point that you can score only because of the solid work you've done in the paper. This new idea draws out the implications of your thesis so that readers continue to think about it after they've finished reading. The paper ends, but your ideas go on.

Provide a Gentle Landing. Keeping people hanging is all right in a mystery story or on a Ferris wheel, but not in an academic paper. Be sure your readers know when you are finished.

Concluding your paper merely affirms the principle of closure dear to human beings: you initiated a discussion and invited readers in; now you owe them the courtesy of seeing them to the door. Let your conclusion bring the paper to a gentle, clear, and firm end.

Promise and Delivery Checklist

Internal Check

- Does the paper make a clear promise to the reader?
- Does the form of the paper suit the promise it makes?
- Does the paper deliver on its promise? Can it?
- Does each paragraph develop the thesis or promise?
- Is any paragraph or sentence unrelated to the promise or thesis? Can it be cut?
- Can a reader understand how each paragraph or idea leads to the next?

External Check

- Does the opening paragraph attract a reader's attention? Does it make a reader eager to go on?
- Does the opening contain the promise the paper makes to a reader?
- Does the opening ease the reader into the point of view the paper presents?
- Does the conclusion remind the reader how the paper has delivered on the promises it made?
- Does the conclusion give the reader at least one new idea to think about?
- Does the conclusion bring the reader down to earth gradually?
- Does the paper feel complete?

APPLICATION

1. Read the following introductions to essays, some by professional writers, some by students. Notice how they (1) get the readers' attention, (2) tell the readers what the thesis of the writing is going to be, either directly or indirectly, and (3) move quickly into the exact focus on the subject the writer wants the reader to think about. Be able to discuss the specifics of these introductions with your class.

   A. We live in a country with the highest per capita income ever known to mankind; yet of every 100 of our citizens who reach the age of 65, 95 are flat broke! Of every 100 who reach their "golden years," only 2 are financially independent, 23 must continue to work, and 75 are dependent on friends, relatives, or charity.

      They lost the money game. The money game is not like any other game. You cannot choose whether you'll play. You cannot choose to sit out a hand or move to another game. For this game—the money game—is the only game in town.

      Since you have no choice but to play, then the only intelligent thing to do is to learn the rules and play to win! Losing means spending 20 to 30 years of your life in angry frustration in a state of financial insecurity.—Venita Van Caspel, *The New Money Dynamics.*

   B. "What is my goal in life?" "What am I striving for?" "What is my purpose?" These are questions which every individual asks himself at one time or another, sometimes calmly and meditatively, sometimes in agonizing uncertainty or despair. They are old, old questions which have been asked and answered in every century of history. Yet they are also questions which every individual must ask and answer for himself, in his own way. They are questions which I, as a counselor, hear expressed in many differing ways as men and women in personal distress try to learn, or understand, or choose, the directions which their lives are taking.

      In one sense there is nothing new which can be said about these questions. Indeed the opening phrase in the title I have chosen for this paper is taken from the writings of a man who wrestled with these questions more than a century ago. Simply to express another personal opinion about this whole issue of goals and purposes would seem presumptuous. But as I have worked for many years with troubled and maladjusted individuals I believe that I can discern a pattern, a trend, a commonality, an orderliness, in the tentative answers to these questions which they have found for themselves. And so I would like to share with you my perception of what human beings appear to be striving for, when they are free to choose.—Carl Rogers, *On Becoming a Person*

C. Now that they've taught pigeons to play table tennis and chimpanzees to play word games and computers to play chess, it's becoming quite difficult to distinguish humans from the rest of the landscape. So, if you set out to ask what makes people people rather than animals or machines, by and by you have to look into the subject of music. It appears that the ability to make music is a characteristic of human nature only.

True, birds sing. But their repertoire is very limited, fixed in each species by its habits and family background. Take the starling. Its familiar song of "cheap, cheap, cheap" bespeaks its natural habitat: city halls and bank buildings. Or listen to the melody of the dove—"plop-plop, plop-plop." That is clearly a genetic message, as the original names of the dove reveal. In English, this bird is called the *pigeon,* a word clearly derived from *pig* (meaning "pig") + *eon* (meaning "eternal"). In Spanish, of course, the bird is called *plopaloma.*

Properly speaking, then, birds cannot really be said to make music even though they can do a number on you.—Ward Cannel, *How to Play the Piano Despite Years of Lessons*

D. Teaching ten-year-olds how to play tennis is like teaching them how to play the piano. The only reason they are out on the court is because "Mommy" signed them up. And since learning tennis takes many hours of repetition and concentration, this causes a problem. The ten-year-old has an attention span only long enough to allow his or her little mind to come up with something mischieveous. After the first ten minutes are up, well, Billy and Jim start to fight, Terry puts gum in Nancy's hair, Nancy starts to push him, and the tennis teacher is ready to call it a day.

The trick to solving this problem is keeping the kids from thinking they are being taught. They could be at home watching television or riding bicycles which would be fun. So, the teacher must make learning to play tennis look like fun. That is the key to effective teaching.—Rick Jones

E. Last week while making out my annual report, I noticed something that I had not previously realized. Over the past year Dettmer's Greenery has been slowly declining in profits. So I took out time to consider seriously the problem, and I arrived at two factors which I feel are the reason for this decline. These two factors are low plant sales and improperly budgeted time. I do, however, have several suggestions which could help the company to correct these two problems.—Vicki White

F. An eight-year-old boy at summer camp lies on his bed crying. He feels empty, and he wants to go home. Ten years later, he stares out the window of his apartment with the same desolate feeling. Now, he realizes that he cannot run home, so he searches for some cure for his homesickness.

Most everyone has experienced this feeling at some point in his or her life. It is perfectly normal. It is the type of problem that must be confronted and then solved. As in all problems, there are ways to solve it.—Mark Shelton

2. Read these opening paragraphs from student essays and notice how you respond as a reader. Are you interested? Can you tell what the writer is going to write to you about? Does the writer give you an angle on the subject? Be ready to discuss your answers in class.

   A. What will happen to you the first few days of college life? Once you have settled into your class and study routine, what will you do with spare time for social pleasures? Where will you search for new friends?

      There is no need to look far. Even though most friends made at home and in high school are left behind, there will still be a lot of people around who are looking for friends just like you.

      The first place you probably make a new friend will be. . . .

   B. Chocolate-covered cherries have always been my favorite confectionery. They are always a special treat around our house especially around Christmas. This type of candy is, in my opinion, the best candy ever made. Plus it has a special kind of flavor made of ingredients that I do not particularly care for.

      Christmastime around our house is something special. . . .

   C. "Do you want to go to the show tonight?" "I don't know." "Aw, come on. I don't have anybody to go with." "Well, all right, guess I will."

      Oops, has another "yes" slipped out again when a "no" was intended? Don't worry. It's a common problem many people share. "No" seems to be a word that sticks to the tongue while "yes" blurts right on out and past it. How does a person learn to say "no"?

   D. The small-block Chevrolet V8, without a doubt, has become the most popular engine in America. During the past 22 years, Chevrolet has produced more than 32,000,000 small-block V8's. Since its debut in 1955, enthusiasts quickly recognized the small-block's power-to-weight benefits. This started new development and almost total modification of the small-block. To improve performance, the factory increased the small-block's size from the original 265 inches to displacements as large as 400 cubic inches. They also tested and produced many off-road performance parts at unbelievably low prices.

      But the development of the small-block by the factory was only the beginning. . . .

E. After waiting for what seemed like an eternity for my twenty-dollar steak, I noticed a wisp of smoke float over my shoulder. I glanced behind me to see if the kitchen was on fire and caught a blast of poisonous smoke in my face. The effects of this attack were immediate; my eyes became red and watery and my once-hungry stomach suddenly felt sick and queasy.

   I am sure all of you nonsmokers can empathize with my feelings that night as I was attacked by a foe who was wielding that omnipotent weapon, the cigarette. The physical and mental strain that nonsmokers get from smokers is intolerable. My anticipated pleasant meal that evening was ruined by an inconsiderate smoker. How can we nonsmokers stop this assault on ourselves?

F. Wouldn't it be super if you could just swallow a pill about the size of a vitamin and in a few minutes know everything there is to know about a certain subject? Jump into a machine and have it pop you into the middle of an atom to watch the electrons whirl about you? How about slipping back into the 1800's and seeing Abraham Lincoln and the way he lived his life? Just imagine how much time we wouldn't have to spend in school and how much more interesting learning would be.

   Well, getting back to reality, I think learning is a very difficult thing to get a hold of. It seems that a subject has to be interesting to enable it to sink into our head and stay there for a while. . . .

G. There are many things in this world that are known all over the globe. They are all vague ideas of universal concepts; they are vague because they are interpreted differently by each individual. One of these concepts is love. Love is a human emotion that is expressed in varying ways by different people.

3. Choose two of the introductions above (*A* through *G*) that need rewriting, and rewrite them.
4. Read these conclusions from student essays. Decide if each conclusion meets the three requirements for a good ending:

   Does the ending remind the readers of what has been said?

   Does the ending give the readers one new thing to think about?

   Does the ending provide a gentle completing of the paper so that the readers are not left hanging in the air?

A. To sum up, here are the steps you should follow if you are interested in installing solar heating in your home. First, see your banker and see what kind of loan you can get. Next, talk to your local power company; some companies help citizens install the system. Some even put in the system free of charge so long as the owner lets them collect data from it. If your power company will not help you with your system, then see if you can find a nearby installer of solar equipment, or do it yourself. Design a system and its installation around your loan. Get your loan for as long a period as possible; the longer the loan the more likely it is that a solar system will pay for itself. And, finally, start installing the system knowing that you are one of a growing number of people who are tired of paying high utility bills and tired of worrying if they are going to be warm this winter and who have turned to the sun for their energy needs.

B. Campus life is not, then, an individual effort. It is learning, studying, and making conversation and friends. Look around, smile, and be friendly, because friends are one of the greatest assets a college student has.

C. Time management includes more than just studying and having fun. Good time management should tell you when to get up, when to go to class, what to do in between classes, and everything else almost. Good time management is the efficient use of the time you have. Therefore, good time management is very important to college students, especially freshmen.

D. With the use of these new parts and the parts perfected in the past, it is now possible to reach over 2 horsepower per cubic inch in the small-block. Each year the power-to-weight ratio has increased, but can this go on forever? Can the Chevy small-block engine continue to improve and stay the favorite of most Americans for the years to come? Even if it can't, the Chevy small-block has already achieved more success than any other American-made engine, and it will not soon be surpassed.

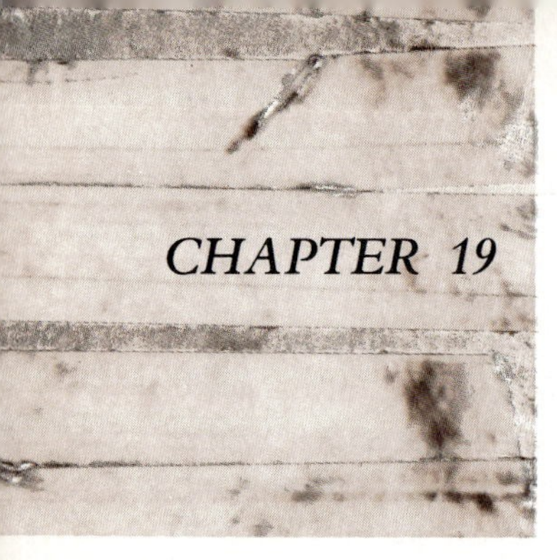

CHAPTER 19

Making Paragraphs Work

Paragraphs are conveniences. They bind sentences together in ways helpful to both writers and readers. At one time, writers were encouraged to treat paragraphs as separate, intricately crafted units of writing answerable only to their own standards of unity, coherence, and emphasis. Students especially were given the impression that writers spent time choosing elaborate paragraph patterns before they ever set to work on a paper. In fact, very few professional or business writers work this way, consciously designing their paragraph structures. Instead they treat paragraphs as dynamic components in the larger mechanism of the paper itself. Paragraphs are crafted to do something in the paper, to introduce a subject, expand on an idea, show a shift of thought, explore a contrast, highlight a piece of dialogue, house a conclusion. The essence of paragraphing is structured motion.

Paragraphs in an essay are somewhat like components in a stereo system. Alone and separate, they may contain plenty of technology, but they're also mute and useless. But take that amplifier and connect it to an equalizer, turntable, speakers—and suddenly there's an orchestra playing in the living room. This chapter will give you a detailed look at how paragraphs operate within papers—the two major jobs they have, the responsibilities they share for making ideas move and flow like music. The point is not to focus on paragraphs for their own sake, but to enhance the completing stage of writing—when attention to paragraphs can pay off in more successful writing.

WHAT A PARAGRAPH IS

The root word for *paragraph* originated in Greece, where the term *paragraphos* meant a mark a writer put in the margin of a manuscript to set off part of a text. (*Para* = "beside"; *graph* = "mark.") Since these early writers didn't indent the way we do today, or actually write in paragraphs as we know them, they used these marks in the margins to draw the readers' eyes to certain key points. Our contemporary use of paragraphs is not too far removed from this.

Think of a paragraph as a container that holds words and sentences that you want to keep together for some reason or other. Since *paragraph* is a term for the *container* that holds sentences and words, it stands to reason that the container can be used for different purposes. It's like having a jar that can contain berries or cherries or marbles or milk, or having a jar that you could use to prop up a window at your beach cabin or use as a magnifying glass. Paragraphs are similar. Sometimes they are containers for thought units, and sometimes they perform a function that serves the writer. Let's look at these two uses of paragraphing.

TWO KINDS OF PARAGRAPHS

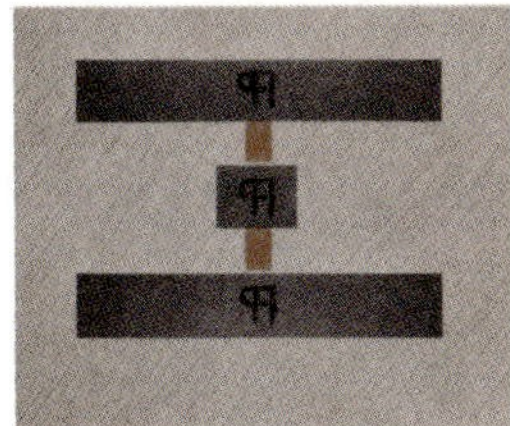

Topic Sentence paragraphs present content *within the paragraph* in a way that defines or limits the reader's thoughts; contains a chunk of *thought;* provides the reader with a feeling of *completeness and satisfaction* by paragraph's end.

The Topic Sentence paragraph takes one main idea and develops it. The topic sentence (sometimes stated, sometimes implied) tells the readers what you are about to discuss, focuses the readers' minds on that particular thing, and then provides enough information to prove or explain or illustrate or otherwise develop that main idea. Thus it is possible to break a Topic Sentence paragraph down into two parts: the *topic sentence* itself (the main idea, either stated or implied) and the *additional sentences* (directly related to the topic sentence and developing it). Since the information in a paper is carried by topic sentence paragraphs, they are essential to clear writing.

Function paragraphs direct the reader in *how to read* the essay; help keep the reader interested; allow the writer to emphasize or elaborate on certain points; and let the writer show style in writing.

The Function paragraph is a different matter entirely. In it, you won't find one main idea set forth and developed. In fact, at times a Function paragraph may be only one sentence; it's a "paragraph" only because it is indented. Often a series of Function paragraphs, taken all together, do indeed make up a single, related thought, but the writer chooses to break that chunk into smaller units. Some of the most common uses for Function paragraphs are these:

1. To add drama to the writing, keeping the reader's attention.
2. To make transitions.
3. To set off conversational dialogue and questions.

4. To break up a paragraph that seems too long (or to keep all paragraphs in the piece of writing about the same length).
5. To accommodate the author's personal writing style.
6. To emphasize a point, to develop an example, or to add details.

The descriptions of the two paragraph types are not exclusive. That is, it's possible to have a Topic Sentence paragraph that is also dramatic, and it's possible to have a Function paragraph that adds details. So the qualities that both paragraph types share overlap. Yet in terms of *purpose* or *use* or *function,* the two types are quite distinguishable. The Topic Sentence paragraph operates over and over, the same way. And Function paragraphs nearly always look and act like Function paragraphs and not at all like Topic Sentence paragraphs.

THE TOPIC SENTENCE PARAGRAPH

The Topic Sentence paragraph presents and develops a point or thought within the paragraph, defines or limits the reader's thoughts, and provides the reader with a feeling of completeness.

All essays must have several good Topic Sentence paragraphs; these paragraphs let you focus and limit attention to the issue you want the reader to think about. The Topic Sentence paragraph also provides the reader with a sense of *satisfaction* or *completeness* because it conveys the information or content of your message. A good Topic Sentence paragraph will never leave your reader guessing. It will also never let the reader's mind wander from your subject.

By putting the main points of your message into Topic Sentence paragraphs, you can be sure that your reader knows what you are trying to say. Topic Sentence paragraphs spiff up untidy thoughts and present them in a controlled, predictable, orderly form. They state the message clearly, leaving nothing for the reader to guess about.

That sounds a bit marvelous, a bit miraculous. Imagine having the reader think what *you* want her to think about, rather than what *she* prefers to think about! Well, it is wonderful, but it is also quite *systematic* and a "miracle" that anyone can repeat again and again, once the principles are understood.

Watch how a Topic Sentence paragraph operates:

Here's a word: **Sea** I write it down, and you read it.

Then you "see" in your mind's eye whatever the word makes you think of. Perhaps a vacation you took at the beach, a program you saw on TV, the time you were in the Navy, jogging on sand, a storm, whales, *Moby Dick,* or drowning. You think of whatever *you* think of; all I've done by writing down the word is to stimulate you to remember.

I add a few more words, giving you a phrase:

The Dead Sea

Now what has happened?

I've limited your thinking, directed it to what *I* am thinking about the word *sea.* Instead of entertaining any personal memory that you might remember connected with the word *sea,* now you are limiting your thinking (momentarily at least) to *The Dead Sea.* Maybe you think of the Dead Sea Scrolls. Or you might think, "Isn't that where you can float more easily than on the ocean?" or "I don't know anything about the Dead Sea." Whatever happens, you concentrate on *The Dead Sea* instead of just *sea,* simply because I have given you more information. I'm narrowing your attention.

Now, watch this. I give you a whole sentence:

The Dead Sea is not a sea at all.

What will probably happen when I write this sentence is that you will stop looking into your own memory for something you know about the Dead Sea and will instead pay attention to me because I've caused you to be interested in what I have to say. If you aren't actually interested, at least I've limited the things that at the moment you are thinking about *seas* and have directed you to the thing about seas that I want to say to you. And, of course, this is the purpose of all communication from one person to another: getting the other person's attention.

So, the Topic Sentence paragraph allows you to direct and control the reader's attention to what you want to communicate.

But is the sentence enough?

I've just written to you, *The Dead Sea is not a sea at all.* You're interested. I have your attention. What if I don't go on? How long would I keep your attention? If I added nothing to that sentence, you would be perfectly within your rights to say, "Well, what about it?" or "So what?"

Thus, if I want to keep your attention and get a complete message across to you, I have to add more sentences to this one. So that's what I do:

> Despite its name, the Dead Sea is not a sea at all. It is actually a lake. The lake ranges in depth from 33 meters in the north basin to 2 meters in the south basin. The lake is 45 miles long by 9 miles wide. The two basins which make up the lake were joined in biblical times by a neck of land which could be crossed on foot; today that neck of land is submerged and the lake looks like one continuous body of water.
>
> —Harvey Arden

You can see now how a paragraph works. I can't deliver my complete message unless I give you enough additional information. Maybe the single sentence *Despite its name, the Dead Sea is not a sea at all* would be enough for me, the writer, if I know all the facts about it already. But if I want another person to believe or pay attention to what I say, I have to provide enough information—enough sentences—so that the reader will feel *complete* and *convinced* when the paragraph is finished.

TOPIC SENTENCE PARAGRAPH:
A group of sentences that are connected one to the other to cause the reader to know some particular point the writer is making; the smallest unit of writing that a writer can use to get a *developed message* over to the reader.

It is ironic that the more information you give, the tighter you pull the circle of your reader's attention. The single sentence alone won't say enough. It's only when you put sentence to sentence that you can tell the reader any *meaning* about the subject. With each additional sentence, you're drawing your reader more and more into your circle of information. And you're directing—in fact controlling—what he or she thinks about your subject. A Topic Sentence paragraph can really put you in command and let you give the reader exactly the information you've chosen.

APPLICATION

1. Practice limiting your reader's thoughts by adding more information organic to your topic sentence. You can do this by pretending to be both the writer and the reader. Start with a single word. Write down what you think of when you see the word:

   Geography:

   Now, add some words to the single word (*geography*) and make a phrase that limits the reader's thinking:

   Phrase about *geography:*

   Now turn the group of words into a sentence:

   Sentence about *geography:*

   Do you see how with each step you are drawing a tighter circle around what your reader will think? You are directing the reader to what *you* want to say instead of letting the reader explore his or her random thoughts.

2. Do the same activity with the word *architecture*. Begin by listing the random thoughts you have about the word.

   Architecture:

   Add some words to *architecture* that make a phrase to limit the reader's thinking:

   Phrase about *architecture:*

Now turn the group of words into a sentence:

Sentence about *architecture:*

3. Take each of the following words through the same three steps. Notice every time how the writer can direct and control the reader's attention by giving additional information.

   mountain technology work equality children

Checking for Flow: Looking at Topic Sentence Paragraphs

Now let's apply this information about Topic Sentence paragraphs. If anything needs improvement in Topic Sentence paragraphs, it is probably in one of these three areas:

Principle 1: Tell the Reader Clearly What the Paragraph Is About

The Topic Sentence paragraph is named for its chief characteristic: the *topic sentence.* In a word, the topic sentence tells the reader what the paragraph is about. All other sentences in the paragraph *relate* to the topic sentence, by explaining or developing or giving additional information. The topic sentence, then, is absolutely necessary for a paragraph to deliver a developed message. More accurately, it is the *order* and *structure* of the topic sentence that are absolutely necessary. How does it order and structure? In two ways:

1. The topic sentence directs your readers to think about that aspect of the subject that you want them to consider. (Remember the Dead Sea examples earlier.)
2. The topic sentence also orders your own thoughts.

The topic sentence in a Topic Sentence paragraph works like a classifying system. It puts together thoughts that belong together. What determines whether they belong together is the *topic sentence.*

Here is how it works. Look at this example about the Anasazi Indians, who built the famous cliff dwellings in Colorado:

> *The Anasazi were builders and settlers on a large and permanent scale, and it is for this that they are best remembered.* At a time many centuries before the European discovery and settlement of the Americas, the Anasazi had developed a complex civilization of large and closely related communities. They erected massive and multistoried apartment buildings, walled cities, and cliff dwellings of shaped and mortared sandstone. They were dedicated farmers who planted, tilled, and even irrigated their crops, putting by the harvest to see them through the year. They were creative craftsmen of pottery and jewelry, and practiced a highly formalized religion in distinctive cere-

> monial chambers. The permanence and stability that they saw in their lives was reflected in the homes they built, but for reasons not yet completely understood their civilization lacked the durability of the building. The Anasazi abandoned their homeland, leaving the great stone cities and familiar farmlands for other areas in the Southwest, eventually to mix in the amalgam of modern Pueblo.
>
> —Donald G. Pike

Because the topic sentence is what it is—*The Anasazi were builders and settlers on a large and permanent scale, and it is for this that they are best remembered*—the reader can see immediately why the six other sentences in the paragraph belong there. The topic sentence is the "leader," and gathered around it are the sentences that constitute the rest of the group. The topic sentence is the "boss" or "director" and determines everything else that goes into that particular paragraph.

You can now see why it is necessary that you have a topic sentence for the paragraph. Without a topic sentence, there's nothing to direct the readers to a particular aspect of the subject, and there's nothing to hold the sentences together as a group. A paragraph without a topic sentence looks like this:

> Jogging is a fast-growing sport. Sports really contribute to good health. There is a new sports magazine on the market this month. Playing ball was a sport done thousands of years ago in primitive societies. People get injured in sports every year. Tennis players do not have a wide variety of shoes available to them. Sports can be expensive.

Reading that jumble of sentences, you feel as though you were being pushed from this to that, never knowing what was coming next. There was not a single "leader" sentence in the bunch that directed your thoughts and held all the other sentences together.

How *could* this paragraph become a good Topic Sentence paragraph? In fact, it's impossible to use all these sentences in one coherent paragraph; the best you could do is choose *one* of them, make *it* the topic sentence, and add the necessary sentences to develop the point.

> Playing ball was a sport done thousands of years ago in primitive societies. In fact, at Chichen Itza, an ancient Mayan Indian ruin on the Yucatán Peninsula in Mexico, you can still see the long ball court, the rings through which the ball was thrown, and the murals showing the two teams playing the game. The guides at Chichen Itza will tell you, too, how the winner of the ball game was rewarded. He was sacrificed to the rain god because that god deserved the very best. And by winning the game, he had proven he was the best.

It is in your own best interest to have topic sentences in your Topic Sentence paragraphs. Since your whole purpose is to get a message across to another person, you need to do everything possible to make it *easy.* Remember that the reader gets impatient. The reader wants to *know* quickly what you are going to talk about. Remember, too, that the topic sentence helps *you* too because it sets up an expectation that the rest of the paragraph can fulfill.

APPLICATION

1. Here are some sentences that could be good topic sentences for a Topic Sentence paragraph. Do a quick mini-discovery draft of a Topic Sentence paragraph to see what sentences will best "unwrap" each one.
   A. Paying bills has its humorous side.
   B. Working can be hazardous to your health.
   C. Mathematics is part of daily lives.
   D. Few Americans understand how the economy works.
   E. Transportation problems limit our lives.
   F. A woman who works has two exciting lives.
   G. Going to college as an adult requires special skills.
   H. Working and going to school at the same time is a drag.
2. Here are some "additional" sentences that might be added to a topic sentence. Write the *topic sentence* that will tie each unit together.
   A. Red makes you feel aggressive and alive. Blue, on the other hand, can be calming or it can be depressing. If you wear yellow, you will probably feel cheerful, if for no other reason than because people say, "You look cheerful today dressed in yellow." Black can look smashing and chic, or it can look drab, depending on how you accent it. Probably the worst color to wear at all is gray. You just fade into the crowd.

      Topic Sentence:

   B. When the day is cloudy and gloomy, I get depressed. Even if I have a busy day planned, the gloominess of a day without sunshine makes it difficult for me to function effectively. But rainy days don't depress me at all. Sometimes, though, they make me angry—especially when I have to do a lot of walking that day. I hate to arrive at work soaking wet. Other times, rainy days cheer me up. There is nothing as refreshing as a rain shower after several days of hot, muggy weather. My best moods, however, occur on warm, sunny days. The brightness of the sun lifts my spirits; I feel energetic and ready to work. The only problem then is that I'd rather be outdoors than indoors.

Topic Sentence:

C. Some advertisers suggest that their cigarettes will make you masculine or feminine. Marlboro and Virginia Slims ads are good examples of this. Others would like us to believe that their cigarettes will bring romance into our lives. Their ads feature happy couples usually strolling hand-in-hand; no doubt, we are to assume that the cigarette was instrumental in forming the romance. Still others claim that their cigarette is refreshing, that its taste will make you feel springtime fresh. Now that we know cigarette smoking may cause lung cancer, some advertisers try a logical appeal by comparing tar and nicotine levels; the smart smoker buys the cigarette with the least tar and nicotine and the best flavor. Actually, the smart person enjoys the ads and buys no cigarettes!

Topic Sentence:

Placement of the topic sentence in a topic sentence paragraph. Where does the topic sentence go in the paragraph? Usually it is placed in one of three places:

1. At the beginning
2. At the end
3. Nowhere—it's just "understood"

1. Placing the topic sentence at the beginning. By far the most common location for the topic sentence is at the beginning of a Topic Sentence paragraph. It is easy to appreciate the advantage of putting it there. The reader knows *immediately* what you are going to talk about. And *you* have a constant reminder too—from the very start—of what to concentrate on in this paragraph.

Here are two paragraphs written by college students. Both writers took pains to let the reader know *immediately* what they were going to talk about. See how their topic sentences signal the readers about what is going to be discussed.

> *Without a doubt, the small-block Chevrolet V8 engine has become the most popular automotive power plant in all aspects of motor sports.* Its power-to-weight benefits were quickly recognized by enthusiasts, and its development continues even today. During the past 22 years its size has grown from the original 265 cubic inches to displacements up to 400 (not to mention what a few hot rodders have been able to come up with). Not only has the size increased, but virtually every part of the

> engine has been modified in one way or another to improve performance. Special light weight cylinder blocks and heads have been produced by manufacturers throughout the country. Even the Chevrolet factory has been caught up in the sharp demands for better performing parts. They actually developed several magnesium cylinder blocks that weighed only 35 pounds, but they proved unusable and never reached the market. The Chevrolet people and other companies continue to work on ideas of saving weight so that the Chevy V8 will retain its popularity.

> *What happens when ducks swallow lead?* The pellets pass through the digestive tract to the gizzard where they are converted to a soluble form and absorbed by the bloodstream. Lead causes a reduction in oxygen supplies to all tissues. It interferes with the body's ability to break down glucose, leading to weight loss. Lead also disrupts the production of hemoglobin and anemia is the likely result. This imbalance in blood chemistry impairs the functioning of the liver and heart and causes severe damage to these organs. The external symptoms are an extreme loss of weight, wing droop, refusal to eat, a tendency to seek isolation and cover, and loss of the ability to walk or fly.

2. Placing the topic sentence at the end. One good reason for putting the topic sentence at the end of a paragraph is to keep the reader in suspense and, therefore, interested. The reader reads on to see what you are going to say when you get through, *but only if what comes first is really compelling.* Imagine a business or professional person picking up a book that started "You should learn how to type." Do you think the person would be interested in reading on? But imagine how it would be if the writer approached the subject by beginning the paragraph differently.

> All around us, every day, hundreds of millions of units of information travel all around the globe. From Bangkok to San Francisco, from Paris to Perth Amboy, this information rides the electronic waves that are changing and permeating the modern world. Nowadays, most people would find their lives greatly simplified by the use of computers—the "airline" that transports this wealth of information. And there is only one factor, aside from money and the fear of trying something new, that prevents the average business or professional person from benefiting from the computer goldmine: *not knowing how to type.*

The reader is much more likely to be willing to read on because the writer built up to the main point.

Another reason for putting the topic sentence at the end of a paragraph is to build point by point toward the conclusion so that the reader will be prepared to agree by the time he or she arrives. This type of paragraph is sometimes called *inductive,* since it induces the reader through a series of specific details toward a conclusion that draws those details all together. Here is an example:

> The Tarzan legend interests us for many reasons, not the least of which is that this human child was reared by apes. Wolves also, according to documented accounts, have raised humans (who grew to be more feral, more wolflike, than human). And stories abound of abandoned cubs of one species being taken in by nursing mamas of another. I myself know a ten-year-old cat who routinely washes her kittens—one of whom is a large three-year-old collie. *So nature herself tells us that it is "natural" to adopt a child of another race.*

The first example, about computerized information, shows how a reader can be teased into reading further. This example shows how a reader can be taken, one step at a time, toward a particular conclusion. The first sets out to trap interest; the second sets out to trap agreement.

3. Placing the topic sentence nowhere—having it "understood." Sometimes you may feel that the reader will know the main idea in the paragraph without being told. In fact, sometimes formally stating the main idea is artificial and stiff, so you put in only the specific details.

In the following example, the writer is describing New York City's subway system. No one sentence says so; therefore the main idea of the paragraph is just *understood.*

> It's a world unto itself down there—dark and drafty on the platforms, garishly bright and sweaty-hot (from all those bodies pressing together during rush hour) in the cars themselves. For some, the subway is "just a way to get from here to there," but for others it is, as they say, "an experience." Here is a typical subway experience: you spot an entrance and head quickly for it, glad for the chance to escape the rain/noise/pollution/what have you. Once inside, you convert your coins into round tokens with upside-down "Y"'s stamped out. You put your tokens into the slot of the turnstile, push mightily, and the arms of the turnstile allow you to enter. (On a bad day—i.e., when the crowd is massive, or angry, or just generally disgruntled—comparisons with the Gates of Hell are hard to resist.) You descend, or ascend, to the track on which your train will, eventually, come, steering clear of the gum that has not yet grown hard and stiff, the still-smoldering cigarette butts, the piles and puddles of questionable droppings—and you emerge on the platform. While waiting for the train, you have time to notice the visual decorations: giant ads that sport mustaches and various ingenious curses; general signs of decay that an old structure denied of daylight is probably

entitled to; and, most blatantly, the train graffiti. Some people see this testimony to the invention of spray paint as shocking and vandalistic; others see it as art. Whichever side you're on, you may not be able to see out the windows, which bear just as many boasts, curses, and comic-book-style decorations as the metal surfaces. Once on the train, you sit—if you're lucky—in a seat made of hard orange plastic (the older cars have wicker seats—these are unraveling, slashed by knives, or both). Or you stand, fighting openly or surreptitiously with other flailing fists for a handhold on the bar above the seats. If you lose out on the bar (or the straps that hang from it), you will have to use your sea legs to stay erect as the train lurches wildly from one bend to the next. Or, if you are in the thick of the sardine-can phenomenon known as rush hour, you will be kept vertical by the sheer pressure of bodies surrounding you. But you may not make it to—and out—the door when the train gets to your stop. (Assuming, of course, that you can *see* your stop from the painted windows.) Once you manage to get yourself out of there, you can try to get the brand-new wrinkles out of your permanent-press suit, dust yourself off, shake yourself into place, and ascend, or descend, the steps to the street—glad for the chance to be out in the rain/noise/pollution/what have you.

It's very important to recognize the difference between a paragraph with an implied or understood topic sentence, such as the one above, and a paragraph that is just a collection of unconnected sentences. If you are in the slightest doubt, put in the topic sentence. That way you are *certain* not to go wrong.

APPLICATION

1. Finding the Topic Sentence: Pick out the topic sentence in each paragraph below. If the topic sentence is implied, compose an appropriate sentence that describes the paragraph.
   A. The alcohol-drunk driver usually finds it hard to hide his condition, if stopped by the police. But the pot-high driver often believes he can "come down" and carry on a seemingly normal conversation with a police officer. This apparent ability to "hide their high" gives many pot smokers confidence that they can drive stoned.

      —Peggy Mann

   B. The room in which I found myself was very large and lofty. The windows were long, narrow, and pointed, and at so vast a distance from the black oaken floor as to be altogether inaccessible from within. Feeble gleams of encrimsoned light made their way through the trellised panes, and served to render sufficiently distinct the more prominent objects around; the eye, however, struggled in vain to reach the remoter angles of the chamber, or the recesses of the vaulted and fretted ceiling. Dark draperies hung upon the walls. The general furniture was profuse, comfortless, antique, and tattered. Many books and musical instruments lay scattered about, but failed to give any vitality to the scene. I felt that I breathed an atmosphere of sorrow. An air of stern, deep, and irredeemable gloom hung over and pervaded all.

—Edgar Allan Poe

C. In democracies, by definition, all human beings should have a say about technological developments that may profoundly change, even threaten, their lives: nuclear power, genetic engineering, the spread of microwave systems, the advance of satellite communications, and the ubiquitous use of computers, to name only a few. And yet, in order to participate fully in discussions of the implications of these technologies one must have training in at least physics, psychology, biology, philosophy, economics, and social and political theory. Any of these technologies has profound influence in all those areas. Because most of us are *not* so trained, all discussion takes place among our unelected surrogates, professionals and experts. They don't have this full range of training either, but they do have access to one or another area of it and can speak to each other in techno-jargon—"tradeoffs," "cost-benefits," "resource management"—and they therefore get to argue with each other over one side of the question or the other while the rest of us watch.

—Jerry Mander

D. When we first saw the barracks apartments, I told myself I would never live there. Five minutes later, we were turning the key to an apartment in one of those horrible buildings. (None of the nicer apartments were vacant, and we needed a place that day.) The first thing I didn't like was the stove that faced the door as you entered the apartment. Walking right into the kitchen as you came in reminded me of the crowded ghetto apartments I've seen on television. Then the couch looked like something you'd find in a cheaply furnished, rundown bus station. It was a gaudy orange vinyl and had no arms, and only two people could sit on it at a time because it was so small. There was no backboard on the bed, and the dresser drawer was made of brown, ugly metal. In the bathroom sink, there were separate hot and cold water faucets. I hated every thing about that apartment—but we lived there for three years!

E. I think the stature of humor must vary some with the times. The court fool in Shakespeare's day had no social standing and was no better than a lackey, but he did have some artistic standing and was listened to with considerable attention, there being a well-founded belief that he had the truth hidden somewhere about his person. Artistically he stood probably higher than the humorist of today, who has gained social position but not the ear of the mighty. (Think of the trouble the world would save itself if it would pay some attention to nonsense!) A narrative poet at court, singing of great deeds, enjoyed a higher standing than the fool and was allowed to wear fine clothes; yet I suspect that the ballad singer was more often than not a second-rate stooge, flattering his monarch lyrically, while the fool must often have been a first-rate character, giving his monarch good advice in bad puns.

—E. B. White

Principle 2: Make Sure That Every Sentence in the Topic Sentence Paragraph Is Related to the Topic Sentence

In the process of writing, ideas can pop up anywhere, sometimes surprising even you, the writer. Often these surprising ideas are so original or intriguing that you veer off in happy pursuit of them. This is fine in the creating stages of writing—in fact, it is even desirable because you may discover some worthwhile point. But when the writing process gets down to the completing stage, you must carefully examine each Topic Sentence paragraph to be sure that the reader doesn't get unintentionally surprised. Sudden veering off can be fun for the writer but confusing for the reader.

Because thoughts are as involuntary as they are deliberate, it's useful to have a means of testing whether they are behaving—or dashing off in all directions. For example, this paragraph from a student paper shows how the writer's thoughts veered while the paragraph was in progress.

> The sand dunes on the Oregon coast are as much fun as a carnival ride. You get into a modified pick-up truck, and the driver, who is probably 35, acts 14. He races up the dunes, stops suddenly, then takes off so fast that the truck—and you—leap several feet into the air. One man in our truck lost his glasses and his cigarette lighter on one of those leaps. His wife got very angry because the man could not find his belongings. The sand was so white and the truck had gone so far before the driver could hear us yelling "Stop!" that the glasses and lighter were nowhere to be seen. The wife wouldn't talk to the man all the way back to the ticket office. The spirit in the back of the truck just wasn't the same after that accident. The man was mad at the truck driver, and his wife was mad at him.

What has happened here? The writer began with a good topic sentence: *The sand dunes on the Oregon coast are as much fun as a carnival ride.* The next couple of sentences give additional information about *why* the dunes are like a carnival ride. But then the writer veers off course: after telling about the man who lost his glasses and lighter, the writer gets onto a different topic—anger and resentful feelings associated with loss of the articles. Suddenly we've been shunted from *fun* to *anger.* And although there is some connection here—the articles got lost and the anger came up during the dune buggy ride—the writer has not stayed on the topic as announced in the topic sentence.

The paragraph could be made to flow easily by giving some attention to the topic sentence. Here's the revised version, with all the sentences relating to the topic sentence.

> The sand dunes on the Oregon coast are as much fun as a carnival ride. You get into a modified pick-up truck with a driver who is probably 35 but acts 14. He races up the dunes, stops suddenly, then takes off so fast that the truck—and you—leap several feet into the air. One man in our truck lost his glasses and his cigarette lighter on one of those leaps. The driver will also spot another truck in the distance. The two will run right toward each other, swerving only at the last minute to avoid a head-on collision. Once our truck ran to the top of a dune, and suddenly there was nowhere to go. The dune went straight down so suddenly that you couldn't see the bottom at all. We all thought we were sailing off into the far-blue yonder and said our last goodbyes. When the ride was over, we all jumped off the truck saying, "I'll never do that again," but in fact we could hardly wait to get back in line to take the ride again.

Here the writer sticks to telling *why* the truck ride on the dunes is so much fun. The writer doesn't get sidetracked onto the story about the man's glasses or his wife's anger. Everything in the paragraph connects to the topic sentence.

APPLICATION

Determine which of the paragraphs below stay on the topic and which stray. Rewrite the ones that go off the topic.

1. Successful cooking can't be done quickly. The good cook reads recipes carefully *before* using them, and he rereads them as he goes along. He must assemble needed ingredients—or go out and buy them if they aren't available in his kitchen. He must gather utensils, and when the

specified utensil isn't available, he must try to come up with a suitable substitute. As he begins the recipe, he measures patiently and exactly and adds things in the order specified. He follows instructions exactly, beating, cooking, and mixing for specified periods of time; he knows that failing to do this may result in a less than perfect product. Then, he cooks the whole thing for as long as the recipe says—not five or ten minutes more or less. After everything is mixed and cooking, he takes time to clean up right away. Bowls, measuring spoons, beaters, and measuring cups must be washed. Unused ingredients must be returned to their proper places. Sometimes the kitchen floor must be mopped to clean up spilled flour or broken eggshells. But for the person who enjoys cooking, all this is time well spent.

2. These days, deciding how to spend your leisure time requires wisdom. If you watch television, you must determine which programs are worth watching and which should be turned off. Sometimes I think the people who produce TV programs aim to insult the public. There's nothing on but silly, unrealistic "sitcoms," violent, unrealistic adventure series, or ridiculous game shows. Do the producers think we have no taste when it comes to TV viewing? Do they think we don't use our minds when we watch television? The least they could do is offer something realistic. Sometimes I get so mad, I seriously consider getting rid of my set.
3. What I like most about going to college is the chance to meet new and exciting people. My roommate is one of the nicest persons I've ever met. He is goodnatured, understanding, and generally easy to get along with. There's only one thing I don't like about him—he studies too much. He gets up early to study and stays up late. I can't sleep when his study lamp is on. And I don't appreciate being awakened at 6 A.M. by his alarm clock. I sure wish he'd ease up on his studying. He'll end up going through college without having any fun—and I'll go through college without enough sleep!
4. The Paris Peace Accord signed in January, 1973, by the United States, South Vietnam, and North Vietnam effectively ended the American military presence in South Vietnam. The President of South Vietnam, Nguyen Van Thieu, signed the document reluctantly since it permitted more than 300,000 North Vietnamese troops to remain in his country. With the treaty, the United States had managed to extricate itself from the longest, most frustrating war in its history, but South Vietnam was left in an untenable position—worse than it had been in when the French pulled out in 1954. The communists, in effect, had won this time, but the Soviet Union would face an almost identical dilemma fifteen years later when it was compelled to negotiate a retreat from Afghanistan. There the might of Soviet arms was insufficient to defeat a native people's struggle for autonomy.

5. Plato and Aristotle represent opposing dimensions of Western cultural consciousness. Plato is the mystic, the idealistic dreamer who strives for unity and perfection in another world. He provides the philosophic framework for a religion and art directed to worlds beyond our own. Aristotle is the voice of reason, the eye turned to this world, examining, naming, categorizing, and counting. He is the scientist, the logician, the sober controller of earthly forces. Of course, neither represents the whole of consciousness. Figures like Cicero and Cleopatra, Caesar and Abraham are also powerful symbolic characters on the stage of history. No one can say just how influential any one person can be.

Principle 3: Always Give the Reader Enough Information

The danger here is that the writer always knows more than the reader and can easily underestimate the reader's need to know. *A confused or unsatisfied reader is a lost reader.* If a writer raises the expectations of the reader and then doesn't fulfill them with enough information, the reader resents what feels like a set-up. It's like a hotel that advertises deluxe accommodations when it has only canvas cots.

Here are two versions of a paragraph that illustrate this principle. The first version clearly does *not* give enough information:

> Cooking southern food is something anybody can learn to do. The most important thing the cook has to learn is to be patient. The cook must also learn to think imaginatively. Finally, someone cooking southern food must think big instead of small.

This paragraph is almost provoking in its skimpiness of detail! Why is *patience* important? What makes *imagination* necessary? And what on earth does the writer mean by "think big instead of small"? This is a prime example of a paragraph in which the writer knows more than the reader *and* isn't telling enough.

Now see what happens when the writer rewrites the paragraph, this time *making sure* that the reader knows what the topic sentence means:

> Cooking southern food is something anybody can learn to do. The most important thing the cook has to know how to do is to be patient. Almost all southern dishes cook for an enormously long time. Black-eyed peas simmer for half a day. Chicken and dumplings take hours. Green beans are cooked until they are pearl gray. The cook must also know how to use meat for seasoning, because almost all southern vegetable dishes are seasoned with meat. Green beans and black-eyed peas are cooked with fat-back or salted pork. Bacon grease is put into corn bread. Biscuits are made with lard. Finally, someone cooking southern food must think big instead of small. A southern meal is likely to have at least two meats, four or five vege-

> tables, three pies, and several cakes. And the portions are large, too. So the cook has to make plenty. With these characteristics, however—patience, imagination, and willingness to think big—anybody can cook southern food.

These details added to the revision bring life to the paragraph and let the reader *know* what the message means. What makes this principle—*always give the reader enough information*— so important? There are two primary reasons:

1. *Readers do not remember general statements very long at all.* What they do remember are images, specifics, "pictures" that the writer gives them. This is why the topic sentence is not enough within itself. It's the same principle at work when a set of instructions contains both written information *and* a picture: you have a much better chance of understanding how to put an appliance together. And this is what you are doing in paragraphs when you give specifics to back up the topic sentence. You are giving the reader a double opportunity of getting the message: one way with the general topic sentence and another way with the specifics you give that paint pictures for the reader.

2. *Readers are more likely to get the message if you give it to them several times.* Not only are you sending it in two different ways—through a topic sentence and through back-up details—but you are also repeating it. And you can hope that at least *one* of those times the reader will get it. This isn't because readers aren't smart. It's just because the communication process has to operate across space, time, and distance, and without the communicator being present. That makes communication difficult.

How much is enough? How can you know what is *enough* information? There is no formula that answers this question. *Who your readers are* is part of the answer, because how much they already know will determine how much you have to explain. So, as you look at your Topic Sentence paragraphs, see whether you have given enough information to make as good a guess as you can about *what your readers will need to be told.* This will be an estimate on your part; and if you are undecided about whether they will or won't know something, go with the *won't* because it is better to give too much information than too little.

Methods for giving enough information. Following are some ways to add information to your Topic Sentence paragraphs so that the readers will be satisfied.

1. Illustrations, examples, and details. Here are some Topic Sentence paragraphs that illustrate this method of providing information. Isabella Bird, an adventuresome Englishwoman traveling alone in the West in the late 1800s, wrote a fascinating account of her travels in a book called *A Lady's Life in the Rockies.** In the Topic Sentence paragraph she uses an example full of *details* to be sure the reader "gets the picture."

> But oh! what a hard, narrow life it is with which I am now in contact! Charlmers came from Illinois nine years ago, pronounced by the doctors to be far gone in consumption, and in two years he was strong. They are a queer family. . . . They have one hundred and sixty acres of land, a "Squatter's claim," and an invaluable water power. He is a lumberer, and has a saw-mill of a very primitive kind. I notice that every day something goes wrong with it, and this is the case throughout. If he wants to haul timber down, one or other of the oxen cannot be found; or if the timber is actually under way, a wheel or a part of the harness gives way, and the whole affair is at a standstill for days. The cabin is hardly a shelter, but is allowed to remain in ruins because the foundation of a frame house was once dug. A horse is always sure to be lame for want of a shoe nail, or a saddle to be useless from a broken buckle, and the wagon and harness are a marvel of temporary shifts, patchings, and insecure linkings with strands of rope. Nothing is ever ready or whole when it is wanted. . . .

2. Description. This method of adding information in Topic Sentence paragraphs answers such questions as "What does it look like?" "What does it feel like?" When you *describe,* you actually picture the object, person, or event for the reader. *You draw it with words.*

In this excerpt from *The Shirley Letters,* the writer—a cultivated woman—describes the interior of her log-cabin home.

> The room into which we have just entered is about twenty feet square. It is lined over the top with white cotton cloth, the breadths of which being sewed together only in spots, stretch apart in many places, giving one a birds-eye view of the shingles above. The sides are hung with a gaudy chintz, which I consider a perfect marvel of calico printing. The artist seems to have exhausted himself on *roses;* from the largest cabbage, down to the tiniest Burgundy, he has arranged them in every possible variety of wreath, garland, bouquet, and single flower; they are of all stages of growth, from earliest budhood up to the ravishing beauty of the "last rose of summer." Nor has he confined himself to the colors usually worn by this lovely plant; but, with the daring of a great genius soaring above nature, worshiping the ideal rather than the real, he has painted them brown, purple, green, black and blue. It would need a floral catalogue to give

*From *A Lady's Life in the Rocky Mountains* by Isabella L. Bird. New edition copyright © 1960 by the University of Oklahoma Press. Reprinted by permission.

you the names of *all* the varieties which bloom upon the calico; but, judging by the shapes—which really are much like the originals—I can swear to moss roses, Burgundies, York and Lancaster, tea roses, and multi-floras.

3. Definition. At times you may want to *define* a term or process, to add information in a Topic Sentence paragraph. Look at the way defining helps you understand the following excerpt; the Topic Sentence paragraph defines in order to give the reader enough information:

> The mountain dulcimer is a small, wooden, fretted instrument that is usually held on the lap while being played. The shape of the body may be a teardrop, a slender hourglass, or some unique variation. Likewise, the sound holes may vary in shape, from simple circles to hearts, clubs, or treble clefs. It has a raised fretboard—up to an inch from the body—on which three or four strings are tensed. These are attached at both ends—to stabilizing pegs at the bottom, and to tuning pegs at the top. Each string is tuned in relation to the other, according to the mode that one chooses—Ionian, Aeolian, Mixolydian, Dorian, Lydian, or Phrygian. The fourth string is often used as a drone—that is, it is tuned to the third string—which produces a haunting, resonant sound.

4. Explanation and analysis. Here are a couple of Topic Sentence paragraphs that use *explanation* to give the reader enough information. They come from a *Road & Track** article on the best cars in the world. *Road & Track* had two categories for this article, "Best Cars in the World" and "Best Car in Each of Ten Categories." These two paragraphs *explain* what those categories mean:

> <u>For the "Ten Best," we reasoned that some cars are "best" for one reason and some are "best" for another.</u> So, if we established rigid criteria for the ten best, we would be restricting the final list in ways that would end up favoring one group or one type. And this, we didn't want. Each car that belonged on this list did have to be "best" for a specific reason, however, although it did not have to be a "best" for the same reason as another. We also decided that the cars on the Ten Best list need not be models that were sold in the U.S. Just because our benevolent and protective government has decreed that some of the world's best cars should be denied to Americans, we did not think this was a sufficient reason for a particular model's exclusion if we agreed that it qualified otherwise as one of the Ten Best.

*From "The Ten Best Cars in the World, 1971," *Road & Track,* August 1971. Reprinted by permission of *Road & Track* magazine.

> For the "Best of Category," the criteria were more restrictive. Basically, the basic criterion was a judgment as to how well the car fulfilled the function for which it was intended in comparison with its direct competition. To make this decision it was of course necessary to include all the various facets that go into such an evaluation: engineering, assembly quality, handling, braking, reliability and so on. For the categories, we also restricted eligibility to those cars on which we had performed one of our normal road tests; that is, to those models that are available for sale in the U.S. at this time.

5. Facts and figures. Another way to develop a Topic Sentence paragraph is to use *facts* and *figures* when appropriate. The only purpose of any form of development is to give the reader enough information so that she or he will believe what you say, agree with what you say, listen to what you say, notice what you say. *Statistics* and *factual information* will often add the weight to your assertions that will swing the reader your way. Here is a paragraph which uses facts and figures to develop the topic sentence.

> A food crisis exists in Ethiopia. As many as 10 million people in that country may be close to starvation as a result of the severe drought. The official government estimate of the number of people affected by the drought is 7.3 million. This figure is based on the number of people registered for emergency food aid. The 10 million estimate includes the hungry people of Eritrea and Tigre provinces, hard-hit by the drought and by heavy fighting, and others who are too weak to leave their villages and go to the relief camps. Many relief workers, including some government officials, estimate that, by the end of 1985, more than 900,000 people will have died as a result of hunger and hunger-related disease in Ethiopia.

6. Repetition. You may be surprised to learn that at times *repetition* is an excellent device for developing a Topic Sentence paragraph. Often, repetition merely bores. And some writers may repeat simply because they don't have anything else to say—they said all they had to say in one sentence and hadn't anywhere else to go. By repeating, they at least fill up the page!

The kind of repetition we are considering here, however, is *valuable development* of the message you are sending. Since readers do not have a long memory for the points you are making, you can develop the reader's mind in case they have been forgotten. The example here shows how valuable *repetition* can be when used in the right way:

> People who get fitted with their first pair of contact lenses are often very excited, delighted, and grateful to see so effortlessly after many years of wearing thick, heavy glasses. *But they need to be responsible,*

> *too, especially in terms of cleaning their lenses.* After a normal day of wear, lenses are coated with a film of natural chemicals secreted by the eyes. If this film is not washed off with a solution made for that purpose, the lens will get brittle and possibly scratched, making it unwearable. Also, the coating obscures clear vision, like a dirty windshield on a car. So it is really important to take care of lenses every night by cleaning them carefully with a lens-cleaning solution suitable for the particular kind of lens. Well-kept lens are more comfortable, and last much longer.

7. ***Comparison and contrast.*** A common way to help your reader "see" what you mean is to *compare* it to something else showing how the two things are alike, or to *contrast* it with something else, showing how your idea is different from something else. Putting two things up together can throw light on the point that you, the writer, really want to get across. Look at the way Annie Dillard uses a *comparison* of Nature with a children's puzzle to develop her thoughts:

> It's all a matter of keeping my eyes open. Nature is like one of those line drawings of a tree that are puzzles for children: Can you find hidden in the leaves a duck, a house, a boy, a bucket, a zebra, and a boot? Specialists can find the most incredibly well-hidden things. . . .

8. ***Narrative.*** "Once upon a time . . .": you can never fail to get a reader's attention if you *tell a story,* but in addition to that, a narrative can help you *explain* or *illustrate* the point you are making in a Topic Sentence paragraph. In the second paragraph here, Thomas Merton uses a story to let the reader know what he means by the paragraph which has come immediately before.

> The rain I am in is not like the rain of cities. It fills the wood with an immense and confused sound. It covers the flat roof of the cabin and its porch with insistent and controlled rhythms. And I listen, because it reminds me again and again that the whole world runs by rhythms I have not yet learned to recognize, rhythms that are not those of the engineer.
>
> I came up here from the monastery last night, sloshing through the cornfield, said vespers, and put some oatmeal on the Coleman stove for supper. It boiled over while I was listening to the rain and toasting a piece of bread at the log fire. The night became very dark. The rain surrounded the whole cabin with its enormous virginal myth, a whole world of meaning, of secrecy, of silence, of rumor. Think of it: all that speech pouring down, selling nothing, judging nobody, drenching the thick mulch of dead leaves, soaking the trees, filling the gullies and crannies of the woods with water, washing out the places where men have stripped the hillside! What a thing it is to sit

absolutely alone, in the forest, at night, cherished by this wonderful, unintelligible, perfectly innocent speech, the most comforting speech in the world, the talk that rain makes by itself all over the ridges, and the talk of the water courses everywhere in the hollows!

Nobody started it, nobody is going to stop it. It will talk as long as it wants, this rain. As long as it talks I am going to listen.

APPLICATION

1. Undeveloped Paragraphs
   Each of the paragraphs in these two passages is undeveloped. Using any of the methods discussed previously, rewrite each paragraph so that the topic is developed fully for the reader.
   A. Although a college degree is a form of success in itself, only the individual can determine if that degree is the beginning or the end of the road. A person must want success in order to attain it.
      In today's highly specialized and technical society, a university education is practically the only way to open doors of opportunity. Most good jobs require college degrees. But once on the job, a person must be willing to work hard and be the best that he can be.
      Although a university education is not the only requirement for success, it is a necessary part of the make-up of a successful individual.
   B. Euthanasia would prevent prolonged mourning by family and loved ones. It would ease the enormous financial burden that a family must bear in order to keep a person alive on life support systems.
      This financial strain combined with the worry and sadness of having a person in the family in this condition brings strains on the rest of the family. These combined pressures often cause breakups in family life and sometimes lead to divorce.
      No family should suffer these misfortunes and in most cases if a family is close, euthanasia will prevent this problem.
2. Topic Sentence Paragraph Review
   The following paragraphs do *not* follow the three principles about writing good topic sentence paragraphs.
   (a) What principle is missing in each paragraph?
   (b) Revise each paragraph so that the message has a better chance of working.

THREE PRINCIPLES FOR TOPIC SENTENCE PARAGRAPHS:
1. Tell the reader clearly what the paragraph is about.
2. Make sure every sentence relates to the topic sentence.
3. Give the reader enough information.

A. "No" is just a simple, one-syllable word used to express a negative answer. Agreed, the word "no" is easy to say, but to answer someone directly with it changes the entire situation.

B. Education concerning the harmful effects of smoking should be increased. This can be done through the schools, starting with health programs for children at an early age. Some schools have initiated such programs, but a more widespread and intensive approach must be employed.

C. Gardening of vegetables is one hobby that is money-saving; not many hobbies can claim this. It is also fruitful, literally. Gardening of vegetables is relatively easy if you approach it in the right manner. First, you must have the proper location and tools. Pick a site that gets plenty of sunshine, is wind free, and preferably enclosed. You then must have some tool that breaks up the soil. I would recommend investing in a small tiller. You will also need an efficient watering system and common tools such as a hoe and garden rake.

D. Jogging requires determination. When a runner first begins, a thousand reasons come up for not going out. It will be too cold or too hot. Or the runner won't have any spare time. It is quite difficult to run in hot weather, and a runner has to train for it. The best thing to do is to run in the cool part of the day, stay in the shade, run slower, and drink something cold upon the return from the run. Running in cold weather just requires bundling up warmly but be careful not to wear too many clothes because your body gets hot fast when you are jogging.

3. Paragraphs Representing All Three Types of Errors
Explain how the paragraphs below violate all three principles of paragraph writing. Then explain how each might be corrected.

A. We are going to have to face the situation. We all have been brainwashed into the society we are by a variety of sources. Television is the main contributor of propaganda, followed by the government, other mass media, public education, the term "the American Dream," your neighbors, big business and labor, and maybe even your own mother.

B. Although it was hard for the man working long hours and not getting paid a high salary, the woman's day was not easy. The average wife in the fifties stayed at home and cooked, cleaned and waited for her husband to come home. There is nothing wrong with this except for the fact that there was no diversion except for the radio. The television did not yet exist. The average couple had only one car which the husband would take to work. This meant the wife was stuck at home all day. To buy groceries, the wife would walk and either carry the bags home or pull them in a small cart. Although a couple starting out in the 1950s had a hard financial struggle, they appreciated all they had worked for.

C. To me the university is a place where I can go to fulfill my dream in life. Granted, the university is not for everyone—just those who want it. A carpenter, construction worker, a farmer have no reason to attend universities, but a doctor, scientist, businessman, or teacher all have to continue their education in universities, which sometimes can be expensive.

THE FUNCTION PARAGRAPH

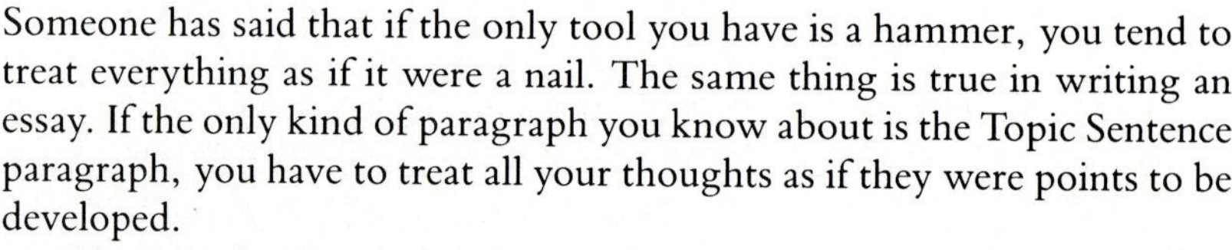

Someone has said that if the only tool you have is a hammer, you tend to treat everything as if it were a nail. The same thing is true in writing an essay. If the only kind of paragraph you know about is the Topic Sentence paragraph, you have to treat all your thoughts as if they were points to be developed.

Fortunately, this isn't the case.

As wonderful, useful, and necessary as the Topic Sentence paragraph is, it isn't the only kind, even though it is the most commonly known. There are other uses of paragraphs—and you see many of them in magazine articles and in books—that are *not* topic sentence + development. Rather, they are *Function Paragraphs,* paragraphs that do things other than give the reader information about a topic sentence.

FUNCTION PARAGRAPH: **Paragraph to keep the reader alert and interested, to dramatize or quicken the pace.**

The Function paragraph guides the reader through the piece of writing, keeps the reader's interest whetted, and expresses the writer's personality, whims, style, and purposes.

Function paragraphs are amusing, quirky, and fascinating to learn about, but the main thing is that they are *useful.* Knowing about Function paragraphs, you aren't confused when you look at writing in books and magazines and find paragraphs that don't begin with a new thought and furnish a developed message. More importantly, however, when you know about Function paragraphs you can discover new ways of controlling your writing and directing your reader, and will find new possibilities for putting energy, personality, and variety into your writing.

Function paragraphs work like the time signatures and notations on a piece of music. They assist you in orchestrating the essay and in telling the reader how to read it. Following are some ways to use Function paragraphs.

1. Function Paragraphs Add Drama and Get the Reader's Attention. Often when people really want to get someone's attention, they will shout, "Listen to me!" Or they will use their hands in a dramatic gesture to keep the listener's eyes on them. When you are writing, of course, you can do none of these things, so you have to depend on other means to get the reader's attention. Function paragraphs will do this for you. See how Isabella Bird uses a one-sentence Function paragraph to set up the reader in anticipation for what is coming next.

> I shall not soon forget my first night here.
>
> Somewhat dazed by the rarefied air, entranced by the glorious beauty, slightly puzzled by the motley company, whose faces loomed not always quite distinctly through the cloud of smoke produced by eleven pipes, I went to my solitary cabin at nine, attended by Evans. It was very dark, and it seemed a long way off. Something howled—Evans said it was a wolf—and owls apparently innumerable hooted incessantly. The pole-star, exactly opposite my cabin door, burned like a lamp. The frost was sharp. Evans opened the door, lighted a candle, and left me, and I was soon in my hay bed. I was frightened—that is, afraid of being frightened, it was so eerie—but sleep soon got the better of my fears. I was awoke by a heavy breathing, a noise something like sawing under the floor, and a pushing and upheaving, all very loud. My candle was all burned, and, in truth, I dared not stir. The noise went on for an hour fully, when, just as I thought the floor had been made sufficiently thin for all purposes of ingress, the sounds abruptly ceased, and I fell asleep again. My hair was not, as it ought to have been, white in the morning!*

That first sentence is so catchy that we tend not to even notice that it is a paragraph all by itself. You read "I shall not soon forget my first night here" and dash on to find out about that night and what was so unforgettable about it. Of course the author *could* have put that sentence with the next paragraph and thus have made *one* unit instead of *two*. And it would certainly have fit the rules for Topic Sentence paragraphs, too. But look at the drama that would have been lost!

Here's another example of a Function paragraph used for drama.

> After the tour I stopped at the refreshment stand at the base of Masada and found myself sitting across from a rather elegant-looking white-haired woman. "Excuse me," she said, "would you happen to know where I can find some mud?"
>
> Mud?

The one-word response to the woman's request dramatizes Harvey Arden's astonishment. And we get it with a punch, which would have been lacking if the author had replaced that single word with a sentence or two that *explained* how he felt. Furthermore, the single word contributes to the lean, swift movement of the passage, as contrasted with the loss of impact that would have resulted if there had been several lines of explanation. It's the difference between someone who tells a joke and lets it go, and someone who explains the punchline for fifteen minutes.

*From *A Lady's Life in the Rocky Mountains* by Isabella L. Bird. New Edition copyright © 1960 by the University of Oklahoma Press. Reprinted by permission.

> must be related to what has gone before. . . . Clear problem-statement is important because it allows a development related constantly to both aspects of any problem: that which exists and that which is desired.

APPLICATION

Explain which of the paragraphs in the following passages are Function paragraphs. Describe what their function is in each passage.

1. Try to remember a time when you *first* read a book or heard a radio show and then *later* saw a film or a television program on the same work.

   If you read, say, *Gone with the Wind, Roots, Marjorie Morningstar* or *From Here to Eternity,* or heard any radio show such as "The Lone Ranger" first, you created your own internal image of the events described while you read or listened. You imagined the characters, the events and the ambience. You made pictures in your mind. These pictures were yours. Of course, they were influenced by the author—what he or she told you—but the creation of the actual image was up to you.

   Marjorie Morningstar was an image in your mind *before* you saw the film. Then you saw the film with Natalie Wood playing Marjorie. Once you had seen Natalie Wood in the role, could you recover the image you had made up?

   —Jerry Mander

2. Style is organic to the person doing the writing, as much a part of him as his hair, or, if he is bald, his lack of it. Trying to add style is like adding a toupée. At first glance the formerly bald man looks young and even handsome. But at second glance—and with a toupée there is always a second glance—he doesn't look quite right. The problem is not that he doesn't look well groomed; he does, and we can only admire the wigmaker's almost perfect skill. The point is that he doesn't look himself.

   This is the problem of the writer who sets out deliberately to garnish his prose. You lose whatever it is that makes you unique. The reader will usually notice if you are putting on airs. He wants the person who is talking to him to sound genuine. Therefore a fundamental rule is: be yourself.

   —William Zinsser

3. I have never been as scared as I was that day.

   We had driven to the top of the mountain to get a better view of the lake. We scrambled out of the car and ran to the edge of the mountain, being careful not to get too close lest we tumble down the steep, rocky side. As we returned to the car, Mike casually pointed to the darkening, swirling clouds above. Those weren't ordinary clouds. Herman shouted, "That's a tornado forming and about to touch down right on us!"

We didn't know what to do. If we stayed on the mountain, the tornado was sure to hit us. We tried driving down, but the swirling leaves and dust on the dirt road ahead told us the tornado was right in front. After frantically—and futilely—signaling for help on his CB radio, Herman decided to risk the drive down. We made it safely, but a few minutes later we heard on the radio that it had touched down on the other side of the mountain, killing several residents of a mobile home park.

4. Come on, admit it.

   You've been living with someone for a while now and you sometimes think you've made a mistake, a big mistake. There are things you want to do that you can't because the person you are living with gets in the way.

   You feel cheated. You're missing alot. You can't stand thinking about it because it hurts so much. Sometimes you just want to be alone, free to be and do whatever you want.

   —David Viscott

SOME FINAL OBSERVATIONS ON PARAGRAPHING FOR FLOW

In the completing stage you look at your writing to see what you can do to make it move faster, interest the reader more, be better connected, or emphasize what you want remembered. You check all the Topic Sentence paragraphs, to see that they are in good order. You see if you want to add any Function paragraphs. You may need a *transition paragraph* to get the reader from one point to another. You may notice places you could use a little drama—maybe wake up the readers and keep them interested. Perhaps one of your thoughts could use another example, and you'll put in a Function paragraph to highlight that extra information.

Make those decisions according to what you believe is best for the reader and for your material. But remember: little writing in the real world is ever one Topic Sentence paragraph after another. Real messages usually don't fall into these neat packages. Function paragraphs add interest and assure flow. You will want some if for no other reason than to sound like *yourself* when you write instead of like some dull "voice of the past."

This doesn't mean, however, that you can ignore rules for paragraphing. You can't just paragraph anywhere and everywhere—with no rhyme or reason—and have your writing work. *If* you are conscious about *why* you are paragraphing—*what purpose each paragraph serves*—then you do get to paragraph wherever you want to. But if you paragraph without conscious thought, the result will inevitably be a disjointed, undeveloped, uncommunicative piece of writing.

There is, then, truth to the saying, "You learn the rules in order to know how to break them." You learn Topic Sentence paragraphing and Function paragraphing to know how to be individual and independent in using them. *But you have to know the basic concepts thoroughly.* You won't be able to fool anybody by claiming, "Oh, I just felt like putting a paragraph there." Strange paragraphing only wastes your time, because the whole purpose of writing—to get a message across to someone else—will have been lost. So be fair to yourself. Learn paragraphing and be honest in its use.

For some, a sense of paragraphing comes naturally—it's like having a sense of rhythm about dancing. In such cases, the paragraphs tend to almost shape themselves with a natural and pleasing variety. For other people, paragraphs are more a matter of conscious design. They are added after the content of the paper has been written and then rewritten at least once. The final version, though, inevitably reveals the personal preference and style of the writer. For example, you may have noticed that people who depend on lots of one-sentence paragraphs often talk with their hands too! And writers who produce long, detailed paragraphs are often long-winded talkers—and may have a reputation for being "heavy" and "serious." The balance between "too breezy" and "too heavy" isn't usually taught—in fact, it usually isn't even discussed in many texts. Yet sophisticated writers somehow learn about such things, and the discovery almost inevitably extends the range of a writer's possibilities.

As you do the completing stage of your essay, watch for the flow of the message. Sometimes a Topic Sentence paragraph will be most appropriate, other times a Function paragraph will work just right. Just keep your eye out for ways of moving the essay along smoothly and continuously; that's the point of it all.

Here is a portion of the essay on the Dead Sea, which we have quoted in this section. The beginning of the essay has been annotated so that you can see exactly how professional writers combine Topic Sentence paragraphs and Function paragraphs in their writing. Beginning with paragraph (5), you should attempt to supply your own annotation or notes—your own analysis, in other words—similar to those provided for paragraphs (1) to (4).

You will observe how much (or how little) rhyme and reason there is to how professional writers use paragraphs. When you finish, you'll understand that there is no firm rule about paragraphing. Yet at the same time, you'll have a broader concept of how paragraphs can be used effectively in your own writing.

THE LIVING DEAD SEA Harvey Arden/*National Geographic Staff*

(1) FUNCTION PARAGRAPH:
To get the reader's attention. The two-sentence introduction sets the scene and gets the essay moving swiftly. Writer gets reader's attention by being a little mysterious as he begins.

(1) Getting to the bottom of it all is not so difficult. If you happen to be in Jerusalem, as I was one rainy November, you need only hail a taxi and ask to be taken to the Dead Sea—the lowest spot on the surface of the earth.

(2) TOPIC SENTENCE PARAGRAPH:
Main idea is Dead Sea; rest of sentences develop this main idea.

(2) It's only a half-hour drive from Jerusalem's 760-meter spiritual height to the Dead Sea's netherworldish shore—399 meters (1,309 feet) *below* sea level. Snaking through sere Judaean hills where Abraham and Jesus once walked, you pass a sign that says "SEA LEVEL" in Hebrew, Arabic, and English. It may vaguely occur to you that there aren't too many places in the world where you can dip below sea level in a taxicab and keep going, but such thoughts are now shunted out of mind by the fact that your ears have begun to pop, your head is ringing slightly, and the wool sweater you'd snuggled into back in Jerusalem's 10° C (50° F) chill has become uncomfortably warm.

(3) FUNCTION PARAGRAPH:
To break up a long paragraph.

(3) Your Israeli driver, Shlomo, informs you that this new-looking road was modernized by Jordan's King Hussein just before the six-day war of 1967 brought the West Bank under Israeli military control.

(4) FUNCTION PARAGRAPH:
To make transition. This paragraph hooks a new train of thought onto previous remark. The paragraph also allows writer to give additional detail about the road.

(4) "Nice of the king," Shlomo remarks wryly, and you slouch back in your seat just a bit uncomfortably at the thought that this is occupied territory. Before 1967 only the southwest quadrant of the Dead Sea belonged to Israel. An Israeli in West Jerusalem, unable to cross into Jordanian territory, had to take an hours-long round-about drive through Beersheba to get to the Dead Sea. Nowadays, using "King Hussein's road" across the West Bank, it's just a short trip. . . .

(5) Off to the left a splash of green brightens the ocher landscape. "That's Jericho," Shlomo says. "Oldest known town in the world. Been there 10,000 years. And that's the River Jordan just beyond, where Jesus was baptized by John. Over there"—he points to some caveriddled cliffs to the right—"is Qumran, where most of the Dead Sea Scrolls were found. And see those mountains? One of them is Mount Nebo, where Moses died. Joshua then led the Israelites into the Promised Land right down there, across the Jordan above the Dead Sea."

(6) He smiles. "It's easy to believe in the Bible when you come to a place like this."

(7) Ten minutes later you reach the Dead Sea shore at a former Jordanian spa called the Lido. Like most first-time visitors, you cross the salt-encrusted beach to the water's edge, crouch down, poke one finger through the oily-looking surface, then gingerly put it to your tongue.

(8) *Arghhh-h!* The taste is as strong and stinging as lye. "Worst-tasting stuff in the world!" Shlomo laughs, and you don't argue. . . .

(9) Despite its name, the Dead Sea is not a sea at all. It's actually a lake with a deep northern basin 331 meters (1,086 feet) deep, and a smaller southern basin averaging only about two meters deep. The two, totaling 75 kilometers (45 miles) long by 15 kilometers (9 miles) wide, are joined across a now submerged neck of land that could be crossed on foot in Biblical times, when the water was lower. . . .

(10) Nor is the Dead Sea "dead." While it's true that fish can't live in it, scientists have discovered in its waters a number of halophilic—salt-loving—microorganisms. One of them, *Halobacterium halobium,* has recently been found by U.S. scientist Dr. Walther Stoeckenius to yield a purple pigment that is the only known biological substance other than chlorophyll capable of photosynthesis—the conversion of sunlight directly into energy.

Polishing Sentences

Chapter 4 presented three basic ways of adding energy to sentences: (1) combine choppy sentences, (2) add details, and (3) place descriptions in the right place. This chapter will demonstrate several other ways of building and refining sentences—to give them more variety and sophistication. Sentences are not isolated parts of an essay subject to limitless and arbitrary manipulation. Like paragraphs and words, sentences must support the larger concerns of a writing situation: audience, purpose, social circumstance. Yet sentences do have a life of their own; they cannot be precisely governed or predicted. They reflect the pulse of conversation within and around you; the sentences you write today will differ from ones you produce tomorrow—even if you are addressing the same issues. They may carry contrary images, favor different verbs, respond to offbeat rhythms, mimic different voices.

Because sentences are so variable, they offer many opportunities for managing strategies and moods. You *can* consciously do things to sentences to make a paper read more smoothly, move more dramatically, seem serious or lighthearted. You can write sentences that convey a sense of balance, harmony, thoughtfulness—or exactly the opposite. Time spent learning about sentences pays off, however, not in a list of facts about clauses and coordinators, but in an instinct you develop for the way words and ideas mesh. And that is what this workshop chapter is about: learning to craft sentences with the same imaginative energy that you bring to creating ideas.

VARY SENTENCES

One key way to add interest and energy to your writing is to vary the structure of your sentences.

Varying Basic Patterns

Linguists tell us that basic English sentence patterns are few and simple, like this:

Cows	eat.	
Cows	eat	grass.
Grass	is	green.

We rarely use such simple patterns in regular conversation or writing. Our "real" sentences are longer—they carry more information. We vary the basic patterns and add information to them through a process called *expansion,* adding single words or groups of words here and there.

This is an example of such an expansion:

John has a job.

Finally, John has a job.

After three months of hunting, John has a job.

John has a job after three months of hunting.

Although he spent three months looking, John finally has a job.

When you are revising for energy in your writing, check to see whether you use the simple patterns over and over again. If you do, you can probably count on your readers getting bored. *Give them some variety.* You can vary your sentences by modeling the variations after some of the ones that follow. Take a simple, basic sentence like:

Green pepper is good in spaghetti sauce.

Now look at the variations you can make of this basic pattern:

To make really good spaghetti sauce, you should add green pepper.

With green pepper added, spaghetti sauce is much better.

By adding green pepper, you can really make good spaghetti sauce.

Spaghetti is better with green pepper in the sauce.

That green pepper which has been added makes this spaghetti sauce better.

The spaghetti sauce, with green pepper added, is better.

The spaghetti sauce, which has had green pepper added to it, is better.

Just for practice, see how many variations you can make of this sentence:

A good dictionary improves writing.

You can even make a kind of game out of seeing how many ways you can write a sentence—sometimes just by moving one word.

ONLY I saw Howard Smith in the morning.

I ONLY saw Howard Smith in the morning.

I saw ONLY Howard Smith in the morning.

I saw Howard Smith ONLY in the morning.

I saw Howard Smith in the morning ONLY.

Each shift produces a slight variation. Making a game of it, and keeping alert for the various implications of each combination, you can enjoy revising your sentences for energy, and maybe even have fun. The bonus for you, besides an increased mastery of sentence varieties, is that you'll have gained a technique for helping the reader stay interested.

Varying Sentence Openers

Sometimes a sentence opener that works just fine on its own loses power when repeated again and again. For example, look at this paragraph:

> He said that now was the time for all good students to come to the aid of their school. He said that funds are needed, and that there are many ways to raise them. He said that if all students do their part, all will be well.

By varying the sentence openers, you can turn this yawn-maker into a sentence that sustains interest. For example:

> Now, he said, was the time for all good students to come to the aid of their school. Funds are needed, and there are many ways to raise them. If all students do their part, he is sure that all will be well.

Can you see how simply varying the ways each sentence begins adds energy, movement, and interest? Which paragraph would be more likely to get your attention—and action?

Varying the Order of Words

Sentences whose words don't all follow the same pattern are much more interesting than sentences whose words follow an identical pattern. For example, here is a sentence made up of words that follow only a single order:

> He raised the window. He looked out the window. He saw his friend. He waved to his friend. He threw down the key. He did not see his friend. He listened for a sound. He heard the key turn in the lock.

By ordering each sentence in an identical way (subject-verb-object), the writer bores the reader. But what if the word order were *varied* from sentence to sentence? It might come out like this:

> He raised the window and looked out. He saw, and waved to, his friend, and threw down the key. No longer seeing his friend, he listened for a sound. In the lock, the key turned.

Merely varying the order of the words—and adding a few transitional words—is enough to turn a monotonous string of sentences into a connected, flowing, energetic paragraph.

APPLICATION

1. Rewrite these sentences, consciously varying the basic patterns you find there. See how many different kinds of sentences you can include.

   It was the last track meet of the season. The state championship. I was going to long jump and run the mile relay. Now the long jump is the first event at any track meet, so I got there early. The long jump started at 10:00 and went on until 12:30. Then the mile relay was at 5:00. I got to the field at about 8:30. I ran around the track four times to loosen up and stretch out. All this took about an hour. By 9:30 the stands were packed, and that's when this terrible nervousness hit me. I realized that over 2,000 people would be watching me as I would run down the runway and take my jump. I got a cold sweat; my entire body was shaking worse than jello in an earthquake. Then everyone started giving orders at once. My two other teammates were telling me what to do and what not to do. The official was telling me to get ready to jump. My coach was yelling at me to get a good jump the first time, and the crowd in the stands was going crazy because we were about to start. As I stepped out onto the runway, my entire mind and body went blank. I couldn't see anything or anybody except the long jump pit 104′ 6″ down the runway. My head was pounding, and all I could hear was the blood rushing through my body. I waited a second, said a little prayer and took off. It felt like I was moving in slow motion. My legs felt like lead weights. My arms didn't want to move the right way, and I thought I'd never get to the end of the runway to the take-off board. Finally, I saw it closing in on me.

2. All the sentences in this paragraph begin with the same words. Rewrite the sentences—aiming for a noticeable increase in energy in the writing—by varying the way the sentences begin.

The afternoon was hot. The boy felt lazy. The flies were buzzing in his ears. The fish were calling. The plow felt heavy in his hands. The sun was hot. The boy made a decision. The boy left the field and went fishing.

3. Every sentence in the paragraph below has the same order: first the subject, then the verb, then the object or prepositional phrase. Vary the order of words in these sentences to add life to the writing.

   We left to go home. The others left to go to the game. Everybody agreed to meet at our house. Everybody came to the house after the game. We made pizza. Everybody had fun. We didn't know the whole story, though. A storm was in the wind.

CHANNEL INFORMATION FOR EMPHASIS AND STYLE

In almost every city, certain streets stand out. They are the great channels of life and energy that direct people to places of power, commerce, artistic achievement. No matter where you live, you can name such key venues: Broadway, Fifth Avenue, Michigan Avenue, High Street, Euclid, Pennsylvania Avenue, Peachtree Boulevard. But cities need more than just their major roads. They require far more intricate patterns of commerce and motion, lots of highways, interstates, alleys, freeways, and neighborhood streets—all interconnected, all working to make the town alive.

Sentences are a bit like that: certain sentences and clauses are main avenues, other clauses and phrases are the supporting arterials. Each pathway of information depends upon the other.

Writing effective sentences often means channeling information strategically so that key ideas cruise the main avenues while supporting notions follow on parallel streets or take crosstown routes, feeding into the traffic at just the right intersection. One method of channeling sentence information is to use *coordination* and *subordination* for clarifying relationships within sentences. For creating a style that says "this avenue of information is special," there are the techniques of *parallelism* and *repetition and rhythm*. All of these techniques—discussed in the following sections—give sentences energy and direction.

Coordination and Subordination

In delivering a message to a reader, you need to make clear which information, of all the information you are handing over, is the most important. You don't have to call attention to your intention in a plodding way—"What's important to me is. . . ." Instead, you can combine two sentences into one.

Each boat had a tall mast.

Each mast had a billowing sail.

can become: Each boat had a tall mast with a billowing sail.

Not only is the result of this combining sleeker and more mature, but it also shows what's important and what's not. This technique, *combining to show emphasis,* lets you control what the reader notices *and* highlight important thoughts efficiently and energetically.

COORDINATE: EQUAL
co-partner
co-worker
co-owner

SUBORDINATE: SECONDARY
subfloor
substitute
subcommittee

"Coordinate" comes from the Latin *co-* (equal) and *ordinare* (to arrange in order). "Subordinate" comes from the Latin *sub-* (below) and *ordinare.* Thus *coordinate* is of an "equal order," and *subordinate* is of a "lower order."

Coordinate you can associate with co-partner or co-worker, someone you are equal with, someone in the same position as you. *Subordinate* you can associate with subfloor or a substitute player in a ballgame, someone less important than the main players.

When two sentences in your writing are of equal importance, they are *coordinate.* When the thought in one sentence is more important than the thought in the other, the less important one is *subordinate* to the more important one.

Why do you need to know this? Because when you are revising for energy and are combining sentences to emphasize what you want the reader to notice, you will have to consider coordination and subordination, even if you don't use precisely those words.

Coordination. Coordination—*linking together words, groups of words, or sentences of equal type and importance*—puts energy into your writing. Look at how this works with *words:*

Two subjects are supposed to be the hardest for freshmen.

One is math.

The other is English.

Linking the two words *math* and *English* makes perfect sense—they have equal value in the sentence: they are "of equal hardness for freshmen." That can be crisply expressed in this combination:

Math and English are supposed to be the hardest subjects for freshmen.

And that handles it. Here is the way sentence combining works with *phrases:*

He spent the evening typing his essay.

He also spent the evening studying for his chemistry test.

Linking the two phrases, *typing his essay* and *studying for his chemistry test,* cuts out extra words and suggests that his evening was divided between the typing and the studying.

He spent the evening *typing his essay* and *studying for his chemistry test.*

The same principle applies to *clauses:*

John went to the concert for two reasons.

One reason was that he had nothing else to do.

Another reason was that he had sort of promised his sister he would go.

Notice how sentence combining streamlines this example:

Since he had nothing else to do and *had sort of promised his sister that he would go,* John went to the concert.

You can also combine whole sentences:

I had planned to spend the afternoon in the library.

I took a nap instead.

I had planned to spend the afternoon in the library, but *I took a nap instead.*

COORDINATING CONJUNCTIONS:

and	**so**
or	**yet**
nor	**either/or**
for	**neither/nor**
but	

Adding the word *but* allows the reader to move more quickly through the information and makes the two sentences one thought. Coordination in your writing does two things:

1. By combining words and groups of words, you avoid repetition that steals energy from what you write.
2. By combining whole sentences, you reveal the relationship between the thoughts.

When sentences are joined by a conjunction that shows that the sentences are equal, the reader knows that one sentence is as important as the other. This example should make it perfectly clear:

John doesn't plan to go to college.

He believes that experience in the working world is more valuable than an academic degree.

Looking at them, we can *infer* that the second is somehow related to the first, but we have to imagine the inference—the writer gives no clues, merely sets forth two sentences, period. But look what happens when the sentences are linked in a way that shows, explicitly, how the two items are related:

John doesn't plan to go to college, *for* he believes that experience in the working world is more valuable than an academic degree.

In the combined form, you *know* that the second sentence explains the first, *and* that the two ideas are of equal importance.

Subordination. Using *coordination* is like setting up a democracy, with everybody having an equal vote in the matter. *Subordination,* though, is more like a monarchy; royalty matter more than commoners in that system. Subordination puts energy in your writing by clearly emphasizing what is important and by displaying that importance in a way that the reader picks up clearly.

Music provides an example of subordination, since it is the *variation* in music that makes it interesting, not the sameness. Music moves from "important" chords, with lots of instruments, to relatively "unimportant" notes, with only one or two instruments. And the important notes or chords usually get played more loudly—and are held longer—than the unimportant ones. A good example is Beethoven's Fifth Symphony, the famous "V for Victory" symphony. The familiar pattern is three short notes followed by an "important" note: ta-ta-ta-DA. Then it repeats: ta-ta-ta-DA. Between these two full and massive statements there is a dramatic pause.

Can you imagine how boring that symphony would be if every note were the same and given equal value:

Ta-ta-ta-ta-ta-ta-ta-ta-ta-ta-ta-ta-ta- . . . ?

Puts you to sleep just reading it, doesn't it? There would be little interest because the listener would have no way of hearing the theme the composer built the symphony around. The notes would sound as flat and boring as a faucet dripping. It's the change in pace, the shift in emphasis, the *subordinating* of some sounds to others that give the music its form. You wouldn't be interested in it if there were no "less important" spots in the music to let the "more important" spots stand out.

SUBORDINATE CONJUNCTIONS
TIME: **when, after, whenever, while, before**
PLACE: **where, wherever**
CAUSE: **because, since, in order that, so that**
CONTRAST: **although, though, while**
CONDITION: **if, unless, since, as long as**

You've seen this same kind of subordination and shift in emphasis in photography, in painting, in architecture. We all soon tire of looking at pictures if there is no focal point, no main thing to see. One reason home slide shows bore most people is that the shots are usually the same—scenic views with no subordination of the background to a more important item/person as the focal point. In fact, almost anything we examine has some parts that deserve emphasis, others that serve best by being in the background. With subordination, you can determine the "foreground" and "background" of your message in writing, too. The variety gives emphasis *and* relief.

By subordinating one sentence to another when you combine them, you carry your reader's eye to the thing you think most important, and at the same time you show the relationship of one part of the sentence to the other—something that can help the reader move easily through the essay.

Parallelism

When you hear the word *parallelism,* maybe you think of how First Avenue runs in the same direction as Second Avenue, or how "parallel lines never meet." In writing, however, parallels are used for a specific effect: you set up the reader's expectations; then at last satisfy them.

Let's examine some parallel sentences written by Mary McCarthy, to see what we can discover about order and expectation/fulfillment, two important aspects of parallelism:

> Sheridan was then about six years old, and this [tin] butterfly immediately became his most cherished possession—indeed, one of the few he had. He carried it about the house with him all the next week clutched in his hand or pinned to his shirt, and my other two brothers followed him, begging him to be allowed to play with it, which slightly disgusted me, at the age of ten, for I knew that I was too sophisticated to care for tin butterflies and I felt in this whole affair the instigation of my uncle.

In the second sentence, the parallelism looks like this:

> He carried it about the house with him all the next week
> *clutched in his hand*
> or
> *pinned to his shirt,*
> and my other two brothers followed him, begging him to be allowed to play with it, which slightly disgusted me, at the age of ten,
> for
> *I knew* that I was too sophisticated to care for tin butterflies
> and
> *I felt* in this whole affair the instigation of my uncle.

The parallelism is in the arranging of the sentence to have neatly recurring patterns or parts:

> *clutched in his hand* **or** *pinned to his shirt*
> *For I knew . . . and I felt . . .*

The effect of parallelism can be *swift* and *punchy,* as in this sentence by Malcolm X:

> In those days only three things in the world scared me: jail, a job, and the army.

The effect, likewise, can be formal and elegant, deliberate and thoughtful. Look at Adrienne Rich's sentence:

> For the first time in history, a pervasive recognition is developing
> that the patriarchal system cannot answer for itself;
> that it is not inevitable;
> that it is transitory;
> and that the cross-cultural, global domination of women by men can no longer be
> denied
> or
> defended.

PARALLEL: **having comparable parts, readily recognized similarities; having the same tendency or direction; moving consistently by the same intervals; near similarity or exact agreement in particulars.**

Parallelism was a device well known by Winston Churchill, and he became a master at using it:

> We shall not flag or fail, we shall go on to the end, we shall fight in France, we shall fight on the seas and oceans, we shall fight with growing confidence and growing strength in the air, we shall defend our island, whatever the cost may be, we shall fight on the beaches, we shall fight on the landing grounds, we shall fight in the fields and in the streets, we shall fight in the hills; we shall never surrender.

And Lincoln, in the Gettysburg Address, managed in few words to produce writing so resonant and enduring that readers are shocked again and again to discover that the entire address is only 266 words long. In fact, the main speaker of the occasion was Edward Everett, who later wrote to Lincoln, "I should be glad if I could flatter myself that I came as near to the central idea of the occasion in two hours as you did in two minutes." The whole piece contains only three paragraphs. It is the last that is so full of parallelisms and so richly enduring:

> But, in a larger sense, we cannot dedicate—we cannot consecrate—we cannot hallow—this ground. The brave men, living and dead, who struggled here, have consecrated it far above our poor power to add or detract. The world will little note nor long remember what we say here, but it can never forget what they did here. It is for us, the living, rather, to be dedicated here to the unfinished work which they who fought here have thus far so nobly advanced. It is rather for us to be here dedicated to the great task remaining before us—that from these honored dead we take increased devotion to that cause for which they gave the last full measure of devotion; that we here highly resolve that these dead shall not have died in vain; that this nation, under God, shall have a new birth of freedom; and that government of the people, by the people, for the people, shall not perish from the earth.

Whether in the speech of presidents or prime ministers, or in the musings about a child's toy, parallelism moves with stately force. Since

Avoid Mismatched Parallelism

No: Drivers need to know about starting a car, stopping a car, and periodic maintenance.
Yes: Drivers need to know about starting, stopping, and maintaining a car.

the human mind responds to rhythm and order, the reader automatically reacts to the tempo of the parallel parts of sentences. Readers get started with the order you set up in the first piece, then move on with you quickly and satisfactorily through the second, and even third, parallel constructions. You have also set up an expectation for the reader, at least by the second parallel item, and by continuing with that pattern you are fulfilling the reader's subconscious expectations and giving pleasure, even though the reader may not actually know why.

Repetition and Rhythm

As a drumbeat energizes music, repetition of words and phrases gives power to your writing by carrying the movement along. Repetition is aesthetically pleasing—readers respond to repetition in writing like listeners respond to rhythm in music.

Here are some examples.

> So many urbanites have a country fantasy, spun from within windowless offices. They soothe themselves with images of wooded glens, blue ponds, and laughing cows. But they know nothing of the hard work of chopping wood from their own trees, and they know nothing of the hard work of draining their own ponds, and they know nothing of the hard work of feeding, sheltering, and milking those laughing cows.

Here, the writer leads off with two relatively short sentences, then builds a longer one with a series of three clauses, each introduced by "they know nothing of the hard work of." This sentence could have been condensed like this:

> They know nothing of the hard work of chopping wood, draining ponds, and feeding, sheltering, and milking cows.

Certainly that would be correct enough, in terms of combining basic elements and compressing them into the most direct, least wordy message. Yet that would lose the ease of motion, the tone of speaking from experience, the picture painting in the original version. The rhythmic version sounds like the writer feels passionate about the subject and has her own story to tell; the condensed version sounds like the writer is a more distant expert who is explaining something. The first is casual, approachable; the second rather formidable. In both, the rhythm and the repetition (or absence of it) produce the effect on the reader.

Here is another sample, this time by Theodore Sorensen. It describes young John Fitzgerald Kennedy, but notice how much information is compressed into the first sentence ("At the age of twenty-three . . ."), how the second sentence carries out the same idea but in much briefer form ("At the age of thirty-five . . ."), and how the third sentence—short, unadorned, tart—expresses the point Sorensen means to emphasize ("But he had little interest . . .").

> At the age of twenty-three he had expanded his highly regarded senior thesis—representing, he wrote his father, "more *work* than I've ever done in my life"—into a distinguished book on *Why England Slept,* a well-reasoned and well-regarded analysis of that nation's lack of preparedness for the Second World War. At the age of thirty-five he continued to be widely read in history, biography and politics. But he had little interest in abstract theories. He primarily sought truths upon which he could act and ideas he could use in his office.

"Dancing in all its forms cannot be excluded from the curriculum of all noble education; dancing with the feet, with ideas, with words, and need I add that one must also be able to dance with the pen?"

—Nietzsche

This kind of repetition and variation will often provide your writing with a splash of style; your readers will probably also stay with you longer and much more happily.

Here is a longer passage written by E. B. White, one of the best essayists and stylists America has produced.

> [1]It is a miracle that New York works at all. [2]The whole thing is implausible. [3]Every time the residents brush their teeth, millions of gallons of water must be drawn from the Catskills and the hills of Westchester. [4]When a young man in Manhattan writes a letter to his girl in Brooklyn, the love message gets blown to her through a pneumatic tube—*pfft*—just like that. [5]The subterranean system of telephone cables, power lines, steam pipes, gas mains, and sewer pipes is reason enough to abandon the island to the gods and the weevils. [6]Everytime an incision is made in the pavement, the noisy surgeons expose ganglia that are tangled beyond belief. [7]By rights New York should have destroyed itself long ago, from panic or fire or rioting or failure of some vital supply line in its circulatory system or from some deep labyrinthine short circuit. [8]Long ago the city should have experienced an insoluble traffic snarl at some impossible bottleneck. [9]It should have perished of hunger when food lines failed for a few days. [10]It should have been wiped out by a plague starting in its slums or carried in by ships' rats. [11]It should have been overwhelmed by the sea that licks at it on every side. [12]The workers in its myriad cells should have succumbed to nerves, from the fearful pall of smoke-fog that drifts over every few days from Jersey, blotting out all light at

> noon and leaving the high offices suspended, men groping and depressed, and the sense of world's end. [13]It should have been touched in the head by the August heat and gone off its rocker.

This paragraph beautifully illustrates *effective repetition*. The whole paragraph is a response to the assertion that it is a miracle that New York City works at all. In substantiating that claim, White arranges the paragraph into two "groups," the first beginning with sentence 3 and the second group beginning with sentence 7. The first group is tied together by the repetition of *time* tags:

> *Every time* the residents brush their teeth, . . .
>
> *When* a young man in Manhattan . . .
>
> *Every time* an incision is made in the pavement . . .

Sentence 7 sets up the pattern that is repeated throughout the remaining sentences: what *should* have happened to New York. Thus White produces a kind of sleight-of-hand: he chronicles the chaos and nonsense that, for him, make New York "implausible," and offers a welter of details that *shows* what he means—and yet he manages, through careful repetition of patterns, to present that picture of chaos in a way that gives the reader a sense of coherence and control about the writing. He manages to create, with his paragraph, almost the same effect that he is describing about New York—it's too chaotic and complicated to work, yet not only does it work, it does so dynamically and wonderfully.

People often ask how much consciousness is needed to produce such masterpieces, and how much is simply the result of natural art or genius. It's a good question but essentially unanswerable. Certainly E. B. White has demonstrated his abilities more often and more highly than most of us are likely to do. Yet that's no reason or excuse for not gaining as much mastery as we are able to. After all, it is *training* that extends whatever native art or genius we possess, whether for running, writing, or playing the violin.

And, of course, it is possible for all of us to extend what we possess. That's just another form of "learning," after all. Here's a good example from a student paper of what can happen when an "ordinary" person decides to gain energy by using balance and repetition.

> A hero is someone whom we all admire and respect. Either he has performed some spectacular task or he has set an example that is worthy enough for others to follow. Such a man needs not to have done something of earth-shattering importance, though he may be more easily recognized as a hero for doing so. He may be a man who has walked on the moon, or he may be a father who is gentle but firm. He may have climbed Mount Everest, or he may be a patient

schoolteacher. He may have saved the lives of his fellow soldiers in combat, or he may have cared for a child's scraped knee. No one says a hero has to have done something of worldwide significance.

The point of this passage is to *contrast* the two concepts of heroism. By using *balance* (he may be *this* or he may be *that*), and *repetition* of this pattern through three sentences, the writer effectively uses structure to reinforce meaning.

Avoid the Passive Voice

The passive voice changes the normal order of sentences. In an active sentence, the subject is also the person or thing that performs the action:

> A drunk driver struck a student on his way to school this morning.

A passive version of the sentence rearranges the action:

> A student on his way to school was struck by a drunk driver this morning.

Notice, however, that it isn't just word order that has changed. Although the message of the sentence remains the same, the focus is different in each. In the active sentence, the drunk driver is the focus; in the passive sentence, the student becomes the focus. This capacity for varying focus makes passive voice a resource to writers.

Unfortunately, many writers misuse and overuse passive voice. Passive voice also involves changing an active subject—drunk driver—into a prepositional phrase of agency—*by a drunk driver.* Sometimes, though, the agent can be omitted to create an impersonal tone:

> Students are asked to proceed to the gym immediately after lunch.

Who does the asking? Presumably, the principal, but the statement seems far more authoritative if the agent is omitted than it does when the agent is retained:

> Students are asked *by the principal* to proceed to the gym immediately after lunch.

In this next sentence, the passive voice is used without the phrase of agency:

> It is believed that some parts of the world will suffer massive food shortages this century.

Here, the passive voice might have been used for one of the following reasons:

1. The writer is the one who believes that we will suffer food shortages, but to create an aura of authority and to sound impressive, he avoids a personal reference in an active sentence:

I believe that some parts of the world will suffer massive food shortages this century.

2. It could be that demographers or farmers are the ones who have predicted the shortage, but by leaving out the agent—it is believed *by demographers* or *by farmers*—the information in the sentence seems absolute and factual rather than speculative.

When it is used consciously to create a desired effect as in the sentences above, the passive voice is a valuable resource in writing. However, the passive voice is frequently used carelessly and indiscriminately, contributing to wordiness and reducing energy. A passive sentence usually requires more words than an active sentence:

Active: The president asked Congress to carefully consider the results of the bill before overriding his veto. (16 words)

Passive: Congress was asked by the president to consider carefully the results of the bill before overriding his veto. (18 words)

Two additional words will not make your writing excessively wordy, but when sentence after sentence is passive, the extra words add up.

Another effect of using the passive voice is a reduction in energy. Remember that the verb is the heart of the sentence. Passive verbs are formed by combining a form of *to be* with the past participle—*was* asked, *is* expected, *will be* hired—and *to be* is a colorless, empty verb. It merely links; it shows no action. So, unless you are deliberately using a passive voice to focus on the complement rather than on the subject, make your writing vigorous by preferring active verbs.

Passive voice can also make your writing awkward. In the following sentence, the writer's attempt to be impersonal by avoiding a second-person pronoun and his inadequate focus on *difference* contribute to the awkwardness of the sentence:

The difference between your insurance benefits and your hospital bill will be required to be paid upon discharge.

Rewriting the sentence with a different focus eliminates the awkwardness and wordiness:

Upon discharge, you will be required to pay the difference between your insurance benefits and your hospital bill.

The difference between your insurance benefits and your hospital bill must be paid upon discharge.

As you edit your papers, question the appropriateness of every passive verb. Could the information in that sentence be conveyed more directly and more naturally in the active voice? If it can be, then revise the sentence.

FINAL OBSERVATIONS ABOUT POLISHING SENTENCES

You want your writing to *move*. To *dance*. To *have life*. At times this energy will just seem to occur naturally when you write. And at other times—and more this way than not—you have to revise your writing to make it jump. You can think about this kind of revising for energy like choreographing a dance or orchestrating a song. Like mixing a record album in the studio after the songs are recorded, it's a chance to make the writing just the way you want it.

APPLICATION

Coordination

Rewrite the following groups of sentences using coordination to link clauses, phrases, and words.

1. Many times speaking to a crowd can be fun.
   It can be nerve-wracking.
   It can be time-consuming.
   It can be frustrating.
2. To save money Andrew's parents have decided not to travel to Yosemite this summer.
   They will spend a few weeks at a local lake instead.
3. Americans constantly criticize their leaders.
   They don't make an effort to vote in national elections.
   They forget to vote in local elections.
4. Many people consider a college education vital for success in the business world.
   Few professionals have reached their positions without at least one degree.
5. The energy crisis made many people seriously consider their driving habits.
   Many people bought smaller cars that use less gas.
   Many people did more walking and bicycling.
6. John had to make a decision about the summer.
   He could go to the local community college and gain some extra hours toward his degree.
   He could work full-time for his uncle's construction firm.
7. Wearing clothes that are in style is very important to some people.
   Others don't seem at all concerned about their appearance.
   They wear jeans and T-shirts everywhere.

8. Everywhere you look you see people jogging.
   You see people walking.
   You see people climbing stairs instead of riding the elevator.
   More and more people are growing conscious of the importance of good health.
9. Julie knew she could easily get tickets to tonight's rock concert.
   She knew that if she went she wouldn't study for Friday's chemistry exam.
10. Doing your own car repairs saves you money.
    It can be as personally rewarding as a hobby.

Subordination

Rewrite the following groups of sentences using subordination wherever possible.

1. Mark hates housecleaning.
   He claims he's basically a neat person.
2. You can chop the vegetables for the stew.
   I can brown the meat and prepare the gravy.
3. We want to visit the college campus next month.
   We want to make sure we have chosen the right courses.
4. John's uncle may offer him a job in his grocery story.
   John may have a job this summer.
5. The rain may stop soon.
   We may have to cancel the picnic scheduled for tomorrow.
6. Most people seem willing to cut down on their use of electricity, gas, and heating fuels.
   They don't want energy conservation to interfere with their established life-styles.
7. We spent the afternoon in the library working on our history project.
   We all went out for pasta.
8. Old movies seem to get more popular every year.
   They offer plot and drama that modern movies often lack.
9. Editing involves grammar and punctuation rules that are hard to remember.
   Many students don't enjoy editing.
10. For many students, writing is fun.
    They are more interested in expressing their ideas than in following rules.

Parallelism

Transform each group of sentences below into a sentence that contains parallel elements.

1. My grandmother bakes cookies and cakes for all of our birthdays.
   She manages a business.

She gardens.
She models.
My grandmother is a remarkable woman.

2. Studying requires determination.
It frequently means sacrificing fun times.
To study effectively, you must have a serious attitude toward your education.
3. A good teacher is someone who thinks of each student as a person.
He is willing to spend additional hours at school to counsel troubled students.
He doesn't care if class discussions veer toward a relevant topic not scheduled for discussion.
4. Walking whenever possible shows that a person is concerned with good health.
Exercising regularly shows a concern with good health.
Watching the kinds of foods you eat is important if you want to be healthy.
5. I expected to feel independent when I moved away from home to go to college.
I knew I would enjoy making my own rules.
I expected to feel grown-up about paying my own bills.

Repetition and Rhythm

Rewrite these sentences in a paragraph illustrating repetition for emphasis.

1. My grandfather was a man of remarkable energy.
He canned the fruit and vegetables which grew in his garden in the summer.
In the early spring, he always planted a garden in his backyard.
When autumn came, he made fruit wines—some to drink right away, some to save for winter.
He helped shovel snow when necessary.
2. It was an unprecedented time in the history of the country.
The president had resigned.
The office of the president had never before yielded so dramatically to public pressure.
The voting public had at no other time exercised its democratic privileges with such results.
Criminal accusations had never before tainted the president himself.
The public had never felt so deceived by the leader they had elected.

Identify what creates the rhythm in this passage by Charles Dickens:

> It was the best of times, it was the worst of times, it was the age of wisdom, it was the age of foolishness, it was the epoch of belief, it was the epoch of incredulity, it was the season of Light, it was the

season of Darkness, it was the spring of hope, it was the winter of despair, we had everything before us, we had nothing before us, we were all going direct to Heaven, we were all going direct the other way—in short, the period was so far like the present period, that some of its noisiest authorities insisted on its being received, for good or for evil, in the superlative degree of comparison only.

Passive Voice

Explain how the use of passive voice makes these sentences awkward. Rewrite each to make it more vivid.

1. By this definition, it can be seen that heroes are very influential in American society today.
2. Technology is pointed out by the author as being one of the basic causes of the schizoid condition.
3. The topic is taken very seriously by the writer and the persona that she uses (which is both serious and full of resentment) expresses her seriousness.
4. But a stand was taken by him, and whether he is right or wrong, this fact cannot be ignored.
5. Through the activities of Sir Thomas More, it is seen that in order to live in society a person has to give up part of himself.

CHAPTER 21

Style: Words and Images

You are writing for a television generation. That means your readers are visually oriented; they are more accustomed to seeing something occur than reading about it—whether it be a space launch, a presidential inauguration, or the World Series. To hold the attention of such readers, you'll need to cultivate strong details and vivid expressions, remembering, perhaps, the observation of Alexander Smith: "Memorable sentences are memorable on account of some single irradiating word." In short, you have to use words to draw pictures.

Selecting words carefully and finding sentence structures suited to them leads to the development of *style*. Style in writing is hard to pin down. It's something like a person's signature or way of dressing—hard to define, but easy to recognize when you see it. ("That hat is *you!*") As you develop as a writer, you'll acquire rhythms, structural devices, thought patterns, and vocabulary choices that mark your personal style. But style is not like a fingerprint—something you are born with and cannot change. You *can* refine your habits to make your writing more lively, mature, and interesting. That's what this chapter is about.

LEVELS OF STYLE

Even a personal style varies according to the level of formality demanded by a particular writing assignment. A formal style suits a writer who wants to be serious, impressive, or impersonal; an informal style brings the writer, reader, and subject matter closer together; a colloquial style imitates the ease and casualness of conversation. Such descriptions are frustratingly vague, however, because they are no more than attempts to define boundaries of a vast and ever-changing territory. Style cannot be reduced to formulas or plotted on a graph. We can define some of the factors that determine whether a style feels formal, informal, or colloquial. Word choice, for one, makes a significant difference.

To understand how words create style, you need to know a bit about the history of the English language. It developed from the languages of the Germanic tribes that invaded England and Scotland between A.D. 450 and 800. The ordinary words in our vocabulary—prepositions, articles, and basic nouns and verbs such as *man, woman, food, bread, ride, give, sleep*—can be traced to the languages of these tribes. Linguists refer to these everyday words as the Anglo-Saxon core of the language.

English borrowed heavily from languages all over the world, but especially from Latin, Greek, and French. After the Norman invasion of 1066, a large body of French words was borrowed. In general, this French influence refined the English language. For example, English speakers began to make distinctions between meat served at the table (French) and the animal from which it came (Anglo-Saxon): *cow* and *beef, pig* and *pork, lamb* and *mutton.* A large body of borrowings from Greek and Latin entered the language through the influence of scholars. Latin was the language of scholarship until the Renaissance, so books were written and all serious scholarship was conducted in that tongue. Consequently, words from Latin and Greek were used then as they are now to add dignity and formality to writing. Words like *fortitude, abdomen, resuscitate, transition* began to appear as synonyms for their more homely Germanic counterparts. That was the beginning of style through diction.

In the list below, notice the difference among Anglo-Saxon, French, and Latin words of approximately the same meaning:

Anglo-Saxon	*French*	*Latin*
begin	commence	initiate
end	finish	conclude
kingly	royal	regal
time	age	epoch

Style becomes more formal as you shift from Germanic to French to Latin words. Familiarity with these levels of diction may help you become more flexible in writing. You don't have to be a word scholar in order to write effectively, but you should know why one word seems more formal than another. Also, you should realize that impressive, formal words may not always be right for the message you are trying to convey. If *heart attack* fits your context, don't try to make your writing more impressive by using *cardiac arrest* instead.

Besides levels of diction, several other techniques affect the formality of writing. Using first-person and second-person pronouns always reduces formality. Referring to yourself as *I* and to the reader as *you* makes your writing less formal; frequently it is the mark of a colloquial or a conversational style. However, you must be careful not to misuse the first- and second-person points of view so that your tone becomes inappropriately "chatty."

The deliberate use of passive voice instead of active is another technique for making writing formal. And the use of abstract words rather than concrete words also contributes to formality.

As you read this passage by Henry Boettinger, notice how the level of diction and the other techniques we've discussed affect style:

> Ideas are not truly active if they remain locked in a single mind. Our need to transfer them to others forces us to consider why and where we want them to go, and how we want them to get there. This demands orientation towards the audience. "Audience" in its narrow sense, of course, assumes a *hearing* of the message. While the human voice is the most powerful method of communication, we will use "audience" in the broader sense, as the group aimed at regardless of the form used. Our objective is to get an idea accepted, and usually a mixture of methods—letters, memos, or reports as well as talks, conferences, and formal presentations—will be necessary if the idea is to have more than a trivial impact. The same principles and approaches are applicable to all forms, and the over-all play should use whatever combination best does the job. We will go into the strategy and tactics involved in some depth later.

You are correct if you think that the diction and style here are informal, perhaps almost casual. But can you explain how the author achieves that effect? First, notice that he uses first person: "our need," "forces us to consider why and where we want them to go," "we will use," "our objective." However, notice also that overall the tone is not casual; there is no indication of "chumminess" or colloquialness. The writer uses first person to refer to himself and to writers in general, not to establish chumminess with the reader. The result is a friendly, yet businesslike tone. Notice also that all the sentences are in the active voice, giving the passage vitality and contributing to the informal effect. Finally, the level of diction is informal; there is a mixture of Anglo-Saxon and Latin and Greek words.

Let's analyze a second passage, this by Frank Smith:

> Reading is an act of communication in which information is transferred from a transmitter to a receiver, whether the reader is a scholar deciphering a medieval text or a child identifying a single letter on a blackboard. Because of this basic nature of reading, there are insights to be gained from the study of theories of communication and information; there are concepts that are particularly useful for the construction of a theory of reading, and a terminology that can be employed to increase the clarity of its expression.

> The present chapter will be particularly relevant to the following aspects of reading: reading is not a passive activity—the reader must make an active contribution if he is to acquire the available information. All information acquisition in reading, from the identification of individual letters of words to the comprehension of entire passages, can be regarded as the reduction of uncertainty. Skilled reading utilizes redundancy—of information from a variety of sources—so that, for example, knowledge of the world and of language will reduce the need for visual information from the printed page.

You probably noticed how many words in this passage end in *-ion*. These are abstract nouns that refer to ideas and intangible things: *information, communication, construction, expression, contribution, acquisition, identification*. There is nothing wrong with *-ion* words, but using them too often leads to overreliance on the passive voice (abstract nouns and passive voice tend to occur together) and to consistent use of weak verbs such as *is, are, will be*. The result can be abstract writing that is difficult for the reader to understand.

A second notable feature of the passage is its frequent use of passive voice: "information is transferred," "insights to be gained," "a terminology that can be employed," "all information acquisition can be regarded." The passive voice contributes to formality and frequently to abstractness in thought.

Finally, the third person point of view contributes to the formality of the passage. There is neither a perceptible writer nor a specific intended reader. Both writer and reader remain unspecified and distant from each other because of the use of the third person.

These analyses should not suggest that one kind of diction or one particular style is always superior to all others. By studying the passages closely, we can understand better how writers use words to create certain effects. The main consideration that makes one kind of diction appropriate and another entirely wrong is the author's purpose.

APPLICATION

In the passages below identify the words and techniques that contribute to informality, formality, or colloquialness.

1. Writers are driven by a compulsion to put some part of themselves on paper, and yet they don't just write what comes naturally. They sit down to commit an act of literature, and the self who emerges on paper is a far stiffer person than the one who sat down. The problem is to find the real man or woman behind all the tension.

For ultimately, the product that any writer has to sell is not his subject, but who he is. I often find myself reading with interest about a topic that I never thought would interest me—some unusual scientific quest, for instance. What holds me is the enthusiasm of the writer for his field. How was he drawn into it? What emotional baggage did he bring along? How did it change his life? It is not necessary to want to spend a year alone at Walden Pond to become deeply involved with the man who did.

This is the personal transaction that is at the heart of good nonfiction writing. Out of it come two of the most important qualities that this book will go in search of: humanity and warmth. Good writing has an aliveness that keeps the reader reading from one paragraph to the next, and it's not a question of gimmick to "personalize" the author. It's a question of using the English language in a way that will achieve the greatest strength and the least clutter.

—William Zinsser

2. How is aim determined? Obviously, it is partly determined by the cultural context and the situational context in both of which the text of the discourse is a part. This means, of course, that the intent of the author of the text partially determines the aim of the discourse.

   But it would be dangerous to adduce author intent as the main criterion of the aim of a discourse, for often a discourse does not achieve the author's intent—"That's not what I meant at all," says the character in Eliot's "Prufrock." And again we may not have the author's intent available to use in recorded form; or, especially in propaganda and literature the expressed "intent" of the author may not at all be the real intent. The fallacy of judging the intent of a work by the intent of the author has been called the "intentional fallacy."

—James Kinneavy

DENOTATION AND CONNOTATION

Your choice of words in writing, your *diction,* helps determine your style because of the varying denotation and connotation of words. Words have straightforward and explicit meanings—what we sometimes call "dictionary definitions." These definitions, which attempt to describe a thing or an idea *in itself,* represent the *denotation* of a word. But words also have meanings that exist in the thoughts, feelings, cultures, and associations of individuals and groups. These additional layers of meaning, called *connotations,* surround a word and expand its impact beyond a simple dictionary meaning.

In many cases, words or phrases can be relatively neutral; that is they lack any *positive* or *negative* connotations. In many countries, for example, the words *red, white,* and *blue* are just that—words that denote three colors. In the United States, however, the terms immediately take on patriotic connotations as we think of the American flag, fireworks, the Fourth of July, the National Anthem, and so on: we cheer for the *red, white,* and *blue.* For most people, a phrase such as *railroad crossing* lacks powerful connotations; it's simply a place where a railroad track intersects a highway. But in a neighborhood where several fatal accidents have occurred at a particular railroad crossing, the phrase may be charged with anger and political activity. *Railroad crossing* becomes a rallying term for citizens concerned for the public safety. A particular situation or *context* thus may give special meaning to an otherwise neutral expression.

Political words and phrases are particularly rich in connotations that shift according to the audience and writer. Consider the impact of the following terms, how some seem negative, some positive, and some variable depending upon the group using them: *supply side theory, trickle down economics, Voodoo economics, prayer in schools, right to life, pro-choice, military preparedness, militarism, war-monger, freedom fighters, liberal, comparable worth, fascist, gun control, affirmative action, reverse discrimination.* You can probably think of dozens of similar terms. Such words partially define the social, political, and professional groups we belong to; in learning the connotations of such terms we absorb the ideas and values of the community that uses them.

Words of political and social significance are far from the only ones with powerful associations. As you become sensitive to the connotations of words, you'll discover that English offers an extraordinarily rich palette with which to illuminate your ideas. A notion as ordinary as walking can be described by a dozen terms or more, each with its own feelings and associations: *amble, plod, stroll, perambulate, tread, lumber, hike, march, hobble, troop, step, leg it,* and so on. Notice how connotations spread out from a word, giving it character and even physical associations:

Saunter	*Shuffle*	*Trudge*
what you do in summer	soles scraping the ground	heavy feet, shoes
dapper, well-dressed folks	hands in pockets, uneasy	sad, tired, so weak
happy, pleasant	baggy pants	heavy, burdened
easy, graceful	slowly	lamely, painfully
whistling	gray day	dismal, cold

As a writer, you must strive to exploit the connotations of the words you are using *for a given audience.* An allusion to "mystery meat," for example, may win a chuckle from dormitory residents who have dined regularly on amorphous clumps of animal matter, but the same phrase might not be well received at a convention of restaurateurs. Don't be afraid to experiment with phrases, or to explore connotations. It is, frankly, bad strategy to rely only on the small word or the common expression when you are in control of a better one. You know well enough that words of similar denotation are not always synonymous: *lean, thin, gaunt, skeletal.* So simply exercise caution when you replace a common word with a more specific one:

> Sally Field gave a *lively* performance in the film.
>
> Sally Field gave a *manic* performance in the film.

If necessary, use a dictionary to discover the connotation of an unfamiliar word, or ask someone familiar with it. Don't shy away from the right word.

APPLICATION

1. Below are pairs of words with similar denotations but different connotations. Discuss the differences and compose sentences using each of the words appropriately.

    contemporary/high-tech
    head honcho/chief executive
    downpour/gully washer
    hearsay/scuttlebutt
    brawny/beefy
    learning facilitator/teacher
    lie/misstatement
    attractive/seductive
    dismiss/sack
    athlete/jock
    home/domicile

2. Some words, phrases, and names come quickly into fashion. For a time, everyone uses them, knows what they mean, and associates them with interesting events, fads, or concepts. At the time this exercise is being penned, some of the *buzz* words and phrases are:

    budget deficits
    kinder and gentler
    tabloid television
    leveraged buyout
    Read my lips
    CD-ROM
    build-down

What words or phrases are in vogue as you read this? What do you associate with these words? How often do you find yourself employing them?

3. A thesaurus is a "tip-of-the-tongue" book: you know there is a word for saying exactly what you mean, but you can't think of it now. But you can't treat all the synonyms a thesaurus may list for any given term as equals. Under *prosperity,* for example, *Roget's International Thesaurus* (3rd edition) lists:

prosperousness	well-being
thriving condition	comfort
success	welfare
ease	

These are all plausible alternatives to the word *prosperity,* but not exact equivalents. The same thesaurus also lists some more colorful synonyms:

the life of Riley	bed of roses
Easy Street	fat of the land
fleshpots of Egypt	purple and fine linen

These terms have their appropriate contexts—often in colloquial speech: "Winning the lottery put Harriet on *Easy Street*"; "Since retiring my dad has enjoyed *the life of Riley.*" But such applications are rather limited.

As an exercise, browse through a large thesaurus until you find several entries that intrigue you with the variety of their synonyms. Then write sentences in which you use as many of the suggested terms as possible, being sure that you place the terms in an appropriate context. Notice which words or expressions might be considered archaic, clichéd, or unsuitable in most situations.

For example, an entry for *fat* might include *heavy, obese, portly,* and *corpulent:*

Despite his diet, Don still felt *heavy* after a run.

Dr. Bronowski classified her patient as *obese.*

Alex was a pleasant lawyer, ruddy, *portly,* and prosperous.

Alex was a nasty lawyer, red-faced, *corpulent,* and flush with money.

After you have completed the exercise, check whether the synonymous terms could be interchanged. Why or why not?

4. Underline the words or phrases that contribute notably to the vividness of the passages below. Discuss their connotations.

   A. When my son and I arrived at the pigyard, armed with a small bottle of castor oil and a length of clothesline, the pig had emerged from his house and was standing in the middle of his yard, listlessly. He gave us a slim greeting. I could see that he felt uncomfortable and uncertain. I had brought the clothesline thinking I'd have to tie him (the pig weighed more than a hundred pounds) but we never used it. My son reached down, grabbed both front legs, upset him quickly, and when he opened his mouth to scream I turned the oil into his throat—a pink, corrugated area I had never seen before. I had just time to read the label while the neck of the bottle was in his mouth. It said Puretest. The screams, slightly muffled by oil, were pitched in the hysterically high range of pig-sound, as though torture were being carried out, but they didn't last long: it was all over rather suddenly, and, his legs released, the pig righted himself.

In the upset position the corners of his mouth had been turned down, giving him a frowning expression. Back on his feet again, he regained the set smile that a pig wears even in sickness. He stood his ground, sucking slightly at the residue of oil; a few drops leaked out of his lips while his wicked eyes, shaded by their coy little lashes, turned on me in disgust and hatred. I scratched him gently with oily fingers and he remained quiet, as though trying to recall the satisfaction of being scratched when in health, and seeming to rehearse in his mind the indignity to which he had just been subjected. I noticed, as I stood there, four or five small dark spots on his back near the tail end, reddish brown in color, each about the size of a housefly. I could not make out what they were. They did not look troublesome but at the same time they did not look like mere surface bruises or chafe marks. Rather they seemed blemishes of internal origin. His stiff white bristles almost completely hid them and I had to part the bristles with my fingers to get a good look.

—E. B. White

B. My first car ever was a two-toned '61 Rambler station wagon, green on bottom, white on top, and bounded by a dented strip of rusty metal. The front seat ran the width of the car; it had a tan criss-cross weave, something like the New York subway seats, and scratchy vinyl to the touch. On the passenger end, the stuffing was constantly threatening to burst and overflow, to dribble down onto the floor, surge up onto the dashboard, and riproar crescendingly through the windshield. Passengers could ride at their own risk.

I loved that car. We went through a major rite of passage together—my learning to drive. I wept when it died.

That was the car that sat so uncomplainingly in the snow drift the winter of '67—the winter it snowed so much that we wore our shades at night to protect the eyes from even the memory of the sun's glare on the icy white streets. The drift was what piled up, over days, around an innocent-looking fence post meant to keep cows in and cars out. The cows had long since gone indoors to await the eventual rebirth of their pasture, now blanketed and sleeping. Only I, my hands lusting for the wheel (my brain sleeping along with the summer clover), thought it necessary to venture out of my warm, tousled, langorous bed; don my orange thermals, two pairs of socks, and every scarf ever knitted by my mother during her stopping-smoking era; thaw the Rambler's door lock with a lighter; and jubilantly jump on in to go out for a spin.

I spun; I twirled; I plowed right into that fence post disguised as a vanilla cotton-candy cone. It took the nearest farmer's plow to undo the suction and get me back on the road again. Rambler's soul was sweet—she forgave, but she got tired. There were a few more scrapes like that, and before the winter was out, Rambler's rambling days were over. No car since—no fuel-savvy Honda, no hydraulically magic Citroen, no Plymouth convertible of my teenage dreams, no matter how sleek or snazzy or expensive—has ever equalled my one, my only, my first love, that green-and-white Rambler. Rest in peace.

5. Revise the vocabulary of the following selection by correcting words you believe have the wrong connotation or by replacing neutral words with more connotative expressions. These paragraphs are a highly exaggerated compilation of the worst forms of abused connotation.

(1) The differentiation between good students and destructive ones in elementary and secondary educational institutions is not so much intelligence as why they do things. (2) Good students often get themselves involved in pranks and skirmishes with the administrative powers out of a desire to be devilish. (3) Truly destructive individuals perform their dastardly deeds out of malice, seeking to aggrieve or vitiate other individuals or to dismantle school stuff for the sheer relish of observing havoc and ruination. (4) They practice defenestration, deface walls, intimidate teachers, smoke dope, and lay siege to the other people's junk in lockers.

(5) Enlightened pedagogues should deal with truly malicious rascals by doling out the severest forms of retribution with celerity. (6) First-time miscreants should be ensconced in study hall; more severe perpetrators should be threatened with extra homework or have their knuckles cracked with a good stiff ruler. (7) Habitual offenders can be dealt with through suspension or—toughest break of all—expulsion.

(8) Better students who occasionally deal in academic tumult should be suitably chastised by forces of academic law and order, but it is probably not necessary to really kick chins unless their misde-

meanors threaten to set a pattern of silliness and frolic throughout the academic community. (9) Such behavior should be stomped out in the bud before it spreads like wildflowers.

CONCRETE AND ABSTRACT LANGUAGE

As you revise, make your language lively and specific. Don't describe *school spirit* as "the good feeling all of us had that we could accomplish anything if we pulled together." Write about it as the confetti choking the halls after a basketball championship, or the torn program in a tearful cheerleader's hand after a defeat. *Punctuality* needn't be "a factor involving the faithful adherence to restraints on time"; readers will probably understand the concept better as your Uncle Joe punching the time clock at the factory the same minute every night shift for ten years. And *democracy?* Imagine what some writers would do with that dry term. But here's how E. B. White defined it during World War II:

> Democracy is the recurrent suspicion that more than half of the people are right more than half of the time. It is the feeling of privacy in the voting booths, the feeling of communion in the libraries, the feeling of vitality everywhere. Democracy is a letter to the editor. Democracy is the score at the end of the ninth. It is an idea which hasn't been disproved yet, a song the words of which have not gone bad. It's the mustard on the hot dog and the cream in the rationed coffee . . .
>
> —"Democracy"

You might be reluctant to write about *democracy* in such a way—thinking you should be more abstract and serious in academic writing. Yet White trusts his readers to recognize the simple acts and feelings that make the grand political concept meaningful to most Americans.

In many situations, of course, a definition like White's is inappropriate. In a dictionary or encyclopedia for example, White's details would be regarded as inaccurate and distracting. Outside the United States, the definition might seem quaint and provincial. In a classroom debate comparing the merits of democracy and oligarchy, the score at the end of the ninth and mustard on a hot dog will seem like trifles compared to other issues. Many circumstances *do* call for language that is abstract and general; we often think in abstractions. When scientists formulate theories, theologians shape treatises, or philosophers explore concepts, they want their ideas to have wide application. So the scientist discusses *gravity,* not the falling apple that clobbered him into considering the theory; the theologian expounds on *poverty,* not on the holes in his own robes. And the philosopher proves in the abstract that *causality* does not exist, ignoring the bruise she suffered kicking the pop machine.

Unfortunately, many writers rely on abstract language only. They want everything they compose to sound as important as the Magna Carta and so they write with all the liveliness of a reference book. They compose long essays about handicapped children without mentioning their personal experiences with such kids. They criticize the system of grading at their school without listing a single specific complaint. They talk about their friends and their hometowns without mentioning any names or places. They expound pompously on sportsmanship, never commenting on the nasty clip that angered them enough to write an essay. The details go unmentioned while the prose plods on. You've read writing like this:

> Sportsmanship is the key to athletic endeavor. No matter what the athletic endeavor you are engaged in is, it requires sportsmanship to make it really and truly worthwhile. We, as a society today, value sportsmanship and all that goes along with it. Sportsmanship is a key to success and to happiness in business and life as well as in athletic competition. Without sportsmanship, we could not have the society we value so much today. . . .

Now compare what happens when the writer chooses words with muscle and backbone:

> My neck snapped back and I was dazed for half a minute, sore for a week. The official missed the clip; no penalty was called; no points were scored because of it. All my opponent had done was hurt me. And for what? For the pleasure of watching me stagger to my feet, wondering where I was? His coach, no doubt, had mentioned sportsmanship, but. . . .

Often just one detail per paragraph ("My neck snapped back . . .") can make a huge difference to a reader searching for a spark of insight, for evidence of an idea treated with integrity and passion. Trust your readers enough to write about the simple things in your experience as you explore even the most important ideas.

APPLICATION

1. Define one of the following terms as a dictionary might (maximum length: about 50 words) and then by specifying details the way E. B. White defines democracy (aim for 200–300 words):

justice	philosophy
baseball	prejudice
greed	hope

science	music
coach	mathematics
politician	truth
free enterprise	pain

2. As you work at making your writing vivid, avoid the following words. Usually, they only approximate your meaning because their denotation is rather general. Search instead for nouns, verbs, and adjectives that say exactly what you intend.

a lot	lots of	several
aspect	matter	situation
factor	nature	terrible
fine	nice	terrific
great	phase	thing
interesting	pretty	variety
item	provide	various
large		

In the sentences below, identify vague words that detract from precision in meaning. Explain how each sentence might be improved.

A. Jones Hall is really a nice dorm; I love it there. And my suitemates and roommates are really super-nice. I had pretty good luck for just pot luck.
B. You should see all the construction work they are doing on campus. It sure makes everything a hassle.
C. This is a great place to attend school.
D. All my teachers are real nice and they really seem like good teachers. They also appear to be very understanding.
E. I rented a video of *Places in the Heart* about a young widow who triumphs over adversity. It's the kind of movie I'll never forget. I keep wondering what I would have done had it been me.
F. You wouldn't believe the changes going on here. They tore everything up and built new stuff.
G. The author showed a small town in Minnesota and its people through the use of both irony and satire.
H. Hunting has a moral issue, especially when it is viewed as a sport.

3. The following paragraphs from a student paper represent a fine attempt at writing vividly. Notice the specificity of the adjectives and verbs. Notice, also, however, that the writer tends to use the weak verb *have*. Revise the passage applying what you've learned about exact diction.

> The two young men had hired a small motorboat and were on their way to experience some of the wonders—physically and emotionally—of the ocean. They had no real knowledge of the sea, except for the small pieces of information they had picked up from

novels and the stories they had heard old fishermen recite; but they were sensible people with good brains. What could possibly go wrong?

As the boat raced through the thick green waves toward the horizon the boys sat rigidly at the back. One of them had his hand tightly clenched to the tiller but was not guiding the boat in any particular direction. The wind tore through the youths' tangled hair, and slapped viciously at their faces, but the excitement had such a hard grip on their hearts it was impossible to even consider slowing down. The boat continued further and further as if it were trying to reach the horizon; but as it got nearer, the horizon tormentingly slid out of their reach.

Suddenly a huge wave hit both of the boys full in the face. The blow was so fierce it jerked their heads back and caused them to lose control of the boat. It spun around wildly for a split second and then the engine coughed twice and died. The two boys looked at each other with panic on their faces, and then one began to laugh and the other immediately joined him. They were shocked at how completely absorbed they had been in the speed of their craft, but they were scared of showing their feelings.

TRITE DICTION

Vividness in writing is reduced by trite diction. Trite phrases and clichés were once fresh and original, but they have lost their vividness through overuse. Trite expressions slip into our speech too easily. When we're talking and an exact expression evades us, we reach for the nearest cliché. But remember that oral speech is much more general than writing, so triteness in casual speech is not as big a problem.

In writing, however, triteness is something to avoid. One writer has described clichés as blank checks that a writer gives to the reader hoping the *reader* will fill in the meaning. Trite diction has a lulling effect on the reader. Since the expressions are familiar to everyone, the reader exerts less effort in following the writer's thoughts. Furthermore, since the expressions are predictable and overused, the reader may conclude that the thought is also unoriginal.

Avoid such clichés and trite expressions as:

out of the horse's mouth	rude awakening
pretty as a picture	nip in the bud
whistling in the dark	apple of his eye
well-rounded education	can't judge a book by its cover
in this day and time	fresh as a daisy
in the nick of time	blind as a bat
giant step	easy as pie

APPLICATION

1. Trite diction is not always the result of using clichés. Sometimes triteness is due to the use of nouns and verbs or nouns and adjectives in well-worn combinations. In the following sentences, the underlined words are examples of these combinations:
   A. The sun was glaring down on all our greased bodies and giving us the most professional tan we had ever had. The water was refreshingly cool and a gorgeous shade of blue. All good things must end, and we decided to go to our rooms, clean up, and enjoy some night life.
   B. While the figures are staggering, there are still a few ways to soften the college tuition crunch.
2. In the exercise below, identify clichés and trite expressions. Rewrite the paragraphs, substituting original expressions for the trite ones.
   A. When it comes to unforgettable characters, Alan Jones takes the cake. Alan is my best friend and can usually get us into some pretty wild circumstances. He is about five foot nine, with wide shoulders and slim build. Alan is a tad bit vain about himself, but I guess everyone is nowadays. I am not sure how we met each other, but it was a few years back and really not of significant importance. We were both the same type people: silly, easy-going, and mischievous. Alone, each of us was like a firecracker without a fuse, docile, yet together we were like an acetylene torch to dynamite. Alan played baseball in high school and coached a little league team after classes.
   B. Back in high school getting a good job for the summer was no easy matter. Sure, jobs at malls or in fast-food restaurants were a dime a dozen, but I wanted a real job—something that might have relevance to a future career. One summer I pounded the pavement for weeks, but kept coming up empty. Then my friend Brian told me about this great job he had heard about. It was for an office assistant at a downtown law firm. It sounded like the opportunity of a lifetime. When it came time for my interview I was really nervous, but convinced myself to go through with it. The guy who interviewed me was stiff and formal and had no sense of humor. When it was over he shook my hand but told me not to hold my breath. He said they were looking for someone older, preferably a law student. At first I was disappointed, but then I got really mad when I found out that my buddy Brian got the job. It turned out his uncle was someone of importance in the firm and had pulled

some strings for Brian. You could say that this was my introduction to the ups and downs of the business world.

C. These days, people must really pinch their pennies if they want to see a movie. Many people have opted to rent movies rather than shell out big bucks and stand in long lines to see a new release in a theater. Of the movies available for video rental, I strongly recommend *Stand and Deliver.* This movie is based on the true story of Jaime Escalante, a hispanic man who came to East Los Angeles to teach math to hispanic students. The high school is in a rough neighborhood and is full of tough kids who don't want to learn. But Escalante won't take no for an answer. He pulls a few rabbits out of his hat to gain the students' attention, and eventually makes the school one of the tops in the nation in A.P. Calculus. Featuring some talented newcomers, *Stand and Deliver* will fascinate you, make you laugh, and make you cheer for Jaime Escalante. *Stand and Deliver* is your best bet for great home video entertainment.

PART 4 Special Applications

This section will show you how to apply the writing process to such special situations as

- organizing your thoughts and words for an essay examination
- writing effective business letters
- writing a résumé and job application letters that help you land the job you want
- developing papers about literature that explain and critique
- meeting the special audience expectations entailed in writing for the sciences

Material this far back in a thick book may resemble the options list in a brochure for a car you're thinking of buying. Wouldn't it be great to order the antilock braking system, the towing package, and the Bose stereo—but they seem pricey and out of your league. Better stick with the basics, right? Sure you can live without ABS brakes—until an ice storm turns roads to roller rinks.

Look more closely at the material in this chapter and you'll discover that the special applications discussed here are, in fact, luxury items *only* until you really need them. Sure you can forget about essay exams or résumés—until you have to write one.

The fact is almost everyone who attends an academic institution sooner or later takes an essay examination. Yet how often do students think of a test as a specific kind of writing with conventions and strategies that can be learned? Not often enough. Students usually plunge into their bluebooks knowledgeable about the subject of the exam, but wholly unprepared for writing about it; they expect instinct to guide their responses to instructors' questions. Chapter 22 suggests that you don't have to rely on instinct alone when facing an essay examination.

Chapter 23 gives you advice about writing a business letter. No matter what your job or profession (even if you don't have a profession), you'll be writing letters to deal with people at the phone company, the gas company, the insurance company, the catalog store, maybe even the IRS. Or you may end up working for one of those institutions and you'll have to reply to all those customers, consumers, and taxpayers. To do it right requires skill and strategy. But once again, you are dealing with a specific kind of writing with its own conventions and guidelines. You can *learn* to write a much better letter than one you'd produce on instinct alone.

One of the most important letters you'll ever write—and probably quite soon—is the job application. Accompanied by a proper résumé, the job application letter is your first step into the profession or employment of your choice. You can't afford to look like a novice, even if you are. That's why you need the information in Chapter 24; you should assume that others competing for that job have already learned what's there.

If you plan to do further studies in English literature, ever have to report on a book for another discipline, or just love to read and then tell others about what you've read, the suggestions in Chapter 25 will help you write effective analyses and critiques of literary works. You may even find yourself writing such analyses for professional or popular publications.

Another professional and academic area in which strong writing skills are crucial is science. Lab reports and scientific papers, abstracts, and reviews of other scientific reports all have to be both precise *and* readable. Chapter 26 not only introduces the conventions of writing for the sciences but also shows you how to apply the writing process so that you convince readers that your scientific research and results are reliable.

So here you have them—five special applications for your writing skills. Take advantage of the keys to these applications offered in the following chapters.

CHAPTER 22

Writing the Essay Examination

"Essay Test"—the very words chill the collegian's soul. Most students seem to prefer "fill in the blank" or "bubble the circle" examinations, which require little more than choosing among pre-packaged alternatives ("multiple guess") or deciding whether something is right or wrong ("true or false"). Now, if you think about it, *those* are the tests that really *are* scary: you're at the mercy of facts, facts, facts. If you've been lucky enough to study the right material in the right manner, you'll probably pass.

But what happens if you know the material generally, but not the specific items selected for the test? In such cases, you end up looking less knowledgeable than you are because the format of the text dictates what answers you may provide. And those answers usually test your grasp of materials, not your ability to use what you have learned.

Essay examinations are different. They give you more opportunity to control the agenda of a test, to emphasize your strengths, to prove your ability to organize and present information. With so-called "objective" tests, there's not much you can do if you don't have specific answers for the questions posed. With an essay examination, you'll be able to respond intelligently if you've done the reading, studying, and thinking that's required. You aren't at the mercy of memory alone. In fact, you've got a powerful ally whenever you sit down to take an essay test: your ability to create, shape, and complete a piece of writing. Controlling the process of writing means that you'll almost always have something to say (creating), you'll know how to arrange the material logically and effectively (shaping), and you'll know how to give your thoughts clarity, energy, and punch. So there's actually little to be worried about.

Like any specialized form of writing, essay examinations follow certain conventions that can be learned and mastered. This chapter explains some of those conventions.

THE PURPOSE OF THE ESSAY EXAMINATION

No, the purpose is not to make you suffer, but to determine what you have learned and what you can do with that knowledge. You don't have to come up with a topic—that's furnished by the instructor. You do have to write a coherent essay in appropriate academic style to show your command of the subject you were taught and the readings you were assigned. Here are some tips for preparing for and taking an essay examination:

1. Study. Nothing glamorous about this suggestion, but you can't beat it as a way of preparing for an examination—or for soothing your nerves. Nothing confers confidence like doing the required work and reading. When you come right down to it, learning takes time and effort. If you want to do well, expect to study *hard.*

It also makes sense to study *well*—to learn as efficiently as you can in the time available. Focus on those questions an instructor is likely to ask. You've observed your teacher in class. What subjects are favorites? What approach does he or she typically take to an issue? What sorts of issues are typically discussed in class? Rather than learning every fact you can, concentrate on key ideas and how they relate. When possible, study with a group; discuss major points, talk about the subject, trade likely questions, brainstorm possible answers. Even if the actual questions are nothing like those you've come up with, you'll find yourself remarkably fluent on many important topics.

2. Read the examination questions carefully. Unfortunately, many students get stuck right at the beginning by not reading the test questions carefully. Yet a patient look at what you are expected to do will yield real benefits. Before you even raise your pen to plunge into the test-taking, ask yourself, "What does this question really tell me to do?" Unless you know what is expected, you will ramble. Once you know what you are to do, however, you can organize your thinking and writing. So one secret of successful exam-taking is: *don't write until you know what you're being asked to write about.*

How do you find out? The wording of the question itself will tell you. Are you being asked to explain, discuss, evaluate, summarize, analyze, classify, illustrate, or something else? The directions tell you what kind of writing to do. In fact, you've already done these kinds of writing. "Explain," "illustrate," and "discuss" are other terms for Writing to Tell. Remember the *how-to* essay, the *personal perspective* essay, and the *information* essay? "Evaluate" suggests the *evaluation* essay, the *problem-solution* essay, and the *assertion-with-evidence* essay. In short, once you identify the kind of writing required, you will be able to use the writing skills you already have.

3. Get an overview. Instead of jumping into the first exam question and writing about it, feverishly, for 50 out of the allotted 60 minutes, look over the entire exam carefully. If you have several topics from which to choose, pick the one(s) you feel most confident about. Allot time according to the importance of each question. Figure out how much time you can afford to spend on each answer.

THE CREATING STAGE

By now whenever you begin to write you probably think "Creating stage—how can I find something to say?" Well, this assignment is different: you don't have to come up with a topic (the instructor's question does that for you). In this case, the creating stage is actually a recovery stage—it's where you retrieve from your memory what you have put into your mind while studying. It works a little bit like a computer: information typed into a computer is stored on a plastic disk. This disk can be removed and later re-inserted; by pressing certain keyboard keys, you tell the computer to retrieve—to bring back—the information you stored previously. While we can't just push a button on ourselves and get instant retrieval, we *can* expect that what we learned will still be there. It's a question of learning how to call it forth.

The best creating technique to use during a test is whichever helps you recall what you have already studied. No amount of looping or cub-

1. **Relax.** Take deep breaths, roll your head from side to side, stretch your spine, extend your fingers, and get the kinks out. Anxiety and shallow breathing go together—if you change your breathing, you will reduce or eliminate anxiety.
2. **Talk to yourself kindly and confidently.** Instead of saying, "It's no use, I'll never get through this," try "I'm a smart person, and I'm sure that as I get into writing I'll know what to do."
3. **Stay alert, not hypnotized.** Staring at anything long enough—even a piece of paper—will get you a little glassy-eyed. If you're successfully hypnotized—if you're on a roll and your writing is working for you—then ignore the following suggestion. But if you are feeling empty and anxious, break the spell: move your eyes around the room slowly, noting different shapes and colors. Feel the temperature of the air on your hands. Look out the window. This will encourage your retrieval system to work better.

ing will give you material for an answer unless you've stored some ideas to being with—"nothing will come of nothing."

Pay attention to the question your instructor has posed. Underline its key verb and you'll likely have the structure you'll need for guiding your answer:

compare and contrast the economic systems of . . .

describe the life cycle of the . . .

analyze the motives for . . .

illustrate the effect of . . .

explain the causes of increased homelessness . . .

Each of these terms suggests a pattern to fill in and a structure for your answer. To fill that pattern you might try the following three basic creating techniques:

The Reporter's Formula

When the examination question asks you to *discuss* or *explain* a topic, the reporter's formula may be the most reliable tool for creating. Simply arrange the questions in the reporter's formula in an order appropriate to your answer: *who, what, where, when, why,* and *how.* You need not respond to each question individually; instead, use them to check that you've covered all the critical points. In the heat of an examination, it's easy to forget to mention who you are talking about, when key events occurred, or why things happened as they did. As you are finishing an essay question, return to the reporter's formula and ask yourself that critical question one more time.

Listing

When it comes to nailing down ideas, a list has the simplicity and power of a hammer; you couldn't invent a better tool for working under pressure. Get your thoughts out on paper in pencil or ink as quickly as possible. Don't be hypercritical or languid; time's too much a factor to be elegant. If you don't like an item in your list, just cross it out. The point is to get everything down. Just making the list will trigger associations, generate ideas, and jog your memory.

Brainstorming

Under the pressure of an exam, brainstorming becomes advanced listing. Set your thoughts flowing by writing non-stop on a scratch sheet. Don't be critical; the best way of resisting really dumb or irrelevant ideas is to see them in black and white. Watch your time. Once you've put your ideas in rough shape, go back over the prose you produced, underline the key ideas, and enter the shaping stage.

THE SHAPING STAGE

The shaping stage is the critical step in writing an essay answer. There are several givens you can be almost certain of:

1. The instructor will be bored reading the tests.
2. The instructor will get very tired of reading the tests.
3. The instructor will already *know* everything in the answer and will be trying to determine whether you know the material.

Audience as Shaper: Instructor as Audience

Responding to an essay question creates an unusual communication situation. For once, you don't have to earn your reader's attention; you're probably going to get more than you may really want. (Instructors are, after all, paid to read tests, and most do their job conscientiously.) You can count on your teacher reading your essay to the end.

You *can't* count, however, on the instructor's not getting tired or bored or confused or becoming convinced that you don't know a thing (all affecting your grade). So the Shaping Stage is extremely important in the presentation of your answer. You should have these objectives:

1. To prove immediately that you know the material.
2. To be very clear.
3. To be as organized as possible.
4. To be as specific as possible.
5. To come across as an individual and a (rather) distinct personality.

Start with a Thesis

In shaping essay answers, begin immediately with a sentence that tells the instructor what you are going to discuss. *This will be the topic sentence or thesis sentence of your answer.* (In fact, your entire answer will probably be one long topic sentence paragraph or a series of topic sentence paragraphs.) Most exam questions don't come right out and give you the thesis. Instead, they narrow the field—they tell you what *not* to write about. You're the one who will develop a thesis. The best time to develop one is before you begin writing—not after. Otherwise you (and your instructor) will wander in a maze of random thoughts.

You need not begin the answer with the same kind of attention-getting opening you use in essays when you have to attract your reader's attention. What is paramount here is the *subject matter.* The instructor is by and large uninterested—at this time particularly—in your personality or individuality except as they play off the subject matter. The instructor *is* interested in knowing that you know the material, so you must make that clear immediately.

The next thing to do in the essay answer is give the information. If you can put it in a series of three to five points, give these swiftly and clearly. Then for each point give an example or two. *Be specific.* Quote as many facts, give as many examples, as you can in the time allowed.

Form

Even though you won't have time to get fancy, you can still come up with a perfectly good form. How? The answer lies in the question. If you are asked to "Compare and contrast" A and B (that is, how are they the same and how are they different?), you would first describe A in terms of characteristics 1, 2, and 3, and then describe B in terms of the same characteristics—1, 2, and 3. That takes care of how they are the same. Then you would discuss how they are different.

If you are asked to "Trace the development of *x*," you would use a *time order:* first this happened, then that happened, then the next thing happened, all the way up to the conclusion.

If you are asked to "Show how *u* resulted in *v*" (or "Show how *v* was the result of *u*"), you would use a *cause-and-effect* order: this cause led to that effect (switch to time order here—via event #1, event #2, etc.), or this effect was due to these causes.

And so it goes. You can rely on your experience writing full-fledged essays to get you through this part.

Don't Pad. It's always a temptation to simply fill up the paper with words, any words—but avoid it. An instructor who has read between 15 and 50 exams on the same subject has a finely tuned "baloney meter." It's better to take your best guess than to just take up meaningless space writing nonsense.

Don't Show Off. You likewise may be tempted to insert material that isn't called for, just because you know it—especially if you're not sure if your answers are any good. The best advice is: *don't.* Most instructors aren't wowed by extraneous information—they tend to see it as the smokescreen it is. You're better off focusing clearly on what you do know, and keeping to the thesis.

What To Do if You Think of a New Point While Writing

Writing itself often generates new ideas, retrieves information you had forgotten, and stirs up your thinking. If this happens while you are writing an essay test answer, *put a quick note to yourself in the margin* (you can scratch it out later). After you've finished the point you're making, look for a minute at your list and think where your new idea might fit best. The important thing is not to run off with the new thought in the middle of what you are saying. Instructors are no different from other humans—

they like order. They need to be able to see where you are going. Rambling answers will confuse and perhaps even annoy them.

You can always add your afterthoughts by inserting them above the line, using a caret (‸) to indicate where they go. Another way is to add the new material at the end of your answer, draw a neat box around it, and make a note at the appropriate place in the essay to tell the instructor to turn to the boxed paragraph(s) on page X.

THE COMPLETING STAGE

You won't have a leisurely amount of time to do your completing, so fine points have to go by the boards. Still, it pays to budget your test-taking so that you save the last 20 percent of your allotted time to complete your essay as best you can.

What, under the circumstances, might "best" be? That you attend to the most significant details—the ones that will make it easy for your instructor to follow your thoughts. So toward the end, before you are quite ready to hand in your blue book, look your essay over and ask yourself these questions:

- "Have I stuck to my thesis?" Wandering off the topic is confusing to writer and reader, both. It's better to present a shorter, more coherent essay than a longer, more aimless one.
- "Are my answers complete?" Have you presented enough evidence to let the reader agree with your thesis, or at least see how you arrived at it? Writing a sketchy, "that's the way it is because I say so" response won't convince the instructor that you really understand the material. You need to give explanatory details, to guide the reader toward your conclusion.
- "Have I used topic sentences and topic sentence paragraphs?" When you write an essay exam, emphasize the topic sentences; like the thesis, they tell the reader what you are writing about. In a regular essay, you would use both topic sentence paragraphs and function paragraphs; in a test essay, you use primarily topic sentence paragraphs, because you have a lot of information to pack into a short period of time. While function paragraphs add flow, drama, and other qualities to any piece of writing, these characteristics can be sacrificed to the more pressing need for coherence and clarity.

  "Have I made sensible transitions from one paragraph to the next?" Going easy on the function paragraphs doesn't mean dispensing with transitions altogether. Your job is to guide the reader—to deliver your message in such a way that it is received. One way is to insert *signal words*—words that direct the traffic of your reader's attention, such as *however, although, consequently, similarly,* and so on. Another way is to use *parallelism* where appropriate—for example, "The initial step is. . . . The second step is. . . . The final step is. . . ." The easier you can make it for the reader to follow your train of thought, the better off you (and your instructor) are.

- "Have I included enough examples and illustrations to make my thesis come alive for the reader?" In a regular essay, you might come up with anecdotes and other colorful illustrations to flesh out your abstract ideas. In writing a test essay, however, you don't have that time. Solution: use the very facts and figures you have studied. They will work fine, and in the process also demonstrate to the reader that you know the material. In addition, some exams ask you to offer your own experiences—for example, "Discuss Erik Erikson's stages of identity, and apply these stages to your own life." In this case, your own experience constitutes a legitimate illustration.
- "Are the examples and illustrations that I've chosen relevant?" One last concern: be selective about which illustrations and examples you offer. If the question causes five examples to spring to mind, use the two or three most likely to back up your thesis. Go for quality.

What To Do if You Don't Know the Answer

Never leave a question blank. Even if you don't know specifics for an answer, **write something.** Two things can serve as sources of answers: (1) looping on class discussions, and (2) points you know about other matters that might be applicable to the question.

If you cannot remember a single thing from the text on the subject, looping may provide you with ideas. Decide how much time you have to spend on the question and divide that by thirds. Plan to loop for the first third. Loop on class discussions. (Then use the other two thirds of the time to write the answer.)

I remember the professor saying . . .

I remember being in class and . . .

When you've finished the looping, look it over and underline points made in class that you might somehow relate to the question. You may not be able to develop these points from textual material fully, but you can give *examples* that *you* make up.

Don't panic. Even if an answer isn't absolutely applicable to the question, you will very likely get some points for writing an organized response. This is better than getting nothing.

What To Do if You Run Out of Time

The best thing to do, of course, is not to run out of time. Watch the clock closely. Divide the number of questions into the number of minutes and be precise about sticking to the allotted number of minutes. (Do the questions worth the most points first and give them the most time.) Just give up the illusion that on an essay exam you will get to tell everything you know about a subject. (In fact, many professors intentionally make the exam longer than the time allows.)

But if you do run out of time anyway—what to do? You have some options:

1. Pick the question you know most about—among all the questions left—and concentrate on that one for the time you have left. Be content to write a brilliant answer to this question in lieu of superficially answering several of the questions left over.

2. Write one or two sentences on all the questions you have left. If there isn't one question that you could shine on, go through each question left over and write a few lines—of course, the best facts, examples, details, and so on that you possibly can muster—on each one. This will show your professor that you knew some of the material at some level.

3. Outline your answer(s) to the questions left over. Instead of fully developing the answer, let your professor know in an introductory sentence that you have run out of time and are going to outline the answers you would have fully developed if you had had time.

Finally, no matter which of the options you choose, when you run out of time, tell your professor in a note on the exam. This courtesy cannot hurt your situation. Most professors appreciate your letting them know that the clock caught you.

Appearance

The way your answer *looks* on the paper will be important in your instructor's grading. Remember these facts of life:

- The instructor will have many papers to grade.
- The instructor will already know the material.
- The instructor likes order.
- The instructor will respond more favorably to neatness and correctness.

Be realistic. If a reader has to squint to read your writing, you're the loser. If the words are misspelled, this can annoy your instructor immediately. Save yourself enough time to look over the paper:

- Be neat.
- Write legibly and use a pen.
- Check spelling.
- Be sure you have written complete sentences.
- Read over what you've written to be sure that it makes sense. Is a word left out? Too many words put in? Did you write one word when you meant another?

You will defeat your own purpose if you write frantically to the last minute and don't leave yourself time to look over the answer.

SUMMARY

1. **Study with the exam in mind.** Thinking ahead to what questions the instructor might ask will help you organize your thoughts, even if you are asked different questions. (And if you are asked the same ones you came up with, you have a big head start!)

2. **Come prepared.** Try to sleep the night before. Wear comfortable clothes. Bring 2–3 working pens, scratch paper—and a watch.

3. **Read the questions carefully before writing.** Look for clues in the wording of the question itself—"Discuss," "Analyze," "Explain," "Evaluate," and so on.

4. **Read through all the questions before writing.** This lets you know what's ahead (and subconsciously prepare for it). It also lets you lead with your expertise—when you start by answering the question you know best, you feel confident and calm.

5. **Take time to create before you write the answer.** Even if everyone around you is writing furiously, use a creating technique to discover what you are going to say before you start writing.

6. **Give complete answers.** Don't just declare your thesis, explain it.

7. **Finish in time to look over the answer.** You may find this difficult because of the temptation to write to the very end. But remember, the instructor doesn't want to know *everything* you know. If you select from what you know and present this selection intelligently, you'll get the grade you want.

8. **Be in charge yourself.** Don't let the test situation panic you or control you. Be calm, or you'll probably forget even the few facts that you think you do know. An essay test situation is simply a time for you to show your instructor something that he or she expects you to know. Take advantage of this opportunity. Organize; and write with the instructor in mind.

APPLICATION

1. Here are two examples of essay examination answers that received an *A* grade from the instructor. Read them and be able to discuss why you think the instructor liked them.

Exam Question: *Discuss the use of the pointed arch in Gothic architecture.*

Student's Answer:

A. List made by student before beginning answer (appears in margin of test paper):

Pointed Arch

1. Allowed irregular spaces to be covered.
   Example: a. Rhomboidal bays of ambulatory
   b. Polygonal chapels of French Chevet
   c. Polygonal chapter-houses of England
2. Made possible use of ribs
   Example: a. St. Denis Abbey Church
   b. Cathedral of Canterbury
   c. Cathedral of Salisbury
3. Made possible rectangular bays
   Example: a. Church of Sainte Chapelle
   b. Cathedral at Amiens

B. The answer itself:

Thesis
Topic sentence
Parallelism: *"first"*

The use of the pointed arch had a great significance to Gothic architecture. The first and most important task it accomplished was allowing an irregular area to be covered by arches and vaults. The round arch required a square vaulting bay, but the pointed arch with its extreme flexibility allowed almost any shape that was necessary. The arch allowed the steepness of the arches to vary, and this let the builders adapt the shape to whatever design might be included in the blueprint. Examples of irregular areas covered by this method are

Examples

the rhomboidal bays of the ambulatory, the polygonal chapels of the French Chevet, and the polygonal chapterhouses of England.

Topic sentence
Parallelism: *"second"*
Examples

The second achievement of the pointed arch was making possible an intricate system of vaulting ribs which served both structural and aesthetic purposes. The idea of the Gothic builder was to make a vault like a skeleton by use of the projecting ribs. Examples of the use of ribs can be seen in all Gothic cathedrals. Three such examples are the St. Denis Abbey church, the Cathedral of Canterbury, and the Cathedral of Salisbury.

Topic sentence
Parallelism: *"Last"*
Examples

Last, the pointed arch also made possible the rectangular as opposed to the square bay. This caused the total weight of the building to be distributed over twice as many points. The horizontal divisions, or bays, that were once present are then lost causing the eye to see the church nave as one smooth continuous aisle, as seen in the Church of Sainte Chapelle in Paris or the Cathedral at Amiens.

Summary

These three uses of the pointed arch were very important because they allowed Gothic architects to achieve the structural and aesthetic qualities that Gothic architecture is noted for.

Exam Question: *How did the Peloponnesian War affect Greece?*

Student's Answer:

A. List made in margin of test before writing answer.
   1. Ended 404 B.C.
   2. Defeated Athens
   3. Left Greece powerless
   4. Sparta & Thebes (2nd half of 4th century B.C.)
   5. States lost liberty to Philip of Macedon
   6. Life structure changed
   7. The individualism approach to life was taught
   8. Independence of city-state relationship lessened
   9. Final effect of Greek civilization spreading around the world

B. The answer itself:

Greece was affected by the Peloponnesian War in several ways. First, Greece was left defenseless and weak after the defeat of Athens. This weakness allowed Sparta and later Thebes to control Greece. As a result, in the latter half of the fourth century B.C., Greek states lost their liberty to Philip of Macedon.

Second, with this loss of liberty, the entire structure of Greek life was changed. The original balance between the city-state and individual was destroyed. Basic simple views concerning man and the state were changed into political and social upset and turmoil. The attitudes about life changed and became more self-centered and individualistic.

Third, as a result of this individualism, the state-individual relationship soon dissolved. Greek attitude also changed, leading to the search for knowledge of the world. Through this search, the Greeks experienced a time of human discovery.

Finally, it is easy to say that the Peloponnesian War was a powerful influence on the developments in Greece. But even though the country was adversely affected, in the long run and in a round-about way, the Peloponnesian War caused Greek civilization to spread around the known world. This was because Philip of Macedon's son was Alexander the Great, and everybody knows about his conquering the world. In this conquering, he took Greek civilization with him.

2. Here are two examination questions written by other students. Read each and write or discuss the strengths and weaknesses of the answers.

Exam Question: *Explain why the oceans are not filled in and the earth is not a slush on the surface.*

Student's Answer:

A. List made before answering:
   1. Subduction
   2. Plate tectonics
   3. Deposition
   4. Erosion

B. The answer itself:

With all the sediment from erosion flowing into the oceans, how come the oceans are not filled in and the earth surface a slush pot?

One reason is the simple idea called subduction. Subduction is a simple idea; the sheet of rock from one area is going or being forced under another. Along the west coast of South America this is evident. The Andes Mountains are a side effect of this.

Second, the way these rock plates can be explained is an idea called plate tectonics. This idea states that there are rockplates on the surface of the earth, and they are constantly colliding and something has to give. The Himalayas are a good example.

A third reason to examine is the fact that all around you are deposition of material from erosion and volcanic activity, not to mention thrust of mountains over time. Rivers are constantly flowing with large amounts of sediment. The Amazon River. The island of Hawaii is a volcanic mountain. You can see the accumulation, but the disappearance is not quite so apparent.

Fourthly, erosion is happening at an unbelievable rate. With all this erosion, the oceans should be filled in. Take the Mississippi River for instance. In the last one thousand years it has built up a seven kilometer river delta. If you multiply this by one thousand times for the whole earth and take into account the depths, the oceans should have been filled in at least twenty-five million years ago. Subduction is the best guess.

Exam Question: *List four major engineering achievements prior to the twentieth century and discuss their importance.*

Student's Answer (no list made):

The first major engineering project was the irrigation system. This idea enabled the Egyptians to farm many miles of nonproductive land. Secondly, and just as important, was the building of roads. The Romans built roads mainly for communication, not transportation. Their army was constantly changing, and roads were vital to their success. The third development was the refinement of steel. This was a significant step to modern engineering, since it allowed production of machinery. The fourth design was a result of refinement of steel. It was the invention of the steam engine. This was very useful since it gave man an alternative energy source to slavery.

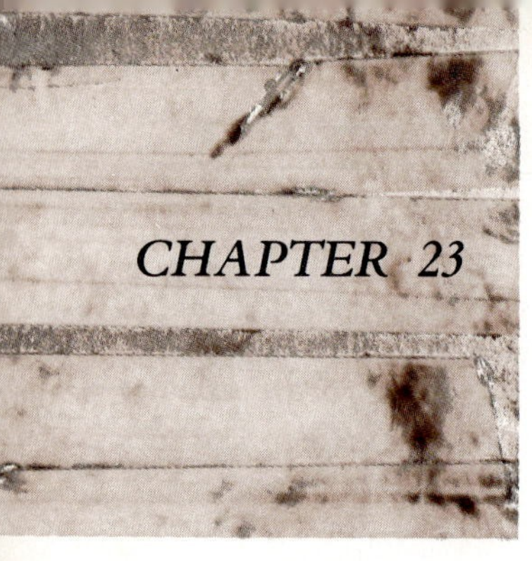

CHAPTER 23

Writing the Business Letter

Not many years ago, "business" meant blast furnaces along the Monongahela River or noisy foundries along the Rouge River. Today the wheels of industry seem to churn out more paper than steel—reams of paper. We've becoming an information society as much as a manufacturing one. That means most everyone writes.

What we write are business letters, whether or not we work in industry. A business letter is simply the form of communication appropriate when people talk to institutions. When you write to (or for) a company, a school, an organization, a church, a political group, you'll follow the conventions of the business letter.

ELEMENTS OF A BUSINESS LETTER

The following sections discuss the key elements to consider when writing a business letter.

Purpose and Tone

A business letter should be businesslike and efficient: you are a person writing to somebody for some definite reason. That reason should be spelled out as early as possible, preferably in the first paragraph of the letter. The first paragraph makes a promise; the rest of the letter delivers on that commitment.

The tone of a business letter should be crisp and factual. You want to sound like someone who knows what's going on and who can get a job done. Don't hesitate, don't whine. Show the strongest, most competent side of yourself or the institution you represent: be serious, dependable, confident, capable, effective, and trustworthy.

Organization

Information in the letter should be clearly arranged, point by point. Each paragraph should develop a single issue or concern. Use lists and indention to highlight important information. Make it as easy as possible for a reader to see the relationship between your main point (the opening paragraph) and supporting information (subsequent paragraphs). Comparable ideas should be treated in parallel form. Try to say everything you must in a single page. Don't waste a reader's time.

Be explicit about requests, queries, or recommendations. Don't keep readers guessing about your intentions or purposes. Furnish clear and accurate information. Any errors can cost time and money, whether you are ordering an item from a catalog or providing a potential customer with warranty or price information.

Use the reporter's formula to check that you've provided all the facts a reader needs: *who, what, where, when, how,* and *why.* One method for checking the completeness of a letter is to consider how good a business record it might be in the future. Could a reader consulting a file two years from now understand the purpose of your letter? (Remember that most letters these days are routinely copied; they go on file somewhere.)

Here is a sample letter that demonstrates clear organization:

Sample "Order" Letter:

1401 Marble Hill
Newton, Pennsylvania 99222
October 10, 1990

Denver Auto Parts
16 Chambers Place
Denver, Colorado 22446

Dear Sir,

Please send me the following parts from your September catalog:

one rear window gasket seal, part #3320756	(page 27)	$ 19.75
one "handy-jack" hydraulic lift, #740	(page 3)	98.00
one *VW Specialties Catalog*	(page 50)	3.95
	TOTAL:	$121.70

Enclosed is my check for the full amount. Please ship my order as soon as possible to the address above.

Sincerely,

André Worth Vergara

André Worth Vergara

Audience and Style

The level of the writing must be appropriate to your reader's understanding. This is especially true if you are better informed than your readers; you must make the adjustment to their level of knowledge and vocabulary so that you don't write over their heads. But don't bore them with a rehash of commonplace information.

Keep sentences short and direct. Use familiar words rather than exotic or unnaturally formal expressions (for example, *use* rather than *utilize; think* rather than *conceptualize*). Avoid artificial attempts to sound

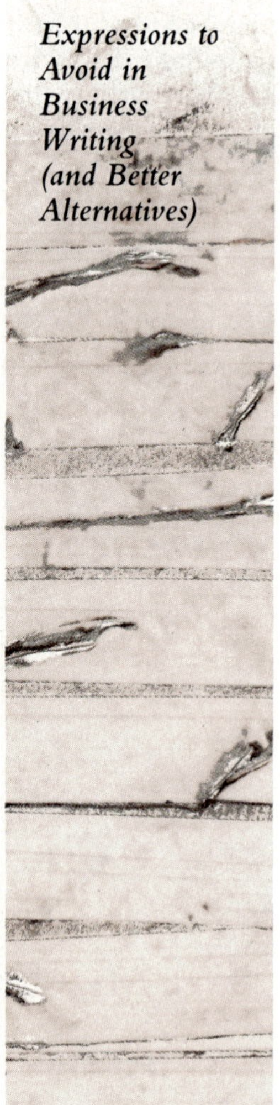

Expressions to Avoid in Business Writing (and Better Alternatives)

as a means of (to)
at the present time (now)
at your earliest convenience (soon)
avail yourself of this opportunity (try)
be cognizant of (recognize)
concerted effort by all parties (effort)
due to the fact that (because)
during the course of (during)
enclosed you will find (here is)
grant permission to (allow)
has the ability to (can)
in accordance with said agreement (as we agreed)
in light of the fact that (since)
in the event that (if)
in the process of -ing (-ing)
initial start-up (beginning)
is reflective of (reflects)
it is my desire that (I hope)
it is recommended that (we recommend)
necessary corrections (corrections)
on the grounds that (because)
on the occasion of (when)
possess an understanding of (understand)
pursuant to (regarding)
regardless of the fact that (although)

impressive or intimidating. Avoid the buzzword, the excessively technical expression used for its own sake: *optimal ergonometrics; incremental revenue enhancements; multiprogrammatic systems monitorization*. In short, write plain English.

Appearance

The appearance of a business letter delivers a message almost as important as its content. If a letter has ample margins (1″ or 1½″ all around), a conventional arrangement, accurate typing, and a professional look, it will be taken seriously. So when writing a business letter, take the time to do it right. Check spelling and usage carefully. Use a fresh typewriter ribbon and good quality paper of standard size (8½ × 11) and color (white). If available, use the company letterhead. Avoid smudges, erasures, and strikeovers.

Format

Business letters follow conventional structures to ensure that essential information is included and to make access to that information easy. Most business letters follow a modified block form, with each block providing specific information. (See the business letter template on the next page.)

You'll notice that the return address (1) and the close, signature, and typed name (7, 8, 9) are lined up together, and that the address, greeting, and body all line up together (2, 3, 4, 5, 6). Each block is separated from the others by double spaces except for the signature (8), which appears in the 4 spaces between (7) and (9).

You also have the option of lining up *all* the blocks on the left, including (1), (7), (8), and (9). This would be a full block letter.

Each of those blocks serves the writer: you can expect to find in each block its appropriate piece of information. Check to see that it is clear and accurate. And each block serves readers, too. Since every letter will be in that form, the readers don't have to start from scratch every time the mail appears in the "In" basket. So the form simplifies the task for everyone.

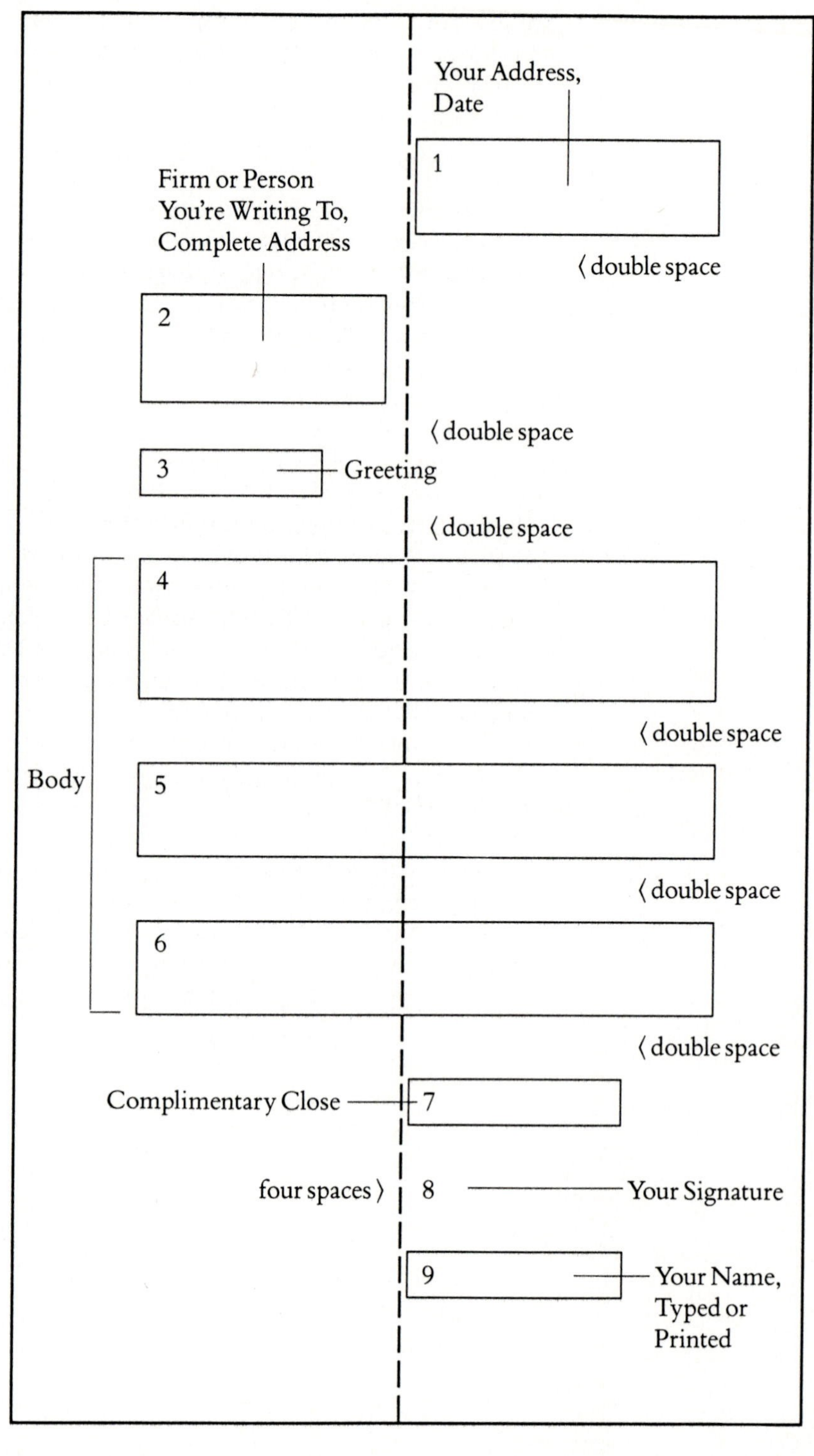
Your Address,
Date
1
Firm or Person
You're Writing To,
Complete Address
⟨ double space
2
⟨ double space
3
Greeting
⟨ double space
4
⟨ double space
Body
5
⟨ double space
6
⟨ double space
Complimentary Close
7
four spaces ⟩
8
Your Signature
9
Your Name,
Typed or
Printed

Block 1—Heading. It includes the address of the person sending the letter followed by the date.

Juliet Capulet
102 Whigham Dr.
Toledo, OH 43615
2 May 1991

Block 2—Inside address. It provides the name and address of the person or institution to whom the letter is addressed.

Tennwear Corporation
606 Carter Avenue
Urbana, IL 61802

Block 3—Salutation. The greeting is followed by a colon in business letters, not a comma. Common titles—such as Mr., Mrs., Ms., Dr.—are abbreviated, but others are usually spelled out in full (Dean, President, Professor, Reverend).

Dear President Bush:
Dear Sister Mary Eugene:
Dear Professor Skully:
Dear Mr. Lim:
Dear Mrs. Smythe:
Dear Ms. Washington:

When you don't know a particular person at a company or institution, your greeting can be simply:

Dear Sir or Madam:

Blocks 4, 5, 6—Body of the letter. This is where you contract your business. Arrange the items to highlight important information. Use the opening paragraph to make a commitment or promise. Then be sure subsequent paragraphs fulfill that promise. These blocks can be indented five spaces or typed without indention. In either case, it is visually attractive to skip a space between paragraphs.

Block 7—Complimentary close. Like the greeting, the complimentary close is a conventional expression. Only the first word in the closing is capitalized; the expression is always followed by a comma. Here are just a few possible closings:

Respectfully yours,
Yours very truly,
Yours truly,
Sincerely yours,
Sincerely,
Yours sincerely,
Best regards,

Block 8—Your signature. Sign the letter in ink just after the complimentary close.

Block 9—Your name, typed or printed. Because signatures are often illegible, type your name under the signature and, when appropriate, include a title or position.

Yours sincerely,

Juliet Capulet
Activities Director

KINDS OF LETTERS

There are basically three kinds of business letters: those that *inform* (this includes good news, bad news, and neutral news), those that *persuade,* and those that *request* information or action (this includes orders, applications, and queries). Informative and persuasive letters follow the strategies of *telling* and *changing* discussed in the Portfolio section of this book. Letters of request—and responses to them—are a bit different, so they will receive special coverage here. But first, consider a principle that all good business letters follow: *the you attitude.*

The "You" Attitude

Compare these two statements:

1. "We are proud to open our new store, our third in Savannah."
2. "We are happy to open our new store in your neighborhood to serve you better."

The first is no doubt true—people have good cause to be proud of opening a new store, especially if it's their third. But that statement comes from the position of the *writer*—not the *reader.* We're glad they are proud—but what's that to us? The second, however, has the *you attitude.* Their happiness (not pride) is about being in *your* neighborhood, and the store is there to serve *you* (not to add another store to the chain). This difference is what is called the *you attitude.* All it means is to think in terms of the reader's benefit and then write in such a way that the reader's benefit is emphasized and highlighted. What are the reader's needs, concerns, interests?

One of the experts in writing with the *you attitude* is L. L. Bean, the famous catalog company in Freeport, Maine. Less skillful people might have said something like, "Fly vest. Lightweight construction. Designed for wading. Contains twelve pockets, rod loop and two D-rings. Made of 100 percent nylon mesh. Snap-closing front. Made in Korea. Machine washable." In fact, if you read a lot of mail-order catalogs, some of them are not much more effective than that. But not Bean's. Here's their version:

Featherweight Fly Vest

Mesh construction is light in weight and provides ventilation on hot summer days. Shorty design for wading, tubing, or sitting down in boat. Twelve pockets, rod loop and two D-rings keep a full day's accessories at hand.

Made of 100% nylon mesh with taped seams for durability. Snap-closing front. Made in Korea. Machine Washable.

0488KH Featherweight Fly Vest, $39.50 ppd. Two colors: Navy. Tan. Sizes: S(34-36), M(38-40), L(42-44), XL(46-48), XXL(50-52).

It reads like an effective advertisement that stirs up responses in the reader. "Featherweight fly vest" suggests, right off, that they are speaking to a special audience and know exactly who that audience is, what they think about fly vests, and what they value: "light in weight . . . provides ventilation . . . shorty design for wading, tubing, or sitting down in boat." And the specific details reassure you that they know what they are talking about. So do the details about the material and design, "Twelve pockets, rod loop and two D-rings keep a full day's accessories at hand. . . . taped seams for durability." The material is presented clearly, vividly, from the point of view of the reader.

Requests

In a sense, *requests* and *orders* are similar in that both ask somebody to do something. Yet someone sending in an order is, in effect, merely responding to an invitation—an announcement, or an advertisement, or even a visit or call from a salesperson. A *request,* though, is usually something you generate on your own because of something you need or want. For example, it's not uncommon for students, doing research projects, to write to government agencies for special information. Most of us have had occasion to ask someone else for advice—a professor, a friend, an expert. When we write requests in letter form, there are a few simple considerations that help things move along smoothly.

REQUESTS:
(1) Be clear and specific.
(2) Encourage an answer.

Be Clear and Specific. If you make your requests too vague or too broad, you won't get the answers you need. If you write to a computer manufacturer and ask for "information on computerized offices," you may get back a set of irrelevant statistics, or ads for equipment you don't need, or something else that does not address your concerns. The more specific your request, the more useful the answer will be. So rather than asking a scattershot question about "information on computerized offices," narrow your focus—what is it about computerized offices that you want to know? How many terminals your office would need to accomplish X type of task? How to train current personnel in computer use? How to tie in to other information systems in other cities? How to replace certain jobs with computers? The more specific and precise you can be, the more likely you are to get what you want.

Encourage Response. Just because you ask doesn't mean that those you ask will oblige you with an answer. A request that's clear, specific, and polite will help to "enroll" them in your project, cause them to be sympathetic and to lend a hand. Other ways of encouraging response are by *telling who you are* and by *explaining how you'll use the information you're requesting.* The more "real" you are for them and the more understandable your request, the more likely they are to do what you're asking them to do.

Following is an example that will show you these elements in action. The requests are *clear* and *specific,* the writer *identifies* herself and *explains* her purpose in writing and *tells* how the information will be used.

No model will serve any and all occasions, but with some alterations, this one will do fairly well. Here's the outline form:

Paragraph 1: identifies writer and project.

Paragraph 2: establishes that writer is not merely idle (she has already researched the library, for example); justifies the request (the additional information will add to the material already gathered); tells what will be done with the information; offers to share a copy.

Paragraph 3: tells how many questions there are (*four,* not "a few"); presents the questions in numbered, itemized form; asks clear, specific questions.

Paragraph 4: says when the material is needed; acknowledges the reader's assistance.

It's clear, complete, forthright, and polite. There's no guarantee that an answer will be forthcoming, but there's certainly a good chance.

Sample "Request" Letter

128 Hill Drive
Reno, Nevada 55555
February 5, 1990

Ms. Elizabeth Elk
Channel 3-TV
One North Main Street
Reno, Nevada 55554

Dear Ms. Elk:

I am a sophomore education/psychology major at the University of Nevada and am writing a paper for one of my classes on the effect of TV commercials on children under age six.

I've had excellent luck with my library research, and now I want to add current information from our local TV stations, like Channel 3. I will share my report with other members of my class and I've written to the local TV magazine to see if they might publish all or part of it. I would of course be pleased to send you a copy if you would like to have one.

Would you please spend a few minutes answering these four questions?

1. Is there a person on your staff in charge of ads for children's programs? If so, could I please have the name?

2. Is there a network policy about the kind, number, subject, or treatment of commercials for children's programs? If so, may I have a copy?

3. Are there criteria that you at Channel 3 have developed (perhaps in addition to the network's) covering children's commercials?

4. Is there anything you think I should know about children's commercials—any studies or guidelines or data which I haven't asked about? If so, would you please let me know what they are (and if available, please send me copies).

My paper is due in five weeks, so I would appreciate your response as soon as possible. Thank you for your assistance in this matter.

Sincerely,

Mary Bloom

Mary Bloom

Responses

As with a letter of request, a letter of response needs to be clear and specific. Don't make your reader do any guesswork or fill in the gaps.

How to Say Yes. When you're giving a "yes" response, it pays to do enough creating to produce a strong—and maybe even original—*you attitude* that will strengthen the relationship and contribute to further good feelings.

The same principle holds when you're simply announcing good news: put the good news in the most prominent place in the letter—right out front. If there are details, they can follow.

> Congratulations: You've just won our annual Anniversary Sale-A-Bration drawing!
>
> I'm please to inform you that you have been accepted to graduate school at State University.
>
> Let me be the first to congratulate you on your promotion.

Even such a simple event as an announcement can also be the occasion for a "second sale" approach, an approach that will lead to future good relationships. The more you take advantage of such occasions, the more effective you'll become at business writing.

How to Say No. When it's necessary to say *no* in a letter, it's advisable to have a *positive* tone. You don't want to appear negative, hostile, or indifferent. You wouldn't say, for example,

> I received your so-called letter about your silly complaint.

Even if the letter was strongly written—even if it made you furious—you still want to keep your response calm. What you hope is that you can somehow handle the situation. If you cannot, you can at least avoid aggravating it. Say instead,

> Thank you for your letter of May 23 about your new Arctic air conditioner.

The first principle of saying *no* in a letter is to keep the tone calm and positive.

The second principle is to avoid saying *no* until you've covered all the facts and reasons for refusing. That way, you can show that you do indeed have facts and reasons, and that you've considered them thoughtfully. That arrangement will help the reader keep an open mind about it, too, since he or she will have to read through the letter to find your answer. And if you think about it, putting the refusal first and then following it with the reasons may make it seem as though you made up your mind first, then thought up the reasons.

Here is a sample "no" letter. It follows both principles quite well.

Sample "No" Letter

Truebuilt Company
22 Industrial Parkway
Brunswick, New Jersey 00234
March 5, 1990

Lawrence Medici
444 Camden Way
Canton, Ohio 44432

Dear Mr. Medici:

We received your letter and your Truebuilt clock-radio model number 3220. Our shop test showed that the clock did, indeed, make the grinding noise you describe in your letter. The problem appears to be a worn gear.

As you know, at Truebuilt we stand behind our work, and we are completely devoted to customer satisfaction. Your clock-radio model 3220 is a fine product, and once the gear is replaced, it should give satisfactory service for many years to come.

In your letter, you request that we repair the clock at our own expense, and we would be happy to do so if the item were under warranty. But because we have no record of your having registered this radio with us, nor is there a sales receipt from you showing date of purchase, we feel you will understand why we cannot agree to repair it at our own expense.

However, we would be pleased to do the repair for you at our regular shop rate. We estimate the repair at about $7.00, which is the lowest cost that will permit us to do a satisfactory job. Our specially trained technicians can quickly have the clock-radio in tip-top shape. Or, if you prefer, we can return the radio to you as is.

Please let us know what you'd like us to do. We look forward to serving you and to making your Truebuilt clock-radio a continuing source of satisfaction to you.

Sincerely,

Harry G. Berg

Harry G. Berg
General Manager
Truebuilt Company

The first paragraph established receipt of the clock-radio and the accompanying letter and gives agreement about the problem. Paragraph 2 develops the "second sale" approach, reminding the customer about Truebuilt's integrity and concern about its products. Only in paragraph 3 does the letter indicate refusal—and even there it presents the reasons carefully first and even avoids the word *refuse*. Paragraph 4 suggests an alternative—Truebuilt will repair the clock for a nominal amount. The closing paragraph sounds a cooperative note and stresses the customer's satisfaction. Mr. Medici may or may not continue on good terms with Truebuilt, but he's much more likely to than if he had gotten back a letter saying something like:

Dear Customer:

You were in error to return the Truebuilt clock-radio to us. We do not repair any appliance which is not under warranty. Our records show that you did not register the radio and that, therefore, we are not obligated to repair it.

Sincerely,

Remember: no matter what the content of the letter, stress the positive whenever possible.

APPLICATION

1. Revise the following sentences to remove wordiness, jargon, and buzzwords.
   A. In relationship to development of fruit, studies have shown, and actual practice proved, that some crops will divert all their attention in the form of water and nutrients into the enlargement of the ripening fruit, and to supply excess water to the plant can mean the difference in producing small or large fruit.
   B. Large corporations are able to invest large amounts of capital into a project because money is available in large corporations or is easily obtained from financial institutions alert for investment opportunities.

C. Implementation of this overall operative factor will almost guarantee multiple interactive criteria and will certainly systematize these performance areas.

D. In conclusion, I would like to wind up this paper by making this final point at the end, namely, that management creates an environment where people can efficiently reach or accomplish desired goals.

E. Bicycles that are neglected can be needlessly difficult to ride or they can cause expensive breakdowns or injury to the rider.

F. The purpose of this report is to inform the reader about the effects of television advertising on your children and what one can do about it.

G. Federal agencies have recognized that children have a hard time distinguishing between commercial and program material. A number of documented studies show that children under 8 years of age have difficulty comprehending the difference. They watch commercials just the way they watch programs.

H. The air was filled with enthusiastic awe. The film mesmerized the audience with skydivers plummeting from great heights, performing aerial acrobatics and complex formations with the agility and finesse of a ballerina. After the film, candidates with fists full of legal tender, impatiently queued, wondering if they would make this week's first jump course.

2. Make the presentation of this information more effective by changing it from narrative form to itemized format.

A. All parachutes have four major parts: (1) The canopy, a nylon air retarding device, displaces the skydiver's weight over approximately two hundred square feet and allows a descent at a slower rate of speed. Most circular canopies have twenty-eight "gores," or pie-shaped panels, sewn together to form a hemisphere. (2) The harness, strapped onto the skydiver, makes it virtually impossible for the jumper to be separated from the rest of the parachute. (3) A container holds the canopy until the jumper pulls the ripcord. (4) Suspension lines, usually seven hundred fifty pound test nylon material, connect the canopy to the harness.

B. Steel storage bins come in 6, 7, 8, and 9-ton sizes. They cost $54,000 for the 6-ton size, and $108,000 for each of the 7, 8, and 9-ton sizes. Steel flat warehouses come in the same sizes. They cost $25,600 for the 6-ton size, $29,000 for the 7-ton size, $34,100 for the 8-ton size, and $38,400 for the 9-ton size.

C. Several factors have caused the rise in the cost of owning a new home. Property taxes have gone up, and so has insurance. Building costs have gone up. Mortgage costs have also increased. Utilities are also higher than they used to be.

3. Read the following letter and discuss its strengths and weaknesses. After the discussion work together to revise the letter.

Circle Seven Ranch
P.O. Box 1177
Santa Fe, New Mexico 87501
February 6, 1989

Mr. Jeb Yargus
Star Route One
Santa Fe, New Mexico, 87501

Dear Mr. Yargus:

The following dead animals have been found on the land leased by you:

4 calves	Block 40
1 cow	Block 50
1 calf	Block 7, under barn

Remove these animals at once and dispose of them either off the ranch or where Mr. Levitt indicates to you. If the animals are not removed by two days from tomorrow, we will remove them, and you will be charged $100.00 per carcass in accordance with Article VIII of the lease signed by you on the 30th of September, 1985.

Sincerely,

Padgett Jarrell

Padgett Jarrell

4. Write to a real firm and order three or more items. Use the standard block form for your letter. Itemize the things you are ordering, and specify serial numbers and prices. If you are ordering from a catalog, cite the date and page number. Arrange the elements in a clear and logical manner.

5. Criticize the form and content of the following letter. Circle all those areas which need to be corrected.

June 3, 1987
Angus Macklin
2852 E. 102 St.
Cleveland, Ohio 44106

Ms. Charnelle Brown
Office of the Attorney General
State of Ohio
Columbus, Ohio 43210

Dear Ms. Brown,
Pursuant to the letter I recently received from you concerning my complaint against the Build 'Em Cheap Muffler Company, you sure weren't much help!

I would have expected you to be already cognizant of the fact that this company is a rip-off joint that refuses to repair the damage incurred by my vehicle due to the installation of their muffler upon said vehicle backwards.

Their attitude seems to be "So sue us if you want your money back." I was hoping that a concerted effort on the part of the Attorney General's office in the form of a letter warning the Build 'Em Cheap Muffler Company that their practices might get them into trouble might persuade them to take immediate action to refund my money.

It is my desire that you might write such a letter at your earliest convenience due to the fact that I am a taxpayer who fully deserves the assistance of the Office of the Attorney general.

Your prompt action in this matter will be appreciated.

Very truly yours:

Angus P. Macklin

Angus P. Macklin

6. Write a letter of request for something you actually want to receive. Be sure to encourage an answer to your letter. Getting the item or information, of course, will be the greatest test of the effectiveness of your request. You may actually encourage the company to send the information or item quickly if you put the right kind of encouragement into the request letter.

7. Imagine that you are president of a company that sells hiking gear. You have just received an order from a customer for a down jacket. You run your business according to the *you attitude*, and you intend to have this customer order something again. Write a response letter that makes the customer feel really thanked and which will bring another order at some time in the future to your company.
8. Write a response letter in which you must tell a customer *no*. Aim at the same time to keep the customer's good will. Use the *you attitude*.

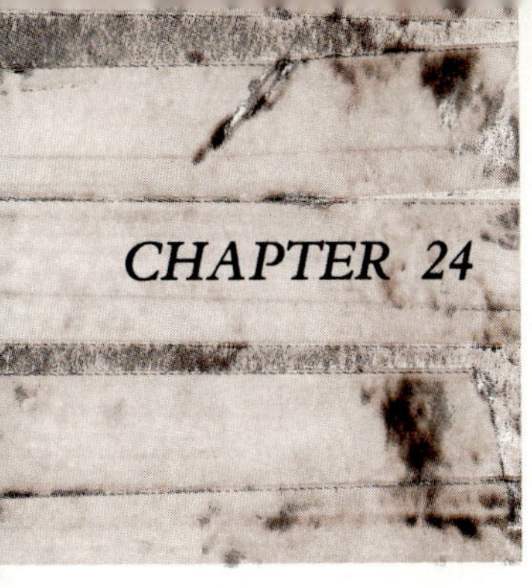

CHAPTER 24

Writing the Job Application and Résumé

When you're applying for jobs, you have two valuable tools: the letter of application and the résumé. Both follow conventions in form, appearance, and organization. And both deserve your time and attention so that they present you to a prospective employer as someone who is qualified and worth hiring.

Imagine the person getting your job application letter, seated behind a desk piled high with incoming mail. She opens one letter after another and they all seem the same—dull, preprogrammed, mechanical. Imagine her boredom after 199 letters. But then she opens yours. It's original, personal, charming, even inviting. It has, of course, all the conventional information, but in addition, it conveys authority, personality, and competence. Suddenly, you're a serious candidate with a job interview.

Does the scenario sound overly dramatic? Perhaps, but it occurs often enough to merit your attention. And it demonstrates that even in a situation as impersonal as a job application letter, you need an edge that writing ability can supply.

CONVENTIONS OF THE JOB APPLICATION LETTER

The job application letter has three parts matched to three basic questions.

MESSAGE

1. **What do you want to say?**
   I want this job.
   I'm qualified for it.
   You'd be well off to hire me.

AUDIENCE

2. **Whom are you saying it to?**
   Someone who does the actual hiring.
   Someone who screens applicants but doesn't do the actual hiring.

PURPOSE

3. **What do you want out of it?**
   I want my letter to look better than the others.
   I want to establish my qualifications.
   I want this job offered to me.

DO CREATING ON:
I want this job.
I'm qualified.
You should hire me.
I'm writing to ______.

The way to say "I want this job" is to simply say that, although you can use some creating techniques to come up with something a bit more individualized and effective. The way to say "I'm qualified" is by giving evidence (or information) about three areas of your life: school, work, and activities. And you make your letter presentable by adhering to the conventions of shaping and completing (all of which is covered in the pages that follow).

But first, it is important to be clear about the areas in which you are going to develop information. Any *creating* you do will produce material usable in *both* letter and résumé, thus serving double duty.

Creating

Use creating techniques to develop answers to the question, "What do I want to say?"

I Want This Job. *Come right out with it.* Once you are certain that you want the job, you needn't feel self-conscious saying so.

Notice that reference is to *this* job, not *the* job or *a* job; it's important to sharpen the focus. You're writing to a *particular company* in a *specific location* with a *unique product*—so don't tell them that you'd like to find *some* work *somewhere.*

Here are four creating activities for *I want this job.*

1. **List the reasons you want *this* job.**

Write as fast as you can for 3 to 5 minutes, and don't stop. Produce as many reasons as you can. Don't worry whether the reasons are good. You are writing to get the ideas flowing, to make original and strong connections.

You probably have reasons right now—but everybody else probably has the same reasons, especially if they concern salary, location, and promotion. So it's worth a few minutes to do some creating here. In the end you may still come up with the same old three—salary, location, and promotion—but even so, there's a greater chance that you'll have a personal way of expressing it—and that will help your letter stand apart from the crowd.

2. **List everything you can think of about *this* job.**

Again, write as fast as you can for 3 to 5 minutes. This activity helps get the job itself in focus and will help you to see what skills, knowledge, and attitudes it requires and to relate your own qualifications specifically to the job.

3. **Ask all the questions you can think of about this job.**

You're turning up information from a different point of view; you'll discover information about both you and the job that you can use later.

4. **Do cubing on *this* job.**

Move swiftly through the cubing activities.

This formal procedure will ensure that you examine the job from at least 6 more points of view—and will produce more and different information.

I'm Qualified for This Job. Everyone who applies for the job will claim to be qualified; what's needed is *evidence* of this qualification. The three most common areas of qualification, usually, are *education, work experience,* and *interests.* Since almost every other letter will have a wooden, mechanical recitation on these points, your task is twofold: to **come up with *your* qualifications** and to **present them interestingly.** That's a tall order, since the "rules" governing applications are a bit restrictive. Again, though, *creating* processes will help.

1. **Do *cubing* on *my qualifications for this job.***

Move around your own qualifications as you go through the six steps: *defining, comparing, associating, describing, analyzing,* and *arguing.* Begin to get "out of your own skin" a little, to see yourself as someone else would see you.

This develops a sense of how you look as a candidate—how others see your strengths.

2. **Do *looping* on *I'm qualified for this job.***

Let this different process bring up different areas, resources, awarenesses. Some repetition is natural, but keep looking for new material to emerge.

3. **Review your life, like a movie, swiftly (about 10 minutes) and jot down every event that might have any bearing on your qualifications for this job.**

Consider family activities, interests, projects. Any travel? Adventures? Inventions? Scrapes? What sorts of things did you do? How do others relate to you? What do you never do?

You'd Be Well Off to Hire Me. Whenever some writers get to this spot in their own letters, they get a sinking feeling; after all, there are so many other applicants—who in the world would possibly want to hire *them!* But once again, *creating* processes come to the rescue.

1. **List all the things you might be able to do for the company if you had *this* job.**

List *all* of them, and don't worry about whether they are "good" or "bad." See yourself from the company's viewpoint and develop an impressive list so that it actually begins to seem as though they *would* be well off to hire you.

2. **Complete this sentence at least 20 times (35 is even better): "On this job, I intend to . . ."**

Think of all the things you really mean to do on that job. Clarify your intention to be serviceable on this job, and you'll begin to see the value you really do offer.

Here is a final assortment of things to make lists about. Spend 10 or 15 minutes on each of these—they are much more specific than the earlier creating activities—and they'll very likely provide information for the rough draft of your letter and résumé.

1. **List all the *jobs* you've ever had, whether you were paid or not.**

What kinds of tasks did you do? What regular chores? Where did you help out? What did you do there? How would that relate to what you might do on *this* job?

2. **List all the times you've taken any *initiative,* taken the lead.**

Were you captain at team sports? Leader in organized activities—Scouts, Kiwanis, Bluebirds, Businesswomen of America?

Think of childhood.

Grade school.

High school.

College.

3. **List all the times you've been *successful.***

What did you win? What awards? What acknowledgements?

Prizes? Ribbons? Medals? Certificates?

What records did you break? Contests?

What do you do well that everybody knows about?

What do you do well that few people know about?

4. **List all the things you like to do.**

How do you like to spend your time?

What hobbies? Trips? Interests? What gives you pleasure when you spend time at it? What do you enjoy finding out about?

When you finish these creating activities, you will have a *lot* of material. Some of it will be worthless, some it may be something you never would have thought of before, and some of it—much, probably—will be very useful indeed, once it is sorted out.

Shaping

Shape your letter to develop your sense of audience and purpose.

I'm Writing to ____. You've developed plenty of material so far, and you can sort it into the three basic groups: *education, work, interests*. The next question is: *what do you keep and what do you discard?*

To deal with that question, begin with a sense of audience. Remember that somewhere, on the other end of the mail route, there's a real person, sitting at a desk, holding a letter-opener, about to slit your envelope. The more clearly you can visualize that person, the greater your chances of surviving the operation. Having a specific person in mind will help you (1) select and order the material and (2) acquire the tone most effective for that particular person.

To whom are you writing? Essentially, it comes down to two types:

1. Someone who does the actual hiring.
2. Someone who screens all the incoming mail and then passes a few along for the "hiring" person to consider.

Unless you're writing directly to the head of the laboratory, the owner of the store, the foreman at the cannery, chances are that you won't be writing to the person who does the hiring. Instead, you'll be writing to a "screening person"—someone whose job it is to keep nearly everyone out (and thus to save the time of the person who will actually offer the job). Large corporations, businesses, and industries will almost always have a personnel department—and if they do, you can be sure you'll be writing to the screening person. For the screening person, you'll need to be more distant, professional, cool, controlled. For the hiring person, you can probably afford to show a bit more personality, be a bit more direct and affable.

First Paragraph: Make It Hook and Hold. The first paragraph is the place to display your best and brightest credentials. It is probably *the* paragraph, of the whole letter, that counts the most. To start fast, be sure it contains everything it should: how you found out about this job (and which one you're applying for if there is more than one); your "hook"—the particular connection or claim, edge, or leverage you have that other applicants don't; and an instant, thumbnail summary of your qualifications.

FIRST PARAGRAPH:
How you heard;
which job;
your "hook";
your qualifications.

That first paragraph establishes who you are—and remember that a busy reader may very well take the short-cut of deciding everything on that one paragraph. You have four to seven lines to put forward your strongest (1) **reasons for wanting this job,** (2) **qualifications for this job,** (3) **connections with this job.**

You'll want to sort through those piles very carefully now—but don't take more than about 20 minutes.

The usual order for presenting this information is:

- how you heard about the job
- which job you're applying for
- your "hook"
- your qualifications.

However, there's no hard and fast rule about this. You can vary that order to present your own case most strongly. If you heard about the job from an influential person, put that information out early. If your training is particularly thorough, mention that right away. If your experience is especially rich, then that's what you want to put first. Here are some sample first paragraphs. These writers are all successful in writing openings that connect them to the job in a way that the reader will regard as special.

Sample Application Letters: First Paragraph

SAMPLE 1:
Mention a name

In a conversation with Mr. Charles Thompson on March 12, I learned that several positions will be available for junior auditors this September. I am very interested in working in this position with Ernst & Whinney because of the excellent fringe benefits offered and the opportunities for advancement.

SAMPLE 2:
Response to ad, specific job

I am writing in response to your ad in Monday's *Hartford Chronicle* announcing the opening for a degreed accountant with banking experience.

SAMPLE 3:
Mention a name and education

During Eastern Transmission Company's orientation meeting at Howard University, your personnel director, Mr. Crockett, expressed a need for graduates with a B.B.A. degree in accounting. I will receive this degree in May and am interested in the accounting experience that your company would provide.

SAMPLE 4:
Personal contact, name, education

I spoke to you at our last AIFD meeting, and you suggested I write and apply for part time work this summer and next fall. Jim Johnson, my major professor, and I both felt that working in your florist shop would give me the experience I need to compete for the better design jobs after graduation.

SAMPLE 5:
Name and experience

Ms. Linda Goldstone, one of your business associates, informed me of a job opening in your firm this summer. Working in Denver the last few summers, I have heard of your reputable marketing department and am very interested in filling the vacant position.

SAMPLE 6:
***Everything!* Mentions work, person, education, experience, plans**

Last summer I worked in the Information Systems department of your company under the supervision of Walt Arp. As a Computer Science major at the University of Wisconsin, I had basic understanding of computer systems and a knowledge of Fortran and PL/I languages. While I was working at Michigan-Wisconsin, Mr. Arp instructed me in the COBOL language and seemed very pleased with the programs I was able to produce as a result of his instruction. I would like to work for your firm again this summer and would prefer to work in Mr. Arp's division if possible.

If you are writing directly to the person doing the hiring, you are a bit freer to play up why you are applying for *this* job. If you know something favorable about the person, the job, the company, the product/services, work it in *if appropriate*. It's always legitimate to acknowledge a person or a laboratory or firm for their actual accomplishments, but it's more appropriate to do that to the person doing the hiring than to the person doing the screening. The first is more likely to respond than the latter.

EDUCATION
courses
research
honors
awards
distinctions
field trips
teachers

Paragraph on Education. For the body of the letter—after the introduction—you'll probably allow one paragraph to discuss each group of qualifications: a paragraph on education, another on work, and a third on interests. Of course your résumé will carry the full details: schools, degrees, courses, places where you worked, dates—all that. So all you want to do in the paragraph on education is to give the highlights.

If you have taken any courses particularly relevant to this job, mention them. If you've had many courses related to this job, select only those most likely to make the best impression. And be sure to mention them by name, not by course number. *History 205* hardly tells anybody anything; *Colonial American History* tells a good deal more. If the relationship between the course and the job isn't completely obvious, explain the connection: "Because of the course in Colonial American History that I took last semester, I have developed a particular interest in working as a gunsmith at Williamsburg this summer."

If you have done special research projects in the area or related areas, mention them. Be sure to include any honors or awards, any distinctions that demonstrate your particular qualities. Field trips? Work with a distinguished professor? Whatever it is, get it into this paragraph if it is connected to school and relevant to this job.

Sample Paragraphs: Education

SAMPLE 1:
Connects coursework to job application

> I am majoring in poultry science and have taken several courses in basic agriculture economics, breeding, feeding, and marketing. As part of my program, I served an internship at a broiler production farm similar to yours. My résumé (enclosed) contains more details about my education and special training. I'm sure you will see that I am well qualified to work for your company.

SAMPLE 2:
Handles problem of what to say when you haven't yet had many courses

> As a sophomore marketing major at Rutgers, I have begun to sample courses in theory, research, methodology, and techniques. I look forward to continuing my education, and in the meantime am looking for opportunities to apply my formal education to actual business situations. My association with your firm could prove a valuable experience for both of us.

Notice that this student might have said something to the effect that, "Since I'm only a sophomore, I haven't really gotten into the coursework very deeply yet." However, keeping the *you attitude* here, she has managed to write about her education as a series of opportunities, most of which lie before her. A nice job, and a model for converting a liability (little education) into an asset.

SAMPLE 3:
Lists courses by title
Selects 3 titles from the many he might have mentioned

> In my academic program I have concentrated on financial accounting, with a strong emphasis in oil and gas accounting. Specific courses I have taken that relate to your industry are:
>
> Accounting Problems: Oil and Gas Accounting
> Advanced Accounting
> Accounting Theory
>
> These courses and others have provided me with a strong background in business.

Paragraph on Work. Your work experience is evidence for the qualities you hope to convince the reader you possess—qualities of employability. Any job—babysitting or pumping gas, volunteer nursing or carrying newspapers—shows that you are willing to hang in there day after day, steady and reliable. If you're an older adult, with many jobs over the years, you may need more than a paragraph to do justice to your career. If you've moved through a series of jobs to positions of increasing responsibility, say so. If you earned recognition or set performance records unusual for a person of your age and experience, don't keep it a secret.

Most applicants will *say* they have certain qualities; you want to be sure to give *evidence* for *your* claims. Your creating activities have probably produced plenty of material, even though you may not actually have had a job that paid. If you haven't had a regular job, discuss the kinds of things you did do—help out in the lawnmower repair shop, tend the neighborhood grocery, start up a day-care program for little kids in your apartment building, and so on. Consider *anything* that might be related to work—activities, attitudes—*anything*. If you think it demonstrates reliability, tenacity, and imagination—*mention it!* And if you truly have nothing to say about work experience, you may want to leave this area blank and concentrate your energies elsewhere.

WORK
jobs
responsibilities
positions
helping out
experiences
similarities

Be sure to arrange the work material in some sensible order. A jumbled hodge-podge won't impress the reader. Orderliness will. List the details chronologically, or in some other way that makes sense.

Sample Paragraphs: Work

SAMPLE 1:
Previous work with same firm

My previous employment with Gulf Oil will allow me to start this job already understanding the computer system and able to operate at top efficiency. I have already completed Gulf's orientation course and the JCL course given to new employees in Gulf's Computer Department, so I am familiar with your computer system.

SAMPLE 2:
Previous similar work, mentions résumé

As my résumé shows, I have worked part-time and summers all through high school and my first two years of college. All these jobs were in the field of retail selling and have provided me with a fairly wide background, so that I can quickly adapt to special kinds of selling. My performance was consistently in the top 20 percent for salespeople in similar areas. In addition, I won three sales contests and was recognized at the annual Hupley's Incentive Banquet.

SAMPLE 3:
Shows advantages of part-time work

For the past three summers, I have been employed by the M. David Lowe Personnel Agency. As a temporary, I was exposed to a wide variety of jobs including receptionist to a Japanese steel company, receptionist to an advertising agency, law firm secretary, and mail sorter/deliverer for a major oil company. I learned how to rapidly adapt to the frequently changing job requirements of temporary work.

SAMPLE 4:
Emphasizes background related to job skills

As my résumé shows, I was married shortly after high school and have spent the last 15 years successfully managing a family of six. This has involved careful financial planning; efficient management of time, scheduling, sequencing of activities; supervision of education of four children; raising funds for PTA, managing two School Board campaigns. These experiences, plus considerable skill in interpersonal relations, have prepared me to make a significant contribution in marketing Isen Household Products.

This last sample shows what can be done when a person is determined to find background experiences that do, indeed, prepare him or her to make a significant contribution.

Paragraph on Interests/Activities. Finally, if you have any outside activities that might also be of interest or accomplishments not connected with either school or work, group those together. If you are writing to a screening person, you might want to leave this information for the résumé. If you're writing directly to the hiring person, it is more likely that you'd want to include it. Information about activities is almost always included on a résumé sheet; it is optional in the letter of application.

If, for example, you have an uncommonly large stamp collection, you might mention it; acquiring and arranging and keeping track of so much detail might well demonstrate qualities the employer is looking for. If you run five miles a day, rain or shine, that's probably evidence of a strong will and a healthy constitution. Being politically active or deeply religious may or may not help; keep in mind whom you're writing to and consider what the reaction might be. If you're skilled at team sports, chances are you'll be considered a good candidate for membership in the firm; if you're a voracious reader, chances are you'll be thought to have some potential as a researcher. If you love to work with numbers or solve problems or lead Girl Scout troops, that may be worth mentioning too. Just go ahead and sort through everything in the *activities and interests* pile. Whatever you come up with, be sure to relate it to *this* job.

Sample Paragraphs: Interests/Activities

SAMPLE 1: **Job-related activity, personal contact**

In addition to my coursework, I am also involved in several extracurricular activities. I am active in the Marketing Society and have arranged for guest speakers to address our group. I also belong to the Century Singers, a choral group at this college. Through this organization, I met Ms. Bradley and assisted her in promotion efforts for this year's spring concert.

SAMPLE 2: **Job-related activity**

As you know, I am a member of AIFD, Student FTD, and California State Florists' Association. I have also worked with student floral concessions in the Floriculture club and this has taught me many sales methods and basic skills. I have participated in the California Allied Florists' design contest and scored well on my arrangement.

SAMPLE 3: **General activities**

I enjoy both group and individual activities. In high school I was a member of the Plano Wildcat Marching Band, the concert band, the German Club and the National Honor Society. At Clark College I have been active in jogging—20 to 30 miles a week—and have been treasurer of the Snow Ski Club for three terms.

Conclusions. With the body of the letter taken care of, you can now wrap the whole thing up. Your conclusion is the final image you leave with your reader, so you should take almost as much care with it as you did with your introduction. Keep it brief and crisp. Close with a snappy recapitulation of *why this job* and *your qualifications* and *your desire for the job.*

Then ask for a specific date for an interview or a response. Many applicants close weakly by saying they are "available" for an interview (who cares?) or that they "hope" they hear (who wants to waste away on hope?) or else they thank the reader for spending time with this letter (as though the letter weren't worth the time). Asking for a specific date for the interview is professional. It sounds strong, assured, and puts the burden on the reader *to respond.* Here are three examples of effective conclusions, each asking directly for an interview:

Sample Paragraphs: Conclusions

SAMPLE 1:
Phone

I would like to meet with you the week after final exams, May 12–May 19, if that is convenient. I can be reached after 5:00 at 846-3010 or at work at 845-1031. If I am not there, leave a message and I will return your call. I am looking forward to hearing from you.

Sincerely,

SAMPLE 2:
Phone (Notice that "can be contacted" is not as effective as the paragraph above.)

I am very interested in discussing your summer job vacancy with you and will be in Chicago May 5. I would like to make an appointment for 2:00 P.M. and can be contacted at (613) 845-6256. I will be looking forward to hearing from you.

Sincerely,

SAMPLE 3:
Time, place, date

I will be visiting San Francisco Friday, May 4, and have made plans to visit your office between 8 and 11 A.M. Will you be available to talk with me then? I am looking forward to meeting you and your staff.

Sincerely,

SAMPLE 4:
Benefit to employer

I will be employed by Ms. Rachel Harper, of your department, during this summer (May 14–August 25). I would like to meet with you sometime during the last two weeks of May to discuss the job openings in the Systems Operation division and how my experience and education can benefit your department.

Yours very truly,

Completing

CHECKLIST FOR COMPLETING

Mechanics: names, dates, ZIP codes, punctuation.

Completeness: introduction, body, conclusion.

Style: tone positive and strong, phrases clear and natural, parallelism OK.

Appearance: layout on page, margins, typing, quality of paper.

Once you have the content and form taken care of, give your draft a final going-over. Check that the balanced phrases are parallel in form. Check for spelling, punctuation, capitalization, and other such mechanical errors. Check for odd or awkward phrases too. Be careful to eliminate "hoping," being "available," or thanking the reader for considering such a weak and unworthy candidate as your humble self. Be sure the addressee's name is spelled correctly. If you don't have the name already, the campus placement office can help you find it. Check the dates, the ZIP codes, and the punctuation for greeting and closing. Are there good clear indentions for the new paragraphs (5 spaces) or a double space between them? Is the conclusion strongly stated? Did you remember to type your name and leave room for the signature too?

When you've finished checking, your rough draft will probably really *look* rough. Rather than go straight to the finished copy, you may want to type the draft once more, this time to see how the margins will look, how the letter will balance on the page. With a clean "rough" draft in front of you, you won't have to make any decisions—or guesses—while you're typing the final copy.

Because the occasion is important (you *want* that job), you must be sure to give the letter the best appearance you can. Be sure the ribbon is fresh—crisp and black is what's wanted here. If you're not a good typist, find somebody who is. This letter should be clean all the way through, with no typos, erasures, strikeovers, or dabs of correction fluid. One campus newspaper advertises some typists who say, "You don't pay for any page with a typo. We guarantee our work." That's the kind of typist you're looking for.

Be sure to use good quality paper, too. The *appearance* of your letter gives off messages. Are you flimsy dime-store stock or high quality bond? Are you crisp and clear or gray and faded? Are you right on target, complete and accurate, or are you covered with erasures, strikeovers, and paint-outs? Take pains to make the *appearance* of the letter say what you want it to say about you. You wouldn't appear for an interview with hunks of your hair whacked out and wearing sneakers with a toe or two peeping loose. So don't present a letter that looks like that either. Let it express the competent, attractive, dynamic **you.**

With a carefully developed message, a clear purpose, a real audience, and an attractive appearance, your letter will represent you powerfully and effectively—just the way you want it to.

Here is a sample letter of application. Note how it gives all the required information.

Sample Letter

P.O. Box 8499
Richland Terrace
Digby, Georgia 30205
March 12, 1990

Mr. Robert Pennington, Supervisor
Davidson's Personnel Department
817 Round Street
Atlanta, Georgia 30307

Dear Mr. Pennington:

Kim Bradley, Assistant Buyer of the Home Appliances department in your downtown store, referred your name to me. While conducting a tour of her department on January 15, Ms. Bradley informed me of Davidson's summer intern program for college students pursuing business degrees. As I live in the Atlanta area from May to September and am a marketing major at the University of Georgia, I would like to become an intern for Davidson's during those summer months.

For the past three summers, I have been employed by the M. David Lowe Personnel Agency. As a temporary, I was exposed to a wide variety of jobs including receptionist to a Japanese steel company, receptionist to an advertising agency, law firm secretary, and mail sorter/deliverer for a major oil company. I learned how to adapt rapidly to the frequently changing job requirements of temporary work.

Currently, I am taking marketing courses on consumer behavior, promotion, and retailing. My extra-curricular activities include membership in the Century Singers, a choral group at the University of Georgia. Through this organization, I met Ms. Bradley and assisted her in promotion efforts for the 1990 spring concert.

The enclosed résumé will give you further information about my education and will provide a list of references.

I will be in Atlanta from May 14 to May 23. Would it be possible for me to interview with you or another member of the personnel management on May 16? Prior to those dates, I can be reached by mail or by phoning 404-789-3333.

Sincerely,

Rita King

Rita King

RÉSUMÉ

RÉSUMÉ:
Gives, in outline form, the data about your education, work experience, and activities that will be of interest to an employer.

It will probably be good news to learn that your résumé is much less demanding than the letter of application. There's almost no more "creating" to go through; practically all you do is fill in the boxes.

A résumé in fact has only two qualities: accuracy of information and aesthetic appeal.

The first of these—accuracy of information—is all but taken care of through the writing you've already done for the application letter. The aesthetic appeal is handled through shaping work on the form provided—that is, *don't try to get it all right the first time.* Use the first draft to get the material logged in accurately and the second draft to experiment with layout. When you're satisfied that the information is complete and accurate and the layout is accessible and crisp, then you're ready for the final draft that makes it all look polished.

How, then, *should* it look—and what *does* go into a résumé? Take a look at the model.

Résumé: Model 1

As the diagram on the opposite page shows, there is nothing mysterious or difficult about the résumé. The subheads show the reader where to find the crucial information. All you need to do is take care to place the information in a visually attractive arrangement. Following the diagram is a résumé worked out on this model.

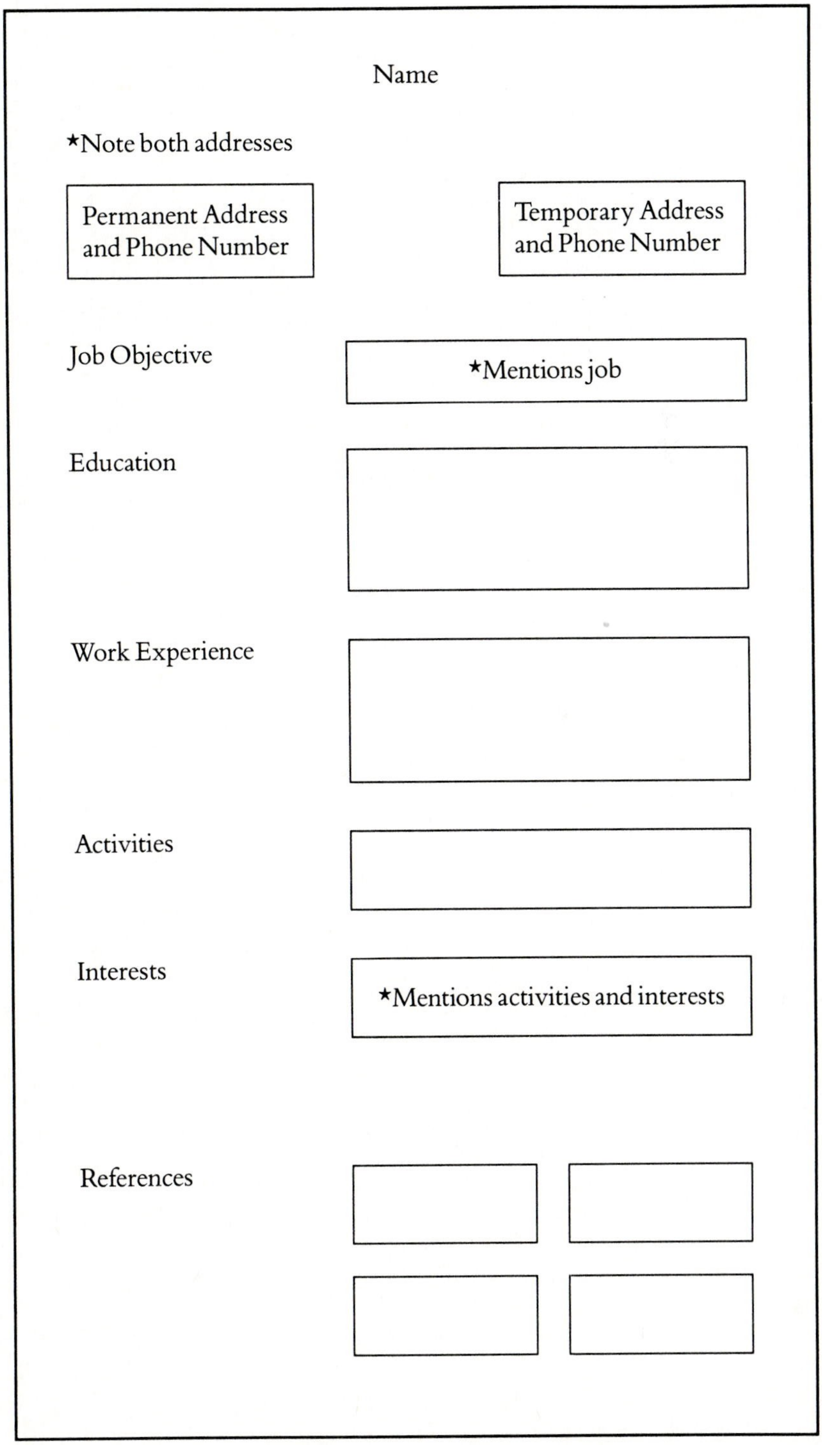

Name

*Note both addresses

Permanent Address and Phone Number

Temporary Address and Phone Number

Job Objective

*Mentions job

Education

Work Experience

Activities

Interests

*Mentions activities and interests

References

Sample Résumé: Model 1

James Franco Spaghie

Permanent Address	Temporary Address
1700 Brighton	Star Route E
La Habra, CA 90631	Orono, ME 04469
Telephone: 213-843-7107	Telephone: None

JOB OBJECTIVE	A position of responsibility in the Controller's or Treasurer's office of a large oil company, with eventually qualifying for general management positions.
EDUCATION	Fox High School, Fox, Georgia 30002 Graduated 11 out of class of 467
	Emory University, Decatur, Georgia Candidate for B.B.A. degree in May 1990, with a 3.4 average. Majored in accounting (emphasizing financial accounting) with courses in marketing, finance, management, business analysis, and economics. Received Dean's list honors for 4 semesters.
PREVIOUS EMPLOYMENT	Framed houses for seven consecutive summers from 1983. Supervised work crew in 1988. Subcontracted sheetrock and roofing work myself in 1988 and 1989. Worked as full-time cashier and stocker for The Kroger Company while a senior in high school.
ACTIVITIES	Fox High School Member of Mountaincat Marching Band, concert band, German club, and National Honor Society.
	Emory University 3 term treasurer of the Sport Parachute Club. Member of Accounting Society, Snow Ski Club, Pre-vet Society, and the DeKalb County Corvette Club.
INTERESTS	Jogging, skydiving, current events

REFERENCES	Dr. Amanda Pace Accounting Department Emory University Decatur, GA 30322	Jack Borne P.O. Box 808 Hazelhurst, GA 30916
	Dr. Sid Marshall Entomology Department Emory University Decatur, GA 30322	Dr. Ann Lorr Accounting Department Emory University Decatur, GA 30322

Résumé: Model 2

On the next page is a second résumé model, followed by a completed résumé. There are a variety of models, so choose a résumé style that pleases you and follow that model.

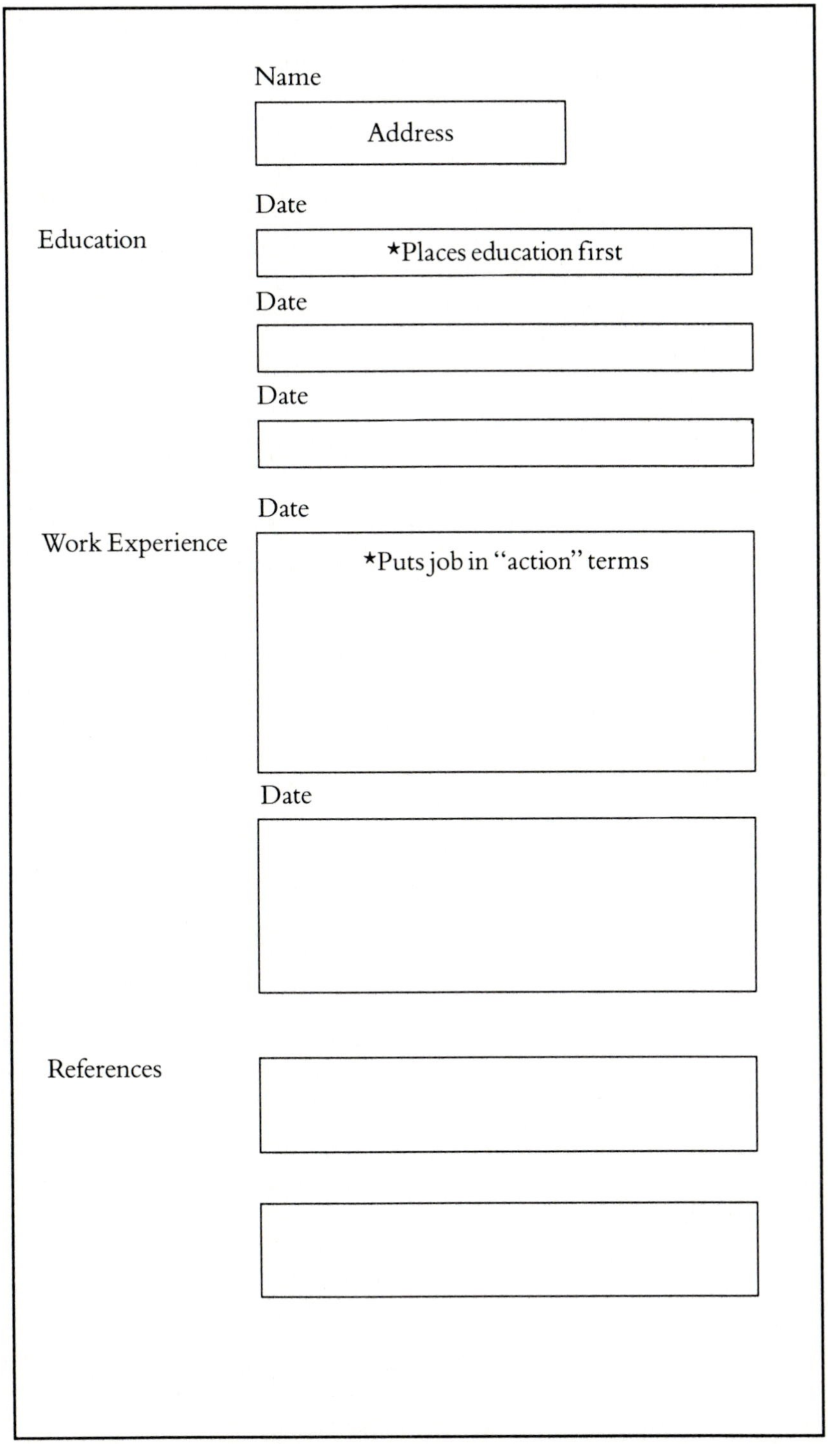

Name

Address

Date

Education

*Places education first

Date

Date

Date

Work Experience

*Puts job in "action" terms

Date

References

Sample Résumé: Model 2

RÉSUMÉ

BARBARA WALKER
201 Lee Street
Walla Walla, Washington 99362

Education

1982–86:
Walla Walla High School
Graduated May 1986.

1986–88:
Walla Walla Community College
Graduated with A.A. degree, June 1988.

1988–90:
University of Washington, Seattle
Graduated with B.B.A. in Accounting, August 1990.
Passed CPA Examination, November 1990.

Work Experience

1988–present:
Seattle Student Finance Center
—Handle daily deposits ranging from $2,000 to $50,000.
—Verify checks written against the accounts.
—Post transactions electronically and manually.
—Balance all transactions at end of each day.
—Assist in preparation of monthly financial statements.
—Train new workers.

1986–June to September and December:
Accounting Assistant at Reserve Equipment Company.
Olympia, Washington
—Prepared employee payroll checks.
—Reconciled monthly bank statements.
—Performed duties of Accounts Payable Clerk.
—Filed and answered telephones.
—Posted and balanced various ledgers of parent company and its subsidiaries.

References

Sue Stewart, Supervisor
Seattle Student Finance Center
P.O. Box Z
Seattle, Washington 99330

Sherrie Harper
Reserve Equipment Company
40 N. Bledsoe Avenue
Olympia, Washington 99345

What, then, is there to know about résumés?

1. All of them look pretty much alike, and yours will need to look like the rest of them.
2. People reviewing them will expect information to be organized conventionally so that they can quickly find what they want to know.
3. Résumés are used for quick reference, and they'll probably be used so during the interview.

And that's pretty much it. Once you know the basic formats, you have some latitude, so long as you keep the design uncluttered. The basics about education and work experience must be there, with your name and address, and two to four references. Information about health and marriage, interests, and activities is optional.

Try to keep your résumé to one page. Busy people don't want to be bothered with more than one page, so edit it down to that size if you can. Sometimes you can get more information by adjusting the layout—narrower margins will give you more information per line, for example, and lists that run in double column take up less space than a single column stretching down the page with white space going to waste on both sides.

If your résumé begins to look cluttered, edit out some of the details. Remember that it is supposed to be an outline that gives the basic facts of your life—the facts an employer might find useful in deciding whether to hire you. And remember that the résumé has a partner in the letter of application. The résumé gives the essential; the application letter highlights and emphasizes, points up and interprets. The two go together; divide the responsibilities between them. Team them up and score.

APPLICATION

1. Write a job application letter and a résumé.
   A. Aim for a job you'd really like to have: a part-time job while you are in school, a summer job, or a full-time job you might pursue when you graduate.
   B. Do appropriate *creating* activities on your reasons for wanting the job and your qualifications for it.

C. Arrange your information in groups labeled *education, work experience, interests/activities.*
D. With your audience in mind, select the details you will use.
E. Do a rough draft for order, completeness, and appearance.
F. Do a completed, final version.
G. Exchange application letters and résumés with members of your writing group. Critique them from the point of view of a potential employer.

CHAPTER 25

Writing About Literature

In writing about literature you're *not* trying to *compete* with it; you're trying to understand it, to *complete* its meaning for you as a reader, to encourage someone else to explore its depths. You want to express your own feelings, inform others of new treasures (or clunkers), or persuade readers you've untangled a mystery. In this respect, writing about literature is just like writing about car repair, or profit projections, or the causes of the Civil War, or any other subject: you need to gather your information, make some decisions about your purpose and audience, and select a strategy that will suit them. Then you organize your material, couch your message in the language your readers will expect you to use, and proceed as you would on any other writing project.

PURPOSE AND AUDIENCE

The literary paper may serve either of two purposes. You may write to *explain* an element of a work, or you may write to *convince* someone else to agree with your interpretation of the work. Explanation is informative writing; and convincing is persuasive writing.

A paper about literature will be most effective if you keep some special audience expectations in mind. *The audience does not want to read a long plot summary.* Simply telling a reader *what* happens in a work is not the same as writing *about* what happens—about the *techniques* the author applied or *how effectively* those techniques come together in the work. Have a clear thesis in mind. The reader should be able to figure out what the thesis is in the first paragraph or so of your paper.

The audience would like your paper to have a focus. However no paper can cover *every* possible interpretation of a work, so don't try to discuss how Mark Twain creates *all* the characters in *Huckleberry Finn* in a six-page paper; focus on one or two characters to show Twain's techniques.

The audience wants to know how you arrived at your interpretation. This means that the reader will be interested in the points you make, but would like to see either direct quotations or paraphrases from the work to back up your assertions, just as readers do in the assertion-with-evidence essay.

SELECTING A STRATEGY: THE FORM YOUR WRITING WILL TAKE

Just as it does in other kinds of writing, your purpose and audience will help you determine which form—*explication, close reading,* or *literary criticism*—you'll use. You are probably familiar with these forms, but the labels for the forms may be new to you. The explanation of an element of a literary work is called a *close reading* or an *explication;* and the interpretation is usually called *literary criticism* or *critical writing.* ("Criticism" does not mean you have to find something "wrong" with the work; rather it means that you approach it with a critical eye.) Each strategy is suited to a different purpose, and you'll want to choose the one that best suits the assignment and your own approach to writing about the piece of literature.

Explication

When you explicate a piece of literature, you unfold its meaning, proceeding carefully through a passage, sometimes line by line and sometimes even word by word. A good explication requires close attention to details of the text, so that your audience can see beauties or depths in the text which they may have missed in constructing their own readings. Explications work best with smaller works of literature. It is more common to see the explication of a short poem, a small passage, a key scene, a crucial conversation, an opening or a closing, than to see the explication of a full novel or short story, or of a longer narrative poem.

Close Reading

Another form of literary response is the *close reading;* one might call it the literary critical paper in miniature. In the close reading paper you traditionally examine the *function* of some very specific element of the work; the function of one of the characters, of a setting, of a key scene, of a piece or pieces of physical description, or of a recurring image or symbol. Sometimes this will be expanded into a comparison and contrast structure—"Governesses in *Moll Flanders* and *Jane Eyre*"; "Clock Images in the *Cantos* and *The Wasteland.*" You will, through this structure, show two kinds of understanding; first, that you understand why the author put the element in the work; and second, that you understand how the work would be different if the element were not there.

Literary Criticism

Close reading expanded into a substantial essay becomes *literary criticism* or a *critical paper.* Such papers may take a slightly sharper argumentative edge; more persuasive strategies are generally used, since the paper has broader ambitions and must argue its thesis more closely. In the critical paper the writer marshals the best relevant ammunition available, picking and choosing carefully to drive points home. It is not unusual to see such a paper contain metrical or stylistic analysis, close readings, explication, or a discussion of historical circumstances if any of these can cast light on the argument.

TERMS USED IN WRITING ABOUT LITERATURE

In writing a paper in any field, it is important to use technical terms correctly. Literary analysis has a number of key terms that need to be understood precisely.

Plot

Plot describes a sequence of events, with a beginning, a middle, and an end. The beginning of the plot, or *exposition,* tells who the characters are, where the action is set in time and place, and what the characters are doing at the start of the work.

Creating Stage: Questions About Plot

How do events relate to one another, or to the whole work?

In what order are events arranged?

If the work doesn't proceed in time order, why not?

Why are certain events placed next to each other in the story?

What confrontations or conflicts take place in the work?

Why are these confrontations included? How are they worked out?

Why has the author omitted certain actions?

Do the actions have a basis in historical fact? If so, how have they been altered in this work?

What advantage does the author gain from arranging the events in the way they are ordered?

Do events take place the way we expect them to? If not, what is the effect on us?

What forces—internal and external—cause the events to unfold as they do?

Exposition alone does not provide action—the story needs a *complication*. This is what occupies the middle of the plot. Complication usually derives from *conflict* among the characters or between the characters and their worlds or within the characters' own minds and hearts. These conflicts interrupt, disturb, change, or threaten the world described in the exposition. The conflict usually becomes more and more intense, resulting in some *climax,* where the action reaches its peak. It may be hard to identify an exact climax; for instance, in *Othello,* some readers feel the climax arrives long before Othello strangles Desdemona. It is after that point in the tale that the complications and consequences of the plot are revealed. After the climax, there comes a clarification or solution called the *denouement*.

Characters

Characters populate literature, and the techniques the author uses to create them are called *characterization*. Authors have many resources for creating characters: they can describe a character's physical appearance, thoughts, manner of speech, background, or deeds; or they can use a "mirror effect" by showing a character's effect on other characters, what other characters say or feel about the character, or how the lives of other characters are affected by the first character's actions. Most authors use a combination of these strategies. The central character in a work is usually called the *protagonist;* the characters who oppose the protagonist or play off of that character are called *antagonists*.

Other labels for characters describe how and how deeply they are drawn, or how they act. Characters described in much detail are called *complex;* characters described very shallowly, or who are predictable, are called *simple* or *stereotypes*. Characters who grow and change in the course of the plot, and who take action to resolve it, are called *dynamic;* characters who remain relatively unchanged or inactive are called *static*.

Creating Stage: Questions About Characters

Are the characters dynamic or static? Complex or stereotypes?

What kinds of people are the characters?

How do they behave?

What are their values?

What kinds of emotions do they display?

How do the major characters grow or change in the course of the plot? How does this affect the outcome of the work?

Do you identify as a reader with a particular character in the work? How does the author make you do this?

Why do particular minor characters appear in the work?

Deciding about characters is often a matter of deciding about their *motivation,* the reason a character appears to have for making or not making a particular choice of action. Sometimes the motivation is *external*—that is, events, places, or the times force a character to make a decision. And sometimes the motivation is *internal,* stemming from a character's thoughts, morals, or desires. Often characters are stirred by *hidden motives* which the author hints at and which readers must infer from the text.

Setting

Setting includes the place, time, and context in which action takes place. This combination is sometimes called the *social context* of a work. When you are aware of the social context you can better detect what the author's attitude is toward it (respectful, apathetic, sarcastic) and what the significant symbols or meaningful "set decorations" are (for instance, in a Western we expect guns and horses and ten-gallon hats). Understanding the setting and its conventions helps readers better create their own reading of the work.

Point of View

Point of view involves two decisions an author makes in telling a story: the *perspective* from which the story is told and the *attitude* the teller will convey. Perspective has several forms:

- First person. The author tells the story in the voice of one of the characters, who speaks from an "I" perspective. The character may reveal events as they unfold, or may retell events which have already taken place. Sometimes the first-person narrator is involved in the events; at other times he or she may be an outside observer, describing how things appear to him or her.

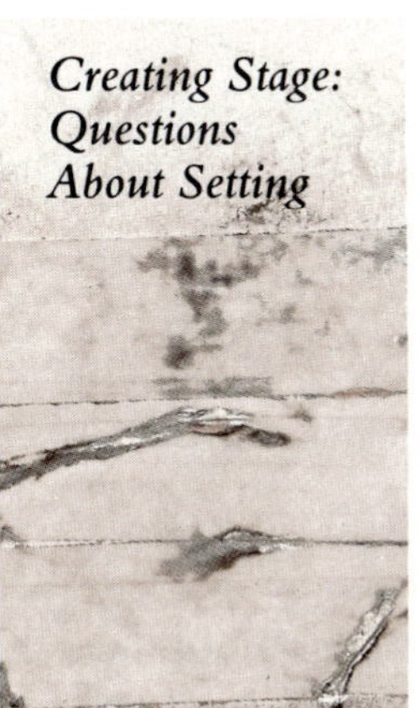

Creating Stage: Questions About Setting

When and where does the work take place?

Why was such a setting chosen?

How would the work be different in another setting?

How are events influenced by the setting?

How are characters influenced by the setting?

How is the mood influenced by the setting?

How believable is the setting?

Is the setting realistic or symbolic? Why?

If the setting is not in the "here and now"—what parallels can you draw between it and the here and now?

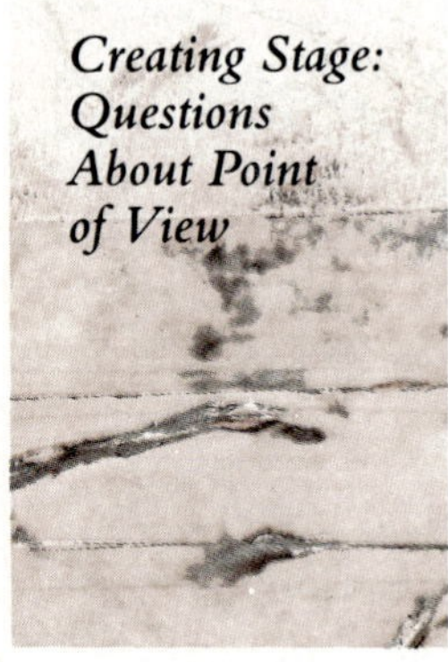

From which of the four points of view is the work told?

What are the advantages and disadvantages of choosing that point of view?

What is the relationship of the narrator to the work?

Is the narrator a participant in events or a describer of them?

Is the narrator speaking as events happen or after some time has passed?

Does the narrator understand what has gone on?

Can you believe what the narrator has told you?

- Third person limited. The author tells the story from the point of view of one of the characters, but the reader is limited only to this character's knowledge. The story is told from a "Darcy said" or "Lear knew only that" perspective.
- Third person omniscient. The author assumes the narrative voice and tells the story, again in third person, but knowing everything that will happen and able to convey that knowledge to the reader. Among the clues for this kind of narration are phrases like "Although Gloucester didn't know it, Edmund was plotting" and "It was to be their last night together. . . ."
- Dramatic. The story's action is presented through the characters' words and actions, as in a stage play or movie; readers know only what they can perceive from these clues.

Point of view also involves the *attitude* of the author. Clues to the attitude can come from the language (slangy or stuffy), from remarks the speakers make (sarcastic or admiring or snobby), or from the style (jarring or flowing, journalistic or florid).

Structure

Structure is the framework that holds a work together. Depending on the individual work this frame may be evident to even the most casual reader, or so subtle that many rereadings are necessary to perceive it.

Usually a work will have an obvious *external* structure; chapters, books, passus, cantos, acts and scenes, stanzas, rhyme schemes, or combinations of these. There are also many kinds of *internal* structure an author can choose. Among the most common are organization by *time,* by *space,* by *character conflict,* and by *layout.*

In organization by *time,* the author attempts to guide the readers' responses by shaping the sequence of events. Mysteries, for instance, usually start with a crime, and then proceed through the investigation to the

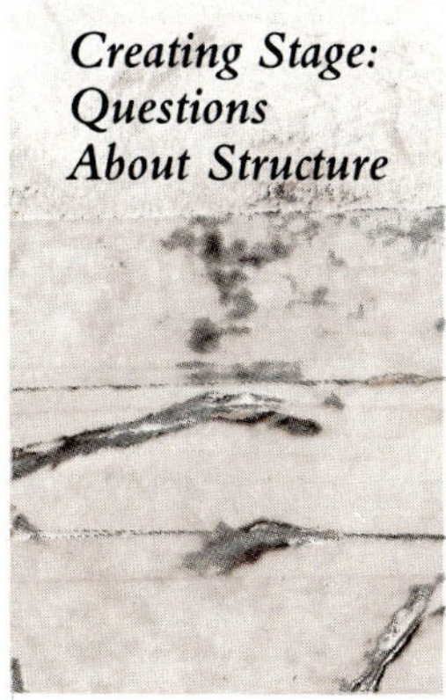

As a reader, how do you perceive the work's structure?

Do some parts contribute more than others?

What kind of structural arrangement has the author chosen?

What advantages and disadvantages does this give the work?

Does it support any other elements of the work, such as theme or style?

Which is more important, the form or the content of the work?

How do the identifiable features of the form (such as chapters, stanzas, acts, rhyme schemes) affect your perception of the work?

final revelation of "who done it." In other works, the author may choose to start at some key episode, and then fill in the background through flashbacks; this focuses your attention on the unravelings of plot.

Organization by *space* is generally concerned with geographic bounds. All of the action may take place within one room, one small town, one country. Alternatively, the action may roam the world over before the work is completed. Another possibility is a base to which the main character returns repeatedly from action that takes place in other locales.

Organization by *character conflict* is sometimes called organization by *incident*. It takes familiar patterns: "Boy meets girl; boy loses girl; boy finds girl." This kind of structure almost always has a key *conflict* or *confrontation;* and the whole structure revolves around this conflict.

Language

Language makes a distinctive contribution to literature. Important terms to know include:

Metaphor (and related techniques). Metaphor enables a writer to make new, significant, or unexpected comparisons to expand the audience's understanding or appreciation of a subject. Metaphor is both a general term for this category, and a specific device; the comparison of one thing with another using the verb *to be;*

> Time *is* but the stream I go a-fishing in.

Simile is the same kind of comparison using the prepositions *like* or *as:*

> . . . the evening is spread out against the sky / *Like* a patient etherized upon a table.

Anthology is an extended metaphor that proceeds through several sentences. It is used to persuade readers that what is true about one of the things being compared is also true about the other thing being compared:

> Baseball is not life itself, although the resemblance keeps coming up. . . . Old fans, if they're anything like me, can't help noticing how cunningly our game replicates the larger schedule, with its beguiling April optimism; the cheerful roughhousing of June; the grinding, serious unending (surely) business of midsummer; the September settling of accounts, when hopes must be traded in for philosophies or brave smiles; and then the abrupt running-down of autumn, when we wish for—almost demand—a prolonged and glittering final adventure just before the curtain.
>
> —Roger Angell

Symbols. Words, objects, or sometimes characters that have meanings beyond the literal one are called *symbols*. The white whale in *Moby Dick,* for instance, can stand for many things besides Ahab's adversary. In the hands of a skilled author a symbol can contribute enormously to the theme and the work's overall effect on readers; in the hands of a less-talented author, the symbols can stick out like sore thumbs. Some symbols have become *universal:* the forbidden fruit of the Garden of Eden, for instance. When you find a symbol being used, look particularly for emotional and thematic overtones; these are often the "other meanings" that symbols convey.

Images. These create mental pictures, helping readers to perceive emotions and feelings without actually having the experience the images describe. In Housman's "To An Athlete Dying Young," the victory parade is described in a series of *concrete images* that help readers imagine what such an event feels like to the participants:

> The time you won the town race
> We chaired you through the market-place;
> Man and boy stood cheering by,
> And home we brought you shoulder-high.

Images can also be *impressionistic*. Without providing specific detail they can convey emotional effect:

> The Soul has Bandaged moments—
> When too appalled to stir—
> She feels some ghastly Fright come up
> And stop to look at her—
>
> Salute her—with long fingers—
> Caress her freezing hair—

How does the language suit the work?

Do particular characters use particular kinds of language or figures?

How noticeable is the language? Does it seem natural and integrated in the work, or does it seem imposed?

How appropriate do the figures seem?

If some of the images seem unlikely, what effect does the author gain by using these?

What adjectives would you use to describe the language used in this work?

What kinds of wordplay are used in the work? What do they contribute to the overall effect?

How does the use of language contribute to your response to this work?

Here Emily Dickinson chooses impressions rather than specific pictures to convey a sense of horror and paralysis.

Wordplay. The use of multiple meanings to direct a reader's response is called *wordplay.*

Most often it takes the form of *punning*—twisting familiar meanings or expressions—such as Oscar Wilde's "Work is the curse of the drinking class" or Shakespeare's famous plays on the word *honest* (meaning both truthful and chaste).

Theme

Theme is the chief generalization the work makes, the central insight into human experience it tries to offer. Almost all stories try to raise some key point or convey some dominant idea, though it may be presented in a number of ways.

In some works, such as Aesop's *Fables,* the theme is presented *explicitly* through the moral at the end of each Fable:

"It's an ill wind that blows nobody good."

In most works, however, the theme will be presented *implicitly,* through the subject the work discusses, the ways in which characters speak and act, and the conflicts and confrontations that take place.

Not all works have a theme; some, such as Edgar Allan Poe's *Cask of Amontillado,* exist only to create suspense and tension. And the theme of some works defy agreement; for instance, Shirley Jackson's *The Lottery*

Creating Stage: Questions About Theme

What seems to be the idea the work presents?
Are there other ideas that are subordinated to this main idea?
What issues does the work consider?

has nearly as many interpretations as it has had readers. But in most works readers can find some central points of agreement; those points of agreement are usually the theme (or themes).

Style

Style is a literary term difficult to define; it can refer to an author, a work, or a historical period. And really, style is a combination of all three: works are composed by authors working in particular periods of history. Perhaps the best way to define *style* is to call it the flavor of a particular author's writing, or of a work, or of a literary period. It is influenced by the words the author chooses, the speed at which the plot progresses, the ways in which incidents are arranged, the arrangements of sounds, the way in which words are placed on the page, and a number of even less tangible effects. And an author's style can vary from work to work, or even within parts of a work.

First, you can look at the *level of diction* the writer uses. Does the writer choose stuffy, formal language or informal, slangy language? Are the verbs and adjectives in everyday use, or do you need a dictionary and thesaurus to interpret them? Does the writer choose a formal dialect of English, or some less-familiar or prestigious one? Look at the combination of words: are they arranged in short, staccato phrases and sentences such as a journalist would use, or are they grouped in long, labyrinthine sentences? The answers to these questions will help you begin to describe style.

Next you can look at the speed with which events in the work take place. Does the action unfold quickly, with one incident hard on the heels of another? Or does the action take place through a series of conversations around a coffee pot? Are the incidents and speeches interrupted by long passages in which the author discusses what has just happened?

Arrangement also affects your perception of the author's style. Do events occur in a straightforward fashion? If the work uses a time structure, do events take place in a linear fashion, from beginning to end, or are they arranged out of sequence? Or do they appear chaotically unarranged? Do events build to a climax, causing suspense and tension, or do they proceed in a leisurely fashion to a predictable conclusion?

Sound also contributes to your impression of a style. The author may use poetic sound effects like *alliteration* (the repetition of consonant sounds such as "*d*aylight's *d*auphin, *d*apple-*d*rawn Falcon"), *assonance* (the repetition of vowel sounds such as "the *u*nderstanding n*o*t to l*o*ve each *o*ther"), or *consonance* (the repetition of similar consonant patterns with different vowels, such as "*w*hy *w*ouldst thou *r*ude on me thy *wr*ing-*w*o*r*ld *r*ight foot *r*ock?"). Key words may be repeated several times in a sentence or passage; depending on how skillfully the repetition is handled, this can contribute to the dramatic effect or lull the reader to sleep.

Finally, the way words appear on the page have an effect—perhaps subliminal—on the reader. Does the writer observe the accepted etiquette for spelling and punctuation, or, like e e cummings, does the author flout the conventions? Does the author use deliberately exaggerated spellings such as *nacherly* for "naturally" to indicate dialect? Even the way conversation looks on a page—many short lines with lots of white space—can affect your impression of the speed with which a work progresses, and the style that it displays.

When you write about style, you must take care to choose terms—especially adjectives—that carry your precise connotations. To call Hemingway's style "journalistic," for instance, means you associate it with the conventions of newswriting: short sentences, relatively commonplace diction, easily-read sentences. (Actually, if you look at Hemingway's style closely, you'll find he writes many long, complex sentences, but since the words and clauses are generally short, the effect is not changed.) But there's a great difference between the "simplicity" of a style like Hemingway's and the "simple" style of Dick-and-Jane stories. A word like *simple,* then, may not be as accurate to describe Hemingway's prose as one like *spare, bare,* or *straightforward.* Take some time to consider your descriptive words carefully; as Mark Twain once noted, the difference between the almost-right word and the right word is like the difference between a lightning bug and lightning.

Creating Stage: Questions About Style

What sorts of words, phrases, images, or symbols occur throughout the work?

Do they fall into patterns you can describe or predict?

Do any of these words, phrases, images, or symbols coincide with significant events or parts of the work?

Why might the author have chosen to do this?

Is there irony in the work?

APPLICATION

1. In your journal, summarize the plot of one of your favorite stories. (If you are stumped for ideas, pick a favorite fairy tale or folk legend.) Use the Creating Questions for Plot to identify at least four aspects of the plot about which you could write a critical paper.
2. Select at least three descriptions of people from your journal. Use the Creating Questions About Character to further explore what you know about them. Then write a new journal entry about one of these characters.
3. Share two or three of your favorite passages of literature describing settings with members of your class, and carefully note their responses. From what you learn from each other, as a group develop a list that illustrates the advantages and disadvantages of the types of settings you prefer. (For example: Gothic settings allow for good atmosphere and use of diction, but they can be stereotyped and hackneyed; and they remind some readers too much of bad horror movies.)
4. Choose a passage from one of your favorite works of literature and try rewriting it from another point of view (for instance, *Pride and Prejudice* in first person, or *The Color Purple* in third-person omniscient). How does changing the point of view change your response to the work?
5. With a group of classmates, brainstorm a list of as many possible structures for poetry, prose, and drama as you can remember. Are there limits to the structure of literary works? If so, what are they?
6. One good way to get a "fix" on an author's language and style is to try to imitate it; this helps you see what kinds of words, structures, and ornaments a writer uses. There are even national contests for imitations of Hemingway (a fine writer) and Edward Bulwer Lytton (one of the nineteenth century's worst writers, the originator of the phrase "It was a dark and stormy night"). Below are two imitations of Hemingway's style written by students who were trying to characterize it for themselves. Read them and try to identify the characteristics they're imitating.

   A. It was the very first time I had walked in these woods since I was very young and they made me feel clean and good and whole again. The cabin had appeared in front of me like a blemish on the face of the mountainside and I swung the door open. The air felt cool and stagnant and heavy.

      Lost in my thoughts I did not hear her approach. She knocked softly.

      "Mein Rabbit died. I'm afraid the mountain was too much for it. Can you help me?"

"I had a dog once," I offered as I gathered a spade to bury the beast.

"No, nein," she stammered, "Mein Volkswagen, mein Volkswagen."

"Of course, my dear. Let us go to Harry's. A little drink will be good." Poor child, I thought. She must be bereaved after losing Volkswagen, her pet rabbit.

I dropped the spade and we walked down the mountain toward Harry's. On the way the stars shone brilliantly, but rain loomed on the horizon.

B. In the autumn of that year we lived in a dorm in the town that looked across the trees and Ridge Road to the large parking lot. Beside the dorm there were paths of red brick. Students hurried by the dorms and down the paths and the leaves they kicked covered the brick on the paths. In the woods beside the paths were squirrels and chipmunks, brown and furry in the pine needles, and the wind was cool and swiftly moving through the trees. The Saturdays in the fall too were busy and the rain fell often during that season and we saw students slipping along the paths and the chipmunks hiding and leaves, wet from the rain, piled together on the paths.

Sometimes in the sunshine we saw groups of alumni marching under the window and children going past pulled by their mothers. There was much traffic in the morning and many monitors on Ridge Road with orange vests of authority putting up sawhorses blocking the entrances into the large parking lot. To the north we could look up a hill and see a forest of pine trees and behind it a large stadium. There was fighting in that stadium too but it was not always successful.

7. Write an imitation of the language and style of one of your favorite authors. Discuss the particular characteristics you were using as models with classmates.

EXAMPLE The Literary Explication

The following is an explication of "An Occurrence at Owl Creek Bridge," a commonly studied short story in introductory English literature classes. Written by Ambrose Bierce, "An Occurrence at Owl Creek Bridge" is one of the most famous of American short stories. Bierce (1842–?1914) came from a family very much involved in the Civil War, and served with great bravery in the Union forces. After the war he settled in San Francisco where, as an investigative reporter, he exposed corruption in the railroads and in carpetbagger government officials. Gradually becoming disgusted with mankind and all its works, he composed works laden with horror and irony, mocking the fear of death he saw all around him. At the age of seventy he disappeared while studying bandits in Mexico, and is presumed to have died there.

Diane, the student writer, was asked to explicate some element of this work for an essay late in her Freshman Writing course. After writing about the story in her journal and reviewing the Creating Questions, she decided to focus on the structure and the concrete language Bierce used—or seemed to. Noteworthy characteristics are highlighted to help you see the writing process at work. As you read the essay, try to identify the possibilities the writer is suggesting to you.

Emphasis: On the short story itself.

Purpose: To explain Bierce's use of structure and language

Context: Written late in her Freshman Writing course

Circumstance: Due in two weeks

Writer-Reader Relationship: Written by someone with insights into the story to an instructor already familiar with the story

HINTS OF REALITY

Ambrose Bierce, in "An Occurrence at Owl Creek Bridge," relates the last few moments of a condemned man's life. The story, which spans some small number of seconds, actually appears to be longer. Filled with attention-grabbing details, the passages play with the reader's sense of time. Bierce also successfully interrupts the action with background information, taking the reader's attention away from the plot. However, even in the midst of these diversions, Bierce supplies evidence through intense detail and definite wording which implies exactly what is happening.

thesis

explication will move carefully through text

The opening scene places the reader directly into the action with Peyton Farquhar on Owl Creek Bridge about to be hanged. A victim of deception by a Federal scout, Farquhar was taken captive while trying to destroy the bridge. Before dropping to his death, he fantasizes about es-

only 2 sentences of plot summary—just right

cape and reminisces about his family, only to be brought back to reality—the sharp pain in his neck, darkness, and death.

Content ¶ describes Bierce's technique

This ¶ was developed using "Language Creating Questions"

Though the beginning and end are fairly straightforward, the purpose of the middle of the story (Section 2) is not clear on a first reading. Bierce first builds up the action by describing the bridge and its occupants, climaxing in "The sergeant stepped aside." But suddenly he interrupts with background to the story, hindering the reader's sense of the passage of time. Bierce soon resumes the action with Farquhar's descent (Section 3). The reader is taken in by Farquhar's dream of escape. Even though Bierce tells us "As Peyton Farquhar fell straight downward through the bridge, he lost consciousness and was as one already dead," our hope of and belief in his escape is very much alive. But Bierce's diction continually implies the truth. In the passage "then all at once, with terrible suddenness, the light about him shot upward with the noise of a loud splash; a frightful roaring was in his ears, and all was cold and dark" there is the suggestion of death. The words "cold and dark" are generally associated with morbid thoughts and death; however, since we are told he was "*as* one already dead" [emphasis mine] rather than that he was actually dead, we assume he is still alive and, possibly, capable of escape.

the explication moves ¶ by ¶, sometimes even sentence by sentence or word by word, through the text to make Bierce's technique apparent

Bierce also suggests the possibility of escape in the next paragraph. He implies that Farquhar has freed his hands and describes the strength which allowed him to do so: "What splendid effort!—what magnificent, what superhuman strength!" The term *superhuman* implies that his efforts were not credible, yet the reader is still caught up in the reality of his dream.

Bierce further tries the reader's credibility in the details of Farquhar's escape. In the midst of it, he appears to be keen and alert; he uses all his senses and relates what he sees and hears: "He looked at the forest on the bank of the stream, saw the individual trees, the leaves and the veining of each leaf—saw the very insects upon them, the locusts, the brilliant-bodied flies, the grey spiders stretching their webs from twig to twig." These intricate details cause the reader to believe more and more deeply in the reality of Farquhar's escape; the reader sees concrete objects to which he can relate, sweeping him into believing in the truth of the dream. But these visions are impossible without a telescope and microscope; how can a man underwater see such things? Bierce deliberately uses extremely small objects in his description to stress the absurdity of someone actually seeing these objects. For instance, he uses "grey spiders stretching their webs from twig to twig." He establishes credibility by choosing *grey* spiders, not white, black or yellow. Then he chooses the action of stretching the webs. Seeing a spider's web, much less seeing the spider stretching it, is highly improbable at that distance; most people don't see a spider web in front of their faces until they walk into it. And in

the "Setting Creating Questions" helped Diane develop this chunk of her paper

this line, Bierce uses a twig, the smallest unit of the tree, rather than a branch or a limb. When the reader thinks about the line, he sees how highly improbable it is that Farquhar actually sees these things and how much more likely it is that he is dreaming about it. However, caught up in the idea that Farquhar is escaping, the reader does not take note of these extraordinary powers of vision.

As if this phenomenal act of vision was not enough to undermine the notion of Farquhar's escape, Bierce emphasizes the acuteness of his other senses through "[t]he humming of the gnats that danced above the eddies of the stream, the beating of the dragonflies' wings, the strokes of the water spider's legs." Not only is Farquhar's sight superhuman, but now his hearing is too. Again the objects described are very minute and the sounds produced would normally be inaudible to the human ear.

While Bierce lures the reader into believing Farquhar's escape, he continues to drop hints of the truth. Another visual observation which should cause disbelief is "the man in the water saw the eye of the man on the bridge gazing into his own through the sights of the rifle." How could Farquhar see the man's eye, obscured by the rifle sights, from such a distance? Bierce deliberately makes the man in the water, not the man on the bridge, the focus; all the attention is on Farquhar and the perceptions of *his* mind. Bierce again uses definite, small details to give the impression of concreteness and reality. He even states that it was a *grey* eye which the saboteur saw, giving the reader an even more specific detail to grasp.

Aside from these details of incredible senses, Bierce chooses adjectives which question Farquhar's true whereabouts. For example, "the wind made in their branches the music of aeolian harps"; these harps are usually heard in heaven. "The water, the banks, the forest, the now distant bridge, fort and men—all were commingled and blurred. Objects were represented by their colors only—that was all he saw." These passages should convey to the reader that something is definitely wrong; the man who was seeing and hearing so phenomenally is now seeing objects as blurs and hearing not bugs but harps. Finally Bierce hammers the readers with reality in one final clue: "He could no longer feel the roadway beneath his feet!" When one is being hung by the neck, "unsteadfast footing" is guaranteed.

The reader has been led through the same fantasy Bierce has created for Farquhar. Through his techniques of interruption and minute, concrete description, Bierce involves the reader in the planter's dream of escape. If the reader had only paid heed to those hints, he would realize that when Farquhar springs forward to fall into his wife's arms, he is actually falling to his death.

Writing for the Sciences

Writing for the sciences entails special emphases:

- You must write to tell *and* to change.
- You must emphasize the *message,* not the presentation or the writer.
- You must meet special audience expectations.
- You may need to use graphic illustration (such as tables, graphs, and pictures) to support the text.

Basically, all writing about science concerns these common issues: What is the problem? How was the problem studied? What was discovered in the study? What do the results mean? Readers of scientific writing expect to find this information. They expect to find it in (1) a conventional organization suited to the writer's purpose; (2) clear, concise, appropriate, and understandable language; and (3) a form which is both accepted by the scientific community and that persuades them that the information is correct. To meet these expectations, you use special approaches at each stage of the writing process.

CREATING

Writing in the sciences is fundamentally a practical matter. Your purpose will be historical, pedagogical, or persuasive. For any of these purposes, the creating stage is essential.

Often, the creating method you'll turn to is *reading and researching,* since you'll be consulting other works in your field (for instance, the experiments, observations, and theories of others), and making observations of your own in the field, classroom, or laboratory.

Brainstorming and *list making* are also important parts of writing about the sciences. Often, professional scientists point to informal "bull sessions" or "think-through" discussions as the sources of key ideas.

SHAPING

There are three frequently used forms of science writing: the *lab report* or *scientific paper,* which draws generalizations based on observations and/or experiments; the *abstract,* which summarizes a longer work; and the *review,* which provides evaluation of published work or general knowledge about a problem.

The Lab Report or Scientific Paper

The *lab report* or *scientific paper* describes the results of the writer's research and observations, and uses *induction* to tie those results to general principles about the field. Though there is a strong element of informative writing in these papers, the overall purpose is to persuade: you want to convince readers that your results are accurate, and that your conclusions are correct.

Most lab reports or scientific papers contain four categories of information:

1. An *introduction* to the problem.
2. A description of the *materials, methods, procedures,* and *theories* used to study the problem.
3. A description of the *results* or *observations* made in the study.
4. A *discussion* of the results.

The introduction. The *introduction* has four jobs to do. In it you must present the nature and scope of the problem, review the pertinent material already published to give the readers a context, and identify the methods that you used to study the problem. And, most importantly, you must state the conclusions the paper will lead to or the hypothesis the paper will prove.

Materials, methods, procedures, and theories. This section is frequently neglected by both writers and readers—and yet it is crucial to the paper. It explains in detail how you conducted the research that you describe in the paper. The steps and ingredients must be identified in enough detail so that readers can decide whether the research was properly conducted, and can duplicate the experiments if they need to.

The results. The *results* are the focal point of most science writing: they tell your readers what evidence you found. Your results section should achieve two goals: it should give an overall description of the experiments, without repeating the exact detail of the materials and methods section, and it should present the data in an organized and understandable manner. Usually data are presented in a two-part format: tables, graphs, or photographs organize the raw material, and the written text highlights the key findings.

Visuals such as tables, figures, graphs, and photographs are important resources in a results section. All visuals should have clear titles, and reference numbers or labels (e.g. Figure 1, Table 2) that tie them to the place where they are discussed in the text. They should contain no information that is *not* discussed in the text. Label all rows, columns, pictures, and sectors. A picture, as the Chinese proverb goes, is worth a thousand words; so is a visual—if the readers can decipher it.

The discussion. The *discussion* is the persuasive section of science writing; here you convince your readers that your interpretation of the evidence is correct by supporting your thesis intelligently and phrasing your argument carefully. Here you put your data into perspective to show what your research has proven. If your research agrees with other published work (or with the results you were expected to achieve in a laboratory experiment), say so—and, if possible, show how your results further the understanding of your subject.

If your results don't agree with the expected ones, then identify and discuss the points of discrepancy: who is more likely to be right, the authors of previous work, or you? Why? Can you identify any reasons why your results don't match your expectations? ("The fact that we spilled two test tubes full of distillate seriously affected our yield.") Show your readers you understand the implications of your work and the consequences of any differences.

The Abstract

The *abstract* provides a concise (100 to 250 words), highly structured, accurate summation of the contents of some other published document, and it is usually prepared by the author of that document. Abstracts are written for busy people who need to know the gist of a longer document to decide whether to read the entire work.

The abstract may be published with the article it summarizes, or it may be published separately. In the abstract, you highlight what your full-length piece of writing accomplishes: you identify the problem and solution, name your principal objectives and methodology, summarize your results, and state your conclusions. Since the abstract is often removed from the work it summarizes, either in a collection of abstracts or in a data base, it must be understandable without the accompanying article.

The American National Standards Institute in 1979 approved a set of guidelines for writing abstracts. In paraphrase, here is what they recommend you do when writing an abstract:

1. Make the abstract as informative as the nature of the document allows, so that readers can decide quickly whether they need to read the entire document. Use key words, phrases, and sentences that reflect the most important information in the larger document. Key words, or "descriptors," help readers find these abstracts in a computerized data base.

2. Make the abstract self-contained so that it can be read without the full document to clarify it. Use standard terminology, and define unfamiliar terms, abbreviations, and symbols the first time they occur in the abstract. Summarize the information provided in visuals.

3. State the purpose, methods, results, and conclusions presented in the original document, either in the order in which they occur or in an order which highlights the results and conclusions the document provides.

4. Write clear, connected sentences, using active verbs and the third person whenever possible. Rework topic and thesis sentences in the original to provide a coherent text. Restrict your abstract to one paragraph, usually of fewer than 250 words, unless you are abstracting a long report or thesis, where you may use up to 500 words (preferably on one page).

5. If the abstract is to appear elsewhere than at the beginning of the document it summarizes, provide a full bibliographical reference at the end of the abstract to the longer work. Use the bibliographical form appropriate for the field of the work. (See pages 532–33 for a list of bibliographic authorities for the sciences.)

The Review

The *review* summarizes, synthesizes, analyzes, and reorganizes a large body of information for readers; therefore, it is fairly long, up to fifty pages. In a review you tell readers all the important points about the subject and provide a framework in which to see that information. Reviews are essential to busy readers who lack the time to keep up with everything published in their fields; they are also assigned frequently by teachers to give students a thorough survey of the material in a field. So the review must address key principles and important issues in the subject, and must include the work of leading researchers.

Reviews also evaluate the work that has been done on a subject, find the strengths and weaknesses in the work, and sometimes go on to project what new work needs to be done or to suggest what other information readers need to gather.

Unlike lab reports or abstracts, reviews have no prescribed forms. Many scientists think of reviews as question-and-answer structures. The introduction explains the need for an understanding of a subject and poses a question or series of questions on a subject (What is our current understanding of X?). The discussion that follows answers the questions in order, usually following a narrative (chronological) order, a general-particular order, or a process order.

The conclusions you draw from a review will probably be brief. Generally they sum up for readers what *is* known about a subject, and, just as importantly, what *is not* known. Sometimes you must compromise to present a very technical subject to nonexpert readers, but if you do your job well, you can provide valuable information to all your readers.

COMPLETING

To complete your lab report, abstract, or review, you must revise it by selecting language that the readers expect and can understand.

The Writing Must Be Clear

As in any other writing, science writing requires precise and sharp language. It won't do to say "The solution was put into a big flask;" your readers want to know *how* the solution was put into its container, and *what kind* of container was used: "The solution was titrated into a 500 ml Erlenmeyer flask at a rate of 125 ml/minute." In the second sentence, the readers know *precisely* how the procedure was handled.

The Writing Must Be Concise

Just as in the other kinds of writing you've practiced, scientific writing values *quality* above *quantity*. So phrases such as "It might be hypothesized by the reader that" and "While it has not been possible to provide definite answers to the questions proposed by this study" must be reduced to "One might hypothesize that" and "While this study provides no definite answers." Make every word count!

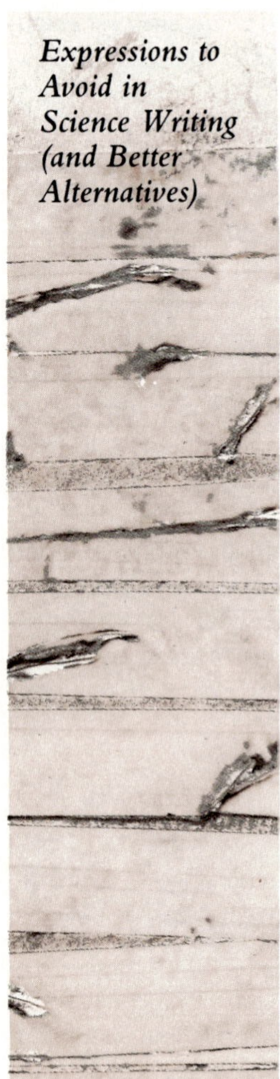
Expressions to Avoid in Science Writing (and Better Alternatives)

at all times (always)
at an early date (soon)
despite the fact that (although)
due to the fact that (because)
facilitate (help)
first initiated (begun)
for the purpose of (for, to)
for the reason that (since, because)
give an indication of (indicate)
has a deleterious effect (damages, harms)
in order to (to)
in the amount of x units (x units of)
in the range of x to y (between x and y)
in view of the fact that (because, since)
methodology (method)
optimum (best)
support a conclusion that (show, conclude)
resume again (resume)
reduce down (reduce)
succeed in doing (do, accomplish)
undertake a study of (study)
within the realm of possibility that (possible)
it is interesting to observe that (delete the entire phrase! If it weren't interesting, you wouldn't include it!)

The Language Must Be Appropriate for Your Readers

If you're writing about medicine for doctors, you'll want to use medical terminology; but if you're writing about medicine for laypeople, you'll want to use language that they can understand. Compare these two descriptions of the common cold, for instance:

> During the initial stages of the rhinitis, the nasal mucosa is thickened, edematous, and pale gray to red, depending on the degree of hyperemia. The nasal cavities are narrowed. The turbinates are enlarged. The mucosal surfaces are covered by a thin watery to mucoid discharge, which is relatively clear in the developmental stages. When such an acute reaction persists for a period of days, bac-

terial infection modifies the character of the discharge and produces an essentially mucopurulent to sometimes frankly suppurative exudate. . . . Histologically, during the initial phases, the reaction is one of extreme edema. The tissue takes on a loosely myxomatous appearance and is sparsely infiltrated with neutrophils, lymphocytes, plasma cells, and eosinophils. This edema is more marked in the polyps. . . . There is secretory hyperactivity of the mucous-secreting submucosal glands. In the stages of frank bacteria infection, the leukocytic infiltrate is considerably augmented and becomes predominantly neutrophilic. (Robbins: 881)

In the initial stages of a cold, your nose will be "runny," discharging a fairly clear fluid. Your eyes, nose, throat and face will look swollen, as if they're retaining fluid. As the cold develops, the discharge from your nose will get thicker and more opaque, your nose will "run" harder, and your eyes may run as well. If these fluids were examined under a microscope, you would see a higher number of infection-fighting cells.

The first example is full of specialized, scientific language; most lay readers would need a medical dictionary to decipher even the first sentence. But it's specific language that doctors can use for a diagnosis. The second example is much easier for most readers to understand. It contains the same information as the first example, but it is directed to a different group of readers.

The Writing Must Be Understandable

Often, this principle is brought to readers' attention when it is violated: carelessly edited scientific writing is full of statements such as, "Examination of the client's child yielded underdeveloped limbs in no apparent distress." To avoid such "stylistic infelicities" which may mar science writing, keep these principles in mind:

1. Since science writing focuses on the message, not the sender, use the third person whenever possible and avoid the use of first person whenever possible. Write "The results suggest that . . ." rather than "Our results suggest that . . . ," which implies that the results would be the same for any investigator.

2. Keep verbs consistent. Generally, use the so-called historical present tense: "The data *suggest* that lithium carbonate is an effective agent in the treatment of certain forms of clinical depression." The past tense may be used in the materials and methods section of a lab report: "The solution *was refrigerated* for 24 hours at 2°C."

3. Avoid the passive voice. Once, nearly all science writing employed the passive: "It was hypothesized that the bases would pair in al-

ternate fashion." Now, however, many journals in the sciences encourage writers to find ways around the passive voice, in an effort to avoid wordiness and awkward prose: "Hypothetically, the bases would pair in alternate fashion."

4. Use complete sentences. Many scientists use fragments and phrases to record information in research notebooks—which is fine—but then transfer those same fragments and broken phrases to their formal writing, which is less admirable. Incomplete statements can lead to ambiguities and questions—and thus to confused readers.

5. Make sure modifiers are in the right places. Often the ambiguities (and unintentional humor) in science writing comes from misplaced, unclear, and dangling modifiers in sentences. Consider this laboratory manual instruction: "Keep stirring the toxin solution until green." Who's green—you or the solution? Double-check your modifying phrases to see that they are placed close to the noun or pronoun they actually modify to prevent your readers from becoming confused.

The Form of Documentation Must Be What Your Readers Expect

While in many college science courses your instructors will ask you to use the American Psychological Association style explained in Chapter 14, other fields require special kinds of documentation. Here are the most familiar guides to documentation styles used in other fields:

Biology

Council of Biology Editors, Style Manual Committee. *Council of Biology Editors Style Manual: A Guide for Authors, Editors, and Publishers in the Biological Sciences*. 5th ed. Bethesda: Council of Biology Editors, 1983.

Chemistry

American Chemical Society. *Handbook for Authors of Papers in American Chemical Society Publications*. Washington: American Chemical Society, 1978.

Geology

United States Geological Survey. *Suggestions to Authors of the Reports of the United States Geological Survey*. 6th ed. Washington: GPO, 1978.

Linguistics

Linguistic Society of America. *L.S.A. Bulletin,* December issue, annually.

Mathematics

American Mathematical Society. *A Manual for Authors of Mathematical Papers*. 7th ed. Providence: American Mathematical Society, 1980.

Medicine

International Steering Committee of Medical Editors. "Uniform Requirements for Manuscripts Submitted to Biomedical Journals." *Annals of Internal Medicine* 90 (Jan. 1979): 95–99.

Physics

American Institute of Physics, Publications Board. *Style Manual for Guidance in the Preparation of Papers.* 3rd ed. New York: American Institute of Physics, 1978.

EXAMPLE *The Scientific Review*

Alice wrote the following scientific review based on library research for her biology class. The paper opens with an abstract summarizing its content.

> ***Emphasis:*** On the information itself
>
> ***Purpose:*** To explain three categories of ecological relationships and to help readers understand their importance.
>
> ***Situation:*** Presented for class discussion
>
> ***Circumstance:*** Deadline—two weeks
>
> ***Writer-Reader Relationship:*** Informed person to interested readers

SYMBIOSIS: PARASITISM, MUTUALISM, AND COMMENSALISM

Abstract

Symbiosis is the coexistence of life forms in an ecological relationship, where the coexistence may be positive, negative, or neutral. The three major categories of symbiotic relationships are parasitism (negative), mutualism (positive), and commensalism (neutral). The paper defines these categories and provides botanical and biological examples of each category to facilitate understanding.

Ecology is the study of the relationships of organisms and their environment. Ecology is not only concerned with stopping pollution and preventing other environmental disturbances, but deals with intimate relationships between members of different species. As proclaimed by one biologist, "the glory of England was due to its old maids!" He reasoned in the following manner:

> Healthy British men are nourished by roast beef. The cattle that supply the roast beef feed on clover. Clover is pollinated by bumblebees. Bumblebee nests are destroyed by field mice. The number of field mice in any area depends on the number of cats. Since old maids keep cats, the number of old maids ultimately determines how much roast beef is available. (Allen and Baker 1968, p. 471–2)

This is strange, but it emphasizes an important principle of ecology: that life is composed of more intricate relationships than people realize.

In order to study the relationships between organisms, ecologists select a well-defined area, an ecosystem, comprised of the sum total of all types of organisms in addition to the non-living or organic environment with which they interact. Within an ecosystem, a series of checks and balances guarantees that no one species will increase its number to an extent that would threaten the survival of the others. Thus, stable ecosystems are so diverse that it is next to impossible to map out every interaction. These interactions that bind the environment together are called symbiosis.

Symbiosis is the coexistence of life forms in an ecological relationship essential for the function of plants and animals, where the interactions may be positive, negative, or neutral. (Herreid 1977, p. 236) Parasitism, mutualism, and commensalism are the three major categories of symbiotic relationships. In parasitism, one organism benefits while the other is affected, in most cases through disease. Mutualism is a partnership beneficial to both organisms involved. In commensalism, on the other hand, one partner, the commensal, benefits while no harm is done to the host.

In parasitism, one organism actually harms the host or in some sense lives at the expense of the host. Some parasites, facultative, can exist either as parasites or free-living parasites. However, some parasites are obligate and cannot complete their life cycles without the participation of the required host or hosts. Most parasites cause disease throughout the environment. Parasites can be found throughout the environment on or in domestic and wild animals, blood-sucking insects (mosquitoes), various foods, contaminated water or soil, and other humans. (Boggs 1973, p. 902) Even though these parasites may cause serious diseases in man, they do not necessarily cause them in other hosts. The deadliest pathogen is one that is the most poorly adapted to the species affected; thus, parasites can be ideally adapted if they are allowed to grow and reproduce within their host. Not only are there disease-causing parasites, there are also parasites that act as predators, accurately characterized in the category of Brood parasitism. (Boggs 1973, p. 903)

Worms infect millions of people each year as parasites. For instance, there is the pork roundworm, *Trichinella spiralis.* This worm utilizes two hosts, the pig and the human. The worm is found in unsanitary places, garbage. The pig eats the garbage and introduces the parasite into its system. While in the pig's system, the parasite's life cycle is completed. Human infection depends on ingestion of encapsulated larvae in striated muscle of the human through inadequately cooked pork. These parasites live within the small intestine, eating nutrients necessary for the survival of the host as well as the parasite. The introduction of the parasite into the human can be prevented by cooking pork well or freezing it for 24 hours or more at −10 degrees Celsius or below. (Herreid 1977, p. 236)

Unlike pathogenic parasitism, brood parasitism is a relationship through which there is a substitution of the parasite's young in place of the host's young. (Boggs 1973, p. 904) This is a very unusual relationship found primarily in species of birds and insects. This substitution occurs undetected by the host adults; the parasite brood then eats the provisions intended for the brood they replaced. Brood parasitism is displayed among such birds as the Black-Collared Barbet and the Lesser Honeyguide. (Boggs 1973, p. 903) In this relationship, the female honeyguide lays her eggs in the nest of the host, the barbet. When the honeyguide's eggs hatch, the young honeyguide uses its hooked beak to kill the host's young. Thus, in killing the host's young, the honeyguide makes it possible for the young honeyguides to take the place of its victims and be raised by the barbet's parents.

Mutualistic relationships are partnerships between two organisms where both organisms benefit. Many times, in mutualistic relationships, a physiological dependence has evolved in which one cannot survive without the other. (Norton 1981 p. 159) Mutualism, like parasitism and commensalism, occurs widely among most of the principal plant and animal groups, including the diversity of physiological and behavior adaptions.

A very common example of mutualism is expressed in termites and protozoa living within the esophagus. Termites cannot digest cellulose fibers contained in the wood, because they do not secrete the enzyme *cellulase,* which catalyzes the process. However, the protozoa do synthesize cellulose, using the wood eaten by the termites as nutrients. While they are nourished by the fermented products secreted by the protozoa, the termites are fed. The protozoa benefit by living in a secure environment within the termite's gut, constantly supplied with food, and provided with a low oxygen environment. (Roberts and Schmidt 1981, p. 6) In this example, the protozoa and the termite are both necessary to keep each other nourished and living. If either the termite or the protozoa die, then the other will also die. Thus, these two organisms are mutually interdependent on one another. This microbe-animal relationship can be found not only in termites, but in a wide variety of animals that have the same partnership with bacteria or yeastlike organisms.

Another mutualistic relationship can be found among lichens (lichens are composed of either a fungus or alga), fungi, and algae. Lichens grow on such inhospitable surfaces as bare rocks, tree barks, and soil. The lichen's relationship with fungi and algae is very complex and not completely understood. But what is known is that each partner seems to provide a necessary component for the survival on the hostile surfaces mentioned above. The algae supply the organic material (containing carbon) by photosynthetic activity, producing glucose and sugar alcohols. The fungi, however, supply inorganic nutrients in the forms of phosphates and metal ions extracted from the underlying substrate. In this friendship, the algae live within the fungi to prevent it from drying out. In turn, they both work together to support the survival of the lichens. This mutual support is so great that it allows lichens to survive in areas as far north as the Arctic Circle where no other forms of life are known to exist. (Norton 1981, p. 160)

A radically different type of mutualism is expressed between ants and aphids. Many kinds of ants depend on aphids for their food supply. The ants "milk" the aphids by stroking them with their forelegs and antennae. Responding to this activity, the aphids excrete honeydew droplets, which are partly digested plant sap that has passed through their guts. In return for providing the food for ants, the aphids are in turn protected by the ants from parasitic wasps, predatory beetles, and other natural enemies. (Boggs 1973, p. 902)

Commensalism is a relationship between two or more organisms where one partner, the commensal, benefits while no harm is done to the host. (Herreid 1977 p. 236) Commensalism is widespread throughout the animal and plant kingdom, especially common in the marine invertebrates. Generally speaking, the commensal derives food, protection, and transportation from its partner. The commensalistic relationship can be classified into two types: continuous contact and non-continuous contact. (Cheng 1970, pp. 13–14)

A commensal that is in continuous contact with its host may be attached to a surface or retained in a cavity. (Cheng 1970 p. 13) Some of these commensals include varieties of the epiphyte plant. Spanish moss, for example, is an epiphyte. Spanish moss grows perched in horizontal branches or hanging like festoons. Using the trees only for points of attachment, Spanish moss manufactures its own food through the process of photosynthesis. Therefore, Spanish moss does not harm its host directly, but sometimes indirectly as it grows so abundant that it breaks branches or stifles the tree's growth.

Frequently, many kinds of organisms will inhabit tissues and cavities of larger plants and animals. Living within these organisms, the microorganisms administer no harm to the host, but live "without paying rent." *Escherichia coli,* a very common bacteria living within the human colon, is one of these microorganisms. *E. coli* is supplied with a variety of undigested food and secretions that help it complete its life cycle without disturbing the host. In effect, the commensal and host are "eating at the same table." (Cheng 1970, p. 15)

Commensalism without continuous contact is a more varied category than commensalism with continuous contact. This is readily displayed between animal commensals and plant hosts through the interactions of many birds, insects, and animals that use trees or other plants for shelter or breeding sites without hurting them. An example of this intermittent contact is displayed by remora fish and sharks. In this relationship, the remora fish attaches to the underside of the shark by its dorsal fin that has been modified through evolution as a suction disc. The sucker releases at will to let the fish swim about and pick up fragments of food remaining from the shark's meal. Many times more than one sucker is attached to the shark. Not only is there structural modification, there is also synchrony of the nervous impulses of the remora with those of the shark. This means as the shark finds food to prey on, certain nerve impulses are released. The remora fish, while attached to the shark, receives the impulse from the shark and prepares to salvage the pieces of the shark's meal. (Cheng 1970, pp. 14-16)

One of the most fascinating and colorful relationships is found between the clownfish, *Amphiprion percula,* and large tropical anemones. The anemones use stinging nematocysts to catch prey or kill or injure dangerous predators. The clownfish lives within the tentacular zone of the anemone but is not injured by the stinging nematocysts. It has been theorized that the commensal fishes produce a protective coat over themselves. This coat protects them from being stung. The anemones protect the clownfish by providing shelter and killing the clownfish's predators with their nematocysts. In addition to the shelter and protection, the clownfish also shares the food of the anemone. (Cheng 1970, pp. 15–16)

These examples are just a few of parasitism, mutualism, and commensalism, but the differences are clear. Parasitism causes diseases in the host that is infected by the antagonistic organism; mutualism is a beneficial partnership between two organisms; and commensalism benefits one partner, the commensal, while no harm is done to the host.

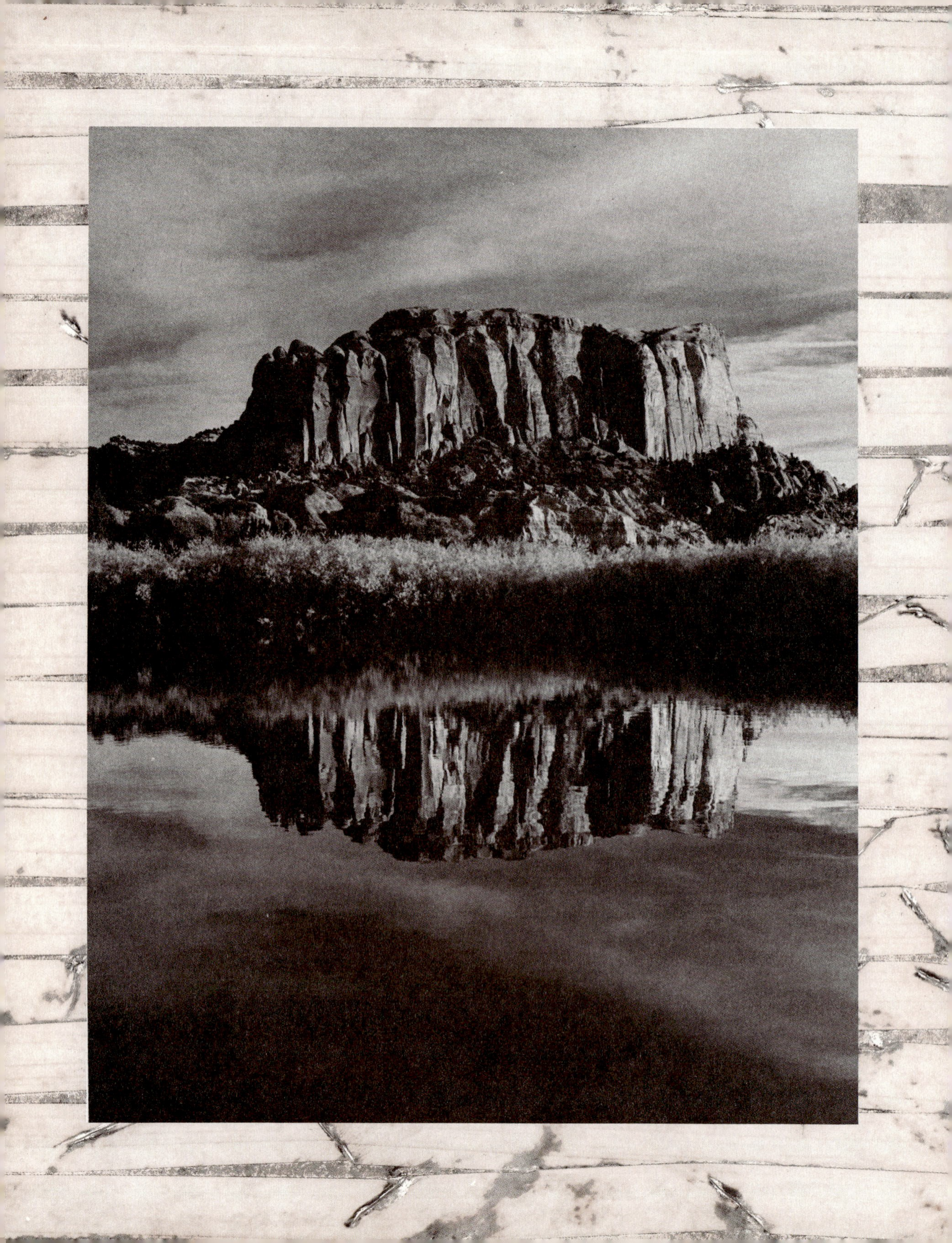

PART 5 Writing Handbook

In the final section of this book you have the opportunity to

- review key grammar terms to help you better understand language and how it works
- identify and learn how to correct errors that make sentences go off track
- master key components of the editing stage: punctuation, spelling, capitalization, numbers, and abbreviations
- become familiar with a brief guide to usage and with standards of "correctness"

For a thorough review of grammar or for detailed advice about usage, it's probably best to consult a comprehensive English handbook such as *The Scott, Foresman Handbook for Writers* or *Handbook of Current English.* This section is not designed to replace these reference tools. Instead, it examines several key aspects of grammar and usage specifically from a writer's point of view.

Chapter 27, "Parts of Speech," for example, explains just what you need to know about key grammar terms: what a noun does to make it different from a verb, what an adjective does that an adverb cannot, how a demonstrative pronoun differs from a relative one, and so on. Understanding these terms and concepts will give you a vocabulary for describing what makes sentences work—or fail. Memorizing grammar terms for their own sake won't improve your writing; understanding how the language works might.

Chapter 28, "Major Sentence Errors," follows logically from the same principle. You need to understand how sentences work in order to avoid major sentence errors. Sentences can go off track in many ways, but the problems grouped in this chapter are those which have historically challenged apprentice writers—comma splices, run-on sentences, fragments, faulty predication, and agreement errors. Logically, these issues might have been raised in Chapter 20, "Polishing Sentences," but the focus there is on making sentences stronger, not avoiding errors. If you worry too much about making mistakes, you might never write a sentence. But there also comes a time to make sure sentences are right; Chapter 28 provides that opportunity.

Chapter 29, "Mechanics," is about punctuation, spelling, and the basic guidelines on capitalization, numbers, and abbreviations. The grouping is a bit arbitrary, but these are all key components at the editing stage. Punctuation is a predictable sequel to a chapter on sentences. In fact, some of the more common sentence errors—the comma splice and run-on—are actually problems of punctuation. But punctuation should not be looked at as a problem; instead, think of punctuation as signals that guide a reader through a sentence. Sure, you have to be careful to use them correctly, but learning to send the right signal isn't terribly difficult. Spelling is perhaps more troublesome to master than punctuation. Readers react strongly to errors in spelling; they regard such mistakes as signs of carelessness or ignorance—even when they are not. So along with some tips on spelling comes this piece of advice: buy and *use* a good college dictionary.

Chapter 30 provides a "Glossary of Usage," a brief guide to such sticky matters as the difference between *bad* and *badly* and *good* and *well.* Consult the list as you need it, but also take time to read the introductory section on "correctness." It may give you a clearer idea of how language works.

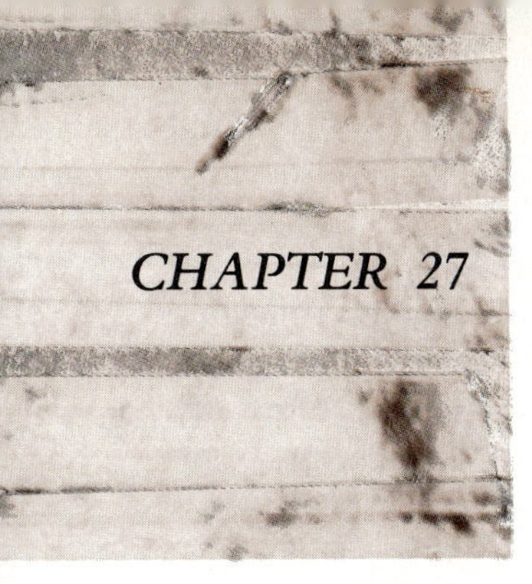

Parts of Speech

Why should you know what a part of speech is? If you had never learned that a noun is the name of a person, place, thing, or idea, wouldn't you still be able to speak and write English? You certainly would. You would have internalized the rules for making English sentences and for using English words just by listening to others speak. But even a person who has never studied grammar formally can tell you that only certain words can occur in certain positions in a sentence. When you study parts of speech, you learn why this is so.

Words are assigned to specific parts of speech according to the functions they perform in a sentence. While many function as the same part of speech in every sentence (for example, *the, beside, of, Susan, he*), most may function as several parts of speech. Look at this list of words: *arm, star, table, position.* Most of us would readily agree that they are all nouns since they all name things. But in actual use they can be several parts of speech, as these sentences illustrate:

Armed with a yellow pad and a dozen sharp pencils, Mike decided to begin his theme.

Mom plans to buy an *arm*chair for Dad.

She *starred* the agenda items in order of their importance.

I want the gold *star,* not the silver one.

After a fruitless three-hour meeting, the frustrated committee voted to *table* the motion.

I found an antique *table* lamp at the auction yesterday.

Resigned to an afternoon of studying, she *positioned* herself under the oak.

The administration has issued *position* papers on a number of issues.

If you were to insist that each of the words above could be used only as a noun simply because it names an object, you would give up some creative uses of the words. Understanding the function that each part of speech performs can help you use words imaginatively and purposefully. This is why studying parts of speech is valuable. To know how to use English creatively, you must understand how words work together to create meaning.

In studying parts of speech, you study the internal structure of English, and studying the internal structure of anything helps you appreciate the whole much better. Those who understand what goes on under the hood of a car understand why a car runs smoothly, why it won't start sometimes, why it jerks strangely. Those who know how to sew understand what's wrong with a garment when "it just doesn't fit right." The same is true of words: knowing something about parts of speech enables you to see why a sentence doesn't sound right—and it helps you fix it so that it does sound right.

Words in English are classified into eight parts of speech: noun, pronoun, verb, adverb, adjective, preposition, conjunction, and interjection.

NOUNS

Although this is not a complete definition, a noun names a person, place, thing, or idea. Nouns can be divided into two broad categories: proper nouns and common nouns.

1. A proper noun names a specific person, place, thing, or idea. Proper nouns are always capitalized.

William Shakespeare	the Netherlands
Van Halen	Jupiter
The Queen Mary	the Revolutionary War
Cincinnati	the Washington Monument
King Henry	the Sphinx

2. A common noun names a person, place, thing, or idea that is one of many others in a class. Most nouns are common.

girl	sky
toy	universe
railroad	mind
honesty	theory
pillar	growth

Notice that these nouns name very different things. Is *honesty* a naming word in the same way *toy* is? What does *growth* name?

Clearly, nouns can be quite different from each other. To help us identify the differences among them, we can assign *features* to nouns.

Noun Features

1. Nouns may be abstract or concrete. Abstract nouns name ideas, events, and other things that are intangible.

joy	Civil War	category	style
sadness	Christianity	marriage	motherhood

   Concrete nouns name things that are tangible, that can be touched, felt, seen, or experienced in some way.

   pencil   hamburger   house   cat

2. Nouns may be human or non-human.

man	Robert Redford	girl	waiter
nurse	Pooh	Nefertiti	zebra

3. Nouns may be masculine or feminine.

lion	daughter	peacock
tigress	widow	widower

4. Nouns may be animate or inanimate. Animate nouns name living things.

   mammal   goldfish   engineer   teacher

   Inanimate nouns name nonliving things.

   rock   ocean   chair   mountain

These features are important because they restrict the kinds of words that nouns may combine with to form meaningful sentences. Certain verbs must have animate nouns, others only abstract nouns, and so on. When you ignore the features of a noun, you may produce an awkward sounding sentence like the following one:

> Any person absent from the polls would have meant that the candidates' chances were not so good.

This sentence is awkward because the verb—*would have meant*—should take an abstract, nonhuman subject instead of the concrete, human *person*. Revision should clear up the problem:

> Even one person's absence from the polls would have meant that the candidates' chances were not so good.

Now the abstract subject *absence* fits the verb.

Noun Functions

Nouns have two basic functions in sentences: they may be subjects or objects. As a subject, a noun announces the topic of a sentence or a clause. In the following sentences, the nouns that function as subjects are underlined:

> The president will make an important foreign-policy statement tonight.
>
> Ribbons and plumes decorate this hat.
>
> The window opens from the side.
>
> When the sudden rainstorm ended, the swimmers returned to the lake.

As an object, a noun completes the meaning of a verb or verbal (verbals will be discussed in detail under *verbs*) or it joins with a preposition to form a prepositional phrase. The nouns used as objects are underlined in these sentences:

1. Object of the verb:

    I finally finished my term paper at 3:00 A.M.

    The president vetoed the tax reform bill.

2. Object of a verbal:

    Typing that paper was hard work.

    I still plan to write a book someday.

3. Object of a preposition:

    During its last session, Congress gave itself a raise.

    I asked the movers to place the couch against the wall in the living room.

Noun Identifiers

Nouns can be made *plural,* and they can be made *possessive.* (There are some exceptions, but this is a general rule.) Nouns are usually made plural by adding *s* or *es.*

> taco/tacos beach/beaches radio/radios

Some nouns are irregular, and their plurals are exceptions.

> ox/oxen foot/feet knife/knives

Usually, a noun is made possessive by adding an apostrophe and an *s: 's.*

> fire/fire's (warmth) writer/writer's (desk)

Making a noun possessive is one of the hardest things for apprentice writers to get right. You have to decide whether the noun is going to be plural possessive or singular possessive (this merely means that you have to know whether you are talking about one thing/person or more than one). The placement of the apostrophe in the possessive depends on whether the word is singular or plural.

The boy's gloves (singular possessive)

The boys' gloves (plural possessive)

APPLICATION

1. Pick out the nouns in the following passage and describe their functions in the sentences.

    People in Oregon can get fresh shrimp any time of the year. They can also get salmon, tuna, and oysters. Prices will be highest in January–March. Most markets will prepare the fresh fish for you, and some markets will even dry or can the fish if you have no way to preserve it at home. The old fishing villages along the coast are some of the best sources for seafood and fish.

2. Identify the nouns in the following sentences:

    A. Haley's Comet is something I won't get to see in my lifetime.
    B. Stress can give you ulcers.
    C. Her manner suggested she was tired.
    D. The combination of apples, raisins, and syrup was a delicious dessert.
    E. The cats slept on the windowsill by the side of the house that was nearest the sun.

PRONOUNS

Pronouns are usually defined as noun substitutes because they frequently replace nouns mentioned earlier in a sentence or in a previous sentence. As noun substitutes, pronouns are important in reducing redundancy in sentences. For example:

John broke his leg as he was climbing down the mountain.

We know that each pronoun refers to John, but it would be frustrating and redundant to rename John each time we refer to him.

John broke John's leg as John was climbing down the mountain.

An important function of the pronoun, then, is to make communication more efficient by eliminating unnecessary repetition of nouns.

Pronouns are considered noun substitutes for another reason: they perform the same functions nouns do. They serve as subjects of sentences and clauses or as objects of verbs and prepositions.

This is my favorite book. (subject)

I refuse to go to that class one more time. (subject)

I explained to *him* why *I* was not going. (subject of sentence and clause and object of preposition)

You don't mean *that,* do you? (object of the verb)

My jeans are different from *those.* (object of preposition)

Because of their close relationship to nouns, pronouns could be considered a kind of noun, and many grammarians and linguists classify them as such. However, they perform so many functions that they must be considered a separate part of speech which can be broken down further.

Personal Pronouns

I, you, he, she, it, we, they, me, him, her, us, them. These occur in the same positions as nouns, but notice that the form of the pronoun changes with its function in the sentence. If it is used as a subject, the *nominative* form is used.

I answered the telephone when *you* called.

They said to put the packages over here.

But when the personal pronoun serves as an object, the *objective* form is used.

I will tell *them* all the nice things you said.

Tell *us* all about the conversation.

Naomi will take a trip with Jere and *me.*

Possessive Pronouns

My, mine, his, her, hers, its, our, ours, your, yours, their, theirs. As indicators of ownership or possession, these pronouns function just as possessive nouns do. Essentially, they modify the nouns with which they appear.

his friends   our books   my story

Reflexive Pronouns

Myself, himself, herself, itself, yourself, ourselves, themselves. Reflexive pronouns occur *only* when a noun and pronoun or two pronouns in the same simple sentence or clause clearly refer to the same antecedent.

This is why the pronoun is called reflexive: it is grammatically and semantically bound to the noun or pronoun it refers to. These sentences illustrate that reflexive pronouns must refer to a noun or pronoun in the same simple sentence.

> Mary considers Mary a good person. → Mary considers herself a good person.
>
> Johnny's mother had warned Johnny to behave Johnny's self before she spanked him. → Johnny's mother had warned him to behave himself before she spanked him.

Reflexive pronouns may also be used as *intensive pronouns* to provide emphasis to a noun or pronoun.

> Linda herself liked the short story.
>
> We painted the ceiling ourselves.
>
> I myself did all the fish-cleaning.
>
> The boys themselves did all the cooking.

Notice that in each case, the intensive pronoun could be omitted without detracting from the meaning of the sentence. It simply makes the noun emphatic.

Relative Pronouns

Who, whose, whom, which, that, when, where, wherever. These pronouns may replace nouns in relative clauses. Like all other pronouns, relative pronouns are *referents;* that is, there is always a noun to which the pronoun refers.

> The story *that* I worked on yesterday is still not finished.
>
> The street *where* Susie Young Stewart lives is hard to find.
>
> I remember the man *who* told me how to get there.

In the first sentence, *that* refers to *story;* in the second, *where* refers to *street,* and in the third, *who* refers to *man*. Notice that the relative pronoun is always the first word in the relative clause.

Demonstrative Pronouns

This, that, these, those. Demonstrative pronouns function as nouns or as modifiers.

1. Nouns:

   > *This* is not what I meant by "a cookout."
   >
   > What did she mean by *that?*
   >
   > Which of *those* did you want?
   >
   > *These* are the best shoes I've ever owned.

Notice that demonstrative pronouns are somewhat vague when they are used as nouns. Out of context, you don't know what any of these pronouns refers to. In the context of longer passages of speech or writing, demonstrative pronouns always refer to a specific noun.

2. Modifiers:

   Those flowers are the freshest ones in the shop.

   These students turned in all their papers on time.

   If you like exciting mysteries, read *this* book.

Interrogative Pronouns

Who, which, what, whom, whose. Interrogative pronouns are used in questions to represent the information that is unknown.

Who is the man in the yellow hat?

Whom do you plan to walk home with?

What are you planning to write your term paper on?

Which boy won the marathon?

Like relative pronouns, interrogative pronouns often appear at the beginning of the clause or sentence since it is the unknown information that is the focus of the sentence. Unlike relative pronouns, however, the referent for these pronouns is unknown.

Indefinite Pronouns

Each, everyone, anybody, either, some, somebody, one, no one, several, everybody, any, all. Indefinite pronouns may function as nouns or as modifiers.

1. Nouns:

   Give me three copies of *each*. (object of preposition)

   Some think that good ideas can be found even in dreams. (subject)

   No one answered the door. (subject)

   Anybody can answer that. (subject)

Indefinite pronouns have no specific antecedent, but they are pronouns because they clearly function as noun substitutes. This set of pronouns is useful when specificity is not important to the meaning of the sentence.

2. Modifiers:

   Several students stayed late at the library.

   One girl said she hated reading *all* novels.

   They ordered *several* cases of soft drinks for the picnic.

APPLICATION

Identify the pronouns in the following sentences:

1. Our house has a solar collector on the roof.
2. Several people asked whether the car's electrical system has its own self-correcting mechanism.
3. Whoever was here left a lot of papers behind.
4. The place where they shot the movie is right over here.
5. That was it.
6. Ours are not the best clubs, but they work fairly well.
7. Richard considers himself a good musician.
8. Their time was short; we asked them if they would begin the program at once.
9. Those bright red rain boots are just what I want. Do you have any?
10. Either of them will be fine, but I prefer the red one.

VERBS

The verb is the heart of the sentence because it contributes to and affects meaning more than any other element in the sentence. It determines the number of nouns needed to make a sentence meaningful. It determines the time and the quality of the action. It sometimes focuses the reader's attention on a particular part of the sentence. So it is not enough to define the verb as an action word. It merits study as a unit in itself to see how it differs from other parts of speech, and how it contributes to communication.

Verbs in English have four principal parts that form the basis of the tense system: present, past, perfect, present participle. Tense refers to the way we indicate *when* an action occurs. English really has only two tenses, past and present, but adding helping verbs and modals (to be discussed later) makes the time and quality of the action more specific and gives the illusion that there are more than two tenses.

Verbs may be *regular* or *irregular* depending on how the principal parts are formed. In regular verbs, the past and perfect are formed by adding *-ed* to the present.

Present	*Past*	*Perfect*	*Present Participle*
press	pressed	pressed	pressing
cross	crossed	crossed	crossing
pass	passed	passed	passing
alert	alerted	alerted	alerting

In irregular verbs, the past and perfect sometimes show changes in the main vowel, and sometimes the past and perfect forms are entirely different from the present.

Present	*Past*	*Perfect*	*Present Participle*
go	went	gone	going
say	said	said	saying
lie	lay	lain	lying
write	wrote	written	writing
do	did	done	doing
is	was/were	been	being

Principal parts are important in understanding how time (tense) is expressed by the verb. *Present* expresses action going on right now.

I *pass* by his house every day.

He *is* ill today.

The past expresses completed action.

He *crossed* the street without looking.

She *wrote* a long paper.

The perfect also expresses past action, but the addition of *have* as a helping verb changes the *aspect* (quality) of the past action. Helping verbs will be discussed in more detail under *Auxiliary*.

He *has done* all he can do.

I *have crossed* that bridge many times.

The present participle is used with a form of *be* to convey the sense of continuing action or future action.

He *is going* home today.

She *is* upstairs *dressing* for her important job interview.

Auxiliary (Helping) Verbs

The principal parts alone allow only limited distinctions of time and quality in action. To increase the range of action expressed by the verb, we use auxiliaries—special verbs that work with the main verb of a sentence. English has two kinds of auxiliaries: *helping verbs* and *modals*.

Helping verbs are forms of *have* and *be* used with the perfect and with the present participle to change the quality rather than the time of the action. Notice how a helping verb changes the quality of the past action in these sentences:

Past: I saw the most boring movie last year.

Past perfect: I had seen it before, so I didn't go again.

Present perfect: Since I have seen this movie before, I won't go to see it again.

Similarly, the addition of *be* to the present participle changes the *aspect* of the action.

Since she moved to another state, she is writing home twice a week.

We are now passing by the capitol.

Helping verbs can be used together to further qualify the verb.

He has been watching TV for three hours.

The meaning of the verb *has been watching* is quite different from the simple past—He *watched* TV for three hours. The expanded meaning occurs by combining the perfect (*have* + perfect) and the progressive (*be* + present participle).

Modals are special kinds of verbs used with any of the principal parts to express the mode of the action. The modal indicates whether action is possible, permitted, required, or desired. The list of modals is short.

can	may	must	will	shall
could	might	ought	would	should

Things to remember about modals:

1. Modals always appear before the main verb.

   I *can* call you later, when I have time.

   He *will* call me when he's ready.

2. When modals are used with helping verbs, the perfect or progressive markers (*-ed* or *-ing*) follow the modal.

   He could have *been* a good writer if he had tried.

   You should have been *studying* instead of sleeping.

3. Modals must be used with other verbs; a modal alone does not express action. Try writing a sentence using only *shall* or *might* as the verb. You can't, because by leaving out the verb, you leave out the heart of the sentence. Certainly, there are times when modals appear alone.

   Mary asked me to come to her party. I said I *might* if I finished all my work by then.

   In context, readers realize that *go* is the understood verb in the second sentence. Only when the context is understood do modals appear alone.

The possibilities allowed through combinations of principal parts, helping verbs, and modals, demonstrate the versatility of English verbs.

He writes home every week.

Until this month, he had been writing home every week.

He has written more letters in two months than I have in two years.

We should write home more often.

I will write my parents tomorrow.

If I'm too busy, I may write the next day.

I must have been writing my paper in the library when you called.

Notice that the combinations reveal a rigid ordering of the main verb, helping verbs, and modals. The modals and helping verbs are optional, but when they are used, they must be ordered like this:

1 (modal) **2** (*have* + perfect) **3** (*be* + present participle) **4** verb
One may be used without the other, but the order must remain the same:

(modal)	(have + perfect)	(be + present participle)	verb
will		be writing	
(modal)	(have + perfect)		verb
could	have written		
(modal)			verb
may			write
	(have + perfect)		verb
	had		written
		(be + present participle)	verb
		are writing	

Notice that only the first word in the verb phrase indicates tense.

Present perfect: have written

Past perfect: had been writing

Past perfect: could have been writing

You can never have two indicators of time as these ungrammatical verb groups have.

could had written   can are writing

You recognize the ungrammaticality of these verbs because you know that in English only the first verb element indicates tense. This is one of the rules of English syntax.

APPLICATION

Describe the verbs in the following sentences as fully as you can. Indicate the tense and the kind of auxiliary in each.

1. They are playing ball in the yard.
2. The grade on the paper seemed to be what upset her.
3. We could have seen the moon if we had moved over just a few feet.
4. Have you looked for your watch under that vase which Mother just moved?
5. The walls are full of pictures that were painted by famous people.
6. Some people see little reason to add up their check balance each week, but I find that it is absolutely necessary if I am to keep track of how much money I have.
7. Various changes in the weather caused the vines to ripen more slowly; therefore, this was not a good year for wine.
8. When he saw what I had written, he jumped for joy.
9. We have already priced the land and found that the cost is unreasonable.
10. Do you anticipate any speeding up of productivity?

Subject-Verb-Complement (S-V-C) Combinations

One of the most important functions of the verb is to indicate the number of nouns needed to complete the meaning of a sentence. You know that there must always be a noun to function as the subject for the verb, but some verbs also require one noun, two nouns, or an adjective as a complement (completer of the action). These verb-noun combinations are classified as intransitive, transitive, or linking.

1. When an action verb is complete without a complement, it is an *intransitive* verb.

   I was *talking* with my mother on the telephone.

   Our teacher *vacationed* in Rome.

   To get my exercise, I *walk* to school every day.

2. When an action verb requires a noun or nouns to complete its meaning, it is a *transitive* verb.

   We were talking *business*.

   I walk *the dog* every day.

   He hit *the ball* farther than he ever had before.

   The president will almost certainly veto *the bill*.

The noun following the verb in these sentences is a direct object, but some verbs take an indirect object as well as a direct object.

IO DO
My sister taught me the alphabet when I was three.

IO DO
He gave me a beautiful bouquet of roses.

To test for an indirect object, simply reword it as a prepositional phrase that indicates at whom the action of the sentence is directed.

My sister taught the alphabet to *me*.

He gave a beautiful bouquet of roses *to me*.

A small group of verbs requires two objects, a direct object and an objective complement which may be either a noun or an adjective.

The committee chose a thoughtful *president*.

She considered him *a genius*.

We painted the hall *red*.

3. When the complement renames or modifies the subject, the verb is a linking verb. There are two kinds of linking verbs in English: *be* verbs and verbs that deal with the senses or with states of being. What makes the complement of a linking verb different from the complement of a transitive verb is that it may be a noun (predicate nominative) or an adjective (predicate adjective). Furthermore, this complement carries most of the meaning in a sentence whose verb is a linking verb. The function of the linking verb is to show identity between the subject and the complement, so the verb itself carries little meaning and conveys little or no action. Notice how important the italicized complements are to the meaning of these sentences with *be* as a linking verb:

   Mary was *sick* today.

   The truth is *that I just didn't have time to do it.*

   Truth is *evasive.*

   Note the italicized complements of the linking verbs:

   The heroine remained *cheerful*.

   She became *despondent* when her dog died.

   In his baggy pants and narrow ties, he seems *unconcerned* about style.

   I feel *awkward* every time I talk to him.

APPLICATION

Identify the verbs in the following passage as transitive, intransitive, or linking. Pick out the complements for the transitive and linking verbs.

> Just past the area known as Lasseter's Country, heavy clouds began to bustle over the horizon. Down it came. It rained cats and dogs. It rained elephants and whales, and it hailed. Within an hour the track was a running river and we were all drenched, though the camels soon grew accustomed to the flapping of their orange raincoats.
>
> Camels have feet like bald tires. They simply cannot cope with mud, and leading them over precariously slippery patches is painful and exhausting to both driver and animal. In the midst of the storm Dookie, my best boy, my wonder camel, who was last in line, suddenly sat down with a thud and snapped his noseline.
>
> I went back to him and tried to get him up. He refused. I shouted at him and had to kick the poor beast until he groaned to his feet. To my horror I saw that he was limping. It looked as if the trip was over.
>
> —From *National Geographic* (May, 1978), p. 589.

Active and Passive Voice

One way to provide focus in a sentence is to change the usual subject-verb-complement order. With an action verb, the subject functions as the doer of the action and the complement as the receiver of the action.

> Bill (doer) threw (verb) the ball (receiver) powerfully to the second baseman.
>
> As my father looked over my shoulder, I began to clean my room.
>
> The principal asked the boys to help him move the desk.

Ordinarily, the doer is the focus of the sentence because he or she appears before the verb and the complement, but when you want to change the focus, you may change the *active* sentence into a *passive* sentence by putting the receiver of the action in the subject position.

> The ball was thrown powerfully by Bill to the second baseman.
>
> The boys were asked to help move the desk by the principal.

The change from active to passive voice is a variation of the regular order of the sentence. The formula for this change is simple.

1. Transform the subject of the sentence into the agent of the action by rewriting it as a *by* prepositional phrase: by Bill, by the principal.

2. Move the direct object (the receiver of the action) into the subject position.
3. Rewrite the verb using a form of *be* (*was, were, is, are*) and the perfect principal part: threw → was thrown, chased → were chased.

APPLICATION

Pick out the passive and active verbs in the following passage.

> Some "inborn" defects—some defects that are the direct consequence of an individual's genetic makeup as it was fixed at the moment of conception—are said to be of *recessive* determination. By a recessive defect is meant one that is caused by, to put it crudely, a "bad" gene that must be present in both the gametes that unite to form a fertilized egg, i.e., in both spermatozoon and egg cell, not just in one or the other. If the bad gene is present in only one of the gametes, the individual that grows out of its fusion with the other is said to be a *carrier* (technically, a heterozygote).
>
> Recessive defects are individually rather rare—their frequency is of the order of one in ten thousand—but collectively they are most important. Among them are, for example, phenylketonuria, a congenital inability to handle a certain dietary constituent, the amino acid phenylalanine, a constituent of many proteins; galactosaemia, another inborn biochemical deficiency, the victims of which cannot cope metabolically with galactose, an immediate derivative of milk sugar; and, more common than either, fibrocystic disease of the pancreas, believed to be the symptom of a generalized disorder of mucus-secreting cells. All three are caused by particular single genetic defects; but their secondary consequences are manifold and deep-seated. The phenylketonuric baby is on the way to becoming an imbecile. The victim of galactosaemia may become blind through cataracts and be mentally retarded.

VERBALS

Although the verb usually functions as the predicate of a sentence, certain verb forms can serve as nouns and adjectives and adverbs. When a verb functions as a different part of speech, it is called a *verbal*. There are three kinds of verbals in English: *participles*, *gerunds*, and *infinitives*.

A participle is a verb used as an adjective. You can recognize participles when you note the use of the perfect form or the *-ing* form of a verb to modify some noun or pronoun in the sentence. In each of these sentences, the italicized phrases are participles that modify the noun serving as the subject:

> The *evaporating* mist made the morning seem like a dream.
>
> *Walking through the street,* Tom could see the damage the flood had done.
>
> The *tired* man trudged to another job interview.

A gerund is a verb used as a noun. You can recognize a gerund when you notice an *-ing* form (the same as the present-participle form) of a verb used in a position generally filled by a noun.

> *Studying* makes me sleepy.
>
> *Going to the lake and spending the day fishing* is my idea of a good time.

An infinitive is usually formed by adding *to* to the present verb form. Infinitives function as nouns, adjectives, or adverbs.

1. Noun:

   > *To quit* now would be unwise.
   >
   > He plans *to finish* his work tonight.

2. Adjective:

   > The best way *to write* is to isolate yourself from all distractions.

3. Adverb:

   > He is drinking special shakes *to gain* weight.
   >
   > *To sleep* comfortably and soundly, drink warm milk before going to bed.

As these sentences illustrate, verbals may be either single words—*evaporating, studying, quitting*—or phrases that include an object or an adverb—*to gain weight, to finish the work, walking through the street, to sleep soundly and comfortably, going to the lake.*

APPLICATION

Identify the verbals in the following sentences as gerunds, participles, or infinitives. For each verbal, explain its function in the sentence and identify its object where there is one.

1. Concentrating on your subject is the most important component of studying.

2. I began to read hurriedly so that I could finish.
3. To avoid this, I usually take breaks while studying.
4. Approaching the field, we again dismounted and cautiously began to search the area by foot.
5. Conforming can be harmful if it causes someone to lower her own standards.
6. To be a hero, one must drastically change the flow of history and the lives of all that come into contact with him.
7. Being accustomed to noise, we ignored the sounds of the siren.
8. Focusing on the bird, we realized it was a bald eagle.
9. The capacity to manipulate the genes of living things certainly represents an ethical crisis.
10. To succeed in college you must be willing to devote much time to studying.

ADJECTIVES

Adjectives are modifying words. Their function is to restrict the meaning of a noun by making it more specific, by describing it, or by indicating its characteristics. By adding adjectives to a noun, you make the subject more specific, which is desirable because the amount of information conveyed to a reader is increased.

1. Modification occurs on the level of words, phrases, and clauses.

    the *healthy* girl (word)

    the girl *with the rosy cheeks* (prepositional phrase)

    the girl *who sat in the dentist's office* (clause)

    the house *where I live* (clause)

2. Single-word adjectives usually occur before the nouns they modify.

    the blue bird   the old house   rush-hour traffic

    the rushing stream   the busy professor

3. Adjective phrases and clauses occur after the nouns they modify.

    the tropical bird *with the brilliant red and blue feathers*

    the busy professor *whose briefcase seemed to bulge at the seams*

    rush-hour traffic *that wastes several hours of a worker's day*

4. Predicate adjectives occur after *to be* verbs and linking verbs.

    The meal was *delicious*.   I feel *fine* today.

    His clothes look *wrinkled*.   She remained *adamant*.

Although there are many words that we automatically qualify as adjectives—*fast, correct, brown, first, pretty, ugly, high*—the English language allows us to form adjectives in several ways.

Adjectival endings may be added to other parts of speech.

-y	sticky	gummy	sunny	chewy
-ful	beautiful	bountiful	colorful	awful
-ive	vindictive	instructive	conductive	restive
-al	verbal	provincial	proverbial	herbal
-ic	ironic	economic	metallic	gastric

Sometimes other parts of speech serve as adjectives without an added ending.

collect textbook	*wall* hanging
food processor	*desk* top
lawn mower	*lawn* chair

Frequently, when other parts of speech, especially nouns, are used as modifiers, the words tend to be perceived as a single unit. For instance, in the following phrases and in most of those above, it is difficult to determine whether the structure is an adjective plus noun or simply a compound noun:

lawn mower   brick wall   china cabinet

In either case, the phrases were originally formed by joining a noun used as an adjective to another noun in a modifying relationship.

As you saw in the discussion on verbs, participles are verb forms used as adjectives.

the *traveling* companions	the *condemned* prisoner
the *tired* man	the *assigned* essay
the paint *peeling* off the walls	the clothes looked *wrinkled*

The degree of modification can be altered through comparative and superlative forms.

the tallest boy	the happiest girl
a most fortunate incident	the more appropriate answer
the hungrier man	

Adjectives are important in writing because of the effect they have on style and meaning. They qualify and restrict the meaning of nouns, but they can also make reading tedious. Think of all the books you have read in which the author gets involved in lengthy descriptive passages. When you are in a hurry to get on with the story, you frequently skim over these "colorful" passages. However, adjectives do not make writing good or bad. The effectiveness of adjectives depends on the writer's purpose.

In newspaper writing, for instance, adjectives are considered undesirable. The goal in news reporting is objectivity, and descriptive words detract from objectivity. Journalists concerned primarily with conveying information limit their use of adjectives so as to keep their own impressions out of the objective news account. Notice how the writer of the wire story below limits the use of adjectives:

> The world's first "test-tube baby," delivered by Caesarean section a week early because of a threat of blood poisoning, is in excellent condition, her doctors said Wednesday.
>
> Gynecologist Patrick Steptoe assured a news conference that the 5-pound, 12-ounce daughter of Mrs. Lesley Brown, 30, was in excellent condition despite the mild emergency that led to the decision to operate. She was born at 11:47 P.M. Tuesday night at Oldham General Hospital.

However, when objectivity is not as important, adjectives contribute to the vividness of the writing:

> From the luscious coolness of a freshly cut watermelon to the fragrance of an abundant blueberry bush, the pleasures of summer fruits abound. This is the season to savor perfectly ripened peaches, sweet but slightly tart raspberries, the richness and color of a bunch of green grapes, and delectably juicy cherries—each taste a fond reminder of one's first encounter with these memorable flavors.
>
> —From *Gourmet* (August 1978), p. 30.

Adjectives may be the most misunderstood part of speech. When writing is dull and colorless, an easy remedy seems to be to add adjectives. But, sometimes, adjectives add nothing to writing. If adjectives are vague or general—good, great, wonderful—writing is no more vivid than it is without the modification. Adjectives, then, should be used carefully, deliberately, and consciously. In themselves, adjectives are neither good nor bad. It is only in context that they are useful and effective.

ADVERBS

Adverbs, like adjectives, are modifying words, phrases, or clauses. They add specificity to the action in a sentence when they modify verbs, but they can also modify adjectives and other adverbs. The following sentences show the variety of functions and positions that adverbs (or phrases and clauses serving as adverbs) can take:

> *Finally,* my mother agreed to let me go.
>
> *Fortunately,* she also agreed to help me pay for my expenses.
>
> We agreed to have our picnic *in the park.*
>
> *During the dinner,* they stopped me in the kitchen.
>
> I learned much about literature *when I took Professor Smith's course.*
>
> *To lose weight,* I plan to stop eating desserts.
>
> She didn't want her dog to run without a leash *because she thought it was unsafe.*

These sentences show that adverbs may occur in many different positions in a sentence. Frequently, when an adverb occurs at the beginning, it is called a *sentence modifier* because it modifies the whole sentence rather than the verb alone. Notice the difference between the use of *finally* and *fortunately* in the sentences above. An adverb that modifies the verb can be moved closer to the verb without making the sentence sound awkward, but the sentence adverb sounds best in initial position:

> My mother *finally* agreed to let me go.
>
> She also *fortunately* agreed to help me pay my expenses.

Fortunately, the sentence modifier, sounds most natural in initial position, but *finally,* which modifies the verb, may be moved to different positions without creating awkwardness. The sentence adverb comments on the action conveyed by the entire sentence.

Sentence adverbs also occur as transitional words, as in the following example:

> The wedding was scheduled to take place in her grandfather's garden. The reception, *however,* was to be held at the most elegant hotel in the city.

However links the two sentences by pointing back to the previous sentence and by signaling to the reader that the second sentence is a contrast to the first. This type of sentence adverb is a conjunctive adverb.

The examples show that adverbs may occur as words, phrases, or clauses. For the writer, this fact means an additional resource in conveying meaning and information to the reader. The writer's choice of a particular level reflects the specificity she or he wants to convey. Notice how each level adds specificity to the meaning of this sentence:

I plan to work at an after-school job	tomorrow.
	during summer vacation.
	as soon as school is out.

Adverb Forms

Adverbs occur in a variety of forms. Many words are considered adverbs simply because they convey the sense of time or place:

still	only
now	there
today	south

But adverbs may be formed by adding *-ly* to an adjective. These are generally adverbs of manner because they tell how something is done:

quickly	colorfully
slowly	hopefully
convincingly	

Like adjectives, adverbs also express degree through comparative and superlative forms:

most convincingly	liveliest
more slowly	lonelier

Finally, there are some adverbs which modify other verbs and adjectives by intensifying their meaning rather than modifying them. Appropriately, these are called *intensifiers*. The words in italics in the following sentences are intensifiers:

We read the chapter *fairly* quickly.

Everyone agrees that she is a *very* cheerful young woman.

He is *somewhat* reluctant to talk about his past.

I'm *quite* sure I won't be able to devote *too* much time to this.

APPLICATION

Pick out all the adverbs in the following sentences, indicating what they modify and identifying them as single word, phrasal, or clausal adverbs or as intensifiers.

1. A brief study of oriental horticulture will also be made.
2. There are quite a large number of borrowed words in our language.
3. When he first went to France, communicating was rather difficult.
4. To complete his assignment, he plans to spend most of the weekend in the library.

5. Unfortunately, our smoke alarm did not sound that night.
6. My chemistry professor plans to drop our lowest grade to reduce the effect of our bad grades.
7. He was up all night writing his paper. However, he plans to sleep late over the weekend.
8. By planning your time carefully, you might be able to go camping and to finish your paper this weekend.
9. It is hard to think independently and to act individually in our society.
10. As they approached the city, they could begin to see the bright lights on both shores.

PREPOSITIONS

Prepositions are words or groups of words that indicate relationships between the object of the preposition and some other word(s) in the sentence. Prepositions function as indicators of time, place, cause, manner, agency, association, or other relationships. Usually, prepositions occur in phrases that function as adverbs or adjectives, as the following sentences illustrate:

Tom lives *by* a drive-in theater.

She sat *beside* me *at* the movies.

In the summer, I'll be working full time *at* our local drugstore.

To me, a summer job is a good way to prepare *for* a full-time job *after* graduation.

In spite of her mother's refusal, Frances went anyway.

When the object is separated from its preposition, the sentence may end in a preposition. For many people, this construction is one of the worst grammatical sins in the English language. There is really no logical reason for claiming that it is incorrect to end a sentence with a preposition. We hear and use sentences like these all the time:

Who are you going to the party *with?*

Who are you mailing that *to?*

That's something I won't put *up with*.

Notice how stiff the sentences sound if they are revised to avoid the preposition at the end:

With whom are you going to the party?

To whom are you mailing that?

That's something with which I won't put up.

The objection to ending sentences with a preposition is that it makes the sentence sound informal and casual. Ending a sentence with a preposition is not a grammatical but a stylistic matter.

Verb Particles

Certain prepositions have become so closely associated with certain verbs that the verb and preposition form a verb unit.

> Would you *look up* this word in the dictionary?
>
> *Call* me *up* when you want to talk.
>
> I can't *make out* what number this is.
>
> We took three prospective buyers to *look over* the property.

In these sentences, *up, out, over* don't function as ordinary prepositions because they don't link an object noun to another part of the sentence. The prepositions are merely bound to the verb in such a way that they change its meaning. *Look* is quite different from *look up, make* is quite different from *make out,* and *look* is quite different from *look over.* Prepositions that are part of the verb are called verb *particles.*

However, not all prepositions that seem to be bound to the verb are particles. In the sentence we looked at above—*That's something I won't put up with—put up* is not a verb plus particle; it is an idiom, a frozen expression of the language. A true particle can be separated from the verb without affecting the verb-particle bond and without affecting meaning:

> I *looked* the number *up*.
>
> They spent three hours in *looking* the property *over.*

CONJUNCTIONS

Conjunctions join words, phrases, and clauses. *Coordinating conjunctions* join grammatically equal elements.

> *Rita* and *her teacher* met to discuss her grades.
>
> They spoke *politely* but *heatedly.*
>
> *She tried to get him to help her,* but *he refused to do it.*
>
> I love to sit outside *early in the morning* and *late in the evening.*

Notice that in each of the sentences, the conjunction joins elements of the same grammatical rank: two nouns, two adverbs, two independent clauses, two prepositional phrases.

There are only a few words that function as coordinating conjunctions:

and	or
but	nor
for	(sometimes *so* and *yet*)

When coordinating conjunctions occur in pairs, they are called *correlative conjunctions.*

> *Neither* Tommie *nor* Rachel is going.
>
> *Not only* did he pass his chemistry test, *but* he *also* got an A on his English paper.

Correlative conjunctions include *either . . . or, neither . . . nor, not only . . . but also, both . . . and, not . . . but.*

Subordinating conjunctions join unequal elements. In fact, the function of these conjunctions is to show a dependent relationship between two clauses.

> Because I *stayed late to help the boss,* I was given an extra day off.
>
> Although I *was nervous that the canoe would spring a leak,* it stayed dry *when we took it out to the middle of the lake.*

Subordinating conjunctions are important in making writing more efficient, for they enable the writer to condense thoughts expressed in separate sentences into a single sentence that shows how the thoughts are related. They express relationships of time, place, cause, opposition, similarity, contrast, addition. Furthermore, the occurrence of a subordinating conjunction is a clue that the clause following it must be linked to an independent clause. Therefore, knowing that subordinating conjunctions signal dependence should help you recognize and avoid sentence fragments.

The following are some of the words that function as subordinating conjunctions:

after	when	whenever	unless
although	because	wherever	through
as	so (that)	while	when
as if	before	though	that (when introducing
if	how	even though	noun clauses)
before	since	until	

Conjunctive Adverb

He had eaten a big breakfast. However, when he smelled the food, he realized that he was hungry again.

In this sentence, *however* does not indicate a grammatical relationship between the two sentences. It is not necessary to make the sentence grammatical, and it could be left out without affecting the fundamental meaning. Conjunctive adverbs are communication aids; they make logical (not grammatical) relationships between sentences that would be only implicit otherwise. They are aids to coherence.

Here are some conjunctive adverbs:

however	moreover
furthermore	nevertheless
henceforth	therefore

INTERJECTIONS

When you interject something, you interrupt the usual flow of a thought or sentence or conversation. That is exactly what interjections do—they interrupt the usual grammatical flow of the sentence. Interjections are not grammatically bound to the sentences they appear in, but they do add expressions of surprise, emotion, or anger. In the following sentences, the interjections are italicized. Notice that the commas set them off from the rest of the sentence both grammatically and semantically.

Oh, I didn't know you were waiting for me.

Good grief, Charlie Brown, won't you ever learn?

Hallelujah, I passed the exam!

Interjections should be used sparingly in writing. Although they emphasize speech effectively, they sometimes seem overdramatic, archaic, or out of place in writing.

APPLICATION

Identify the conjunctions in the following sentences as coordinating or subordinating or as conjunctive adverbs.

1. Political responsibility means that the issues must be dealt with and that each voter must rise to the occasion to decide upon these issues.

2. Although many will disagree with this opinion, I believe that the Supreme Court should hold a place today as one of the few respected and concerned institutions in our country.
3. Indeed, what history truly shows, if one can but see it, is that heroes also have that special inner quality that sets them apart from the rest of mankind, that makes them glow with an inner glory all their own.
4. History shows that real heroes are not merely brave or courageous, for bravery can be feigned and courage taken from a bottle.
5. Many people have convictions, but they are too afraid of being judged by others to act upon these convictions.
6. If I am reading or studying an assignment, I try to concentrate very hard on it. Sometimes, though, this is hard when I am reading or studying for a long period of time.

SENTENCES

There are three kinds of sentences to be aware of: simple, compound, and complex. This is a well-known way to classify sentences. A *simple* sentence has only one independent clause (that is, it is grammatically complete all by itself), and no dependent clauses. For example:

> The boy found the ball.

A *compound* sentence has two or more independent clauses and no dependent clauses. The independent clauses are joined by a coordinating conjunction (such as *and, but, or* and so on) or by a semicolon.

> The leaves are turning yellow or they are turning red.
>
> The crowd was cheering; my brother was up at bat.

A *complex* sentence has one independent clause and one or more dependent clauses.

> When I say "hi," [dependent clause] I expect to get an answer. [independent clause]
>
> I have pictures [independent clause] that are beautiful to look at. [dependent clause]

Clauses and Phrases

Sentences are made up of single words, clauses, and phrases. What is the difference between a clause and a phrase?

A *phrase* is a combination of two or more words that form a meaningful unit within a sentence, a clause, or another phrase. It lacks a subject, a predicate, or both. There are noun phrases, verbal phrases, prepositional phrases, participial phrases, gerund phrases, infinitive phrases—in short, what kind of phrase you have depends on what else appears in the sentence.

Noun phrase:	The wet road
Prepositional phrase:	On the road
Participial phrase:	Having driven on the road
Gerund phrase:	Driving on the road
Infinitive phrase:	To drive on the road

An independent clause contains a subject and a predicate, which together form a complete expression.

Mae *laughed* because she felt so happy.

He liked fish, but *he didn't like to catch them.*

A dependent clause also has a subject and a predicate, but it functions as part of a sentence. It is connected to the independent clause by a connecting word that shows its subordinate relationship. This connecting word can be a relative pronoun (who, which, that) or a subordinate conjunction (although, since, because, after, when, if, and so on).

She laughed *because she felt so happy.*

APPLICATION

For the following sentences, identify the phrases and clauses. Also, distinguish between dependent and independent clauses.

1. I will love you till the end of time.
2. I run because I think it is healthy.
3. I like to run, but I mostly like to do it in my dreams.
4. Skiing on the slopes is exciting.
5. The man who taught me to ski is an expert.
6. Since I was taught by an expert, I should be good at it.
7. Having been taught by an expert, I should be good at it.
8. I'm a novice, but I don't care.
9. After falling down the slopes, I brush myself off.
10. The bright slopes are beautiful at dusk.

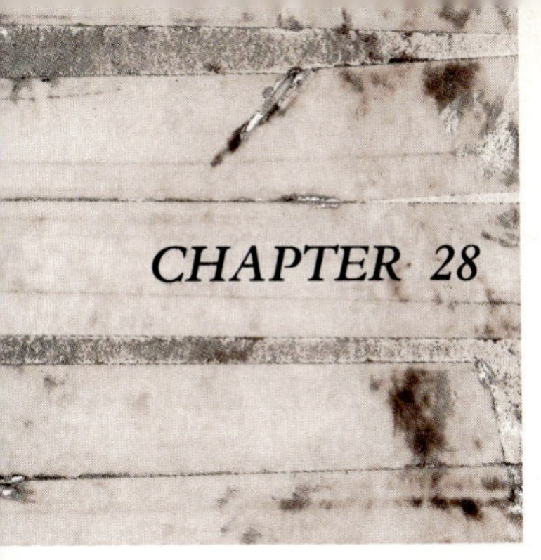

CHAPTER 28

Major Sentence Errors

A few of the rules governing sentences are quite rigid; when they are broken, the clarity of a message may be compromised. So checking your sentences to catch these syntactical and grammatical errors is an important part of the completing stage. What follows is an examination of some common sentence errors: comma splices, run-on sentences, fragments, faulty predication, and agreement errors.

GLOSSARY OF BASIC TERMS

Before editing your sentences, you may want to review these key terms. A *clause* is a group of words having a subject and a predicate. That is, it has something which it is about, and it gives information about that something. An *independent clause* is one that can stand alone as a sentence. It's sometimes called a *main clause,* because it contains the chief information in a sentence. But *independent* is a better name for it, because it helps you remember that this clause doesn't need any help to convey information to the reader.

A *dependent clause* cannot stand alone. Although it contains a subject and a predicate, some other word is present, such as a subordinating conjunction or a relative pronoun, which makes it rely on some other independent clause for its context. Dependent clauses often function as adverbs or adjectives, and sometimes as nouns. Although these are sometimes called *subordinate clauses, dependent* is a better name for them because it reminds you that this kind of clause depends on outside help to make sense.

A sentence is an independent clause with all its modifiers. It expresses one complete unit of information through its subject and predicate. Sentences are classified by how many independent and dependent clauses they contain:

> If there is one independent clause and no subordinate clauses, we call the sentence *simple*.
>
> If there is one independent clause and one or more subordinate clauses, we call the sentence *complex*.
>
> If there are two or more independent clauses joined by a coordinating conjunction, we call the sentence *compound*.
>
> If there are two or more independent clauses joined by a coordinating conjunction, and at least one of the independent clauses contains one or more dependent clauses, then we call the sentence *compound-complex*.

Phrases are groups of related words that lack either a subject or a predicate, or both. You can have adjective phrases, adverb phrases, prepositional phrases, and even noun and verb phrases. Phrases, however, can *never* stand alone as complete sentences.

The *subject* is the topic which the sentence is about. It consists of a headword (either a noun or a pronoun), called the *simple subject,* and all of the other adjectives, adverbs, and nouns that modify it. If the sentence uses a clause rather than a noun as its subject, the sentence is called *headless*.

The predicate is the assertion that a sentence makes. It consists of a *main verb* and its *auxiliary verbs,* which together are called the *simple predicate,* and any *complements* or *modifiers* which occur in the sentence. The simple predicate plus its complements and modifiers is called the *complete predicate*.

COMMA SPLICES

Comma splices occur when you join two complete sentences (independent clauses with all their modifiers) with a comma rather than a coordinating conjunction or when you fail to separate two sentences with either a period or semicolon.

> They could not afford to buy a house, however they put a downpayment on a condominium.

Here the writer has joined the two independent clauses with a comma. How can such a mistake be remedied?

By replacing the comma with a stronger punctuation mark:

> They could not afford to buy a house. However, they put a downpayment on a condominium.

> They could not afford to buy a house; however, they put a downpayment on a condominium.

By converting one of the independent clauses into a dependent (subordinate) clause:

> Since they could not afford to buy a house, they put a downpayment on a condominium.

By connecting the independent clauses with a coordinating conjunction and appropriate punctuation:

> They could not afford to buy a house, but they put a downpayment on a condominium.

Comma splices are serious errors because they suggest to your readers that you can't tell the difference between independent and dependent clauses. In other words, they suggest that you can't recognize a sentence when you see one.

What causes comma splices? Generally, three situations may cause this error. First, if two sentences are very closely related, the urge to join them may be strong. For instance, when describing steps in a process, you may find it natural to write:

> First you blend two eggs and one cup of sugar, next you beat in a teaspoon of vanilla extract.

However, this breaks the rule. When your ideas are closely related, it's best to replace the comma with either a semicolon or a coordinating conjunction and punctuation.

Second, when two sentences are joined by a modifier that could belong to either sentence, a comma splice often results. Having that modifier in the middle of the two sentences sometimes makes you forget that they're still two separate sentences and have to be punctuated as such.

> Look at this sentence, for instance, the modifier could go with either independent clause.

In such constructions, it's usually best to use a semicolon or period to separate the modified sentence from the unmodified one. A rewrite of the example above would look like this:

> Look at this sentence, for instance; the modifier could go with either independent clause.

The third cause of comma splices is confusion of conjunctions and conjunctive adverbs. When conjunctions join two clauses, they usually follow commas. Since conjunctive adverbs often work like conjunctions, it's natural to try to punctuate them the same way. But conjunctive adverbs are *modifiers;* they can be moved around in the sentence for effect. Compare these two sentences:

> Personal income rose 4.5 percent, but savings declined 3 percent.
>
> Personal income rose 4.5 percent, however savings declined 3 percent.

The first sentence is correct because it uses a comma and a conjunction, *but,* to join the two clauses. The second sentence is incorrect, because it uses an *adverb* following the comma. The second sentence could be rewritten as follows:

> Personal income rose 4.5 percent, savings, however, declined 3 percent.

or

> Personal income rose 4.5 percent, savings declined 3 percent, however.

To correct a comma splice when a conjunctive adverb is used, it's generally most effective to replace the comma with a semicolon:

> Personal income rose 4.5 percent; however, savings declined 3 percent.

APPLICATION

Pick out the comma splices in the following sentences. Identify the cause of the error, and revise the sentence to remedy the error.

1. "Faith" has two meanings, in one context it means that we believe that something exists.
2. He gets his point across aggressively, his style is very appropriate.
3. We know this isn't true, why should we believe it.
4. There is a distinction between "house" and "home," clearly they are not synonyms.
5. It feels as if there will be rain before long, even the air smells damp and humid.
6. The journalist has two choices, he can either read all the material available and digest it himself or he can consult an expert for advice.
7. An aura of excitement crackled through the stands, the field was charged with electricity.
8. She could not find the answer in the textbook, thus she turned to her teacher for help.

9. In the beginning learning to use the computer was frustrating, now I feel more confident with it.
10. First you add 25 ml of sodium hydroxide, next you stir the solution for ten minutes.

RUN-ON SENTENCES

Similar to comma splices are *run-on* or *fused* sentences, in which two independent clauses are joined without any punctuation or conjunctions. These are serious errors, because your readers will have difficulty in separating the fused elements.

A *run-on* sentence looks like this:

> Some people call natural disasters acts of God others call them examples of bad fortune.

Here, as you can see, the writer wanted to give two explanations for natural disasters, and ran the two sentences together. How can you fix run-ons?

By separating the two sentences with a period and capital letter:

> Some people call natural disasters acts of God. Others call them examples of bad fortune.

By using a semicolon to separate the two sentences:

> Some people call natural disasters acts of God; others call them examples of bad fortune.

By using conjunctions to join the two sentences clearly:

> Some people call natural disasters acts of God, while others call them examples of bad fortune.

By rewriting the sentences to omit repeated elements:

> Natural disasters are called acts of God by some people and examples of bad fortune by others.

What causes run-ons? Such errors sometimes occur when you change your mind about a sentence as you draft it, and then don't revise the sentence. This leads to run-ons like this one:

> One method of prenatal diagnosis is amniocentesis is the sampling of fluid in the womb for birth defects.

Here, the writer started to write about an example, but changed her mind and defined the term in the same sentence. In revising, she didn't notice that the sentence was trying to do two jobs at once. Run-ons of this sort are best solved by separating the two sentences, or by converting one of the independent clauses into a dependent clause:

> One method of prenatal diagnosis is amniocentesis. This is the sampling of fluid in the womb for birth defects.

or

> One method of prenatal diagnosis is amniocentesis, the sampling of fluid in the womb for birth defects.

A second major cause of run-on sentences is failing to separate two closely related ideas. This is the case in the following sentence:

> Flossing your teeth is important this prevents the buildup of tartar and plaque.

The best remedy for such run-ons is to separate them with either a semicolon or a comma and conjunction:

> Flossing your teeth is important; this prevents the buildup of tartar and plaque.

or

> Flossing your teeth is important, because this prevents the buildup of tartar and plaque.

A third cause of run-on sentences is fusing two short sentences which have the same subject. When two short sentences refer to the same person, place, or thing, a pronoun often serves as the subject of the second sentence. Somehow, this signals the brain to link the sentences. But if the linking is done without punctuation or a conjunction, it results in a run-on:

> Frisch won the Nobel Prize for his research he described the dances of honey bees.

Here the subject of the second short sentence, *he,* clearly refers to the subject of the first sentence, *Frisch*. But even though the ideas are closely related, sentence rules still apply. Same subject run-ons can usually be revised by subordination or by punctuation with a semicolon:

> Frisch won the Nobel Prize for his research describing the dances of honey bees.

or

> Frisch won the Nobel Prize for his research; he described the dances of honey bees.

APPLICATION

Identify the run-ons in the sentences below, and decide what caused them. Then revise the sentences for grammatical correctness.

1. Truth is imponderable you cannot be sure it exists.
2. Astrology is misleading it is a form of self-delusion.
3. Mary lived in New Jersey was where she was born.
4. The cat stared out the window he was intently watching birds.
5. The computer is a powerful tool in education it has many applications.
6. Our team is the conference champion automatically receives a bid to the post-season tournament.
7. The nucleus of atoms contains many particles more are being discovered every year.
8. Mathematics is my favorite subject in school especially is calculus.
9. Some Mazda cars employ the Wankel Rotary engine was developed to avoid some of the problems piston engines have.
10. The Surgeon General reported in 1964 that smoking causes cancer he urged the banning of cigarette ads.

FRAGMENTS

Fragments occur when you punctuate a dependent clause as if it were an independent clause, in effect making it into a sentence. Again, this suggests to the reader that you don't understand what a sentence is; furthermore, it also implies that you don't recognize the connections between your ideas. Consider these examples:

> Creationists argue against evolution. Citing the Bible as their evidence.
>
> They espouse a new theory of science teaching. Which they call "creation science."
>
> Many scientists have argued against "creation science"; notably Stephen J. Gould and Lewis Thomas.
>
> But creationists want evolution taken out of high school science texts. Because it violates their religious beliefs.

In all four examples, the writer has separated elements that belong together. The result is a fragmentation of information. How can fragments be remedied?

By incorporating separated phrases into the independent clause, usually with a comma:

> Creationists argue against evolution, citing the Bible as their evidence.
>
> Many scientists have argued against "creation science," notably Stephen J. Gould and Lewis Thomas.

By joining the separated parts of a complex sentence, usually replacing the period or semicolon with a comma:

> They espouse a new theory of science teaching, which they call "creation science."
>
> But creationists want evolution taken out of high-school science texts, because it violates their religious beliefs.

What causes fragments? Three situations seem to cause writers to separate dependent clauses from the rest of their context. First, sometimes a complex sentence is incorrectly split before the subordinating conjunction or the relative pronoun. This results in fragments like these:

> I bought a Honda Accord. Since *Consumer Reports* gave it a high rating.
>
> She was wearing a seat belt when she crashed. Which probably saved her life when the car rolled over.

Such fragments are best corrected by integrating the dependent clause into the sentence, usually with a comma preceding the subordinating conjunction.

> I bought a Honda Accord since *Consumer Reports* gave it a high rating.
>
> She was wearing a seat belt when she crashed, which probably saved her life when the car rolled over.

A second cause of fragments occurs when a sentence ends with a list of specific examples or names. Often, these lists—composed of phrases, not independent clauses—begin with a signaling word like *particularly, usually, such as,* or *especially.* This yields fragments like this:

> He cited shows with a high level of violence. Such as *Magnum P.I., Hunter,* and *The Equalizer.*

Such problems are corrected by incorporating the list into the sentence, preceding the signaling word with a comma:

> He cited shows with a high level of violence, such as *Magnum P.I., Hunter,* and *The Equalizer.*

A third common cause of fragments is a phrase beginning with an *-ing* participle. Since many nouns end in *-ing,* our minds sometimes confuse the verb forms that end in *-ing* with nouns that can be the subject of the sentence. Compare these two instances:

> Cher shows many talents. Acting is one of them.
>
> Cher shows many talents. Acting in movies like *Suspect* and *Moonstruck.*

In the first example *Acting* is a noun, referring to *talents* in the first sentence. But in the second example *Acting* is a verb participle, modifying what she *shows.* That's a fragment, and must be corrected:

> Cher shows many talents, acting in movies like *Suspect* and *Moonstruck.*

APPLICATION

Identify the fragments in the examples below, and determine what caused them. Then revise the fragments for grammatical correctness.

1. Mr. Hunter lived alone in the house down the hill. Until one night his car skidded on ice and ran into a bridge.
2. Lennon lived in semiseclusion at the Dakota; tending to his son, preparing the meals, and managing the household.
3. There are few Jewish people in South Carolina. Constituting less than one percent of the religious community there.
4. If you look at the street you can find especially unlovely people. People with purple hair, three earrings per ear, etc. People who demonstrate their nonconformity through ugliness.
5. So there they are. Two individuals who share a common search for knowledge and success.
6. Many cars are named after wild and dangerous animals. Like the Cobra, the Jaguar, the Cougar, and the Bronco.
7. Serfs were basically slaves. People who devoted their lives to manual labor and gained only subsistence.
8. They are afraid that television will control their lives. As it did in Orwell's *1984.*
9. The quality of life today is a matter of some importance. Important because we have become wary of the cost to future generations.
10. Many other species are in danger. The tiger, the blue whale, the orangutan, the peregrine falcon, and the California condor, for instance.

Although you should try to avoid fragments in your writing, you should know that they sometimes can be employed to gain readers' attention. If you examine advertising, you'll see that fragments are used often to create the short, snappy rhythm that advertisers love: "Less filling! Tastes great!" Sometimes, too, fragments can catch readers off guard, hooking them by surprise: "In the next 72 hours, three women will die in this country. Die at the hands of their husbands." And sometimes fragments can draw us into a writer's mood, helping us understand the frame of mind of characters described: "He lay there in the bed. Staring vacantly at the ceiling. Occasionally rolling his eyes. Whimpering once in a while, as if in pain. Reacting infrequently to undetectable stimuli. They told me he was brain-dead."

Should you use such fragments? This is a touchy subject in academic writing. Under the influence of advertising and the so-called "New Journalism" of Tom Wolfe and others, fragments have gained popularity as "minor sentences." But in most cases, they are unacceptable in academic writing. Try this rule of thumb: Use deliberate fragments sparingly, and only in situations where you really want to gain the audience's attention. But make sure there are no *unintentional* fragments in your paper, or the readers will be confused, wondering which fragments you intended, and which you didn't. Unless you know your readers very well, it's probably best not to take chances with their reactions in an academic situation. If you're considering using deliberate fragments, first get the reaction of an editing group. If they have doubts, you can bet your readers will too.

FAULTY PREDICATION

Faulty predication, a mismatch between the subject, the verb, and the complement, is a common sentence error. These three elements not only have to be grammatically compatible but also have to fit together logically. This error is hard to detect. Even though something seems to be wrong with the sentence when you read it, the meaning may come across anyway. In the following sentences, you can understand what the writer means, but the subject-verb-complement relationship is illogical.

Her job paid her well.

Clearly, her job does not have money of its own; her employers, not her job, pay her.

The subject of Dana's paper was about acid rain.

In this sentence, a superfluous *about* causes faulty predication. You can say that her subject was acid rain, or that her paper was about acid rain, but not both.

Some errors in predication occur when an adverb phrase is forced to function as a noun phrase:

> An episiotomy is when the skin is cut to help a woman deliver her baby.
>
> The reason you lost the election was because you didn't address the issues.

Frequently, the verb *be* (is, was, were, am) signals equality between the noun and the complement, so the complement must be grammatically equivalent to the noun. These sentences should be rewritten so that a noun or noun clause after the linking verb shows equivalency between the subject and the complement, or so that superfluous words are eliminated:

> An episiotomy is the incision made to help a woman deliver her baby.
>
> You lost the election because you didn't address the issues.

APPLICATION

Identify the predication errors in the following sentences, and determine what caused them. Then rewrite the sentences for grammatical correctness.

1. Bad nutrition during pregnancy causes low birth-weight babies.
2. The reason she dances so well is because she has taken lessons for nine years.
3. The last Democratic victory in a presidential election was when Jimmy Carter won in 1976.
4. King's assassination in 1968 caused more riots.
5. Her sultry good looks are part of her popularity with teens.
6. On the other hand is Madonna who substitutes underwear and provocative dancing for meaningful messages.
7. It was because of the way Joel wrote the paper that the teacher suspected plagiarism.
8. The first reason for this lawsuit is because my client was injured falling down the icy steps.
9. The first live test of an atomic bomb was used against the Japanese in 1945 to end the war.
10. Knowing how to protect myself in an emergency is a good reason for studying judo.

FAULTY MODIFICATION

Modification, one of the best means of expanding the basic sentence pattern, sometimes causes sentence errors. It should always be clear to the reader what sentence element a modifier refers to. As with most sentence errors, there may be no great loss of meaning when misplaced modifiers occur, but the resulting awkwardness or ambiguity may distract the reader or may create an unintentionally comical sentence. Consider, for instance, this sentence from a crafts magazine:

> Stitched on six-count Herkimer cloth, your child will enjoy this rewarding project.

We know that the writer meant to have the project, not the child, stitched to the cloth. But that message gets lost in the giggles as we imagine the picture this faulty modifier conjures up. That's not a reaction writers want from readers. How can faulty modifiers be corrected?

By slight revision to move the modifier nearer the word it modifies:

> Your child will enjoy this rewarding project stitched on six-count Herkimer cloth.

To avoid errors in modification, place the modifier as close as possible to the word it modifies. And always make sure that there is a word to be modified. Your goal in effective modification should be to make your meaning clear to the reader. Don't force your readers to decipher your meaning or to correct mentally the sentences they are reading.

What causes faulty modification? Sometimes modification problems are caused by dangling participles. For instance, consider these two sentences:

> Having had surgery Thursday, Karl Nelson's career is now in jeopardy.
>
> Meals were served to the homeless eaten in shelters and soup kitchens.

The problem here is that the participial phrases do not point to the words they should modify. Revision can correct the errors:

> Having had surgery Thursday, Karl Nelson now finds his career in jeopardy. (Nelson, not his career, had the surgery.)
>
> Meals eaten in shelters and soup kitchens were served to the homeless. (Meals, not the homeless, were eaten.)

Another cause of modification problems is the misplaced introductory phrase, which may not have a word or phrase in the independent clause as its referent:

> Rich in human detail, Gill argues that Wright played many roles in his short life.

The problem here is that the introductory phrase doesn't seem to go with any part of the sentence. Again, slight revision can correct the sentence:

> Rich in human detail, Gill's biography argues that Wright played many roles in his short life. (Gill's book contains the rich detail.)

A similar kind of problem is caused by the misuse of a prepositional phrase. Here the prepositional phrase is attached to a word other than what it's supposed to modify, causing unintentional misunderstanding:

> Some cable networks develop their own programs, such as HBO, ESPN, and Cinemax.

Here, the problem is caused by the placement of the prepositional phrase. We're led to believe that *such as* will be followed by names of programs; instead, we're given the names of cable networks. To avoid this sort of awkwardness, the sentence should be rewritten so the prepositional phrase is closer to the word it modifies or so it accurately modifies the word it follows:

> Some cable networks such as HBO, ESPN, and Cinemax develop their own programs.

or

> Some cable networks develop their own programs, such as HBO's "Live at the Comedy Store," ESPN's "Sportscenter," and Cinemax's "On Stage."

APPLICATION

Identify the faulty modifiers in the following sentences, and determine what causes the problem in modification. Then rewrite the sentences to conform to grammatical and logical rules.

1. Once you have removed all the mildew the musty odor should disappear, unless some of it is down inside the walls where you can't see it.
2. Even if the writers' strike ends immediately it will take four months to produce new television shows, which is not likely.
3. The former All-American suffered through a year of pain, frequent visits to four different doctors, surgery to remove a bone spur that was rubbing on his leg, and rehabilitation.

4. Montezuma is the only coffee packed in a vacuum bag fresh from the roaster.
5. *Nostratic* is the name used for the language of the earliest Indo-European people, which existed around 12,000 years ago.
6. Bidialectalism is an issue in Honolulu which is sweeping the state of Hawaii.
7. The Pilgrims learned from the Indians, baking beans and planting corn.
8. Breaking all records, the hundred-meter dash was very exciting.
9. When it rose from the depths of the sea, the balcony framed a perfect sunrise.
10. Since he left most of it to a museum, Monet's artwork is rarely obtained by private collectors.

AGREEMENT PROBLEMS

Rules of agreement affect the relationship between subject and verb and between pronoun and antecedent. Agreement simply means that a singular subject must have a singular verb, a plural subject must have a plural verb, and that a pronoun must match its antecedent (the word it refers to) in number (singular or plural), in gender (masculine, feminine, or neuter), and in person (first, second, or third). Usually, agreement occurs automatically when you speak and write. For example, when you say, "My dog likes to chase cats," you know that since "dog" is a singular noun, the verb "likes" must be singular, too. However, if you had said, "My dog and my ferret like to chase cats," you would have used a plural verb, "like," to match the compound subject, "my dog and my ferret."

What causes agreement problems? Problems in agreement between subject and verb occur when it's not clear whether the subject is plural or singular. Notice how subtle agreement errors can be:

> Examples of this sort of editing appear throughout the text and offers only a limited perspective to the readers.

At first, the sentence sounds correct. The sentence communicates its message, but in writing, it's hard to overlook the compound verb—*appear* and *offers*. The second verb should be plural—*offer*—to agree with the plural subject.

> Examples of this sort of editing appear throughout the text and offer only a limited perspective to the readers.

Compound subjects joined by *or* and *nor* often cause agreement problems:

> Neither Huck nor Tom speak of Jim's predicament.

The sentence sounds acceptable, but the conjunctions *nor* and *or* suggest singularity: not both, but one or the other speaks. The verb, therefore, must be singular.

> Neither Huck nor Tom speaks of Jim's predicament.

Indefinite pronouns—*each, every, any, anybody, one*—cause similar agreement problems, especially when there is a prepositional phrase between the subject and verb:

> Each of the programs help students edit their papers.
>
> Only one of the desserts are worth eating.

In these sentences, the plural object of the preposition has influenced the verb choice. *Programs* and *desserts* are so close to the verb that they seem to be plural subjects. To avoid this error, simply remember that *each, none, any,* and other indefinite pronouns are singular:

> Each of the programs helps students edit their papers.
>
> Only one of the desserts is worth eating.

Prepositional phrases affect other kinds of subjects as well:

> Many aspects of Muti's newly recorded version is similar to Haitinck's earlier recording of the symphony.

If you take out that prepositional phrase, you notice that the subject—*aspects*—is plural, so the verb should be *are,* not *is.*

Agreement problems also affect pronoun reference. Remember that a pronoun is a noun substitute. Usually, the sentence contains a noun to which the pronoun refers, and the pronoun must reflect the grammatical features of that noun. If the noun is plural, the pronoun must be plural; if it is feminine, the pronoun must be feminine. Most of the time, pronoun agreement presents few problems, but some sentence constructions make pronoun agreement difficult to achieve. As in subject-verb agreement, indefinite pronouns cause problems here too:

> Everybody registered their cars on Thursday.
>
> Someone left their books on the desk.
>
> Does everyone want tickets for the balcony?

You hear constructions like this all the time. There is really no problem in communicating meaning; the problem is grammatical. Indefinite pronouns like *everybody, anyone, anybody, someone, no one, one, each* are considered singular, so they must be matched by singular pronouns. In speech, the agreement problem is not disturbing. However, in writing, the lack of pronoun agreement may distract the reader. To achieve agree-

Mechanics: Punctuation, Spelling, Capitalization

The mechanics of writing can seem trivial. Even a novice writer knows that it's far easier to correct a spelling error or a faulty comma than to resolve a problem in development or organization. It certainly makes sense to deal first with the larger issues of writing—purpose, audience, subject—and then, as deadlines loom, to turn to the mechanics. But sooner or later, it's time to sandpaper away the surface problems and give papers a glossy finish. Why? Because readers will dismiss your well-researched and thoughtful paper if it looks like it was written at the last moment. They won't believe your statistics if you can't punctuate a sentence; they won't be persuaded by your arguments if they don't trust your spelling.

PUNCTUATION

Punctuation is a system in which marks and symbols signal to readers the writer's intentions about how a sentence should be interpreted. They tell readers how you meant to link ideas and words together. In speech, you "punctuate" your sentences with pauses, rises in voice pitch, intonation, modifications in speed of utterance, facial gestures, and hand motions. In writing, punctuation compensates for the absence of these visual and vocal clues to meaning. Commas, periods, semicolons, dashes, parentheses, underlining, and other marks of punctuation help the reader follow your train of thought.

ELEMENTS OF PUNCTUATION

Element	*Function*	*Examples*
Apostrophe ’	Use the apostrophe to show possession, to mark the place where letters are omitted, and to indicate the plural of numbers and letters.	
	Possession:	
	An apostrophe is used with an *s* to form the possessive case of some nouns.	Barbara’s life-style
	With compound nouns, the last noun takes the possessive to show that they both own something.	Bert and Ernie’s capers
	When each noun possesses something (individually), then both nouns are possessive.	Jack’s and Jill’s pails
	With singular nouns that end in *s*, you can form the possessive by adding only an apostrophe or by adding an apostrophe and an *s*.	a waitress’ job, an actress’ costume a waitress’s job, an actress’s costume
	Use only an apostrophe for plural nouns that end in *s*.	a secretaries’ meeting, students’ reports
	Add only an apostrophe to nouns that end in multiple consecutive *s* sounds.	Charlies’ tricks, Jesus’ parables
	Don’t use an apostrophe with possessive pronouns.	yours, its, his, ours, whose, theirs
	Omission:	
	An apostrophe marks where letters or numbers have been left out of a word or date.	I’m, I’ll, can’t, back in ’43
	Plurals:	
	Apostrophes indicate the plural of numbers.	6’s, 70’s, seven 1,000’s
	An apostrophe with an *s* shows the plural of a word as a word.	You had seventeen *you’s* in that paragraph.

Element	*Function*	*Examples*
	If a term is all capital letters or ends in a capital letter, you don't need an apostrophe for the plural.	I'll have six B.A.s before it's all over. Eight ADDs are enough for that computer program.
Bracket [ ]	Brackets are used to set off material that is your own inside quotation marks which surround someone else's words.	"The trio [Kingston Trio] will appear at the Bottom Mark Sunday, November 12," read the announcement in the paper.
Colon :	A colon is a punctuation mark of anticipation that halts the reader, then connects the first statement to the following one.	
	A colon can connect a series or list to the sentence.	I have four classes: math, biology, English, and history.
	A colon can link one statement to another to develop, illustrate, explain, or amplify it. When used in this way, the colon can even link two sentences.	Any large cafeteria can have two related problems: it must fix enough food but not too much, and it must keep the food from spoiling.
	A colon can introduce a stacked list.	The following courses will be offered in the fall: Math 103 Math 209 Math 308 Math 104 Math 210 Math 309
	A colon adds emphasis to a phrase that completes a sentence.	There's only one thing I want for Christmas: a new camera.
	Colons can separate chapters and verses as well as hours and minutes.	Genesis 1:1 9:30 A.M.
	In proportions, colons represent ratios.	$8:4 = 12:x$
	A colon can follow salutations in business letters.	Dear Sir: Dear Ms. Geoffry:
	When using colons with quotations, capitalize the first letter of the first word of the quotation if the quote originally began with a capital letter.	The sign stated: "No shoes, no shirt, no service."

Element	*Function*	*Examples*
	A colon always goes outside quotation marks.	These are qualities he calls "good": wine, women, and song.
	If you quote a statement that ends with a colon, drop the colon and add ellipses.	"Any large cafeteria can have two related problems . . . ," an author contends.
Comma **,**	A comma can link, enclose, separate, and show omissions.	
	To link: Place a comma before a coordinating conjunction (*and, but, or, nor, for, so, yet*) when it combines two sentences (independent clauses).	The food was good, and the company was even better.
	(Some handbooks suggest that the comma can be omitted if the sentences are short, if there is no complicated punctuation in them, and if the sentences won't be misread. You will always be safe, however, if you insert the comma. This will obviate your having to make an individual decision each time.)	
	To separate: Commas separate introductory elements from the rest of the sentence.	During the first game of the series, we had four runs, six hits, and no errors. Finally, I'm finished. Yes, I know I'm excited.
	The comma may be omitted if the introductory clause or phrase is short and does not cause confusion without the mark of punctuation. It will never be wrong, however, to insert the comma.	When you go I will go.
	Commas separate items in a series.	The library offered books, magazines, journals, and newspapers.
	The comma before the final item in a series is optional.	We had stories to tell of Indian pueblos, spicy food and hot summer nights.

Element	*Function*	*Examples*
	No comma is needed if all items in a series are joined by *and.*	We saw Porsches and Jaguars and Broncos on the lot.
	A comma joins two coordinate modifiers. (To identify coordinate modifiers, see if they can be switched and the meaning stays the same.)	Her romantic, optimistic view of life encouraged us.
	A comma separates a nonrestrictive element that comes at the end of the sentence.	They all like to watch old movies, especially if they can eat popcorn.
Dash ——	When typing, use two hyphens (--) to indicate a dash.	
	A dash can indicate a sharp turn in thought.	That marks the end of that class—unless I failed the last test.
	A dash can add emphasis to a pause.	I'll get the job done—after I take another break.
	Dashes can set off an explanatory series or an appositive series.	Two of the applicants—Scott and Jan—will be offered jobs.
	Dashes can add emphasis to a parenthetical element (an item inserted in the sentence that isn't essential to meaning).	Only one person—you—can control what you say.
Ellipses . . .	Ellipses are a punctuation mark that shows you've left out some words.	
	When you quote only part of a statement, insert ellipses to show where you've left the information out.	
	Use three dots to indicate a break in a continuing sentence.	"Work . . . is the privilege of all citizens," the politician explained.
	Use four dots to indicate the end of a sentence.	"It's best not to tell. . . . I certainly never would," she said.
	Remember: it's not fair to leave any important information out of a quotation or to pull words from a quotation and change the meaning.	

Element	*Function*	*Examples*
Exclamation Point !	Exclamation points are a punctuation mark used at the end of sentences to indicate surprise, anger, or emphasis.	She's married! Hell, no, I'm not giving in! I'll never do that again!
Parentheses ( )	Parenthetical information is played-down and de-emphasized: it may not be essential to a sentence, but it may be interesting or helpful to the reader.	Many American presidents (for example, Dwight Eisenhower) were military leaders. CUNY (City University of New York) offers a variety of programs.
	Punctuation: Parenthetical material does not affect the punctuation of a sentence. If a parenthetical clause comes at the end of a sentence, for example, the period to end the sentence would go outside the parentheses.	I like some history courses (American), but hate others (ancient Greek).
	When numbering a series of items in a sentence, use two parentheses, not one.	I'll eat (1) potatoes, (2) meat, (3) carrots, and (4) gravy.
	When a complete sentence is enclosed in parentheses, the end punctuation goes inside the parentheses.	I want to know (They did not tell me.) what I've got to do to improve.
	If you have an item that you need to set off with parentheses inside of a parenthetical idea, use brackets.	I want to know (you can tell me [if you want to]) . . . .
Period .	A period indicates a full stop at the end of a sentence.	Louganis won the gold medal.
	A period is used with an indirect question.	She asked if I liked the opera.
	A period is used after an *acceptable* sentence fragment.	Did you enjoy the festival? Very much.
	A period always goes inside the quotation marks.	"Daffodils often grow on hills." That was the statement made by the horticulturist.

Element	*Function*	*Examples*
	Use periods after initials in names.	John F. Kennedy, Dr. E. K. Hambrick
	Use periods between dollars and cents.	$54.98
	Use periods with abbreviations.	Inc., Ms., M.D., Ph.D.
	Use periods following the numbers or letters in lists or outlines.	I. A. B.
Question Mark ?	Use a question mark at the end of a sentence that asks a question.	What do you think you're doing?
	With quotations, when the writer who is doing the quoting is asking the question, the question mark goes outside of the quotation marks.	Did he say, "I know exactly what I'm doing"?
	When the quotation is a question, the question mark goes inside the quotation marks.	She asked, "What do you think you're doing?"
Quotation Marks " "	Quotation marks enclose direct repetition of words.	
	When you quote anything word for word from another source, enclose those words in quotation marks.	The report said, "Too many high school graduates are going to college."
	If a quotation is longer than four lines, indent all of the lines of the quotation ten spaces from the left margin, double-spaced. Don't use quotation marks with indented quotations.	
	If a quotation is more than one paragraph (and it is not indented because it's not more than four lines), put quotation marks at the beginning of every paragraph but at the end of only the last paragraph.	"I can't pay the rent; I can't pay the rent. "My kids are hungry. "My house is cold. "My husband left me. "I can't pay the rent."

Element	*Function*	*Examples*
	If you have a sentence with a quotation within a quotation, use single quotation marks (the apostrophe key on a typewriter) on the inside quote.	She asked, "Did I hear him say 'Get lost'?"
	Use quotation marks to indicate titles of short stories, magazine and newspaper articles, and songs.	"The Catbird Seat" "An Occurrence at Owl Creek Bridge"
	Always put periods and commas inside closing quotation marks.	He said, "I'll go." The sign read, "Do not enter," but they decided to investigate further.
	Always put colons and semicolons outside closing quotation marks.	The hero said, "I'll pay the rent"; that surprised me. These are my favorite "classes": lunchtime, study hall, and rest period.
	For all other punctuation: if the punctuation is a part of the quotation, place it inside the quotation marks; if the punctuation is not a part of the quotation, place it outside the quotation marks.	
	See *question marks.*	
	Words used in a special way or words to which the writer wants to draw attention for some reason are put in quotation marks.	"Teasing" your hair is bad for it.
Semicolon **;**	A semicolon can join two sentences that are close in meaning. It indicates a greater pause than a comma but not as great a pause as a period. Semicolons can also add clarity to involved sentences.	
	Use a semicolon to join closely related sentences.	I want to go; he doesn't.

Element	*Function*	*Examples*
	Use a semicolon to join closely related sentences combined with a conjunctive adverb.	I want to go; however, he doesn't.
	Use the semicolon to divide series in sentences that have several series.	Please make these changes in the brochure copy: "communications" to "communication"; "phone" to "call"; "promises" to "results."
	Use a semicolon to separate sentences joined by a coordinating conjunction if the sentences already have commas.	In most cases, I would order steak, baked potato, and salad; but today I think I'll order fish.
Virgule/Slash /	A virgule or slash is used to separate two things which belong together as choices or to separate lines of poetry that have been run together.	Do you know the either/or rule? Roses are red / Violets are blue / Sugar is sweet / And so are you.

APPLICATION

Fill in the blanks in the sentences below with appropriate punctuation marks. Be able to explain your reason for each choice. In some sentences, several marks may be used to perform the same function; and some of the blanks will remain empty.

1. Pidgin___ a spare___ direct___ and often delightfully irreverent patois___ is spoken by native Hawaiians___
2. It is___ for many young Hawaiians___ a crucial link to a rich past___ that is all too quickly being bulldozed away___
3. Many Hawaiians wonder if it is good___ that their native language be allowed to die out___
4. Pidgin is composed of elements of many languages___ English___ French___ Japanese___ Hawaiian___ and Indian___ to name a few___
5. For many youngsters in Hawaii___ Standard English is a foreign language___ that they learn in school___
6. Some people think that poor spellers have a mild form of dyslexia___ but that doesn___t explain why good readers can read words but not write them___

7. Another group blames the English language itself___ because it mixes elements from so many languages___ that spelling rules just don___t apply___
8. The National Education Association___ NEA___ has formed a panel___ to study spelling reform___
9. Their purpose___ according to a spokesperson___ is to examine ways of simplifying English spelling___
10. Wouldn___t it be wonderful___ if English had consistent spelling rules___

Put the apostrophe in the correct places in these sentences.

1. Its true that that persons hat is the funniest Ive ever seen.
2. The childrens playroom is painted orange and yellow.
3. Their parents reactions were not surprising.
4. Give everything its due.
5. Wherever you go, its not going to be home.
6. Her friends summer plans are still up in the air.
7. Tommies chickens are laying eight to twelve eggs a day.
8. Thats amazing.
9. That is Malcolms or Freds motorbike.
10. Her mother-in-laws plane arrived right on time.

Punctuate the following sentences:

1. Wherever you go whatever you do remember me.
2. In the dim twilight of the evening stars peeked out and we said hello.
3. If not watched carefully misplaced modifiers are likely to squint dangle become misplaced or otherwise behave badly.
4. Youll feel like giving them a good shake and sending them to bed without supper.
5. Sadly they put the flag at half mast.
6. Here are your color choices blue white pink purple and red.
7. My choice is for the tall glass her choice is for the short one.
8. When you see them and they see you what will you do?
9. Whatever else happens I will be at the party on time I really want to see everybody arrive.
10. Stop and see the caves whatever you do George and Nell urged.

SPELLING

Spelling mistakes are among the most difficult errors to detect when editing your work. In detecting punctuation errors and sentence-structure problems, you at least know when an error is likely to occur; you can train yourself to watch for it. For instance, you can look for structures that might lead to comma faults. But how are you supposed to know whether you've misspelled a word?

Some handbooks suggest that you check every word you are not sure of. If you think that advice is illogical, you're right. It is based on the assumption that we can intuitively guess which words may be spelled incorrectly. Sometimes, we can. The assumption may be valid with difficult terms (*entrepreneur, aggravate*) and with words most of us wouldn't even attempt to spell without a dictionary (*bourgeoisie, fluorescent, mnemonic*). But writers don't typically mangle difficult words; more often it's the ordinary terms that cause problems (*address, a lot, separate, receive*).

Unfortunately, poor spelling suggests carelessness. When you spell *all right* as *alright* or the possessive pronoun *their* as *there,* you'll aggravate your readers, who have a surprisingly low tolerance for such miscues. Spelling errors can sting like fire ants. Job application letters or business memos that contain misspellings may leave you unemployed; if the doctor mistakenly gives you medicine for *hypo*tension rather than *hyper*-tension, you might never have to worry about spelling again. Fortunately, just about anyone *can* learn to spell.

What Causes Misspellings?

When you write or type quickly, your mind may jump several words ahead of your fingers. You find yourself omitting, reversing, or leapfrogging letters you intended to put down. Such errors are tolerable in a draft as long as you can decipher the crippled words; but the errors must be removed before you hand your final version over to readers.

Words that sound alike but are spelled differently (homophones) cause many spelling problems. You know quite well that *two, too,* and *to* have different meanings, but if you don't sort out the words in your final draft, you'll confuse and annoy your readers.

Some homophones which commonly plague writers are:

are/our	loose/lose
forth/fourth	led/lead
past/passed	whether/weather
principle/principal	capital/capitol
here/hear	sight/site/cite

Some words that are spelled similarly have significant differences in meaning. Words like *affect/effect* and *access/excess* may look similar, and you may pronounce them nearly the same, but they have very different meanings. The only way to distinguish these words is to look them up and commit them to memory. The *Glossary of Usage* in this Handbook contains some of the most troublesome words of this kind.

Some English sounds have many possible spellings. One thing which makes English hard for foreign speakers to learn is the inconsistency of its spelling system. There are at least two ways to spell the /ənt/ sound:

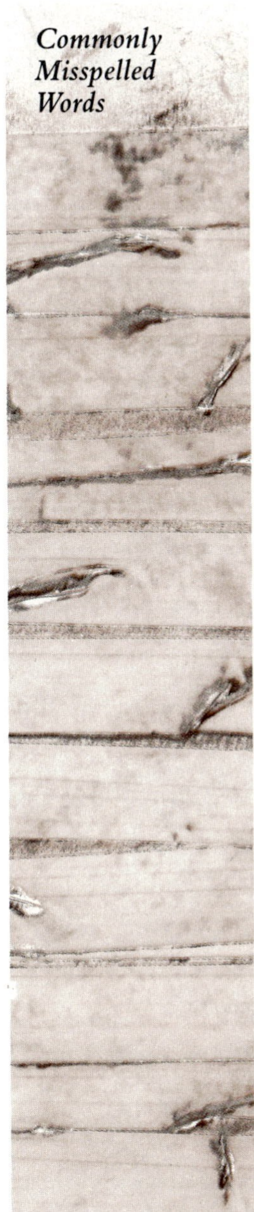

Commonly Misspelled Words

accept, except
access, excess
accommodation
acquire
adapt, adopt
affect, effect
all together, altogether
altar, alter
angel, angle
believe
benefited
berth, birth
born, borne
calendar
capital, capitol
censor, censure
choice, choose, chose
cite, sight, site
coarse, course
complement, compliment
congratulations
correspondence
council, counsel
counselor
dairy, diary
decent, descent
definite
description
desert, dessert
desperate
dining, dinning
dyeing, dying
elicit, illicit
embarrass
emigrant, immigrant
environment
equipped, equipment
exceed
excite
existence
fare, fair
formally, formerly
forth, fourth
forty
grammar
guarantee
hear, here
holy, wholly
hungry
independent
instance, instants
irrelevant, irreverent
it's, its
knew, new
know, no
knowledge
laboratory
later, latter
lead, led
loose, lose
luxurious
maintain, maintenance
moral, morale
necessary
ninety
occasion
occurred
past, passed
personal, personnel
perform
precede
presence, presents
principal, principle
privilege
proceed
prophecy, prophesy
quiet, quite
receive
referring
respectively, respectfully
right, rite, write
schedule
separate
similar
sophomore
staid, stayed
stationary, stationery
success
suit, suite
superintendent
than, then
their, there, they're
threw, through
to, too, two
vain, vane, vein
weak, week
weather, whether
who's, whose
worse, worst
writing

-ent and *-ant*. There are many ways to spell the /əl/ sound: *-le, -el,* and *-al* to name a few. When the adverb ending *ly* is added to a word, is it spelled *-ly* or *-ally?* When certain words are turned into adjectives, do you use the suffix *-ible* or *-able?* When the vowel /ə/ isn't stressed, do you spell it *a, e, i, o* or *u?*

Unfortunately, there's no systematic way to beat these rules; you either must memorize the word or look it up every time you use it. Some word-processing programs have spelling checkers that identify curiously spelled words, and there are calculator-sized spelling banks available. But these only help when you're near your computer or the batteries are charged; they're not foolproof. And they can't tell whether you've written *prank* when you meant to write *drank.* It's best to *learn* how to spell your demons yourself.

How can you correct misspellings? Fortunately, most of us don't misspell every word; rather, certain words or sound categories give us trouble. *Keeping an error log,* a list of the words you misspell, will help you identify your own spelling demons. When you read, *pay attention to the spelling of unusual words, or words you use in speech but rarely in writing:* naive, facetious, triskaidekaphobia, and so on.

In addition, *learn the five "fouls"* that cause many simple spelling errors:

1. *ie/ei.* If you didn't learn this rhyme in grammar school, memorize it now: *I* before *E,* except after *C,* or when sounded as *A,* as in *neighbor* and *weigh.* There are some notable exceptions to this rule, such as *weird, leisure, height,* and *foreign.* However, this rule will help you spell words like *achieve* and *receive* without difficulty.
2. *Final e + suffixes.* This rule works differently for vowels than for consonants. For vowels, when the suffix begins with a vowel, drop the final e: write + ing = writing; envelope + ing = enveloping.

   Exceptions to this rule occur if the word ends in *-ce* or *-ge.* In those cases, keep the final e:

   outrageous　　noticeable　　knowledgeable

   For consonants, when the suffix begins with a consonant, keep the final e:

   tasteful　　falsehood　　careful　　niceness

   Exceptions to this rule include some words that end with *j* and *g* sounds. In these cases the final *e* is dropped:

   judgment　　abridgment　　acknowledgment　　argument

   These exceptions aren't systematic, so you need to memorize them.
3. *Final consonants + suffixes.* When a suffix beginning with a vowel is added to short words or to short syllables that are accented, double the final consonant:

   referred　　handicapped
   shipped　　winning
   bugged

When a suffix beginning with a vowel is added to a final syllable that ends in a consonant but isn't stressed, don't double the vowel:

ending targeted visiting plunderer

When a suffix beginning with a consonant is added to a word ending in a consonant, don't double the final consonant:

development witness capful

4. *Final y + suffix*. Change *y* to *i* except when the suffix is *-ing:*

   happiest noisier pliable

   Exceptions include plying, spying, and whinnying.
5. *Final c + suffix that begins with a vowel*. Change *c* to *ck:*

   frolicking trafficker
   panicking colicky

There are many more rules of English spelling, but these are the ones that will help you prevent the misspellings that occur most frequently.

APPLICATION

1. There is at least one misspelled word in each of the following sentences, and sometimes there is more than one. Find the misspellings and correct them. Also, check the pronunciation to be sure you can pronounce them correctly.
   a. Higher incomes yield more social priveledges and better success in our society.
   b. The coyote is the subject of many legonds atributing to him various abilitys.
   c. The coyote ganed the image of the sneeky, cunning killer because he is extreamly smart.
   d. It is necessary to clerify what the author means by equality.
   e. Thinking independantly is the very thing that brings Winston to his downfall.
   f. This generally results when there is a drought, a suvere winter, or the ocassional lean year, when through no explainable reason there is an extream lack of wild game.
2. Choose the correct spelling for each of the following words.
   a. separate, seperate
   b. definately, definitely
   c. judgement, judgment
   d. privilege, privelege
   e. devide, divide
   f. embarass, embarrass

g. pronounciation, pronunciation
h. memento, momento
i. fourty, forty
j. oposition, opposition
k. grammar, grammer
l. acheive, achieve
m. calender, calendar
n. preceed, precede
o. occurance, occurrence
p. arguement, argument
q. existant, existent
r. similiar, similar
s. writting, writing
t. recieve, receive
u. professor, proffessor
v. aggrivation, aggravation

MECHANICS

Mechanics are rules that standardize certain features in writing. In some cases they provide signals to the reader; but in most cases, mechanics are simply conventions that standardize things like capitalization, the use of numbers, and abbreviations. Some guidelines, such as the rules that deal with punctuation, may be easier to remember than others, such as those for using numbers. Fortunately, you don't have to memorize any of these rules. You can find them quickly in this book and in most handbooks about writing. It is important that you observe these rules, though, because readers expect you to follow conventions even on items that don't substantially affect your message.

Capitalization

1. Capitalize the first word of every sentence.
2. Capitalize proper nouns.

Names of Persons, Monuments, Museums, Buildings

Jesus Christ
the Library of Congress
the Lincoln Memorial
W. E. B. DuBois
Elizabeth Cady Stanton
the Sears Tower

Names of Places

India   West Virginia   Philadelphia

Names of Vessels

the *Mayflower*   *Freedom 7*   the *Monitor*

Events and Periods

the Dark Ages   the Inquisition   Reconstruction

3. Capitalize names of deities.

Apollo   Buddha   Allah

4. Capitalize titles before and after names.

Dr. William Walling	Professor Barbara Tuchman
the Rev. Jesse Jackson	Ms. Marsha Tucker
Capt. John Smith	Queen Elizabeth II
President George Bush	Art Cox, D.D.S.

5. Capitalize the first word and all other words except short prepositions, conjunctions, and articles in the titles of literary works, movies, and works of art. Capitalize prepositions over five letters long.

Portrait in Grey and Black	*Lonesome Dove*
"Annabel Lee"	the *Mona Lisa*
Star Wars	*One Flew over the Cuckoo's Nest*

6. Capitalize names of recognized groups and organizations.

Democrats	National Rifle Association
Jaycees	National Organization for Women
Republicans	Daughters of the American Revolution

7. Capitalize specific course names.

   Math 218   Psychology 101B

8. Capitalize directions when they refer to specific geographic areas.

   Edward Abbey writes about the Southwest.

   She's from New England.

9. Avoid unnecessary capitalization.

   I am taking a *sociology* course.

   Princeton is *northeast* of Philadelphia.

   He studies members of the lower *middle class.*

   Chris is a rising *junior.*

Abbreviations and Symbols

Use abbreviations and symbols sparingly and carefully in your writing. Few abbreviations and symbols are acceptable for the kind of writing you do in academic courses, but if you notice the writing you are exposed to every day—newspapers, magazines, textbooks—you will see that abbreviations and symbols are rarely used there, too. In general, writers avoid abbreviations because they make writing seem casual and unpolished. That is why you should avoid such abbreviations as *dept., apt., Tues., inc.*

in your writing. Don't write: *I have an appointment with the head of the math dept. Weds.* In some cases, abbreviations are permissible. The following guidelines should help you use abbreviations properly.

1. Abbreviate titles when they are part of a name.

   Mrs. Ronald Reagan   Lt. Col. Oliver North
   Dr. Martin Luther King

2. Organizations that are more commonly known by initials than by the full name may be abbreviated.

   AFL-CIO   SALT
   NASA   OSHA
   NATO   NOW

   When you are not sure whether your audience will recognize the acronym, write out the whole name the first time you refer to it; you can use the initials for subsequent references.
3. Abbreviate the names of states only when they are part of an address. If you are referring to Willowbrook, Illinois, in the text of your paper, do not write Willowbrook, IL.
4. Latin abbreviations such as etc., e.g., and i.e. are permissible in most writing.
5. Other acceptable abbreviations include the following:

   A.M.   B.C.
   P.M.   rpm
   A.D.   mph

6. Many abbreviations have become common through everyday use: TV, CB, CD, stereo, C.O.D. Use them only if they fit the tone of the particular piece you are writing.
7. Use the dollar sign ($) only for exact sums or for estimates of very large sums such as $4.83 or $1.6 billion, but write "about three dollars."
8. Do not use the ampersand (&) as a substitute for *and* in your writing unless it is part of an organization's name, as in Harper & Row.
9. Spell out percent (%) and cents (¢).

   The survey shows that only 9.6 *percent* of all college freshmen are financially independent.

   The price of ground beef has gone up 50 *cents* a pound in one month.

Numbers

Figures used in the text of your writing should be spelled out most of the time. Follow these guidelines for using numerals correctly:

1. Spell out numbers from one to ten. In very formal writing, spell out all two-digit numbers.

   We have to read *five* books this semester; we may choose from a list of 25 novels.

2. Use figures to indicate exact sums, time, large figures, and dates.

2:30 A.M.	1961	203,431
$8.65	500 B.C.	

3. Avoid beginning a sentence with a figure. If you can't rewrite the sentence so the figure is not at the beginning, then spell out the number.

   Avoid: 1963 marked the beginning of an important era in American life.

   Write: In 1963, Americans began an important era in politics.

4. Numbers from 21 to 99 are hyphenated when spelled out: thirty-five, ninety-seven. Make sure you learn how to spell these: forty (not fourty), ninety (not ninty).

Italics

Indicate italics in handwritten and typed work by underlining. Use italics in the following instances:

1. to indicate foreign words

   writ of *habeas corpus, in absentia.*

2. to indicate emphasis

   What do you mean *he* saw it?

   It was Tom, *not* Bob, who wrote the winning essay.

3. to refer to words as words

   Penultimate is one of my favorite words, but I hardly ever get to use it.

4. to indicate titles of literary works, works of art, movies, ships

   The Queen Mary *The Agony and the Ecstasy*

   The Wizard of Oz

Apostrophe

The apostrophe is a mark of punctuation. Unlike other marks discussed under punctuation, it is used to punctuate single words while commas, semicolons, periods, and colons are used to punctuate sentences. It is a difficult mark to use correctly because it has no equivalent in speech. Commas and periods are comparable to pauses in speech, but there is no oral equivalent for the apostrophe. Consequently, this mark is easy to omit or misplace. Fortunately, the rules for using the apostrophe are few and relatively uncomplicated:

1. Use an apostrophe in contractions to indicate that letters have been omitted.

   haven't   doesn't   she's   we'll

2. Use an apostrophe and *s* to indicate possession.

   Tom's car   this week's menu   the boy's illness

   Remember that in forming plural possessives, the apostrophe goes after the *s*.

   the students' unrest   our professors' homes

   two weeks' notice

   Also remember that irregular plurals form the possessive just as if they were singular.

   children's clothes   women's organizations

   Words that end in *s* may be punctuated as possessives in two ways.

   Mr. Jones' car   Mr. Jones's car

   Choose the form that you feel most comfortable with. Finally, remember that no apostrophe is required for possessive pronouns.

   his   theirs   ours   yours

   It's means *it is;* the possessive pronoun *its* requires no apostrophe.

3. Use an apostrophe to indicate the plural of symbols, letters, and words.

   You have too many *you*'s in this sentence.

   The *e*'s in your typewritten work look like *o*'s.

Hyphen

The hyphen is another mark of punctuation that applies to words rather than to whole sentences. (Make sure you do not confuse the hyphen with the dash. On the typewriter, the dash is formed by striking the hyphen key twice. In regular handwriting, you can simply make the dash longer than the hyphen.) The hyphen has two main uses: it indicates compounds and word division.

1. Use a hyphen between parts of compound words.

   all-night attorney-general
   semi-official mother-in-law

   Compound adjectives are usually hyphenated.

   pistol-packing hero blood-thirsty beast
   hard-hearted villain

   If you are not sure whether a compound should be hyphenated, check the dictionary.

2. Use a hyphen with certain prefixes.

   Hyphenate words formed from a prefix and a proper noun.

   all-American anti-Communist

   Hyphenate to avoid two identical vowels next to each other.

   re-emergence anti-industrial

   Hyphenate prefixed words to distinguish them from words spelled the same but without the hyphen.

   re-create/recreate redress/re-dress
   re-cover/recover

3. Hyphenate to indicate word division at the end of a line, but observe these guidelines:

   a. Do not divide words of one syllable like *changed, known,* or *through.*
   b. Do not separate a suffix or syllable of less than three letters (*-ed, -le*) or a one-letter prefix or syllable (*a-, e-, o-*).
   c. Separate hyphenated words (*father-in-law, less-known, all-night*) only at the hyphen.
   d. Do not divide a word on the last line of a page.

Quotation Marks

1. Use quotation marks to indicate that you are employing someone else's exact words. Always use quotation marks when you directly quote a source in your writing.

   Robert Lewis contends that the project "remains valuable, even though its application is limited."

2. Use quotation marks when writing dialogue.

   "What did Randy say about me?" asked Mary Margaret.

   "He thought you looked great in that pink dress," I replied.

3. Use quotation marks when you intentionally use a word in a novel way or when you want pointedly to indicate sarcasm, irony, or humor.

   Perri Klass worried about the "good students" in her class.

   He coined the term "neutron" to label these new particles.

4. Observe these guidelines when punctuating quotations:

   a. When a quotation ends in a period, question mark, or comma, place the mark inside the quotation marks.

      She replied, "If you want me, just whistle."

      Sherlock Holmes never actually said, "Elementary, my dear Watson!"

   b. Semicolons and colons are placed outside the quotation marks.

      Fitzgerald remarked that "the rich are different than you and I"; however, many think he didn't really mean it.

      Martin Luther King told his people "I have a dream": a dream of equality, of access, of belonging.

   c. When a question mark or an exclamation point is not part of the quotation, it goes outside the quotation marks. Periods, however, are always placed inside the quotation marks.

      Did Tony Bennett sing "I Left My Heart in San Francisco"?

      The referee grasped his hand and yelled "the winner"!

      What would you do if I said, "I don't care"?

Glossary of Usage

Grammar and usage are not the same thing. Grammar is the systematic description of a language on the levels of sound (phonology), words (meaning or semantics), and sentences (syntax). Grammar describes how language users put sounds together to make words and put words together to make sentences. When we list parts of speech, verb paradigms, or sentence patterns, we deal with aspects of grammar. Grammar does not include pronouncements about what is right and wrong. That's the prerogative of *usage*.

The concept of *correct* usage arises from attempts by grammarians to limit changes in English; despite the fact that living languages—like English—inevitably change. When books of English grammar first appeared in England and America in the eighteenth century, the English language had already been evolving for more than a thousand years—from the Old English (A.D. 449–1100) of *Beowulf* and the Anglo-Saxon Chronicles to the Middle English (1100–1500) of Chaucer to the Early Modern English (1500–1700) of Shakespeare and on to more recent forms. As education became more widespread among all social classes (and changes in language more noticeable), people concerned with language tended to regard any changes in English as evidence of deterioration and decline.

Early grammarians sought to arrest this imaginary decline by formulating principles that defined "correct" English. In doing so, they imposed many illogical rules upon the language. The rule prohibiting double negatives, for example, was made by a mathematician and the one forbidding a preposition at the end of a sentence by scholars of Latin—who tried to impose the grammar of that classical tongue upon English. By the eighteenth century, grammar had become *prescriptive* rather than descriptive. The authors of these early grammars believed it was their duty to impose order upon English and to tell people (to prescribe) how to use the language correctly. Inevitably, they branded certain linguistic practices as incorrect.

Since then, however, grammarians have grown to realize that *usage*—not abstract principles of logic or consistency—determines acceptability and appropriateness in language. Usage is the way people regularly and persistently talk and use language. If people throughout the country recognize and use *ain't* to mean *are/am not,* then books of grammar and dictionaries must *recognize* the occurrence of the form. Recognizing a certain linguistic form is not the same thing, however, as accepting it as correct in all contexts.

So usage—understood as determining when a particular form or word choice is accepted in a given situation—has become a regular part of writing instruction. Formal study of our language makes us more attuned to matters of context and appropriateness. *Ain't,* for example, may be used in spoken language in casual conversation, but it does not regularly appear in academic conversation or writing; similarly, the apostrophe in possessives is often missing in signs and advertisements (mens room; Kellys Restaurant), but the omission is considered an error in business and academic writing. Conventions and usages like these are what writers need to understand to avoid using forms out of context. If usage sounds suspiciously more a matter of social convention and style than stringent grammatical laws, you are right. Usages change more slowly than fashions, but they do simply reflect what most speakers, readers, and writers regard as acceptable.

Usage actually covers two different areas. First, it deals with functional varieties of the language—with slang, colloquialisms, and casual, formal, and informal styles. Almost any variety of English is acceptable in the appropriate context. Look at this passage from the opening of Mark Twain's *Huckleberry Finn:*

> You don't know about me without you have read a book by the name of *The Adventures of Tom Sawyer,* but that ain't no matter. That book was made by Mr. Mark Twain and he told the truth, mainly. There was things which he stretched, but mainly he told the truth. That is nothing. I never seen anybody but lied one time or another, without it was Aunt Polly or the widow, or maybe Mary. Aunt Polly—Tom's Aunt Polly, she is—and Mary and the Widow Douglas is all told about in that book, which is mostly a true book, with some stretchers as I said before.

No one would deny that Huck has used incorrect grammar and slang throughout this passage. Yet, many people consider this one of the greatest books in American literature. Why do we accept Huck's (or Twain's) incorrect grammar and usage? Because we recognize that Twain was manipulating language to make his readers see Huck as an uneducated, naive boy. In writing, then, the writer's purpose has much to do with determining what is acceptable and appropriate.

A second concern of usage is to explain why certain words are frequently misused. Similarities in spelling and meaning often lead to confusion of words like *affect* and *effect, allusion* and *illusion.* Usage also covers stubborn grammatical problems like the appropriate use of *who* and *whom.* Consequently, this chapter includes a list of words that present usage problems with explanations on how to handle those words correctly.

DIALECTAL VARIETIES OF ENGLISH

One problem that often falls under the heading of usage is the appropriateness of dialectal varieties of English. The problem is serious because of the social and political implications of saying that one dialect should be preferred to all others.

A dialect is a variety of a language spoken by a particular group of people bound by political, social, economic, professional, or geographic ties. Some of the most familiar dialects of English are Black English, Appalachian dialect, and Southern dialect. However, dialects of sorts also exist among professional and occupational groups, such as doctors, educators, lawyers, and construction workers; all have their own varieties of language characterized by words, ideas, and attitudes unfamiliar to people outside their group.

Dealing with dialectal varieties of English in the schools and in society is a problem because of the implication that certain dialects are "nonstandard" and therefore inappropriate for all situations. Many educators believe that it is the responsibility of the English teacher to eradicate nonstandard dialects and to teach all students to use standard English because it is understood by more people and is appropriate in a wider variety of situations. Unfortunately, no matter how noble the intentions of educators are, the implication that nonstandard dialects are inferior to standard English still remains.

One observation that might help reduce the problem created by dialectal varieties of English is the recognition that dialects represent oral language. Nonstandard dialects appear inferior when they are written because they reflect pronunciations and sentence patterns that are quite different from standard written English. Writing is an artificial form of communication because it represents an attempt to put speech on paper. Consequently, there are codes (rules) that apply to written language that don't apply to speech.

In writing, dialectal varieties are valuable in fulfilling the writer's purpose, as we have seen in Mark Twain's creation of Huck's character.

However, Twain's use of nonstandard dialect was conscious and deliberate. It is only when dialectal varieties are used in inappropriate contexts that they are considered wrong—but notice, it is the *use* of the dialect, not the *dialect itself,* that is inappropriate.

The failure to recognize the oral nature of dialects and the reluctance to admit that nonstandard dialects are appropriate in some situations have made the issue of nonstandard English a political and social problem. It won't be solved until more people—including politicians, educators, and citizens—understand that there are no absolutes in the use of language. Grammatical correctness and dialectal appropriateness are determined by the situation, and the situation includes such variables as context, the writer's intentions, and the makeup of the audience.

GLOSSARY OF USAGE

accept, except Easily confused because of similar spelling and pronunciation. *Accept* is a verb meaning *to receive.*

She was delighted to *accept* the award on her sister's behalf.

Except is a preposition meaning *with the exclusion of.* (*Except* can also be a verb meaning to leave out.)

Everyone wants dessert *except* me.

adapt, adopt Two distinct, different verbs. *Adapt* means *to change something to fit a new purpose.*

He *adapted* his beliefs about reincarnation to her religious beliefs.

Adopt means to *accept something as one's own without change.*

He *adopted* Mary's beliefs about life after death.

advice, advise Both refer to helping someone with a difficult decision or a problem. *Advice* is a noun.

His *advice* was to take the course now.

Advise is a verb.

He *advised* me to take the course now.

affect, effect Frequently confused because of similar spelling and meaning. *Affect* is a verb meaning *to influence.*

I'm not sure how this drug will *affect* you.

Effect is a noun meaning *a result.*

The most common *effect* is dizziness.

affective, effective Easily confused. *Affective* is a technical, psychological term for *emotional.*

> Educators claim that the *affective* domain influences a student's learning process.

Effective means *producing the intended result.*

> The drug was *effective* in getting rid of Pat's cold.

ain't Controversial. Generally considered nonstandard but used by many educated speakers in casual speech. Inappropriate in formal writing and in classroom writing, unless it is deliberately used to create a particular stylistic effect.

all ready, already *All ready* is an adjective phrase meaning *everything is ready.*

> We were *all ready* to go on the trip when we discovered it was snowing.

Already is an adverb meaning *by this time* or *prior to some designated time:*

> Have you done your assignment *already?*

all right, alright Should be two words. The one-word form is incorrect.

allusion, illusion Frequently confused and misused.
Allusion is a reference.

> It is frustrating to read something filled with *allusions* that I don't recognize.

Illusion is a deceptive impression.

> He had the *illusion* that no studying was required.

alot should be two words—*a lot.* Colloquial; should be avoided in formal and classroom writing.

among, between *Among* refers to at least three items.

> The new teacher had expected to find more than ten enthusiastic writers *among* all five of her classes.

Between refers to two items.

> She couldn't decide *between* her new red dress and her favorite blue dress.

amount, number Frequently misused. *Amount* refers to a total quantity not considered in units.

The *amount* of homework I have each night is increasing.

Number is used with enumerated, countable items.

The *number* of assignments in my English class is more than I expected.

as, like *As* is a conjunction, so it should introduce a clause.

She didn't clean up her room *as* I asked her to.

Like is a preposition.

I want a pair of jeans *like* Ernestine's.

bad, badly Frequently misused. *Bad* is an adjective, *badly* an adverb.

Avoid: I feel *badly* about forgetting to call you.
Write: I feel *bad* about forgetting to call you.
Or: He performed *badly* in his recital.

being as, being that Colloquial expressions; use *because* or *since* instead.

Avoid: *Being as* I may be late. . . .
Write: *Since* I may be late. . . .

beside, besides Both are prepositions. *Beside* means at the side of.

He sat down *beside* her.

Besides means in addition.

He doesn't have much to do tonight *besides* his homework.

but that, but what Colloquial expressions that should be avoided in writing. They are redundant; use *that* alone.

Avoid: There is no question *but that* he'll go.
Write: There is no question *that* he'll go.

can, may *Can* expresses ability or power.

They *can* finish tonight if they hurry.

May refers to permission, opportunity, or willingness.

They *may* not be able to finish that tonight.

can't help but Colloquial expression acceptable in speech but not in writing.

> Avoid: I *can't help but* worry about him.
> Write: I *can't help* worrying about him.

cite, sight, site Easy to confuse in meaning and spelling. *Cite* means to quote as an authority or example.

> She *cited* Professor Green's book as the source of her ideas.

Site refers to a building or a piece of land.

> Construction *sites* usually detract from the attractiveness of the surrounding area.

Sight refers to landmarks or things to see.

> Did you see all the *sights* in London?

continual, continuous *Continual* means recurring at intervals.

> We've been unable to have our picnic because of the *continual* rain this summer.
>
> *Continuous* means uninterrupted.
>
> This afternoon it rained *continuously* for two hours.

convince, persuade *Convince* means to win agreement.

> I *convinced* John that the movie was worth watching.

Persuade means to move to action.

> I *persuaded* John to go see the movie with me.

could of Incorrect form that shows interference from speech.

> Avoid: Sheryl *could of* called last night if she had known you were here.
> Write: Sheryl *could have* called last night if she had known you were here.

device, devise *Device* is a noun.

> This *device* is supposed to cut down the phone bill.

Devise is a verb.

> I must *devise* a way of getting out of here by midnight.

different from, different than The correct grammatical form is *different from,* but *different than* is appropriate in some cases.

These jeans are *different from* the ones I ordered.
It tasted *different than* I had expected.

enthuse, enthused Back formation from *enthusiastic.* Widely used, but many grammarians and English teachers still object that it is colloquial.

farther, further *Farther* is an adverb referring to literal distance.

We hadn't driven to the cabin in years. Today it seemed *farther* out of town than it did when I was a child.

Further refers to distance only figuratively.

They had discussed the problem in two four-hour meetings. *Further* discussion was postponed to give the committee a chance to rest.

fewer, less *Fewer* is used in comparing quantities that can be counted separately.

I have *fewer* clothes than she has.

Less is used in comparisons involving amounts or quantities that aren't enumerated.

The Joneses make *less* money than we do.

good, well Ordinarily, *good* is an adjective.

This pie tastes *good.*

And *well* is an adverb.

He did the work *well.*

But the words are interchangeable when they refer to the state of one's health.

Aren't you feeling *good?*

Aren't you feeling *well?*

hopefully A sentence adverb used much as *fortunately* is used.

Fortunately, the war ended before too much destruction occurred.

Hopefully, the war will end before many lives are lost.

However, many object that *hopefully* means "I hope that" or "It is hoped that," and they argue that those phrases should be used instead of the adverb. Its use is widespread, although it should probably be restricted to speech and informal writing.

imply, infer Confused frequently because both deal with judgments about what others say. *Imply* refers to what a statement means.

> Your criticism *implies* that the book is not worth reading.

Infer means to take an implication; it refers to a judgment made by a speaker or a listener.

> From your criticism, I *infer* that it would be a waste of time to read that book.

irregardless Common in speech, but a nonstandard variant of *regardless.* Logically, the two negative affixes—*ir-* and *-less*—should not occur in one word.

its, it's *Its,* the possessive pronoun, requires no apostrophe. *It's,* a contraction for *it is,* requires an apostrophe.

lend, loan Purists and traditionalists frown on using *loan* as a verb, but it is used frequently in speech.

> Would you *loan* me a quarter?

In writing, use *lend.*

> Would you *lend* me a quarter?

lie, lay Verbs related in meaning; frequently confused because of an overlap in their principal parts: *Lie* is an intransitive verb meaning to recline; *lay* is a transitive verb meaning *to place* or *set down.* They share the same form for the past principal part of *lie* and the present of *lay.*

Present	*Past*	*Perfect*
lie	lay	lain
lay	laid	laid

Use them in the following senses.

> I want to *lie* down when I get home.
>
> Yesterday, I *lay* in bed until 9 o'clock.
>
> I haven't *lain* in bed that late for a long time.
>
> Please *lay* the book on the table carefully.
>
> Yesterday, you *laid* it on the edge and it fell off.
>
> I should have *laid* it down myself.

loose, lose These two words are often confused because of their similar spelling. *Loose* is an adjective meaning unrestrained or a verb meaning to unfasten.

> My bicycle chain is *loose.*

Lose is a verb meaning to misplace.

If I don't tighten it, I'll probably *lose* it.

lots, lots of Colloquial expression that should be avoided in writing.

may be, maybe *May be* is a verb form: an auxiliary + verb *be*.

We *may be* going to New York soon.

Maybe is an adverb.

Maybe he's going sooner than he thinks.

myself Should be used only as a reflexive pronoun, never as a substitute for *I* or *me*.

Avoid: If you want a ride, call either Gabriel or *myself*.
Write: If you want a ride, call either Gabriel or *me*.

prejudice, prejudiced Use these words carefully. If you use it as a participle, make sure the *d* appears.

The defendant feared the jury would be *prejudiced* against him.

principal, principle Homophones that frequently are confused. As a noun, *principal* means a leader or chief or head.

His *principal* was pleased with the drama coach's choice.

As an adjective, it means *main*.

My brother, Frank, will play the *principal* character in the school play.

Principle is a noun that means theory, concept, or rule.

The law of diminishing utility is one of the *principles* you study in an economics class.

proved, proven Commonly used interchangeably as the past participle and perfect forms of *prove*.

After working five hours, he has finally *proved* his algebra problem.

Proven may be used as an adjective (past participle) but not as the perfect form. The correct perfect form is *proved*.

My grandmother claims this is a *proven* remedy for colds. [proved would be inappropriate here]

raise, rise *Raise* is a transitive verb meaning to lift up.

He *raised* the box above his head.

Rise is intransitive and means to get or go up.

I saw it *rise* above his head.

real, really Common in colloquial speech, but should be avoided in writing when used as intensifiers. *Real* may be used in formal writing to mean *actual* or *true*.

sensual, sensuous Frequently confused. *Sensual* means *carnal,* or having to do with sex, as in *sensual thrill*.

Sensual feelings appear without our permission.

Sensuous refers to the senses.

The baby, Sarah, was delighted by *sensuous* impressions.

set, sit Verbs that are sometimes confused. *Set* is transitive and means to put something down.

Set the book on the table.

Sit is intransitive and means to occupy a place by sitting.

He invited me to *sit* by him.

shall, will Many people still claim that *shall* is the only correct form to use with the first-person pronoun.

I shall go to town tomorrow.

However, it sounds formal, and it bears connotations of commands or prophecy.

Thou *shalt* not steal.

I *shall* return.

Will is appropriate in most contexts. However, in questions, *shall* can be used without too much formality.

Shall I join you?

should of Incorrect form due to interference from speech. The correct form is *should have*.

unique Means one of a kind but is frequently used in the sense of "unusual" or "rare."

Going to Europe was a *unique* experience.

The objection to the use of *unique* is that its "original" meaning has been lost or obscured through overuse.

used to Be sure the *d* is there. Since *d* and *t* merge when you use the phrase in speech, it's easy to forget that *used* is a past participle or a past form and must end in *d*.

He *used to* run four miles every day.

He is not *used to* getting up so early.

who, which, that Relative pronouns that are frequently used interchangeably. *Which* and *that* should refer to inanimate or animate, nonhuman objects; *who* should be used when referring to persons.

who, whom Relative pronouns frequently used interchangeably. *Who* should be used when the relative pronoun is the subject of the clause, *whom* when it is the object.

the young man *who* will marry my sister

the young man *whom* my sister will marry

would of Incorrect form that reveals interference from speech. The correct form is *would have*.

Index

Abbreviations, 601–2
Abstract, in scientific writing, 527–28
Abstract language, 448–49
Abstract nouns, 441, 543
Accept/except, 610
Active voice, 555–56
  use of, 440
Adapt/adopt, 610
Adjectives, 141, 558–60
  comparison of, 559
  infinitives used as, 557
  in how-to essay, 141
  predicate, 558
Adopt/adapt, 610
Adverbs, 141, 560–62
  conjunctive, 566
  infinitives used as, 557
  in how-to essay, 141
Advice/advise, 79, 610
Aesop, 517
Affect/effect, 79, 610
Affective/effective, 611
Agreement, between subject and verb, 582–85
Ain't, 611
Alliteration, 519
All ready/already, 611
Allusion/illusion, 611
Almanacs, 228–29
Alot, 611
Already/all ready, 611
American Chemical Society, documentation style for, 532
American Institute of Physics, documentation style for, 533
American Mathematical Society, documentation style for, 532
American National Standards Institute, 528
Among/between, 611
Amount/number, 612
Analogy, 355
  in evaluation essay, 197, 198
Analysis
  in assertion-with-evidence essay, 182
  in break-down organization, 353
  in cubing, 315
  in persuasion essay, 212
  in problem-solution essay, 153
  in topic sentence paragraphs, 403–4
Angell, Roger, 516
Antagonist, 512
Anthology, 516
APA style
  for books, 292–94
  for doctoral dissertation, 296
  for incorporating documented materials, 272–73
  for long quotations, 274
  for master's thesis, 296
  for nonprint media, 296–97
  for parenthetical references, 269
  for periodicals, 294–95
  for professional meeting papers, 296
  for reports, 295–96
  for reviews, 296
Apostrophe, 587–88, 604
Appearance, of business letter, 475
Application, in cubing, 315
Arden, Harvey, 387, 417–18
Argumentation, 315
As/like, 612
Assertion, in thesis, 44–45
Assertion-with-evidence essay, 92, 176–89
  audience for, 179–80
  completing stage of, 185–87
  creating stage of, 179
  delivery in, 180
  editing, 187
  example of, 187–89
  organization in, 180–82
  paragraphs in, 185–86
  peer-editing in, 182–85
  promise in, 180

Assertion-with-evidence essay (*continued*)
  reasons for writing, 176–77
  sentences in, 186
  shaping/drafting stage of, 179–82
  thesis in, 180
  words in, 187
Association, in cubing, 315
Assonance, 519
Atlases, 228–29
Attribution, 275–76
Audience
  in assertion-with-evidence essay, 179–80
  in business letter, 474–75
  and choice of English, 10
  in essay examination, 457
  in evaluation essay, 195–96
  in how-to essay, 136–37
  identifying, 35–36
  importance of, in writing, 308–9
  in information essay, 164
  involving, 41
  in job application letter, 490
  in literary essay, 508–10
  in personal experience essay, 114
  in personal perspective essay, 126
  in persuasion essay, 209–11
  in problem-solution essay, 150–51
Author, attitude of, 514
Author card, 227
Auxiliary verbs, 550–52, 570

Bad/badly, 612
Balance and repetition
  in evaluation essay, 203
  in personal experience essay, 120
  in personal perspective essay, 130
  in problem-solution essay, 156–57
Basic terms, glossary of, 569–70
Bate, Walter Jackson, 61
Bean, L. L., Catalog Company, 478–79
Being as/being that, 612
Beside/besides, 612
Between/among, 611
Bibliographies, 229–30
Bierce, Ambrose, 521, 522–24
Biographical references, 229
Block quotations, 274–75
Body of letter, 477
Boettinger, Henry, 440
Booklists, 230–31
Bracket, 588
Brainstorming, 15–16, 28
  in essay examinations, 456
  in persuasion essay, 209
  in problem-solution essay, 149
Break-down order, 353–54
Bureaucratic phrases, eliminating, 69
Burke, Billie, 302
Business Index, The, 228
Business letter, 472–88
  appearance of, 475
  audience for, 474–75
  elements of, 472–78
  format of, 475–78
  kinds of, 478–84
  listing in, 472–73
  organization of, 472–73
  purpose of, 472
  reporter's formula in, 473
  request letters, 479–81
  response letters, 482–84
  style of, 474–75
  tone of, 472
  "you" attitude in, 478–79, 500
Business writing, expressions to avoid, 474
But that/but what, 612

Can/may, 612
Cannel, Ward, 380
Can't help but, 613
Capitalization, 600–601
Card catalog
  author card, 227
  subject card, 226–27
  title card, 228
Caspel, Venita Van, 379
Cather, Willa, 104
Cause and effect, 349–50
  in persuasion essay, 212
  in problem-solution essay, 152
Celebrity endorsements, 271
Center of gravity sentences, 21
Chaining, 18–20, 28
  in how-to essay, 135
Chaix, Marie, 104
Character conflict, organization by, 515
Characterization, 512
Characters, 512–13
Chronological organization, 116
Churchill, Winston, 428
Cicero, 327
Circumlocutions, avoiding, 69, 71

Circumstance
  in writing to change, 94
  in writing to express, 89
  in writing to tell, 91
Cite/sight/site, 613
Clarity, of thesis, 46–47
Clark, Walter, 102
Classical invention, 325–29
  circumstance, 326, 329
  comparison, 325, 326, 328
  definition, 325, 326, 328
  in evaluation essay, 195
  example of, 330–36
  guides for, 326
  in information essay, 163–64
  in persuasion essay, 209
  relationship, 326, 328
  testimony, 326, 327, 329
Classification, 353
Clause, 569
  dependent, 568, 569
  independent, 568, 569
  subordinate, 426, 565, 569
Clichés, 131, 451
Climax, 512
Close reading, literary response as, 510
Colon, 78, 588–89
Comma, 78, 589–90
Comma splices, 570–72
Common nouns, 542
Communication models
  transformation, 32–33
  transmission, 32
Comparison
  of adjectives, 559
  in cubing, 315
Comparison/contrast
  in evaluation essay, 197
  in persuasion essay, 212
  in relationship order, 354–55
  in topic sentence paragraphs, 405
Complement, 554, 570
Complete predicate, 570
Completing stage, 2, 7, 53–82. *See also* Editing; Revising; Proofreading
  in assertion-with-evidence essay, 185–87
  editing in, 72–80
  in essay examination, 459–62
  in evaluation essay, 202–3
  finishing in, 80–82
  in how-to essay, 141–42
  in information essay, 169–72
  in job application letter, 500–501
  paragraphing for flow in, 415–17
  in personal experience essay, 118–20
  in personal perspective essay, 130–31
  in persuasion essay, 216–17
  in problem-solution essay, 156–57
  proofreading in, 82–83
  revising in, 54–72
  in scientific writing, 529–33
Complex sentence, 567
Complication, 512
Complimentary close, 477
Compound sentence, 567
Computer-printed paper, 81–82
Concrete language, 448–49
Concrete nouns, 543
Concrete words, replacing vague words with, 66–67
Conflict, 512, 515
Confrontation, 515
Conjunctions, 564–66
  coordinating, 425, 564–65
  correlative, 565
  subordinating, 426, 565, 569
Conjunctive adverb, 566
Connotation, 442–44
Consistency, in how-to essay, 142
Consonance, 519
Content notes, 268, 269–70
Continual/continuous, 613
Contractions, 130
Convince/persuade, 613
Coordinate clauses, 130
Coordinating conjunctions, 425, 564–65
Coordination
  in assertion-with-evidence essay, 186
  in how-to-essay, 142
  in personal experience essay, 120
  in problem-solution essay, 156
  of sentences, 423–26
Correlative conjunctions, 565
Could of, 613
Council of Biology Editors, documentation style for, 532
Creating stage, 5, 12–45
  in assertion-with-evidence essay, 179

Creating stage (*continued*)
  characteristics of, 5–6
  definition of, 5
  in essay examination, 455–56
  in evaluation essay, 193–95
  in how-to essay, 135–36
  in information essay, 163–64
  in job application letter, 490–93
  in personal experience essay, 113–14
  in personal perspective essay, 125
  in persuasion essay, 208–9
  in problem-solution essay, 148–50
  and procrastination, 8
  in scientific writing, 525–26
Creating techniques, 14
  brainstorming, 15–16, 28, 149, 209, 456
  chaining, 18–20, 28, 135
  classical invention, 163–64, 209, 195, 325–36, 344
  cubing, 125, 150, 179, 209, 315–19, 344, 491
  for job application letter, 490–93
  list-making, 16–18, 28, 113, 135, 193, 194, 456, 472–73, 490–91, 492
  looping, 20–27, 28, 113, 125, 135, 149, 163, 179, 194, 209, 491–92
  noticing inside purpose, 337–39, 344
  reading and researching, 39–41, 163, 179, 209, 345, 525–26
  reporter's formula, 14–15, 28, 113–14, 149–50, 163, 456, 473
  track switching, 135, 150, 179, 195, 319–24, 344
Critical paper, 511
Cubing, 315
  in assertion-with-evidence essay,179
  example of, 316–19
  guides for, 315–16
  in job application letter, 491
  in personal perspective essay, 125
  in persuasion essay, 209
  in problem-solution essay, 150

D'Angelo, Frank, 325
D'Angelo, Gary, 55–57
Dash, 78, 590
Debased verbs, 70
Deduction
  in assertion-with-evidence essay, 181
  in general-specific order, 352
  in persuasion essay, 212
  in problem-solution essay, 153
Definition
  in general-specific order, 351
  in topic sentence paragraphs, 403
Delivery
  in assertion-with-evidence essay, 180
  in evaluation essay, 196–97
  in how-to essay, 137
  in information essay, 164–65
  in personal experience essay, 115
  in personal perspective essay, 126
  in persuasion essay, 211
  in problem-solution essay, 151
Demonstrative pronouns, 547–48
Denotation, 442–44
Denouement, 512
Dependent clause, 568, 569
Description
  in cubing, 315
  in discovery draft, 39
  in spatial order, 350–51
  in topic sentence paragraphs, 402–3
Descriptive words, placement of, 64–65
Details
  adding, to sentences, 64
  in topic sentence paragraphs, 401–2
Device/devise, 613
DeVries, Peter, 8
Dialectal varieties, of English, 609–10
Dickens, Charles, 436–37
Dickinson, Emily, 517
Diction
  avoiding trite, 451
  level of, 518
Dictionary, 79, 231
Different from/different than, 614
Direct object, 554
Direct quotations, documenting, 266
Discovery draft, 39–43
  expanding into working draft, 247–48
  for research paper, 244–45
  writing technique for, 39–43
Documentation of sources. *See also* APA style; MLA style
  guides to, 532–33
  in research paper, 265–67
Dylan, Bob, 266

Edited American English, 10
Editing, 7. *See also* Completing stage; Peer-editing
  in assertion-with-evidence essay,187
  in evaluation essay, 203
  find-the-errors step in, 77–80
  get distance step in, 75–77
  in how-to essay, 142
  in information essay, 172
  in personal experience essay, 120
  in personal perspective essay, 131
  in problem-solution essay, 157
  and procrastination, 8
  read aloud step in, 77
  reasons for, 72–74
  in research paper, 248–50
  techniques in, 74–75
Effect/affect, 79
Effective/affective, 611
Elbow, Peter, 20
Ellipses, 590–91
Emerson, Ralph Waldo, 39
Emphasis
  in writing to change, 93
  in writing to express, 88
  in writing to tell, 90
Encyclopedias, 231–32
English language
  history of, 439
  varieties of, 10, 609–10
Enthuse/enthused, 614
Essay, 5–11
  approach of, 6
  assertion-with-evidence, 176–89
  audience for, 6
  beginning of, 40
  completing stage of, 7
  creating stage of, 5
  end of, 40–41
  evaluation, 190–205
  foundation of, 6
  information, 160–75
  middle of, 40
  personal experience, 111–22
  personal perspective, 123–32, 176
  persuasion, 206–18
  problem-solution, 145–59
  purpose of, 6
  shaping stage of, 6
  structure of, 6, 40–41
Essay examination, 453–466
  adding new material to answer, 458–59
  appearance of, 461–62
  audience for, 457
  completing stage of, 459–62
  creating stage of, 455–56
  form for, 458–59
  hints for surviving, 455
  purpose of, 454–55
  shaping stage of, 457–59
  thesis in, 457–58
  tips for taking, 454–55
Essay writing, comparison of, and journal writing, 109–10
Evaluation essay, 92, 190–205
  audience in, 195–96
  completing stage of, 202–3
  creating stage of, 193–95
  delivery in, 196–97
  editing of, 203
  example of, 203–5
  organization in, 197–98
  paragraphs in, 202
  peer-editing in, 198–202
  promise in, 196–97
  reasons for writing, 190–91
  sentences in, 202–3
  shaping/drafting stage of, 195–98
  thesis in, 196–97
  words in, 203
Everett, Edward, 428
Examples
  in assertion-with-evidence essay, 182
  in break-down order, 354
  in topic sentence paragraphs, 401–2
Except/accept, 610
Exclamation point, 591
Explanation, in topic sentence paragraphs, 403–4
Explication, 510
Exploratory writing, 13–14
Exposition, 511–12
External check, and promise and delivery, 362, 375–78
External standards, 193, 195

Fabun, Don, 61, 62
Facts and figures, in topic sentence paragraphs, 404
Farther/further, 614
Faulty modification, 580–81
Faulty predication, 578–79
Fewer/less, 79, 614
Find-the-errors step, 77–80

First person point of view, 116, 130, 513
Flashback technique, 116
Form. *See* Organizational patterns
Format
  of business letter, 475–78
  incorporating documented material into, 270–75
Foucalt, Michel, 101
Fragments, 575–77
Frye, Northrop, 21
Full block letter, 475
Function paragraphs, 385–86, 408–14
  definition of, 408
  in information essay, 169
  in personal experience essay, 119
  in persuasion essay, 216
Further/farther, 614

General-specific order, 351–52
Gerund, 557
Get distance step, 75–77
Glossary, of usage, 607–18
Good/well, 614
Grammar, 607
Gross, Theodore, 63

Habits, 8
Handwritten paper, 80–81
Harnetz, Aljean, 302–3
Harrison, George, 297
Heading, 477
Helping verbs, 550–52
Hemingway, Ernest, 519
hopefully, 614
How-to essay, 90
  audience for, 136–37
  completing stage of, 141–42
  creating stage of, 135–36
  delivery in, 137, editing in, 142
  example of, 142–44
  organization in, 137–38
  paragraphs in, 141
  peer-editing in, 138–40
  promise in, 137
  reasons for writing, 133–34
  sentences in, 141–42
  shaping/drafting of, 136–38
  thesis in, 137
  words in, 142
  writing, 135–44
Hughes, Richard, 104–5
Hyphen, 604–5

Idea, 37, 39
Illustrations, in topic sentence paragraphs, 401–2
Images, 516–17
Imply/infer, 615
Incident, organization by, 515
Inconsistencies, 79
Indefinite pronouns, 548
Independent clause, 568, 569
Indexes, 232–33
Indirect object, 554
Induction
  in assertion-with-evidence essay, 181–82
  in general-specific order, 351, 352
  in persuasion essay, 212
  in problem-solution essay, 153
  in scientific paper, 526
Infer/imply, 615
Infinitive, 557
Information essay, 90, 160–75
  audience for, 164
  completing stage of, 169–72
  creating stage, 163–64
  delivery in, 164–65
  editing, 172
  example of, 172–75
  organization in, 165
  paragraphs in, 169–70
  peer-editing in, 165–68
  promise in, 164–65
  reasons for writing, 160–61
  sentences in, 170
  shaping/drafting stage of, 164
  thesis in, 164–65
  words in, 171–72
Info Tech, 228
Inside address, 477
Intensifiers, 562
Interjections, 566
Internal check, and promise and delivery, 362–75, 378
Internal standards, 193–94, 195
International Steering Committee of Medical Editors, documentation style for, 533
Interrogative pronouns, 548
Intransitive verbs, 553
Invention, 14. *See also* Creating stage
Irmscher, William, 9
irregardless, 615
Isaacson, Walter, 299
Italics, 603
It's/its, 79, 615

Jackson, Shirley, 517
Jacobi, Ernst, 67
Jagger, Mick, 297
Jargon, stereotyped, 69
Job application letter. *See also* Résumé
  audience for, 490
  completing stage of, 500–501
  creating stage of, 490–93
  message of, 489
  purpose of, 490
Jones, Rick, 380
Joseph, Chief, 61
Journal attitude, 110
Journal writing, 95–110
  comparison of, and essay writing, 109–10
  to collect things, 101–2
  to give meaning to events, 107–8
  to imitate good writing, 103–4
  to keep record, 96
  to sharpen powers of observation, 98

Kelly, James B., 299
Kennedy, John F., 217
Kettering, Charles, 340
Key words
  as reminder signs, 58, 60
  as transitions, 55
King, Martin Luther, 216
Kinneavy, James, 442

Lab report, 526–27
Lahr, John, 303
Language
  abstract, 448–49
  concrete, 448–49
  consistency in, 248–50
  in literary essay, 515–17
  in scientific writing, 530–31
Lay/lie, 615
Lend/loan, 615
LeRoy, Mervyn, 303
Less/fewer, 79, 614
Library
  card catalog in, 226–28
  reference material in, 228–39
Library guides, 229–30
Library of Congress, 226
Lie/lay, 615
Like/as, 612
Lincoln, Abraham, 217, 428
Linguistic Society of America, documentation style for, 532
Linking verb, 554
Listing, 16–18, 28
  in business letter, 472–73
  in essay examinations, 456
  in evaluation essay, 193, 194
  in how-to essay, 135
  in job application letter, 490–91, 492
  in personal experience essay, 113
  in personal perspective essay, 125
List of Works Cited, 270
Literary criticism, 511
Literary essay
  audience for, 508–10
  characters in, 512–13
  example of, 522–24
  language in, 515–17
  plot in, 511–12
  point of view in, 513–14
  purpose of, 508–10
  setting in, 513
  strategy for, 510–11
  structure in, 514–15
  style of, 518–19
  terms used in, 511–19
  theme in, 517–18
Loan/lend, 615
Looping, 20–23, 28, 114
  in assertion-with-evidence essay, 179
  in evaluation essay, 194
  in how-to essay, 135
  in information essay, 163
  in job application letter, 491–92
  in personal experience essay, 113
  in personal perspective essay, 125
  in persuasion essay, 209
  in problem-solution essay, 149
  student example of, 24–27
Loose/lose, 615–16
Lots/lots of, 616

Maclean, Norman, 106
Main verb, 570
Make-it-look-good step
  computer-printed paper, 81–82
  handwritten paper, 80–81
  manuscript form, 80–82
  proofread step, 82–83
  typewritten paper, 81
Mander, Jerry, 396, 414
Mann, Peggy, 395
Manuscript form. *See* Editing
Marginal notes, making, in editing, 76

Problem-solution essay (*continued*)
creating stage of, 148–50
delivery in, 151
editing in, 157
example of, 157–59
organization in, 151–53
paragraphs in, 156
peer-editing in, 153–56
promise in, 151
reasons for writing, 145–46
sentences in, 156–57
shaping/drafting stage of, 150–53
thesis in, 151
words in, 157
Process, 348–49
Procrastination, 8
Promise
in assertion-with-evidence essay, 180
in evaluation essay, 196–97
in how-to essay, 137
in information essay, 164–65
in personal experience essay, 115
in personal perspective essay, 126
in persuasion essay, 211
in problem-solution essay, 151
Promise and delivery
external check, 362, 375–78
internal check, 362–75, 378
Pronouns, 545–49
demonstrative, 547–48
indefinite, 548
interrogative, 548
personal, 546
possessive, 546
reflexive, 546–47
relative, 547
Proofreaders' marks, 83
Proofreading, 82–83. *See also* Completing stage of research paper, 250
Proper nouns, 542
Protagonist, 512
Proved/proven, 616
Psychological message, in problem-solution essay, 157
Punctuation. *See also* Specific marks of
elements of, 587–94
errors/omissions, 77
inaccurate use of, 78
Punning, 517
Purpose, 39
of business letter, 472
of job application letter, 490
of literary essay, 508–10
in writing to change, 93
in writing to tell, 90

Question mark, 592
Quintilian, 60
Quotation marks, 592–93, 605–6
Quotations, for research paper, 274–75

Raise/rise, 616–17
Read aloud step, 77
Reader. See also Audience
giving information to, 141, 401–6
importance of thesis to, 47
Reading and researching, 339–41, 345
in assertion-with-evidence essay, 179
best uses for, 341
guides for, 340
in information essay, 163
in persuasion essay, 209
in scientific writing, 525–26
Real/really, 617
Recursive, process of composing as, 52
Redundancies, 67
References
APA style, 271–73
MLA style, 271–72
placement of, 271–73
Reflexive pronouns, 546–47
Relationship, 212
Relationship order, 354–55
Relative pronouns, 547
Reminder signs, 54, 58–60, 186, 202
Repetition, 429–32. *See also* Balance and repetition
in persuasion essay, 217
in topic sentence paragraphs, 404–5
Reporter's formula, 14–15, 28
in business letter, 473
in essay examinations, 456
in information essay, 163
in personal experience essay, 113–14
in problem-solution essay, 149–50
Request letters, 479–81
Research. *See* Reading and researching
Research paper, 219–303
APA documentation style for, 292–97
attribution, 275–76
conducting research for, 222
determining thesis for, 245

discovery draft, 244–45
documentation of sources, 265–67
example of, 250–64
finding and evaluating, 238–39
incorporating documented material into format of, 270–75
list of works cited, 270
MLA documentation style for, 276–92
note taking, 239–41
parenthetical references in, 268–69
plagiarism, 297–301
strategic approach to writing, 243–50
use of library for, 225–39
use of quotations in, 274–75
using sources in, 265–67
where to put reference, 271–73
Research process, 222–25
Research report, 93
Response letter, 482–84
Résumé, 502–7. *See also* Job application letter
Review, in scientific writing, 528–29
Revising, 7, 54. *See also* Completing stage
for flow, 54–60
for punch, 66–71
Rhythm
in evaluation essay, 203
in personal experience essay, 120
in personal perspective essay, 130
in persuasion essay, 217
Rise/raise, 616–617
Rogers, Carl, 379–80
Run-on sentences, 79, 573–74

Salutation, 477
Sassoon, Beverly, 59
Sassoon, Vidal, 59
Schell, Jonathan, 298
Scientific paper, 526–27
Scientific writing, 525–36
abstract in, 527–28
completing stage of, 529–33
creating stage of, 525–26
documentation for, 532–33
example of, 533–36
review in, 528–29
shaping stage of, 526–29
Semicolons, 78, 593–94
Sensual/sensuous, 617
Sentence(s), 567–70
adding details to, 64
in assertion-with-evidence essay, 186
avoiding passive voice in, 432–33
center of gravity, 21
combining choppy, 62–64
complex, 567
compound, 567
coordination, 423–26
in evaluation essay, 202–3
expanding, 420–21
in how-to essay, 141–42
in information essay, 170
parallelism in, 427–29
in personal experience essay,119–20
in personal perspective essay, 130
in persuasion essay, 217
in problem-solution essay, 156–57
and repetition and rhythm, 429–32
revising, for energy, 62–65
run-on, 79, 573–74
subordination, 424, 426
varying, 419–22
Sentence combining, 130, 186
Sentence errors, 569–85
Sentence fragments, 79
Sentence modifier, 561
Set/sit, 617
Setting, 513
Shall/will, 617
Shaping/drafting, 2, 6, 30–31
in assertion-with-evidence essay, 179–82
audience in, 35–36
discovery draft, 39–43
in essay examination, 457–59
in evaluation essay, 195–98
in how-to essay, 136–38
ideas in, 36–37
in information essay, 164
in job application letter, 493–99
preliminary agreements, 31–34, 35–37
in personal experience essay, 114
in personal perspective essay, 126–27
in persuasion essay, 209–13
in problem-solution essay, 150–53
purpose in, 32–33
in scientific writing, 526–29
thesis in, 43
Shelton, Mark, 380–81
Shirley, Dame, 106
Should of, 617
Sic, 274

Sight/site/cite, 613
Signature, 478
Simile, 515
Simple predicate, 570
Singer, June Flaum, 73
Sit/set, 617
Site/cite/sight, 613
Situation
  in writing to change, 94
  in writing to express, 89
  in writing to tell, 91
Slash, 594
Smith, Frank, 440–41
Sorensen, Theodore, 430
Sources
  finding and evaluating, 238–39
  in research paper, 265–67
Space, organization by, 515
Spatial order, 350–51
Spelling, 595–99
Stafford, William, 96
Standard American English, 10
Standards of evaluation, 193–96
Steward, John, 55–57
Strategy, for literary essay, 510–11
Structure, 514–15
Style, 438, 518–19
  avoiding trite diction, 451
  of business letter, 474–75
  concrete and abstract language, 448–49
  connotation, 442–44
  denotation, 442–44
  levels of, 438–41
Subject, 570
  agreement with verb, 582–85
Subject card, 226–27
Subject-verb-complement (S-V-C) combinations, 553–54
Subordinate clause, 130, 569
Subordinate conjunctions, 426, 565, 569
Subordination
  in assertion-with-evidence essay, 186
  in how-to essay, 142
  in personal experience essay, 120
  in problem-solution essay, 156
  in sentences, 424, 426
Symbolic writing, 516
Symbols, 516, 602
Synthesized information, documenting, 266–67
Taboos, 8–10
Tenses, need for consistency in, 80
Texts, definition of, 2
That/who/which, 618
Theme, 517–18
Thesaurus, 79
Thesis, 43–48
  assertion in, 44–45
  in assertion-with-evidence essay, 180
  clarity of, 46–47
  determining, for research paper, 245
  distinction between topic and, 43
  in essay examination, 457–58
  in evaluation essay, 196–97
  in how-to essay, 137
  importance of, to reader, 47
  in information essay, 164–65
  organizing, 51–52
  in personal experience essay, 115
  in personal perspective essay, 126
  in persuasion essay, 211
  in problem-solution essay, 151
  technique for writing good, 43–48
  writer as insider in, 45
Third person point of view, 130, 441, 514
Thoreau, 98, 107
Time, organization by, 514–15
Time order, 348–50
Time value, in writing to change, 94
Title card, 228
Tone, of business letter, 472
Too/two/to, 79
Topic, distinction between thesis and, 43
Topic sentence, placement of, in topic sentence paragraph, 392–95
Topic sentence paragraph, 169, 385, 386–88, 389–91, 392–95, 397–98, 400–406
  analysis in, 403–4
  comparison and contrast in, 405
  definition in, 403
  description in, 402–3
  details in, 401–2
  examples in, 401–2
  explanation in, 403–4
  facts and figures in, 404
  giving reader enough information in, 400–406
  illustrations in, 401–6

narrative, 405–6
placement of topic sentence in, 392–95
relationship between topic sentence and other sentences, in, 397–98
repetition in, 404–5
topic sentence in, 389–91
in writing information essay, 169
To/too/two, 79
Track switching, 319–21
in assertion-with-evidence essay, 179
in evaluation essay, 195
example of, 321–24
guides for, 320–21
in how-to essay, 135
in problem-solution essay, 150
Transformation model, 32–33
Transition paragraph, 415
Transitions, 54, 55, 58, 170, 186, 202
Transition signal words, 59
Transitive verbs, 553–54
Transmission model, 32
Trevelyan, G. M., 58
Twain, Mark, 509, 519
Two/to/too, 79
Typewritten paper, 81
Typos, 77

Unique, 617
United States Geological Survey, documentation style for, 532
Usage
concept of correct, 607–9
glossary of, 610–18
Used to, 618

Vague words, replacing with concrete words, 66–67
Verbals, 556–57
Verb particles, 564
Verbs, 549–52
agreement with subject, 582–85
auxiliary/helping, 550–52
intransitive, 553
linking, 554
transitive, 553–54
using action, 68–69
using vitiated, 70
Virgule, 594
Viscott, David, 414–15
Visuals, in scientific writing, 527
Vitiated verbs, 70

Well/good, 614
Which/that/who, 618
White, E. B., 397, 430–31, 445–46, 448
White, Vickie, 380
Who/which/that, 618
Who/whom, 618
Will/shall, 617
Wordplay, 517
Words
in assertion-with-evidence essay, 187
avoiding circumlocutions, 69, 71
avoiding redundancies, 67
commonly confused, 79
connotation of, 442–44
denotation of, 442–44
eliminating unnecessary, 68
in evaluation essay, 203
in how-to essay, 142
in information essay, 171–72
in personal experience essay, 120
in personal perspective essay, 131, 171–72
in persuasion essay, 217
placement of descriptive, 64–65
in problem-solution essay, 157
replacing vague with concrete, 66–67
using action verbs, 68–69
Working draft
expanding discovery draft into, 247–48
revising, 248
Works cited, 268
list of, 276–77
Would of, 618
Writer, as insider, 45
Writer-reader relationship
in writing to change, 94
in writing to express, 89
in writing to tell, 91–92
Writer's block, 12–13
Writing
formality in, 438–41
identifying purpose of, 32–33, 87–94
strategic approach to, for research paper, 243–50
Writing handbook, 539–40
Writing portfolio, 86–87
definition of, 3
guides for collecting, 87
purpose of, 3

Writing process, 5–7
  assertion-with-evidence essay, 176–89
  completing stage of, 2, 7, 53–82
  creating stage of, 12–45
  evaluation essay, 190–205
  how-to essay, 135–44
  information essay, 160–75
  personal experience essay, 111–22
  persuasion essay, 206–18
  problem-solution essay, 145–59
  research paper, 219–303
  shaping stage of, 2, 6, 30–52
Writing to change, 87, 92–93
  circumstance in, 94
  emphasis in, 93
  motivation for, 93
  purpose in, 93
  situation in, 94
  time value in, 94
  writer-reader relationship in, 94
Writing to express, 87–88
  circumstance in, 89
  emphasis in, 88
  motivation for, 88
  situation in, 89
  writer-reader relationship in, 89
Writing to tell, 87, 89–90
  circumstance in, 91
  emphasis in, 90
  motivation for, 90
  purpose in, 90
  situation in, 91
  writer-reader relationship in, 91–92
Writing Without Teachers (Elbow), 20

Yearbooks, 228–29
Yes, letters that say, 482
You attitude, in business letters, 478–79, 500
Yourcenar, Marguerite, 39

Zinsser, William, 414, 442

Acknowledgments

LITERARY

Chapter 2

Pages 20–21 Material on Looping is drawn from *Writing Without Teachers* by Peter Elbow, Oxford University Press, 1975. Used by permission of the author.

Chapter 4

Pages 55–57 From *Together: Communicating Interpersonally, Second Edition,* by John Stewart and Gary D'Angelo. Copyright © 1980 by Newbery Award Records, Inc. Reprinted by permission of McGraw Hill Publishing Co.

Pages 67, 68–69, 70 "Redundancies," "Bureaucratic Phrases and Alternatives," "The Words in Parentheses . . ." and "Vitiated Verbs" from *Writing at Work* by Ernst Jacobi. Reprinted by permission of Ten Speed Press.

Chapter 5

Page 96 From *Writing the Australian Crawl* by William Stafford. Copyright © 1978 by The University of Michigan. Reprinted by permission.

Page 101 Excerpt from Michel Foucault, "How We Behave," *Vanity Fair.* Excerpted from *Michel Foucault: Beyond Structuralism and Hermeneutics* by Hubert L. Dreyfus and Paul Rabinow. Copyright © 1982, 1983 by the University of Chicago. All rights reserved. Reprinted by permission.

Page 104 Willa Cather, *Death Comes for the Archbishop*. New York: Alfred A. Knopf, Inc., 1927.

Pages 104–105 Richard Hughes, *High Wind in Jamaica*. Harper, 1929.

Page 105 Excerpted from *West with the Night,* copyright © 1942, 1983 by Beryl Markham. Published by North Point Press and reprinted by permission. All rights reserved.

Pages 105–106 Excerpt reprinted by permission of Farrar, Straus and Giroux, Inc. from *The Habit of Being* by Flannery O'Connor. Edited and with an introduction by Sally Fitzgerald. Copyright © 1979 by Regina O'Connor.

Page 106 From *The Shirley Letters* by "Dame Shirley," (Louise Clappe). Copyright © 1983 by Peregrine Press, a division of Gibbs M. Smith, Inc. Reprinted by permission.

Page 106 From *A River Runs Through It and Other Stories* by Norman Maclean. Copyright © 1976 by the University of Chicago. Reprinted by permission of the publisher.

Page 106 Harry Mathews, *Country Cooking and Other Stories*. Burning Deck, 1980, 52–53.

Page 107 From "River" by Eugene McDaniels. Copyright © 1973 by Lonport Music Corp., Inc.

Chapter 14

Page 235 Entry from *Readers' Guide to Periodical Literature,* 1987. Copyright © 1987 by the H. W. Wilson Company. Material reproduced by permission of the publisher.

Page 236 Entry from "The New York Times Index," 1987. Starting Lotte Company of Japan. Ending . . . new demands of wealth. Copyright © 1987 by The New York Times Company. Reprinted by permission.

Page 298 From *The Fate of the Earth* by Jonathan Schell. Copyright © 1983 by Jonathan Schell. Originally appeared in *The New Yorker.* Reprinted by permission of Alfred A. Knopf, Inc.

Page 298 Excerpt from "Vermont Bans the Bomb," *Time,* March 15, 1982. Copyright © 1982 Time Inc. Reprinted by permission.

Pages 298–299 Excerpt from "Thinking About the Unthinkable," *Time,* March 29, 1982. Copyright © 1982 Time Inc. Reprinted by permission.

Page 299 Excerpt from "A Deadly Dilemma," *Time,* April 12, 1982. Copyright © 1982 Time Inc. Reprinted by permission.

Part 3

Page 306 "Exploring the Labyrinth of the Mind" by James Gleick, August 21, 1983, *The New York Times Magazine*. Copyright © 1983 by The New York Times Company. Reprinted by permission.

Chapter 16

Page 326 From *The Little Rhetoric* by Edward P. J. Corbett. Copyright © 1977 Scott, Foresman and Company.

Chapter 18

Page 379 From *The New Money Dynamics* by Venita Van Caspel. Copyright © 1978 Reston Publishing

Company, Inc. Reprinted by permission of Simon & Schuster, Inc.

Pages 379–380 "What is my goal in Life? . . ." is excerpted from *On Becoming a Person* by Carl R. Rogers. Copyright © 1961 by Carl R. Rogers. Reprinted with the permission of Houghton Mifflin Company.

Page 380 "Now that they've taught pigeons . . ." is excerpted from *How to Play the Piano Despite Years of Lessons* by Ward Cannel. Copyright © 1976 by Ward Cannel. Reprinted by permission of Crown & Bridge, Publishers, Paterson, NJ 07504.

Chapter 19

Pages 387, 417 "The Living Dead Sea" by Harvey Arden from the February 1978 issue of *National Geographic Magazine*. Used by permission.

Pages 389–390 Reprinted from *Anasazi* by Donald G. Pike and David Muench. Copyright © 1974 by American West Publishing Company. Used by permission of Crown Publishers, Inc.

Pages 396, 414 Excerpts from pp. 70 and 241–242 in *Four Arguments for the Elimination of Television* by Jerry Mander. Copyright © 1977, 1978 by Jerry Mander. By permission of William Morrow & Company.

Page 397 Excerpt from "Some Remarks on Humor" copyright 1941, © 1969 by E. B. White from *Essays of E. B. White* copyright © 1977 by E. B. White. Reprinted by permission of Harper & Row, Publishers, Inc.

Pages 405–406 From "Rain and the Rhinocerous," Thomas Merton, *Raids on the Unspeakable*. Copyright © 1965 by the Abbey of Gethsemani, Inc. Reprinted by permission of New Directions Publishing Corporation.

Pages 413–414, 440 Reprinted with permission of Macmillan Publishing Company from *Moving Mountains* by Henry M. Boettinger. Copyright © 1969 by Henry M. Boettinger.

Pages 414, 442 From *On Writing Well* by William Zinsser. Copyright © 1976 by William K. Zinsser. Reprinted by permission of the author.

Chapter 20

Page 430 From p. 14 of *Kennedy* by Theodore C. Sorenson, 1965, Harper & Row, Publishers, Inc.

Pages 430–431 Excerpt from "Here is New York" copyright 1949 by E. B. White from *Essays of E. B. White* copyright © 1977 by E. B. White. Reprinted by permission of Harper & Row, Publishers, Inc.

Chapter 21

Page 442 "How is aim determined? . . ." is excerpted from *A Theory of Discourse* by James Kinneavy, 1975, Prentice-Hall, Inc.

Pages 445–446 Excerpt from "Death of a Pig" copyright 1947 by E. B. White from *Essays of E. B. White* copyright © 1977 by E. B. White. Reprinted by permission of Harper & Row, Publishers, Inc.

Chapter 23

Pages 478–479 Featherweight Fly Vest copy courtesy of L. L. Bean, Inc., Freeport, ME.

Chapter 30

Page 608 Excerpt from *The Adventures of Huckleberry Finn* by Mark Twain. Doubleday, 1960.

PHOTOS

Cover: Takahashi Rikio, *Niwa (Movement B2)*, 1985. Reproduced by Courtesy of the Trustees of the British Museum.

Page xxii © Jonathan A. Meyers
Page 84 © Gail Russell
Page 304 © Jerry Jacka
Page 454 © Jonathan A. Meyers
Page 538 © Jonathan A. Meyers

ILLUSTRATIONS

Background art by Sally Havlis
Marginal art by Candace Haught